TRIUMPH OF TREASON

This book has been designed in a Victory Format. Smaller type and margins produce fewer pages which permit a vital saving of paper and labor in the manufacture of a wartime book.

TRIUMPH
of TREASON

"Contre nous de la tyrannie..."

by

PIERRE COT

· ZIFF-DAVIS ·
PUBLISHING COMPANY

CHICAGO · NEW YORK

Translated by Sybille and Milton Crane

"To my comrades of the Popular Front

who will carry on to its goal

the struggle against Fascism and Hitlerism

begun the sixth of February, 1934"

"*We want an order of things where the citizen is subordinated to the magistrate, the magistrate to the people, and the people to Justice.*"

ROBESPIERRE: Address at the
Convention on February 5, 1794.

Contents

INTRODUCTION   1

PART I

ORIGINS AND DEVELOPMENT OF THE RIOM TRIAL

CHAPTER 1   CAUSES OF THE TRIAL   11

Vichy's Need To Defend Itself   11
 The Indispensable Scapegoats   12
 "Preserve the Honor of the Army"   14
 "Save the Fifth Column"   16
 Overwhelm the Leaders of the Popular Front   18
The Hate of the French Fascists and Reactionaries   21
 The Case Against Me   24
  Opposition to the French Nationalists   27
  Opposition to the Capitalist Monopolies   30
  Opposition to European Fascism   34
  Opposition to the Croix de Feu and the Cagoulards   38
  My Position in the Popular Front   40
 The Case Against Gamelin, Jacomet, and La Chambre   41
 The Necessary Vengeance of French Fascism   44

CHAPTER 2   THE FRENCH DEFEAT   45

Principal Causes of the Defeat   46
 The Isolation of France: the Collapse of the Franco-
  Soviet Pact   47
 The Military Weakness of France: the Mistakes of the
  General Staff   53

The Moral Disunity of the French People: Fifth
    Column Activity   60

Theories Advanced To Explain the Defeat   69

The Aging of the French Nation   70

The Policy of the Popular Front   70

Conversion of the French Bourgeoisie to Fascism   70

Weakness of French Democracy   73

The Cagoulard Affair   77

A Hypothesis To Be Verified by History   80

CHAPTER 3   THE POPULAR FRONT   81

The Origins of the Popular Front   82

The Work of the Popular Front   87

The Overthrow of the Popular Front   92

Consequences and Responsibilities of the Popular Front   99

The Role of the Popular Front in French Politics   102

CHAPTER 4   THE VICHY GOVERNMENT AGAINST JUSTICE   104

The Organization of the Supreme Court of Justice   107

Unconstitutionality of the Supreme Court   109

Arbitrary Character of the Procedure   110

The Conduct of the Riom Trial   114

Grounds for the Accusation   114

Limited and Mutilated Debates   117

Advance Condemnation by Pétain   123

Instructions to the Press and a Secret Dossier   127

Truth on the March   130

The Attitude of the Judges   136

The Witnesses' Testimony   139

Adjournment Sine Die   143

PART II

REFUTATION OF THE ACCUSATIONS BROUGHT BY
THE VICHY GOVERNMENT

CHAPTER 5 THE ECONOMIC PREPARATION OF THE WAR   151

Economic Policy of the French Conservatives   154
Economic Policy of the Popular Front   156
Vichy's Thesis for the Failure of the Popular Front's
Economic Policy   160
   "Weakness" in Repressing Labor Agitation   161
   Nationalization of War Industries   162
   Application of New Social Legislation: the Forty-Hour
   Week   164
Actual Causes for the Failure of the Popular Front's Economic
Policy   169
   Supplementary Depression of 1934-1935   169
   Desertion of Employers and Capital   171
   Excessive Caution of the Government   173
Homage to Léon Blum   175

CHAPTER 6 THE MILITARY PREPARATION OF THE WAR   177

Decadence of the Army   178
   Pétain as Minister of War   181
   The Irretrievable Delay   185
   Daladier's Efforts to Overcome the Errors of His
   Predecessors   187
Military Morale   191
   Morale of the Troops   191
   The Fascist Officers   196
   Politics in the Army   198
The Status of Matériel   199
   Daladier a Match for Goering   202
   Armament Programs Determined by the Doctrine   207
   Matériel Kept for the Germans   210

CHAPTER 7 THE ROLE OF THE MILITARY IN THE
            DEFEAT   213

French Military Doctrine: The Continuous Front   214
     The French Conception of War   215
     The German Conception of War   219
     Conservatism of the French General Staff   225
     Consequences of French Military Conservatism   228
The German Military Doctrine: the Schlieffen Plan   232
     Failure of the Plan in World War I   233
     The New Version of the Plan and Its Application   237
The French Defense   241
     The Mistakes of the High Command   245
     Military Leadership   255
          Pétain's Influence   256
          Gamelin and Weygand   262
          Daladier   267

CHAPTER 8 AVIATION AND THE FRENCH DEFEAT   274

Air Power in the Battle of France   276
     Quality of Personnel and Matériel   276
     Quantity of Planes in Active Service   277
     Productive Capacity Feeding the Air Forces   280
     Organization of the Aerial Forces   281
The Employment of the Aerial Forces   283
     German Methods   284
     French Methods   286
The Cause of the Defeat in the Air   289
     Economic Factors   289
          Capacity of Production   290
          The Volume of Credits   293
          Distribution of Credits and Resources   295
     Diplomatic Factors   297
          International Air Agreements   298
          French Purchases Abroad   299
     Military Factors   301
          The Doctrines of Air Warfare   302
          Those Responsible for the Misuse of the Air Force 304

CHAPTER 9   AVIATION POLICY OF THE POPULAR FRONT   307

Political Aspect: The Functions of the Air Ministry   308
My Work as Minister of Aviation   309
Why I Didn't Resign   316
Social Aspect: Aeronautic Reforms   318
Economic Aspect: Nationalization of the Aeronautic Industry   320
Reorganization of the Aeronautic Industry   321
Effects of Nationalization   326
Military Aspect: Organizaton of the Air Force   330

CHAPTER 10   THE INTERNATIONAL AVIATION POLICY   336

Policy Toward the Spanish Republic   336
Acceptance of the Nonintervention Policy   337
Development and Consequences of the Nonintervention Policy   347
Aid to Republican Spain   351
Collective Security and Rapprochment with the Soviet Union   356
Difficulties in Negotiating a Franco-Soviet Alliance   357
Importance to France of Aerial Collaboration with Russia   359
Answers to Vichy's Accusations   364

PART III

CONCLUSION

CHAPTER 11   THE FUTURE OF FRANCE   369

Significance of the Riom Trial   369
The Algiers Committee of National Liberation   374
The French People   387

APPENDIX   397

Introduction

T HIS BOOK IS WRITTEN on behalf of those whom the Vichy government attempted to try at the Riom Court. It is more especially written on behalf of my friends, Léon Blum and Édouard Daladier.

These men have been silenced by the Vichy government. No one knows exactly what has happened to them since April, 1942. They were arrested in the summer of 1940 and charged with responsibility for the French defeat. Not until February, 1942, were they brought before the Supreme Court of Justice at Riom. After six weeks of public hearings, a law was enacted by the government to impose on the Court the adjournment *sine die* of the trial. The edict proclaimed that supplementary information was necessary to expose more fully the defendants' "breaches in the fulfillment of their governmental offices." It was mere pretext, for new information was never sought. Instead, the Vichy government sent the accused from Riom to the other end of the country, to Portalet, an ancient fortress, lost in the heart of the Pyrenees, in a snowbound valley, a day's trip from any center of communication.

In December, 1942, Hitler's jailers replaced Pétain's. In 1943 uncon-firmed rumors spread that Blum and Daladier had been transferred to Germany. Even if these rumors were untrue, Pétain's most dangerous adver-saries were cut off from the rest of the world.

They have been buried alive in a new Bastille, worse than the one destroyed on July 14, 1789, with only two ways of exit open to them—death, or liber-ation by the French people after the defeat of Fascism in Europe.

Why did the Vichy government halt the trial in this manner? Because, even before a court controlled by dictatorship, accused persons have been allowed to present their defense and to speak—and Pétain and Laval were afraid of Blum's and Daladier's revelations.

Until the eve of the Riom trial, Pétain felt perfectly safe. All precautions had been taken to assure the condemnation of the men allegedly responsible for the French defeat—Blum, Daladier, and their "accomplices." The judicial travesty had been prepared and planned carefully. For a year and a half, clever propaganda had been carried on throughout France and the world, calumniating the defendants and the republican regime they represented. This propaganda had borne excellent fruit, principally outside France, for many democratic governments, imitating Pontius Pilate, affected to strike a balance

1

between the accusers—adversaries of political freedom and "collaborators" of Nazi Germany, and their victims—champions of democracy and anti-Fascists. An exceptional Court, composed of judges appointed because of their political bias and devotion to Pétain's regime, was created. Finally, in October, 1941, interfering with the march of "justice," Marshall Pétain sentenced the defend-ants, in advance of trial, to life imprisonment, thus depriving the Court of what little freedom of consideration and judgment it possessed.

In spite of these precautions, the Riom trial turned against the Vichy government. Marshal Pétain, General Weygand, and Admiral Darlan were obviously not of the intellectual stature of Blum and Daladier. When the accused were given the opportunity to address the Court, not only did they challenge the Prosecuting Attorney, but they attacked their accusers. They shook the whole structure of the charges. It became clear that if the respon-sibilities for the French defeat were to be weighed and shared, Pétain's and Weygand's responsibilities were greater than Daladier's in the military field; the Fifth Column was guiltier than the democratic regime in the political field; big business and the pro-Fascist haute bourgeoisie were guiltier than the Popular Front in the economic field.

A new political atmosphere was created rapidly by the attitude of Blum and Daladier at Riom. This atmosphere was felt both inside and outside France. After June, 1940, the French government ceased to appeal to reason, justice, law, or humanity. Pétain had erased from the French political vocabu-lary the democratic motto: Liberty, Equality, Fraternity. Taking the stand at Riom, Blum and Daladier used these words, and the world heard again the classic language of French democracy. In the statements of the accused—attacks against the Vichy government rather than defense of themselves—the echo of the French Revolution resounded. The true France appeared again; not the reactionary France, fettered to the credo of the *ancien régime,* whose spokes-man was Marshal Pétain, but a generous country of toilers and thinkers, vint-ners and artisans, scientists and workers; the France of 1789, 1793, 1848, and of the Popular Front, her face turned toward the future, less mindful of her own wealth, comfort, or destiny than of the progress of mankind; France, the champion of liberty.

This true France, speaking through Blum and Daladier, told the Vichy government hard and unpleasant truths. She defied Hitler to destroy her spiritual independence and moral unity. She proclaimed her indomitable faith in the final defeat of Fascism, in the birth of a new and free Europe. Priority of ideal over interest, predominance of reason over force, equality of men before the law, fraternity of all races and nations—these were the precepts proclaimed at Riom and heard throughout the world. The Riom trial showed that the French spirit was not broken even when in chains.

The Vichy government was alarmed by this discovery, which was a counter-current to its "National Revolution." Pétain realized, but too late, that the Riom trial was a blunder, an obstacle to his partnership in Hitler's New Order. Would it not be better to postpone the trial or force its denouement? The Marshal hesitated. Hitler did not. The trial was to be stopped at once. "The

2

Vichy government does not realize its exact position," said Hitler, and Pétain bowed before this sneer. Laval, a more faithful Fascist, replaced Darlan as head of the Vichy cabinet; the trial was adjourned indefinitely, and the accused were sent to Portalet. The tragicomedy of Riom was over, but the farce had lasted long enough to let Hitler, Pétain, and the world understand that the flame of the French Revolution was still burning.

Léon Blum and Édouard Daladier, the champions of French democracy at Riom, are now silenced and imprisoned. As freedom of press and speech has not existed in France since June, 1940, no one in the nation can protest their imprisonment or present their defense to the public; no one can uphold their charges against Marshal Pétain and the government of Vichy, political beneficiaries of the military defeat of France. It is my duty to continue the battle for them.

I, too, stand accused before the Court of Riom. I have been accorded a great honor by Marshal Pétain, his government, his Prosecuting Attorney, and his Council of Political Justice. They place me on the same level with Blum and Daladier. I stand with the scapegoats of the republican regime and the Popular Front—and I thank the Vichyites for it. I am prouder of this distinction than of the decorations I won on the battlefields of 1914-1918, because I believe that the spiritual frontiers of France must be defended even more strongly than her physical frontiers. I can now add a new title to the ones I have earned in a long fight against Hitlerism and Fascism, a fight which began long before June, 1940, and which has been the raison d'être of my life.

During my public life I committed mistakes. But I have never voluntarily been absent from a battle against Fascism. In French politics I fought, in turn, against the Royalists, the Croix de Feu, the Cagoulards, the conservatives and the reactionaries of every stamp. I was a partisan and militant of the Popular Front and remained unswervingly faithful to its ideal. I saw in the Popular Front the legitimate heir of the French Revolution. I believed that only the alliance of all popular forces, Communists included, would bring about the birth of a new democratic France.

In the international field I opposed the Japanese government when it attacked Manchuria; Mussolini when he invaded Ethiopia; Franco when he betrayed the Spanish Republic; Hitler when he destroyed Czechoslovakia. I supported the League of Nations, collective security, the Franco-Soviet Pact. I was thus an unrepentant sinner, according to the canons of the Fascist church, and I largely deserved the wrath of the Vichy government.

Marshal Pétain was not the first to write my name on the black list and to make it a symbol of anti-Fascism. Hitler denounced me as one of his foremost adversaries in the speeches he delivered in September, 1938, the eve of the Munich Pact, for trying to transform Czechoslovakia into an air base for French and Russian bombers; Eduard Beneš, Joseph Stalin, and I were the authors of an international plot organized by the warmongering anti-Fascists against peaceful Nazi Germany. I shall return to the alleged plot later; but I might say now, that in the light of later events, I have often regretted that the criminal intentions Hitler ascribed to us did not have a better basis in fact. If we had trampled out the nest of Nazi vipers, our crime would have spared the world untold tragedy.

Hitler's denunciation singled me out for attack by his French accomplices. A few days after Hitler's speech I met my friend Marx Dormoy, former Minister of the Interior in Blum's cabinet. Dormoy, who had denounced the notorious Cagoulard plot, said to me: "If Hitler ever becomes master of Europe, we shall have a Fascist government in France, with Marshal Pétain as its leader. The first three democrats to be arrested or assassinated will be Léon Blum, you, and myself." He was almost right. He was killed in September, 1941, while under the "protective arrest" of Marshal Pétain's police; his assassins have yet to be found or punished. Blum has been in prison for more than three years; and if I had been in France, I, too, would have been imprisoned or, more probably, assassinated.

It was to continue the fight that I remained abroad. I left France at the end of June, 1940. I was in England when the Vichy press and radio announced that I would be prosecuted before the Court of Political Justice with Blum, Daladier, Paul Reynaud, Georges Mandel, General Maurice Gamelin, and several others. Where did my duty lie? I consulted not only my French friends, but some important statesmen then in London who were familiar with my activities. All agreed that, if I returned to France, I would be recognizing Vichy's right to judge and condemn the French democratic leaders; in short, that I would be recognizing the legitimacy of the Vichy government.

In September, 1940, when I was charged, I had just arrived in the United States. Guy la Chambre, who succeeded me as Minister of Aviation in 1938, was accused at the same time, and decided to return to France. I respected his decision, whatever his motives, but I did not feel obligated to imitate him. I had another task to carry on.

I would have returned to France only if I could have ameliorated the physical or moral situation of the other defendants. No one can seriously contend that my return would have had any such effect. Blum and Daladier still would have been silent if I had been their fellow prisoner in Portalet, and I still would have been incapable of acting and speaking for them. Moreover, had I followed La Chambre, I should have had no opportunity to appear before the judges of Riom. I should not have been given the slightest chance to defend myself, much less to attack my accusers. The "punishment of my crimes"—i.e., my murder—had often been demanded by Charles Maurras, leader of l'Action Française, and by the Cagoulards. A few days before Pétain's request for an armistice, the German radio broadcast that I had been "executed by French aviators and patriots"; this news item, repeated at various times, constituted an appeal to potential assassins. The fate of Dormoy was in store for me— unless my enemies would have chosen a more discreet device and announced in the press that I had committed suicide.

These were the main motives for my decision: to avoid making things easy for my enemies; to defend my friends of the Popular Front and the ideal of the French people; to expose what I know of the machinations that led France to defeat and Pétain to power; to continue my battle against Fascism.

I shall return to France when I can submit myself to judges deriving their powers from the French people.

This book is not intended to be an objective and complete analysis of the causes of the French defeat nor of the collapse of the republican regime. The time has not yet come for such a task, and the best scholars today lack both the perspective and the necessary documents to reach definitive conclusions. Military and diplomatic archives have yet to be published; the memoirs of contemporary statesmen have yet to be written. A man who would dare to judge and condemn under these circumstances would show a childish frivolity of mind or a criminal intellectual dishonesty.

The events of June, 1940, were the logical outcome of mistakes piled up during twenty years. These mistakes were committed in various ways and degrees by all political parties and social classes. Some did wrong; others let wrong be done. In addition, the events of June, 1940, grew out of international disorder which France was not alone in provoking: France paid for American isolationism, British conservatism, Anglo-Saxon red-baiting; she followed China, Ethiopia, Spain, and Czechoslovakia on the list of victims of "appeasement," a policy practiced not only in Paris, but in London and Washington, too. Only the historians of the future will be able to establish the hiearchy of French errors and of international blunders.

But I must give my opinion about the events I witnessed. I must take my part in the collective testimony. I was for many years a member of the French cabinet, a leader of the Popular Front, and for a longer time a member of the French Parliament. I knew Pétain, Weygand, Darlan, Laval, and their accomplices.

I will try to report truthfully and impartially what I saw, and, in the language of the French *Code d'Instruction Criminelle,* "speak without hate nor fear." I hope I can succeed. I must warn my readers that my opinion is provisional, capable of qualification or change; a witness cannot be a judge.

It is my conviction that six men—Léon Blum, Édouard Daladier, Guy la Chambre, Maurice Gamelin, Pierre Jacomet, and Pierre Cot—cannot be held solely or mainly responsible for the French defeat. No one can maintain that the complex problem of the fall of France can be summed up in the single case presented by the Vichy government to the Riom Court. Scapegoats, not criminals, were prosecuted at Riom.

I am not so naïve as to claim that we, the scapegoats of the defeat, were all blameless. We were not supermen, but fallible men. Winston Churchill once declared in a broadcast that he had committed three mistakes; Hitler replied, with heavy irony, that he, Hitler, had committed nine hundred and forty-seven. Hitler was right. One cannot act or govern without making numerous mistakes. The more one acts, the more mistakes one makes. A statesman's greatest fault is to refuse the risks of action through timidity or fear of responsibility and of error.

What matters is not the list of errors of detail, down to the slightest, that we, the men accused by the Vichy government, committed, but the appreciation of the ensemble, direction, and main line of our policy, and since our penal responsibility is questioned, the honesty of our intention. With respect to the latter, I can prove our blamelessness without difficulty. Not we, but our adversaries, repeated, "rather Hitler than Léon Blum"; not we, but our accusers, awaited Hitler's victory, to crush French political freedom and democracy; they, not we, came to power in the time of our country's catastrophe; they alone were the beneficiaries of the defeat.

I shall point out my faults and those of the other defendants, for I could not do otherwise without betraying what I consider the truth. I must repeat with Cicero: *amicus Plato, amica magis veritas.* Those who know me can testify that I never blindly followed all the policies of the government. Not always did I agree with Blum, and there were many issues in which I did not support Daladier, and more in which I did not support La Chambre. I should merely weaken the value of my testimony if I pretended that I approved of Blum's attitude during the Spanish war, of Daladier's at Munich, or of La Chambre's policy in the Air Ministry. French democrats have no need to be concerned; while I shall express my opinion freely, I shall in no way endanger my co-defendants.

The Riom trial was a paradox. If we were guilty—politically, not penally—it was for what we did not do and for acts that were not included in Vichy's accusation. It was not Blum's social and economic policies which hindered France's industrial development in 1936-1937, but the obstinacy of the industrialists and financiers who opposed the popular majority. It was not Daladier who prevented France from building a modern and well-equipped army with motorized divisions and a first-rate air force, but the members of the General Staff, who had been indoctrinated by Pétain and Weygand. It was not La Chambre nor I who imperiled France's aerial security, but the generals who did not believe in aviation and the diplomats who destroyed the spirit and substance of the Franco-Soviet Pact by handing Czechoslovakia to Germany. Blum had erred in yielding to the British government in the case of the Spanish Republic; Daladier, in not retiring a politically ambitious Marshal of eighty-three and in permitting Georges Bonnet to strike an accord with Neville Chamberlain; La Chambre, in dissolving the parachute battalions; and I, in not driving more Fascist generals and technicians out of French aviation.

I shall plead guilty—not to the things with which we have been charged, but to the error of leaving too much power and initiative in the hands of those who have accused us. I shall plead guilty for my friends and myself; I shall accuse our accusers, without hate, without passion, but without indulgence. We are not the only ones who must answer for our acts and errors before history and the French people. When the responsibilities of the various governmental groups in France are weighed, the men of the Popular Front will be able to hold their heads high before the men of Vichy.

Whether the Vichy government wanted to or not, it committed a far-reaching political act by initiating the Riom trial. This act will be its Nemesis, as surely as the murder of the Duke of Enghien was Napoleon's and as the guilt for the Dreyfus case pursued the predecessors of Pétain and Weygand at the head of the French Army. The Vichy government made the laws which will be applied to its leaders by the French people. Only when its mistakes and ours are compared and weighed, will the true meaning of the Riom trial be revealed.

The Riom trial must be assigned its correct place in the politics of France. It was a moment in the unfinished battle between the forces of liberation and those of reaction, a battle which goes back to the French Revolution. Its historical interest, from this point of view, lies in the demonstration that the conflict between the *ancien régime* and the Revolution has not ended; the Vichy government is the actual expression of the *ancien régime,* and the Popular Front a modern version of the French Revolution.

The Riom trial went beyond France's history. It was also a moment in the world conflict between Fascism and liberty. Blum and Daladier stood not only against Pétain and his government, but also against Hitler and his disciples all over the world. Thanks to them, France is present in the ideological war in which civilization is at stake.

The reactions created by this double aspect of the trial—the struggle for and against the Revolution, the struggle for and against Fascism and imperialism—will determine the future of France and, therefore, of Europe. A study of the Riom trial may help us to a better appreciation of French democracy, to a more complete understanding of the dangers of Fascism, to a more accurate prevision of the destiny of our epoch.

PART I

ORIGINS AND DEVELOP-
MENT OF THE RIOM TRIAL

*"Against us, the bloody banner of
tyranny is raised. . . ."*

LA MARSEILLAISE

In organizing the Riom trial, the Vichy government wished to show the world that the Third Republic and the Popular Front bore the guilt for the defeat of the French Army. By adjourning the trial *sine die,* it admitted that it was incapable of proving this charge. Even in the eyes of Vichy's friends, the Riom trial was a blunder.

Why was this blunder committed? Marshal Pétain and his acolytes undoubtedly underestimated the caliber of their adversaries; they believed that their judicial machinery would have no difficulty in overwhelming Blum and Daladier, two men imprisoned for eighteen months and slandered daily by the official propaganda. They miscalculated. Blum and Daladier proved so much greater than their foe that they reduced to silence the hue and cry against them.

But a crude psychological error does not explain why Pétain decided, first, to try the republican regime through the leaders of the Popular Front, and then, after the trial had begun, to stop it. The causes of this contradiction must be sought in the origin and the development of the trial—the object of the first part of this book.

Causes of the Trial

1

THE OFFICIAL CAUSE of the Riom trial was the defeat of France. The Supreme Court of Justice, organized by a law of July 30, 1940, was ordered by the Vichy government to try those it considered "mainly responsible for the defeat."

A study of the causes of the defeat might at least have preceded the choice of "those mainly responsible for the defeat." In June, 1940, most Frenchmen thought not only that the war had been badly prepared and badly conducted, but that the country had been betrayed; true or false, these ideas should have been closely examined and thoroughly analyzed. The world was less surprised by the defeat of the French armies than by the circumstances of that defeat, its extent and suddenness, and by the consequences, notably the feeble resistance of French democracy and the establishment of a government prepared to collaborate with Hitler.

VICHY'S NEED TO DEFEND ITSELF

Vichy never tried to determine objectively the causes of the defeat. Without taking the time to conduct a preliminary investigation, the Vichy government proclaimed the exclusive responsibility of certain Popular Front ministers, to whom it added a few secondary figures. Having decided on an official doctrine, Pétain forbade its criticism, discussion, or opposition.

As neither the Constitution nor the Penal Code gave the government any right to try those whom it wanted to attack, a law was hastily drawn in July, 1940, not by Parliament but by Pétain. It established the Supreme Court of Justice to try "the ministers, former ministers, or their immediate subordinates . . . accused of having committed crimes in the exercise of their functions, or attendant on the exercise of their functions, or of having betrayed the duties of their offices." In less than two weeks, on August 13, 1940, the Supreme Court of Justice was prepared to function; its judges had been appointed, and the Prosecuting Attorney brought charges before the Court that "ministers, former ministers, or their civil or military subordinates . . . had betrayed the duties of their offices in the acts which contributed to the change from a state of peace to a state of war before September 4, 1939, and in those acts which eventually aggravated the consequences of the situation thus created." A month later, the Prosecuting Attorney declared that he had discovered the authors of these infamous acts and demanded the indictment of Daladier, La Chambre, and myself, as well as of General Gamelin and Con-troller-General Jacomet. In October, 1940, Blum's name was put on the list of "those responsible for the war." At that time, in fact, it was for having "contributed to the change from a state of peace to a state of war," and for having "aggravated the consequences of the situation thus created" that we were indicted, which was strange in the case of Blum and myself, who had not been cabinet members since the beginning of 1938. To repair this error, it was later declared that we had "contributed to the change from a state of peace to a state of war" by neglecting preparations for the war in 1936 and 1937. At the same time and under other pretexts, the Vichy government indicted Georges Mandel and Paul Reynaud before the Supreme Court of Justice, while Jean Zay, Pierre Mendès-France, and Pierre Viennot, also former members of the Popular Front cabinet, were called before other courts.

These indictments reveal a great and clumsy haste. Had the Vichy government really been convinced of the responsibility of the Popular Front ministers in the war and the defeat, it would have gone to work less quickly. When we were indicted, in September and October, 1940, it was impossible for Vichy to have studied the causes of the war or of the defeat, or even the actions of the Popular Front ministers. This was because the government had abandoned Paris at the beginning of June, 1940. In the rush of a departure which resembled a flight, most of the ministerial archives had been gathered quickly, loaded on trucks, and scattered to the four corners of the country. Many documents were lost, and those remaining had not yet been collected and reclassified. How was it possible to study and evaluate the acts of the Popular Front ministers "committed in the exercise of their functions or attendant on the exercise of their functions," without government archives and administrative dossiers for the periods during which these ministers were in office?

The true causes of the Riom trial, therefore, had little to do with the causes of the defeat. A moment's reflection will show why a dummy trial of scapegoats was substituted for a serious trial of those responsible.

The Indispensable Scapegoats

The Vichy government was born of defeat. Its members were the political profiteers of defeat. Only defeat had allowed them to establish and maintain themselves in power, suppress civil liberties, and throw themselves headlong against the will of the people into the policy of collaboration. Had it not been for the defeat, Pierre Laval, already the most unpopular man in France, Weygand, a general conquered without fighting, Baudoin and Lehideux, rep-resentatives of big business and private interests, and other gentlemen of little importance, could not have become members of a French cabinet in 1940.

Marshal Pétain's friends point to the fact that the French Parliament gave him a large mandate. But no one in France, not even Pétain himself, considers this mandate the basis of the power that he exercised after July, 1940. In a strong article written in 1940, Professor René Cassin, member of General Charles de Gaulle's National Committee, demonstrated the illegal character of the Vichy government. In its tragic meeting of July 10, 1940, the French Parliament had conferred an "irregular" mandate on Pétain. The act which conferred this mandate was engendered by fear: a third of the deputies, regularly elected in 1936, were absent. Some had been thrown into concentration camps and deprived of their rights because they were Communists; others had embarked aboard the *Massilia* for North Africa; still others were in German-occupied France. The senators and deputies who voted power to Marshal Pétain did so under the threat of seeing all France occupied by Hitler's troops. They were blackmailed in the most shameful way. Laval took charge of this task; a book written by one of his friends, Jean Montigny, gives abundant proof of the constant pressure Laval exercised on the President of the Republic and on Parliament on behalf of Pétain.*

Even if the French Parliament's mandate to Pétain were in order, it was only a limited mandate. Pétain was to be a kind of trustee, appointed to execute the will of the French people and to establish whatever new institutions the people might wish to create. He was to govern as a non-partisan arbitrator, in charge of preparing a constitution which the people would accept; this constitution was to be put in force and supervised (*appliqué*, in the text of the law) by new Assemblies, elected as quickly as possible; the Senate and Chamber were to continue their existence until the election of these new Assemblies. These texts were explicitly stated in the mandate: the people remained sovereign; Marshal Pétain was to be only a temporary administrator whose duties were to maintain order, to represent France to the world, and especially to let the French people heal their wounds and choose their new representatives freely.

Never was a public mandate violated more deliberately. Instead of being a faithful trustee of the French people, Marshal Pétain used his power to establish a dictatorial government, based not on popular sovereignty but on the *Führerprinzip*. "Authority no longer comes from below," he declared in a speech broadcast on August 12, 1941, "it is that which I entrust or which I delegate." Louis XIV was not more absolute. Ministers, civil servants, the military, all were obliged to swear an oath of fidelity to the person of Marshal Pétain. The constitution drafted by the Marshal, which made him absolute master of France, was never submitted to the people. He did not try to hide from the world that the French people as a whole disliked his regime and his policy. "The authority of my government is questioned," he said in the same address, "but in 1917 I put an end to mutiny; in 1940 I put an end to rout; today it is from yourselves that I want to save you."

* Jean Montigny, *Toute la Vérité* (Clermont-Ferrand: Éditions Montlouis, 1940).

And, as in 1917 Marshal Pétain had shot the mutineers, he now sent to concentration camps and handed over to the Gestapo those Frenchmen who refused
to bow before him.

In so far as this authoritarian conception of power was in contradiction
with the mandate that had been given to him by Parliament, Pétain became
a mere usurper. He was in the position of a tenant who, having rented a
house, behaves like an owner, selling or destroying that which does not belong
to him. This point was made clear in August, 1942, by Édouard Herriot,
President of the Chamber of Deputies, and Jules Jeanneney, President of the
Senate, who jointly addressed a letter to Pétain, denouncing his abuse of power.
This letter was published in the Anglo-Saxon and Soviet newspapers, but it
did not receive proper attention. Because of their functions, Herriot and
Jeanneney were acting on behalf of the French Parliament, from which Pétain
claimed to hold his power. They demonstrated that France no longer had a
legitimate government; they solemnly warned the world that the Vichy government no longer had the right to speak and act in the name of France.

This letter of Herriot and Jeanneney is an important document for the
appreciation of the French political situation. Given the circumstances, it was
a courageous thing to do.

Born of the defeat and dependent on it for the establishment of their
dictatorship, the Vichy rulers had to find scapegoats in the summer of 1940 for
that defeat. It was for them a matter of necessity. They feared that the French
people would seek those guilty of the defeat among those who profited by it.
To anticipate this, men and names had to be made the prey of public opinion.

What men and what names? That is what has to be examined.

"Preserve the Honor of the Army"

First of all, it was necessary to "preserve the honor of the Army." General
Weygand thundered these words like a command. He used, unconsciously,
the same terms that leaders of the French Army had invoked during the
Dreyfus affair to prevent public opinion from discovering their criminal
mistakes. "Preserve the honor of the Army," to French military men, is to
secure by every means—including those outlawed by moral law and the
Penal Code—the defense of the military corporation.

The question of the responsibility of military leaders in the military defeat
of France either had to be evaded or posed in distorted terms. To "preserve the
honor of the Army," the scapegoats of the defeat had to be chosen from the
political personnel of the Third Republic.

In truth, at the end of June, 1940, the question of who was responsible was
in everyone's mind. In the two weeks preceding the armistice, I was in touch
with the crowd of refugees that slowly and painfully followed the roads south-
ward. In the offices of the prefects, in the town halls, restaurants, and relief
centers, I listened to many conversations, received many confidences, heard

many opinions. Opinions differed on governmental policy, but all agreed in denouncing the blunders of the French General Staff. The country was unanimous, not against Blum, Daladier, or me, nor even against Laval, Pierre-Étienne Flandin, Georges Bonnet, or Jacques Doriot, but against the generals who had been incapable of understanding the conditions of modern warfare and who were guilty of not knowing the rudiments of their profession. "Just as before 1914 they had prepared for the war of 1870," the people said, "before 1939 they prepared for the war of 1914."

The severest condemnation came from the soldiers. Lost on the roads in pursuit of dispersed divisions and phantom regiments, thrown together with the refugees whose uncertainties and anxieties they shared, the men in uniform cursed the conduct of their leaders. They repeated that they never had been schooled in the techniques of modern warfare, especially in the combined use of tanks and aviation, and they were amazed at the ineptness of their commanders in the battles of May and June. They asked why the Meuse and Seine bridges had not been blown up before the arrival of German motorized columns; why Paris had not been defended street by street, as the Spanish Republicans had defended Madrid (and as the Russians were to defend Stalingrad); and they wanted to know why more than half of the tanks and airplanes had been left in the rear—in Orléans, Toulouse, Lyon, North Africa —instead of being massed for a counterattack that might have changed everything. They knew that the depots were bursting with the cannon, airplanes, and equipment they had needed

One began to hear quoted the disturbing remarks with which General Weygand had tried to persuade the cabinet to ask for an armistice: that he needed his tanks to master the revolutionary elements, if it should become necessary. That is to say, the Commander-in-Chief of the French Army preferred fighting French workers to throwing all his forces against the German troops. The soldiers praised the bravery of certain leaders—Giraud, Lestien, De Gaulle, Lucien, Delattre de Tassigny, and many others—but they declared that most of the officers had been the first to flee. "They left in automobiles and we left on foot," they said, talking about those officers, faithful followers of l'Action Française, Je Suis Partout, Gringoire, and other Fascist newspapers which had said in various forms, during the winter, that this was a democratic war and consequently did not interest them.

These statements circulated throughout the country, especially among the working classes and in petit bourgeois circles, which in France have always shown a quicker and sharper intelligence than other social groups. The criticisms of the General Staff were perhaps exaggerated, but confused as they were, they represented popular opinion. By June, 1940, not one man, unless he were directly involved, would have defended the General Staff. The most indulgent spoke of incompetence, the most severe of betrayal—and the latter were in the majority. Moreover, available information about war prisoners indicated that these unfortunates were still more bitter against their leaders than were their comrades in France. Their anger was legitimate. It was inex-

15

plicable, after all, that the General Staff, after deciding to abandon Paris and thus opening the east to the Germans, had not ordered the troops which occupied the Maginot Line to fall back toward the south. More than a million men, the best of the French Army, were caught in the German trap, a disaster which could have been prevented by an order from General Weygand. The most plausible explanation of this "error" occurring spontaneously to the prisoners of war, was that General Weygand, fearing the fury of his soldiers more than he did the enemy, and preferring the defeat of France to revolutionary outbreaks, allowed the youngest and most ardent men of the French Army to be locked up in German prisons rather than see them scattered through France. Thus France was covered by a great wave of anti-militarism, scorn for the stupidity of the General Staff, and deep resentment against certain leaders who were considered particularly suspect. Gagged by Marshal Pétain, and with only censored newspapers to read, France was not free to express any opinion; but the people were unanimous in thinking that the Army leaders had not been up to the level of their task. An impartial inquiry, not exempting the General Staff, would have been the normal outlet for public feeling.

Vichy neither could nor would order such a dangerous investigation. By its composition, the government of Vichy was representative not of the French people but of the General Staff. Its first cabinets were headed by Pétain, the spiritual leader of the French Army, the man who had played the most important part in the preparation of the war and in the formation of the General Staff. And these cabinets were composed largely of members of the General Staff—General Weygand, General Pujo, Admiral Darlan, General Huntzinger, General Bergeret, and Admiral Platon. As the French proverb says, "the wolves do not eat each other!"

Thus the first problem which faced the government of Vichy, confronted by the political and psychological consequences of the military defeat, was to divert to political men the ever-growing anger against the leaders of the Army. The French growled: "We have been betrayed or deceived by the generals"; proclamations and propaganda were to transform this into: "The generals were admirable, but you have been betrayed and deceived by your own representatives." Every device had to be employed to replace the reality of military responsibility by the legend of political responsibility.

"Save the Fifth Column"

But what political men should be chosen to bear the onus of the defeat?

Here again, the choice was determined by circumstances. On the one hand, the government wanted to destroy democracy and establish in France a Fascist political regime and a corporate economic system. Marshal Pétain's object in taking power (or, as he pompously said, making his country the gift of his person) had not been to permit the French nation to heal its wounds, come to itself, and determine freely its own political, economic, and

16

social institutions; his publicly avowed purpose was to overthrow the repub-lican regime, suppress local and governmental civil liberties, "purify the French nation by punishing it," and bring France back to the social and religious disciplines of the *ancien régime*. To achieve this purpose, Marshal Pétain and his ministers were not satisfied with the support of the German government; they also needed the support of French enemies of democracy and of the Fascist organizations. On the other hand—and herein lay their difficulty —a spirit of animosity was growing in popular circles against these same anti-democratic and Fascist elements, based on a growing awareness that the Fifth Column had played a preponderant part in the disaster, a part as grave and sinister as that played by the incompetence of military leaders.

In June and July, 1940, most of the French people were less concerned with the public utterances of Marshal Pétain and his ministers than with the pro-Fascist and pro-Hitler tendencies of the supporters of the new govern-ment. Most of the ministers were unknown. The Marshal's backers included all the enemies of the Republic, all the men whom the French people had learned to distrust: Maurras, the doctrinaire of *l'Action Française,* who had incessantly praised Fascist regimes; Flandin, who had telegraphed congratula-tions to Hitler after the rape of Czechoslovakia in September, 1938; Marcel Déat, who, in August, 1939, had written the notorious article asking the French soldiers "not to die for Danzig"; Bonnet, who had destroyed the Franco-Soviet Pact by his negotiations with von Ribbentrop; Colonel Casimir François de La Rocque and Jacques Doriot, leaders of the two largest Fascist and anti-Semitic organizations; and Laval, who already symbolized "collaboration with the New Order," whose intrigues and negotiations with Mussolini and Franco were known, and whose intrigues and negotiations with Hitler were suspected. Moreover, the French people saw that every true patriot in public office refused to support Pétain and his government—not only Communists and Socialists, but also conservatives and liberals, such as Jeanneney, President of the Senate; Louis Marin, disciple of Poincaré and leader of the French conservatives; Champetier de Ribes, head of the Catholic group of the Democrates Populaires, and Herriot, whose talent and thought incarnated so brilliantly the patriotic tradition of the French Revolution.

To their astonishment the French people saw Pétain slowly fill the most important posts of authority in local, departmental, and central administra-tions with men who had taken part in the Cagoulard plot, with those who had repeated the infamous refrain "rather Hitler than Léon Blum," and even with some of those who before or during the war had been arrested for treason-able domestic and foreign activities. The people were applying to the govern-ment the old proverb, "tell me who your friends are and I'll tell you who you are." They were alarmed to see Vichy employ for its most delicate missions Ferdinand de Brinon, Jean Montigny, Jean Goy, Jean Luchaire, and Gaston Henry-Haye—members of the Comité France-Allemagne, an organization which, before the war, had been inspired and financed by Otto Abetz, after 1940 Hitler's Ambassador in Paris. They learned with fury that on the night

17

of the armistice, when France was in mourning, Frenchmen and Frenchwomen of the aristocracy, high finance, and industry had drunk at Bordeaux to the defeat which had rid them of the nightmare of democracy and of the Popular Front. The people understood that the Fifth Column in France, as in Spain, had opened the door to Hitler's agents. And they watched with awe the agents of the Fifth Column become masters of France, the France of Pétain, Weygand, and Laval.

The new rulers of France soon realized the danger which was threatening them and their friends. To establish French Fascism, Fascism had to be rehabilitated; to suppress democracy, democracy had to be dishonored. To achieve its ends, the Vichy government had to "preserve the honor of the Army," and save the honor of the French friends and accomplices of Hitler and Mussolini. The scapegoats would be useful not only to mask the *military* errors of Pétain, Weygand, and their generals, but also to cover up the *political* crimes of Laval and his accomplices. Because the French grumbled "we have been betrayed by Hitler's agents and deceived by the partisans of Fascism," the Vichy propaganda had to repeat incessantly: "The traitors are not the men you accuse. Hitler's partisans are good patriots, friends of peace, as the partisans of Fascism are good citizens, friends of order; but you have been precipitated into war and deceived by those democrats who were blinded by the hate of Fascism and dominated by Judeo-Communist influences." By every means, the reality of Fascist treachery had to be replaced by the legend of democratic irresponsibility.

"Overwhelm the Leaders of the Popular Front"

Like Balzac's *peau de chagrin,* the list of scapegoats for the defeat necessarily grew smaller and smaller. After passing from military men to civilians, Vichy passed from political men in general to anti-Fascists in particular. To choose political men known for their anti-Fascist activities was to attack the ministers of the Popular Front. By a series of deductions and calculations that had nothing to do with justice, but in which were involved the lowest tricks of political *combinazione,* Marshal Pétain decided that it was a political necessity to lay the blame for the defeat on the Popular Front. His decision, however, revealed a lack of political sense, forcing the government into an impasse, from which the suspension of the Riom trial hardly extricated it. His decision also showed a certain shortsighted Machiavellism, a kind of small-town horse trader's shrewdness, in that he succeeded in imposing his views not only on the minds of Frenchmen favorable to Fascist ideas, but also on that part of Anglo-Saxon public opinion which was still unaware of the ideological unity of Pétain and Hitler.

It was evidently not a question of trying the Popular Front ministers as a group. Among these ministers, a small number, carried away by their ambitions or their pacifist illusions, felt the contagion of appeasement and participated in or applauded the request for an armistice; such were the cases of Camille Chautemps, former Premier, of Charles Spinasse, former Minister of National Economy, and of Paul Faure, former Minister of State and General Secretary of the Socialist party. The government of Vichy wanted to flatter these men in order to use them. Chautemps was entrusted with a mission to the United States; Faure was made a member of the Conseil National; Spinasse became the editor of a paper which proposed to reconcile Socialism and Pétainism—as Hitler had tried to reconcile Socialism and nationalism. The list of scapegoats had, therefore, to be carefully prepared.

Pétain and his ministers were spared the trouble of drawing up this list of victims. It had long been in existence, and the Fascist organizations merely handed it to the government—*their* government. The list of "the first political men to dispose of" in the event of a Fascist coup had been prepared by the authors of the Cagoulard plot. It included the names of men who were considered especially dangerous, those capable of organizing popular resistance to Fascism, and against whom the Fascists had sworn revenge. This list, a vertiable honor roll of French democracy, was shown to me in 1937 by Marx Dormoy, who had discovered the Cagoulard plot. On the list were: Léon Blum, Édouard Daladier, Pierre Cot, Jean Zay, Marius Moutet, César Campinchi—all Popular Front ministers; to these names were added the leaders of the Confédération Générale du Travail, the great French labor union—chiefly Léon Jouhaux, Racamond, Costes, Doury, and Neumeyer; and the leaders of the Communist party—particularly Maurice Thorez, Jacques Duclos, Gabriel Peri, Ramette, Guyot, and Cachin. We were to be the Cagoule's first victims. After Munich, the Cagoulards added Paul Reynaud and Georges Mandel, who deserved this honor because of their anti-Hitlerian policy.

What has become of the men on the list? To understand the Riom trial this question must have an answer, and the answer throws a tragic light on the indictment of Blum, Daladier, and myself. The Vichy government has tracked down and pursued all those whom the Cagoule—in the words used by Maurras in *l'Action Française*—promised to "destroy like dogs," and has thus carried out the dirty work of the Cagoulards.

Jouhaux, the chief of the C. G. T., and the leaders of the Communist party could not be brought before the Court of Riom because they had not held governmental posts; hence other methods of "liquidation" were employed. Jouhaux was placed "under the surveillance of the police"—that is, he was arrested and held without trial. Communists who were caught were thrown into concentration camps. After Hitler's attack on Russia, the principal Communist leaders—Péri, Semard, Sampaix, and others—were handed over to the Gestapo and massacred, and prices were put on the heads of Thorez, Ramette, Duclos, and Guyot. Since Mandel and Reynaud had neither belonged to Popular Front cabinets nor had been Ministers of National Defense, an infamous accusation was used for their arrest: that of having speculated with the national currency and of having misappropriated public funds. Dormoy was assassinated. Zay was condemned, under pretext of desertion, to ten years in prison. Moutet was about to be arrested, when a friend warned him and he had time to flee. The indictment of Campinchi was difficult, since all his acts as Minister of the Navy bore the signature of Admiral Darlan, an important member of the Vichy government; Campinchi died at Marseille from an operation. Blum, Daladier, and I were accused of having betrayed the duties of our offices, and Marshal Pétain declared us responsible for the defeat of France.

If the reader reflects on these facts, if he consults the Fascist and pro-Fascist newspapers from February 6, 1934, to June 17, 1940, it will become obvious that the motive for accusing us was vengeance. Blum, Daladier, and I organized the Popular Front with the leaders of the Communist party. Without us, the Popular Front would not have existed, and without the Popular Front, the Republic would have been overthrown before 1940. If we were named scapegoats for a defeat in which Fascism played a decisive part, it was not because of the inadequacy of French military preparation during the rule of the Popular Front; it was because we defended democracy, denounced the criminal activities of the Fascist organizations, and created the Popular Front to oppose them more successfully.

My statement is easily proved. The Popular Front government was organized in June, 1936; on this date according to Marshal Pétain and the Prosecuting Attorney's list of charges at the Court of Riom, our so-called injurious activity to the interests of national defense began. But the hate of the Fascist organizations and the fury of the Fascist newspapers had been directed against us long before this time, and our arrest and sentence had been demanded from February 6, 1934 on. Why this particular date? Because on that date, a mob led and inspired by the Fascist organizations, particularly l'Action Française and the Croix de Feu, had tried to invade the Chamber of Deputies, form a provisional government, and overthrow the republican regime. Blum, Daladier, and I had organized the opposition to this Fascist coup. The 6th of February has become a historic date in the war between Fascism and democracy. Since then we have been the men most hated by the Fascist organizations and by the French disciples of Hitler and Mussolini. Long before the Popular Front government could have concerned itself with national defense, our fate was sealed, and Fascist newspapers thus early called for our trial by a political tribunal, even for our assassination.

"To the gallows with Léon Blum, Daladier, and Pierre Cot! Death to the assassins of February 6th! To the High Court with Léon Blum, Daladier, and Pierre Cot!" How often were those words spoken and printed between February, 1934, and June, 1936! According to l'Action Française, Gringoire, Le Jour, and other Fascist and reactionary papers, we were "assassins" and "executioners"; I was a "bloody scamp," Daladier a "killer," Blum a "hyena." Maurras, today Pétain's political adviser, ordered his partisans to "prepare their carving knives" for us. Fascist hatred had reached its climax before June, 1936, nor did the manner in which, after that date, we prepared the national defense increase it. In fact, I received more threats and endured more attacks between 1934 and 1936 than between 1936 and 1940. Had Fascism triumphed in France before its power was broken by the Popular Front, Blum, Daladier, and I would have been tried or assassinated. We would not then have been blamed for failing to give the French Army necessary weapons; some other pretext would have been found.

As it was, however, Vichy had to bring us before its Supreme Court of Justice and demand our conviction. Its political philosophy and the exigencies of its partisans forced it either to organize a judicial parody or to have us assassinated.

To understand the imperative character of this obligation, the place held by the Vichy government on the French political chessboard in July, 1940, must be considered. Marshal Pétain had the confidence of Hitler and of the Fascist and reactionary groups. But the governmental team which surrounded him was, in the eyes of the authentic Fascists, a group of amateurs, not of professionals. General Weygand, Admiral Darlan, the civil servants, and the bankers around them, and Laval himself, had remained in the background during the political battles of 1934 and 1936. They were known to be hostile to democracy and partisans of an authoritarian regime, but during the growth of the Popular Front, they had encouraged the soldiers of the Fascist cause only as the old men of Troy had encouraged the soldiers of Priam, from high up on the wall. They did not have the political experience of a Doriot, a De la Rocque, or a Maurras, veterans of the anti-democratic struggle.

The old-guard Fascists had the impression that they were being used to pull the chestnuts out of the fire for the generals, industrialists, and politicians who composed Marshal Pétain's government. The governmental team, therefore, had to make itself acceptable to the French Fascist leaders on whom it depended to organize the police and to recruit the guards for their concentration camps, the personnel for their youth camps. To obtain their co-operation, it was necessary to pay, and as it is easier in Fascist countries to persecute innocents than to carry out a program, Vichy ordered the Riom Court to condemn us. To establish authority over its partisans, the Vichy government had to throw Christians to the lions; consequently, it had to accuse them of having burned Rome.

The hate which the Fascists had sworn against the leaders of the Popular Front after February 6, 1934, as well as the fear of defeated generals—apprehensive of blame—was thus at the bottom of the Riom trial.

THE HATE OF THE FRENCH FASCISTS AND REACTIONARIES

I have often pondered the causes of this hate. I have tried to fathom the state of mind of the French Fascists, which, for a democrat, is as difficult to do

21

as it is for a civilized man to understand the state of mind of Hottentots. I have wondered why I became, with Daladier and Blum—and perhaps even more than they—their *bête noire*. I have tried to discover by what chain of circumstances I earned "either this excess of honor or this indignity." If I now offer the result of my reflections, it is not to give a résumé of my political life; it is because a brief study of the role of hatred in contemporary French politics seems essential to an understanding of these politics. For such a study my "case," as a French diagnostician or an Anglo-Saxon lawyer would say, is characteristic. I could take as well the cases of Blum or Daladier; but I shall reserve that analysis for the account of the Riom hearings. Moreover, in examining my own political career, introspection will, I believe, aid rather than hamper me.

Before proceeding, however, I must make two general observations. The first is a simple paraphrase of Clemenceau's biting quip: "The men of the Right are easy to recognize; they are not only stupid but the wickedest." The violence of the Right appears throughout contemporary political history. The French are a civilized people, but we need only think for a moment of the past to understand that this civilization is the product of a long effort and conceals a latent violence—the horrors of the wars of religion, the excesses of the revolutionary period, the cruelties of the White Terror, the bloody punishment of the Communards by the Versailles generals in 1871. We know from experience that since the French Revolution hate has been the almost exclusive prerogative of the extreme Right—hate, and its sister, injustice. The French worker is naturally good; the peasant is naturally indifferent; but, on the whole, the French bourgeois is naturally egotistical and cruel. In 1871, when the Commune of Paris, which held its power from the majority of the people, was conquered by the army of Versailles, 100,000 workers fell; the workers' population of Paris was reduced by 30 per cent; 20,000 men, women, and children were executed without trial by the soldiers of Marshal Mac-Mahon and General de Gallifet. It was the greatest slaughter in French history; the massacre of St. Bartholomew had claimed only 5,000 victims, and the French Revolution, during the Terror, fewer than 10,000.

"The men of the Right are wicked," and, even under the Third Republic, their wickedness had opportunities to show itself. Not to speak of the Dreyfus case and the cloud of anti-Semitism which descended on France at that time, we may recall that Combes and Jaurès, before the last war, and Briand and Herriot, in the post-war period, were prey to the most disgusting attacks from the conservative and reactionary press. If we except certain German periodicals which helped prepare Hitler's advent, I can think of nothing more vile than the files of *l'Action Française* since the beginning of the twentieth century, or those of *Gringoire* in the last decade. Poincaré himself, yes, Poincaré, the conservative and nationalist, because he had committed the crime of being a republican, did not escape the foul slanders of Léon Daudet and Maurras. It has always been an honor in France, occasionally a sad honor, to be the opponent of the nationalists and reactionaries. The best champions of democracy have known this honor, and some, like Jaurès and Salengro, have died for it.

My second observation is based on a phrase in one of Harold Laski's recent books: "The basis of Fascism is hate."* Every time that Fascism or its related doctrines have developed in a country, political hatred has risen to fever pitch. I leave open the question whether Fascism is the cause rather than the effect of hate. The fact remains that Fascism makes use of hate and that hate alone creates the atmosphere essential to its growth. Fascism, as Laski points out, has always been directed or utilized by shameless adventurers with no scruples, and the substitution of instinct for reason in political thought and public opinion explains why Fascism engenders so much hate. No one has more successfully appealed to instinct than Hitler—national instinct, race instinct, corporative instinct, professional instinct; no one has so bitterly mocked the superiority of reason and the dignity of the individual. Fascism is a far less developed doctrine than democracy or Communism, both of which are based on reason. Fascism evokes primitive instincts, and the primitive man always gives personal forms to his feelings, symbols, and myths. The gods of primitive peoples are gods of flesh and blood, gods with beards, holding thunderbolts. Similarly, Fascist catechisms teach boundless admiration of the chief, devotion to his person, and hatred for his enemies. The Fascist, like the savage, must love and hate, whereas civilized men must think and understand. We must not be astonished to find so much hatred in the disciples of Doriot and the partisans of Pétain; if they did not hate their opponents so violently, they would not be such good Fascists.

During my political career I saw hate grow among Rightist political organizations. Why? Simply because my career developed from 1928 to 1940, the period when the conservative bourgeoisie was being corrupted by Fascist theories. When I entered Parliament, French reaction was still kin to liberalism; in 1940 it was Fascist. Yet in 1928 the men of the Right were already wicked men. At that time, to be sure, hate was cultivated systematically only by the partisans of l'Action Française. This was natural, since Maurras' doctrine, in Mussolini's own words, was one of the bases of Fascism. Not until February 6, 1934, were the cruelty and brutality so characteristic of Fascism grafted on to the natural "wickedness" of the Right. Colonel de la Rocque and the members of his Croix de Feu adopted Hitler's methods as best they could. They began to hunt republicans, Socialists, and Communists. It was impossible to hold a public meeting in a large city without running the risk of attacks, fights, stabbings, shootings, and, often, fatal brawls, provoked by organizations of the extreme Right.

I speak from personal experience, having been attacked several times. In 1935, at Aix-les-Bains, the hall in which I was speaking was raided by the Fascists, who wounded several people and threw an acid grenade at me in an attempt to blind me; I was hit in the ear, and have been slightly deaf ever

* Harold Laski, *Reflections on the Revolution of Our Time* (New York: Viking Press, 1943).

23

since. In February, 1936, Blum was attacked by Royalists during the funeral procession of Jacques Bainville, one of their leaders. He suffered a head injury and would have been killed, had it not been for the intervention of bricklayers working nearby. Shortly afterward, a democratic deputy, Elbel, was attacked and lost an eye. I could multiply these examples and quote the Fascist newspapers' calls to violence and murder. *Cui bono?* Finding a fertile soil in the traditions of the French Right, hate, as an epiphenomenon of Fascism, grew freely and rapidly.

It appears that the German soldiers were surprised to find so much brutality in the French disciples of Hitler who welcomed them in June, 1940. Let us hope that the French Fascists have not attained the degree of sadism, the enjoyment of cruelty, and the technical perfection in applying torture that characterize the agents of Heinrich Himmler. I want to believe, with all my heart, that even those Frenchmen whom the Fascist passion has led furthest astray will always be revolted by these degrading methods. But certain refugees who have escaped from concentration camps, certain Spaniards obliged by the Vichy government to work on the construction of the Dakar railroad, have stated that they were as severely treated by Vichy's jailers as by Hitler's. Whether it be German or French, Fascism always brings out the worst instincts of human nature; it rapidly demoralizes those who abandon themselves to its perversion.

The Case Against Me

In reviewing a career which attracted so much Fascist hatred, I will summon up my years of battle. Perhaps I shall not state the most important things, for a man is generally the poorest judge of matters relating to his own life, but I shall state what seem to be the most important. I shall speak of the things to which I dedicated my best energies, of the ideals which I upheld, and of the obstacles I encountered. I do not ask for approbation, but for understanding. I do not say, "I was right"; I say, "this is what I did."

For more than twenty-five years I have studied or practiced politics. I was thirty-two in 1928 when I was elected a member of the Chamber of Deputies, a post which I held until June, 1940, without interruption, re-elected regularly by strong majorities in Savoy. I did not enter public life unprepared. As Professor of Public Law and International Public Law, I had taught certain branches of political science, which I applied later as a member of Parliament and of the cabinet. After four years at the front in the first World War, I had finished my studies at the Universities of Grenoble and Paris, receiving the titles of Doctor of Laws and Doctor of Political and Economic Sciences; having completed certain research projects at the Thiers Foundation, I had been accepted at the Concours d'Agregation des Facultés de Droit et des Sciences Politiques, which gave me the right to teach in a French University. I had been, in turn, professor at the University of Rennes and attorney at the Court of

Appeals in Paris. Then Poincaré, who had become interested in me (probably because I opposed him), asked me to work with him as a member of the Judicial Committee in the Foreign Affairs Department. Some years later I had the opportunity, as a specialist in Public Law, to take part in studies that dealt with certain administrative reforms undertaken by the Ministry of the Interior. Thus I was able, before entering Parliament, to observe the machinery of French administration.

It was, in part, through family tradition that I entered politics. My father and grandfather, who belonged to the petite bourgeoisie of Savoy, had fought for the Republic at a time when this required courage. In the language of their time, which has changed little in France, both were "Reds," which meant democrats, fighting against the "Whites," which meant royalists and reactionaries. Both had held various elective posts in Savoy. At the time of the Dreyfus affair, my father fought against clericalism; but he died in 1900, when I was only five years old, and my very pious mother gave me a Catholic education. Thus in my origin was that double tradition, the contradiction of which explains the political history of the French people.

When I entered Parliament, the democratic ideal of the French Revolution dominated my thought. I was elected deputy under the banner of the Radical-Socialist party, the democratic party whose chief inspirer was Herriot. Our ideas corresponded, in general, to those which the American New Deal was to present some years later. We were confirmed democrats, who saw the solution to post-war problems in a pacific extension of the democratic principle to social, political, and international problems. There was more idealism than realism in this desire. We underestimated the power of the reactionary forces in France and in the world. We did not realize how much the evolution of capitalism had already weakened democracy. We had read the works of Marx, but we had not understood them. There was a good deal of childishness in our political concepts.

What attracted me to Parliament was foreign rather than domestic policy. I had no taste for electoral committees or for party quarrels. The war had developed in me, as in many men of my generation, a profound horror of nationalism and militarism; we put our faith in the development of international institutions and the League of Nations. I had taken part in the activities of the Institute of International Law at the Hague and of the School of International Relations at Geneva, directed by Professor Alfred Zimmern. With all the ardor of youth, I believed (as I do today) in the necessity and possibility of international collaboration. Those who have not lived through this period, who did not participate in the first efforts—I was going to say babblings—of the League of Nations, cannot understand the enthusiasm which at that time animated the young professors, students, and statesmen (Beneš and Titulescu were then less than forty years old!) who, after the first World War, tried to realize the great dream of the soldiers and peoples of all nations: peace and disarmament.

Such was my state of mind when I was first elected representative from

Savoy to the Chamber of Deputies. I soon became interested in the administrative side of public life. From 1928 to 1940 I was not only a member of the Chamber of Deputies, but also mayor of my little mountain village and *conseiller général* of Savoy. The exercise of these functions was my real school of political science, and I maintain that a man cannot govern a state if he has not previously been trained in the practice of local government. In Parliament my political activity was concentrated on international affairs.

In 1929 Aristide Briand named me a member of the French delegation to the League of Nations, a post in which I remained for four years. I was also a delegate to the Disarmament Conference. In 1932 I was appointed Undersecretary of State for Foreign Affairs in the Paul-Boncour cabinet. In 1933 I became Minister of Aviation, and it was in that post that I witnessed the French Fascists' uprising of February 6, 1934. After February the 6th I participated in the democratic opposition to the Doumergue cabinet (in which Pétain was Minister of War), and later to the Flandin and Laval cabinets. It was during this time (1934-1936) that the Popular Front was conceived. After the elections of 1936 I became a member of the Popular Front cabinet and again took part in the government of France until the beginning of 1938; at that time I refused to enter the Daladier cabinet, of whose foreign and economic policy I disapproved. Thus, in the course of my political career, I was a member of seven different cabinets.

The hatred of the reactionaries, and later of the Fascists, was aroused against me by the accidental circumstances of my parliamentary and governmental career more than by the development of my political thought, which moved constantly toward the Left.

My political thought, as I have said, was founded on the principles of the French Revolution. I cannot describe or even summarize it here. I have always believed that the principles of the French Revolution were the best expression of the political genius of the French nation. I saw in that Revolution a period of grandeur and nobility such as France had never known before and has never known since. I thought the principles of the Revolution had to be developed and applied to the problems of modern life. I did not consider them fixed and lifeless formulae, but seeds cast into the hearts and brains of men, seeds whose growth must bring harvests, ever richer and more fruitful. I thought that economic and international democracy had to be added to political democracy. The more deeply I plumbed the heart of French politics, the more fully did I realize that there could be no political or international democracy without economic democracy. The richer my administrative and governmental experience became, the more I was convinced that universal suffrage alone was insufficient for the realization of the ideal of the French Revolution, that social equality must be the cornerstone of political liberty, and that the economic structure of society must be changed to build a true democracy.

For twelve years, in French and international public life, I fought for these ideas. In the course of this fight I encountered a resistance all the more strong, since I not only opposed doctrines, but challenged powerful interests. I have seen the slow paralysis of the democratic state through the play of economic forces, or rather through the use made of economic power by those who controlled that power. If I look back over my own past, if I reflect on the most recent periods of the battle which the forces of progress and the forces of reaction have been fighting for centuries in France, I find so many reasons for the French Fascists and conservatives to hate me that I am hardly surprised to find their propaganda pursuing me even into exile. The heirs of those who urged the assassination of Jaurès, the admirers of the assassination of Matteoti, and the murderers of the Roselli brothers and of Marx Dormoy could not leave me in peace. I have disturbed them in the past and I continue to disturb them now. They know that in spite of their calumnies, popular elements in France do not consider me one of the men responsible for the French defeat, but merely a man who has fought on every front in the struggle against Fascism. I have united all reactionaries against me, because I did my best to unite all popular elements against them. To justify this general statement, I should like to show in what manner I deserve the fury of the French nationalists, the rancor of the large capitalist organizations, the rage of the European dictators, and, finally, the hatred of the Fascists who support the Vichy government.

Opposition to the French Nationalists

I aroused the anger of the French nationalists in the very first years of my political activity. In their eyes, my chief crimes were my desire to have France aid the German Weimar Republic, and my work to make the Disarmament Conference a success.

In 1928 I belonged to that group of Frenchmen who thought that the peace of the world was in a large measure dependent on the reconciliation of French and German democratic forces. This was Briand's program. The reconciliation was difficult; it encountered serious obstacles on both sides of the Rhine, chiefly those of nationalism. If the German nationalists, supported and financed by German heavy industry, thought only of revenge, the French nationalists, supported and financed by their own heavy industry, thought only of profit. The former wanted to destroy by violence the most legitimate clauses of the Versailles Treaty, while the latter tried to enforce its most absurd provisions.

The Versailles Treaty deserved neither the excessive criticism nor the dangerous fetishism which surrounded it. It was an imperfect work, therefore perfectible; it contained good and bad elements, based rather on economic and psychological ignorance than on viciousness or perversity. It was a mediocre treaty. By a loyal and progressive application of the League of Nations Pact, the treaty could have been amended and made to evolve toward the complete reconciliation of the former belligerents. To this end, however, precautions should have been taken against the imperialism of the Junkers and the nationalism of the Comité Français des Forges. To cite a few examples without going into details, it would have been necessary to put into operation the procedures of Article 16 of the League of Nations Pact (which foresaw collective sanctions against an aggressor), of Article 8 (which foresaw general and controlled disarmament), and of Article 19 (which foresaw the peaceful reconsideration of treaties that might become inapplicable, and of international situations endangering the peace of the world). Similarly, it would have been necessary to wipe the reparations slate clean, because the existence of that problem alone threatened the economic and financial equilibrium of Europe. All that would have been possible, had there been the will to do it.

A program of collaboration between French and German democrats, based on a reciprocal understanding of political and economic realities, was certainly more reasonable and more in the interest of France than the follies recommended by the French nationalists. But this would not only have wounded the nationalists' vanity, it would also have menaced their interests. Those whom the public called "cannon merchants" had no desire to see a policy of international collaboration and controlled limitation of national armaments replace a policy of huge war budgets and, therefore, of huge profits. Their interests coincided with those of the military class, which, in every country, desired the maintenance and development of permanent armies. What they wanted was not war, for they feared the revolutions which wars might engender, but the threat of war. A certain degree of international tension, supplied by Franco-German rivalry, was essential for their profits. I remember that Briand once said: "A battleship, to me and the common people, is a man-of-war, but I know persons to whom a battleship is one billion francs: three hundred millions in raw materials, three hundred millions in work, and three hundred millions in profits—and these last three hundred millions are worth defending."

Using the worst demagogical method, fear, the French nationalists sabotaged any rapprochement between France and the Weimar Republic, when such a rapprochement might have succeeded. At their instigation, France refused to give Chancellor Gustav Stresemann and Dr. Heinrich Brüning what she later gave Hitler. The partisans of reconciliation with the German democrats were dragged through the mud by those same men who were to become the agents of the Fifth Column and the partisans of collaboration. Because we demanded the fair application of the League of Nations Pact, including the article relating to the reconsideration of treaties, our patriotism was questioned. All the advocates of the League—Herriot, Paul-Boncour, Jouvenel, Blum, and especially Briand—were accused of jeopardizing the security of their country. If I was one of those more bitterly attacked, it was merely because, being younger, I took a more active part and gave my thought a more trenchant and less prudent expression.

My second crime, according to nationalist rules, was still greater. The attacks of the nationalists, militarists, and journalists inspired by the cannon merchants reached their culmination when I participated in the Disarmament

Conference as member of the French delegation, as Undersecretary of State for Foreign Affairs, and finally as Minister of Aviation. The work of the Conference was directed by Arthur Henderson, whose deputy was Philip Noel Baker, now a member of the Churchill cabinet. I proposed a project of aerial disarmament which implied the suppression of national air forces, the control of commercial airplanes (to avoid their being used as bombers), and the creation of an International Air Force under the control of the League of Nations. I believed, and I still believe, that this plan would render war impossible. The project met with the opposition of the French General Staff, and General Weygand, its chief, protested against my activities to Daladier, then Minister of War, who told him to keep his mind on war preparations and not to meddle with the country's foreign policy.

A few months later I created a scandal by proposing that the French delegation support a project submitted by the American delegation for the suppression of "offensive arms"; General Requin, our military expert (whom we shall meet again at the Riom trial), declared that there were no "offensive arms" and that, at any rate, heavy cannon and tanks were "defensive arms." I caused further scandal by supporting Litvinoff's definition of aggression. The hate of the General Staff and of the nationalists for me reached its climax in the spring of 1933. The only member of the French government present at Geneva, I thought it necessary to make Hitler unmask his batteries by suggesting a reasonable proposal in which the question of disarmament was bound to that of control. In a speech before the plenary meeting of the Conference, I asked that France and Germany agree to have short-term armies, organized on the model of the Swiss militia; such armies being truly democratic, their organization would have led to the disappearance of the military castes which have been a danger in Europe for so long.

I had, of course, obtained the approval of Daladier, President of the Council, and Paul-Boncour, Minister of Foreign Affairs, before making this proposition. My speech provoked the rage of the Hitlerian and Fascist press. As I was still young in French politics, I was surprised to note that the rage of the French nationalist papers far surpassed that of the German press. The most violent attacks appeared in the *Journal des Debats,* a paper controlled by the Comité des Forges, whose foreign policy was inspired by the notorious De Brinon, the friend of von Ribbentrop and Abetz, and *l'Echo de Paris,* a conservative paper representing the policy of the General Staff. Daladier informed me by telephone, the day after my speech, that General Weygand again had protested against my attitude, saying it "ran the risk of making possible an agreement on the question of disarmament."

To support the cause of general and controlled disarmament and the organization of an International Air Force, it was necessary to contend not only with German ability but the stupidity of the French military men. Within the French delegation itself, my influence was secretly opposed by certain military experts who preferred to follow the instructions of General Weygand rather than those of the government. Other experts, more aware of international problems and less provincial in their outlook, believed in the necessity of settling the disarmament question. Among the latter was an officer of the Corps de Controle, Controller-General Jacomet, a specialist in financial and administrative problems, who contended that international control of armaments could be organized. He put forward an extremely ingenious project which the Subcommittee of Control had adopted. This adoption deprived the French General Staff of its best pretext for refusing to agree to armament reduction. Weygand has since nourished a profound hatred for Jacomet, whom he accused of "betraying the cause of the Army." Jacomet was brought before the Court of Riom in 1942, and I am convinced that Weygand's hatred was one of the principal reasons for his indictment. As the French proverb goes: "Vengeance is a dish that is eaten cold."

Thus, from 1933 on, through my activity in Parliament and at the League of Nations, I have succeeded in antagonizing Hitler and in attracting the fury not only of Weygand but of the cannon merchants and the French nationalists.

Opposition to the Capitalist Monopolies

The anger of the capitalist organizations was soon added to the fury of the nationalists. These organizations have played an increasingly important part in French public life during the last twenty years; they have subsidized all Fascist and pro-Fascist movements and they have inspired and paid for the campaigns directed against those statesmen who, faithful to the democratic doctrines, tried to realize the will of the people. Herriot, whose efforts in 1924 and 1925, to use his own words, "were smashed on the wall of silver," experienced, before Blum, the political power of French capitalism.

As in all preceding economic regimes, capitalism has had its advantages and its disadvantages; it has constituted an important stage in the history of humanity. But, like every other economic regime and every other institution, capitalism obeys the law of evolution. During the period 1920-1940 the evolution of capitalism—substituting great business combines for free competition and thus favoring the concentration of capital and the development of private monopolies and trusts—constituted, without doubt, a danger to democracy. To study the importance of this danger to French democracy, one need not resort to Marxist theories; it suffices to observe, without prejudice, the functioning of French governmental and administrative institutions. In the recent past the mechanism of these institutions became more and more impaired by the weight of great economic concentrations, which operated in three directions.

First, French economic life was dominated by a powerful financial oligarchy, at the top of which was the Bank of France. A beneficiary of privileges which went back to Napoleon, the Bank of France was the absolute master of public and private credit. The State was obliged to bow before its requirements to meet the needs of its Treasury, and the Bank of France, even more than Parliament, had the power to make and break cabinets and ministers. Not only Herriot and Blum, but Clemenceau and Flandin had pointed out the Bank's abuse of power. Second, public opinion, basis of a democratic regime, was not expressed, because 90 per cent of the newspapers and radio stations were under the control of the capitalist organizations. These organizations were occasionally competitors, but they were always united, by virtue of a "gangsters' agreement," when there was a question of fighting the social or international policy of democratic governments. Before the official censorship of the Vichy government, the French press had known the unofficial censorship of the Havas Agency. Third, the mass of French workers—badly protected against the abuses of their employers until 1936—was threatened more and more by unemployment, while the mass of artisans, small producers, and small businessmen was rendered more and more powerless by the pressure of trusts and monopolies. These groups no longer enjoyed that minimum of social security and independence essential to the operation of democratic institutions. For all these reasons, obvious to anyone who knew French life before the war, the State and the individual, the two poles of democracy, were steadily losing their independence and their liberty.

If I had confined myself to a denunciation in general terms of the contra-diction between French political democracy and French capitalism, if I had asked for State control over the economic life of the country, or even the transformation of the social regime, I would have found myself in the same situation as most Socialists and democrats; my ideas would have irritated rather than disturbed the capitalist profiteers who knew their own power. Their irri-tation became anxiety, then hate, when circumstances led me to apply the democratic doctrine. Within a few years I had occasion to commit two crimes in the eyes of the French capitalists: I had caused a few of their leaders to be imprisoned and I had suppressed certain of their sources of profit by the "nationalization" of the aeronautic industries. Let us examine these crimes.

It was partly chance which led me, from the very first months of my govern-mental career, to take a position against certain capitalist interests. In Febru-ary, 1933, I succeeded the great mathematician Paul Painlevé as Minister of Aviation. Painlevé was very ill and died some months later. While he had been in office, he had decided to expose a scandal which was beginning to preoccupy political and aeronautic circles—the scandal of the Aéropostale, an aerial navigation company connecting South America and France. Thanks to the courage of its pilots—who included Mermoz and Saint-Exupéry—this company had written numerous glorious pages in the golden book of French aviation. That it had rendered France great services it would be unjust to deny. But the enterprise had fallen into the hands of a financial group which was more powerful than scrupulous. The directors of this group belonged to one of the most authentic of the "200 Families," the Bouilloux-Lafonts. Their power derived from their political connections as well as from their wealth and undeniable cleverness. One of the Bouilloux-Lafonts was Vice-Presi-dent of the Chamber of Deputies, and Aéropostale had as its lawyer Pierre-

Étienne Flandin, former Minister of Finance, future Premier, future admirer of Hitler, and future Minister in the Vichy government. The financial administration of the Aéropostale showed certain irregularities, which its directors hoped to cover up by using their political connections and their savoir-faire. They encountered an obstacle in the conscience of a civil servant of the Aviation Ministry, M. Emmanuel Chaumié, Director of Commercial Aviation, who has since died in an airplane accident. To get rid of this obstacle, the directors of the Aéropostale attempted to dishonor Chaumié by using a grossly fabricated forgery. Painlevé defended Chaumié, who was exonerated. When I became Minister of Aviation, one of the directors of the Aéropostale was liable to prosecution before the *Cour d'Assises* for forgery, and others to prosecution before the *Tribunal Correctionnel* for various misdemeanors committed in the administration of the enterprise.

I did no more than my duty. I felt no animosity toward the Bouilloux-Lafonts, but I refused all requests to let the affair be "fixed." A crime is a crime; the rich and powerful should be judged in the same way as the weak and poor; and justice, according to Chancellor d'Aguesseau, should be given "according to laws and not according to men." I visited Painlevé in the little sickroom where this great scholar was still carrying on his research on the eve of his death. "Those people are very powerful," he told me, "but it is necessary to put an end to their machinations." The hand of justice fell on the guilty; they were convicted and sentenced. The Aéropostale was liquidated.

The directors of the Aéropostale served their sentences; they have paid their debt to society, and no one now has the right to attack them. I have spoken of this case only because it belongs to contemporary political history. It was the first time in French parliamentary history that a young minister had brought into court people holding such high places in the triple hierarchy of money, society, and politics. This hierarchy has never forgiven me. For many of its members, the scandal consisted not in the commission of the crime, but in the prosecution of the criminals. By demanding the application of the regulations of the Code, I had violated the rules of the game, according to which a criminal of a certain class is not a real criminal. This was made very clear to me. Painlevé was right. Those people were powerful.

The Aéropostale affair obliged the administration to reconsider, in its entirety, the problem of commercial aviation. The major scandal of the Aéropostale had its counterpart in the minor scandals of certain other air lines. Beneficiaries of concessions and subsidies, these companies had organized a vast network of private monopolies which permitted them, without running any risks, to earn great profits to the detriment of the state. A law, passed several years before, which I had helped to draft as a member of the Aeronautic Commission, permitted the government to institute reforms. In spite of the resistance of private interests and the attacks of the press, this law gave me power to organize a national company, uniting all French air lines under state control. This was the Compagnie Air-France, whose establishment saved the state several tens of millions annually, and became the statement of a primary formula of "nationalization." The Compagnie Air-France was the first attempt in France to create a company jointly financed by private stockholders and the state; it was an imperfect experiment, but certainly superior to private monopoly. This formula has at present been outgrown by events; but in 1933 it constituted a political and economic innovation, and the big capitalist organizations understood what this threat meant to their interests.

At this point I should like to address some parenthetical remarks to the American public. American democrats have such deep affection for economic freedom that they generally oppose state intervention in the economic domain. I do not intend to discuss their point of view. I should simply like to point out that opposition to state intervention in the economic domain has always been less strong in Europe than in America for a very simple reason. American capitalism grew up under conditions different from European capitalism. Capitalism found in America liberty of space and possibilities of expansion which Europe lacked, so that, until very recently, American capitalism was still in its "pioneer" stages. European capitalism, however, grew up in small states with restricted frontiers, where monopolistic organization developed rapidly. We have had to choose between private monopoly with its abuses and public or state monopoly. In America it is possible to have several competing air lines because the clientele is large and the distances vast. The same situation would be impossible in France or Germany. Until now it has been possible, although difficult, to maintain the competitive system in America to a certain degree; in Europe it has become impossible.

I left the Ministry of Aviation in February, 1934. The capitalist organizations and big business were not sorry to see me go. In one year I had earned their hatred, first, by proposing to the League of Nations a project for the creation of an International Air Force and the suppression of national air forces, which had aroused the anger of the nationalists and of the cannon merchants; second, by having the courts convict certain influential members of one of the 200 Families; and third, by reforming commercial aviation through the substitution of a national company for private monopolies. During this year an Air Force, independent of the Army, had been organized. General Weygand had opposed this project, and on this count as well as on the others, the nationalist press set its dogs on me. The reader should by now begin to understand the "case" against me and to see why I reaped such a harvest of hate. In one year I had broken a record.

To explain more fully the anger of the great capitalist organizations, I must now turn to the "nationalizations" which the Ministry of Aviation practiced in 1936 and 1937.

In June, 1936, as a result of the general elections, a Popular Front government came into power in France. The Popular Front was the French version, *mutatis mutandis,* of the American New Deal; and the hostility of French capitalist circles to the Popular Front government can be gauged by recalling the hostility of American "big business" to leaders of the New Deal.

Nationalization of war industries played a part in the Popular Front program. I had taken part in the formulation of this program and in the orientation of public opinion. Nationalization was prompted by the desires of the country. It had been demanded not only by the Popular Front, but also by most of the political parties and by the war veterans' organizations. It was accomplished by a law which Chamber and Senate voted almost unanimously. By nationalizing the aircraft factories, I simply executed the mandate given me by Parliament, the legal interpreter of the will of the people.

The Ministry of Aviation applied in its nationalizations new formulae, which were considered good and were used later to nationalize the railroads and to organize the Compagnie du Rhône.

Opposition to European Fascism

And yet all these violations of the canons of capitalism were evidently my minor sins. If I had committed no other crimes and remained quiet, I might perhaps have found grace, not in the eyes of Marshal Pétain and General Weygand, but in the eyes of Laval and Flandin, who have, over those military men, the advantage of intelligence over stupidity. What made my case a hanging matter was my fight against Fascism, in both domestic and foreign policy. I have always been, and I remain, an unrepentant anti-Fascist; that is why I have always figured on the death lists of l'Action Française, the Croix de Feu, and the Cagoulards.

It was by taking part in the battle for collective security and the Franco-Soviet rapprochement that I opposed Hitler, Franco, and Mussolini.

The organization of collective security was the necessary extension of the League of Nations Pact. The League should not have limited its action to the organization of collective security; but it could not have been anything if it were not, first of all, a vast mutual-aid society, an association of nations binding themselves to respect and to apply international law. No society can exist without policemen, and the ancients were right to represent justice as a woman holding scales in one hand and a sword in the other. Just as force without justice is tyranny, so justice without force is utopia. "Force and justice must be joined," said Blaise Pascal. Full of these ideas, I asked, when Japan invaded Manchuria, that the French government take the initiative in bringing international sanctions against Japan by putting the French fleet at the disposal of China. André Tardieu, then Premier, laughed in my face.

After 1933 it was clear that Hitler's ambitions threatened the peace of Europe and of the world. Germany was well-equipped and heavily populated; therefore, if events required, it was necessary to be able to oppose her with the front of collective security. The establishment of this front depended on the participation of all peoples who did not accept the Fascist doctrine. Russia was in the front line of anti-Fascism. During the Disarmament Conference I had become friendly with Maxim Litvinoff, indefatigable champion of "indivisible peace"; had the democracies only listened to him, world peace would have been preserved. Invited to Russia by the Soviet government, I arrived in

Moscow in August, 1933, accompanied by a mission of military and technical experts, who were to study "the bases of a rapprochement between Soviet and French aviation." I was the first French minister to make an official trip to Soviet Russia, which followed an unofficial one that Herriot had just made. His visit had succeeded in dissipating certain Russian prejudices against the French Republic, prejudices that were only natural if one remembers France's aid, from 1918 to 1922, to all White Russian adventurers who fought against the young Soviets. Our aeronautic mission was greatly impressed by the industrial and military might of the Soviet Union. This was no superficial impression, for the mission included officers and engineers who could hardly be suspected of sympathizing with the Communist doctrines, such as General Barrès, Inspector-General of the Air Force, and M. H. Caquot, general director of aeronautic construction, member of the *Institut de France*.

To every honest man, it was apparent that the developing Soviet power was the only force that could be compared to the growing might of Hitler; to have Russia join the collective security movement was a decisive factor for peace. At the end of my trip the Soviet government asked me to transmit confidentially to the French government a proposition for the negotiation of a security pact. On our way to Paris we stopped at Prague, and Eduard Beneš, then Minister for Foreign Affairs of Czechoslovakia and the best political mind of the European democracies, greeted me with these words: "At last France has understood that the line of defense of her own security must pass through Moscow." The proposition of the Soviet government was the normal conclusion of my trip; the French government had obviously not sent one of its ministers and the highest authorities of the Air Force to Soviet Russia merely to give them an opportunity to eat caviar, drink vodka, and attend a magnificent ballet on the French Revolution. Hitler was right when he said that it was during the summer of 1933 that the first stones were laid for the Franco-Soviet Pact, which Louis Barthou was to negotiate in 1934, Pierre Laval to sign in 1935, the French Parliament to ratify in 1936, and Georges Bonnet to violate and wreck in 1938.

I laid the first stone, but Herriot remains the great champion and supporter of the Franco-Soviet Pact in France, as Litvinoff remains the initiator and father of the Pact. I was merely one of Herriot's co-workers in the daily political struggle to create a policy which alone was capable of offering solid resistance to Hitler. The purpose of this policy was not to "encircle" Germany, for neither Russia, France, nor Czechoslovakia ever intended to leap at the throat of the German people. The Pact was an instrument of peace; it threatened Germany only if Germany intended to threaten the peace of the world—that is, in the same way that the police, by their existence, threaten a bandit. I might also add that the French democrats who went to Russia were as impressed by the economic, social, and political achievements of that nation as by the spectacle of the Soviet armed force. No people, no regime, in the contemporary world has been able to realize an effort comparable to that of the Soviet Union. For my part, I have always believed that a synthesis of the spirit of the French and of the Russian Revolutions can give Europe a formula capable of renewing its political ideology and rejuvenating its democracies.

The military capacity of the Soviet Union was at that time of particular interest to the French nation; that it why we tried to negotiate and ratify the Franco-Soviet Pact and then to perfect this Pact by a military alliance. Russia wanted this alliance, which had been envisaged in the first negotiations, but certain elements of the French government opposed it, pretending that it was essential not to irritate Hitler. In the second part of this book we shall have occasion to examine the steps taken in 1936 and 1937 toward the military development of the Franco-Soviet Pact; and I shall tell what political and military authorities opposed these efforts.

Let us return now to the facts we were examining. Czechoslovakia formed, from the aerial point of view, a bridge or landing-stage between France and Russia. A network of military agreements, between France and Czechoslovakia on the one hand, and between Czechoslovakia and Russia on the other, was a substitute for the Franco-Russian alliance, which France obstinately refused. In 1936 and 1937 I did all I could to reinforce this network. Military agreements bound France to Czechoslovakia, and some of these agreements bore my signature. Hitler was not entirely wrong in accusing me, on the eve of Munich, of wanting to place Czechoslovakian bases at the disposal of French and Russian planes; he merely forgot that the object of these agreements was not to make an attack on Germany possible, but to let France, Czechoslovakia, and Russia put into operation the mechanism of collective security in the framework foreseen by the League of Nations Pact. Any French Minister of Aviation, mindful of the security of his country and appreciating the need for defense against Hitlerism, would, I think, have practiced the same policy. Given Hitler's plans against Czechoslovakia and the Ukraine, it was natural for him to consider me a dangerous opponent and to unleash his propaganda against me. The French pro-Fascist and reactionary press began to denounce me as an "enemy of peace," the "agent or accomplice of Stalin and Beneš," a "warmonger," and a "firebrand." It was understood that I was all these things, and Hitler a peaceful lamb.

It was not only my governmental activity in favor of the Franco-Soviet rapprochement that aroused the European dictators; Mussolini and Franco, in their turn, had specific reasons to resent me.

After 1935 the mass of the French people understood that the aggressive policy of the Fascist dictators was a menace to France and to peace. They felt as one with the victims of these aggressions, and knew that after Ethiopia, Austria, Spain, and Czechoslovakia, France ran the danger of suffering under the yoke of Fascism. They were far more patriotic and farsighted than those rich bourgeois whose hatred for the Soviet Union and concern with their immediate interests made them side with Hitler, Franco, and Mussolini.

I was taking an ever greater part in the action of the French anti-Fascists. In 1935, after Mussolini's invasion of Ethiopia, a committee was formed in

France for the defense of the Ethiopian people and the application of sanctions to Fascist Italy. This committee chose me as its president. At about the same time the various organizations which supported the cause of collective security decided to form a vast union of the pacifist forces, capable of mobilizing public opinion against the fomenters of international unrest. The "International Peace Campaign" came into being. Thanks to the activity of Louis Dolivet, today Executive Secretary of the Free World Association in New York and editor of the magazine of the same name, the I. P. C. became a great success; it soon included the Confédération Générale du Travail (which then mustered six million members), the Union Fédéral des Anciens Combattants (a war veterans' organization with a million and a half members), the associations for the League of Nations, all democratic organizations, etc. It extended beyond the frontiers of France. Groups of the I. P. C. were set up throughout Europe —except, of course, in the Fascist countries—in Soviet Russia, China, and India; the International Committee of the I. P. C. included the names of Mme. Chiang Kai-shek, Nehru of India, and J. M. Tchervnik, general secretary of the Russian trade-unions. I was elected co-president of the international organization with Lord Robert Cecil, whom I had met in Geneva at the League of Nations. We had participated together in many an international congress. From 1936 on I was closely associated with this man, one of the noblest figures in contemporary politics. There is nothing of which I am prouder than of the friendship which ties me to him. In 1937 he received the Nobel Peace Prize and never was a distinction more highly deserved. This great Englishman has given all his life, his activity, and his authority to the cause of peace among peoples and among men. Under his leadership the I. P. C. became the world's most active movement in favor of collective security. However, like the democracies, we were unable to prevent war, not because our principles were bad, but because in 1939 the forces of war were more powerful, although less numerous, than the forces of peace.

The Fascist dictators cannot forgive me for having been the defender and friend of the Spanish Republic. This was one of the charges brought against me by the Vichy government at the Court of Riom. When this activity is added to my activity at the head of the I. P. C. and to my work for Franco-Soviet rapprochement, it is obvious that I did my utmost to arouse the irritation of the European dictators and to deserve the hatred of the Fascists. There would have been no justice, in the Hitlerian sense of the term, if the Vichy government, when it inaugurated its policy of "collaboration with Hitler's New Order," had not declared me guilty of having "betrayed the duties of my office in the acts which determined the passing from a state of peace to a state of war." Either the responsibility for the European war falls on Hitler, or else it falls on the partisans of collective security and universal peace; and since there is no question of Vichy believing in the guilt of Hitler, I had to be included on the list of those responsible for the war.

Finally, I have deserved the hatred of the French Fascists on the same score as my friend Marx Dormoy, who was assassinated, and Roger Salengro, who was driven to suicide by an atrocious campaign of calumny. Even if I confine myself to the narrow field of French domestic policy, I cannot blame the Fascists for considering me their "public enemy number one."

Three events earned me this honor.

In the first place, I remain, for the French Fascists, one of the "assassins" of the 6th of February, 1934. On that day, the Fascists and pro-Fascist organizations, particularly l'Action Française, the Croix de Feu, and the Jeunesses Patriotes, had mobilized their troops and tried to invade the Chamber of Deputies. They used as a blind the notorious Stavisky affair—with which, incidentally, no member of the government then in power was accused of being involved. The immediate pretext was the government's dismissal of Jean Chiappe, Prefect of Police, who had at least equivocal relations with the swindler Stavisky. This displeased the Fascists, whose friend and protector Chiappe had been. The object of the demonstration, which quickly degenerated into a riot, was to force a cabinet which had the confidence of the Parliament, to resign and give way to a provisional government. This provisional government was to suppress democratic liberties in the name of "order" and to establish a so-called regime of authority. The Fascist uprising all but succeeded. The government's duty was to oppose this barefaced plan of replacing the power of Parliament by the power of the mob. The police tried to halt the attack of the demonstrators, and, to avoid being overwhelmed, had to resort to the use of arms. It took all necessary precautions not to spill blood uselessly; the mob comprised several hundreds of thousands, tightly packed; fewer than twenty were killed and about one hundred wounded. The nationalist press declared that the government had machine-gunned an unarmed crowd. A Parliamentary Committee of Inquiry, including members of extreme Rightist parties, established the baselessness of these accusations. But the Fascist organizations and the reactionary press tried to arouse public opinion against the "assassins of the 6th of February." Three names were denounced with particular violence: Daladier, President of the Council; Eugene Frot, Minister of the Interior; and Pierre Cot. Since then the Fascist organizations have pardoned Frot for having done his duty on the 6th of February as a reward for his support of Bonnet's policy of appeasement and of Vichy's policy of collaboration.

As Minister of Aviation, I obviously had nothing to do officially with the maintenance of order or the direction of the police. But I had already aroused the anger of the nationalists and the capitalists, and I was considered, rightly or wrongly, one of the die-hards of the cabinet; thus I was chosen— even then!—as a scapegoat. The charge was so fantastic that the Committee of Inquiry did not even ask me to appear as a witness. My part in the 6th of February had been limited to approving the government's action and recommending that the President of the Council and the Minister of the Interior use the means given them by law to put an end to the inflammatory campaigns of the monarchist and Fascist press. I had pointed out that the proclamation of a state of siege would permit the seizure of newspapers and the re-establishment of peace and order. My advice was not followed, and, on February 7th, the Daladier cabinet resigned. The Fascists had not overthrown the government, but they had nevertheless made their point, since the cabinet formed by Gaston Doumergue included men such as Laval, Flandin, Marquet (who was also to become one of Pétain's ministers), and Pétain himself. The Doumergue cabinet in 1934 was a preface to the Pétain government of 1940, and left the way open for the agitations of the Croix de Feu, at that time the largest of the Fascist groups. The chief, Colonel de la Rocque, together with the "victims" of February 6th swore to revenge themselves on Daladier, the other "assassins," and me.

In the second place, the French Fascists consider me one of the leaders of the Popular Front. The Popular Front was the spontaneous reaction of the French masses against Fascist agitation, the riposte to the "mobilizations" ordered by Colonel de la Rocque. By making me a symbol of the 6th of February, the Fascists destined me to become a symbol of the Popular Front. Convinced of the Fascist danger, I had been one of the first democrats to recommend the union of all anti-Fascist elements. I took part in the activities of the Popular Front, as did all the democratic and Socialist deputies of the same political generation: Zay (convicted and imprisoned by the Vichy government), Mendès-France (convicted and imprisoned), Dormoy (assassinated), Salengro (driven to suicide), Viennot (convicted and imprisoned by the Vichy government), Pierre Bloch (arrested and imprisoned by the German authorities), and many others, not to speak of the innumerable militant syndicalist and Communist workers on whom the hand of Vichy also has fallen.

In the third place, the French Fascists hold me partly responsible for the proceedings brought against the Cagoulards, whose plot against the state had been uncovered by the French police in 1937. The Cagoulards had borrowed their methods from Nazi terrorists and their costume from the Ku Klux Klan. They had formed a Secret Anti-Revolutionary Committee (C. S. A. R.), which received arms from Germany and from Italy; they perpetrated outrages (the bombing of the Quartier de l'Étoile) and murders (the assassination of the Roselli brothers), as a result of which their activities were in part discovered. I had to concern myself with the Cagoulards, because their propaganda had penetrated into aeronautic circles. One of the chief Cagoulards was General Dusseigneur of the Air Force. The judicial authorities decided to arrest and imprison him. I was asked—sometimes threateningly—to obtain the release of that general, whose imprisonment apparently wounded the honor of the Army. I replied that if an honor had been wounded it was not the Army's but only that of General Dusseigneur, who had participated in a plot against a state whose servant he was. Just as I decided to let justice take its course in the Bouilloux-Lafont affair in 1933, so I decided to let it take its course in the Dusseigneur affair in 1937. Many anonymous letters informed me of the impending vengeance by the heads of the Cagoule. I cannot blame the French Fascists for keeping their word, nor can I be surprised at seeing Vichy execute that vengeance.

My Position in the Popular Front

Such is the résumé of my political life. I want to make it clear that I have not told the story of my career out of vanity. If I state that I was a figure symbolic of the fight against Fascism, it is not because I demand rewards for my activities. I do not want to imitate those refugees and emigrés who claim to have seen, understood, and prophesied everything. Having been a minister only seven times, and a member of Parliament only twelve years, I leave it to those who belonged neither to Parliament nor to a cabinet to explain to the State Department and to the Foreign Office the secrets of French politics, the importance of the missions with which they were supposedly entrusted, and the confidences which they received. I leave it to those civilians or generals who never knew the peasants and workers of France to speak in their name. So much the worse for those who listen to these empty barrels! Personally, I was only a man at grips with the difficulties of thought and action—a man with his pettiness, weaknesses, and errors, a man no different from others.

Circumstances have played a great part in my life. They have largely determined the general line of my development, and I owe more to them than to myself. Events rather than studies have shaped me. Anyone with my intellectual discipline, confronted with the same problems, would have had the same reactions as I; and the way in which I dominated or was dominated by these reactions has been chiefly a matter of temperament. My life has been simple, if not calm. When I was only twenty, war had already taught me to hate nationalism and militarism; these lessons, together with my training in political science, made me an active supporter of the League of Nations. The Aéropostale affair and my first governmental experiences, added to my studies of public law, brought home to me the contradiction between political democracy and capitalism. Economic and demographic statistics of France and Germany taught me that the front of collective security with the Soviet Union was the only effective obstacle with which Europe and the world could oppose the dangers of Hitlerism. The attitude of the Fascists and nationalists after February 6, 1934, showed me that in France "the men of the Right are wicked men" indeed; and the political history of my country proved to me that in 1936, as in 1848 during the MacMahon regime, and from 1894 to 1906 during the Dreyfus affair, it was necessary to unite the forces of the revolutionary workers with those of the liberals and democrats to check the activities of these "wicked men." These truths, evident to me from the beginning, became ever stronger and clearer; they brought me to the front line of the war against Fascism and Hitlerism. If I were asked how I became Vichy's "enemy number one," I might answer, with some irony, that it happened all by itself!

The preceding pages are not a plea but an explanation. I do not say that I was right to have a certain attitude, but rather that given this attitude, it was natural that I should figure on Hitler's and Pétain's death list of enemies.

I add that while I regret my errors, I regret none of the acts which won me the anger of the nationalists, reactionaries, Fascists, and Cagoulards. Like many others, I could have chosen the easy way; but I grew up in the mountains, where one often has to take the steepest path to avoid the avalanche. I am only sorry not to have fought the enemies of French democracy more bitterly. I do not regret sending airplanes and arms to the Spanish republicans; I only wish I had sent more. I do not regret my policy toward the Soviets; I only wish I could have carried it to a successful conclusion. I say, with Corneille, "if I had it to do over, I would do it again." As I do not regret my anti-Fascist activity, I cannot regret its consequences. I prefer to be a political refugee, carrying on in exile the fight against Fascism, rather than a dishonored partisan of the policy of collaboration inaugurated by Pétain and carried on by Laval.

A French proverb says that one has the friends one deserves; if it is equally true of one's enemies, I am proud of mine.

The Case Against Gamelin, Jacomet, and La Chambre

These reasons explain the charges against the men of the Popular Front. They do not at first glance explain the charges against General Gamelin, Controller-General Jacomet, and La Chambre, who was my successor in the Air Ministry.

These men must be considered minor figures; they were accessory defendants, whose indictment was a necessary prelude to the indictment of the three men of the Popular Front: Blum, Daladier, and myself.

It was impossible to avoid bringing General Gamelin before the Court of Riom, for it was he who had been officially in charge of the preparation of the Army after 1936 and who was responsible for the direction of military operations until the beginning of June, 1940. General Weygand, Chief of the French General Staff at the time of the defeat, gave the excuse that he had found a difficult and even desperate situation. "They called me too late," he said; "three months sooner I could have organized the defense of France." It was necessary to convict Gamelin to preserve the military prestige of Weygand and to explain why Weygand had been so easily conquered and why he had recommended the armistice as early as June 12, 1940. Moreover, not to try Gamelin, Chief of Staff of the French Army after February, 1936, would have meant making the situation easy for Daladier, Minister of National Defense after 1936. Daladier would merely have had to point out that all the acts in the preparation of the war for which he was blamed bore the signature of

Gamelin, had been executed by Gamelin, and involved Gamelin's responsibility far more than his own. Even in a Fascist country the ridiculous has its limits. Finally, even if General Gamelin had been a weak man at the head of the French armies, he had been loyal; he had refused to associate himself with the Fascists and the Cagoulards; he had been an avowed partisan of agreements with Soviet Russia; in September, 1938, he had drawn up a report showing the strength and weakness of the French military situation and concluding that Czechoslovakia could and should be defended. Hence, Vichy, eager to please Hitler, had good reason to resent the honest Gamelin.

After the first hearings at Riom, General Gamelin declared that "to keep the honor of the Army intact" he would not answer any of the judges' questions. This declaration was generally interpreted as indicating Gamelin's adhesion to Vichy's official doctrine of mandatory reticence concerning the responsibility of the military men in order to bring out more forcefully the responsibility of the political men—a policy which was imposed on the French press. Perhaps General Gamelin merely wanted to reserve for his future memoirs the revelations which would display the stupidities or treasonable activities of the Marshal and those generals who accused him. Perhaps he feared to irritate Pétain by drawing him into the trial. The indictment of General Gamelin involved vengeance, the vengeance of Fascists against a loyal man, and of Hitler's friends against the partisans of the entente with Russia; it involved the necessity of trying the Chief of Staff in order to try the Minister of National Defense; and it involved the compliance of all the military men with Pétain's order of silence so that "the honor of the Army"— the honor of Pétain, Weygand, Corab, and other Fascist generals—might be preserved.

The case of Controller-General Jacomet was more complicated and revealed a greater degree of Machiavellism. Few persons understood his indictment. As General Secretary of the War Department, Jacomet had been in charge of purely administrative problems. He had merely executed the decisions of his chiefs. The Council of Political Justice, which prepared the decision that Marshal Pétain handed down on October 16, 1941, against "those mainly responsible for the defeat," declared that Jacomet "did not appear as one of the men principally responsible . . . and that there was no way to apply to him Constitutional Act No. 7"—in other words, there was no way to punish him. One must therefore know the in and outs of French administration to understand why Jacomet was imprisoned. His indictment before the Court of Riom had two explanations. First, Vichy wanted to eliminate a witness who would have been dangerous for the prosecution and valuable to the defense. Having been in control of war manufactures, Jacomet easily could have demolished Vichy's thesis by showing that all the deficiences with which Blum, Daladier, La Chambre, and I were charged were actually caused by the hesitations and incomprehensions of the General Staff and the Supreme War Council, of which Pétain was the most influential member. Jacomet could have proved without difficulty that if the French Army lacked tanks, airplanes, anti-aircraft guns, it was because the Supreme War Council had not done its work and had not, at the proper time, asked for the kind of armament which the development of the German Army had made necessary. According to French procedure and contrary to American and English law, a defendant cannot be heard under oath; he cannot be a witness. By indicting Jacomet, Vichy deprived Daladier of his best witness. The Vichy government violated the Penal Code, but it knew the *Code d'Instruction Criminelle* well enough.

The second reason for Jacomet's indictment was the vengeance of the military in general and of Weygand in particular. I have already indicated the role Jacomet played at the Disarmament Conference in 1932 and 1933. Weygand never forgave him for having tried to make the control of armaments possible; in Weygand's eyes, even to take the Disarmament Conference seriously was lese majesty against the Army.

Finally, to reach me, Vichy had to try La Chambre, who was not a Minister of the Popular Front, nor even a supporter of the Popular Front. He was a young liberal bourgeois, heir to an immense fortune and brought up in great luxury. In 1928 he had been elected member of Parliament for Ille et Vilaine. He became friendly with Daladier, who appointed him Minister of Aviation in 1938 after the fall of the Popular Front. Before this time he had opposed both the Communists and the Socialists. As Minister of Aviation, he fought the policy of the Popular Front; he opposed the support of the Spanish Republic and the Franco-Soviet rapprochement, and was a partisan of Bonnet's appeasement policy. Moreover, having left France in July, 1940, for the United States, he hastened to make statements to the press in favor of Pétain, who repaid him by accusing him of having "betrayed the duties of his office." It was therefore surprising to see La Chambre accused in a trial so obviously directed against the Popular Front leaders.

Vichy could not accuse me without accusing La Chambre, for its thesis was that the inadequacy of French aerial armament was the result of bad policy practiced since June, 1936. Between June, 1936, and June, 1940, I was Minister of Aviation for less than nineteen months, whereas La Chambre had held that office for almost two and a half years. Moreover, I left the Ministry of Aviation in January, 1938, two and a half years before the defeat. Since the average life of a combat plane is three years in peacetime and only a few months in wartime, even by forcing matters to an extreme, it would have been difficult to hold me solely responsible for the situation. Vichy at least had to pretend to associate my successor with my mistakes.

La Chambre committed no graver mistake than to believe in Pétain. A real farce was enacted to persuade him to leave the United States and return to France: if he consented to throw all the blame on me he was promised liberty and the return of his confiscated property. Once he had been imprisoned, all those promises were forgotten, to avoid political difficulties. (All this in spite of the declaration in October, 1941, by Pétain's Council of Political Justice affirming "there was no basis for detaining administratively Guy la Chambre"!) In 1942 the Supreme Court of Justice ordered his "provisory release," but Marshal Pétain refused to have the court order executed. Seriously ill and regretful, La Chambre is dying slowly in the prison of Bourrassol. With no other reason than hatred for my policy and for the Popular Front, Pétain has thrown one of his own partisans into prison—an innocent man at that. The ways of the Fascists are not attractive.

The Necessary Vengeance of French Fascism

Thus the Vichy government had reasons for bringing all of us before the Court of Riom—reasons which had nothing to do with the war or the defeat. Under a dictatorial and Fascist regime, such reasons are sufficient excuse to accuse and convict political enemies. "He who wants to drown his dog accuses him of being mad." The Riom trial took place not in a free country under the rule of law, but in a Fascist state, subject to the caprices of an eighty-six-year-old soldier, the servant of Hitler. For such a trial to have truth as its objective would be a disconcerting paradox; the object of Fascist political trials is always vengeance, never justice.

It can happen, although rarely, that vengeance may coincide with the demands of justice. The fact that Blum, Daladier, and I have been leaders of the Popular Front and enemies of Fascism explains our accusal, but it obviously does not mean that we are not guilty for the war and the defeat. The preceding pages have shown that appearances are against the Vichy government, but appearences are not enough. The Riom trial was the trial of the scapegoats, but it might at the same time have been the trial of the guilty. A broad examination of the causes of the French defeat will show that this was not so. The problem was not even touched by the Court of Riom. The trial of those responsible for the defeat is still to be held.

The French Defeat

2

NAZI GERMANY was a totalitarian state of eighty millions; France a capitalist democracy of forty millions. Experience has shown not only in France, but also in England and America, that democratic capitalist regimes are not as well-equipped to prepare and wage total war as the totalitarian states. This general observation does not admit a general conclusion that National Socialism is superior to capitalist democracy, for the value of a political and economic system cannot be measured in terms of its capacity to wage war. Genghis Khan was the greatest conqueror and ablest soldier of his era, yet his victories contributed little to the advancement of humanity.

Before a list of the guilty can be drawn, numerous preliminary studies must be made; and these studies presuppose the publication of diplomatic and military archives relating to the preparation and the execution of the war. From available material, however, we do know that the problem of the causes of the defeat, when the details are studied, is singularly complicated. We do know that the causes of the defeat were many, because the causes of the weakness of France in 1939 and 1940 were many. Some of these causes were inevitable. No statesman, had he Napoleon's genius and Louis XIV's absolute power, could have transformed an agricultural country of forty million inhabitants into an industrial country of eighty million inhabitants. Other elements could have been altered, but the causes resulted from a long series of mistakes for which all the democracies and not France alone must be blamed. In France avoidable mistakes were aggravated not by the action of a single political party, but by all the parties that were successively in power.

Finally, we must add treason to the inevitable and avoidable causes of French weakness. This treason cannot be fully exposed so long as Hitler dominates Europe and controls the Vichy government.

Complete and definitive explanations for the French defeat cannot be attempted at present. It is possible, however, to show the complexity of the problem, which must be approached with the prudence and moderation which were absent in Vichy's action. I would not presume to say: "Here is the truth." I propose only to clarify the known facts, to present certain aspects of the problem, to formulate hypotheses, and to offer my own interpretation of what occurred. Because of my intimate association with the events, I do not ask the reader to accept my interpretation without reflection and criticism. I do not pretend to judge men, but to study facts and offer my testimony. That, for the moment, is the limit of my task.

Marshal Pétain might have shown himself to be a great and honest man, if only he had asked all Frenchmen to ponder the lessons of the defeat in silence, and to seek in themselves—the Marshal not excepted—how each had contributed to this defeat, through indifference or egoism, through blindness or self-interest, through passion or thoughtlessness, for all Frenchmen are guilty, in varying degrees. By accusing six men and convicting them without a hearing, Pétain has been culpable of base dishonesty. This appears even in a general review of the problem of the defeat.

France was defeated twice—politically and in the field. The military defeat, in the middle of June, 1940, was not dishonorable; it is never dishonorable to be conquered when one is the weaker. After Waterloo, Napoleon remained a great general. But the political defeat was dishonorable. It began in the middle of June, 1940, with the refusal of the Pétain government to keep France's agreements and continue the fight in North Africa, and it had its climax on October 16, 1940, with Pétain's historic declaration that "to maintain French unity, he had decided to take the way of collaboration." The events which followed this declaration, including the total occupation of France in 1942, have been only the necessary and logical steps of dishonor. Such a word, applied to an old Marshal of France, may shock us—but it is not too strong. Of all the governments representing nations conquered by Hitler, only the Pétain government preferred collaboration to exile. It stooped so low as to have its courts condemn as traitors those who continued to fight the enemy under the leadership of General de Gaulle.

PRINCIPAL CAUSES OF THE DEFEAT

I see three main reasons for the military and political defeat of France.

The essential cause of the defeat was the isolation of France, resulting from the failure of collective security. Deprived of her indispensable alliances, with only the aid of England, France could have resisted, but she could not have won the war. The determining factor was the rupture of the Franco-Soviet Pact, a Pact which guaranteed France a perfect security in that it obliged Germany to choose between peace and a two-front war. The annulment of this Pact gave Hitler his opportunity.

The second cause was the weakness of the French Army. The military defeat became a rout, primarily because of the intellectual inferiority of a General Staff which could neither prepare for nor direct the war.

The third cause was the moral disunity of the French nation and, more specifically, the moral collapse of the ruling classes. This played a particularly important part in the political defeat. With her armies beaten on the continent, France could have continued the fight in North Africa and in her

Colonies, but the government and the General Staff preferred the risks of an entente with Hitler to those of Franco-British solidarity. The decisive factor was the activity of the Fifth Column in certain social and political circles of the haute bourgeoisie.

Let us examine these reasons. Then, asking ourselves whether these causes are interrelated, we shall see whether it is possible to find a common denominator for the events which helped transform the great country of the French Revolution into the disgraced and gagged France of Pétain.

The Isolation of France: the Collapse of the Franco-Soviet Pact

France was conquered because in September, 1940, she did not have indispensable allies. Had the diplomatic situation been different, in spite of the other causes of her inferiority, France would have been able to defend herself and avoid defeat. Conversely, given the state of military and political agreements existing in 1939, even if France had not been served so badly by her superannuated generals and her Fascist industrialists, her armed forces would have been beaten on the European continent.

France's military weakness, compared to Germany's strength, made a war without allies unthinkable. The number of Frenchmen who could be mobilized was half that of the Germans; the number of qualified workers, the quantity of tools, the availability of natural resources and industrial equipment—in short, all that makes a country able to produce—were in the ratio of approximately one to three. With the same effort and using the same methods, France could not have opposed Germany on the battlefield with more than one French soldier as against two Germans, and one French cannon as against three German. Consequently, the cornerstone of French security was collective security. This categorical imperative, resulting from necessity, was understood perfectly by Herriot, Briand, Paul-Boncour, and Blum, by Reynaud and Mandel, and, to a lesser degree, by Poincaré the jurist and Tardieu the nationalist. With collective security France could have barred the way to aggressors, prevented the conquests and extensions of Fascism, and played the part of a generous protector to Eastern and Central Europe. She might have saved China, Ethiopia, the Spanish Republic, Czechoslovakia—and even herself—if she had had the right to ask for the same assistance she should have given others. On the other hand, all that weakened the bonds of collective security, nullified the League of Nations Pact, and contributed to the success of aggressor states, brought about the isolation of France and prepared the conditions of her defeat.

We know what France's choice, or rather her choices, were. After 1919 France worked with all her might for the organization of collective security; she wearied the League of Nations' Assemblies and Committees with her insistence on the problem of security. Later, however, France let the Fascist powers destroy, stone by stone, what she had constructed so painstakingly.

47

Sanctions were not properly imposed against Italian or Japanese aggressors, the Spanish Republic was abandoned, Czechoslovakia was betrayed. France neglected her duties, her partners, and her agreements in such a way that by 1939 she had lost the majority of her friends. She could hardly hope to be treated better than she had treated them. She entered the war with only Poland and England on her side. The Polish Army resisted magnificently, but its fight, without Soviet backing, was clearly hopeless. England sent France more soldiers, airplanes, and arms than the French General Staff had asked for or anticipated; but Chamberlain's England was incapable of playing its traditional policeman's role on a continent where Hitler had been given every means of arming himself and defying the police.

What France lacked in 1939 was the support of Russia. Because this aid was the *sine qua non* of collective security, it was the *sine qua non* of French resistance. French diplomacy should have done everything to insure this aid. Had Russia been tied to France in September, 1939, the war would have been won in 1940. It is an historical fact, shown by the Napoleonic campaigns and especially by the wars of 1870 and 1914, that without a Russian alliance, France has always been defeated in Europe, but when allied with Russia, she has always been victorious.

In September, 1914, France was saved by Russian intervention. The German armies, having gone through Belgium and crossed the Meuse, had invaded northern France and were preparing a move first to the south and then to the east, in order to complete the vast encirclement which spelled victory. The French armies, defeated at Charleroi, were incapable of opposing this strategy. It was then, at the request of the French government, that the Russian armies attacked East Prussia. To meet the Russian threat, the German High Command had to remove two army corps from the western front and send them hastily to the eastern front, thus disorganizing its operational plan and its transportation arrangements. To shorten the advancing line, the German High Command ordered its troops to march toward the east of France before reaching the Seine; its armies moved east, leaving Paris to the south, thus giving Joffre and Galliéni the opportunity for a counterattack, which became the victorious Battle of the Marne. The Battle of the Marne was decisive. Germany lost the first World War in 1914 because the Russian soldiers sacrificed themselves in East Prussia to relieve the French. Winston Churchill, speaking of these events in his memoirs, emphasized that the Russian Army had not completed its mobilization when it attacked at that moment. The Russian Army had understood in 1914 that one must run great risks and launch an offensive even under dangerous circumstances, when it is essential to help an ally threatened by encirclement or destruction.

Russian aid was essential to France in 1914. What was true in 1914 was still more true in 1939, because the German and Russian armies had become relatively stronger, and the French Army relatively weaker. After the experience of the Franco-German war of 1939-1940 and of the Russo-German campaigns of 1941-1943, it is evident that a military agreement between the Soviet Union and France would have prevented the outbreak of the war in 1939 and certainly the French defeat in 1940. Two arguments support this opinion.

The first argument is based on the doctrine of the German General Staff (expressed in numerous books and magazine articles between 1920 and 1939). One of the constants of this doctrine has been that a two-front war is an insoluble problem for contemporary Germany when one front is held by the Russian Army and the other by the French. The insolubility of the problem rests on general and permanent factors which have little to do with the organization of the Russian Army or the intelligence of the French High Command, but which involve geography, German supply lines, the extent and precariousness of transport in Eastern Europe, the difficulties of occupying and controlling vast territories in Eastern Europe, and the immensity of Russia. Napoleon lost his Grand Army in this immensity; and the very existence of a Russian front in 1918, on the eve of Brest-Litovsk, when the Russian Army was in complete collapse, kept one hundred Austro-German divisions from being used elsewhere. To avoid being trapped in Russia during a future campaign against the French Army, the German General Staff decided not to commit the mistake of 1914, and resolved not to embark on any venture before separating France from Russia. The second World War could have been avoided by a Franco-Soviet military alliance.

The second argument is based on the comparative strength of the European armies in June, 1940. No statistics are needed to show that Germany never would have been able to throw the necessary airplanes, tanks, and divisions against the French, if at the same time she had been threatened by the Red Army. The facts speak for themselves. In the winter of 1940-1941 the production of German factories was obviously greater than that of Russian factories. Moreover, Germany had captured much war matériel in Europe, but particularly in France. For example, five hundred French tanks were used against Russia. In spite of these favorable elements, Germany was not able to annihilate the Red Army in 1941. Thus the Germans would have been far less able to deal with a two-front war in 1939 or 1940 than in 1914. When the military archives are published, it will be seen that the ratio of force and armaments would have been much more favorable for a Franco-Russian coalition in 1939 than in 1914.

What was true in 1940 was still more true in 1938 before the Munich agreements. At that time France could count on the support of the Czech Army—forty first-line divisions, excellently trained and equipped, ready to oppose Germany with the best armaments in Europe (the products of the famous Skoda works). France could have used Czechoslovakia's strategic position, of which Bismarck had said: "Whoever holds Bohemia dominates Europe." Between France and the Soviet Union, Czechoslovakia formed a sort of bridge; from France or Czechoslovakia, Soviet bombers could menace not only the industrial centers of the Ruhr, but those of eastern Germany—Chemnitz, Silesia, Munich, Vienna, and Berlin. The accords of Munich modified this situation. The French and British cabinets gave Hitler a free hand in Czechoslovakia, and impressed Russia and the whole world with their thoughtlessness and shortsighted egoism, thereby opening the way for the dissolution of the Franco-Soviet Pact.

The idea that the Soviet government was solely responsible for the annulment of its Pact with France is hypocritical. Here again, we must wait for the publication of the French, Russian, and German archives to know the whole truth, but the established facts and published documents now available show that on August 23, 1939, when Stalin signed his famous pact with von Ribbentrop, French policy and diplomacy had left him no alternative.

The Soviet Union was above reproach during the entire period between the signing of the Franco-Soviet Pact in 1935 and the signing of the Russo-German Pact in 1939. Russia had remained faithful to the principles of collective security and to the letter and spirit of the Franco-Soviet Pact. She had constantly proposed negotiations of technical and military agreements with France to reinforce the Pact and facilitate its execution.

Until 1939 France refused these propositions and let Russia know that she rejected stronger accords. From 1935 to 1939 the Franco-Soviet Pact was attacked unjustifiably and hypocritically in the French press and in Parliament. Partisans of the Pact were accused of being warmongers. After the fall of the Popular Front France indicated that she was not taking the Pact seriously and was trying to escape its obligations. This policy became more and more obvious under Bonnet as Minister of Foreign Affairs, and progressively weakened the Pact, converting it from a perfectly clear alliance into one of those "friendship pacts" which no one took seriously in Europe before 1939.

When the obvious interest of France, confronted by a growing Nazi threat, would have been to strengthen a rapprochement with Russia, French policy did nothing but undermine the Franco-Soviet Pact and violate its spirit. I witnessed, as Minister of Aviation and member of Parliament, this progressive sabotage, and protested against it constantly. The principal stages of this sabotage were these. First, at the time of the Spanish war France gave Russia the impression that her policy was bound to England's; she let it be understood that if she refused to help the Spanish Republic, it was because the Spanish Republic could count on the friendship and help of Soviet Russia. Second, at the time of Munich Russia was left out of the negotiations, although she had as much interest as France in the fate of Czechoslovakia. France showed that, in spite of her formal and solemn agreements, she would never fight to prevent Hitler from extending his domination to the east. Third, two months after the Munich agreements France welcomed von Ribbentrop to Paris and concluded a general accord with Germany, giving France's foreign policy an entirely new orientation. This accord indicated France's desire for a rapprochement with Germany and fatally disturbed Russia. In 1939 von Ribbentrop let it be known that he had Bonnet's assurance of French neutrality in the event of further German expansion toward the east. In 1939, after the outbreak of the war, Bonnet denied this interpretation; but if we are confronted by two liars who do not agree, it is because one is telling the truth. Von Ribbentrop's interpretation of the Pact of Paris was certainly nearer the historical truth than Bonnet's. In short, by her attitude during the Spanish war, by her treatment of Czechoslovakia, and by the signing of the Bonnet-von Ribbentrop Pact, France slowly detached herself from Russia.

At the end of 1938 the Franco-Soviet Pact was no longer a living treaty, but a dead text. Soviet Russia could harbor no illusions about the true intentions of French policy. No one could think seriously that France, who had refused to help Czechoslovakia, would come to the aid of the Soviet Union if Germany again moved to the east. Bonnet's policy had made it clear to the Soviet government that Russia could not count on France. It is difficult to blame Russia for drawing this conclusion from a political situation which was not of her creation and which she had tried to prevent. In addition, during the winter of 1938-1939, Germany hastened to complete the construction of the Siegfried Line. These fortifications, incomplete at the time of Munich, became impassable for the French Army in the course of the winter. By the beginning of 1939 Russia knew that the French Army could not aid her effectively.

What could the Soviet government do? To remain faithful to the Franco-Soviet Pact, after Munich and the Pact of Paris, with Chamberlain as Prime Minister in London and Bonnet as Minister of Foreign Affairs in Paris, was to invite attack by Germany. To denounce the Franco-Soviet Pact in 1939 before accepting von Ribbentrop's proposition would have been more elegant, but fatally elegant; Germany, having achieved the annulment of the Franco-Soviet Pact, would then have attacked Russia before turning on France and England. The Soviet government actually had no alternative but to try one supreme effort with France and England, and to inform the French government discreetly that if this effort failed, Russia, following Bonnet's example, would be obliged to "revise her alliances" and to modify the general course of her policy.

That was precisely what Russia did. The Soviet government asked France for the last time to take her agreements seriously and to negotiate a military accord. France accepted—on condition that England participate in the negotiations. England, in turn, accepted, but with visible repugnance and reticence. British foreign policy was at that time directed not by Churchill and Anthony Eden, who favored an entente with the Soviet Union, but by Chamberlain and Lord Halifax, apostles of appeasement. Similarly, French foreign policy was in the hands of Daladier and especially Bonnet. Interminable exchanges of notes took place between France, England, Poland, and the Soviet Union. Europe's temperature mounted. At last, in July, France and England consented to send a military mission to Moscow; but, as if to show a contemptuous lack of haste in dealing with the Soviet government, the French mission first went to London and from there proceeded slowly to Moscow. When the negotiators arrived, they informed the Russians that they had not the power to make binding agreements, but merely to exchange information. When the time came for a frank discussion of war plans, the Russian General Staff realized with stupefaction that the French and British representatives either did not have such plans or were concealing them out of lack of confidence. After this experience, and with Hitler's attack on Poland imminent, the Soviet government could choose only between being attacked under the worst conditions and signing a Russo-German pact.

The French government knew perfectly well that, if it did not conclude a military agreement with Russia, the Soviet government would have to come to terms temporarily with Nazi Germany. During the war the French government published in a *Yellow Book* the diplomatic documents bearing on the Franco-German crisis. These documents contained certain dispatches sent to the French Minister of Foreign Affairs by our Ambassador at Berlin, M. Coulondre, who had been Ambassador to Moscow before going to Germany. During the winter of 1938-1939 Coulondre asked the French government to conclude a military agreement with Russia in short order, as the only means of avoiding a Russo-German pact. In Paris the Soviet Ambassador did not conceal his anxiety; he informed the French cabinet several times of the importance his government attached to the rapid negotiation of a military agreement; he spoke in private to the most influential members of the cabinet, pointing out the possible consequences of the Franco-Soviet situation. "We want to defend collective security with you," he said, "but don't oblige us, by your appeasement policy, to choose between our security and yours, when a military accord can insure both." I witnessed these repeated efforts of Ambassador Souritz. But no one is more deaf than he who does not want to hear. The fact remains that the Soviet government did warn the French of the danger they were running. Without walking into Hitler's trap and asking for a direct attack, there was not much else that Russia could do.

History will determine who was responsible for the Franco-Soviet break, and it probably will find that the responsibility was shared by many. In the years preceding the war the policy of those who were to become the adversaries and the victims of Hitler, lacked clarity, mutual confidence, and good faith.

We shall return to certain aspects of the Franco-Russian problem in connection with some accusations directed against the Popular Front. For the moment it should be noted that the essential cause of the French defeat was the collapse of collective security and of the Franco-Soviet rapprochement. French security was never greater than when it was founded on the strength of the Red Army and the bastion of Czechoslovakia; and French security was never so precarious as when France lost both Czechoslovakia and the confidence of the Soviets. Before September, 1938, France was in little danger of attack and in no danger of defeat; after August 23, 1939, France was sure to be attacked and in grave danger of defeat.

The publication of the diplomatic archives may fortify this statement to a greater or lesser extent, but cannot disprove it. It is impossible to demonstrate that a Franco-Polish bloc supported by England could be stronger than a Franco-Czech-Russian bloc also supported by England; the latter existed before Munich, but was deemed inferior to the virtues of appeasement.

Those responsible for the French defeat are principally those men who were either thoughtless or so dominated by their hate of Soviet Russia as not to understand the double and necessary relation of French security and collective security on the one hand, and of collective security and the Franco-Soviet Pact on the other. On the list of "the men principally responsible" we must put in first place those who worked, consciously or unconsciously, for the collapse of collective security and the destruction of Russia's confidence in France.

The Military Weakness of France: the Mistakes of the General Staff

The second cause of France's defeat was the weakness of her Army. Opposed by the German forces, the French Army revealed itself to be inferior, in quality more than in quantity. In 1939-1940 it was far from deserving its country's confidence, a confidence which was based largely on the affirmations of the military chiefs. In July, 1939, speaking at the Exposition of Lille, General Weygand said: "You ask my opinion of the French Army. I will give it to you frankly and truthfully. I think that the French Army is better than at any time in its history; it has first-rate matériel, first-rate fortifications, excellent morale, and a remarkable High Command. None of us wants war, but I can say that if we are obliged to win a new victory, we will win it." Events were to prove the inaccuracy of these forecasts. In September, 1939, the French Army was unable to give Poland decisive aid; in May and June, 1940, it was incapable of resisting the attack of Hitler's troops.

The study of the documents and evidence submitted to the Court of Riom will throw more light on these points. Let us for the moment examine rapidly the questions raised by General Weygand: the morale, the matériel, and the leadership.

What was the morale of the French Army? Napoleon believed that morale was the most important factor in war. "Morale is to armament," he said, "as three is to one." In spite of its technical complexity, or perhaps *because* of it, modern war does not seem to have changed this ratio. Modern warfare requires an almost superhuman effort of each soldier. A battle is no longer the conflict of armed masses on the firing line, where officers can direct the action of each soldier; it is a conflict of mechanical engines, often operating in small units. Each one of these engines—the tank, the airplane, the anti-aircraft gun, the submarine—is manned by a team of a few men, and the relation between the various fighting units is determined by precision instruments, sometimes operated by a single man. Modern battle thus requires the methodical and co-ordinated action of specialists and technicians, each of whom has his particular part to play. More isolated and less interchangeable than in the past, the soldier must have better technical education and higher morale.

Foreign public opinion has a tendency to think that the morale of the French Army was lower than that of the German. The fact is that the latter was composed of fanatics who were well-trained and who were proud to die for their Führer, while the French soldiers were somewhat disillusioned— they had not been told what they were fighting for, and they lacked confidence in their officers, many of whom hated democracy and preferred "Hitler to Léon Blum." The evidence offered at the Riom trial showed that the moral inferiority of the French Army proceeded from a lack of technical education and training, not from lack of individual courage. Soldiers and officers were surprised by a type of war—the Blitzkrieg, whose rudiments their leaders had not taught them. And all evidence disclosed that the morale of the soldiers and of the troop officers was higher than that of the General Staff in charge of directing the war. There is a saying that "the value of a troop depends on its leader"; where the French soldiers were well commanded, they fought with the courage of their predecessors at the Marne, at Verdun, and at Chemin-des-Dames. Moral deficiency was not the principal element in French military weakness.

A more important element of weakness was the insufficiency of matériel at the soldiers' disposal. The Riom trial made curious revelations on this point and proved that France had more matériel than had been supposed, although it was less modern than the German matériel. About 40 per cent of the tanks and 60 per cent of the airplanes were *never used in the war.*

Do we need to emphasize the importance of matériel in modern warfare? In a war of machines, military and industrial strength are linked closely, a connection that appears not only in the manufacture but in the use of arms. In the days of infantry and cavalry battles, the advantage was with agricultural and pastoral peoples rather than with nations of merchants and artisans, because the best cavalrymen and foot-soldiers were recruited from among farmers and horse-drivers. In the days of tank battles and aerial combat, the advantage is with industrial nations, for the modern soldier is a mechanic and a technician, supported by other mechanics and technicians. Germany therefore had a great advantage over France.

The inferiority of French matériel was caused, in part, by pre-war differences in French and German production of war equipment.

First, the productive capacities of French factories in the years preceding the war were about a third of the capacity of German factories. France produced approximately one-third of the amount of steel and aluminum that Germany did. Even if France had concentrated the same proportion of her productive capacity on armament manufacture as had Germany, she would still have produced only one cannon, one tank, and one airplane to Germany's three. Second, according to a study* published by the Foreign Policy Association, Germany spent four times as much as France on national defense between

* William T. Stone, "Economic Consequences of Rearmament," *Foreign Policy Reports,* October 1, 1938.

54

1934 and 1938. This means that Germany concentrated a greater proportion of her productive capacity on war preparations than did France, and that the cost of national defense was twice as much for each of the eighty million Germans as for each of the forty million Frenchmen. The French had "butter" and the Germans "cannon." Third, in planning her national defense and her armament programs, Germany was giving more importance than France to aviation and tanks. France concentrated on other armaments; the French fleet was almost twice as strong as the German, and France, until 1938, had more soldiers and officers under arms than Germany. The result was that, spending four times less for her entire national defense, and maintaining a stronger navy and a larger army than Germany, France built not three or four but five or six times fewer airplanes and tanks than did Germany.

Thus, as always in the case of historical events, the simplest reasons, based on realities, explain the tragic inadequacy of French war matériel.

But the most important factor of French military weakness was the mediocrity of the High Command and of the General Staff. I speak not only of the High Command during or before the war, but of the General Staff as a quasi-permanent institution of French military policy—perhaps of French policy in general. It was an institution with its own methods, traditions, and doctrine. Applied to modern warfare, its military doctrine was invalidated by events and contributed greatly to the transformation of the defeat into a rout.

Broadly summarized, the war doctrine of the French General Staff was that of defense and a war of position, as opposed to the doctrine of offense and a war of movement, the basis for the German *Blitzkrieg*. The French doctrine was taught not only at the Centre des Hautes Études Militaires and the École Supérieure de Guerre—it was included in the military regulations by the General Staff, and developed by such military authors as Generals Debeney, Loiseau, Maurin, and Weygand, to name the most illustrious. Just a few months before the war General Chauvineau presented this doctrine with great talent in a book, *Is Invasion Still Possible?*† He answered his own question in the negative; he foresaw stabilization of fronts and the war of attrition. "The tank has failed as a means of breaking through," wrote this French doctrinal prophet. None other than Marshal Henri Philippe Pétain, the highest military authority in all France, wrote the preface and recommended that all officers read Chauvineau's book.

Chauvineau claimed that the General Staff's doctrine was motivated by prudence and realism; actually it was characterized by archaism and lack of daring. Said to be founded on the lessons of 1914-1918, it interpreted them wrongly and merely expounded the ideas which Pétain had developed before 1914 as a colonel and professor at the École Supérieure de Guerre. Good in its youth, the doctrine had grown old. It failed to allow for the revolution in warfare produced by the discoveries of science and by the progress of industry in general and the internal combustion motor in particular. It failed to allow for the transformation wrought by tanks and airplanes. It was a conservative doc-

† N. Chauvineau, *Une Invasion Est-Elle Encore Possible?* (Paris: Berger-Levrault, 1938).

trine, contradicting the revolutionary conceptions being developed in Germany and Russia and the modern ideas of warfare a few French officers tried vainly to force into the minds of their leaders.

Among these nonconformist officers the most brilliant was General de Gaulle. In 1935, as a commandant, he published his daring book on the use of tanks, the formation of armored divisions, and the creation of a modern army. While Germany attentively studied his ideas, the French General Staff distrusted the young officer who had ventured to have ideas of his own and who was capable of substituting thought for obedience.

The German General Staff, eager for new ideas, encouraged its officers to do historical research and to write intellectual studies and even polemics, while the French General Staff forbade criticism and discouraged thought. The abundance and richness of German military literature between 1920 and 1940 is remarkable compared with the poverty and weakness of French military literature in the same period. The French Army did not think. Its leaders shrugged their shoulders when you spoke to them of German conceptions or Russian methods, when you cited the articles of General Erfuhrt and the books of Major Guderian, or when you mentioned the experience of the Red Army and the lessons of the Spanish war. They were not interested. They lived in a static world and considered every new idea heretical. Colonel Maindraz, Military Attaché at Moscow, was recalled because he claimed that the French Army had much to learn from the Red Army. Colonel Morel, Military Attaché at Madrid during the Civil War, was reprimanded because his reports conformed not to the truth held by the General Staff, but merely to the truth. Thus the French Army went to war in 1939 fortified with a doctrine, theories, and "Regulations" perfectly suited to the conditions of war in 1918.

It is all the more necessary to study the causes of the General Staff's stubbornness and intellectual poverty when one remembers that France almost lost the war in 1914 because of the bad military doctrine of its General Staff, which, as has been said, is always late by one idea and one war. Motorization did not exist in 1914; the generals of Wilhelm II were older and less bold than those of Hitler; and French foreign policy was supported by a Franco-Russian alliance. The French government in 1914 had had time to "retire" the incompetent generals and to rejuvenate the Army. But even then the French military leaders preferred the policy of large effective forces, which the three-year service plan gave them, to the policy of heavy cannon and machine guns, which the democratic parliamentarians demanded. The French soldiers of 1914, dressed in the famous red trousers which made living targets of them, were thrown against German trenches defended by machine guns; in the first months of that war the French Army lost more men than the German Army, although the latter was fighting both France and Russia. Thus the intellectual poverty of the French General Staff had deep roots. From 1918 to 1939 the German generals, chastened by the defeat of 1918, sought in the analysis of the causes of their defeat the avoidance of future errors—while the French generals had become unbearably conceited as a result of the victory of

1918, which they claimed to have won by superiority of methods. Moreover, the average age of the German generals in June, 1940, was ten years below that of the French generals, and experience has taught us that men of fifty can adapt themselves more rapidly to unforeseen situations than men of sixty.

Clemenceau and Foch had both foreseen the consequences of the aging of the French Army. In his later years Clemenceau had protested against the advanced age of the generals and the raising of the age limit until it reached seventy. "What can we do with generals of seventy?" he asked. At the same time Foch pointed out that to maintain a strong French Army in front of a disarmed Germany would favor the spirit of routine and conservatism in this Army. "We will achieve a paradoxical state," he said, "wherein Germany, who is not supposed to have an army, will develop within its cadres a new organization which will correspond to the war of the future, while we, who have an army, will continue it after an existing model which should no longer be of any use." In 1940 the French Army "continued" on that line and was conquered by the modern army built by young German generals.

The General Staff's outmoded doctrine gave the French Army a false conception of modern warfare. And for this warfare the General Staff could not adequately prepare.

The French war plans—which were supposed to envisage all possibilities—obviously did not provide for the breaking force and rapidity of penetration of the German motorized columns. No preparation had been made for the destruction of the bridges over the Seine or the Loire, just as no provision had been made for the defense or abandonment of Paris. Such operations hardly can be improvised; thus, when the French armies were obliged to fall back south of Paris, the artillery was rendered useless because it had no maps of the country where the battle was developing.

The Army had not received the necessary instruction or training to resist the blows of the German armies. The generals who testified before the Court of Riom admitted that they had been surprised by this form of war. How could these generals have taught their officers and troops what they themselves did not know? The ignorance of the leaders and the poor training of the soldiers were the chief causes of the Army's demoralization. Thus, in December, 1939, at the request of General de Gaulle and General Billotte, who invoked the lessons of the Polish campaign, the French decided to create armored divisions out of a part of the tanks which the Army possessed. If these divisions had been formed a year earlier, they could have resisted Hitler's *Panzerdivisionen*—but improvised as they were at the beginning of 1940, they were thrown into battle without adequate staffs, instruction, or training. Similarly, France had no parachute troops in June, 1940; parachute units had been created in 1936, but were dissolved in 1938 and their members dispersed because the General Staff considered them of no military value.

A narrow military doctrine prevented the French Army from having armaments adapted to the necessities of modern warfare. War doctrines determine armament programs; Germany manufactured the arms needed for a war of movement, while France constructed the arms required for a war of position. The Maginot Line absorbed as much concrete and steel as the Siegfried Line, but France started the war with four motorized divisions (of which one was armored) while Germany had ten; France had a 543,000-ton fleet and Germany only one of 233,000 tons, but the French Air Force, in May, 1940, had about 2,100 first-line planes while the Germans had about 6,000. The French Army had the inadequate armament its generals had asked for, instead of the armament required by the necessities of modern warfare. No point was brought out more clearly at the Riom trial. Certain generals complained that they had lacked airplanes; Guy la Chambre forced them to admit that they had at their disposal precisely the insufficient number of airplanes for which they had asked and which figured in the General Staff's plans. Yet the ministers were accused of not having built what the General Staff had not asked for! The Riom hearings also showed that if France did not have dive-bombers, it was because the General Staff had informed the Air Ministry in 1938 that it considered this type of airplane useless.

The General Staff's doctrine proved especially faulty in the actual conduct of the war.

Addressing the Court of Riom, Léon Blum said: "The best prepared and best equipped army will be defeated if the mistakes of its High Command have put it into a strategic position from which it cannot escape, or if its High Command has not inspired it with the will to fight. On the other hand, matériel, however abundant, cannot be everywhere at once; if the doctrines behind the disposal of arms are vicious, if the plans are imprudent, if the forecasts are erroneous, even an army having superabundant matériel may find itself in a state of irremediable inferiority at the place and hour that the enemy surprises it. . . . France and the world will learn with amazement the actual numerical relations between French and enemy matériel at the outbreak of war or at the moment of the German attack."

Blum concluded that it would be necessary to investigate "whether the errors of the High Command had not been the determining cause of the defeat." The Court of Riom refused to undertake this investigation because the Vichy government feared its consequences. While Daladier was irrefutably demonstrating the mistakes of the General Staff, the President of the Court interrupted him, saying: "This demonstration is outside the scope of the trial . . . the trial deals with the inadequacy of the military preparation for war and not with the conduct of operations." For the Court of Riom and for Vichy, it was understood that the French General Staff could make no mistakes, and therefore the conduct of military operations could not be considered among the causes of the defeat.

But public opinion has formulated, in France and abroad, questions which will have to be answered one day, and one may be sure that these questions would have been asked at Riom if the answers would have embarrassed the accused. Why was the Maginot Line not extended to the North Sea? Why was the destruction of the Meuse bridges not ordered by General Corap? In general, why did the High Command take no measures to oppose the advance of German columns? Why were so many bridges, railroads, and gasoline bases abandoned without being destroyed? Why did the General Staff take no measures to prevent the blocking of roads by refugees? Finally, why did not General Weygand order the troops in the Maginot Line and the reserves massed behind the Maginot Line to fall back to the south? Or, if these troops were not all able to retreat in the same direction, why were they not ordered to cross the Swiss frontier, where they could have been disarmed and interned in neutral territory? (Bourbaki did this during the War of 1870 to prevent his men from becoming prisoners of the Germans.) Why had all these mistakes been committed, mistakes which reveal the responsibility of the General Staff and its utter confusion in face of a *Blitzkrieg* which it had declared a military impossibility even after the conquest of Poland?

In spite of the precautions taken by the Vichy government and its magistrates, certain documents mentioned in the debates and certain questions asked by Daladier at Riom lifted a corner of the veil and revealed scraps of the bewildering truth. It was made clear that the French armored divisions were not employed by the High Command as they could and should have been. Daladier quoted the following sentences taken from a report of Colonel Perré, a tank inspector: " 'On the front of the Somme and the Aisne, certain generals had the curious idea of stationing tanks as sentinels on the bridges, depriving them of all support, instead of sending the armored divisions into battle . . . according to clear and precise plans. The armored divisions were wasted, scattered, broken up. That explains why the efficacy of our machines was so different, *although we had as many tanks and armored cars on the battlefield as the Germans.*' " Daladier also quoted a report of General Keller: " 'French tanks were scattered from Dunkerque to Belfort, one battalion and one commander of a tank company at the disposal of every colonel of an infantry regiment.' " It was proved at the Riom trial that the High Command did not throw into the battle all the matériel at its disposal; the depots were bursting with tanks and airplanes—which were later surrendered to the Germans—while the troops lacked armaments. According to General Rivet, Chief of the Information Service at General Headquarters, the Germans used at most 3,900 tanks in their operations against France and at least half of these tanks were inferior in quality (tonnage, armament, and armor) to the French tanks. The French Army had at that time 3,000 tanks in France and 369 in North Africa, and England put 600 tanks at France's disposal, making an allied total of 3,969 tanks to the 3,900 German tanks. According to General Keller's statements, only 2,000 French tanks were used. The same was true of the Air Force. The testimony at Riom of Colonel Chatelain, Chief of the "Special Air Force Storehouse," revealed that a count of all military airplanes in the occupied zone had been made on July 28, 1940, after the armistice; the French Air Force at that time had 4,238 airplanes in France, of which 1,739 were first-line planes. In addition there were in North Africa, 1,800 military airplanes, 300 of them first-line. This made a total of 6,038 airplanes, of which more than 2,000 could have been used for immediate action. In short, the French Air Force had as many airplanes as did the Royal Air Force during the Battle of Britain. Of these 6,000 planes, fewer than 1,000 were used during the Battle of France!

It was then not so much the deficiency in the morale of the troops nor their lack of adequate armament, but the incompetence of the High Command which caused the French defeat. In June, 1940, the French General Staff lost not only the battle; it also lost its prestige.

Deprived of Russian aid, badly prepared for modern warfare, and badly directed on the battlefield, the French Army was bound to be conquered on the European continent. The mistakes that the military leaders had piled up in ten years could not be repaired in a few months. With a different Chief of Staff and a different leader of the government, the defeat might have been limited to the military domain and would not have become a national disaster. Beaten on the Meuse, the Seine, and the Loire, the French Army still could have fallen back, inflicting severe losses on the enemy; at the worst, it would have been possible, with the aid of the English fleet, to organize a second Dunkerque and to send to North Africa the tanks and the planes that General Weygand had hesitated to use against the German Army.

To accomplish this, Weygand and Pétain would have had to be animated by the will to resist and conquer; they would have had to wish ardently for the collapse of Hitlerism and Fascism, for the victory of the democracies. Had they any such wish?

The Moral Disunity of the French People: Fifth Column Activity

One must examine here not the morale of the Army, but the morale of the nation as a whole. "A great European nation," wrote Clausewitz, "cannot be entirely defeated without the aid of internal disunity." Hitler had certainly pondered these words when he ordered the agents of his Fifth Column to exploit all the inherent tendencies of moral, social, or political disunity existing in the countries he intended to dominate. He understood that the "aid of internal disunity" was a still more efficacious element of conquest than it was in Clausewitz' time.

Modern warfare, with its multiple aspects and scientific techniques, has revived the importance of the moral factor as an instrument of victory or defeat. War has truly become "total war"; the entire nation takes part in the struggle, by its military effort and by its economic and intellectual effort, which extends from scientific research to ideological propaganda. Aerial bombardment has broadened what was formerly called "the fighting zone" to the whole territory of a belligerent country. On land and sea, the classic distinction between combatants and noncombatants has disappeared. In modern war not only the army but the whole nation must be fortified against the effects of foreign propaganda and against its own discouragement. In addition, contacts between a modern army and the civilian population have become increasingly varied and frequent. The army is the microcosm of the nation; all social classes, all political parties, all opinions are represented in it.

If the political parties are not united in a single effort, if the social classes are opposed to one another, if the privileged class uses the war to reinforce or maintain its privileges, if the sacrifices are shared unequally and the rewards distributed unjustly, if goods are not conscripted as well as men, one can hardly expect national morale to remain at a high level. Then the morale of the army will quickly reflect the morale of the nation.

Finally, the wars of our time are no longer national wars, but ideological battles; they are more noble, for it is better to fight for a principle than for a bit of land, the possession of a mine or a port. The world fights today for and against Fascism, and for and against liberty. Such a war is, in truth, an international civil war. Germany harbors enemies of Fascism and the Anglo-Saxon countries, enemies of democracy. The battle of ideas goes on in each country, sometimes in the open, more often underground. Under these conditions, the strongest nation is the one where the value of the basic principles of state is least discussed; the weakest nation is the one where the military leaders, instead of obeying the government, criticize its composition, authority, and decisions—thus encouraging their subordinates to question, in turn, the authority and competence of their superior officers.

The morale of France at war was weak in that the French nation was not united behind the government. The Fifth Column provoked a disunity which the common people resisted as best they could and which the government did not fight strenuously enough. The activity of the Fifth Column and the passivity of the government combined to destroy French morale and hastened the defeat.

In September, 1939, the French people entered the war without enthusiasm but with discipline. The mobilization was completed without incident. The men said: "We must finish with *that* once and for all. *That*, to them, meant Hitler's policy of aggression and force. They were not going to fight for Poland or against the German people, but against methods and doctrines which constantly imperiled the peace of the world. The common people, with greater intelligence than their rulers, grasped the meaning of the war. They should be praised all the more for it because they were deeply attached to peace and had suffered greatly from the previous war.

As I am a severe critic of my compatriots when I must be, I have the right to tell the Anglo-Saxons that they are occasionally unjust toward the common people of France—whereas for two years they were indulgent to the Vichy government. They often forget, in judging the behavior of this people, that France had mobilized and lost more men in the course of World War I than any other belligerent nation. The proportion of dead and missing had been, in France, 10.5 per cent of her gainfully occupied male population; the corresponding proportions were 7.8 per cent in Germany, 6.2 per cent in Italy, 5.1 per cent in England, and 0.2 per cent in the United States. The proportion of disabled had been 11 per cent in France and 7.5 per cent in Germany.

Consequently, the number of young men brought up in the horror of war by a disabled father or a widowed mother was greater in France than in Germany. Again, as a result of the defeat, of the peace treaty, of the policy of reparations, and of the Hitlerian doctrine, a great number of young Germans had been brought up in the cult of revenge, while young Frenchmen of the working classes, temperamentally inclined toward conciliation, repeated that the worst international agreement was better than the best of wars.

For a multitude of reasons, then, it was at the same time easy and necessary for the government to explain constantly to the French people why France was fighting at the side of England. France and England were fighting for the principles of collective security and international order, without which peace was impossible; they were fighting to safeguard the law according to which no one alone can determine and enforce justice; they were fighting for democracy and for all the moral and spiritual values which this word represents to an Englishman and to a Frenchman. All these were reasons that could reach the hearts of the French. It was particularly dangerous not to emphasize the ideological aspect of the war, because it was France and England who, to maintain international order, had declared war on Germany. Technically, although an aggression, their action was an international police operation, and not to emphasize this aspect was to play into the hands of German propaganda. This propaganda repeated daily that Germany had been the object of an unjust aggression and that France was fighting England's battle; its most dangerous slogan was: "The English supply the machines, the French supply the men." To counteract this campaign French propaganda should have said: "We are fighting for democracy and international order"; instead, it limited itself to saying: "We are fighting today for fear of being attacked tomorrow."

The French people were offered nothing but the mediocre arguments of preventive war; their cause was cheapened, not ennobled. Moreover, the French were now told about Poland the opposite of what, a year earlier, they had heard about Czechoslovakia; and, as in England, it was the same government that upheld these contradictory theses. The French government failed to oppose Hitler's holy war with a holy war of liberty. Its leaders seemed ashamed to speak of democracy, thus depriving themselves of their best trump for national and international order.

Deprived by her inadequate propaganda of the necessary spur, France, after the first weeks of the war, sank into indifference. Her war did not interest her; during the winter of 1939-1940 France was bored. This indifference proved fertile soil for the Fifth Column.

The activity of the Fifth Column will not be considered by historians as a special phenomenon of French public life, but as an integral part of Fascism. The Fifth Column has appeared wherever Fascism has tried to gain a foothold. It was at work in Spain, Austria, and Czechoslovakia before it turned up in France, and there are Fifth Columns in the United States, India, and Latin America. By the Fifth Column I do not mean only spies and licensed traitors. The Fifth Column includes all who, by accepting Fascist doctrines or methods, become the conscious or unconscious accomplices of a foreign power. Treason and complicity have their degrees and nuances. The General Staff of the Fifth Column consists principally of ambitious men who try to seize power by destroying or paralyzing the democratic system. The body of the Fifth Column is composed of people who think they are saving their country from the "Communist menace" or from "British imperialism," and who do not even know in whose favor their actions are operating. Through hate of the Popular Front, good Frenchmen, or men who considered themselves such, served Hitler gratuitously by doing work to which they would never have consented, had they been offered payment. Why? Because they detested the Republic and democracy more than they loved France. They accepted the idea of the defeat as a necessary evil which permitted them to rid France of the democratic system and to keep in power, in the neighboring countries, the Fascist dictators whom they considered solely capable of maintaining order in Europe. They afterwards became unconscious collaborators of these dictators. They thought they were doing their duty in letting Hitler free France from the "Judeo-Masonic" influence, and Europe from the Communist peril. These people who had never read Marx, considered the "Marxist danger" more immediate than the Hitlerian. They preferred the risks of an entente with a victorious Hitler to the risks of a democratic victory that would cause the collapse of the Fascist dictators in Europe. Considering Hitler in Germany, Mussolini in Italy, and Franco in Spain as knights of an anti-Bolshevist crusade, they became precursors and later partisans of "collaboration with Hitler's New Order."

The history of the Fifth Column in France before, during, and after the armistice of June, 1940, cannot be written for some years to come. The trial of the Fifth Column is the trial for treason which the French people will inevitably demand. Enough evidence has been published already to prove that France was stabbed in the back by those who saw in Hitler the new St. George who would slay the Communist dragon. When Pierre Lazareff, former editor-in-chief of *Paris Soir* (the French newspaper with the widest circulation), reports royalists as saying: "We need the defeat to wipe out the Republic"; when Elie Bois, former editor of the *Petit Parisien* (the most influential political newspaper), reports great industrialists as admitting to him, during the winter of 1939-1940, that a plot had been organized to replace the democratic regime by a "government of authority" and that this plot presupposed a Nazi victory; when Anatole de Monzie writes, in a book* passed by the censor of the Vichy government, that Marshal Pétain said in February, 1940: "They will appeal to me in the third week in May"; when Geneviève Tabouis tells of the work accomplished in the Parisian salons by the Fifth Column's "brigade mondaine"; when Henri de Kerillis, former officer and nationalist deputy, exposes the inroads of the Fifth Column in the conservative and military circles which he knew; when Henry Torrès reveals to us what was going on in the offices of the official propaganda . . . we have every reason to accept their affirmations, which tally so perfectly with the events.

* Anatole de Monzie, *Ci-Devant* (Paris: Flammarion, 1941).

On the eve of the war, in a series of articles published in l'*Europe Nouvelle,* Georges Bidault demonstrated, with striking documents, how the French Fascist press was carrying out the orders of the German propagandists; at the same time the government had been driven by revelations published in l'*Humanité* to expel Otto Abetz, the director of Fifth Column activities in France. No one, of course, can base a definitive judgment against specific persons on these affirmations or revelations. But in the most serious works on the French defeat, in four books of scientific value, written by men of un-questionable intellectual honesty—Jacques Maritain, Yves Simon, Albert Guérard, and Pertinax (André Geraud)—I find the same impression: France was betrayed, France was handed over, France was abandoned by Frenchmen who saw their savior in Hitler. And how could it have been otherwise? Why, of all the European democracies, should France have been the only one with-out a Fifth Column? How could Hitler have neglected to undermine France's resistance before throwing his armies against her?

No, France received no exceptional treatment from Hitler and Fascism. A general plan co-ordinated the activity of the Fifth Columns all over the world. All were recruited from the same circles and had the same social and political composition. The object was the same everywhere: to divide and unnerve public opinion, weaken the resistance of the regime, and prepare a governmental group ready to execute a Fascist coup d'état at a moment of trouble or confusion. The methods were the same everywhere: cultivation of the seeds of disunity which normally exist among free men and in free countries, exaggeration and inflammation of all racial and religious conflicts, all class rivalries, all political antagonisms, gradual conversion of opposition and dissent into hate, creation of an atmosphere of civil war. The means used were the same everywhere: campaigns of calumny against the democratic leaders capable of opposing Fascism (Blum in France, Roosevelt in the United States), the development of anti-Semitism, because anti-Semitism is the first manifestation of racism and contains *in petto* the whole doctrine of Hitler, use of the fear of Communism among the middle classes, because anti-Communism is the best way to prevent the union of all anti-Fascist forces. This last device has been the most efficacious; the fear of Communism has be-come, in European and American politics of recent years, a much more important factor than Communism itself.

The Fifth Column was able to carry on its work because of the feebleness of governmental action against it. The government, of course, took measures against spies and traitors; but these terms were applied only to agents sent directly from Germany, and these agents were the least numerous and danger-ous. No measures were taken against native Fascists and friends of the Nazi regime. The government, counting on their "patriotism," left them a clear field. They benefited by the old policy of concessions and appeasement. Just as the Fascist dictators had profited by the weakness and complacency of the French, English, and American democracies to obtain strategic positions for the execution of their plans before the war, so the French Fascists gained positions during the war to carry out their coup d'état at the moment of defeat. A great network of intrigue enveloped France, its meshes growing ever tighter and stronger.

The government reserved all its harshness for the Communists. After the signing of the Russo-German Pact and the invasion of Poland, it was considered more reprehensible to be the friend of Stalin, with whom France was not at war, than the friend of Hitler, whose armies were preparing to invade France. It was more suspect to be a partisan of Franco-Russian rapprochement than to be a partisan of a Franco-Hitlerian entente.

The measures taken against the Communists, who were doing their duty as well as the rest in the Army and the factories, contrasted painfully with the indulgence enjoyed by the Fascists. These measures were at once unjust, arbitrary, and clumsy. Communist senators and deputies were dismissed from Parliament; other Communists who held public office were ousted, leaving unrepresented those who had elected them. Communist leaders were thrown into prisons or concentration camps. These arrests deprived the workers of some of their leaders, and overlooked the fact that the French working class had always provided the best fighters for liberty. Moreover, under the simple pretext of Communism, and sometimes upon mere denunciation, militant anti-Fascists, who had never been Communists, were molested and subjected to irritating police investigations. A democratic or Socialist worker was frowned upon by the Army which eagerly welcomed into its ranks the young bourgeois of the Croix de Feu and other Fascist organizations. The enemies of the Republic were trusted, while its defenders were suspected. Under such a system the common people began to realize that a vast offensive against the working class was being disguised as an anti-Communist campaign.

Meanwhile, the government's economic and social policy became more and more reactionary. Greater sacrifices were asked of workers than of employers. The right to strike, along with all social legislation, was suspended, but the right to huge profits continued in full force. Right or wrong, the government's policy seemed to be directed against the Popular Front in general and Communism in particular rather than against Fascism in general and Hitlerism in particular. Anti-Communist feeling reached its climax with the Russo-Finnish War; a veritable wave of madness swept over Parliament, where Pierre-Étienne Flandin demanded that France declare war on Russia. As France obviously could not fight Russia and Germany at the same time, this policy would have resulted in peace negotiations with Germany. Daladier, then President of the Council, and General Gamelin, then Chief of Staff, resisted this dangerous move as best they could. But, generally speaking, the Fascists had their own way in the country at large and in the Army. The anti-Communist agitation was a smoke screen behind which was being prepared the great political conspiracy that was to paralyze France and facilitate Hitler's work. By its repressive policy toward the workers and its indulgent treatment of the Fascists, the government prevented the soldiers' war from becoming a people's war—

a transformation which alone could have produced the great burst of en-thusiasm and energy necessary for the conquest of France's internal and external foes.

In spite of the action of the Fifth Column and the inaction of the govern-ment, however, the morale of the common people remained intact until June, 1940. It is a point on which I must insist, because one obtains exactly the opposite impression from most of the books on the fall of France hitherto published in the United States.

These books were written by authors who belong by education, profession, and manner of life to the bourgeoisie, particularly to the Parisian bourgeoisie, the class which was contaminated by the Fifth Column and by Fascism. Today, most of the supporters of the Pétain-Laval government belong to the upper middle class; most of those fighting this government come from the lower classes. The books to which I allude contain scandalous anecdotes about the so-called Parisian high society, but they fail to mention the name of Jouhaux, Secretary of the Confédération Générale du Travail, in which there were a few dozen traitors and five million honest workers worthy of the traditions of the French Revolution. The authors of these books described what they saw; they believed in the decay of France because they saw around them the decay of the French bourgeoisie. None of them had any contact with the workers and peasants who form the immense majority of the French people; none of them ever took part in the great demonstrations of the common people or felt the pulse of the French masses.

The same observation applies to the accounts of certain Americans who, traveling in Europe, made short stopovers in France, or, if they lived in France, described only the most corrupt circles. Just as one cannot judge America in terms of the people who live on Park Avenue, one cannot regard the Parisian haute bourgeoisie as typical of France. It was most unfortunate that the Comité France-Amérique, which undertook to explain France to Americans, should have been directed chiefly by René de Chambrun, son-in-law and parti-san of Pierre Laval. Only Jacques Maritain, in his excellent book *A Travers le Désastre,* pays homage to the fortitude of those he calls the "little people," the French masses. The peasants and workers of 1939-1940 were what they had been in 1914-1918. Greatly disturbed by the spectacle of the Fascist spider spinning its web more and more closely around France, they would have been ready to answer to a great national appeal, had such an appeal been made. To describe their state of mind, I cannot do better than report what was told me by Alexis Leger, former General Secretary of the Ministry of Foreign Affairs. Leger, today a refugee in Washington, tells the following story. When the members of the government, abandoning Paris on Weygand's advice, were moving to Tours before going to Bordeaux, Paul Reynaud's automobile was stopped by hordes of refugees on the roads. The people who stopped him were peasants driving their carts, workers tightly packed into trucks, and pedestrians and bicyclists; they were coming from the north, and had been bombed and machine-gunned by German airplanes. Reynaud was recognized and cries went up. Having been told by his associates that the people wanted peace at any price, Reynaud grew pale when he heard the crowds muttering, until he realized that they were shouting: "Hold fast, Reynaud! *Vive la France! On les aura!*" The French people's last word to Reynaud was to "hold fast," but the advice of Pétain and Weygand was to ask for an armistice. The Fifth Column had not poisoned the common people; it had converted the military leaders.

The Fifth Column played an important role at the time of the armistice. Its activity resulted directly in the request for an armistice and the government's refusal to go to North Africa. The most efficient instruments of the Fifth Column, in this case, were Weygand, Pétain, and Laval.

At the Council of Ministers which was held at Cangé, near Tours, on June 12, 1940, General Weygand urged the government to end the war. His principal argument was that a Communist revolution had broken out in Paris. He stated that Maurice Thorez, General Secretary of the Communist party, was already installed in the Presidential Palace. Georges Mandel, Minister of the Interior, immediately telephoned to the Prefect of Police in Paris, who denied Weygand's statements; there was no disturbance in the city, the population was quiet, and Thorez was not even in France. Mandel turned to Weygand and said: "If one of your officers brought you false information in such a serious situation, I think that you would have him arrested." These facts were reported to me by two members of the cabinet. The same story is told by Hamilton Fish Armstrong in his *Chronology of a Failure.** Either Weygand, knowing his information to be false, was a Fifth Column agent; or else deceived, and preoccupied with the anti-Communist struggle, he had accepted without verification anything that supported his thesis. In the latter case, his thoughtless behavior made him an unconscious agent of the Fifth Column.

At the end of June, 1940, France certainly had enough troops and war matériel to resist in North Africa; the fleet was intact, and, combined with the British fleet, would have had absolute control of the Mediterranean. The Air Force possessed 2,100 first-line airplanes which could have been sent to North Africa without difficulty. France had an army of 400,000 men in Syria and North Africa (Morocco, Algeria, Tunisia), larger, better equipped, and more easily supplied than the Italian Army in Libya. The African Army could have been reinforced by troops and matériel from France, the safe evacuation of which was ensured from both Atlantic and Mediterranean ports by the British and French fleets. A report sent by General Noguès, Commander-in-Chief of the North African Army, informed the government that Germany could not invade North Africa so long as the British and French fleets were in control of the Mediterranean. Albert Lebrun, President of the Republic,

* H. F. Armstrong, *Chronology of a Failure* (New York: Macmillan, 1940).

decided to leave for North Africa with some of the ministers and parliamentarians who were then at Bordeaux, but Laval threatened to establish a dissident government if Lebrun proceeded with his plans. Jean Montigny, Commissioner of Information in the Pétain government in July, 1940, and Laval's partisan, has related this interview between the two men in his book published with the authorization of Vichy.* The parliamentarians who, with official consent, had already sailed aboard the *Massilia* for North Africa, were arrested by governmental order upon their arrival at Casablanca—more Fifth Column activity.

It is hardly necessary to stress the consequences of the decision taken by Pétain, Weygand, Laval, and their accomplices. Had the Pétain government decided to go to North Africa, the whole course of the war might have been different. All of France would have been occupied, to be sure, but her situation would have been that of Norway, Holland, Belgium, Luxembourg, Greece, and Yugoslavia—the situation of every country whose government preferred the hard road of exile to the servitude of collaboration. The situation of the war prisoners would not have been worse; on the contrary, some troops of the east and southeast could have been interned, much to their advantage, in Switzerland for the duration of the war. Furthermore, Pétain and his ministers, unlike other governments-in-exile, would have been on French soil in North Africa. Far beyond having a symbolic value for Britain, they actually would have fortified her position. If the democracies, in June, 1940, could have counted on the French fleet—the most powerful in Europe after the British—2,100 first-line airplanes, the North African Army's strategic position, and all the human, military, and economic resources of the French Colonial Empire, Hitler, Mussolini, and Hirohito would not have had the slightest chance of winning the war. France could have given orders to her African Army and to her fleet to attack the Italian forces in Libya. With the ratio that existed—400,000 Frenchmen against 250,000 Italians—it would have been possible to answer the German victory on the continent by a French victory in North Africa. By throwing all her forces in the balance, France could have turned Hitler's victory into a Pyrrhic victory. Such a policy would have prevented Pétain from destroying the democratic system and might have led to an early fall of the Fascist dictatorships. But the mission of the Fifth Column was precisely to avoid the destruction of the Fascist dictatorships in Germany, Italy, and Spain, and to replace the Third Republic by a "government of authority."

How explain the role played by Pétain and Weygand in that decisive phase of the defeat of France? Why did they act as if they had been agents of the Fifth Column, favoring Hitler's cause both in the decisions they took and in the advice they gave? Why did they follow a line contrary to the French interest?

* Jean Montigny, *Toute la Vérité.*

68

Concerning these men, the hypotheses of treason cannot be accepted without proof. History will search for this proof. Until further information is available, the best explanation for their attitude is their admiration for Fascism and the hate for democracy which had dominated them for many years.

These sentiments led them to overestimate Hitler's force and to underestimate the British capacity for resistance. Winston Churchill was referring to them when he said in 1941: "The French generals declared to their government that within fifteen days the British Empire would have its neck wrung like a chicken." Their admiration for Fascism and for National Socialism made them believe that it was possible to reach an understanding with Hitler; they thought that Hitler, as conqueror, would be satisfied with tearing up the Versailles Treaty and retaking the provinces of Alsace and Lorraine. Pétain spoke of a "negotiated peace between soldiers"; he believed that a France, purged of democracy, should be associated with the direction of the European New Order. Acceptance of military defeat gave them an opportunity to overthrow the Republic and to establish a military dictatorship leading the French nation back to the discipline of the *ancien régime*. They hoped for a monarchic restoration, which they would serve as guides and advisers. They needed military dictatorship to blur the mistakes committed by them and their colleagues of the General Staff. Here facts speak for themselves. As soon as they had seized power amid the confusion of the collapse, Pétain and Weygand, with the help of Laval and Darlan, hastened to suppress all political liberties, gag the people, and set up a Fascist regime.

The question of knowing to what extent Weygand and Pétain were sincere does not interest us. In reading certain of their declarations on the necessity for France to do penance and to purify herself by suffering, it is possible to ask whether their religious and political fanaticism did not blind them to the extent of depriving them of all reason. There always will remain against them the fact that they gave the government false information in order to lead France to abandon the fight, when she still had a large Colonial Empire, the second largest Navy in Europe, an important Colonial army, and first-line planes. Only history will tell if it was through incompetence or treason that they supported Hitler's interests and the Fascist cause.

THEORIES ADVANCED TO EXPLAIN THE DEFEAT

How did France, before and during the war, come to commit so many blunders in her foreign, domestic, and military policies?

Three general explanations have been advanced: the aging of the French nation, the Popular Front, and the rallying of the French bourgeoisie to Fascism.

The Aging of the French Nation

The military and political defeat of France occasionally has been attributed, especially in the United States, to a kind of aging of the French nation, of which the fall in the birth rate is considered the most obvious symptom. It has been pointed out that all great nations have been leaders of civilization, only to be dethroned by younger, more dynamic cultures. The philosopher Ernest Renan, comparing the French Revolution to the Reformation, emphasized that nations who contribute most to humanity are bound to suffer an eclipse. He recalled the general weakening of German civilization in the sixteenth and seventeenth centuries as a result of the strain caused by the Reformation; and he foretold that French civilization would pass into the shadow in the nineteenth and twentieth centuries as a result of the strain of the Revolution. Although it is true that all peoples rise and fall in accordance with the economic and technical evolution which determines their intellectual efforts, these movements are always slow, as is the rhythm of all great human tides. The old age of France manifested itself only in the fields of military science and industrial organization. France's contributions to civilization in the advancement of sciences and liberal arts between 1920 and 1940 were not inferior to those of Germany and Italy. All foreigners who knew France in these years bear witness to the intelligence, skill, and devotion to work of the "little people." Finally, the present resistance of the French masses to Fascism and Hitlerism, their participation in the underground struggle and in sabotage, reveals an energy and courage which cannot be reconciled with the general theory of the nation's old age.

The Policy of the Popular Front

According to Vichy, the Popular Front put France in a state of least resistance. It is already clear that the mistakes of the Popular Front were not at the bottom of all the phenomena we have described. The Popular Front did not bear the principal responsibility for the Munich agreements, the anti-Soviet policy, and the activities of the Fifth Column. It was not the Popular Front which prevented Weygand from throwing against the German columns all the tanks, airplanes, and guns left in the depots. No one, unless he is trying to mask the errors of the appeasement policy, the mistakes of the General Staff, and the activity of the Fifth Column, can charge the Popular Front with the exclusive, or even the principal, responsibility for the defeat.

Conversion of the French Bourgeoisie to Fascism

I consider the rallying of the French bourgeoisie to Fascism the most acceptable explanation. It alone permits us to understand all the aspects and causes of the French defeat and reveals an element of truth in the theory of France's old age. The French people, although no older than the other European peoples, was led by the oldest and weakest of its social classes. This class was too blinded by its own interests to be capable of working for the nation as a whole, and too much fettered by its prejudices to master the problems of modern life. This theory illuminates, furthermore, the mistakes of French foreign policy, which stemmed from the bourgeois horror of an alliance with Russia and its desire to see the authoritarian systems maintained in Germany, Italy, and Spain. It also explains the intellectual inferiority of a General Staff that was the military expression of the bourgeoisie. The General Staff, as demonstrated by the Dreyfus affair, was linked historically with the most reactionary and anti-democratic elements. The last explanation also throws light on the activity of the Fifth Column, four-fifths of whose members were recruited from the bourgeoisie.

This conversion to Fascism was not sudden and complete, but gradual and partial. While the upper bourgeoisie became more and more actively Fascist, the middle bourgeoisie was saturated with Fascist ideology, and a fraction of the petite bourgeoisie was resigning itself to Fascism as to an inevitable fact. The Fascist and pro-Fascist organizations in France before the war— l'Action Française, the Jeunesses Patriotes, the Croix de Feu, the Cagoulards, Doriot's Parti Populaire Français—had an almost exclusively bourgeois membership. The most active anti-Fascist organizations, on the other hand, recruited their members chiefly from the common people. This situation has not changed since June, 1940. The conversion to Fascism resulted from the political and intellectual evolution that began in the last quarter of the nineteenth century. The French bourgeoisie, gradually abandoning its eighteenth century heritage of rationalist and liberal thought, as expressed in a democratic society, regressed toward a hierarchic social order and an authoritarian form of government, such as the *ancien régime* had been. Fifty years ago Charles Maurras, the exponent of the monarchist doctrine, Georges Sorel, the theoretician of syndicalism, and Maurice Barrès, the novelist of nationalism, prepared the way for Fascism. They furnished the bourgeois classes with the arguments, formulae, and metaphors which in our day were used to destroy the republican regime.

As the bourgeoisie was predominant in French politics, this progressive conversion had important consequences. The Third Republic was largely a democracy in name only. Within governmental and administrative institutions the power of the bourgeoisie had grown stronger and stronger at the expense of the common people. The will of the majority was no longer sovereign. Most of the members of the government, most of the civil servants, and all the Army leaders belonged to the bourgeoisie. Unconsciously at times, they behaved less as representatives of the French nation than as representatives of the bourgeois circles to which they were attached by family, education, and way of life; because of them, the governmental and administrative machinery was controlled not by the majority of the people, but by a wealthy minority. France was under the yoke of a bourgeois dictatorship. The bourgeoisie, when it succumbed to the Fascist powers, handed over to them a state well under its control.

This leaning toward Fascism has attacked all the democracies in varying manners and degrees; each nation has reacted differently to it.

Let us consider only the case of capitalist democracy, a democracy limited to the political sphere. Fascism is a disease of the contemporary democratic state or, rather, a stage in the evolution of capitalist democracy. One might say of Fascism and the capitalist democracies what La Fontaine said of the animals who were ill of the plague: "All did not die but all were stricken." Every capitalist nation has defended itself more or less effectively against Fascism, just as human beings during an epidemic differ in their resistance to infection. Until now the democracies that have resisted the Fascist microbe best have been the Anglo-Saxon, Scandinavian, and Swiss democracies, where individual minds have the best tradition and experience of free inquiry, where the critical spirit has never been arrested in its development by the predominance of a military caste, and where, as a result of local government, democratic institutions have the deepest roots. Countries which have been either militaristic, Catholic, or highly centralized have fallen easier prey to Fascism than pacifist, Protestant, or decentralized states.

The causes of the conversion of the middle classes, formerly considered the backbone of democracy, must be sought in an analysis of the structure and evolution of modern society. It is impossible to carry out this analysis conscientiously without borrowing from the methods of historical materialism. It is not at all necessary to go into all the subtleties of Marxism to understand how much the evolution of contemporary society has been linked to the development of the capitalist system. This development, in the course of the last fifty years, has been dominated by the concentration of economic power; modern capitalism has gone from free competitive enterprise to the entente of producers, and from there to monopoly, without a pause.

It is not necessary to be a sociologist to observe the following series of phenomena. First, the concentration of enterprise has modified the composition of the middle class; the small entrepreneur and artisan have been transformed into the "employer" and "technician" in the service of large enterprises. Consequently, to use statistical language, the middle class today includes fewer "independent employers and workers" who desire freedom in their professional habits, and more units in the hierarchy of large capitalist enterprise. The change in the professional groups composing the bourgeoisie has its repercussions in the political and psychological reactions of this class, to the extent to which our habits of thought are dominated and limited by our professional education. A worker does not reason like a peasant, and the head of a department in a large bank does not have the same views as an independent businessman. Men who are fixed in a professional hierarchy bow easily before discipline and are not as good recruits for political democracy as the old independent workers.

72

Second, the concentration of enterprise engenders industrial and commercial agreements; instead of fighting one another, the enterprises, reduced in number, try to come to terms and divide the market. These agreements lead directly to the "corporative system," for "corporatism" means a certain degree of commercial concentration and economic integration sanctioned by law. The tendency toward corporatism has been especially visible in small states such as Portugal and Austria, and in large industrial states where capitalism, after exhausting its possibilities of expansion within the country, found itself deprived of foreign and colonial outlets—the case of Germany. Fascism has been the most natural political expression of corporatism; it is the translation into political terms of the hierarchic principle on which corporatism is founded. It appeared as the capitalists' only alternative to the various forms of Socialism.

Third, the concentration of enterprise, by extending the range of social conflicts, replaces professional worker-employer disputes by much graver class struggles; a strike or a lockout which affects 50,000 workers is far more important than 500 strikes, each of which affects 100 workers. As the class struggle becomes more violent, the fear of revolution grips the bourgeoisie. The existing social order is compromised by its own contradictions; the beneficiaries of this order, fearing the loss of their privileges through the democratic mechanism, search for anti-democratic movements and organizations able to impose "order" and reinforce "authority." These words replace "liberty" and "equality" in their thinking and conversation.

These factors have been sufficient to draw the bourgeoisie from liberalism and bend it towards corporatism. Wounded by the harshness of the modern world, the bourgeoisie is no longer conservative but reactionary. It dreams with bitterness and melancholy of the "good old times." It accepts a radical transformation of political institutions and the abandonment of its liberties in the hope that the ancient order of things will be recreated, an order in which the son of the worker did not have the chance to rise above the son of the employer or of the civil servant. The development of capitalism has thus provoked, in every capitalist country, a favorable climate for the development of Fascism. When a violent crisis occurs—be it a politico-economic crisis in Italy, an economic crisis in Germany, a political crisis in Spain, or an unexpected military defeat in France—the country is ripe for clever demagogues. They take advantage of the situation to undermine democracy by promising to free the middle class from "Judeo-Masonic exploitation" and from the "Communist menace." A frightened middle class accepts the Fascist political revolution as a safeguard against social evolution. This is the cause of the political malady from which all democracies have suffered and to which many have succumbed.

Weakness of French Democracy

French democracy, like all the other democracies, had its strong and its weak points. Its particular character was shaped by economic and social circumstances and, in its most individual aspects, by historical circumstances.

The strength of French democracy came from its revolutionary tradition. Unlike the more peaceful and steady development of the Anglo-Saxon democracies, the French was created by revolutions—the Revolutions of 1789-1793, of 1830, 1848, and 1871. It was a fighting democracy, inspiring Marx to say: "Revolutions are the locomotives of History." All political progress in France sprang from revolutionary battles, and all social progress was accomplished under the threat of revolution. When the French speak of the Revolution without further specification, they mean the Revolution of 1789, and every French democrat thinks of himself as a son of that Revolution.

This democratic tradition has taken two principal forms. The first is the attachment of the petite bourgeoisie to the republican form of government. The common people love the Republic. For one hundred and fifty years, with the patience of a peasant clearing a field, the common people of city and country have devoted themselves to creating the Republic, defending it when it was in danger, re-creating it when it had been destroyed. For it they have fought on the barricades. To save it they have opposed all of the forces of reaction—Church, Army, Aristocracy, and Industry. The second expression of the French democratic tradition has been the political orientation of the labor organizations. Unlike American unions, French labor syndicates have been political forces. They were not limited to purely professional activity; they were not preoccupied exclusively with ameliorating the material situation of the workers by fighting only for higher wages and shorter hours. They concerned themselves with the form of government, the economic system, and with international relations, and always had a political and social program. Without taking a direct part in the electoral conflicts or seeking to be represented in Parliament by a labor party, the syndicates played an important role in the political education of the country and in the political struggle. This tradition has kept the French worker untouched by Fascist propaganda and by the corporative idea. The labor unions were in the front line of the anti-Fascist struggle between 1934 and 1940. They have been the leaders of the underground battle against Hitler and the Vichy government. The attachment of the common people to the Republic and the political power of the labor organizations were the armor of democracy, and this armor would have been sufficiently strong if the military defeat, caused and utilized by the enemies of democracy, had not overturned the political situation to the benefit of Fascism, and permitted Pétain, with Hitler's support, to crush the Third Republic.

The weakness of French democracy has two causes. The first factor is historical: it is the persistence, on the part of the haute bourgeoisie, of an anti-democratic tradition, a fanatical opposition to the extension of the democratic principle. According to the historians, there have been, for the past hundred and fifty years, two France's: one, a liberal and democratic France, the France of the Revolution and of the Declaration of the Rights of Man, and the other, a reactionary, militaristic, and nationalistic France, the France of the Restoration and of the Empire, of the MacMahon regime and of the Dreyfus affair. The two France's have been constantly at war; the adversaries of democracy have never disarmed and have never accepted the political new deal of the French Revolution. For a century and a half, all Frenchmen—consciously or unconsciously, depending on the degree of their political education—have been divided into two spiritual families, partisans or enemies of the Revolution. The political history of contemporary France is the history of the struggle between these two families.

In popular language—which expresses most accurately the feelings of a people—contemporary France has known only two great parties, the "Reds," or heirs of the Revolution, and the "Whites," its adversaries. In all crises, this fundamental distinction has reappeared. The French conservatives, consequently, have been not only guardians of established order and opponents of social progress, but also enemies of the republican system. There are real conservatives in the Scandinavian and Anglo-Saxon countries, but in France, the conservatives, by political tradition, have always been reactionaries, preoccupied with restoring the past rather than adapting themselves to the present. They have supported, in varying circumstances, the King, the Emperor, Marshal MacMahon, General Boulanger, and Pétain. Tomorrow they will support any one who seems capable of delivering them from the democratic menace. They feel that democracy, with its principle of majority rule, represents a threat to their privileges. The French bourgeoisie has always had a small nucleus of men who would do anything to destroy the Republic. During the Revolution this nucleus fomented the civil war in Vendée and helped the armies of England and Austria "try to muzzle the French people"; in 1815 it welcomed the Austro-Russian troops in Paris after Waterloo, as in 1940 and 1942 the adversaries of the Third Republic welcomed Goering and his officers.

This small but permanent nucleus of anti-democrats was the rallying point for French Fascism. Their rallying was largely due to the influence of Maurras, theoretician of absolute monarchy. No man has done more to develop the hatred of democracy and to transform this hatred into admiration for Fascism.

The second circumstance favorable to the development of French Fascism has been the progressive degeneration of the democratic institutions. Few realize how undemocratic these had become.

From its beginning the Third Republic was not very democratic. Its system was fixed by the Constitutional laws of 1875, and Clemenceau once declared that these laws were a "war machine against the Republic." They had been drafted and passed by a National Assembly composed largely of royalists and conservatives. The National Assembly accepted the republican principle because its members, split into rival groups, could not agree on a monarchic formula. Some favored an absolute monarchy and others a constitutional monarchy. The authors of the Constitution of 1875 tried to make the Republic as undemocratic and "unrepublican" as possible, and they succeeded in a great measure. Still more important for the understanding of its constitutional weakness is the fact that the republican regime, from 1920 to 1940, suffered a progressive degradation, resulting not from actual modifications of the constitutional laws, but from their application and interpretation by Parliament.

The republican regime, less and less capable of translating the will of the majority into governmental decisions, became less and less democratic.

This transformation has rarely been described. Since the French Republic was a parliamentary democracy, Parliament had legislative power as well as the control of the executive power, the cabinet being politically responsible to it. The French Parliament, like the British, was divided into two houses, the Chamber of Deputies and the Senate. Only the Chamber was elected by direct universal suffrage. The Senate, similar to the English House of Lords, represented the most conservative elements of the nation—chiefly the middle class and the "rural bourgeoisie." In senatorial elections the rural bourgeoisie had an advantage; those Frenchmen who lived in the country and small towns elected proportionately three times as many Senators as those who lived in the big cities. This gave three times as much political power to the rural and suburban bourgeoisie as to the working population of big cities. The result was that only the Chamber of Deputies was representative of the whole nation (including its radical elements), while the Senate was the political expression of the conservative bourgeoisie.

This created no serious difficulties before the war of 1914. During the 1875-1914 period the political powers of the Senate were less extensive than those of the Chamber of Deputies; it was generally understood that the Senate could not overthrow the cabinet, and that after using its "right of remonstrance," it had to bow before the will of the Chamber in financial matters, since the Chamber had the right to apply the "doctrine of the last word." After the first World War, however, these wise constitutional guarantees were abandoned. The Senate now considered its powers equal to those of the Chamber, caused its will to prevail in financial matters, and claimed the right to overthrow the cabinet.

In practice, the extension of the Senate's political power resulted in legislative paralysis and ministerial instability, in short, governmental impotence. Differently constituted and representing the will of often irreconcilable social groups, the Chamber and Senate were bound to have divergent political orientations. As the cabinet, to exist, needed the confidence of both houses, it was always obliged to seek a compromise between the will of the people and that of the conservative bourgeoisie. When the cabinet's attitude pleased the Chamber, it displeased the Senate, and vice versa. A survey of the many ministerial crises between 1920 and 1940, one of the weaknesses of the Third Republic, reveals that 80 per cent of them were caused, directly or indirectly, by the disagreement between Chamber and Senate on financial matters. Every cabinet that showed progressive tendencies was pitilessly overthrown by the Senate. That was the fate, for example, of the Herriot cabinet in 1924 and of Blum's two Popular Front cabinets in 1937 and 1938, although these cabinets enjoyed the confidence of the Chamber and, therefore, of the country. Professor Guérard, in his book The France of Tomorrow,* without analyzing this constitutional mechanism, states that French democracy had fallen under

* A. L. Guérard, The France of Tomorrow (Cambridge, Mass.: Harvard University Press, 1942).

a "dictatorship of the bourgeoisie." The political instrument of this dictatorship was the Senate; its economic instrument, the Bank of France.

From 1920 to 1940, in three general elections out of four, the French people chose progressive governments; and every time, the wealthy minority, whether by the manipulation of its economic power or through the Senate, compelled these governments to follow a conservative policy or overthrew them. The progressive majority of the "Leftist cartel" elected in 1924, that of the "Leftist coalition" in 1932, and that of the Popular Front elected in 1936 were all broken, not because of a modification of public opinion, but because of the control exercised over the state by the bourgeoisie. Big business rather than the common man dominated the Third Republic.

An important consequence of this "dictatorship of the bourgeoisie" was the increasing impatience of the masses and of organized labor with the Third Republic. The French workers felt that the will of the people was no longer sovereign, that it could never prevail, especially in social questions, against the will of the minority. They felt that the state had lost its independence. After the fall of the Popular Front government, they lost confidence in the possibilities of "reformism" in a democracy constantly obliged to bow before the political domination of big business. Anglo-Saxons have wondered what it was that encouraged the growth of revolutionary parties in France; it was largely the impotence of the democratic mechanism. Revolution appeared as the alternative to reformism.

It was not because it was too democratic, but because it was not democratic enough, that the Third Republic weakened and was conquered. Politics cannot be explained by hypotheses, much less by regrets. But if the French governmental institutions had been truly democratic, the Popular Front cabinets would not have been overthrown; had the Senate not held a reactionary mortgage on Parliament, the French government would have supported the Spanish Republic and would have continued to work for a Franco-Soviet rapprochement—for such was the feeling of the majority. The war and the defeat would have been avoided. When the enemies of democracy attribute the defeat of France to the weaknesses of the republican regime, it must be said in rebuttal that the French Republic was more democratic in 1914-1918 than in 1939-1940: in 1918 France was victorious; in 1940 she was conquered.

The Cagoulard Affair

A majority of the French bourgeoisie unwillingly resigned itself to Fascism, which offended its liberal traditions. A powerful minority, however, adopted Fascism with enthusiasm as a means of fighting the Republic.

Much information and research will be needed to determine to what degree the military and political defeat of France was caused by the conspiracy of this Fascist minority. What has already been demonstrated is that such a conspiracy existed. It was created before the war, and was used by Hitler to smash

77

French resistance; it culminated in the dictatorship of Marshal Pétain; it has been carried on by Fascist organizations in France and in North Africa to prevent the French people from recovering political freedom in the event of an Allied victory.

The conspiracy against the Republic was discovered in November, 1937. During 1936 and 1937 more and more outrages had occurred all over France; bombs had exploded, caches of arms had been found, anti-Fascist refugees had been assassinated. After each crime wave the police uncovered more threads of an important plot. An inquiry was ordered. Many arrests were made. According to a communiqué of the Ministry of the Interior on November 19, 1937, "the documents seized showed that the conspirators were bent on substituting for the republican form of government, a dictatorial regime which was to precede the restoration of the French monarchy." The conspiracy became known as the Cagoulard plot. The Cagoulards (Hooded-Men) had formed a powerful secret association organized on the Hitlerian model by the most dynamic elements of the Fascist organizations. To quote again from the official communiqué, the plotters had collected "a large quantity of war matériel, in large part of foreign origin"; they had "a military set-up patterned after the services of the army. . . their adherents were grouped into divisions, brigades, regiments, battalions, etc. . . with a complete General Staff and a medical corps. . . this showed the organization's character to be prepared unquestionably for civil war." Among the leaders of the Cagoulards were representatives of finance, industry, the Army, and the aristocracy—such as General Dusseigneur, Commandant Loustaleau-Lacau (a collaborator and friend of Marshal Pétain), Duke Pozzo di Borgo, Viscount de Douville Maillefeu, Baron H. Pastré, MM. Eugene Deloncle, Moreau de la Meuse, and others.

The discovery of the Cagoulard plot aroused strong feeling among the people. It was clear that the French Fascists were preparing to imitate the Spanish Fascists by waging a civil war with assistance from abroad. The connections between the French Cagoulards and the German, Italian, and Spanish organizations were proved not only by the origin of their armaments, but by unequivocal documents and by the pattern of their activities. Thus the Cagoulards executed a series of crimes and acts of sabotage planned in agreement with Franco (bombings of trains or matériel destined for republican Spain, the attack on a Loyalist submarine in the port of Brest, etc.); moreover, one of the Cagoulard leaders was a Baron Potters, of Austrian origin, who called himself Baron de Pottière after Laval naturalized him in 1935, and who, according to the French Intelligence Service, was connected with Colonel Nicolai, the chief of Hitler's espionage services. The Cagoulards were subsidized by the great financial and economic organizations, and were in touch with high military figures, among them Weygand and Pétain. The Cagoulard plot was the French version of the Franco insurrection. This was in 1937. In 1940 the Cagoulards formed the staffs of Pétain's new regime. In 1942, when the chances for a Nazi victory began to dissipate, certain leaders of the Cagoule went to Algiers and slipped into the political entourage of the honest and patriotic General Giraud—an entourage which included authentic Fascists, former members of the Vichy government, like Peyrouton and General Bergeret, but very few democrats. Having practiced the policy of collaboration with Hitler in order to defeat democracy, the Cagoulards now experimented with a policy of collaboration with the democratic powers in order to keep the French people in servitude. For the Cagoulards are interested in neither the victory of Germany nor the victory of the Allies; they have but one aim—the defeat of French democracy.

The story of the Cagoulards permits us to touch on the moral and intellectual corruption of the French middle class. The Cagoule was the most dynamic expression of the bourgeoisie's conversion to Fascism. It was Fascism in its purest form, totally unscrupulous, ready to commit any crime and to form any alliance, be it one with Hitler, to reach its goal. But the evil was both older and deeper—the Cagoule was only one of its most visible symptoms. One can follow, year by year, the chief stages in the ever stronger adhesion of the French bourgeoisie to Fascism.

1934: the uprising of the 6th of February is the first manifestation of the conversion.

1935: the reactionary bourgeoisie supports the policy of Pierre Laval against sanctions and the League of Nations; because of this policy Laval is adopted by the bourgeoisie. ("Much will be forgiven Pierre Laval for his policy in favor of Italy," wrote the political editor of *l'Echo de Paris* in 1937.)

1936: the reactionary bourgeoisie begins its campaign against the ratification of the Franco-Soviet Pact; for simple reasons of domestic policy, it fights an agreement which would have been the best instrument of our foreign policy and our national security.

1936-1937: the reactionary bourgeoisie savagely opposes both the policy and the men of the Popular Front; the characteristic phenomenon of this opposition is the campaign of slander which drove to suicide Blum's Minister of the Interior, Roger Salengro. The bourgeoisie supports Spanish Fascism.

1937-1938: the Cagoule affair.

1938: the fall of the Popular Front and the coming to power of Georges Bonnet, whose policy culminates in the Munich agreements and the visit of von Ribbentrop to Paris.

1939: the war and the organization of the Fifth Column.

1940: the seizure of power by Pétain, Weygand, Darlan, and Laval in the confusion of France's defeat.

1941: the collaboration policy.

1942: the Cagoule splits; some leaders go to North Africa to collaborate with the Allies, while the others continue their collaboration with Hitler and Mussolini.

The adhesion of the reactionary bourgeoisie to Fascism was thus the decisive element in the French defeat; it was the cause of causes, the common denominator for the factors of the defeat. It provoked the panic fear of Communism, which prevented France from continuing in the direction of a rapprochement with Russia. It aroused a kind of conservative chauvinism in military circles, which prevented the French Army from becoming a modern army. Men like Pétain and Weygand, instead of concentrating on preparations for the war, thought in terms of a coup d'état. It infused the French bourgeoisie with an admiration for Hitler that engendered the Fifth Column. The Cagoulards were the principal agents of this conversion; they not only professed to, but actually did, prefer Hitler to Léon Blum.

A Hypothesis To Be Verified by History

A historical vantage point alone will permit classification of the causes of the defeat of France in the order of their importance. In my interpretation of the facts, I have limited myself to the formulation of a hypothesis; time and research will be required for its verification, completion, and correction.

The defeat of France appears to me as a tragedy in three acts: it was prepared by France's isolation, chiefly caused by the rupture of the Franco-Soviet Pact; it was consummated by the military weakness of France, chiefly caused by the General Staff's professional and intellectual inferiority; it ended with the fall of the Third Republic and the policy of collaboration, chiefly caused by Fifth Column activity. Each of these determinants played its special role. Yet the three acts form a coherent whole: at every juncture, the treason of the French haute bourgeoisie appears. This class is responsible for the defeat; the Vichy government is merely its instrument.

If this hypothesis is correct, it is not the French people who are responsible for the defeat, but only a small minority of them. It is not the French people who have deserted the cause of democracy and anti-Fascism. Give them the right to speak and their first words will be "Liberty, Equality, Fraternity." Let the friends of France have confidence in the future. When France regains her freedom, she will take her traditional place among civilized nations—on the front line.

The Vichy government has its own hypothesis: the responsibility of the Popular Front. The friends of France must recognize the danger of the Vichy thesis. By accusing the Popular Front, Vichy accuses the French people, for no one can deny that the Popular Front has been the expression of the will of the majority.

The study of the documents and testimony presented at the Riom Court will permit us to choose between the two hypotheses.

The Popular Front

3

T HE ACTIVITY of the Popular Front was by no means limited to the acts mentioned in the list of charges at the Riom trial. The Popular Front will be accorded an important place in French political history for its achievements.

In a general way the Popular Front was the French equivalent of the New Deal. It aroused the same violent opposition and the same eager hope. Like the New Deal, it was both a political movement, trying to realize the aspirations of the people, and a social movement, attempting to correct the principal injustices of the established order and to resolve the contradictions of the existing economic system. Like the Revolution itself, it was founded on the enthusiasm and confidence of the masses. Such movements by their very scope, sometimes commit blunders and excesses, but they have their nobility and their grandeur; they leave their mark on history. Through them alone humanity accomplishes its liberation.

From this point of view, the Popular Front was more a preparation than an achievement. Its official existence was short because its adversaries never allowed it to come to maturity. It was organized in the years 1934-1936. It came to power in June, 1936, as a result of general elections which sent four hundred Popular Front candidates, out of a total of six hundred, to the Chamber of Deputies—the largest majority in French history. The power of this majority was broken at the beginning of 1938 by the combined efforts of reactionaries and domestic and foreign Fascists. But the flame of the Popular Front still burns and its light still guides the hopes of the most active fighters in the underground organizations. The Popular Front lives on as a persistent faith in the hearts of the French people. In January, 1942, Pertinax, a conservative columnist and an opponent of the Popular Front, wrote in the American press that if France were free again, the people would vote for a Popular Front majority; and the modifications which General de Gaulle has been led to make in the administration of his movement, especially in accepting the support of Socialists and Communists, shows to what extent the Popular Front still exists. When Fascism is overthrown, the formulae, names, and doctrines of the Popular Front will have become superannuated, like the formulae and doctrines of the French Revolution. Like the spirit of the Revolution, however, the spirit of the Popular Front will live on. The French nation, having achieved a greater degree of political maturity and understanding of what the battle for human liberation involves, will remember with emotion the beginnings, endeavors, and ideals of the Popular Front; the people will sing its songs and shout its battle cries. The days of the Popular Front will appear as a period of great enthusiasm and generosity; a period of youth and development. The Popular Front was the birth of a new idea; it remains the dawn of a new epoch in the history of France.

A general view of the Popular Front is necessary because in a large section of the foreign press the movement was distorted and caricatured. Many Frenchmen abroad, including refugees from the Vichy government, have participated in this work of distortion without realizing the harm they were doing to the French people. France was never more united than under the Popular Front government, for no political development was ever accepted by so large a majority. The attitude of Frenchmen living abroad is not surprising when one remembers that France, unlike most European countries, has had almost no lower class emigration. French emigrés are principally bourgeois, and it is normal, although regrettable, that they should have brought with them the general reaction of the bourgeoisie, which in thought and interests differs so widely from the common people of France.

THE ORIGINS OF THE POPULAR FRONT

The Popular Front had its genesis in the reaction of the French people to the political and social bias of a part of the bourgeoisie. It was the people's riposte to the Fascist menace and to the Croix de Feu, which became the most important and best organized Fascist movement.

Initially an association of nationalistic and reactionary war veterans, the Croix de Feu became a militant anti-democratic, anti-Semitic, and pro-Fascist organization. Its strength was revealed on February 6, 1934, with the fall of a democratic cabinet, a cabinet that possessed the confidence of Parliament. The Croix de Feu exploited its success by provoking Fascist demonstrations throughout the country, and speedily won over a majority of young reactionaries. Like the Italian Fascists in the days of the march on Rome and the Nazi bands before 1932, its members were organized in military or semi-military groups. Troops paraded in the streets. Gatherings of ten thousand or twenty thousand men would appear overnight in a given place. The secrecy and rapidity of these maneuvers indicated the organizational and financial power of the movement. The Croix de Feu had airplanes and ambulances, uniforms and munitions, and proclaimed openly its preparations for civil war. Like Fascist movements the world over, it was subsidized largely by the great industrial organizations. The only important difference between the Fascist movement in France and German or Italian Fascism was the almost exclusively bourgeois character of its following. In spite of all efforts, the Croix de Feu made no headway among the masses. It was anathema to the healthy common sense and political intelligence of the common people. But the organization was strong enough to provoke the first anti-Semitic outbreaks in North Africa, where it has always been very powerful. Anti-Semitism, anti-Communism, anti-democracy, the narrowest nationalism, military preparation for civil war— these were the characteristics of Fascism in Europe, and these were the characteristics of the Croix de Feu.

The movement was led by a former cavalry officer, Colonel de la Rocque. (The French masses have always distrusted cavalry officers and aristocrats who meddled with politics.) A perfect example of the brainless aristocrat, Colonel de la Rocque, whose speeches and writings reveal a poverty of thought matched only by his contempt for grammar, proclaimed his veneration for Mussolini in 1934-1936. To this he added his admiration for Franco in 1936-1938. The methods the Colonel adopted were Hitler's. He appeared in a powerful automobile, surrounded by motorcycle guards; his "men," wearing Basque berets and leather belts, saluted him with outstretched arms, repeating his name incessantly; he affected a haughty and intense expression and never smiled. He was dangerous, like children who play with matches. Although incapable of seizing power, he could provoke civil war by being the dictator's apprentice. He was known to be the friend of Marshal Pétain, then Minister of War; of General Weygand, then Chief of Staff; and of many other high officials of the Army. He profited by the tolerance—to call it by no stronger name—of the Doumergue, Flandin, and Laval cabinets, which were in power during 1934 and 1935. In 1938 certain dissenting members of the Croix de Feu brought charges against their former leader; in the course of this trial, it was revealed that Colonel de la Rocque and his movement had been on the payroll of these cabinets. André Tardieu, who was called as a witness, added that as early as 1930-1932, when he was President of the Council, he had paid De la Rocque and the Croix de Feu, so that this organization might oppose "revolutionary" labor forces. These facts were still unknown in 1934-1936, when De la Rocque passed for an honest, independent, disinterested man, without governmental connections—a man capable of nothing more than starting civil war under pretext of re-establishing "order."

The agitation of the Croix de Feu produced a profound reaction, particularly among the masses and the intellectuals. After February 12, 1934, the labor unions of the Parisian area, together with the leading parties of the Left, organized a mass demonstration protesting against the riot of the 6th of February. The anti-Fascist feeling of the people was reflected in a day of general strike throughout the country. Nevertheless, the Croix de Feu gradually intensified its war against the workers' organizations and the political groups that did not accept its Fascist ideology. The people became more and more alarmed when police investigations disclosed many Fascist munition depots near the German frontier. Such political agitation and traffic in arms showed ever more clearly the Fascists' threat to France. The French who wanted to remain free, the political and trade-union organization that wanted to avoid the fate of their German and Italian brothers, resolved to unite in order to combat the common danger. Out of this union arose the Popular Front.

The Popular Front also had its social cause.

The economic depression which descended on all the countries of America and Europe between 1929 and 1933 struck France somewhat late and was relatively moderate; the unemployment curve never fell as low in France as in other countries having the same economic structure. In 1934-1935 the crisis was severe for the peasants, for the small officials, and particularly for the workers. As part of the "deflation" policy of the Doumergue, Flandin, and Laval cabinets, wages and salaries were reduced although they already were exceptionally low. French employers had never understood that a policy of high wages has social as well as economic advantages—internal peace and increased purchasing power. French social legislation lagged far behind that of most European countries, and the poorly paid French worker was even more poorly protected against unemployment. Under these conditions, the slightest reduction in salaries was catastrophic; it involved lowering the workers' standard of living, a reduction not in luxuries but in necessities. The decrease in purchasing power affected the sale of agricultural products, and the peasants followed the workers into misery. Between 1934 and 1936 the Medical Inspection of primary schools revealed a serious condition of malnutrition among working-class children. Finally, with an overabundant labor supply from which to choose, employers could discharge and blacklist the active and militant trade-unionists.

In 1934-1936 France was one of the democratic countries in which private wealth was unevenly shared and in which the leveling of classes had made least progress in the last hundred and fifty years. The French Revolution thought it had struck a decisive blow against social inequality when it destroyed the feudal regime; the immense lands of the aristocracy and the Church had been divided and distributed in a more equitable fashion. But large estates had been re-created under the Restoration, and more important, a new form of wealth—movable wealth—had appeared in the nineteenth century and become concentrated in the hands of a small minority. The French aristocracy of wealth was as privileged and parasitical a class as the old landed aristocracy had been. It exacted a share of the national income which nothing could justify.

According to a study by Paul Beik, published in the *Political Science Quarterly* (September, 1941),* 90.5 per cent of the Parisian population, in 1930, owned 4 per cent of the private wealth, while 0.28 per cent owned 44.87 per cent. Between these two extremes of the social scale, there was a wealthy middle class constituting 9.2 per cent of the population and owning 45.97 per cent of the private wealth. The great majority of the people had only

* Paul H. Beik, "Evidence Concerning the Distribution of Wealth in France," *Political Science Quarterly,* September, 1941.

a trifling share in the distribution of material goods. None of the arguments generally advanced in justification of private property—work, social utility, economic interest, superiority of intelligence, cleverness, or thrift—can justify a system which gave three thousand times more to one rich man than to nine-tenths of his fellow men. If one takes the round figures of the Parisian population, one will see that the great luxury of ten thousand was opposed to the poverty of two million (the wage-earners and their families), while a privileged bourgeoisie of two hundred thousand served as a screen which gave the foreign tourist the impression that Paris was a city where the average man was quite well-to-do.

In the provinces, particularly in the small-scale farming regions, the economic inequality was less apparent; but statistics prove that the wealthiest 5 per cent possessed as much as the poorest 90 per cent. This social injustice produced the conditions favorable to the development both of Fascism and of anti-Fascism. The Croix de Feu and the Popular Front won adherents most easily in the large cities, where the division of wealth was more apparent and poverty was more acute. These conditions explain why French Fascism was more bourgeois than Italian or German Fascism, and why it was much more conservative and reactionary. In Paris the aristocracy of wealth—the ten thousand, or the "200 Families"—paid, inspired, and used the Fascist movements; the privileged bourgeoisie—the two hundred thousand—furnished the leaders and followers for these movements; these followers were joined by several thousand of a misled *Lumpenproletariat*, whose existence Karl Marx had already pointed out in his studies on the Second French Republic, but in the case of the Croix de Feu and other Fascist groups, it was chiefly a white-collar *Lumpenproletariat*. The Popular Front, on the other hand, was composed of the under-privileged 90 per cent.

The Popular Front differed from the New Deal in that it united Communists and liberals in a single political organization. This alliance was essential to ward off the Fascist menace. It was made possible by the best and strongest tradition of French politics—the periodic union of all the spiritual heirs of the French Revolution. The Revolution has been an intellectual and moral patrimony shared by all the liberal and radical elements of the French nation. To understand the necessity of the Popular Front, the French democrats had only to recall history; there they found at every political juncture and in all the crises of public life the union of the liberal bourgeois and the revolutionary worker for the establishment or defense of the republican regime. Speaking at the Congress of the Radical-Socialist party at Nantes in October, 1934, Daladier cried out: "Look at our history! Whenever in the past the Third Estate [the lower bourgeoisie] and the proletariat joined forces, the Republic was saved, be it in the Revolution of 1789-1793, the Revolution of 1848, or in the alliance, in the days of the Dreyfus affair, of the revolutionary Jaurès with the liberal bourgeois Waldeck-Rousseau. But where this union crumbled, the result was the coup d'état of the 18 Brumaire or that of the 2nd of December, and the Republic toppled." Political leaders had only to contemplate the reality of French life to know that in city and country alike the true line of political demarcation was again between the "Whites" and the "Reds."

There was little hesitation. The action of the Croix de Feu rapidly created an alliance of the democratic petit bourgeois and the Communist worker, who suffered under the same insults and attacks. Republicans who were most anxious to preserve the liberty and dignity of the individual, Herriot and Paul-Boncour, for example, realized as early as 1934 that effective opposition to Fascism could come only from a "united front" of all democratic and popular organizations. These men knew that the Popular Front was as natural and essential for domestic policy as collective security was for foreign policy; just as collective security was impossible without the co-operation of Soviet Russia, the Popular Front could not be achieved without the participation of the Communist party. This party included the most dynamic and best organized working-class elements, and the fight against Fascism was unthinkable without their co-operation. Between 1934 and 1936, the acceptance by Communists and republicans of the Popular Front was the touchstone for their opposition to Fascism. There was no other way to dam the Fascist tide. Liberals all over the world sympathized at that time with the achievements of Communist Russia, where a new democratic constitution was in preparation; red-baiting had not yet been sponsored by Fascist propaganda. The alliance of French democrats and Communists in 1934-1936 was no less necessary and legitimate than the present-day alliance of the Anglo-Saxon democracies with China and the Soviet Union. Facts are stronger than sympathies or antipathies. No one can reproach the French and Spanish for having learned in 1936, under the stress of internal political exigencies, what other countries learned in 1941, under the impact of international necessities.

Furthermore, French democrats and Communists were united not merely by temporary conditions of the war against Fascism. They both understood that their differences of opinion were less profound than the gulf which separated them from the Fascists. They saw the possibility of coming to an understanding, whereas the contradictions between democracy and Fascism and between Communism and Fascism could never be resolved. The Communists realized that political liberty has been a very strong tradition in the land of the Declaration of the Rights of Man, and the democrats understood that the dignity of the individual might be defended better by the *provisional* dictatorship of the proletariat, which admits neither hierarchy of races nor anti-Semitism, than by the *definitive* dictatorship of Fascist regimes. Democrats and Communists became aware that the best formulae for the future might well be those in which political liberty, as exalted by the French Revolution, would become the crowning of social equality, the basis of the Russian Revolution.

French intellectuals took the lead in this work of reconciliation. Shortly after February 6, 1934, a *Comité de Vigilance des Intellectuels Anti-Fascistes* was organized. It included among its members the greatest names of French science. The leaders of the anti-Fascist crusade were Jean Perrin, winner of the Nobel

Prize for Physics and General Secretary of the Académie des Sciences; Paul Langevin and Emile Borel, both members of the *Institut de France*, and both imprisoned by the Nazis; Dr. Paul Rivet, now in exile; Professor Georges Politzer, shot by the Nazis; and others of equal stature. The greatest French savants took part in the creation of the Popular Front. The glory of French thought, they were also the glory of the Popular Front. Only when Pétain, Weygand, and Laval can invoke such names in their behalf will they have the right to speak in the name of intellectual France.

Favored by French political tradition and profiting by the support of the masses and of France's best thinkers, the Popular Front was created. At first it was a spontaneous organization for defense against Fascism; attacked by the Croix de Feu and Royalists, Communist and Socialist workers and democratic petits bourgeois gave shape to the first form of the Popular Front as a natural reflex. The second stage was the merger of the two great French workers' organizations: the Confédération Générale du Travail, or C. G. T. (non-Communist trade-unions) and the Confédération Générale du Travail Unitaire, or C.G.T.U. (Communist trade-unions). This merger expressed the great desire for unity in the working class as a bulwark against the power and egoism of the employers' organizations. The third stage of the Popular Front was the political alliance of the great parties of the Left—the Radical-Socialist party (corresponding to the American Democrats), the Socialists, and the Communists. These parties—the largest on the French political chess-board—joined by less important groups, such as *la Jeune République*, a political section of democratic Catholics, and by the anti-Fascist political and syndicalist organizations, the C.G.T., the C.G.T.U., the *Comité de Vigilance des Intellectuels Anti-Fascistes*, the *Ligue des Droits de l'Homme*, the Republican War Veterans, and others, drew up a common political program. Continuing the tradition of the French Revolution, the organizers of the Popular Front pledged to stay united as long as the Fascist menace remained in existence.

In 1936 the Popular Front entered the electoral lists in the general legislative elections. Its victory was unprecedented; four hundred deputies out of six hundred! When Pétain, Weygand, and Laval can obtain such a success—in free elections—they will have the right to speak for the French people.

THE WORK OF THE POPULAR FRONT

The true strength of the Popular Front lay in the enthusiasm of the people. To describe the feelings which animated the French people at that time would require the pen of a Zola, and I must limit myself to a few awkward evocations. The Popular Front was more than a political movement: it extended to all forms of social activity and all manifestations of collective life. It touched not only the government but the structure of society. It was a new way of facing political and social problems, and consequently the beginning of a new era in French public life. It was the true expression of the conscience of the people. During what may be called its heroic period—the formative years of 1934-1936—it was concerned chiefly with defending political and trade-union liberties against the attacks of the Croix de Feu; but during its period of achievement—1936-1938—it attacked basic problems and set about reorganizing the nation's collective life. Striking manifestations of its activity were public meetings at which governmental programs were discussed, and the resulting reforms changed the face of France. A purifying breath passed over France, clearing the air of the furious words of Colonel de la Rocque and his followers. A true national unity came into being around the workers and intellectuals, embracing everyone except the small minority already converted to Fascism.

I shall always remember the demonstration that took place on July 14, 1935, in Paris, between the Place de la République and the Porte de Vincennes. In the workers' part of town, where barricades had been built in 1830, 1848, and 1871, seven hundred thousand men and women, French toilers and thinkers, marched for hours in the parade, and took the oath of the Popular Front: "Remain united to conquer Fascism." On the same day, at the same time, in the Champs Elysées and the Avenue du Bois, the exclusive sections where the Parisian playboys lived, Colonel de la Rocque had his men march in military formation. What a contrast between these two parades! On the one side, the crowd of workers, artisans, intellectuals, and scientists, faithful to the traditions of French democracy; on the other, the defenders of the privileges for the 200 Families, ready for civil war, their arms outstretched in salute to their chief. The elements of the drama staged in 1940 were present on that day in July, 1935.

After the general elections of May, 1936, the people's joy broke loose in factories and collieries, in industrial areas and villages. The common people were liberated, liberated by their own action. They looked to the future with confidence. Returning to the traditions of 1791 and 1848, they celebrated by dancing in the streets. Their happiness was healthy and strong, like youth itself. They bore no grudge, and asked only that their adversaries accept the verdict of the majority and respect the laws of the land. Great popular celebrations were organized by the government and the workers' unions; there were youth festivals and work festivals, peace festivals and anniversary celebrations of the French Revolution. During these demonstrations and fetes the French people once more began to sing the *Marseillaise*. Under the Third Republic the *Marseillaise* had lost its meaning by becoming the song of official ceremonies and military bands; the people no longer sang it. The Popular Front restored its life and its primary significance as a democratic and revolutionary song. It became again the song of the Federates, the song that for more than a century had been sung all over the world by exiles and revolutionaries. In the same way the new strength and joy of the people brought about the rediscovery of the old passwords. All France—with the exception of the Fascists—echoed: "Bread, Peace, and Liberty"; "Strong, Free, Happy France"; "Liberty, Equality, Fraternity."

I pity those Frenchmen who did not feel or understand the significance of the Popular Front. I have known nothing more eloquent or moving than those processions, in which the strength and nobility of the French people revealed themselves. The magnificent beginnings of the French Revolution or the famous "banquets" which preceded the events of February, 1848, could not have been more stirring. Those who did not perceive that the Popular Front was the foundation of a true French renaissance, those who saw in the Popular Front only the occupation of factories and sit-down strikes, make one think of those eighteenth-century aristocrats who saw in the French Revolution nothing but the September massacres and the invasion of the Tuileries. The Popular Front was not without blemishes, but we must remember what Clemenceau said about the Revolution: "It is an entity; we must take it with its errors and grandeur, or reject it entirely."

What was the program and what were the principal achievements of the Popular Front?

The program* was drafted in January, 1936, and accepted by the nation in May, 1936. After three years of exile, I still believe this program is a credit to the people who inspired it. Not only did it translate faithfully the wish of the people, but it was well adapted to the political, economic, and social situation of 1936. It is easy to criticize in retrospect a program of action, but if we compare the program of the Popular Front with the plans of the nationalists, conservatives, or Fascists, we will understand why the French people did not hesitate in their choice.

The program of the Popular Front must be appraised in terms of the political situation of 1936. It came neither from the Communists nor from the Socialists; it comprised the reforms which all the organizations and parties of the Popular Front considered necessary. The Popular Front did not propose to bring about a social revolution or to set up a Socialist regime in France. If it contained revolutionary members, these men were all well aware that the conditions essential for the establishment of Socialism did not yet exist in the France of 1936, and they were economically and politically too farsighted to attempt an artificial creation of such conditions. I speak with authority, since I took part in formulating the program of the Popular Front. We knew that the majority of the French people was neither Socialistic nor Communistic, but merely wished to see the government check the Fascists, defend democratic liberties, correct the most flagrant injustices of the existing social regime, and do its best to maintain world peace by organizing collective security. That is what was expressed in the three words, "Bread, Peace, and Liberty," and that is what the program envisaged. As Blum said at the convention of the Socialist party on June 5, 1936: "The mission of the Popular Front is the direction of bourgeois society; the Popular Front must obtain as much order, justice, and fair treatment as this society can give the majority

* See Appendix I.

of the workers and producers." On June 6, presenting his cabinet to Parliament and the nation, he said again: "We are a Popular Front government and not a Socialist government. Our object is not to transform the social system, but to carry out the program of the Popular Front."

The most important points in this program were: "(1) the nationalization of war industries . . . (2) the reduction of the working week . . . (3) the reform of the banking profession and of the system of the Bank of France . . . (4) the reform of the press, through measures preventing the creation of trusts and obliging newspapers to make public the sources of their capital . . . and (5) a foreign policy conforming to the principles of the League of Nations Pact." Work was begun at once to draft the laws and regulations designed to put this program into practice. The Popular Front took power in June, 1936, and the most important laws were voted in August or shortly thereafter.

The social policy of the Popular Front saved France from civil war. When Blum formed his first cabinet on June 5, 1936, political tension between Fascists and anti-Fascists and social tension between workers and employers had reached its climax; violence would have been the next step. Much has been said of the strikes and the occupation of factories which characterized this period of French public life, but it has rarely been mentioned that this wave of strikes preceded the coming of the Popular Front. For example, when I became Minister of Aviation in Blum's cabinet, work was at a standstill in every airplane factory, and the workers occupied the shops. The Minister of Aviation who had allowed this situation to develop was not a Popular Front man, but the notorious Fascist, Marcel Déat. Economic life was suspended throughout the nation. The Popular Front had to deal with an extremely grave situation, for which it was not responsible and which was the inevitable consequence of the political mistakes and economic errors of the Doumergue, Flandin, and Laval cabinets, and of the industrialists' abuses of authority. After having sown the wind, the conservatives let their successors reap the whirlwind. The French employers, terror-stricken, asked the Popular Front government to protect them against the consequences of their own errors. Blum made a successful appeal to the workers' intelligence. Numerous conferences held in the Premier's office between representatives of workers' and employers' organizations resulted in the "Matignon Agreements," which momentarily restored industrial peace. Yet strikes and lockouts continued to appear, provoked for the most part by employers who refused to obey the new parliamentary decrees.

To deal with these conflicts the Popular Front government had recourse to methods of mediation and arbitration rendered obligatory by a law of December, 1936. The government remained impartial in its dealings with workers and employers. The social order of the Popular Front was not the famous "order which reigned in Moscow" in the days of the Czars nor the order of workers cowed by the police, but the more humane order of law and arbitration. No blood was shed. When factories were occupied, there was no material damage; machinery and tooling were respected and carefully kept in order.

During 1937 more than a thousand disputes were peacefully arbitrated; in only fifty-three cases were the decisions rejected, and in forty-three of these, the refusal came from the employers. This policy of wisdom and moderation must be credited to Blum, and it bore fruit in the economic as well as in the social field. In 1935, with Laval as President of the Council, the employers could rely on the use of force, but the index of industrial production fell 8 per cent below that of 1933; in 1937, when Blum was President of the Council, employers and workers had to submit their disputes to arbitration, but the index of production rose 12 per cent above the 1935 level.

The workers' condition, material as well as moral, was transformed by the Popular Front's social policy. The beneficiaries of this policy were the workers, the peasants, and the mass of producers and dealers whose fate is bound to the prosperity of the workers. According to the statistics of the International Labor Office, "the lump sum of wages and salaries" had fallen, under the Doumergue, Flandin, and Laval cabinets, from 191 billion francs in 1933 to 87 billions in 1935. This sum rose to 120 billions in 1937, and the purchasing power of the masses was thus greatly increased. If one compares the cost of living in 1935 and 1937, it becomes clear that the index number of the real value of total wages rose from 91 to 96. This general improvement benefited the class that had been most exploited.

To understand the justification for a general wage increase, one must remember how the French worker was treated before the reforms of the Popular Front. In 1935, when Laval was in power, the average hourly wage of a weaver, in provincial cities of more than 10,000 inhabitants, was 2.90 francs—which, at the current exchange (at that time particularly favorable to France), was about 20 cents an hour, or $9.60 for a 48-hour week; and very few weavers worked more than 40 hours per week. In Paris, where the cost of living was especially high, the average salary of a shop girl was 89 francs per week, or about $5.70. Americans who were in Paris at that time may tell their compatriots whether it was possible to live on such a salary without ultimately suffering physical or moral degradation. In the provinces, some women employed in airplane factories earned 55 francs, or $3.85 per week. The farm worker, whose income was even lower, often lived more like an animal than like a human being.

The elementary duty of every democrat—even beyond the ranks of the Popular Front—was to protest against this state of affairs. The general wage increase was not the sole attempt to improve the condition of the workers. A program of public works reduced the number of unemployed from 431,000 in 1936 to 350,000 in 1937. The 40-hour week was established. A system of collective bargaining was organized under the law. Free compulsory education was extended by two years. Two weeks of annual paid vacation for all workers was initiated and railroad facilities made available to them. Sports, outdoor life, games, and popular theaters were developed. In one year's time France was transformed from one of the most backward countries in respect to social legislation to one of the world's leading exponents of it.

The French worker ceased to be merely a tool and became a human being —a man with time to think, opportunity to learn, leisure to know his country and to take part in the benefits of culture. The family was no longer a machine that manufactured units for the General Staff's regiments and for the employers' factories. French workers went out every week end, on foot, bicycle, or skis, to enjoy the air of their country. The vacation resorts, beaches, forests, and mountains, hitherto reserved for the bourgeoisie, found a new clientele of "paid vacationists." The workers discovered that their country was beautiful, and France, with all her beauties, became the property of her children. Young people, tramping from one youth hostel to another, sang *Marchons au devant de la Vie.* And all France was joyous, unaware that the Fifth Column was already at work and that an aged Marshal was preparing to bring the people back to the hierarchies of the past by way of the concentration camps.

The social policy of the Popular Front was not the policy of a government, of a party, or of a group, but of the French people. The vast majority of this people approved the Popular Front program, which was executed under the control and with the collaboration of representatives of the people. The Matignon Agreements, which inaugurated a new era in worker-employer relations, were signed by representatives of the employers as well as by the Confédération Générale du Travail; the law establishing paid vacations was voted unanimously by the Chamber of Deputies and adopted without opposition by the Senate; the collective bargaining law was voted 528 to 5 in the Chamber, and adopted without opposition by the Senate; the 40-hour-a-week law was voted 408 to 16 in the Chamber, and 182 to 84 in the Senate; the nationalization of war industries was decided by an almost unanimous vote of the two houses. I know of no period in French parliamentary history in which such a degree of national unity was achieved. The application of these laws was controlled in the most detailed fashion by Chamber and Senate Commissions, in which all political parties were represented. When Vichy criticizes my decisions in the Ministry of Aviation, I can answer that these decisions were all approved by the Parliamentary Commissions, and if they were bad, they nevertheless expressed the will of the nation.

THE OVERTHROW OF THE POPULAR FRONT

The Popular Front cabinets were not overthrown by the Chamber, but by the Senate. The first Blum cabinet was overthrown on June 21, 1937, after it had received a vote of confidence in the Chamber, 347 to 246; the second Blum cabinet was overthrown on April 6, 1938, after a vote of confidence in the Chamber by a majority of more than sixty. The votes of the Senate had nothing to do with questions of general or social policy, but only with the financial policy of the Blum cabinet. It is a rule of parliamentary government that in financial questions the house elected by universal suffrage is alone sovereign and should have the "last word." If the Constitution of 1875 had not been a "war machine against the Republic," or if the Constitutional law were interpreted in 1936-1938 as it had been during the first fifty years of the parliamentarian regime, the Popular Front would not have been broken. The lawful representatives of the majority never withdrew their support from the Blum cabinets. The by-elections which took place after April 8, 1938, showed that the country remained faithful to the Popular Front. The conservative bourgeoisie, already partially converted to Fascism, overthrew the Popular Front government in 1938 through the Senate, just as in 1940 it overthrew the Republic through the Fifth Column and established a Fascist dictatorship through Pétain.

The bourgeoisie threw against the Popular Front all its forces—a reactionary press, strong resistance by employers' organizations to social measures, agitation by Fascist groups. No device was neglected. In June, 1937, the Senate overthrew the first Blum cabinet. A new Popular Front cabinet was formed under the leadership of Camille Chautemps, but it differed greatly from the first. Chautemps recalled Georges Bonnet from Washington to be Minister of Finance. Nothing could have been more inauspicious than the choice of Bonnet, enemy of the Popular Front, friend of Otto Abetz, and friend of the Lazard Bank (which was to play an important role in the financial preparation of the Munich agreements), Bonnet in a Popular Front cabinet was like a wolf invited into a sheepfold. The spirit of the Popular Front was broken.

In January, 1938, as a result of a conflict between Bonnet and the Socialist ministers, the Chautemps cabinet was reshuffled and its policy departed still farther from that of the Popular Front majority. In March, 1938, a purified Popular Front cabinet, including neither Bonnet nor Chautemps, was formed by Blum, and the anti-Fascists took heart once more. The Minister of Foreign Affairs was Paul-Boncour, a strong partisan of collective security. But in April, this cabinet—the last governmental expression of the Popular Front—was again overthrown by the Senate. Daladier set up a "concentration cabinet" with the support of certain liberals, such as Reynaud and Mandel, who were opponents of the Popular Front. This cabinet remained in power until February, 1940. The Socialists took no part in it, and I followed their example. In January, 1938, I had left the Ministry of Aviation to become Minister of Commerce. My policy as Minister of Aviation had been directed toward the nationalization of factories, the preparation of agreements with the Soviet Union, and strong opposition to the Cagoulards; it had been attacked violently by the Fascist and reactionary press and had been bitterly criticized by Marshal Pétain in a protest to Chautemps. When Daladier became Premier he asked me to join his cabinet, but I refused. Bonnet was Minister of Foreign Affairs and the cabinet included several representatives of the policy of appeasement, which I was fighting bitterly. I remained faithful to the Popular Front. I thought, and I think today, that it is impossible to fight Fascism without appealing to representatives of all anti-Fascist parties, from bourgeois liberals to Communists.

As I see it now, the essential cause of the failure of the Popular Front was its lack of daring. The development of Fascism, within and without France, demanded the transformation of the Popular Front cabinet into a real "Committee of Public Safety," modeled on the Committees of the French Revolution and capable of making drastic decisions with the support and under the control of representatives of the majority. In exceptional times the government should have resorted to exceptional methods, and in 1936 the war against Fascism should have been treated as having already begun, remembering that "the supreme law was the welfare of the Republic." The Popular Front cabinets preferred to remain within legal bounds, forgetting that this legality was more apparent than real, and overlooking the fact that it was not a truly democratic legality as long as the control of economic activity remained in the hands of a small minority and the Senate was not elected by the majority of the people.

This lack of daring, generally marked by an excessive respect for the Senate's opinion, characterized all forms of governmental activity at that time. It accounted for a few major political mistakes.

The first of these, perhaps the most important, occurred in the realm of foreign affairs. It was the Popular Front government's reluctance to support the Spanish Republic. Since the British conservatives then in power preferred Franco to the Republic, the French government was not willing to compromise Anglo-French relations by uniting with Russia to stem the Fascist tide in Spain. The second was a mistake in domestic policy. The government did not take sufficiently strict measures against the Fascist organizations. To prevent the campaigns of slander—a favorite Fascist device—the Senate was asked to change the law governing the press. The Senate refused. Similarly, proceedings against the instigators of the Cagoulard plot were not conducted with sufficient energy when it became apparent that these proceedings threatened to involve the entourage of Marshal Pétain and certain other military leaders. Officials and officers who had made no attempt to conceal their Fascist sympathies were allowed to remain in public office and in the Army. The third error was that the economic and financial policy of the Popular Front government did not parallel its social policy. There was little use in reducing working hours and raising wages if the measures taken did not at the same time aim to reform the structure of French economy. The reform of the Bank of France, the nationalization of war industries and of railroads should have been only parts of a general plan to substitute state control for control by private trusts. Such a general plan was never accomplished because the majority of the Senate was determined to defend the existing economic system. To re-establish financial security, it would have been necessary to check the freedom of international monetary transactions and to establish stock market control. The Senate preferred to overthrow the Blum cabinet rather than give it the authority it asked. And last, the contradictions of a progressive social policy and of a conservative economic policy placed small business in a particularly difficult situation. To reconcile these contradictions, it would have been necessary to form co-operative groups of artisans and small producers and to grant them the credits they needed for the transformation and modernization of their equipment. Such a policy, however, presupposed state control over the management of credit, and there again, the necessary reforms ran afoul of the Senate's opposition.

At every turn, the Popular Front government found itself opposed by a conspiracy of Fascist and reactionary elements which were united in their hatred for progressive democracy and economic control. This conspiracy should have been broken, for it imperiled the security of the Republic and of France. The Popular Front government attempted to fight it with the inadequate means granted by law. Appealing to the generosity of its adversaries, it asked the Senate for stronger weapons; the Senate refused. In his study on *The Crisis of French Democracy,* Professor Emile Giraud described the French Senate as "an assembly of old men, landholders, and celebrities." Because this assemblage bore no love for the Popular Front, it allowed democracy to perish.

How is it possible to explain this lack of daring, which proved fatal to the Popular Front and to French democracy?

First of all, we must reject one explanation that a part of the French and foreign press has frequently offered. It has been said that the Popular Front government was constantly troubled by labor agitation, artificially provoked by the Communists. Thus stated, this explanation is only a caricature of the truth. It is perfectly true that strikes and occupation of factories created an unfavorable atmosphere for a legitimate transformation of the economic system; they frightened the democratic petit bourgeois, who should have been the natural ally of the Popular Front, and helped the progress of reactionary and Fascist propaganda among the middle classes. But strikes and occupation of factories were an effect more than a cause. The workers did not strike without reason; it was not to their interest to lose wages or to embarrass the government they had elected. The employers rather than the workers were interested in creating social disorders and paralyzing the action of the Popular Front. Certain employers did not hesitate to use *agents provocateurs* to create disturbances—just as the Fascist organizations tried to have the Communists charged with the outrages committed by the Cagoulards. In 80 per cent of the cases submitted to arbitration, it was shown that the conflict resulted from an abuse of the employers' authority or from an employers' refusal to apply the social legislation correctly. Similarly, a report of the *Comité d'Enquête sur la Production,* drafted at the end of 1937, showed that the workers' organizations had accepted all the derogations to the social laws that were asked for national defense. The working class should be praised all the more for giving this proof of its wisdom, because at that time it was hostile to the government's attitude in the Spanish war.

The same is true of the Communists. A certain section of public opinion, picking up the themes of Fascist propaganda, has fallen into the habit of attributing to the Communists the mistakes committed by the workers in general during 1936-1937. This opinion is based on misinformation and reveals a lack of critical judgment. The Communists had to fight two chief enemies within the working class: *agents provocateurs,* paid by the employers' organizations to outbid the Communists and bring about the defeat of the Popular Front's social experiment; and Trotskyites, who were few in number, but very active. Trotskyites had no interest in seeing the success of the Popular Front, the downfall of which their leader had predicted. The Communists constantly opposed Trotskyist demagogy, which the *agents provocateurs* promoted. The French Communists had adopted the tactics of the Popular Front as the best means of checking the development of Fascism. They merely wanted the Popular Front experiment to be carried out under conditions of social justice which would assure the widest support of the working masses. At the beginning of July, 1936, when the number of sit-down strikes was growing dangerously and threatened the economic equilibrium of the country, Thorez, General Secretary of the Communist party, sent out his command. "We must know when to end a strike," he said, and the working class returned to the machines. In 1937, when the reactionary press, distorting certain incidents of the Spanish war, was trying to create a dangerous pro-Franco agitation in Catholic circles, Thorez initiated his policy of co-operation with anti-Fascist Catholics. The Communists did not want to turn the Popular Front into a revolutionary upheaval. They committed mistakes, yet no more than did any other party in the Popular Front, and I can truthfully say that they were faithful to the spirit of the Popular Front. The Popular Front was paralyzed by the treason of its Right wing, not by the inflexibility of its Left wing. The disturbance of the workers and the pressure of the Communists served as a screen for the most moderate and least loyal members of the Popular Front, who had never been its unreserved partisans, to reject its discipline.

It was thus not the intransigeance of the workers which caused a lack of daring in the Popular Front government. The true explanation of this deficiency seems to me at the same time more simple and more complex. I feel no hesitation to express my opinion on this point; as is widely known, I supported the most radical ideas of the Popular Front cabinets. Nor can there be any doubt about my position with respect to the Spanish war, the Soviet Union, the Cagoulards, and the nationalization of war industries. I was attacked violently by the entire reactionary press for the attempted "democratization" of the Air Force and the expulsion of its Fascist elements. I may therefore state freely the results of my observations and reflections.

The timidity of the Popular Front cabinets was, in a large measure, the reflection of the general mistake committed by all democratic governments with respect to Fascism. European and American democrats alike, underestimated the power and danger of Fascism, and it is not certain that all of them, even now, have realized their error. Thus if the Spanish republicans, who were infinitely more courageous and farsighted than the others, had arrested Franco and Gil Robles in the spring of 1936, the Spanish Civil War would not have taken place. The Soviet Union also made a mistake, not when it signed the Russo-German Pact, but in 1940 and 1941 when it miscalculated the probable strength of the Nazis. I give these examples because both republican Spain and Soviet Russia gave proof of greater awareness of the Fascist menace than did the other European or the American countries. Similarly, the General Staffs of all the democratic nations long underestimated the new military doctrines of the Reichswehr. All democrats, in France and elsewhere, erred in their analysis of the conditions which caused the phenomenon of Fascism within a certain form of capitalism.

To be more specific, the Popular Front has been criticized for conducting a lawful reform government instead of leading a revolution. To blame the Popular Front for lacking audacity is hypocritical unless one admits favoring revolutionary methods for a revolutionary end; only those who were revolutionists in 1936 have a right to make such a reproach. Nothing could have been accomplished beyond what was done without breaking the Senate's resistance and smashing the framework of the existing system. The former would have demanded a political revolution, while the latter would have meant social revolution. The simplest and most necessary measures—for example, the purging of the civil and military administration, the suppression of the Fascist press, the prohibition of the export of capital—could not be taken without modifying the existing laws, that is, without obtaining the Senate's consent. And while the Senate approved the social legislation and even certain measures bearing on the economic structure (such as the nationalization of war industries and the reform of the Bank of France), it refused to give the Blum cabinet legal instruments with which to govern more audaciously. What the government needed was to imitate Robespierre, not Roosevelt. It needed to declare "the Republic in danger," to override the vote of the Senate and to govern strictly on the basis of the Popular Front majority which the country had just elected—in short, to proclaim "the dictatorship of the majority."

The dictatorship of the majority is beyond question a form of democratic government. It goes back to the Jacobin tradition of the French Revolution, and to the Revolutionary government of the Convention which formed the First French Republic. The dictatorship of the majority is the only form of democratic government adapted to periods of internal or external crisis, and no democratic state has hesitated to employ it in times of civil or foreign war. It cannot be assimilated to the dictatorship of a man or of a minority, which is an anti-democratic and Fascist form of government. Every democratic Frenchman understands today that the dictatorship of the majority became a necessity after June, 1936—all the more so after the Senate refused a vote of confidence to the Blum cabinet, which had the support of the Chamber of Deputies and the nation, and still more so after the discovery of the Cagoulard plot. The most favorable moment to establish such a form of government would have been the period following the general elections of 1936. But it is too easy to be daring in retrospect. In 1936 no one had enough courage or foresight to advise the Popular Front government to proclaim openly the suspension of legal procedure and to resort to revolutionary methods.

The very composition of the Popular Front made its operation difficult. The Popular Front government had been elected on a reform program, not a revolutionary one. To exercise the dictatorship of the majority, one needed the majority's approval; the country had to be shown that the gravity of circumstances necessitated this dictatorship as the only possible means of executing the desired reforms. It was essential to outlaw the Fascist leaders, conscious or unconscious tools of Hitler. The people had to be weaned away from the Third Republic's tradition of mildness towards its enemies. It may not have been possible to do this. The Popular Front was not composed solely of Socialists and Communists accustomed by their own doctrines to the idea of a provisional dictatorship of the proletariat as a variant of democratic government in times of crisis; the Popular Front also included Radical-Socialists with a strong reverence for law. Among the Radical-Socialists, a large number—Zay, Mendès-France. De Tessan, myself, and many others—were faithful to the Jacobin tradition and believed in the spirit of the law more than in its letter. Others, like Daladier, had a conception of law which was more formal than real; still others, following Chautemps, were ready to seize any opportunity to abandon the Popular Front.

No one knows whether the dictatorship of the majority would have been approved by the majority of the Popular Front electorate. No one can tell what might have been the reaction of a democratic petit bourgeois or a peasant to the spectacle of the Blum cabinet closing the doors of the Senate and turning itself into a Committee of Public Safety. In the course of its march the Popular Front lost part of its troops. The dictatorship of the majority would have run the danger of appearing as a dictatorship of the largest and most ardent fraction of this majority—that is, a dictatorship of the proletariat, and few will maintain that France was ripe for such a move in 1936 or 1937. For my part, I tend to think that the great wave of enthusiasm created by the Popular Front elections would have swept away all resistance. The English proverb, "nothing succeeds like success," agrees with Corneille when he says: *"Nous serions partis cent, mais par un prompt renfort, nous eussions été mille en arrivant au port."* The fact is that most of the representatives of the democratic parties were reformers incapable of realizing that at certain periods of history reform itself, if it wishes to achieve its ends, must use exceptional methods to counter exceptional attacks.

The Popular Front leaders lacked daring because their conception of the general situation and of the Popular Front itself was more static than dynamic. They remained prisoners of a program, formulated in the first months of 1936, which obviously took no account of the Spanish war or the Cagoulard plot. They took it as a contract, whose terms the signatories must observe, rather than as a remarkable statement of a given situation, which had to change. They did not understand that the political scene in France had been altered by the overwhelming victory of the Popular Front, and that the program had been superseded by a powerful explosion that had shaken French political life. In a certain sense the enemies of the Popular Front understood better the significance of this explosion; they knew how great a disaster they had experienced, and they were fearful of its consequences. In 1936 the French reactionaries had almost resigned themselves to the people's leadership in economic and political life; the Fascists felt they were defeated. But the leaders of the Popular Front were like those generals who fail to exploit their success because they had not foreseen that the ardor of their troops would allow them to penetrate deeper into enemy lines.

In June, 1936, the leaders of the Popular Front were left behind by their troops. In writing these lines, I am not forgetting that I was one of these leaders, and I take my share of the collective reproach I address to the cabinets of which I was a member. The question today is whether we have all understood the lesson of subsequent events.

CONSEQUENCES AND RESPONSIBILITIES OF THE POPULAR FRONT

The preceding observations are not a sufficient basis for judgment of the Popular Front, but they are enough to serve as a basis for a better understanding and they make clear its relationship to the tradition of the French Revolution. Moreover, they serve as an indication of the Popular Front's consequences and responsibilities.

In spite of its errors and weaknesses, the Popular Front rendered great services, often underestimated, to France and to all countries fighting Hitlerism.

It opposed the growth of French Fascism from February, 1934, until June, 1940. As long as the Popular Front existed, Fascism was powerless; the unity of the Popular Front had to be destroyed before collaboration with the Nazi order could be initiated by the coming to power of a Fascist government. The Popular Front retarded the victory of French Fascism by six and a half years, a delay which had important consequences. It forced the French Fascists to dishonor themselves by accepting Hitler as a godfather. Without the military defeat and the presence of Nazi armies on French soil, France never would have accepted the yoke of Fascism, just as the Spanish Republic would not have been defeated without German and Italian aid to Franco.

The Popular Front, by its resistance, contributed to the protection of the Soviet Union and the Anglo-Saxon democracies. We have the right to ask certain Frenchmen in London, Algiers, and New York, as well as certain Anglo-Saxon critics of the Popular Front, what would have happened without the resistance of the Popular Front? What would have happened if France had had a pro-Fascist government in 1936, led by Pétain, Laval, Weygand, or any other reactionary, supported by a conservative and Fascist majority? A Fascist or even a reactionary France not only would have abandoned Czechoslovakia in 1938, but would have taken part in the Anti-Comintern Pact; she would have permitted the expansion of Germany to the east and would have supported—as did Mussolini, Franco, and Pétain—Germany's attack on the Soviet Union. Had France been Fascist in September, 1939, England, under the leadership of Neville Chamberlain, would not have declared war on Nazi Germany. After wiping out the Polish Army, the Reichswehr with all its troops would have attacked the Red Army to the applause of reactionaries all over the world. This attack might have taken place in the spring of 1940, and the Red Army, abandoned by the rest of the world, probably would have lost this unequal duel. Once rid of the Red Army, Hitler would have become master of Europe without losing many men or firing many shots; dominating Europe and controlling Russia by the combined action of his Fifth Column and his Army, he could have forced his will on the world, America included, and humanity would have entered upon a period of unparalleled suppression of political liberty.

The fact that France had no Fascist government in September, 1939, was due to the Popular Front. This forced Hitler to change his plans. Although the Daladier-Bonnet cabinet was undermined by the spirit of appeasement, just as was the Chamberlain-Halifax cabinet, French democracy, though weakened, still existed, and Hitler was compelled to throw his armored divisions against the French Army before using them to attack his principal enemy, Soviet Russia. The six years, during which, step by step, the Popular Front fought Fascism, gave the democracies a respite in which to realize the danger and to organize their defense. Without the resistance of the Popular Front and without the diplomatic astuteness of Stalin in 1939, Hitler undoubtedly would have attacked Russia first.

Another great service of the Popular Front was the modification of the very bases of French politics. By its formation, development, and downfall, the Popular Front taught the French people an important lesson. The French masses learned that the enthusiasm which had attended the birth of the Popular Front was not a strong enough foundation for a democratic government that was to realize the sovereign will of the nation. The Popular Front experiment permitted the French to achieve a new degree of political maturity. The subsequent experience of military and Fascist dictatorship has been a painful contrast to it. The masses have witnessed, within a few years, two diametrically opposed forms of government, from whose opposition new political ideas may develop.

These are the lessons taught by the experience of the Popular Front.

First, if the Popular Front could have modified the economic structure of the country, it would have broken the resistance of the enemies of the people—that is, if political democracy had been based on economic democracy. Until now democrats and social democrats have maintained that one could progress from political democracy to economic democracy, whereas it is necessary to begin with the control of economic life by the people's representatives in order to make political democracy function properly.

Second, the experience of the Popular Front showed the dangers of a purely formal conception of democratic legality. The abuses of power committed by the Fascist states and their "interpretation" of law have made the concepts of law and legality more precious than ever. But these concepts must evolve from formalism toward realism. In the field of democratic public law it is no longer possible to consider legal that which merely conforms to the letter of constitutional law; the will of the majority also must be considered. The experience of the Popular Front, supplemented by the experience of Vichy, has led French political thought to new conceptions of democratic legality and of public and administrative law. In a general way, nothing can be considered legal in matters of government and public law if it is contrary to the will of the people; the will of the people expresses itself through the elected representatives of the people; a civil or military dictator (Vichy) or an assembly expressing by its composition the opinion of a political or social minority (the Senate under the Third Republic) does not represent the nation.

Third, the experience of the Popular Front revealed the dangers inherent in certain reformatory doctrines. Reform can ameliorate an imperfect economic or political system provided the system is fundamentally sound, but it cannot transform a fundamentally bad one. Reform corrects, but does not change; it permits a more rapid or more harmonious development of a system, but does not permit either a change from one system to another or the creation of an entirely new one. If France had been an economic and political democracy, the zeal for reform of the Popular Front cabinets would have extracted "the maximum of order, security, and justice" from democratic institutions. Just as the French people had been unable to pass by mere reforms from the *ancien régime* to a democratic regime, or from a monarchy to the Republic, so the experience of the Popular Front established that France could not transform her economic and social structure by mere reforms.

Fourth, the experience of the Popular Front proved that a period of dictatorship is necessary for the achievement of important structural changes desired by the people. Such dictatorship should be democratic, a dictatorship of the majority, under the control of the people's representatives. This dictatorship of the majority was the system of the Assemblies of the French Revolution. In periods of extreme crisis it can become a "provisional dictatorship of the majority of the majority," or a government of the nation by the representatives of the largest class of the nation. In no event, however, can it become the dictatorship of a man or of a minority class without growing into an instrument of oppression and leading to Fascism.

Fifth, the experience of the Popular Front has shown that the historic conditions of the fight for democracy have not changed in France since the time of the French Revolution. The battle is still between the "Whites" and

101

the "Reds," between the common people and those who do not want the French government to be a government of, by, and for the people. As long as there is a minority in France hostile to the democratic principle, the French people will have to remain on guard; and unity, whether within a single popular party or in a coalition of all popular parties, will be the prerequisite for the battle in defense of democracy.

The experience of the Popular Front liberated the French masses from the illusions of reformism. It showed that political democracy cannot work if economic democracy has not been previously established. This presupposes an implacable struggle. The experience of the Popular Front showed that the privileged classes are ready to sacrifice the democratic form of the state when they feel their privileges menaced by the functioning of political democracy. Karl Marx had already given this interpretation to the reaction which followed the Revolution of 1848 and permitted the coup d'état of Napoleon III; Rosa Luxembourg, before 1914, had foreseen the rallying of the bourgeoisie to regimes of authority; and Otto Bauer, former leader of the Austrian Social Democrats, wrote in 1936 that the success of Fascism in Europe had done away with the belief that "it is possible to transform the capitalist order into a Socialist order without a revolutionary jump."

Stripped of their reformist illusions, the French masses under the dictatorship of Pétain have learned the value of political liberty. When tomorrow comes they will know how to use "the dictatorship of the majority" to establish and to maintain the new economic order from which will emerge a true democracy—not "democracy for the minority" but "democracy for the people."

THE ROLE OF THE POPULAR FRONT IN FRENCH POLITICS

As time passes, it becomes easier to judge the Popular Front and to assign to it an exact place in French political history; the details withdraw into the shadow and the peaks begin to emerge.

The Popular Front was the answer of the French people to Fascism. It remains the main witness of France's desire for democracy. The last time that France was allowed to speak freely she did not say, "Fascism and Pétain," but "the Popular Front and Léon Blum." Until there are again free elections in France, the only men who have the right—in the real as well as formal sense of the word—to speak in the name of the majority of the French people are the men of the Popular Front, for the last legitimate Parliament of democratic France was that of the Popular Front.

The Popular Front stirred the soul of the people. It was a magnificent period of generosity, confidence, and enthusiasm. It opened the doors to a better future. It showed the French people a great ideal for which to strive. The ideal was not attained because the French Fascists had the aid of Hitler, but it has kept all its value in the eyes of the workers, peasants, and intellectuals. In the history of the Third Republic, there is no more noble period than the years in which the Popular Front struggled.

The Popular Front united all the adversaries of Fascism. As Fascism was the modern form of the French reactionary tradition, the Popular Front was the modern expression of the tradition of the French Revolution. Once more the liberal petit bourgeois and the revolutionary worker became aware of their kinship. As children of the Revolution they knew where their historic duty lay—to complete the conquests of the French Revolution by adding to political liberty, social equality and the fraternity of labor. They recognized their enemies; they knew that to conquer Fascism in France it would be necessary to fight all forms of political and social reaction, the roots of the evil.

The Popular Front does not belong only to the past. As Blum proudly told the judges of Riom, "a political phenomenon like the Popular Front does not shoot up overnight like a mushroom." When the war is over, the forms, the name, the program, and the methods of the Popular Front will change, but its spirit will remain in the memory of the people, and will become the dawn of a new era.

The men of the Popular Front lacked only daring. How shall we be able to show tomorrow that we have learned the lessons of the past? And how shall we be able to realize the ideas of the Popular Front and of the French people? What shall we need as we again take up, not only in France but throughout the whole world, the task interrupted by the sinister interlude of Fascism? The answer was given by Danton, the man of the French Revolution: *"De l'audace, encore de l'audace, et toujours de l'audace."*

The Vichy Government Against Justice

4

JUSTICE IS THE TOUCHSTONE by which civilizations may be judged. The supreme duty of the state is to assure not order so much as the reign of justice. While justice breeds order, order without justice becomes oppression. Hence it is the first duty of the state to set up disinterested and dispassionate tribunals capable of settling the disputes of individuals and of imposing on all citizens respect for the law. For law and justice are above the state, and even the criminal must be protected against the abuse of authority. To all men justice must assure the same rights, and those rights must be guaranteed by certain basic laws. David Hume wrote that "England's fleet, her power, her monarchy, and her two houses, all have but one aim— to preserve the freedom of the fifteen great judges on the royal bench."[*] And Montesquieu, defending, after Locke, the principle of the separation of powers said that "there can be no liberty as long as the judicial power is not separated from the legislative and the executive. . . . All would be lost if the same man or the same body of leaders, aristocrats or commoners, were to exercise these three powers—the power of making the laws, the power of executing the public will, and the power of judging crimes and settling private differences."[†]

Nowhere is the independence of the judge more essential and more difficult to preserve than in the realm of politics. For tyrannical governments the simplest means of ridding themselves of their political adversaries always has been to have them condemned by docile and pliable judges. "It is an eternal, recurring experience," wrote Montesquieu, "that whoever possesses power is tempted to abuse it to its farthest possible limit. Virtue itself must be kept in bounds. To avoid the abuse of authority, it is necessary, in the natural disposition of things, that power be used to restrict power."[†] While the interest of the public demands the punishment of those who have discharged their functions contrary to existing laws, it requires with equal severity that they may not be condemned in any manner contrary to those laws by their successors in government. Custom and law in all civilized countries have surrounded the mechanism of political trials with safeguards, which citizen and state have an interest in preserving.

The separation of powers, the independence of judges, and the guarantee

[*] David Hume, *The History of England* (London: R. Bowyer, 1806).
[†] C. de Montesquieu, *De l'Esprit des Lois* (Paris: Garnier Frères, 1874).

of penal law have been abolished almost entirely in Fascist countries; no one, therefore, would believe in the justice of sentences pronounced in the name of Mussolini, Hitler, or Franco. Yet it seems that the Pétain government went even further. In a recent book, Pierre Mendès-France, Undersecretary of State for Finances in the second Blum cabinet and a victim of the Marshal's new order of justice, has analyzed the manner in which this justice has been administered since June, 1940. The jury has been abolished. The magistrates, who under the Republic enjoyed independence and life tenure, are now subject to the will of the government, which may appoint, depose, and recall them *ad nutum*. Where the judges formerly swore that they would rule according to the law and to their conscience, they now take an oath of allegiance to Marshal Pétain. Countless special tribunals, usually composed of military men with notoriously Fascist sympathies, have been created to reinforce the judicial apparatus; their sentences require no motivation. *Habeas corpus* no longer exists. The rights of the defense have been reduced to a minimum, and the examination of criminal cases no longer implies a hearing of both sides, since witnesses are frequently threatened with the concentration camp if in their testimony they should not comply with the government's wishes.‡ These revelations of Mendès-France are confirmed by the very laws promulgated by Vichy as well as by accounts of prisoners who have escaped from concentration camps. Before going on to a discussion of the Riom trial, let us dwell for a moment on the general problem of the dishonored justice administered by Vichy. How could that government have stooped so low during the years 1940-1942?

The first answer is that the dictatorship of Marshal Pétain has been the weakest of all European dictatorships; it has rested on a small minority whose numbers are dwindling every day. Since it did not have the people's confidence, it had to institute a reign of terror to maintain itself.

Furthermore, the Vichy government could not destroy the political organization of French democracy without affecting the judicial system. The two are intimately linked, for both are based on the same principles and the same philosophy. It has frequently been remarked that the French have legal minds; it has been said that "they need law as the British need comfort." One of the most remarkable contributions of the French genius to Western civilization has been the elaboration of a system of public and private law which combined in a vast synthesis, Roman law, Christian thought, and judicial custom. For more than a century, the peoples of Europe, America, and Asia have studied this law. This legal philosophy—which in the eyes of Vichy bears the stigma of the French Revolution—actually prepared the way for the Revolution. It expressed itself in the Declaration of the Rights of Man and in the Constitutions of the Revolution; it culminated in the Codes, which, although formulated in the time of Napoleon, had been prepared and inspired by the Revolutionary Assemblies. A still more remarkable fact, and one which reveals the true instinct of the French people, is that for a hundred and

‡ Pierre Mendès-France, *Liberté, Liberté Cherie* (New York: Didier, 1943).

fifty years the principles embodied in the French Revolution have been the basis of all the modifications of French law and of all the important political currents. Having taken up the task of fighting the spirit of the French Revolution, the Vichy government was bound to collide with the principles which dominated criminal law and the judicial organization. To safeguard its control over the French nation, it had to eliminate both the separation of powers, which assured the independence of judges, and the regulations of criminal procedure, which checked abuses of authority.

Lastly, the Vichy government was made up chiefly of men who had only scorn for the law. Aside from the few politicians who, like Laval and Peyrouton, had long been partial to Fascist ideas, and the businessmen, like Lehideux, Pucheu, and Baudoin, who represented the 200 Families, one found principally generals and admirals in Pétain's cabinets. The military class in France has always opposed the judicial spirit; it has never bowed before the need for an independent justice, and has always rebelled against the superiority of reason and law over force and instinct. In contemporary political history nothing illustrates this attitude better than the notorious Dreyfus affair.

This complex case left deep marks on French politics. One cannot understand the intellectual and moral conduct of a Pétain and a Weygand without remembering that at the time of the Dreyfus affair they were both young officers who had received their education and learned the traditions of the French Army from the General Staff then in power. The real tragedy of the Dreyfus case was not the proof that French officers were capable of using false documents to condemn one of their comrades, whose only crime was his Jewish origin; it was rather the realization that the military hierarchy—the General Staff collectively—was not shocked at the revelation of such devices. On the contrary, the leaders of the French Army proved themselves ready to hide the most criminal practices under the cloak of their authority, in order to avoid scandal and preserve what has already been referred to as "the honor of the Army." Captain Dreyfus, a young Jewish officer, had been declared guilty of treason by a court-martial at the request of the General Staff. His innocence was proved indisputably several years later. But, before that time, it was learned that his condemnation had been obtained by the illegal communication to the court-martial of a "secret dossier," of which Dreyfus and his defenders had had no knowledge. The honesty of an officer, Colonel Piquart—whose courage made him the General de Gaulle of his generation—established that the incriminating parts of the "secret dossier" were forgeries concocted by certain General Staff officers. Instead of recognizing its errors, the General Staff stubbornly produced new documents, which, in turn, also proved to be forgeries. The scandal grew to the point where the Dreyfus affair became a major question of policy. The conscience of the French people found itself confronted with the fundamental problem of the relation between state and individual, between justice and authority, in short, with the fundamental problem of democracy. As always in moments of crisis, France split into two camps of different composition, a separation revealing the true line of division in

French politics. As Soltau has pointed out in his *French Political Thought in the Nineteenth Century,* "the Dreyfus case reduced itself to a simple choice between two conceptions of society, which had been struggling since the Revolution for mastery in the French mind: the one based society and civilization on certain elemental individual rights, which no danger of upheaval or reasons of state could shake; the other, based them on authority as external and prior to individual citizens superior to and judge of the rights of these and the desirability of their exercise. It was the Declaration of the Rights of Man versus the *ancien régime,* and it suddenly forced every thinking man to choose the side to which he belonged."*

The Dreyfus affair revealed that military circles shared a political doctrine, or, more precisely, a political tradition, outspokenly reactionary and opposed to the spirit of democracy and the French Revolution. One can therefore understand why, ever since the Revolution, the people have fought the reactionary tradition of the French military caste with an anti-militarist tradition. French anti-militarism has occasionally shocked foreign public opinion, which confused it with anti-patriotism or lack of discipline. In reality, like French anti-clericalism, it is purely political in nature. It is an instinctive defense against the intrusion of the military into political life. The people's instinct is based on historical experience and on the profound conviction, be it true or false, that French military leaders by their turn of mind, upbringing, and professional training are not only poorly prepared for governmental tasks, but generally opposed to democratic principles. If the French are suspicious of "generals" and "priests" in politics, it is because generals and priests in France generally have been adversaries of the Republic. The attitude of certain officers and of many democratic Catholics in the present battle against Fascism demonstrates that this rule has its illustrious exceptions.

Let us return to the Riom trial. No one could expect a Fascist-supported dictatorial government, born of defeat and led by military men trained in the days of the Dreyfus affair, to give its political adversaries the judicial guarantees traditional among free nations. The question, therefore, is not whether the Riom trial was in order or not—it could not possibly have been— but the degree of its irregularity. To find the answer that will locate the Vichy government on the Fascist scale, we shall study successively the organization of the Supreme Court, the conduct of the Riom trial, and the general aspect of the public debates.

THE ORGANIZATION OF THE SUPREME COURT OF JUSTICE

The Riom Court was established in an unconstitutional manner in order to obtain the unlawful condemnation of Popular Front ministers.

*R. H. Saltau, *French Political Thought in the Nineteenth Century* (New Haven: Yale University Press, 1931).

Two incontestable principles dominate the penal law of every civilized nation. The first is that no one may be accused and condemned except in accordance with a precise law specifying the nature of the crime and the severity of the penalty to which the delinquent exposes himself. This is the Roman principle of *nullum crimen, nulla poena sine lege*. The second is the principle of non-retroactivity of penal legislation, according to which no one can be condemned except under a law already in force at the time the criminal act was committed. Both these principles rest solely on reason and common sense; they have been adopted and consecrated by long practice, both in the countries under the influence of Roman law and in the Anglo-Saxon or Germanic countries. One would fall into autocracy if judges were to follow their own will instead of enforcing the law, and one would sink into despotism if the government by means of a retroactive law could decide that the author of an act formerly permitted by law might be punished. Both principles have existed in France since the Revolution. "No one can be judged and punished except in accordance with a law established and promulgated previous to the commission of the crime, and legally enforced," said the Declaration of the Rights of Man in 1791, and the Declaration of 1793 added that "the law which would punish crimes committed before it existed would be a tyranny; the retroactive effect given such a law would be a crime." Article 2 of the Civil Code states that "the law disposes only for the future; it has no retroactive effect." And Joseph Barthélémy, Marshal Pétain's Minister of Justice, commented in 1933, in his *Treatise on Constitutional Law*, on this principle: "An individual commits a deed which is considered illicit; then a law appears which makes this deed an offense and imposes penal sanctions for it. The principle of non-retroactivity of laws prevents the prosecution of the individual, as the past is beyond the reach of the legislator. In this case, the rule *nulla poena sine lege* reinforces for the protection of the individual, the security drawn from the non-retroactivity of laws."*

The Vichy government realized that it could never prosecute the leaders of the Popular Front so long as it observed the elementary rules of French and, I might add, of human law. Blum, Daladier, La Chambre, Gamelin, Jacomet, and I had not committed a single infraction of existing laws. We had merely governed and administered the country in accordance with the will of the people and under the control of Parliament. Unable to find any existing penal law that would cover our actions, the Vichy government had to invent new laws by which it could declare our political activities criminal; without an ex post facto law the Vichy government would have been forced to renounce its revenge on the Popular Front leaders. Yet it had to prosecute us. To find a pretext the government created a new tribunal endowed with exorbitant powers, and invented a new crime and new methods of criminal investigation that deprived the accused of the guarantees provided for by law. These creations were covered by Constitutional Act No. 5 of July 30, 1940, and by the decrees of July 30, August 14, and September 24, 1940. These dispositions were both unconstitutional and contrary to the penal law.

* J. Barthélémy and P. Duez, *Traité de Droit Constitutionnel* (Paris: Dalloz, 1933).

Unconstitutionality of the Supreme Court

The provisions of the Constitution of 1875 pertaining to the responsibility of ministers were evidently what should have governed the trial of the Popular Front ministers, since that Constitution was in force at the time the Popular Front was in power and at the time the trial was ordered.

According to Article 12 of the Constitutional law of July 16, 1875, minis-ters "who have committed crimes in the exercise of their functions" must be charged by the Chamber of Deputies and judged by the Senate which is to act as the high court of justice. This system is similar to the procedure of impeachment as it exists in England and the United States. It imposes on the political assemblies the duty of executing political justice and of doing so in a manner guaranteeing their own competence and impartiality. By entrusting neither a chief of state nor a cabinet with the task of bringing charges against ministers, it avoids the excesses of a spirit of vengeance or party influence to the detriment of true justice. Barthélémy expressed his admiration for this system in his *Treatise on Constitutional Law*: "Political jurisdiction is truly divided between the two chambers; this affords the accused minister an im-portant guarantee, inasmuch as he may be condemned only by the successive votes of both chambers. This solution is in harmony with the tendency of modern law, which considers the twofold examination in criminal procedure— the opinion of the investigating commission and the final judgment—an essential guarantee to the accused."

The law of July 10, 1940, empowering Marshal Pétain to draw up a new constitution, actually stated that "the new constitution must be ratified by the nation and enforced by the assemblies that it is to create." These assemblies did not yet exist, and have never been created by Marshal Pétain. Constitu-tional Act No. 3, promulgated on July 11, 1940—as an application of the law of July 10—specifically assured the maintenance of Chamber and Senate by its first paragraph: "The Senate and the Chamber of Deputies shall continue to exist until the formation of assemblies as provided for in the Constitutional law of July 10, 1940." The Chamber and the Senate had been "adjourned until further notice," but the Chief of State reserved for himself the right to call them into session whenever such a move seemed opportune. If, therefore, the Vichy government wanted to bring charges, it was compelled by the Con-stitution of 1875 and the Constitutional Acts of July 10 and July 11, 1940, to call a session of the Senate and Chamber and leave to them the task of operat-ing the mechanism of political justice.

The Vichy government preferred to violate the Constitution. On July 30, 1940, a new "Constitutional Act" abrogated those articles of the Constitution of 1875 that provide the mechanism of political justice, and created instead a "Supreme Court of Justice," for the specific purpose of judging "ministers, former ministers, and their immediate subordinates, civilian or military, who are accused of having committed crimes or misdemeanors in the exercise of their functions and of having betrayed the duties of their office." Before this Court

109

we were summoned. Daladier's attorney, M. Ribet, and Blum himself demonstrated before the Court, as a point of public and penal law, that the government had violated the Constitution by setting up the Supreme Court of Justice and had applied retroactively to us the laws it had forged. The irrefutability of their demonstration became evident in the embarrassed reaction of Prosecuting Attorney Cassagneau, who, although it was his task to defend and justify the thesis of the government, announced at the hearing of February 23, 1942 that "we are here not to decide whether the laws are constitutional but only to enforce them." Nothing revealed more clearly that the Court of Riom was a tribunal at the command of a dictatorial government.

Arbitrary Character of the Procedure

If the very existence of the Court was a challenge to constitutional law, its composition, its competence, and its mechanism defied both criminal law and reason. To prove this point, let us use a study on the Supreme Court of Justice, published in France by Joseph Magnol, Dean of the Law School at Toulouse and Professor of Criminal Law. Although favorable to the Vichy government, in exposing the new principles of criminal law Professor Magnol underlined the arbitrary character of the measures taken; despite his pro-Fascist sympathies, Professor Magnol was shocked by the texts he was called upon to explain.

Let us examine the composition of the Supreme Court of Justice.

If it was not possible to have the Popular Front ministers tried by an assembly of political men—their peers—they should have been judged by a jury. Until 1940 the institution of the jury for the judgment of criminal cases was about the same in France as in all the free countries of the world. But a jury of independent men would have asked questions embarrassing to the representatives of the General Staff whom it was essential to shield. Hence the Court had no jury. It comprised seven regular and three deputy judges, all appointed by Marshal Pétain. Article 2 of the law of July 30, 1940 ruled that the President and Vice-President of the Supreme Court should be selected from among the judges at the Court of Cassation; the other judges could be chosen from "officers of the first or second sections of the General Staff, or from members or former members of corps constitués [administrative bodies]." Since no definition of corps constitués existed in French law, the government enjoyed perfect freedom of choice and discrimination. In fact, the members of the Court were recruited from the ranks of military and civil servants devoted to the regime, friendly to the General Staff, and resolutely opposed to the Popular Front. The trial showed that among these men those who were professional judges possessed a certain courage and tried to resist the pressure exerted upon them by Marshal Pétain and his ministers.

The texts which determined the Court's realm of jurisdiction were even more eloquent and dangerous than those regulating its composition.

The Court's duty was not merely to apply the law to ministers, former ministers, and their immediate subordinates. The Court enjoyed sovereign power in interpreting the law and determining the penalties of the men handed over to it by the government. I quote Professor Magnol: "In addition to acts provided for in criminal legislation, Article 1 of the law of July 30, 1940, is aimed at certain acts which do not constitute any legal infraction. Thus, in the case of a minister who is said 'to have betrayed the duties of his office,' it is up to the Supreme Court to qualify this fact. In this way, the decree recognizes a supreme power of qualification in violation of the rule of *nullum crimen, nulla poena sine lege*. . . . Article 12 establishes the sovereign power of the Court with respect to the application of penalties. When the act with which the accused is charged is nowhere specified in criminal law, the Court is free to choose the penalty. . . even if it be the death penalty. One might question the possibility of imposing the death penalty in such a case. . . but there is nothing to limit the Supreme Court's freedom of choice among the penalties established by the Criminal Code. . . . The penalty is arbitrary, in the sense in which that word was used in the law of the *ancien régime*."

This return to the arbitrary penalties and legal system of the *ancien régime* is shocking to a democrat. Judges without any political experience were empowered to inflict whatever punishment they wished, even the death penalty, on the adversaries of the dictator, although French criminal law did not define the so-called "betrayal of the duties of governmental office." The Vichy government was not satisfied with bringing France back to the *ancien régime;* it introduced into French law the National Socialist concept of law, in which law and justice are only a means to govern. One can find similar dispositions in the Third Reich, but nothing more drastic. The organization of the Supreme Court at Riom allows us to measure the despotic character of the Vichy government.

This despotism was equally evident in the actual operation of the Supreme Court of Justice. I cannot enter into details of procedure, but a few examples will demonstrate the deliberate effort to deprive political prisoners of all the guarantees to which, in civilized countries, even the most dangerous criminals are entitled.

Among the primary guarantees of an impartial justice is the separation of functions among preliminary inquiry, investigating commission, and judgment. A body of magistrates—police officers, attorneys, or judges—has charge of the preliminary inquiries and of gathering all the particles of information which make up the accusation. The results of their inquiries are then subject to a cross-examination by both sides—prosecution and defense—before a first court or an investigating commission, which by a preliminary sentence decides whether there are grounds for sending the accused before another court for definite trial and judgment. There the accused may be condemned, but only after a public hearing of both prosecution and defense. Though this general

111

scheme of criminal procedure varies slightly in the different countries, the distinction among inquiry, information, and judgment is everywhere maintained.

In France, when a person is accused of a crime, an investigating judge (*juge d'instruction*), who is completely independent, is appointed to examine all charges brought against the defendant, make all necessary inquiries, and receive whatever testimony may contribute to the evidence. If after this first phase of the information the investigating judge decides there are sufficient grounds for a prosecution, he sends the accused before an actual investigating commission (*Chambre des Mises en Accusation*) which plays the same part as the grand jury in Anglo-Saxon countries. The *Chambre des Mises en Accusation* decides, by an act of indictment (*arrêt de renvoi*), whether the accused shall be committed for trial in the court of definite judgment (*Cour d'Assises*).

The very organization of the Supreme Court of Justice was a violation of these traditional rules. The Court's jurisdiction included the preliminary inquiry as well as the final judgment. Moreover, the examining judge was a member of the Court and as such participated in the final judgment; i.e., he judged his own investigation. I should like to forestall any possible suspicion that I may be exaggerating these legal monstrosities by quoting Professor Magnol: "The Supreme Court of Justice has a twofold mission—a mission of investigation and a mission of judgment. That is what distinguishes it from all other courts of law, whose mission is not—at least not primarily— one of investigating the case, for they have attached to them an autonomous body in charge of the preliminary inquiry. The court of final judgment, therefore, cannot assume jurisdiction over any one case, but may rule only on the facts transmitted to it [by the investigating court]. . . . In the case of the Supreme Court of Justice, the matter is different, as no separate investigating body has been set up in connection with it. The Court itself, through one of its members delegated for the purpose, takes charge of the preliminary inquiry, and thus, in a sense, becomes its own investigating commission. . . . The law of September 24, 1940, rules that the Supreme Court must *investigate* [italics M. Magnol's] a case and pass final judgment. The member of the Supreme Court who undertook the inquiry may take part in the final verdict."

Another guarantee of the impartial administration of justice is the right of the accused to a full hearing and to freedom of defense. At every step of the inquiry, the accused must be entitled to know and to discuss freely the charges against him as well as every particle of evidence collected and utilized. If investigations are ordered on a specific point, he must be allowed to take part in them; if an expert's opinion or some other document is added to the dossier, he has a right to discuss it; if a witness is heard, the defendant may know his testimony and, thanks to the procedure which in Anglo-Saxon countries is known as "cross-examination," may in turn question the witness. At every stage of the proceedings, the accused must be assisted by a counsel for the defense, with whom he must be able to communicate freely. The aid of a counsel is, indeed, indispensable to any defendant to protect him against actual abuses and against the devices of a skillful justice.

These judicial guarantees were suspended for the political adversaries of the Vichy government. Freedom of the defense and the guarantee of a full hearing for both sides are specified in the French Code of Criminal Procedure, and the law of July 30, 1940, stated that the articles of the Code of Criminal Procedure would be applied "in so far as they were not contrary to the dispositions of the present law." In the course of the preliminary inquiry, the government realized that it would be dangerous to maintain those customary rules and, by a decree of August 14, 1940, decided that the Code of Criminal Procedure should not be applied in the preliminary inquiry of cases before the Supreme Court. Here again, I quote Professor Magnol: "The Supreme Court is not compelled to apply the rules of the Code of Criminal Procedure except in the phase of final judgment. . . . As far as the initial stages are concerned, notably the preliminary inquiry, it must be admitted that the Court, especially after the decree of August 14, 1940, is sovereign and determines its own procedure. That may possibly have been the purpose of the decree of August 14, 1940. . . . The Court has thus been entitled to decide . . . that the presence of the counsels for the defense at the examination of the defendants during the preliminary investigation, and the communication of the dossier before trial are not required. . . . The defendants can communicate with their attorneys only upon special permission of the examining magistrate, in whose discretion it is to grant or refuse such authorization. It is true that Article 8 of the law of July 30, 1940, rules that the defendants may be assisted by a counsel; yet only in the phase of final judgment are they allowed to make full and free use of that privilege."

Deprived of every legal guarantee during the preliminary investigation, the defendants would thus be entirely at the mercy of an examining judge, who, as has been pointed out, would be their political enemy. This judge could put them into solitary confinement; he could refuse to let them have all documents and other evidence; he could deny them the right to see their counsel. In the words of Professor Magnol: "He could resort to house search and the seizure of correspondence or objects to be produced in evidence, without fear that his actions might be invalidated by his nonobservance of the rules established by the Code of Criminal Procedure, as the latter do not apply to the procedure before the Supreme Court."

A body of men, most of whom a dictatorial government appointed on the basis of their political bias, was thus endowed with absolute power: the making of the law (which allowed them to define, in each specific instance, the "betrayal of the duties of office"), the enforcement of the law (by which they could pronounce even a verdict of death), and the arbitrary investigation of political cases under their jurisdiction.

Even the *ancien régime* never went to such an extreme. Its justice was imperfect, yet not completely arbitrary. The *ancien régime* was absolute monarchy, with its excesses; the Pétain regime has been absolute tyranny, with all its abuses.

THE CONDUCT OF THE RIOM TRIAL

According to the laws which fixed its competence, the Supreme Court of Justice alone had the right to undertake and conduct the trial of the Popular Front. Marshal Pétain was confident that the judges he had appointed for their anti-democratic prejudice would give him the verdict he needed. But it soon became clear that the Court of Riom was taking its work seriously; before condemning, it wished to judge. In spite of their devotion to Pétain, the judges did not intend to be transformed into servants of authority. The Vichy government, dissatisfied, intervened more and more in the conduct of the trial, which became a compromise between Pétain's eagerness to prosecute his adversaries and the scruples of the Supreme Court.

The result of this compromise was not justice, but paralysis. The Court was incapable of either condemning or discharging the accused, and the Riom trial was interrupted by governmental order after long, purposeless debates.

When it came to indicting the Popular Front ministers, the fundamental contradiction between the Court and the government revealed itself.

Grounds for the Accusation

Let us first examine the things of which we were *not* accused. Not one act against honor and decency was brought up against us. I have a right to mention this fact, and on behalf of Blum and Daladier, it is my duty to insist on it, in view of the calumnies of the Fascist propaganda. The Vichy government, with its propaganda methods modeled after Hitler's, has made every effort to discredit us, especially in Anglo-Saxon countries, by letting its agents spread the notion that we were disreputable and corrupt "politicians." It has been rumored that we accumulated large fortunes as a result of political machinations. It was repeated under cover that I was an "agent of Moscow." In the days of the Popular Front, our slanderers, profiting by the lenient press and libel laws, which the Senate so obstinately refused to change, had spread the rumor that Blum, at Lausanne, and I, at Monaco, owned numerous estates yielding large revenues. Those familiar with our mode of living would shrug their shoulders at such insinuations. None of the great democrats escaped slander. Jaurès, honesty personified, was accused of having been in the pay of Germany before 1914. Briand, who until the day he received the Nobel Prize did not have a bank account and had never used a check, was accused of corruption and venality; the same was said of Herriot. The leaders of French democracy have been neither better nor worse than their peers in other countries, but they have been the most defamed.

The French people, so familiar with the proverbial "wickedness" of the men of the Right, have never been deceived by such talk; they know that Blum, Daladier, and I were poorer in June, 1940, than at the time of our entrance into politics. But these calumnies were utilized by reactionary and Fascist groups and were spread abroad. In 1941 an American magazine, *Scribner's Commentator*—which in the same issue contained an article by Laval's son-in-law, René de Chambrun—attacked the Riom defendants, intimating, for example, that I had embezzled certain credit appropriations destined for the Air Ministry. I addressed a letter of protest to the editor of the magazine; it was never printed. On July 25, 1942, I learned that Attorney General Biddle was prosecuting *Scribner's Commentator* for its pro-Axis activities. The leaders of the Popular Front thus had the honor of being criticized by pro-Fascist periodicals all over the world.

Nobody today has the right to harbor even the faintest suspicion against the honesty of the men prosecuted at Riom. With the advantages of dictatorial rule on its side, Vichy has made detailed investigations of our persons, our property, our families, our friends, and of the manner in which we employed credits entrusted to us. Had it been able to discover the slightest irregularity that might have impaired our moral reputation, it would most certainly have publicized it immediately as a powerful weapon against us. The law of September 24, 1940, extended the jurisdiction of the Supreme Court of Justice to "acts of extortion, corruption, and embezzlement" and to instances in which we might have "betrayed the duties of our offices by speculating on the value of national currency or by abusing the funds entrusted to our control." This law was obviously aimed at us. Our prosecutors searched everywhere for evidence, questioned our enemies and slanderers, and stripped our private lives. They found nothing, for there was nothing to find.

Let us examine the actual accusation.

The Vichy government adopted Hitler's thesis that our policy had caused the war. The preliminary indictment (*réquisitoire introductif d'instance*) demanded the opening of investigations "against ministers, former ministers, and their immediate subordinates, civilian or military, who had betrayed the duties of their offices through acts that contributed, before September 4, 1939, to the passing from a state of peace to a state of war, and through such acts as had subsequently aggravated the consequences of the situation thus created." Here again I must insist on one point. Vichy propaganda has spread a rumor among the democratic nations that Pétain opposed Hitler's demand and refused to order the war guilt trial. Certain columnists, in articles written in March, 1941, on the Riom trial, put Pétain on a plane with Blum, and congratulated the old Marshal on having resisted Hitler. Unfortunately for the old Marshal, the truth behind the rumor is explicit in the texts.

The preliminary indictment was an official document drawn up by Prosecuting Attorney Cassagneau, the government representative at Riom. The investigations with which the Court was asked to proceed were nothing but the war guilt trial, inasmuch as we were accused of having declared war. As Blum and I had been out of the government since February, 1938, this meant that our policy at the time of the Popular Front had provoked Germany and brought about the outbreak of the war. That had been Hitler's accusation against me on the eve of the Munich agreements. The same indict-ment was brought against Daladier, La Chambre, Gamelin, and Jacomet, who—at the time of France's declaration of war on Germany—had been, respec-tively, Premier and Minister of National Defense, Air Minister, Chief of Staff, and General Secretary of the Ministry of National Defense. And the same accusation was raised against Paul Reynaud and Georges Mandel—for having "wanted" the war and "aggravated the consequences of the situa-tion thus created"—probably for refusing, throughout June, 1940, the sug-gestions of Pétain and Weygand to ask for an armistice.

Thus the documents published by the Riom Court and the Vichy govern-ment speak for themselves. This government will have to bear the shame for transmitting to the Supreme Court of Justice indictments aimed at absolving Germany by declaring French statesmen guilty of betraying the duties of their offices and steering their country into war.

The Supreme Court of Justice refused to stoop quite so low as to conduct a trial which, in the words of Blum, would have been "the trial of France." It transformed the war guilt trial into proceedings revolving around the re-sponsibility for the country's unpreparedness in the war. To accomplish this transformation, it ignored the first part of the preliminary indictment, which demanded an investigation into the passing from a state of peace to a state of war, and in the second part of the indictment, it suppressed the term "subse-quently." The object of investigation was thus changed to "acts which had aggravated the situation created by the passing from a state of peace to a state of war." By an elaborate construction, the Court decided that such acts might well be found in the insufficient preparation of the war.

As Blum emphasized before the Riom Court, neither he nor I could have been prosecuted except by suppressing the word "subsequently," inasmuch as neither of us was a member of the government subsequent to 1938. It was our "warmongering" policy that Pétain wanted to punish and that the Supreme Court refused to try. Pétain was then obliged to take into con-sideration the attitude of the Court. He had to take new steps. The trial, limited to responsibility for insufficient preparation of the war, might become dangerous for the Vichy government, inasmuch as it might add the names of Pétain and Weygand to the list. The trial had to remain one of scapegoats, it had to remain the trial of the Popular Front, and every pre-caution had to be taken to conceal the true causes of the defeat. Precautions were needed not only against the accused and their defense, but against the Supreme Court itself, which had declined in Marshal Pétain's confidence by refusing to declare the French Republic guilty of having precipitated the war.

The measures taken were: limited and mutilated debate; the judges were reminded of their duty by Pétain's preliminary decision declaring the de-fendants guilty; and the influence of public opinion on the course of the trial was reduced to a minimum.

Limited and Mutilated Debates

The debate was limited to the participation of certain political opponents of the Vichy government in the military preparation of the war. This limitation obviously made it impossible to establish the true causes of the defeat, and it seriously impaired the rights of the defense.

At the outset, in its act of indictment (*arrêt de renvoi*), the Court imposed definitive limitations on the debate, excluding from the trial all questions relating to the conduct of military operations. This decision alone proved the arbitrary character of the trial. At the opening of the session on February 19, Blum addressed the Court as follows:

"By your act of indictment everything pertaining to the conduct of military operations has been eliminated from the debate. . . . One can hardly conceive of a more amazing paradox. Why was this tribunal created? Because the French Army has succumbed in an ill-fated campaign, and because the French people wanted to know why the Army has been defeated in this war. No one can deny that the people's instinct attributed this military defeat above all to military causes. And you who are to establish these causes, you who have drawn so many things into the orbit of this trial, you exclude from it the war. . . . In the debate on the responsibility for the defeat, the war will be absent.

". . . your indictment . . . strikes a blow, equally serious and intolerable, at our defense. You exclude from the trial anything that might involve the military High Command during the war—in other words, everything touching on military doctrines, strategic principles, operations, and the actual utilization of modern equipment. You intend to concentrate the prosecution on the matériel, I might almost say, on the quantitative aspect of armament. Yet even the best prepared, the most generously equipped army, will succumb nevertheless if the mistakes of the High Command have maneuvered it into a hopeless situation or if the weakness of its leadership has failed to inspire it with the will to fight. Again, the matériel, however abundant, cannot abound everywhere at the same time. When the doctrines that determine its employment are defective, when the plans are imprudent, and when speculations prove erroneous, even an army having superabundant matériel may find itself in a condition of irremediable inferiority at the time and place where the enemy's surprise attack has struck. These remarks are obvious to the point of being commonplace, but they are curiously confirmed by your investigation. France and the world will be stupefied to learn the true numerical relation between French and enemy matériel at the outbreak of the war or at the time of the German attack in May, 1940. Hence the question of whether the mistakes of the High Command were not, perhaps, the ultimate cause of the defeat would have to be settled first. That is the direction which you should be following in your investigation if you want to fulfill your task; and that is what I asked of you so urgently over a year ago, in a note addressed and handed to you. Not only have you failed to pursue this essential and interlocutory inquiry . . . but you have, through your indictment, prevented us from raising it in the courtroom."

117

Blum's demonstration was irrefutably logical. Before saying to the leaders of the Popular Front that they were unable to make the French nation produce the modern matériel that its Army required, one had to prove that the defeat was due to a lack of such matériel. To establish whether the principal and ultimate cause of the defeat lay in the military leaders' misuse of the matériel would be precisely what in French law is called *la question préjudicielle,* the question to be solved first, because on its solution depend the answers to all others. To refuse to examine it was to violate the rights of the defense; it was the Supreme Court's first abuse of those rights.

At the hearing of February 20 Daladier took up that question once more. He was not, like Blum, a lawyer. Yet with practical arguments he convincingly demonstrated the manner in which the Court's decision and the limited debate had made it impossible for him to refute the accusations brought against him.

"I can prove," he said, "that in September, 1939, and on May 10, 1940 [the date on which Hitler's offensive against France was launched], the [French] Army was equipped with such matériel as should have made possible a victorious resistance to the German offensive. . . . I can produce figures and irrefutable documents. I shall show the intensity of my effort to assure the French Army matériel equal in quality and only slightly inferior in quantity to that of the German Army, despite Germany's great industrial superiority over France. . . .

"Why was France conquered? Why a defeat so sudden and brutal that the conqueror himself is still surprised at the rapidity of his victory? How is one to arrive at its causes if the government that is condemning me refuses to communicate the military documents and the accounts of operations so indispensable to this discussion? Where is the respect for the rights of the defense if one forbids investigations into the responsibilities for the defeat as soon as the question is no longer one of former ministers but of the commanders who led the armies into battle? Why were so many French tanks and armored cars senselessly dispersed along the entire front, instead of being grouped and organized for rapid and powerful counterattacks? Why were so many arms and munitions left in depots and arsenals, useless to the country's defense, at the very moment the battle was raging? Why was the French front pierced at Sedan, and later at the Meuse, and how is one to explain that formidable surprise which proved the decisive cause of the defeat?

"And how many more painful questions ought to be asked on military operations and on the circumstances under which at Bordeaux, after a dramatic governmental crisis, the decision was made to cease firing and to ask for an armistice? After the affirmations, many times repeated, that the French people would learn the whole truth, why now this obstinate refusal to let me introduce the documents which are kept at the Ministry of War and which alone would completely illuminate the true causes of the defeat? Indeed, it is even stranger when we know that the Pétain government has modified the military code of justice in such a manner as to ensure the impunity of generals who capitulated in open field or who, after their imprisonment, accepted liberation on their word of honor that they would never again bear arms against the enemy. Let us marvel, furthermore, at the declaration of Marshal Pétain's government that passes a retroactive amnesty where it is a matter of investigating military responsibility, and, at the same time, in the search for responsibility among political men, creates a new type of crime, giving it retroactive effect. Thus, if Gambetta were living today, he would probably be in prison, while Bazaine would be in the government."

Gambetta was the democrat who in 1871 saved the honor of France when he declared himself a partisan of resistance and urged that the fight against Bismarck's armies be carried on; his attitude was not unlike that adopted in 1940 by the Popular Front leaders imprisoned by Pétain. Bazaine was the Marshal of France who commanded the French armies at Sedan in 1870; his general attitude was similar to that of Pétain and Weygand in 1940. But after the war of 1870, Gambetta, the patriot and democrat, was honored as a great Frenchman, while Marshal Bazaine was court-martialed.

As early as the first hearing, the government and the Supreme Court of Justice refused to organize a full and fair trial. Furthermore, Daladier revealed—and this is a fact not yet published in England and America— that the Vichy government had modified existing laws for a twofold purpose: to rescue the guilty military leaders and to crush its political adversaries. According to the French military code of justice, every general who capitulates in the field must be judged like a captain who loses his ship at sea. This rule, which is to be found in almost every country since it conforms to the military traditions of all armies, was abolished by Marshal Pétain. Why? Because the condemnation of French generals by independent and competent courts-martial might have rendered more difficult the trial of political men.

Moreover, General Gamelin refused to answer questions addressed to him, and thereby encouraged, as Blum pointed out, the Court's decision not to examine the military aspects of the French defeat. By his silence, Gamelin prevented the raising of any questions involving, even indirectly, the mistakes of the High Command and of the General Staff or indicating the responsibility of the military authorities in the defeat. No one could appraise General Gamelin's part in the preparation of the Army and the conduct of the war without inquiring into the responsibility of his predecessors in charge of army preparations, of his successors, responsible for military operations after him, and of his superiors, who should have inspired and directed his decisions. Gamelin's predecessor as head of the Army General Staff was General Weygand, and his successor was again General Weygand. Moreover, both Weygand and Gamelin were subject to the control of the Supreme War Council, whose virtual chief since the death of Marshal Foch was Marshal Pétain. Pétain was Gamelin's superior in rank. It would have been impossible for Gamelin to defend himself without involving the decisions of Marshal Pétain and General Weygand.

"The attitude of General Gamelin was long to be expected," said Blum. "Now that it is an accomplished fact . . . I doubt whether there is anyone here who has been able to suppress a feeling of pain. . . . He has told you his reasons [for his attitude]. He will not protest against a sentence pronounced on him by a chief who has been the leading proponent of our war doctrine; nor does he want to accuse his subordinates in the courtroom. His silence was dictated partly by Pétain's decision and partly by the Supreme Court's act of indictment . . . which barred from the debate whatever might have involved the question of military leadership during the war."

It was in this way that the Riom trial was limited to the search for "political" responsibilities.

Still another restriction was to remove from the Riom proceedings any possibility of fairness and impartiality.

If the Court was limiting itself to a study of the mistakes committed by political men in their efforts to prepare for war, it should have examined the mistakes of all the premiers and all the ministers of national defense during the period that preceded the war. Its investigations should have covered the entire period of German rearmament, the years 1934 to 1939, instead of concentrating on the period of Popular Front rule. This was another instance where an arbitrary restriction, intended to safeguard members and friends of the Vichy government against being drawn into the proceedings, put a severe curb on the rights of the defense.

At the hearing of February 19, 1942, Blum again furnished the most forceful demonstration. I will limit myself to a summary of it, quoting from the original wherever possible.

"The Supreme Court of Justice," Blum remarked, "is determined to examine only the responsibilities incurred after June, 1936, that is to say, the responsibilities of the Popular Front. Why? . . . Did the rearmament of France suddenly reveal itself as a duty of ministerial office in June, 1936? Or is it, perhaps, that this duty had been admirably fulfilled until June, 1936?

"The Nazi party assumed power in March, 1933. The Third Reich left the League of Nations at the end of 1933 and from that time on rearmed openly." On April 17, 1934, the French government showed that it had lost its confidence in the German government and renounced all hopes for the success of the Disarmament Conference when she sent the famous diplomatic note declaring: "France will herself provide for her security." This gave Hitler a free hand: on March 16, 1935, compulsory military service was re-established in Germany; the German budget for national defense, which in 1934 had been only 381 million dollars, was raised to 2,600 million dollars in 1935 and to 3,600 million in 1936. The year 1934, then, was the time for France to begin rearming if she did not want to let Germany dangerously outdistance her in the armament race.

During 1934, 1935, and the first five months of 1936, France did not have a Popular Front government. As Blum said: "There was a strong government that enjoyed full powers—Gaston Doumergue was Premier, André Tardieu, Secretary of State, Marshal Pétain, Minister of War. [Laval was a member of that government, and General Weygand was Chief of the Army.] There existed at that time not even a trace of modern matériel in the equipment of our fighting units. And yet, what was done? How large were the credits? What was the volume of actual orders? What work projects were undertaken? Only General Denain, the Minister of Aviation, embarked upon the immediate execution of a vast program, but the official files show with what precipitation and incoherence. The duties of the cabinet were obvious and imperative. Were they fulfilled? To judge if they were, one need only refer to the events of March 7, 1936, two years later [the date of Germany's remilitarization of the Rhineland]."

This remilitarization, in violation of the Versailles Treaty, directly threatened the security of France and stirred up violent feeling throughout the country. Many believed, rightly or wrongly, that in permitting Hitler's Germany to rearm the Rhineland, France was fatally weakening herself. The French government began by protesting to Germany; then, overnight, the tone changed. And why? Because the three ministers in charge of national defense and the chiefs of the General Staffs of the Army and the Air Force were forced to recognize and admit the weak condition of the French forces.

"This incident," said Blum, "which was to bear such grave consequences, will suffice to indicate in what condition the [Popular Front] cabinet of June, 1936, found the Army. . . . What had been accomplished between 1933 and 1936? Was it at any time adequate to meet the necessities and the dangers? The disposition of available matériel is even more important than its quantity, and during the campaign [of 1940] the decrepitude and inadequacy of military doctrines and strategic conceptions became tragically evident. But these doctrines and notions had hardly been born together with the legislation of the Popular Front. Long before June, 1936, . . . the doctrine of our invulnerable fronts, the absolute faith in our fortifications [Maginot Line] and in the defense strategy, the distrust of armored cars and, particularly, of the role of aviation in warfare, had been proclaimed, inculcated, and practiced. Documentary evidence abounds, and with what signatures!"

Despite the Court's attempts to stifle the debate, subsequent proceedings were to reveal that the signatures had been notably those of Pétain and Weygand.

"Why then," insisted Blum, "did not the investigation go further back? The act of indictment is silent on this point. The preliminary indictment drawn up by the Prosecuting Attorney resorts to a few peculiarly embarrassed explanations, which might be summarized as follows: 'To assume that their predecessors were guilty would not absolve the accused of their responsibility.' Indeed an unusual conception of justice and equality! Among those guilty of the same crime, one group would thus be punished, while the remainder would be spared deliberately. What can be the basis for this discrimination, if not a political criterion? Is it not evident that, if our predecessors were found guilty, our mistake would at least be attenuated by the fact that we were carrying the burden of a situation which they had transmitted to us? The records would show, on the contrary, that after June, 1936, we did what no one had done before us; the government which I headed put into action a total program to which in size and significance none of the preceding plans could compare. And the dossier proves, furthermore, that the program did not exist merely on paper, but that it was carried out, that it never lacked the necessary credits, and that it was in advance of the time anticipated for its execution when we entered the war. If it was not, by that time, completed, if it was not undertaken on a more methodical industrial scale beginning at the bases of production, the reason has been that it was launched too late; and this tardy beginning is precisely what leads us to the question of responsibilities prior to June, 1936."

Blum's statement is verified by the examination of the French and German budgets for national defense as they were published on October 1, 1938, in *Foreign Policy Reports* by William T. Stone.* This report shows that the French budget, which amounted to 678.8 million dollars in 1933, when Daladier was Minister of War and I was Minister of Aviation, fell to 582.7 million dollars in 1934, when Marshal Pétain was the Minister of War; this budget was raised by the Popular Front to 834.4 millions by the end of 1936, to 909.2 millions in 1937, and it reached 1,092.1 millions in 1938. The Popular Front rearmed France, though perhaps insufficiently, whereas Marshal Pétain had disarmed the country at the very moment that Hitler was launching his rearmament program. In 1934 and 1935 Marshal Pétain's budgets for the Army (Air Force and Navy not included) were below 7 billion francs, while in 1937 and 1938 the war budgets prepared by Daladier amounted to 12 and 16 billion francs respectively. If only Marshal Pétain had been as "bad" a Minister of War as Daladier, or if the conservative cabinets of Doumergue, Flandin, and Laval had been as "incompetent" as the cabinets headed by Blum, the situation of the French forces in 1939-1940 would have been better.

The truth is that the Vichy government had prevented a complete investigation of the responsibilities for the defeat; it had ordered a trial only of the Popular Front ministers—and the Supreme Court had accepted its decision. "To begin investigations for the trial in June, 1936," said Blum, "is to admit that political tactics—perhaps political vengeance—have dictated that choice. I can conceive of no other plausible reason. . . . It is an attempt to unload the responsibility for military defeat on the Popular Front and its labor and social policy and thereby on all democratic institutions." Limited and cut short in this way, the trial was not an instrument of justice, but of reprisal. The Vichy government intended to mask the true responsibilities for the defeat—chiefly those of Pétain and Weygand—and the Court consented to cloak this diversion by its authority. "We shall see . . .," said Daladier on February 20, "where, by whom, and in what manner France was betrayed,"

*William T. Stone, "Economic Consequences of Rearmament," *Foreign Policy Reports,* October 1, 1938.

and his counsel, M. Ribet, declared: "The French people have the right to know why a mysterious screen seems to hide certain high placed responsibilities."

The Riom trial was transformed into a political operation by the fear of a government and by the weakness of its judges.

Advance Condemnation by Petain

Pétain refused to give the trial even a semblance of impartiality or justice. On October 10, 1941, in a decision unprecedented even in the annals of Fascist governments, Marshal Pétain went over the heads of the Supreme Court judges and condemned the principal defendants to life imprisonment—for he could do no more.

On January 27, 1941, by Constitutional Act No. 7, Pétain had established the mechanisms of his government. "The Secretaries of State, high dignitaries and high officials of the State will take an oath before the Chief of the State. They will swear allegiance to his person [Article 1]. They are personally responsible to the Chief of State. This responsibility involves their persons and property [Article 2]. In case one of them should betray the duties of his office, the Chief of State, after an investigation which he shall initiate, may. . . apply to him the following punishments: deprivation of political rights, confinement to residence under guard in France or the Colonies, administrative internment, detention in a fortress [Article 3]." This was the establishment of absolute personal power in all its rigor and with all its possible abuses. Moreover, Article 5 of the new decree declared these dispositions applicable "to former ministers, high dignitaries, and high officials who have held office within the past ten years." This law, too, was retroactive. It allowed Marshal Pétain to strike with impunity at the entire political and administrative leadership of the Popular Front; it permitted him to substitute his action for that of the Supreme Court of Justice and to condemn his political adversaries to "detention in a fortress." Constitutional Act No. 7 was issued at the moment when the magistrates of the Supreme Court, after the first investigations, announced that the culpability of the Popular Front ministers in the preparation for the war was in no way proved. It was at about the same time that Georges Ripert, Dean of the Paris Law School and a member of the Supreme Court, resigned, declaring: "I will not let Marshal Pétain dishonor my white hair." This decree was a means of bringing pressure on the Supreme Court of Justice; if the Court refused to return a verdict of guilty, Marshal Pétain could do so himself. If the magistrates refused to condemn, they in turn, could be indicted for having betrayed "the duties of their office," and the Chief of State could condemn *them.*

Marshal Pétain went further. On September 29, 1941, he created a "Council of Political Justice," charged with rendering opinions on questions relating to the enforcement of Constitutional Act No. 7. This Council was composed of nine members, only three of whom had any political experience: a Senator, Colonel Josse (an old soldier, about Pétain's age); a member of the Chamber of Deputies, Vallin, who was one of the Croix de Feu leaders; and a former deputy, Felix Aulois, a courageous veteran, but blinded by his reactionary feeling and one of Pétain's main supporters. The others were Audollent, Drouat, Percerou, Peretti della Rocca, and Ripert.

More than a year after its creation, the Supreme Court of Justice had not finished the preliminary investigation and had not yet decided that the charges warranted bringing the accused to trial. These practical and judicial difficulties did not embarrass the Council of Political Justice; less than two weeks after its formation, the Council handed Marshal Pétain a recommendation, not only on the culpability of the Popular Front ministers and their "immediate collaborators," but even on the culpability of Paul Reynaud and Georges Mandel, who had been prosecuted and brought before the Supreme Court on the charge of "speculation with the national currency and misappropriating funds." In its recommendation the Council declared that "the indictment of the Prosecuting Attorney of the Supreme Court had been laid before it." It did not even call the accused to give them an opportunity to discuss the charges; it did not even see the documents gathered by the Court during the investigation. It based its decision on the preliminary indictment, a list of charges drawn up, not by an independent judge, but by the Prosecuting Attorney, the representative of the government before the Court of Justice. In the French legal system, a prosecuting attorney is not, as in Anglo-Saxon countries, an elected magistrate representing the people; he is a mere agent of the executive power, obliged to make his written indictments conform to the instructions given him by the Minister of Justice. According to the old rule of our criminal law, "his speech is free, but his pen is in bondage."

The Council of Political Justice, in basing its conclusions on the preliminary indictment, violated the most elementary principle of justice, the right to a hearing. The decision concerning Reynaud and Mandel was taken by a majority vote and that concerning the other defendants was unanimous. Nine men assumed the right to condemn eight others, whom they had not seen, whose depositions they had not heard, and whose trial was still in the stage of preliminary investigation. The Council sentenced Blum, Daladier, Gamelin, Reynaud, Mandel, and me to life imprisonment; adding, with a certain naïveté, that the sentence against me could not be executed because I was in the United States. The Council decided that La Chambre and Jacomet were less guilty than the others accused and gave no ground for the application of Constitutional Act No. 7.

Not less infamous than the proceedings of the Council of Political Justice were Marshal Pétain's condemnation of the accused and his attached commentary.

The commentary was made public in a broadcast on October 16, 1941, sixteen days after the decree creating the Council of Political Justice had been published in the *Journal Officiel*. The Council's decision was delivered on October 10. Ten days to study the records and documents, elaborate an opinion, and formulate conclusions! Six days for Marshal Pétain to study the indictment and make a final decision on the most complicated problems of contemporary history! *Imperatoria brevitas!* The short lapse of time between the creation of the Council of Political Justice and the radio speech effectively invalidated all decisions reached.

Although the Supreme Court of Justice had been declared the competent judicial authority, Pétain assumed the power to condemn, before the public hearings had even begun. He condemned solely on the basis of the opinion given him by the Council of Political Justice, whose stipulations he referred to as "clear, complete, and perfectly justified," although he did not take time to check them. Despite the Council's inability to find grounds for the application of Constitutional Act No. 7 to La Chambre and Jacomet, Marshal Pétain decreed their continued internment in the prison of Bourrassol. Dictators pay no attention to logic.

Pétain's official commentary was an order given publicly to the justices of the Supreme Court. Pétain declared that, in spite of his condemnations, the Riom Court remained in charge of the case and was to "pass judgment within the shortest possible time." He added that the Court's sentence probably would decree penalties harsher than his. He carefully pointed out that the Council of Political Justice had proposed *only* life imprisonment because this was "the heaviest penalty provided for by Constitutional Act No. 7." The Riom Court could do better; it could pass death sentences. "The gravity of the acts with which those principally responsible for our disaster are charged," said the Marshal, "is such that it cannot be masked or hidden by mere political sanctions. . . . The chief culprits, to whom this first sanction is today being applied, may find this sanction transformed into a far heavier penalty by the end of this trial."

Pétain made it absolutely clear to his justices that he expected them to furnish him with a political weapon for his dictatorial propaganda. "The sentence that will conclude the Riom trial must . . . strike at individuals and also at methods, customs, and the [democratic] regime. It will be without appeal. There will be no further discussion. It will mark the end of one of the most painful periods in the life of France." Finally, to prevent any mistake on the part of the justices, he reproved them in a manner, which, coming from the dictator of a Fascist country, might well be called a threat: "I felt that the jurisdictional procedure [of the Riom Court] with its prudence, its delays, and its slow progress, was aggravating the unrest under which the country is suffering. It is that unrest which I am attempting to alleviate by today's decisions. . . . In times like ours each one must assume his own responsibilities. I am setting the example by assuming my own."

Never before, not even in the history of Fascism and despotism, had a Chief of State publicly reproached his Supreme Court for its "prudence." Never before had a dictator interfered in a criminal trial, condemning the accused— his political opponents—without even a hearing, then handing them back to the judges with the words: I am setting you an example; do your duty and do it quickly; the guilt of these men must not be disputed; increase wherever possible the penalties I have pronounced; and in sentencing the men, pronounce your condemnation of the regime whose representatives they were.

Marshal Pétain's decisions and his radio speech of October 16, 1941, deserve being quoted in treatises on public law as flagrant examples of the confusion of executive, legislative, and judicial powers, and of the abusive interference in the mechanism of justice by a despotic Chief of State.

These decisions deprived the Supreme Court of Justice of the last appearances of independence. Unable to acquit the defendants or to condemn them to any punishment lighter than life imprisonment, the Court could not wholly reject the accusations of the Council of Political Justice. To use legal terminology, there existed a "prejudice" against the accused, a prejudice created by one who not only represented the highest authority in the State, but who was also the direct superior of the magistrates of the Court. An official communiqué, issued by the Havas Agency on the eve of Pétain's decision, announced that decision as having been taken "by virtue of his Constitutional rights to full jurisdictional power." Pétain, as Chief of State invested with judicial and executive powers, overruled the Riom Court in the same manner as the judgment of a Court of Appeals might overrule the lower courts. Moreover, the magistrates at Riom had taken an "oath of loyalty to the person" of the Chief of State, and were "responsible [to him] with their persons and their property." Forced to obey *perinde ac cadaver,* they became mere instruments of dictatorial power. Practically and legally, there could be no contradiction between the verdicts of the Marshal and the Riom Court. For the Court to pronounce the accused innocent, or even to declare their guilt attenuated, would have been to accuse Marshal Pétain of having committed an error and an act of injustice, and the judges' oath forbade any such verdict.

Blum and Daladier and their defense protested this advance condemnation before the Court and the public. "The verdict of Marshal Pétain," said Blum, "challenges every free conscience in the world to revolt. Here is something that offends both reason and the written law, something which, I believe I can say, particularly violates the oldest traditions of the French spirit. . . . The fundamental iniquity, the basic fault, affect . . . all the accused present in the courtroom. These men, whom your conscience as judges should obligate you to regard as innocent until the moment of the verdict, come before you already condemned. The highest authority in the State has pronounced them guilty of the same acts, subject to the same criminal legislation, and the sentence it has decreed has already been executed." Blum added these proud and contemptuous words: ". . . the case has been taken out of your hands . . . It is *res judicata* against you as it is against us . . . an indelible mark has been imprinted in advance on your future verdict. . . . You have tried to clear yourselves, to save your independence as judges; you know better than I that you have failed. Or do you, truthfully, feel free to acquit and release the men who, on the same charges, were declared guilty by a Chief of State to whom you have sworn an oath of allegiance? You are aware that he has left you no choice but to punish us even more harshly." The magistrates made no reply; and I imagine that they must have lowered their heads in shame, still feeling the sting where Marshal Pétain had slapped their faces.

Daladier, without Blum's sublety of mind and without his juridical formulae, denounced with equal fervor the sentence with its paralyzing effect on the rights of the defense: "I appear before you not as an accused," he said to the Court, "but as one condemned. I was condemned on October 16, 1941, by the Chief of State, upon the suggestions of a Council of Political Justice appointed by him, without an opportunity to defend myself, without even knowing the list of charges drawn up against me. I was condemned four months before the trial. . . . Is there in all our history a single example of so much contempt for law and justice? . . . We shall see in the course of this trial where, by whom, and in what manner France was betrayed. But I protest against this arbitrary condemnation, which is based on force alone. It will prove an ineradicable stigma on the dictatorial regime which was imposed on a defeated France with the aid of foreign domination, but which shall vanish with the conquerors and be buried in contempt. Three-quarters of a century ago, this kind of sentence was branded by the historian M. de Carne, a member of the French Academy, when he wrote in the *Revue des Deux Mondes* during the Second Empire: 'Cloaking prepared verdicts in legal robes has at all times been the work of certain commissions, whose odious memory would have impaired the honor of French magistracy, were it not that its members, in most cases, had no part in the formation of such political tribunals.' "

And the last word on this point came from Blum's attorney, when he said to the Court: "History, one day, will question your independence."

Instructions to the Press and a Secret Dossier

Public trial and the hearing of both sides are among the guarantees prerequisite to the administration of justice. The "hearing of both sides" implies that the accused has a right to know and discuss freely with the aid of his defense counsel, the charges brought against him as well as the documents, evidence, witnesses' depositions, and experts' testimony utilized against him. A public trial is intended to insure the widest possible control by public opinion, both through the public's actual presence in the courtroom and through the facilities for representatives of the press to report on the sessions and comment freely on the various aspects and episodes of the trial.

These rights become particularly precious in the case of an organized political trial before a group of specially-appointed magistrates instead of a jury of free men; yet neither of these guarantees was fully granted to the adversaries of the Vichy government.

The second hearing of the Riom trial revealed the existence of a "secret dossier," which the Court refused to communicate to the accused and their defense. On February 20, 1942, one of Blum's lawyers, Samuel Spanien, announced its existence. The Prosecuting Attorney finally admitted that the Court was, indeed, in possession of two sets of documents, which neither had been, nor would be, communicated to the defense. One set, he declared, pertained to Communist activities of no interest to the accused; the other contained testimony for the fuller enlightenment of the judges. This was an admission, and no one was satisfied with the explanation. In the first place, the legal rule is absolute and permits of no distinction between documents communicated to the defense and documents reserved to the court. Moreover, had the dossier on Communist activities been of no interest, it undoubtedly would not have been brought into the trial. And finally, there can be no disputing the defendants' right to know and discuss all the testimony that might serve to enlighten the judges—particularly if it originated with Marshal Pétain or certain foreign authorities, as was pointed out by the defense.

The existence of a secret dossier was peculiarly disturbing in a country where the tradition of the Dreyfus affair was still alive and where a trial in which several Fascist governments were interested was being conducted. In his testimony on February 20 Daladier insisted strongly on the stake which Hitler's Germany had in the Riom trial: "The condemnation of the Frenchmen whom she has the audacity to declare responsible for the war was Germany's first demand when she fixed the conditions for an armistice. She has not ceased to be concerned. In a radio address on October 13, 1941, Reichsminister Funk announced to his German listeners that the French government would soon condemn those guilty for the war, thus reaching a new stage on the road to collaboration. He received satisfaction on October 16. It has been the aim of Germany to utilize for her propaganda the verdict pronounced by Marshal Pétain, which she expects to have confirmed and increased [by the Riom Court]." General Franco, too, was interested in the Riom trial, for one of the charges brought against Daladier and me in the preliminary indictment and by the Council of Political Justice was that we had delivered airplanes and armaments to the Spanish Republic.

As long as a dictatorship rules France, no one will ever know the contents of that secret dossier. Nor shall we learn what French or foreign evidence, so essential to the Court, had to be withheld from the accused and their defense.

At the very beginning of the trial, it was evident that the accounts of the press were to be subjected not merely to the regular censorship but to a particularly strict control.

On February 19, 1942, Blum's attorney, Le Trocquer, informed the Court of the instructions that the Ministry of Information had issued to the French press on the eve of the war guilt trial. Ever since the Vichy government's advent to power, the French press had been guided by a series of general or specific "regulations," any violation of which led to the suppression of the newspaper or a penalty for the reporter. On the eve of the Riom trial the press received eight "general instructions."* The object of these regula-tions was to compel the press to publish, instead of objective accounts, articles deliberately unfavorable to the accused and supporting the thesis of the government. The newspapers were instructed to emphasize the responsibility of the accused for the defeat of France; to show that no responsibility whatever fell on the Army or its chiefs; to stress on every occasion the harm caused by the methods of a democratic government to which "the people had fallen victim"; to eulogize the policy of Marshal Pétain, pointing out that "France was forced to create a new regime or perish"; and, finally, to "comment on and expand each day the arguments and refutations issued by the Press Service" of the Ministry of Information.

The trial transformed all French newspapers into agents of government propaganda. Le Trocquer had little difficulty in showing that the press, instead of placing the trial under control of public opinion, was used only to deceive public opinion. In the course of the trial the "general instructions" were elaborated by "special instructions" banning the publication of even the most minor facts that might either support the defense or injure the "prestige of the Army" in general, and of Marshal Pétain in particular. The result of this barrage of general and special instructions to the press was that the majority of newspapers ceased publishing reports and limited themselves to the accounts furnished by the censorship directors.

The control of the foreign press was a somewhat different matter. In all political trials in Fascist Germany and Italy, particularly in the Reichstag fire case, the foreign press had been unrestricted; it had been free to choose its correspondents and to wire its reports without censorship interference. Simi-larly, foreign journalists had enjoyed complete freedom of expression at the Moscow treason trials. Several foreign governments asked Vichy to grant their press the same privileges at the Riom trial. William C. Bullitt, then United States Ambassador to France, used all his influence to obtain for the de-fendants this trifling guarantee, which had become invaluable in view of the disregard for all other rules of justice. It is largely to the credit of the United States government that the Riom trial was not kept entirely secret and that several times the veil was lifted. On February 19, 1942, G. H. Archam-bault, the *New York Times* correspondent, was able to cable, along with his report, the news that "censorship had been lifted entirely for the foreign press."

This concession did not last long. That very same day, four of the ten American correspondents were deprived of their special passes to attend the trial without any explanation. These withdrawals were serious, as they ex-cluded from the courtroom such experts on French politics as Ralph Heinzen of the United Press, Paul Ghali of the *Chicago Daily News,* Melos Most of the Associated Press, and James King of the Trans-Radio Press Service. When a formal protest was registered by the American Embassy, two of the four passes were restored. But on February 21 a passage in a report by Archam-

* See Appendix V.

129

bault was suppressed by the censors. Thus the promised freedom of the press for foreign newspapers had become limited, *ratione personae* and *ratione materiae,* to the journalists whose reports suited Vichy. Despite all restrictions, American correspondents succeeded in enlightening a public which Fascist and reactionary propaganda was trying desperately to deceive. Whoever seeks an impartial picture of the Riom trial in the press reports must do two things. First of all, he must extract from the accounts the truly valuable facts, and to do this he has to be able to read between the lines—an unusual practice in countries where people enjoy a free press. That is, he must make the different cables from Riom complement and complete one another. Second, he must keep in mind the circumstances under which the reports were written and sent. Correspondents, whatever their ability or professional sense of responsibility, were handicapped by the double threat of the censorship bureau and the possibility of having their admission to the courtroom canceled.

Neither the instructions to French newspapers nor the fetters on the foreign press were able to accomplish the purpose of the Vichy government. In France the underground press took on the task of correcting the false information handed out by the official controlled press; its work was facilitated by mouth-to-mouth transmission of news, a system which in most countries under dictatorial rule is as prompt and reliable as in primitive society. Foreign countries had to content themselves with the distorted picture that Vichy's censorship permitted them to see. Yet much of the material which Vichy itself believed unobjectionable was scandalous enough to startle public conscience and to imply the truth behind the Riom trial. Today, narrow-minded reactionaries and the friends of Fascism are the only ones to maintain that the defendants of Riom are more to be blamed for the defeat of France than their accusers.

TRUTH ON THE MARCH

The Vichy government, using every unconstitutional and illegal means, committed countless abuses of power to prevent truth from revealing itself at Riom and from penetrating to the outside world. Yet in defiance of all precautions, truth was to force the doors of the courtroom; its light was to illuminate and guide public opinion and throw into relief Pétain, Weygand, and the agents of the Fifth Column.

It was because truth was on the march that the Vichy government was compelled to postpone the trial indefinitely.

The trial began under circumstances most unfavorable to the accused. In the preceding pages I have analyzed the legal situation; one must also bear in mind the psychological and political conditions. For a year and a half, official propaganda had endeavored to create an atmosphere propitious for the condemnation of the men whom Marshal Pétain had called "those chiefly responsible" for the disaster. "For seventeen months," said Daladier at one of the early hearings, "I have been a prisoner. For seventeen months, without a chance to defend myself, I have been denounced to the French people for having fomented the war and caused the defeat. At a time when I was actually forbidden to answer such attacks . . . the newspapers with official authorization, the Radio Nationale, and the Chief of State himself were representing me to France and the world as 'the man who, one day in September, without daring to consult the Chambers, had declared a war that was lost in advance' and handed over to the enemy a defenseless country.".

In the course of the proceedings, the atmosphere changed. It grew increasingly evident that conscientious and impartial judges would not be able to condemn the men who were being tried. Three circumstances contributed to this change of atmosphere—the statements of Blum and Daladier, the attitude of the magistrates, and the witnesses' testimony.

The powerful logic of Blum and Daladier and the force of their arguments, which overwhelmed the magistrates and everyone in the courtroom, helped more than any other factor to reveal the truth. So much so that a "confidential note" addressed on March 4, 1942, by the director of censorship at Clermont-Ferrand to the editors of all French newspapers said: "I must tell you in all sincerity that the defense of Daladier produced a very strong impression."*

I have already had occasion to quote certain important statements of Blum and Daladier, and there will be more. As far as possible I have aimed at letting the reader appraise for himself the value of these declarations and the moral and intellectual stature of the men who made them. I am the friend of Blum and of Daladier, and according to Vichy, their accomplice. My judgment would seem suspect were I to speak of the nobility and courage which they so often have proved. Men of good faith who read the statements of Blum and Daladier will want to compare their own impressions with the abominable legends spread by Fascist propaganda and by the reactionary press in every country. Let them glance at the declarations of Blum and Daladier and compare them with the speeches of Pétain, to understand that these men are not of the same caliber as he. They ring a different note; they indicate a different tradition. On the one hand, there is French thought with its logic, its strength, and its clarity; on the other, the language of force and hypocrisy, pathetic imitation not of Hitler but of Franco or Quisling.

Blum dominated the Riom proceedings with his intelligence and culture, discussing on its highest plane every question that came before the Court. Blum brought with him into the courtroom the great tradition of French politics, philosophy, and jurisprudence. He represented the spirit of Montesquieu—an earlier magistrate, jurist, philosopher, and writer, who had foretold the French Revolution. As president of the Popular Front Council and head of the largest French political party, Blum had inherited and continued this tradition. Two passages in his first statement will justify this parallel with Montesquieu, even in the eyes of his adversaries—Blum's appeal to the professional conscience of the magistrates of the Supreme Court, and his declaration that the trial of Riom was the trial of the Republic, a trial in which he proposed to uphold the defense till the very end.

* See Appendix V.

"In his message Marshal Pétain said, at the same time that he presented you with the *fait accompli* of his condemnation: 'The proceedings shall be conducted in the open. . . . I have weighed the advantages and disadvantages of it. . . .' Let us arm ourselves with these words as if their purpose had really been to leave to your conscience as judges a free zone. Permit me to tell you, gentlemen, that I, like most of you, have been a judge. For nearly a quarter of a century I was a magistrate. My judicial career was almost completed when, against my wish, I was thrown into public life. I was always attached to the higher courts—the Council of State, the Tribunal des Conflits. I know from experience what the conscience of a judge is, and I dare say I know that of a Supreme Court. Sovereignty for a judge is not so much a comfort and a convenience as a burden. The fact that he feels above himself neither a higher court nor any other power of appeal does not free him; on the contrary, it must only increase his sense of responsibility. Whatever he decides will be definitive, and therefore irreparable. . . . As we appeal to your professional conscience, let us remind you also of your love for your country. Once already your patriotism changed the character of this trial, which was introduced as the trial of those responsible for the war, or, in other words, as the trial of France. You refused to conduct it in that form. The visible result of your refusal is the absence from this bench of Paul Reynaud and Georges Mandel, whose presence would be essential in a debate on the responsibility for the war, and who were aimed at directly in one paragraph of the decree that authorized the formation of the Court; but no investigation has as yet been started against them, nor have they been brought out of their cells at Portalet to keep us company.

"Mind you, however. . . the present trial is no longer that of France—but if it remains what it is, it will prove to be the trial of the Republic. A debate on responsibilities for the defeat from which the responsibility of the military has been deliberately excluded, must needs become not alone a conscious assault on the truth, but a suit against the republican regime. The Marshal's message gives reason to fear that this is precisely what is expected of you. Do you believe that such a debate will serve the interest and the wish of a country that desires the truth and has never rejected the Republic?

"We shall try, therefore—as we can do no more—to substitute for this partisan trial the courageous and objective investigation which the country expects. We shall suggest to you the means. We hope to succeed with your help. But if you were to fail us, we should not lose courage. We should still fight on. Our duty toward the nation—which we mean to fulfill even here—would not be affected by your refusal; on the contrary, it would only become more urgent. For such a refusal would clearly indicate that you, in full cognizance of the situation, are maintaining the proceedings within their present limits and character: the trial of the Republic, which is still the legal foundation of the country; the trial of the democratic regime with its customs and its methods; the trial of the policy of social justice and conciliation of the government over which I presided. It would then be our task to prove to France that she is not the degenerate nation which, having believed in liberty and progress, has to atone for this ideal and submit to punishment. As long as the Republic is the accused, we shall remain at our combat stations as its witnesses and its defenders."

Daladier was not so much the jurist and philosopher as the fighter, the soldier who struggled with his adversaries for every inch of territory, refusing all compromises, and who, at the opportune moment, launched his decisive counterattack. He announced that he would answer Marshal Pétain's accusations against him by exposing, in turn, the one "truly responsible" for the defeat—Marshal Pétain. It was not Montesquieu who spoke through the mouth of Daladier, but Danton, striking fiercely at his enemies.

"I shall reveal," said Daladier, "the actual quantities of modern equipment which I found in use by the French Army when I took over the Ministry of War [in June, 1936]. In 1934, after the French note of April 17, 1934, had made it clear that all efforts at an understanding on disarmament had failed, at a time when Germany announced her intention to rearm and was putting into operation a vast armament program, the French Minister of War, then Marshal Pétain, reduced the armament credits granted to him by Parliament. A year later, in 1935, barely 40 per cent of the credits appropriated [by Parliament] were utilized for the production of war materials. Unfortunately the balance sheet of modern matériel in use by the Army in the summer of 1936 can be drawn up quickly with respect to tanks, modern cannon, fortification equipment, and other items."

Daladier also insisted on the political character of the trial: "As Marshal Pétain said on October 11, 1940, 'the disaster is but the reflection in the military sphere of the weakness and the acts of the former political regime.' The purpose now is to dishonor the Republic, having already destroyed it despite the law voted by the National Assembly [on July 9, 1940]. Was it the Republic that reduced the armament credits in 1934? Was it the Republic that prevented the War Minister of 1934 from matching the German armament plan with a French program? Is the Republic responsible for the professional blunders or the moral failings which we shall discuss in the course of this trial? Neither the Republic nor the institutions of liberty led France to her defeat, but the men who would not put into action the arms and war materials at their disposal.

"But what of it? The truth will blaze forth in the course of this public trial, in spite of all obstacles put in its path. It is up to you to pass judgment on the violations of the law. As for me, I have never in my official capacities had the honor of meeting the judges who today are sitting in the Supreme Court of Justice. But I have faith in their impartiality and I am sure that they will do honor to the noble traditions of French justice. If I were not at peace with my conscience, if I felt responsible for the disaster, I should not have outlived it, as all those who know me well will understand. But because I am sure I have done my patriotic duty, I shall fight for the truth, without concern for my own fate.

"Only knowledge of the truth can give back to the people, who today are being misled by propaganda and partisan feeling, their confidence in the future. Their fighting sons were not cowards. Nor has the French nation forfeited her heroic virtues; her passionate love of freedom has never led to that so-called decadence for which, today, she is asked to atone in resignation. I am convinced that even in this severe and momentous trial, however bitter and painful it may be, the French people will find something to give them hope for their own future."

Particularly in the discussion where the various accusations were taken up point by point, Daladier proved himself an able debater. Nothing will illustrate this more effectively than the oratorical duel between Daladier and President Caous at the hearing of February 28, 1942. An account of it, although prohibited in France, was published in a Swiss newspaper le Sentinelle, and served as basis for a pamphlet widely distributed by anti-Fascist underground organizations in France.

Caous: "M. Daladier, you seriously failed in the duties of your office when in 1933 you caused Parliament to decree the premature retirement, for budgetary reasons, of 5,000 active officers."

Daladier: "True, but you seem to forget that Marshal Pétain, my successor as Minister of War in 1934, enforced the law and retired a great number of officers. Moreover, you probably do not know that the generalissimo of that period, General Weygand, issued a circular letter to that effect, in which he demanded the economical and rapid enforcement of the law. If, therefore, I was guilty of a lack of foresight at that time, why am I the only one to stand in the dock?"

Caous: "M. Daladier, you are accused of not having supplied our forces with a sufficient number of training grounds for troops and tanks."

Daladier: "It was I who caused the appropriation of the first and most generous credits for setting up training grounds in 1933. Unfortunately my successors did not share my concern. Thus in 1933 I brought about a vote of 27 million francs for training camps. In 1934 my successor, Marshal Pétain, reduced these credits by 15 millions and assigned only 12 millions for the purpose. You might ask him his reasons for doing so."

Caous: "M. Daladier, in five years you presided only once at the Supreme War Council. It can be said that you showed no great enthusiasm in that respect."

Daladier: "That is quite possible, but what is one to say of the ministers who, though urged by our generalissimo to summon the Supreme War Council, did not in two years find the time to call a single meeting?"

Caous: "Oh! Oh!"

Daladier: "Here is a document which I submit to the Court. General Weygand made a report in 1935, from which I extract these simple lines that form its conclusion: 'Since May 17, 1934, the date on which I submitted to the Minister of War the reasoned opinion of the Supreme War Council regarding the needs of the Army, I have repeatedly urged the convocation of the Council so that it may make its recommendations on the measures to be taken in order to remedy the deficiencies set forth in that opinion. Such a meeting, the only effective means to action, was never called.' Do you know who were these ministers whom General Weygand was thus informing? They were, first of all, Marshal Pétain and, next, General Maurin."

Caous: "M. Daladier, you made the mistake of remaining too long in favor of the one-year military service, which was inadequate for building up a strong army."

Daladier: "Agreed, but on that point I am in excellent company, for on July 3, 1934, Marshal Pétain announced before competent Parliamentary Commissions that he would not modify the one-year service, and on November 20, 1934, General Maurin made identical statements before these same Commissions. Why, then, do you not treat those gentlemen with equal severity?"

Caous: "We did not possess enough war matériel to enter the conflict. You should have thought of that."

Daladier: "If that were true, it would mean that the production of war materials was begun too late. In that case, I should like you to note something of considerable importance. In April, 1934, Hitler informed all countries of his intention to rearm Germany; and since he meant what he said, he appropriated that same year a budget equivalent to 1,500 million French francs for the German rearmament program. The year before [1933] I had brought about the appropriation of 600 million francs for matériel. It was evident that to retain a margin of superiority over Germany, the duty of my successor [Pétain] in 1934 was to double credits; that indeed was the minimum. What did my successor do? He reduced the credits by 200 million francs, reserving only 400 millions. And thus it happened that, in the year when the Reich created three armored divisions, we ordered no more than seven modern tanks, 130 motor machine guns, and approximately 180 anti-aircraft guns."

Finally, the greatest service that Daladier rendered, or tried to render, to the cause of truth was to demand of the Court the real war guilt trial, that is, the trial of treason and the Fifth Column. He waited to make this appeal until the witnesses' testimony made it possible to show that considerable quantities of modern matériel had been left behind the lines, piled up in the depots where the Germans had found them, while the French troops had suffered from lack of equipment and munitions.

"It has been said and repeated among the people," said Daladier on April 2, 1943, "that during the months preceding the declaration of war and during the war itself, certain military and civilian elements exerted every effort to hamper France's action. Would not that be the explanation of many strange things that we have heard? This explanation was the product of the people's instinct, which in such matters is rarely mistaken. After all the testimony you have just heard to the effect that the supplies which the Army needed to be able to fight had been left in depots behind the lines, I shall—unless the question of why the High Command did not utilize those arms is clarified in the course of the proceedings—ask the Court to order right here an investigation of the activities of a Fifth Column that poisoned the country."

The Attitude of the Judges

Even the justices of the Supreme Court helped the cause of truth—or, more precisely, they did not oppose it so much as might have been feared. Not courageously, but in a timid and passive way, they contributed to the revelation of errors and injustices. The American press complimented them on their correctness and impartiality. I personally have too high a notion of the prerogatives of justice to give unreserved support to this praise.

Acquainted with the traditions of the French judiciary, I expected better of the Supreme Court. I did not believe that Pétain could find professional judges who would form an unconstitutional court, which, by retroactive enforcement of a law, would condemn men accused of a crime that did not exist in the criminal code and would deprive them of the common guarantees of criminal procedure. I thought that at least these judges, having power to investigate, would not refuse the just demand of Blum and Daladier for a full and impartial inquiry that would uncover the share of all parties guilty of the defeat. I hoped that they would leave the accused free to defend themselves and to bring up, in the course of the debate, mistakes of the military command and the treacheries of the Fifth Column. Above all, I did not think that a body of French justices would, without any protest, permit Pétain to condemn the accused in advance, robbing their future verdict of even the appearance of independence. When Blum made his appeal to the conscience of the Court and Daladier protested against having been condemned in advance, the President of the Court ought to have seized that opportunity to affirm before the representatives of the foreign press the impartiality of French justice. He could have answered: "This Court is free. It will take no orders, not even from the Chief of State. It has the right to sentence the accused to death, but it also has the power to acquit; its conscience will decide." A few such words would have raised the judges of the Riom Court to the level of the defendants. While they did not stoop so low as Pétain, the appeal of Blum and the protest of Daladier caused them to do no more than lower their heads and accept the affront without a word.

If the magistrates of the Court lacked greatness, they at least showed some professional conscience. They acted timidly but with probity; they were not heroes but honest men. If they did not give evidence of an indignation which would have added to their stature, neither did they act with dishonorable baseness. Their attitude can be summed up in the statement that they enforced with propriety laws whose principle should have revolted them. They showed that in Pétain's France the judges, on the whole, had not fallen so low as the military. Moreover, before severely criticizing their conduct, we must remember how much more difficult the task of an honest judge is in a Fascist country than in a democratic one. Similarly, it must not be forgotten that certain judges refused to sit on the bench at this trial. After Marshal Pétain pronounced his condemnation, the President of the Supreme Court, M. Lagarde, asked to be relieved of his functions; he was replaced by M. Caous. M. Lagarde's gesture saved the honor of the French judiciary as General de Gaulle's revolt saved the honor of the Army.

What did the Court contribute to the cause of truth?

The Court refused to let the trial become one for the responsibilities of the war, as the government had asked. Marshal Pétain wanted a trial proving that democratic France and not Hitlerian Germany was responsible for the European war; he wanted to base his policy of collaboration with the New Order on a decision rendered by French judges. M. Lagarde was then still President of the Supreme Court, and the Court refused to conduct such an odious trial. The "trial of France" asked for by Germany and ordered by the Vichy government would have disgusted everyone, including some partisans of Marshal Pétain; even certain newspapermen of the extreme Right asked the government not to endanger to that point the national dignity. It was Blum, and not Pétain, who expressed the true feeling of the French people, when at the hearing of March 11, 1942, he demonstrated in the presence of reporters of the German and Italian press that the responsibility for the war fell on the Axis powers. "International public opinion," he said in finishing his observations, "does not need a Supreme Court to find out who are those guilty for the war." Let us be just towards the Riom Court: its magistrates refused to accept the "trial of France."

The Supreme Court of Justice affected to be unaware of the decision handed down by Marshal Pétain on October 16, 1941. It protested against this arbitrary sentence by handing down on October 28 an indictment quite different from the "clear, complete, and perfectly motivated" conclusions approved and sanctioned by Pétain. A comparison of the texts* leaves no doubt on this point. The Court retained only three of the accusations which the Council of Political Justice had handed down against me. The Council had accused me of having limited the Air Force credits, favored insubordination, discouraged the command, disorganized the Air Force, sacrificed the interests of the country to my partisan preferences and, worst of all, aggravated these sinister actions by means of subterfuges and lies, attempting to

* See Appendix III and Appendix VII.

137

deceive Parliament and the nation by thus leading it to believe its security assured. The Supreme Court of Justice abandoned these ridiculous but degrading accusations; it followed the Council only in blaming me for more honorable deeds, among them the enforcement of the law concerning the nationalization of war industries, and the shipment of airplanes to the Spanish Republic; it added that "in the absence of sufficient charges, there was no need to continue with the other accusations"—this legal jargon meaning that the accusations brought against me by the Vichy government and the Council of Political Justice were baseless. This decision gives me the right to treat as slanderers the members of the Council of Political Justice and those who might be tempted to revive their arguments. The Court had the courage to absolve me publicly of certain charges approved by Pétain—for which act I wish to thank its members publicly.

The Court left the accused free during the public hearings to discuss the charges brought against each of them. It did not allow them to extend the trial to the uncovering of the entire truth, yet it respected the freedom of their defense as best it could. The propaganda of the Vichy government in the United States was so skillful that I have often heard Americans crediting Marshal Pétain with what was actually the specific merit of the Court. "The proof that Pétain was not really a Fascist," they said, "was that Léon Blum, Édouard Daladier, and the witnesses at the trial were allowed to speak freely." In saying this they forget that even in despotic states—if the courts are not suppressed altogether—judges have always allowed the accused to answer the charges against them and, in their turn, to question the witnesses. A despotic government can condemn without trial, as did Pétain on October 16, 1941. But when he uses legal channels, he must have recourse to professional judges, men conditioned by certain professional habits and necessities; even the least conscientious among them cannot condemn a guilty man without giving him the opportunity to defend himself. The tribunals of the Inquisition questioned heretics before sending them to execution; Dimitroff, accused of the Reichstag fire by the Nazi government, defended himself freely and was actually acquitted. It was consequently impossible to keep Blum and Daladier from speaking before the Court.

Finally, as it became obvious that the trial was turning to the advantage of the accused and to the confusion of the government, the Court refrained from taking the initiative for suspending the proceedings; a decree was necessary to deprive it of jurisdiction in the case. As the hearings progressed, the judges' attitude toward the accused underwent a noticeable change. All the foreign correspondents pointed out this transformation, which was to the credit of the magistrates. In spite of their political prejudice against the Popular Front leaders and their desire not to displease Marshal Pétain, the Riom judges were sensitive to the sincerity of Blum's and Daladier's declarations. Impressed as they were by the force of the defense and the poverty of the prosecution, they felt ashamed of the role imposed on them; they realized that if mistakes had been committted in preparing for war, all could not be traced back to six men, nor could one blame the accused without condemning Pétain and Weygand at the same time. In a word, the judges themselves succumbed to the truth.

What might have become of the Riom trial had it followed a normal course? No one knows. Perhaps it would have ended in acquittal, or, more plausibly, in condemnations so light as to cast severe blame on Marshal Pétain and his ministers. Whatever the hypotheses and the possibilities, President Caous and the Supreme Court contributed to the advancement of the truth.

Because of this contribution, because of the difficult conditions in which the judges found themselves, one must forget their weakness and remember their honesty.

The Witnesses' Testimony

Contrary to the magistrates, the witnesses contributed *actively* to the revelation of the truth. The witnesses for the prosecution were the only ones to be heard before the suspension of the trial; yet the sum total of their statements represented a much more significant contribution to the defense than to the prosecution.

To begin with, the ignorance and stupidity of the French General Staff became flagrantly apparent. In the absence of Weygand and Pétain, partisans of their doctrine were present to listen to incriminating evidence. On March 18 General Mittelhauser, former Army chief and member of the Supreme War Council, declared that the French Army did not have sufficient officers; Daladier thereupon furnished documentary proof that at the time of mobilization it actually had 4,000 more officers than the German Army, and General Gamelin for once stepped out of his mute role to confirm the figure. President Caous could not help reproaching General Mittelhauser for making such inaccurate statements under oath; to this the General had only one answer, worthy of Colonel Blimp, which aroused general mirth. "I am sorry," he said, "but I read it in the newspapers." Similar hilarity was caused by a statement of General Langlois at the session of April 1. General Langlois was deploring the influence of certain political leaders, whose thought, he said, was "un-French." "Are you referring to me?" retorted Blum quickly. General Langlois, somewhat nonplused, answered that he did not want to be personal and that it was the League of Nations which had poisoned the atmosphere. "If it is the League of Nations you are accusing," said Blum, "I have nothing to say, but the League does not figure among the accused."

Gross ignorance was even more serious than mere stupidity. In March General Lenclud, Army corps commander, maintained that not a single aerial unit had been assigned to his corps; yet on March 24 La Chambre read a letter addressed to the Court by General Lenclud, who admitted that he had been mistaken and that an air squadron had been attached to his corps. In a war in which aviation played a decisive role, General Lenclud had not known of the existence of the air power under his control! On March 24 Lansing Warren telephoned to the *New York Times*: "Several of the generals who testified today professed entire ignorance of German preparations and progress in military science. General Huret, for instance, declared that the French material for pontoon bridges was magnificent, but that they had done nothing for light transports and were unaware of the German use of rubber boats. 'The use of these boats came to us as a great surprise,' he told the Court." At times ignorance took the form of dissembling and thus came close to dishonesty. On March 17 General Besson, Commander of the Third Army and member of the Supreme War Council, declared that the inferiority of the French Army had been particularly "appalling" with respect to air power—implying that the Minister of Aviation was to be blamed for that inferiority; La Chambre, however, compelled him to admit that his army had had at its disposal all the air units demanded by the War Council, which obviously shifted the responsibility from the Air Minister to the military authority.

Furthermore, several statements revealed the degree to which Fascist propaganda had penetrated into military circles. Many officers, in their hatred of the Popular Front, were anxious to blame it for all the inadequacies of French military preparedness. It was the state of mind that produced attacks such as General Langlois' against the political leaders "whose thought was un-French." There were other examples. On April 2 General Hureaux declared that, through the fault of the Popular Front, the military credits incorporated in the budget for 1936 were insufficient, whereupon Blum reminded him that the budget for 1936 had been prepared by the Laval cabinet in 1935 and enacted long before the advent of the Popular Front. On March 24 General Huret claimed that the enforcement of the 40-hour week had retarded the improvement of a turret essential for the equipment of the Maginot Line; when cross-examined, he was forced to admit that that particular work was completed long before the war and that, in fact, he knew of no instance where the enforcement of the 40-hour week had affected the preparation of the war. The most flagrant case of intellectual dishonesty, however, was the testimony of Colonel J. P. Perré. A militant Fascist, Colonel Perré had been placed by the Vichy government at the head of the court-martial at Gannat, a special tribunal set up to deal hastily with so-called Communist and De Gaullist activities.

Testifying at the session of April 1, Colonel Perré maintained that "the riots accompanying the advent to power of the Popular Front in 1936 delayed by six months the production of tanks scheduled in the program of 1935." Blum had no difficulty in proving that the program in operation at the time the Popular Front took over the government had been in no way delayed. Then, as Colonel Perré persisted in his accusation, Blum asked him exactly what program he was referring to, so that one might compare its provisions with the actual output of the factories. Thus driven into a corner, Colonel Perré, much confused, answered that what he meant was not really a program so much as a plan he had worked out in his mind but had never published!

Most of the witnesses' testimony was significant in other respects than as declarations which merely betrayed ignorance, senility, or dishonesty. The charges raised in the Prosecuting Attorney's indictment were all contradicted by the prosecution's own witnesses! According to the preliminary indictment—or the Vichy government—the policy of the Popular Front had demoralized the Army; yet numerous witnesses affirmed that the morale of the troops was as good in 1940 as it had been in 1914, and that only the Fascist officers were demoralized. According to Vichy, the policy of the Popular Front had prevented the Army from obtaining the matériel it needed; it was demonstrated that the production plans drawn up by the General Staff had been executed and that in June, 1940, the French Army had as much matériel as the German attacking forces in France, which, in turn, revealed that the Vichy government had publicized incomplete or inexact figures on the quantities of matériel available in May and June, 1940. The government insisted that the responsibility of the High Command for the conduct of operations did not enter into the case, and again it was proved that part of the matériel had remained in the munition depots in the rear, while the remainder had been used in the most inefficient manner during battle. Thus the witnesses lifted more than one corner of the veil which, as M. Ribet put it, had been thrown over the problem of the French defeat.

Such a result is remarkable if one considers the witnesses—all military men who had occupied important posts. They might all have been held jointly responsible for the inadequate preparation and bad conduct of the war. It was in their interest to unload on the leaders of the Popular Front the total burden of guilt; they were linked by camaraderie and professional solidarity to the General Staff, whose mistakes the defendants were openly denouncing. Moreover, they were all witnesses for the prosecution—*témoins à charge* as they are called in France—who, according to French procedure, have always been heard first. Those who took the stand at Riom had been chosen by the government and the Prosecuting Attorney to prove the statements of the indictment and create an atmosphere unfavorable to the leaders of the Popular Front. In all countries the burden of proof lies with the accuser; the defendant need not prove his innocence, but merely discusses the charges brought against him. At the Riom trial, the witnesses for the prosecution were to have been followed by the neutral witnesses and by witnesses for the defense—civilians as well as military men. Three hundred and fifty witnesses should have been heard; when the trial was interrupted, only fifty had testified. Had the witnesses for the defense been allowed to speak, they would have supplemented the testimony of the witnesses for the prosecution—which, on the whole, had been surprisingly favorable to the accused—and would have completed the revelation that had only just begun.

It would be a grave mistake to believe that all French generals were living in pious admiration of the doctrine of Pétain. People with little knowledge of military affairs need only turn to the statements of General de Gaulle to realize what the best military men thought of the General Staff's methods and its responsibilities. General de Gaulle can hardly be suspected of being a partisan of the Popular Front, but his opinion is that of the best military expert modern France has produced. Had not the trial been suspended, civil servants, statesmen, and military leaders would have appeared to point out mistakes, rectify factual errors, challenge the argument of the indictment, and defend the ministers of the Popular Front simply by assigning the blame where it belonged. General Bineau, Director of Military Studies, would have been compelled to expose the doctrines which the General Staff was teaching at the War College and the different military schools. General Bourret, Army commander and member of the Supreme War Council, who had always been an opponent of the methods and policy of Pétain and Weygand, would have been heard. Among the witnesses would have been General Doumenc, who since 1933 had recommended the formation of motorized divisions, and General Decamp, who had reported to his superiors the activities of the Cagoulards and Fascists. General Maindras would have revealed the intrigues that led to his recall from Moscow; General Morel, the former Military Attaché in Madrid, would have told what scant attention had been paid the reports on new German methods of warfare which he had drawn up on the basis of his observations in the Spanish war. It would take too long to enumerate them all. According to a study by a correspondent for the *Frankfurter Zeitung,* which was quoted at length in a telegram from Berlin to the *Neue Zürcher Zeitung* on April 6, 1942, the prosecution had reason to fear that Generals Weygand, Georges, and Colson themselves—all men in high Army positions—would come and "corroborate the statements of the accused regarding the outdated character of the General Staff."

In the realm of aviation the spectacle promised to be the same. The General Staff officers who in 1936 and 1937, at my request, had worked out projects for the development of the Air Force, would have told how their plans, when submitted to the Permanent Committee of National Defense, were rejected by a decision in which Marshal Pétain participated; they would have mentioned that in 1936 France created units of parachutists, which were dissolved in 1939 because the General Staff saw no need for them. General Jeannaud might have told how he was reprimanded by the Chief of Staff for having dared to indicate in a report in November, 1938, that the aerial defense of the land was inadequate. The engineers and civil servants who in 1937 had drawn up a program for the construction and equipment of numerous aircraft factories would have testified that Georges Bonnet, then Minister of Finance, refused the necessary credits for the execution of the program.

Finally, after the military, there would have been the civilian witnesses. It would, indeed, have been a curious situation. Men who supported Vichy and enjoyed the government's protection would have been obliged to defend the Popular Front against the prosecution, simply to avoid being placed in a compromising position by the accused. Thus Blum was reproached for his economic policy, yet the Minister of National Economy in the Popular Front cabinets had been Charles Spinasse, one of the few Socialists who rallied to the side of Marshal Pétain. I was accused of not having produced enough airplanes—which, indeed, was impossible in view of the limited credits at my disposal; but the Director of Aircraft Production, when I was Air Minister, had been the same M. J. Volpert, who was Deputy (*Directeur du Cabinet*) to Pétain's Minister of Aviation, General Bergeret. If Spinasse and Volpert had

142

been called to the stand, what could they have said? Unfortunately the government's cautious adjournment order prevented the judges from hearing them.

A continuation of the proceedings would have completely smashed an indictment that had already been severely shaken by the testimony of its own witnesses. Let us pay tribute to these witnesses. Fettered by the military hierarchy, for the most part opponents of the democratic regime, they nevertheless had the courage to say what they thought; if they had made mistakes, they redeemed themselves by testifying according to their conscience and the truth. Men such as Girodias, Sthelé, Bernard, and Verdurand showed more courage than either their superiors or the members of the Court. The world will respect these soldiers, who dared to uphold honor, the noblest tradition of their profession.

Adjournment Sine Die

On April 11, 1942, a dispatch informed the world that the Riom trial had been adjourned by order of the Vichy government, and that it would be resumed at an unspecified time, on a different basis.

No one was surprised at the news. On April 2 the Court had adjourned until April 15, supposedly for the Easter holidays. For more than a month it had been known that the government was trying with every means at its disposal to stop the course of a trial that was becoming ever more embarrassing. The Easter holidays were a breathing spell which allowed the government to bring pressure on the Court. The judges were asked to issue a "spontaneous" order for further supplementary investigations and the adjournment of proceedings until they were completed. The Court refused. President Caous replied in effect to the Minister of Justice, who had transmitted to him the government's suggestions: "What you are asking would mean a denial of justice; imprisoned, as they have been, for eighteen months, and condemned in advance by Marshal Pétain, the accused have a right to be judged. Marshal Pétain, in his speech of October 16, 1941, declared that 'the Court not only had unquestionable jurisdiction over the case but, in the national interest, was expected to pass sentence within the shortest possible time.' If he has changed his mind, let him say so himself. We have swallowed enough humiliation. If the government wishes to interfere once more in the course of justice, it is free to do so and shoulder the consequences before history."

On the eve of April 15 a law was promulgated removing the case from the Court's jurisdiction. This decree, which in practice forbade the Court to sit, pretended to enlarge the competence of the Court to include the very political and military questions it had formerly been forbidden to judge. "The trial has been limited merely to the unpreparedness for war," was the comment of the Minister of Justice to a reporter of Paris-Soir, "and a limited trial could at best yield a limited truth. . . . We shall have to begin anew, and this time without blinkers." The decree intimated that the Court, "invested with new powers, would resume and extend its investigation," not mentioning, however, on what basis or at what time. No order to resume proceedings has yet been given; the accused have been returned to the dungeons of Portalet.

This decision proves that the Vichy government was afraid. The acknowledgment of this fear could be seen in an interview given to the press by Joseph Barthélémy, in which he stated that "in order to face exceptional circumstances, we have used exceptional methods. . . . The Riom trial has given the accused an excellent platform which they used to praise political doctrines contrary to that of the Marshal . . . . Certain words spoken might have troubled our relations with a foreign power." Marshal Pétain found himself in the position of the Sorcerer's Apprentice, incapable of dominating the forces he had unleashed. In spite of his power, he was afraid of what Blum and Daladier could say. Why was the government so afraid?

First, because the trial had unloosed in the country a strong wave of emotion. Truth came out bit by bit. In spite of orders to the press, public opinion was informed by those thousand and one ways which in countries under a dictatorship take the place of newspapers and radio. Attorneys, journalists, employees, and police officers—all those who by their different functions entered the courthouse at Riom—reported what Blum and Daladier had said. Newspapers from Switzerland, with accounts far more complete than those of the French press, were smuggled across the border and secretly distributed. Anti-Fascist underground pamphlets published regular reports of the proceedings and revealed Pétain's mistakes in the preparation of the war. Blum and Daladier appeared once more as the best interpreters of French spirit and French thought. The people were enthusiastically moved by these two men who dared oppose an entire regime, who stood up against Pétain and Hitler, and who again spoke the language of democracy. By comparison, the orations of Pétain and his ministers seemed spiritless and dull. Every time Daladier spoke of Pétain, France laughed; every time Blum accused Hitler, France trembled with rage; and when the leaders of the Popular Front spoke of the Cagoulards and the Fifth Column, France understood by whom and in what manner she had been betrayed. At the call of the true leaders of democracy, she regained her confidence in the future. Let us imagine what it must have meant to peasants and workers, soldiers and petits bourgeois, to learn of Daladier's outburst as he spoke of the German generals: "Wait, the hour of victory may yet come for the defeated." Never had Pétain been able to say anything like that. And men, as they walked through the streets, found themselves whistling the *Marseillaise,* which once more, as in the days of the Popular Front, became the song of the Revolution.

The clearest result of the Riom trial was to decrease Pétain's popularity and to place once more at the head of the French nation the leaders of the Popular Front. The reaction of the French people escaped none of the foreign journalists, however isolated they were at Vichy and Riom, however carefully they were watched by friends and spies of the government. On March 16 we find in a dispatch published by the B. N. P. agency at New York: "The former Premiers, Léon Blum and Édouard Daladier, have gained several points by laying the blame on certain words and actions of Marshal Pétain prior to the war, and by attacking bitterly the groups that are preaching collaboration with the Nazis." On March 30 the Associated Press cabled from Vichy: "The Vichy regime apparently seeks to stop with the least possible publicity a trial that from its inception has proved a boomerang, with the defendants accusing the accusers with uncomfortable defiance." On April 4 the correspondent of the *Frankfurter Zeitung* (one of the keenest observers of the trial) indicated that the proceedings up to that point had yielded the prosecution no proof of its indictment: "The only thing that is clear, until now, is that the defendants contributed more to the preparation of the war than to an understanding with Germany. And inasmuch as the proceedings offer the accused an opportunity to attack the political past of the new men of Vichy and to make the responsibility for the defeat fall on those who are now in power, there is a growing tendency to believe that the Vichy government will seek an excuse in order not to resume so disadvantageous a trial after the Easter holidays."

The whirlpool of French public opinion aroused the attention, and finally caused the intervention, of Hitler. The trial he had demanded ever since June, 1940, was a trial of war guilt and not of the responsibility for French military unpreparedness. The Court, however, had refused to institute proceedings in that form, and the Vichy government had been unable to force them to do so. As it was now developing, the Riom trial could only irritate Hitler. Blum and Daladier were flinging back at him the responsibility for the war itself; the debates revealed that, with better leadership and without the treachery of Fascist circles, the French Army could have resisted the attack of the Reichs-wehr; the accused threatened to uncover the role of the Fifth Column in the weakening and the defeat of France; and, finally, two men, indisputably the representatives of large popular factions in France, were proclaiming their faith in the ultimate victory of the anti-Fascist powers. Such a trial, if continued, would obviously harm the prestige of Marshal Pétain, and Hitler, with all his contempt for Pétain—the French Hindenburg—needed him as the rallying point for the numerous Fascist groups in France. A situation had to be prevented in which Pétain would be discredited in the eyes of his troops, and the French people would be aroused at the call of the Popular Front leaders; the courtroom of Riom could not be allowed to become a platform for Blum and Daladier. Hitler informed Pétain that the Riom trial was the test for the Vichy government's ability to collaborate; he made clear that either the government had to maneuver itself out of a perilous situation or the trial would have to be modified.

As early as March 2 the diplomatic correspondent of the D. N. B. (German News Agency) published the Führer's warning. "Authorized German circles," Hitler wrote, "consider the trial as a barometer that will show whether the French are willing to collaborate in the making of a new Europe. . . . A controversy that seems to revolve around the question of whether such and such a general was responsible for the defeat will not help to clarify the atmosphere. What is needed is an answer to the question: why did France declare war on Germany when she knew perfectly well the Führer's desire for peace? . . .

The Riom trial ought never to have been reduced to a mere search for scape-goats, but should have indicated clearly the road that France was to follow." A few days later, in a major political speech, Hitler expressed his "surprise" at seeing that Vichy did not understand more fully the requirements for a policy of collaboration. On March 19 the German radio announced that M. de Brinon, Vichy Ambassador to Germany, had notified Marshal Pétain that the trial would have to be suspended. On March 26 Marshal Pétain met with Laval near Vichy. What followed is well known: in the first days of April Marshal Pétain asked Laval to form a new cabinet, and a law was promulgated depriving the Riom Court of its jurisdiction.

Thus fear—fear of seeing the French people respond to the appeal of the leaders of the Popular Front, fear of seeing the responsibilities of the General Staff and the traitors of the Fifth Column uncovered, fear of Hitler's wrath—required both the return of Laval to power and the smothering of the trial. In chains and behind prison bars, Blum and Daladier were still able to make Pétain tremble.

The Riom trial had begun by an abuse of power—men were sent before an unconstitutional court for crimes unknown in penal law. It was crowned by a further abuse of power—the condemnation by Marshal Pétain of the Popular Front leaders. It ended in still another abuse of power—the Supreme Court of Justice was deprived of its case and the judges were prevented from carrying out their duty. At every stage in the process the separation of powers had been violated and justice ridiculed.

Yet this trial—illegal, incomplete, and without guarantees—gave Blum and Daladier an opportunity to throw some light on the true causes of the French defeat. Appearing before the Court as condemned, not as accused, they had no thought of defending themselves; their only concern was to help reveal a few scraps of the truth. It was not their own fate which preoccupied them, but that of France and of democracy, of which they were the champions and servants. Perhaps for the first time in history, a parody of justice was turned unexpectedly into an instrument of justice, for the true aim of justice is less the punishment of the guilty than the establishment of the truth. Because the Riom trial was suspended, we do not know the whole truth about the causes of the French defeat. But we know far more today than we did in February, 1942, when the trial opened. We may safely assume—without fear that the future will prove us wrong—that the men who were truly responsible for the French defeat were not the leaders of the Popular Front.

To substantiate this statement, we shall next compare, point by point, the accusations of the Vichy government with the facts as revealed at the Riom trial, omitting the cases of General Gamelin and Controller-General Jacomet. Gamelin deliberately withdrew from the debates with no defense, refusing "to compromise the honor of the Army." Jacomet, in the course of his examination, revealed himself as a troublesome witness for the government rather than as a defendant.

The accusations brought against us in the name of the Vichy government were set forth in the Prosecuting Attorney's indictment order. This document detailed every charge that could be brought against the defendants during the trial. It was summarized in the "recommendations" of the Council of Political Justice, which served as a basis for the condemnations by Marshal Pétain on October 16, 1941. But the Court, after examining the indictments and the other prosecution documents, decided that certain charges were not justified. It issued an act of indictment (*arrêt de renvoi*) on October 28, 1941 enumerating the charges for which there existed "adequate suppositions" warranting the ordering of our trial.

The limits of the Riom trial were defined in this document; all other charges, as French law puts it, "had been decided in favor of the accused (*chose jugée en faveur des inculpés*)." The Council of Political Justice had taken from the indictment order all that could be used against the accused, ignoring whatever might aid in their defense, and added certain political and merely whimsical accusations which the indictment order—a somewhat more serious document—had refused to include. The "recommendations" of the Council of Political Justice must be considered not as an objective statement, but as an exaggeration of the Prosecuting Attorney's indictment order.

An analysis of the charges in the indictment must be prefaced by a few general observations, without which it would be difficult to evaluate the responsibility of the Popular Front ministers.

We were accused of neither treason nor conspiracy against the safety of the State nor corruption nor extortion—crimes for which the criminal law provides—but of having "betrayed the duties of our offices." We were ministers of a parliamentarian democracy, which meant that the duties of our offices were to obey the will of the people and to govern under the control of Parliament. Every one of the acts for which the Vichy government blamed us conformed to the program of the Popular Front—to the will of the French people—and was performed under the control, and with the approval, of Parliament. The French parliamentary system provided for the strongest control over governmental and ministerial power by Parliamentary Commissions and administrative checks, such as the Council of State and the Audit Office (*Cour des Comptes*). At times the mechanism was so precise and detailed that it prevented rapid action, but it had no loopholes. Whoever declares that we betrayed the duties of our offices implies that these duties consisted in violating the will of the French people and the Constitution that subjected us to the control of Parliament.

The second observation is based on the nature of political responsibility under a parliamentary system. According to French Constitutional law, this responsibility is "joint and collective"; it extends to all the members of a cabinet or, if one wishes, to all the members of a ministerial group. All the political decisions criticized by the Vichy government were made collectively by the cabinet: the enforcement of the 40-hour week, the nationalization of the war factories, general organization of the Army and Navy, the support—however inadequate—of republican Spain, the policy of conciliation in labor conflicts, the refusal to eject striking workers from factories, etc. Under French law these decisions cannot be left to a single minister, for they involve the responsibility of the entire ministerial team. Consequently, Blum, Daladier, and I were mainly responsible for the policy of the government during the Popular Front period, and Daladier and La Chambre were mainly responsible for the general policy of the government from 1938 to 1940. Three types of responsibility were involved in the trial: Blum's and mine, which was bounded by the Popular Front period; La Chambre's, which fell in the period after it; and Daladier's, which covered both periods. By this I do not mean to blame Daladier in particular or to exculpate the Popular Front cabinets, but to offer certain facts. Indeed, I regret not having committed more political acts which would be considered criminal by Marshal Pétain, whose conception of patriotism and of governmental duties I reject entirely.

The third observation is a corollary of the second; its purpose is to point out Vichy's unwarranted discrimination among the premiers of 1936-1938. Vichy's thesis was that France had been badly prepared for war by the cabinets which were in power during that time; it would therefore be necessary either to prosecute the leaders of all or to prosecute none. During those years France had three Premiers: Blum, Chautemps, and Daladier; yet only Blum and Daladier were prosecuted, although the governmental career of Chautemps was longer than Blum's. No man's governmental authority continued so persistently as Chautemps'. The general policy for which Blum was held responsible was enforced not only by the first Popular Front cabinet, headed by Blum, but also by the second, of which Chautemps was Premier. The Council of Political Justice declared that Blum "was in power in the course of the period preceding the war," because he was "Premier for over a year and Vice-President for more than seven months." What, then, of the man who was Premier for over eight months and Vice-President for over three and one-half years? And how can Blum be blamed for the acts he may have committed as Vice-President when his Premier, Chautemps, was not even questioned as a witness?

The apparent inconsistency of this discrimination was pointed out by Blum, *cum grano salis,* at the hearing of March 10, 1942. Although Chautemps had been a Popular Front minister, he was not prosecuted because he became a collaborator of Marshal Pétain's, first as Minister of State, then as a diplomatic agent to the United States. Like Blum, I want to emphasize that Chautemps did not in any way deserve to be called before the Supreme Court of Justice—but for all the acts charged to Blum, the responsibility of Chautemps was even greater, because it extended over a longer period. The French people will not condemn Chautemps for having been Premier and Vice-President of the Popular Front cabinets, but they will demand that he explain his attitude during the dramatic days that culminated in the request for an armistice.

The accusations brought by the Vichy government can be divided into two categories: those dealing with the inadequate economic and military preparation of France, and directed chiefly against Blum and Daladier; and others, dealing with the foreign and aerial policies, aimed at me and, incidentally, at La Chambre.

148

PART II

REFUTATION OF THE AC-
CUSATION BROUGHT BY
THE VICHY GOVERNMENT

"War was in their hands but a means of getting rid of the Constitution, the mere achievement of a far-fetched conspiracy to destroy Liberty."

ROBESPIERRE: Address on the principles of Revolutionary Government, on December 25, 1793.

The Economic Preparation of the War

5

L ET US BEGIN with an examination of the charges against the Popular Front government relating to the economic and military preparation of the war. The general thesis of the prosecution was: the French Army was crushed by the superior German war matériel; the economic policy of the Popular Front had disorganized production; the 40-hour week, the nationalization of war industries, the "criminal failure to repress working-class agitation" were the main elements of this disorganization; because of the weakness of French economy, the Army could not obtain the matériel which it needed; those responsible for this policy were, in general, the Popular Front cabinets and, in particular, Blum and Daladier. In addition, the French Army was poorly equipped for modern warfare and its morale, "undermined by unpatriotic propaganda," was inferior to that of its adversaries; the men responsible for the technical and moral unpreparedness were: first, Daladier, who, for more than four years had been Minister of War and Minister of National Defense; second, as far as aerial armaments were concerned, La Chambre (Air Minister from January, 1938, to March, 1940) and I (Air Minister from June, 1936, to January, 1938).

The general thesis of the defense was this: you are confusing disorganization with an attempt at better organization. In June, 1936, the Popular Front government inherited a particularly difficult situation. The country was divided and agitated by Fascist propaganda; economic activity and industrial production had been utterly disorganized by the policy of deflation practiced since 1934; the French Army, long neglected, was so disorganized and ill-equipped that it would have been impossible—according to the General Staff's own admission—to oppose Hitler's military occupation of the Rhineland on March 7, 1936. The Popular Front did its best to remedy this situation, and, in a certain measure, succeeded. If its efforts failed to produce better results, the major part of the blame goes to its accusers, who took advantage of the defeat to overthrow the republican regime—the reactionary industrialists and financiers who sabotaged the defense effort and a General Staff which, guided by Marshal Pétain for ten years, refused to believe in the importance of tanks and airplanes. Not only did the defense claim to have ample evidence in support of this argument, but it pointed to the fact that the General Staff— indeed, Pétain and Weygand themselves—either could not or would not use the matériel and armaments at their disposal for the defense of France.

The accusation relating to the economic preparation was principally aimed at Léon Blum.

According to the Vichy government, the economic policy of the Popular Front disorganized industrial production, and consequently armament production. If one considers the texts made public by the prosecution—the act of indictment, the recommendations of the Council of Political Justice, the sentence of Marshal Pétain, or even the Prosecuting Attorney's indictment order—one realizes that the Vichy government did not even attempt to show the defendants' guilt with respect to this point. To cover its acceptance of this accusation without proof, Vichy sought refuge in the following banalities, taken from the "clear, complete, and perfectly motivated" recommendations made to Marshal Pétain by his Council of Political Justice: "Blum showed criminal weakness in dealing with labor agitation which had grave repercussions in war factories; by failing to give arms production the stimulus which the situation so urgently demanded, Blum disorganized production by the nationalization of the war factories, thereby concealing, with his authority, the sinister activity of his Ministers Daladier and Cot." The social reforms of the Popular Front, particularly the enforcement of the 40-hour week, were measures "on which the country might have reached an agreement," but whose true meaning and national purpose were so distorted that they "became instruments of social struggle." The prosecution's papers proved nothing; they did not tell where, when, how, or to what extent armament production was retarded by the action of Popular Front ministers, nor did they indicate the precise responsibility of each minister. So vague and tenuous an accusation did not justify the request for punishment.

If these papers revealed nothing, the witnesses for the prosecution were not much more explicit, and their attempts to demonstrate the responsibility of the Popular Front leaders were very hesitant. Only General Huret, with his story of the turret, and Colonel Perré, author of the famous "plan that he had in his mind," tried to discredit the social legislation voted by Parliament and enforced by the government. The only information bearing on the economic policy of the Popular Front and on the question of its influence on the preparation for the war was offered by Blum and Daladier. I shall make use of these facts, supplemented by others that are easily verifiable, to let the reader judge this aspect of the Riom trial for himself.

No one, of course, can sketch in a few pages more than an outline of the Popular Front's economic policy. It had its merits and its weaknesses, its advantages and its disadvantages. I did not admire it wholeheartedly. The Popular Front will not live in the memory of the French people for its economic policy, which lacked daring and foresight as evidenced in its inability to resolve the contradiction between its social progress and its timid economic achievements. But I think I can do Blum a service by dissipating certain erroneous statements cleverly spread abroad by Fascist and reactionary propaganda.

It must be emphasized that the economic policy of the Popular Front was superior to that of its opponents. An economic policy is judged by general results rather than by details; under the Popular Front, French production actually increased. The propaganda of Vichy has tried to suppress that fact. Americans and many Frenchmen still believe that French economy, perfectly healthy before the coming of the Popular Front, was imperiled by the social reforms of the Blum cabinet. The truth is that French economy was exceedingly weak until the Popular Front reanimated and, in some measure, reorganized it.

This becomes clear from the statistics of industrial production. We shall use these statistics as a barometer of French economic power as we determine whether France was capable, after the Popular Front experiment, of producing the war matériel that her armies needed. The statistics show that in 1933 France satisfactorily emerged from the period of general depression. The general index of production rose from 72.2 in 1932 to 80.7 in 1933, as compared with a rise from 63.8 to 71.9 in industrial production throughout the world (not including the U. S. S. R.). It is interesting to compare this rise to that of the great industrial countries: 85.2 to 88.2 in Great Britain; 52.7 to 62.7 in the United States; 53.3 to 60.7 in Germany; 69.1 to 72.2 in Belgium; 60.2 to 73.7 in Italy; 97.8 to 113 in Japan; 92.7 to 93.8 in Norway; 89 to 91 in Sweden. This favorable situation suffered under the measures adopted in 1934 and 1935 by the cabinets of Doumergue, Flandin, and Laval, with the result that the general index fell to 73.1 in 1935, when Laval was Premier—that is, to approximately 10 per cent less than in 1933, when Daladier was Premier. This decline was serious because, during the same period, the large industrial nations intensified their efforts. The indices rose from 88.2 to 105.6 in Great Britain; from 62.7 to 78 in the United States; from 60.7 to 94 in Germany; from 72.2 to 82.2 in Belgium; from 73.7 to 93.8 in Italy; from 113 to 127.4 in Japan; from 93.8 to 107.6 in Norway; from 91 to 123 in Sweden; and the general world index climbed from 71.9 to 86. The measures adopted by the Popular Front stimulated industrial production and the economic activity of

VARIATIONS IN THE FRENCH GENERAL INDEX OF INDUSTRIAL
PRODUCTION, 1932-1939
(Base: 1929=100)

Year	1932[1]	1933	1935	1937	1938[2]	1939
French Government	Laval-Tardieu (later Herriot)	Daladier	Laval	Blum	Daladier	Daladier
French General Index	72.2	80.7	73.1	81.9	76.1	80.0
World General Index[3]	63.8	71.9	86.0	103.7	93.0	

[1]Lowest point of world economic crises.
[2]Fall of the Popular Front.
[3]Excluding Russia.

the country, and the 1937 index rose 12.0 per cent over that of 1935, as compared with a 20.6 per cent rise in the general world index from 86 to 103.7. The French index fluctuated somewhat in 1938, when the fall of the Popular Front handed the power back to the most conservative elements in the business world, and rose again after Munich, when the intense preparation for war caused a fever of production in all Europe. The variations of the French general index as shown in the table above might serve as an answer to the charges made by the Vichy government against Blum and the Popular Front.

It was in 1934-1935, and not under the Popular Front, that the curve of French industrial production ceased to parallel the curve of world industrial production. This was particularly grave because the industrial production of France declined about 10 per cent while Germany's rose 55 per cent, an advantage which France never could overcome. The importance of this advantage and the weakness of French economy in 1936 have to be considered in evaluating the responsibilities of the Popular Front for the decline of French power before the war of 1939.

ECONOMIC POLICY OF THE FRENCH CONSERVATIVES

The weakness of French economy before the advent of the Popular Front is a fact well known to economists, although insufficiently recognized by the public. It is treated in an excellent article, "The Blum Experiment and the Fall of France," by Henry W. Ehrmann, in *Foreign Affairs* for October, 1941. "In June, 1936," wrote Mr. Ehrmann, "French economy was suffering from progressive emaciation. Whereas other industrial countries had touched the bottom of the depression in 1932, and from that date had begun an almost uninterrupted rise, the upswings in French industrial production had been abortive, with the result that in 1935 the index of production fell to its lowest figure since 1932. Compared to 1932 figures, the volume of industrial production had decreased in France by about 31 per cent, in the United States by 24 per cent, in Germany by 6 per cent. British production had already increased by 6 per cent. On the eve of the 1936 elections, the *Bulletin Quotidien,* a daily publication run by the Comité des Forges, summarized the economic and financial situation in the years just past: 'It was the worst period we have witnessed in times of peace.' "

It was therefore during 1934-1936 and before the social legislation of the Popular Front that French economy was disintegrating, while Nazi Germany with modern methods was creating her war industry, and industrial production was growing throughout the whole world. Without going into details of French economic weakness before 1936, let us say that it sprang from the general conception that French financiers and industrialists had of their role in society; they thought of themselves more and more as "rentiers," as men living on their incomes rather than as producers. Industrialists and financiers wanted greater profits and smaller risks; they asked the state to protect them

154

by customs duties and direct or indirect subsidies, and they shook off the authority of the law. They appeared as a privileged, if not parasitical, group within the nation as they departed further and further from the classic role of the entrepreneur in a liberal economy.

In 1934 and 1935 French economic policy was actually directed by the Bank of France. "There exists in France," Clemenceau had observed, "a power greater than that of the cabinet or Parliament; it is the power of the Regents of the Bank of France." Little by little, the Bank of France had become "a state within the state." It was a private bank exercising a public monopoly ever since the time of the First Empire, a monopoly on the issuance of paper money and the rediscount of commercial values. This bank took gross advantage of a special situation, contrary to French common law: instead of being administered by the representatives of a majority of its forty thousand stockholders like other French commercial organizations, it was directed by a Council of Regents elected by the two hundred most important stockholders. This put the Council of Regents into the hands of a small plutocracy, which was able to control the economic activity and, consequently, the general policy of the country. The Bank of France had complete control of public credit through the device of "advances," which it alone could grant to the Treasury; and it controlled private credit through the rediscounting of commercial values. More and more, it came to extend private credit only to enterprises in which the Regents were interested, and public credit only to cabinets whose general policy it approved. The history of capitalism does not afford another such example of private power. In 1934-1935 this power manifested itself on the political plane. Pierre-Étienne Flandin, Premier at the beginning of 1935, had to give way to Pierre Laval, because Flandin had tried to resist this omnipotence.

The Bank of France was powerful enough to force the acceptance of an economic doctrine whose principal characteristics were the following: a policy of monetary deflation, with a lowering of prices, wages and salaries, and a refusal to devaluate the currency at a time when devaluation had become an international necessity; a lazy and easy-going policy on the part of the employers, who, to keep their large profits, reduced the wages of their workers and obtained customs protection (chiefly by means of import quotas), instead of changing their methods of production and improving their machinery; unfair distribution of private credit, which was restricted to enterprises controlled by the Regents of the Bank of France, and refused to small and middle-sized firms and especially to agricultural associations. This economic policy led to social and political unrest. The employers' abuses of authority and the agitation of Fascist groups caused the birth of the Popular Front in reaction. English and American businessmen who visited French factories in the 1934-35 period know that in general they were poorly managed and equipped, and that their directors made no effort of adaptation and organization comparable to those of great industrial nations such as the United States, Germany, England, and Soviet Russia. Left to its own ways, living in the illusion of an automatic return to prosperity, imposing its will on the government instead of being under its control, the industrial and financial bourgeoisie which directed the economic affairs of the country had not, in 1934 and 1935, received the impetus which would have enabled it to overcome the obstacles of international competition.

ECONOMIC POLICY OF THE POPULAR FRONT

The Popular Front supplied this impetus. After the inevitable gropings of the first months, the Blum cabinet undertook a series of economic reforms which were neither perfect nor complete, but which ameliorated the situation considerably. The plutocratic system of the Bank of France was modified. A plan of nationalization proposed by the cabinet and adopted by the Chamber of Deputies was rejected by the conservative Senate, but under the press of democratic opinion, the latter consented to correct the principal abuses of the earlier system. The Bank was put under some measure of governmental control, the privilege of the two hundred strongest stockholders was abolished, representatives of the great national workers' and farmers' organizations were admitted to the Bank's administration and given a voice in the distribution of private credit and the administration of public credit. After this preliminary reform, the Blum cabinet attacked the other defects of French economy.

The policy of deflation, which had failed in every country where it had been tried, was abandoned; the currency was devaluated to its true rate of exchange, and joined the gold bloc with the English pound and the American dollar, as a result of international conventions. This measure, the most important of the financial reforms, was complemented by a general adjustment of wages to the cost of living.

The shortsighted policy of the French employers was met by lowering tariff barriers, which in 1934 and 1935 had caused a decline in foreign commerce—some import quotas were abolished and others liberalized; and by the initiation of social and progressive legislation, obliging the employers to compensate for the rise in labor cost by systematization of the labor process and a better use of their machinery. Melvin M. Fagen, in an article published in the *New Republic* of September 2, 1940, showed that this policy resulted in an increased productivity of labor (the number of working hours completed rose less than the index numbers of production), and in an effort by the industrialists to renovate their plants. "Although unfriendly to the Popular Front wage-hour legislation," he wrote, "a French engineer, R. P. Schwartz (writing in *Factory Management and Maintenance*), and an economist, Henry Laufenburger (in *La France Economique,* 1937), admit that the inquiries made of various efficiency experts in the mechanical industries indicated the increase in output during 1937 was principally due to nationalization and retooling under the impulsion of higher labor costs. Despite the fact that the work week was shorter and there was no increase in personnel, Schwartz reports, 'in a chain and transmission gear factory, thanks to new equipment installed, the weekly output is now bigger than it used to be under the 48-hour week.' "*

The improved distribution of credit, made possible by the reform of the Bank of France, permitted the strengthening of French economic machinery by the following measures: (1) inauguration of a program of great public works for the construction of roads, ports, hydroelectric centers, dams, railroads, etc.; (2) institution of a system of loans to compensate small industry for the impact of the social legislation, by enabling it to purchase new machinery; (3) nationalization of war industries. As we shall see later, the principal object of this nationalization was the regrouping of factories, the more complete utilization of the means of production, and the creation of new centers of production dispersed throughout the country and sheltered from aerial bombardment.

Collective bargaining and the arbitration of labor disputes were made compulsory. These measures were intended to preserve peace and prevent the sit-down strike from becoming the workers' only answer to the employers' abuse of authority. They staved off civil war in 1936 and permitted the peaceful arbitration of more than one thousand labor disputes in 1937.

This general review of the economic reforms achieved by the Popular Front would be incomplete without some mention of the measures taken to protect agricultural producers, especially by the creation of the Wheat Office (*Office du Blé*) and the development of producers' co-operatives. Actually, the economic policy of the Popular Front was inspired by the experiments of the Scandinavian countries and the United States—a policy of high wages, extensive public works, and improved credit facilities for producers; it was complemented by social legislation under which Frenchmen of every social class and opinion who respected parliamentary law were to be guided and encouraged in the practice of tolerance.

These measures resulted in a considerable increase in production. Compared with that registered in the same years in other countries, this increase may seem inadequate, and we shall have to investigate the causes of this relative inadequacy; but men of good faith will note that it contrasts with the decline of production in 1934 and 1935. The adversaries of the Popular Front have not failed to mention that French production would have risen in just the same way if the conservatives had not been defeated; but to say that, is to oppose a mere hypothesis to statistically established facts. Others maintain that toward the end of 1935 the index of production had a tendency to rise; but they forget to add that this tendency was of short duration. Several months before the advent of the Popular Front, foreign events, especially the remilitarization of the Rhineland, and on the domestic scene the social agitation resulting from the deflation of salaries and Fascist threats, had created a countercurrent. To credit the revival of French economy in 1936 and 1937 to the Popular Front is but an impartial statement of the facts.

It is equally important to ascertain what ends were served by the general increase of industrial production. The thesis of the Vichy government,

* Melvin M. Fagen, "Lesson of France," *New Republic*, September 2, 1940.

157

as stated in the recommendations of the Council of Political Justice, is that the reforms of the Popular Front "became instruments of social struggle . . . by which the moral strength of the country was dangerously weakened." According to Vichy, the workers and, to a lesser degree, the farmers were the only ones to profit by the new situation resulting from the increase in wages and purchasing power of the masses. "The Popular Front's mortal sin," Vichy said, "was to prefer butter to cannon."

Again, the truth is in the statistics. The following table contains figures from the *Statistical Yearbook of the League of Nations* and from the *Yearbook of Labor Statistics of the Bureau International du Travail.* A comparison of the figures yields the following results: (1) a general increase in industrial production of 12.6 per cent from 1935 (Laval) to 1937 (Blum) was accompanied by an increase of 5.5 per cent in the lump sum of wages and salaries computed in terms of real value—which means that the purchasing power of wage earners and officials increased about one-half of the whole of industrial production; (2) the general 12.6 per cent increase in industrial production included a 5 per cent decrease in the production of foodstuffs and an increase of only 10 per cent in textile production—which means that the production of consumers' goods increased 50 per cent less than the totality of industrial production; (3) the volume of basic products serving the armament industry and the industrial equipment of the country increased by about 26 per cent—which indicates that the general growth of industrial production was concentrated much more on reinforcing economy and national defense than on increasing the general consumers' well-being. In the study from which I previously quoted, Melvin M. Fagen gave the following example. "The smelting of iron

INCREASE OF FRENCH INDUSTRIAL PRODUCTION FROM 1935 TO 1937
AS SHOWN BY INDEX NUMBERS OF PRODUCTION
(Base: 1928=100)

	General Index of Production	Lump Sum of Wages in Real Value	Consumer Goods			Products Serving Industrial Equipment And Armament						
			Foodstuffs	Textiles	Average	Iron Ore	Pig Iron	Steel	Mech. Industries	Chemical Products[1]	Machines (Eng.)	Average
1935—Laval	79	91	104	80	92	66	58	66	71	81	64.8	67.8
1937—Blum	89	96	99	88	93.5	78	79	84	88	103	79.6	85.3
Percentage Variation	+ 12.6	+ 5.5	— 4.8	+ 10.0	+ 1.6	+ 18.2	+ 36.2	+ 27.3	+ 23.9	+ 27.2	+ 22.8	+ 25.8

[1]Base: 1929=100

158

ore rose 27 per cent and the production of steel 19 per cent from 1936 to 1937, reflecting the freshened impetus toward industrial mechanization. Indeed, as compared with the iron and steel production in Germany (3.5 per cent), Great Britain (10 per cent), and the United States (13 per cent), France (22 per cent) could show greater progress from 1936 to 1937 than any other country." Moreover, the studies published by M. Jean Dessirier in the *Revue d'Economie Politique* in 1938 and 1939 show that under the Popular Front, the division of private revenues of capital and labor remained about the same—which means that the general growth of industrial production was absorbed by the great tool and armament works. This growth benefited not a particular group, but all classes; it was the first time in many years that a French government had in so large a measure taken cognizance of national interest.

It is therefore as incorrect to charge that the Popular Front preferred butter to cannon as to contend that its economic policy reduced industrial production almost to nothing. A general increase of 12 per cent in industrial production, an increase of 26 per cent in the production of raw materials serving armament manufacture and the industrial equipment of the country cannot be considered negligible. It is true that industrial activity during the same period was rising more rapidly in England (17 per cent), in Germany (25 per cent) and in Soviet Russia (45 per cent), but none of these countries had suffered from an enfeebling system of deflation for two years. If one criticizes the economic policy of 1936-1937, what is there to say of the policy of 1934-1935, when French industrial production dropped about 10 per cent while British production increased 20 per cent, German, 55 per cent, and Russian, 48 per cent?

One cannot study the documents without coming to the conclusion that the economic policy of the Popular Front was superior to that of its opponents.

VARIATION OF THE GENERAL INDEX OF INDUSTRIAL PRODUCTION DURING
THE YEARS 1933-1935 AND 1935-1937
(Base: 1929=100)

Country	1933	1935	Variation from 1933 to 1935, in per cent	1937	Variation from 1935 to 1937, in per cent
Russia	198.4	293.3	+47.8	424.0	+44.6
Norway	93.8	107.6	+14.7	129.6	+20.4
Great Britain	88.2	105.6	+19.7	123.6	+17.0
France	80.7	73.1	— 9.4	81.9	+12.0
Italy	73.7	93.8	+27.4	99.6	+ 6.1
Belgium	72.2	82.2	+13.9	97.0	+18.0
United States	63.9	75.6	+18.3	92.2	+22.0
Germany	60.7	94.0	+54.9	117.2	+24.8
World[1]	71.9	86.0	+19.6	103.7	+20.6

[1]Excluding Russia.

French economy suffered infinitely less from the errors of the Popular Front than from the policy of the Doumergue, Flandin, and Laval cabinets. But Marshal Pétain had been in the Doumergue cabinet, and Laval and Flandin were members of the Vichy government, when action was ordered against the ministers of the Popular Front. It is hardly surprising that among Pétain's precautions against the uncovering of disagreeable truths was an order forbidding the Court to extend its investigation to the 1934-1935 period.

The foregoing arguments constituted an ample justification for Blum and Daladier. But the economic policy of the Popular Front was not above reproach. The weaknesses emerge if one compares the economic expansion of France between 1935 and 1937 with that of the great industrial nations. An accurate measure is given by the table on page 159; yet the insignificance of the faults of 1936-1937 as compared with those of 1934-1935 must always be borne in mind.

What were the causes of this inadequacy and why was France unable to do as well as the United States, although outstripping Italy from 1935 through 1937?

VICHY'S THESIS FOR THE FAILURE OF THE POPULAR FRONT'S ECONOMIC POLICY

According to Vichy, the economic effort of the Popular Front was paralyzed by three factors: the weakness of the government in coping with labor agitation, the nationalization of war industries, and the enforcement of social legislation "diverted from its true end."

To justify the Popular Front ministers in a general way before impartial judges, it would suffice to point out that their hands were not entirely free. Not only had they inherited a poor economic mechanism, but their adversaries, instead of observing the rules of the democratic game, employed every legal and illegal means to multiply their difficulties. The Popular Front ministers did not create economic disorder; they inherited it. The first wave of sit-down strikes had swept the country before the Popular Front came to power. They inherited political as well as social disorder, as agitation of Fascist organizations had grown steadily since February 6, 1934. From every point of view their situation was more difficult than that of the democratic governments of England or America, and the results of their efforts were bound to be different.

It requires more time to repair than to destroy, to change than to improve. Blum made this point forcefully at the hearing of March 11, 1942, when he said: "The Popular Front was not a beginning and one cannot isolate it as one pleases. I shall expose the calumnies and reveal the truth about the Popular Front government when it becomes necessary. I shall show the Popular Front's contribution to domestic and international peace, to material, moral, and political preparation for the defense of the country. But if you think that its policy was evil . . . you should have extended your investigation to those who necessitated it, either by direct action or by inevitable reaction. Seek out its principal authors, of whom we would seem to be mere accomplices. . . . Address your-selves to the champions of gold parity and deflation at any price. They are the harvesters of that misery, suffering, and revolt of the laboring classes of which the elections of May, 1936, were only the expression. . . . Here is the cause of many of the technical difficulties which had to be overcome before the realiza-tion of any programs, and for all the labor difficulties which caused us much trouble. One might draw up a terrible balance sheet of factories temporarily or permanently closed, of plants not kept up or modernized because the profits permitted neither amortization nor development, of specialists exhausted by unemployment and driven to other trades. The Doumergue, Pétain, Flandin, and Laval cabinets had been free to choose their policies. Ours was dictated by theirs. Or rather, our choice was one between the policy we practiced and civil war—civil war which was hardly the way to increase production and avoid foreign war. Our duty—the duty of our office—was to ward off this calamity by reawakening the nation's confidence in free institutions, and thereby show-ing ourselves scrupulously faithful to a program chosen by universal suffrage. A feeble and exhausted economy had to be revitalized by methods contrary to those whose failure had thrown the nation into such a dangerous position. If you think, with the Prosecuting Attorney, that in carrying out this duty we violated the interests of the country, begin by seeking out those who imposed it on us."

The thesis of Blum was that the Popular Front government had a right to plead the existence of attenuating circumstances, and to demand that a hierarchy of responsibility be established between those who had caused the economic disorder and those who tried to repair it. But let us take up in detail the three accusations of the Vichy government.

"Weakness" in Repressing Labor Agitation

It was easy to declare in 1942 that the Popular Front government showed weakness in "the repression of labor agitation." If this means anything at all, it implies that the government should have used the police to evacuate factories held by striking workers. To maintain that the government should have used force to settle labor conflicts in 1936 and 1937 is to ignore the social and political problem of that time and to close one's eyes to the nature and extent of the existing phenomenon.

The enforced evacuation of factories would not have stimulated production as the employers could not have obtained adequate labor replacements; the number of strikers occupying the plants was about eight times larger than the total number of unemployed, and approximately twenty times larger than the number of unemployed capable of replacing the strikers in workyards and shops.

Moreover, the use of force in labor conflicts would have provoked civil war—which at that time, as Blum pointed out at the March 11 hearing, was a more imminent threat than war with Germany. To deny this would be to ignore the state of exasperation to which the French masses had come after two years of reactionary rule and Fascist provocation. At the same hearing Blum emphasized that the French employers had considered him "a savior"; that not one had asked him to use force against the sit-down strikers; that employers, on the contrary, pressed the government to take the initiative in negotiations which resulted in the Matignon Agreements. The debates in the Chamber and Senate on the strikes reveal that not a single deputy or senator, however reactionary, appealed to the government for the use of force.

Finally, the evacuation of factories by the police, which would have been most difficult for any French government to enforce at that time, was morally and politically impossible for a Popular Front government, supported in Parliament and throughout the country by the majority of the French people. Had the government sent police against the workers—who had just grounds for complaint—it would have been overthrown by the Chamber of Deputies, and in a state of divided public opinion, France would have been without a government in the most tragic political and social situation imaginable at that moment. Such conditions would hardly have contributed to the establishment of calm or to the economic strengthening of the country. Negotiation was therefore the only way of dealing with a labor problem unprecedented in French history. In adopting that policy Blum was unanimously approved by the government and supported by the large majority of the nation.

Nationalization of War Industries

It is equally easy in retrospect to declare that the Popular Front government erred in nationalizing the war factories; but it would be more difficult for such critics to demonstrate that nationalization reduced armament production. The Vichy government did not even attempt such a demonstration at Riom. A few observations will suffice to invalidate the charges made against Blum and Daladier on this count.

What exactly was the nationalization of the war factories? To destroy the legend created by Vichy, this is the first question to be asked in general terms. Many imagine nationalization as a radical and revolutionary measure, by which the factories were taken from their owners and given to the workers. In reality, nationalization was the creation, or rather the extension, of an armament industry directed or controlled by the state. This national industry was developed by creating new factories or purchasing some existing plants; in the latter case, the purchase price was determined by negotiation, by arbitration, or by experts appointed by the courts. As all the legitimate interests of the owners were safeguarded, there was no denying the right of the state to create or develop its own armaments industry. Nationalization was all the less revolutionary, since the French state, even under the *ancien régime,* always had owned its arms manufacturing plants and arsenals. Private armament manufacturers began to appear only in the course of the nineteenth century; the rapid development of these private enterprises, especially after 1914, led to actual monopolies for the most important and most remunerative manufactures. Nationalization was a means of striking at these private monopolies, either by opposing to them the competition of nationalized factories or by transforming them into public monopolies. This procedure was in the tradition of French administrative law, and experience showed that it was efficacious.

Furthermore, it must be remembered that the nationalization of war industries was the wish of the whole country. What the French people wanted was a complete nationalization which would have left no private war industries in France. International investigations had denounced the scandalous and dangerous activities of many such enterprises. The nationalization of war industries figured not only in the program of the Popular Front, but had been urged by most of the political parties and by the associations of war veterans, so important in a country which had mobilized and lost a larger percentage of its men than any other belligerent nation in 1914-1918.

The law providing for nationalization of the war industries was passed on August 16, 1936, by almost unanimous vote of the Chamber and Senate. The enforcement of this law was approved not only in political, but in military, circles, as can be seen in the writings of General Mordacq in 1938: "The nationalization of private factories of war matériel—whose wisdom may be disputed from a financial point of view—cannot be attacked from the point of view of national defense. It has permitted us to create an absolutely vital strength of supplementary production, which, on the day we mobilize, will contribute powerfully to our war production."* It would have been impossible for the Popular Front government not to implement an article of its program which was called for simultaneously by its partisans and by war veterans and military authorities.

Finally, nationalization of the war industries was, like Aesop's tongue, good or bad, according to the use made of it. It is childish to think that factories directed by the state are always worse than private factories. Not to leave the field of armaments, we might point out that the best cannon built by France in a century, the 75 mm., was invented and built in state arsenals; furthermore, the war production of the Soviet national plants equals in quantity and quality that of the best privately-owned factories. The defense of Blum demonstrated that the nationalization of the war industries was a powerful weapon against producers' association and trusts, which were a serious obstacle to the fulfillment of programs set up by the General Staff. Numerous examples of the beneficial effects of nationalization as a check on the trusts were offered by Blum, Daladier, and Jacomet; nor were their statements, which were based on information gathered in the course of the investigation, contradicted by President Caous, the Prosecuting Attorney, or the witnesses for the prosecution. Daladier mentioned that when the Schneider-Creusot Company, the most important French manufacturers of war matériel, and the Brandt Company, specialists in modern artillery matériel, had agreed to refuse orders for the construction of war factories in North Africa, nation-

* J. J. H. Mordacq, Les Grandes Heures de la Guerre (Paris: Plon., 1938).

163

alization alone proved the way to break their resistance. He showed that nationalization had made it possible to re-equip with modern machinery ten important factories which had been operating with old equipment and outworn
methods, certain of obtaining huge profits without effort or risk because of
their monopolies.

Blum and Jacomet revealed that the tank construction program could
not be carried out until the Louis Renault Company's monopoly had been
broken by the nationalization law in 1936. They affirmed, without contradiction, that nationalization had made it possible not only to equip existing
factories better, but to create new factories and enlarge the armament industry
according to a general plan without which the preparation and execution of
industrial mobilization would have been far more difficult. It is apparent
that the true block to armament production was not nationalization, but the
existence of private monopolies; in fact, nationalization was the most effective
weapon against the power of the trusts.

The Riom hearings also revealed the true reasons for the campaign against
nationalization. Blum demonstrated by a striking example the methods to
which the cannon merchants had resorted to maintain their monopoly. The
Schneider works, having received orders from the Soviet government for construction of large guns for battleships, deliberately delayed execution of the
order. A director of the firm, who belonged to the Schneider family—one of
the 200 Families—called on M. Vladimir P. Potemkine, the Soviet Ambassador; he explained that the delay was intentional, but that Potemkine's order
would be filled immediately if he would do the Schneider firm a favor; the
Ambassador was to inform Blum that the Soviet government would like to
see the Schneider firm escape nationalization. Blum paid homage to the integrity of M. Potemkine, who contented himself with apprising the Premier
of this strange and most revealing move.

During the Riom hearings no deposition or document was offered to
prove that the nationalization of war industries had disorganized or in any
way delayed armament production; on the contrary, the defendants were
prepared to show how and why nationalization had improved and stimulated
the French armament industry.

Application of New Social Legislation: the Forty-Hour Week

Vichy maintained that French economy was endangered and the manufacture of armaments retarded by the application of the social legislation voted
by Parliament.

Of all the social reforms instituted by the Popular Front, only one can
be criticized seriously: the reduction of the work week to 40 hours. The paid
vacation law also reduced the total period of working time, but this law was
so just and so universally popular that no one had the courage to blame
the Popular Front ministers for it. In a book *Un An d'Audaces et de Contradictions,* a criticism of the economic reforms of the Popular Front, M. E.

Thery, editor of *l'Economiste Français,* spoke in the following terms of the paid vacation law: "The very principle of this reform is indisputably just and its application marks a real social progress. . . . It has been carried out with great skill and awareness of the necessities of the national economy."*

Similarly, the opponents of the Popular Front could have raised objections, from a political point of view, to the provisions of the law of June 24, 1936, which regulated collective labor agreements, assured freedom to belong or to refrain from belonging to a specific union, created workers' delegates in every factory employing more than six workers, and laid down the rules for apprenticeship and hiring. They might also have opposed the law of December 31, 1936, which made mediation and arbitration obligatory in the settlement of labor disputes. But it would be impossible to contend that these measures had weakened French economy and delayed the production of armaments. It was only the 40-hour week which was criticized in Riom.

The question of France's wisdom in adopting the 40-hour week is complicated, and cannot be answered with a simple yes or no. In 1936 this was not only an economic question; it was a social and political problem. It was not certain that calm could be restored in the working class after the employers' excesses in 1934-1935 without enforcing the 40-hour law. Even considered only from its economic aspect, the question was not simple. To try to classify it and to answer the accusations of Vichy, three observations must be offered.

First, it is not the *legal* number of working hours which determines the quantity of work that an economic system can absorb at a given moment, but the general conditions of the market; and it is not only the actual working time which influences production, but the productivity of the labor. At the moment when the 40-hour law was enforced by the Popular Front government, the quantity of work that French industry could absorb was certainly less than 40 hours per week per worker, and the result of the new law was a more equitable division of the burden of labor between the unemployed and the employed worker. The decrees enforcing the 40-hour week were prepared in August and September, 1936, and issued after October of the same year. In September, 1936, there were 420,776 unemployed on relief and 466,124 unsatisfied requests for work; a year later, in September, 1937, when the Committee of Investigation on Production was beginning its work, the figures were 314,553 unemployed receiving aid and 337,376 unfilled requests for employment. The statistics for the unemployed receiving aid included only about two-thirds of the total unemployed in France.

Thus the Committee of Investigation could declare in its conclusions, published about a year after the 40-hour law had been put into effect, that "in a general way, there was no manpower crisis." France was so far from having a manpower crisis that, after the fall of the Popular Front, the Daladier cabinet, yielding more and more to the pressure of industrialists and conservatives, increased the *legal* number of working hours without bringing about any increase

*M. E. Thery, *Un An d'Audaces et do Contradictions* (Paris: Librairie Générale de Droit at de Jurisprudence, 1937).

in the *actual* working time. The employers were unable to profit by the right which they had demanded. In June, 1938, 0.1 per cent worked more, and 21.8 per cent worked less, than 40 hours per week. Nothing could have demon-strated more conclusively that the campaign against the 40-hour week was purely political, and could not be supported by any argument drawn from the actual situation. This fact was pointed out by Melvin M. Fagen: "French labor was putting in a longer week during the first quarter of 1937 (after the 40-hour week had been instituted) than it was during the same period in 1939, when the law had been abolished. In the heyday of the Blum regime, the average work week was almost 5 per cent longer than it was after the law had per-mitted employers to keep their men at their benches up to 50 hours a week."[*]

COMPARISON OF THE LEGAL AND ACTUAL LENGTH OF THE WORK WEEK
IN 1937 AND 1939[1]

Year	Legal Length	Actual Length
1st trimester, 1937	40-hour week with possible exceptions	42.3 hours
1st trimester, 1939	50-hour week or more	40.2 hours

[1]Source: *Bulletin of the Ministry of Labor.* Statistics based on the monthly inquiries in factories employing more than 100 workers.

The system of the 40-hour week was capable of furnishing all the labor that French economy, as it was organized at that time, could absorb. The re-duction of the working day caused a drop of about 25 per cent in the number of unemployed, that is—from the point of view which should have interested the Court of Riom—it made possible a broader training of the reserve of workers who would be needed in time of war. The Daladier-Reynaud decrees which lengthened the work week in a purely theoretical manner had the oppo-site effect; the number of unemployed receiving aid and the number of unfilled requests for work rose, reaching 404,730 for the former and 444,327 for the latter in December, 1938 (instead of 357,856 and 389,626 in December, 1937), and 415,987 and 460,816 in January, 1939. The effects of the 40-hour week were not to reduce the actual work, but to give more workers employment in the same factories and at the same machines.

Second, the institution of the social legislation of the Popular Front, the 40-hour week included, did not provoke the catastrophes that some feared. "If social legislation were the opiate that slowed up production," wrote Mr. Fagen, "the narcotic effect should have been immediately noticed." Yet the effect was exactly the opposite. "Before the Blum regime and the introduction of the 40-hour week (during the first five months of 1936), the average index for metal manufactures was 77. During the first five months of 1937, with the 40-hour week established and with higher wages, the index averaged 90, an

[*] Melvin M. Fagen, "Lesson of France," *New Republic*, September 2, 1940.

increase within a year of almost 17 per cent. Two years later, during the first five months of 1939, after the 40-hour week had been modified and all energies were strained to meet the war emergency, the average rate of production was only 3.4 per cent higher than it had been under Blum."

If the 40-hour week created any difficulties for French industrialists, it forced them to greater efforts of thought, management, organization, and equipment, by which the national economy profited; it was the necessary leaven in the loaf. In the following table I have brought together some index numbers of the total of actual working hours and of industrial output. A comparison of these figures will show that the relation between the actual working hours and industrial production, which had declined between 1933 and 1935 as a consequence of the deflation policy of the Doumergue, Flandin, and Laval cabinets, improved in 1937, after the institution of social legislation; in other words, the productivity of labor, which had fallen in 1934 and 1935, increased in 1936-1937. The figures also show that the productivity of labor declined in 1938 and 1939, when the influence of conservative elements caused the abandonment of the 40-hour week, but that it remained higher than it had been in 1935 and even in 1933, because some of the benefits obtained under the impulse of Popular Front social legislation were not entirely lost. The results are still more striking in metallurgical industry production, the basis of the war industry.

PRODUCTIVITY OF LABOR IN FRANCE FROM 1933 TO 1939[1]

Year	1933	1935	1937	1938	1938 (1st trimester)	1939 (1st trimester)
Index of the total of actual working hours (industrial workers)	73.6	66.8	64.9	65	65.4	67.1
General index of industrial production	80.7	72.5	81.7	76.1	84.3	84.7
Index of metallurgical production	77	71	88	76	90	85

[1]Figures taken from the *Yearbook of Labor Statistics* and the *Statistical Yearbook of the League of Nations.*

Third, the 40-hour law had planned for a system of "derogations" and overtime for industrialists working for national defense. The Riom Court's act of indictment reproached Daladier for having prevented the war industries from operating under this system by his circular letter of July 26, 1936. The hearings showed that in July, 1936, the armament programs instituted before the Popular Front did not even assure 40 hours of work weekly to labor in war industries and that in October, 1936, when new programs had been set up, the circular letter of July 26 was abrogated. The Committee of Investigation on Production declared in September, 1937, that all derogations requested for national defense had been granted. Let us admit for the sake of argument that without Daladier's circular, war production would have been 20 per cent greater in August and September, 1936; who can believe that such an increase in production would have altered materially the state of French armaments in 1940?

Must we conclude from these observations that the 40-hour law was without faults? Not at all. Having noted the good phases of the law, we may now mention its disadvantages, which came not from the principle of the law but from the manner of its enforcement. The inquiry into production in 1937 showed that the first enforcements had been too strict and absolute. As early as April, 1937, Léon Jouhaux, General Secretary of the Confédération du Travail, in an article in *le Peuple,* had pointed out possible disadvantages of a rigid application of the law, and asked that the 40-hour principle be adjusted in different ways to different situations. Greater flexibility would have yielded better results and achieved a greater expansion of production. But on the one hand, the criticisms of the 40-hour week under this heading must be kept within reasonable bounds. The institution of a new regulation of labor is always a long task, requiring successive experiments and modifications. Unless one wants to condemn oneself to failure, it is necessary to establish general rules before foreseeing exceptions to them. A certain degree of rigor was necessary at first, and should have been borne with patience. On the other hand, the inflexibility of the law derived neither from the text voted by Parliament nor from the decrees instituted by the Popular Front cabinet to regulate the enforcement of the law. It was, rather, the result of a somewhat pedantic and formal application of the letter of the law on the part of the Ministry of Labor and the interested parties themselves.

On this point we may accept the evidence of an author who cannot be suspected of sympathy for the Popular Front, M. E. Thery, editor of *l'Economiste Français:* "The decrees for the enforcement of the law were minutely prepared after long consultations of all the interested parties. . . . Very flexible, so that they may be adapted to the infinitely diversified necessities of every profession, they provide, in a general way, for an interim period between publication and application, thereby permitting each of the parties to present to the Ministry of Labor observations which the final decrees will take into account."* Thus the 40-hour week could provoke criticism neither against the principle itself nor against the governmental decrees, but merely against a certain rigidity in the enforcement of details. The measures, it must be repeated, did not affect the industries working for national defense. I mention in passing that the Minister of National Economy, the member of the Popular Front cabinets who might be criticized for not having supervised the enforcement of the social legislation more attentively, was not brought before the Supreme Court of Justice. His name is Charles Spinasse; in 1940 he became one of the chief supporters of Marshal Pétain.

* M. E. Thery, *Un An d'Audaces et de Contradictions.*

ACTUAL CAUSES FOR THE FAILURE OF THE POPULAR FRONT'S ECONOMIC POLICY

The arguments advanced in the name of the Vichy government before the Supreme Court did not explain why French economy did not profit more by the impetus of the Popular Front. Only a complete study of the economic and social situation would have allowed the Court to arrive at the causes, but such a study would have revealed that those principally responsible for the economic weakness of France were not the Popular Front ministers.

Summarized, these reasons were: the confusion caused by the policy of 1934-1935; the desertion of industrialists and capitalists; and a lack of boldness in governmental action.

Supplementary Depression of 1934-1935

French economy, and especially industrial production, had been disorganized and weakened more profoundly than anyone imagined by the "supplementary depression" of 1934-1935, following the "normal" or general depression of all capitalist states in 1930-1932. France—and France alone—found herself in the position of the man who, while recovering from a dangerous illness, is struck by a second attack of the same disease.

France had been moderately hit by the great world depression. In 1932 the general index of industrial production (which had remained at 83.5 in England, 89 in Switzerland, 84 in the Low Countries) fell to 72.2 in France, whereas it reached a low of 52.7 in the United States, 53.3 in Germany, 60.2 in Czechoslovakia (for the year 1933), 60.3 in Canada, 62.5 in Poland, 66.9 in Italy, and 69.2 in Belgium. Certain French enterprises, which would have been eliminated by a more severe depression because of their inadequate equipment, were able to continue in existence by reducing their production. Throughout the world economic recovery was aided by reconstructive measures instituted by industrialists and governments alike. Economic New Deals, under a variety of names and methods, appeared almost everywhere; in all countries the index of industrial production began to rise steadily. In 1934-1935 France, on the contrary, favored its producers less than it did those citizens who lived on unearned income, and as a result, French enterprises experienced the difficulties and discouragements of a second depression which they might have been spared. This second depression was greater than the first because it struck an already weak and barely convalescent organism. The general index of production fell to 73.1 in 1935 as compared with 72.2 in 1932. The period of acute crisis was longer if one considers that the 1934 index was 75.2, while that of 1931 had been 86.4—which means that the average index for 1934-1935 was 74.1 as against 79.3 for 1932-1933.

During that second crisis the "protected" enterprises (private monopolies, state-subsidized enterprises, etc.) were hit relatively more lightly than in 1931-

1932 because they profited by the aid of the Bank of France and the government, to the detriment of the rest of the country. The studies of M. Jean
Dessirier, the best French statistician, showed that the "protected" enterprises
continued to show a profit at the same time that the deflation policy plunged
the mass of the workers and small entrepreneurs into want; this, in turn,
meant that the "unprotected" private enterprises suffered more from the economic policy of 1934-1935 than from the consequences of the world depression.
The following chart shows how the industrial countries came out of the depression and how France in 1934-1935 entered a second depression more
severe than the first:

GENERAL INDICES OF INDUSTRIAL PRODUCTION FROM 1929 TO 1938[1]
(Base: 1929=100)

Year	World[2]	Germany	U.S.A.	Canada	United Kingdom	Belgium	Czecho-Slovakia	Italy	U.S.S.R.[1]	U.S.S.R.[3]	France
1929	100	100	100	100	100	100	100	100	100	100	100
1930	86.5	85.9	87.7	84.8	92.3	88.8	89.2	91.9	131		99.6
1931	74.8	67.6	68.2	71.1	83.8	81.1	80.7	77.6	161		86.4
1932	63.8	53.3	52.7	58.1	83.5	69.1	63.5	66.9	183	135	72.2
1933	71.9	60.7	62.7	60.3	88.2	72.2	60.2	73.7	198	154	80.7
1934	77.7	79.8	68.2	73.5	98.8	73.0	66.5	80.0	238		75.2
1935	86.0	94.0	79.1	81.3	105.6	82.2	69.9	93.8	293		73.1
1936	96.4	106.3	93.6	89.8	115.8	86.7	80.2	87.5	382		78.3
1937	103.7	117.2	102.7	99.5	123.6	97.2	96.3	99.6		292	81.9
1938	93.0	126.2	80.0	90.0	115.5	78.7		98.5	413	313	76.1

[1]Source: *Statistical Yearbook of the League of Nations.*
[2]Excluding U.S.S.R.
[3]Index calculated by the Berlin *Institut für Konjunkturforschung.*

These were the results of France's double crisis. Most enterprises had been
unable to modernize their machinery. Those too small to be "protected" had
seen their reserves wiped out twice because they had been unable to obtain
adequate aid from private credit, which was directed by the Bank of
France and distributed mainly to enterprises in which the Bank's two
hundred largest stockholders were interested. The large "protected" enterprises had also not sought aid, but for different reasons. Rather than incur new

expenses for interest, they found an easier device to maintain their profits: they obtained customs protection and subsidies from conservative governments. Furthermore, the double crisis had affected not only machinery but human beings. The directors of small businesses had lost courage and faith in themselves and in the future. Their spirit of initiative had resisted the depression of 1930-1932, but could not weather the supplementary depression of 1934-1935, and they came to hope that the large monopolistic enterprises would buy them out and leave them at the heads of their factories as employees. They let themselves be driven like sheep to slaughter into a "corporatism" advocated both by the Fascists and "big business," which would have resulted in the complete subordination of French economy to the financial power of the trusts.

Desertion of Employers and Capital

In this frame of mind French employers were incapable of doing their share in France's reconstruction. Their conversion to Fascism was mostly due to their own incompetence, and that incompetence came largely from the bad effects of the two economic crises. By 1936-1937 the entrepreneurs had lost their professional skill. A slow evolution had made them either the fearful employees or the beneficiaries of a privileged class which was defending its positions and interests in the general decadence of economic activity that its own egoism and shortsightedness had produced. The economic recovery of France in 1936-1937 was hindered far less by the government's errors in enforcing the new social and economic legislation than by the mistakes of employers in directing their enterprises. France lacked neither good workers nor good technicians nor even good ministers at that time, but rather courageous employers and competent industrialists.

Henry W. Ehrmann understood this when he wrote: "It is generally agreed, among others by the Official Inquiry into Production, that French industry had chronic defects which raised costs to a much higher level than those in other countries with comparable economies. Insufficient rationalization and inadequate scientific organization of work, lack of standardization and incompetent commercial methods combined to make French industry and commerce especially sluggish under 'depression' conditions. The same factors impeded effective competition on the world market, despite the price advantage created by the Blum devaluation."*

The same general apathy was found among bankers and capitalists. The same avoidance of risk and responsibility, the same shirking of national duty encouraged by Fascist and reactionary propaganda, hindered the financing of the most essential enterprises. Here we are faced by the question of the role and value of private capital in modern economic life. It will become ever more important to know to what extent state control over economic activity and public credit will replace the outworn machinery of savings and private credit.

* Henry W. Ehrmann, "The Blum Experiment and the Fall of France," *Foreign Affairs,* October, 1941.

In the France of 1936-1937 and even 1938-1939 we witnessed a general strike of capital, which had graver consequences for the recovery of economic activity than the sit-down strikes. This strike of capital was intensified by the export of money to foreign countries. It has often been said that the Frenchman's head is Left and his purse is Right, meaning that the Frenchman is progressive and radical in his thinking, but becomes conservative when he has private interests to defend; it also means that intelligence in France is generally Left and capital generally Right. Furious at their unprecedented defeat in 1936, the conservatives and reactionaries tried to oppose political forces with economic measures by transferring their fortunes abroad; as they could not export their lands, estates, or factories, they exported their movable capital, and the bankers of America, England, Holland, and Switzerland never had so many French clients as during the Popular Front regime. The national economy was thereby deprived of indispensable working capital and new funds. Not only were the French bankers and capitalists unconcerned by such considerations, but it was precisely their intention to create difficulties for the Popular Front government. Melvin M. Fagen, in his study in the *New Republic*, noted how the attitude of the Popular Front's enemies impeded the rearmament of France:

"The Popular Front's extraordinary defense program for the expenditure of twenty billion francs in 1937 (almost double the 1935 military budget), including four billion for the northern defense, was supported by all parties in the Chamber. What then followed illuminates the peculiar patriotism of French capital. Such a prospect for increased arms expenditures would, we might expect, lead to business optimism and to what our financial writers call 'a flurry of buying' on the stock market. But the *New York Times* of September, 1936, had a different story to tell under the headline, 'French Arms Plan Spurs Gold Flow.' The news that the government was about to spend millions on defense was greeted with horror by those Frenchmen whose eyes were glued to the daily bond quotations. The New York Federal Reserve Bank, within three days after the announcement of the defense program, received for safekeeping almost twenty million dollars in French gold. During the month of September enough French capital had fled to the United States alone to cover one-half of the entire cost of constructing the defenses along the Belgian front. Each time the government prepared to spend the money that had been authorized for the northern fortifications, the hounds of hell broke loose. Again in March, 1938, when Premier Chautemps asked for an expenditure of fifteen billion francs for this purpose (the money to be spent by a politically independent National Defense Commission with Marshal Pétain as president), the hemorrhage of capital began once more and the franc fell to the lowest rate it had reached since November 11, 1926. The *New York Times* reported on March 9, 1938, from Paris: 'The troubles of the franc, according to bankers here . . . [arise from] the proposal of the Chautemps government to seek approval of a financial plan involving contemplated expenditures of fifteen billion francs for national defense this year.' The next day the Chautemps government was overthrown because it dared to insist that money be spent on guns, tanks, and fortifications. Blum became Premier again for one month—until the Senate refused to grant his renewed requests for defense funds."*

Like the industrialists who were unable to manage their factories, and like the generals, the French capitalists failed in their duty.

Excessive Caution of the Government

The third cause of France's economic weakness in 1936-1937 was the government's lack of boldness. I have already mentioned this fault with respect to the general policy of the Popular Front; I shall return to it only to point out its economic aspects.

In his book *The Economics of War,* published before the United States entered the war, Horst Mendershausen wrote: "The failures of France and of Great Britain in the present war find their explanation not so much in an excessive degree of popular liberties as in the absence of democratic control over influential and privileged groups and in the hesitation of the government to assume economic leadership."† This absence of democratic control caused the failure of the financial policy of the Popular Front. This policy, which was not discussed before the Court of Riom, cannot be examined here. But experience showed that it might have been, in large measure, a policy of constraint, involving a rigorous control of financial and banking operations; not to organize this control was to rely on the good faith of the government's political enemies and the patriotism of the financiers to prevent the bleeding of capital. The political and social condition of France did not permit the bestowal of such confidence on the opponents of the Popular Front.

Similarly, the absence of sufficient control of economic life caused the failure of the Popular Front experiment. In 1936 the Popular Front tried to revive a certain economic liberalism, as the New Deal had done in the United States. It hoped to succeed in this effort by classical methods, especially by injections of credit into the economic machine. It failed because French economy had passed beyond the point where the provisional restoration of a system of free competition would have been possible. In 1936 French economy was already controlled by great private interests, especially by the 200 Families of the Bank of France. Things had come to the point where the state either had to substitute its control for that of these interests or run the risk of being overthrown by them.

Short of returning to a deflationary policy, which was condemned by the country and by events, the only alternative to the policy practiced by the Popular Front would have been the method of four- or five-year "plans" established by the state and enforced under state control. Soviet Russia was the first to use this method. Without the five-year plans Russia would never have been able to achieve in so brief a time and under the most difficult condi-

* Melvin M. Fagen, "Lesson of France," *New Republic,* September 2, 1940.

† Horst Mendershausen, *The Economics of War* (New York: Prentice Hall, 1941).

tions a social and economic transformation without historical precedent. This method, borrowed by Hitler from Stalin, permitted Germany to come out of the economic crisis more rapidly than the other capitalist states, and let Hitler construct the economic instrument which he needed to forge his army. The two modern armies which were built up before 1939 were founded on and maintained by planned production.

This method would have been particularly well adapted to France's situation in 1936. French economy, as we have seen, had been so weakened and disorganized by the general crisis and the supplementary depression that it would have been easier to reconstruct it entirely on new bases than to revive this dying organism for a short time. The Popular Front tried to squeeze the maximum service from the bad instrument which its predecessors had left; it would have been wiser to use the materials to build anew. The same efforts and resources would have yielded France an instrument of work and production more powerful and better adapted to the economic and international situation. There would have been no contradiction between the adoption of such a method and the democratic principle, since the general plan as well as the details of enforcement would have been set up and operated by a democratic government; it would have been possible to create a more democratic basis for our economy by destroying the anti-democratic power of the trusts. Finally, and above all, a planned production would have resolved the contradictions between the boldness of the Popular Front's social ideas and the timidity of its economic achievements. Had the government been more daring in action and showed its economic orientation more clearly, it would have relieved the fear of the masses and petits bourgeois. I like to think that certain industrialists themselves, impressed by the grandeur of the enterprise, would have given their aid more willingly to the Popular Front, had they seen that the government was more resolute, more foresighted, and, in a word, more youthful.

Why was planned production not adopted by the Popular Front government? The reader knows enough about Blum to realize that the Premier of the first Popular Front cabinet lacked neither the physical courage nor the intellectual audacity for the task. I have already answered this question in examining the general policy of the Popular Front. The method of planned production could not be adopted without first breaking the resistance of the Senate and the haute bourgeoisie; and that could have been achieved only by establishing a "dictatorship of the majority" and transforming the cabinet into a Committee of Public Safety. Everyone knows today that such a democratic dictatorship would have saved France and the peace of the world. It would have avoided, four years later, the dictatorship of Pétain, because it would have prevented the defeat that brought Pétain to power. France under a dictatorship of the majority would have remained faithful to collective security; she would have prevented the catastrophes in Spain and Czechoslovakia by her fidelity to the Russian alliance; she would have spared humanity great miseries.

But to establish the dictatorship of the majority, France had to be ready to accept a radical transformation and a pacific revolution. Revolutions are not made to order; history decrees and decides on them, having first prepared them.

HOMAGE TO LÉON BLUM

One would seek in vain in the economic history of the Popular Front for grounds on which to condemn Blum or the Popular Front ministers who sup-ported him. One may or may not approve of the economic policy practiced in France in 1936 and 1937; one may regret such and such a measure and blame its audacities or its timidities. Regrets and reproaches are easy after the fact. We call them in France l'esprit de l'escalier.

But it is impossible to deny that this economic policy was desired by the country, regardless of whether it was superior to the one which preceded it or whether it avoided civil war. It would be unjust to appraise any single fact of this policy without taking into account the difficult and perilous situation of France in 1936, and without considering the precautions the gov-ernment had to take if it was to avoid more serious disturbances. It is impossi-ble not to pay homage to the generosity which animated Blum, to his keen judgment, and to the sincerity of his efforts.

Above all, it is impossible to ignore the facts. In March, 1938, when the Popular Front fell, it left French economy stronger and healthier than it had found it; the factories were better equipped, the output of labor increased, and the index of industrial production had risen 12.6 per cent since 1935. The conservative governments in which Laval, Flandin, and Pétain had figured had achieved exactly the opposite result. That alone fixes their respective re-sponsibilities.

Léon Blum in prison; Pétain and Laval in power! Surely this is a strange denial of reason and justice. Only Hitler's domination of France could make it a reality.

In the course of my life I have come into contact with many French and foreign statesmen; I have never met one greater than Léon Blum, and I have never found another with the same sum of moral and intellectual values. After many years of friendship and close association with him in his governmental work, I still wonder whether the qualities of his mind or those of his heart are more to be admired.

Only barbarians could deny the qualities of his mind. The great range of his knowledge, the natural elegance of his thought, the purity of his language, and the wealth of his culture ally him with those philosophers of the eighteenth century who prepared the way for the French Revolution and with the jurists of the Renaissance, the true builders of the French state. I know nothing more harmonious than his conversation or his manner of reasoning; his mind possesses that alertness which is the mark of true intelligence. There is nothing more powerful than his dialectic; a man of great learning, he proceeds by vast syntheses, advancing from peak to peak in the realm of thought; and this delight in general ideas makes of him an incomparable conversationalist in private life, and a highly talented orator in public life.

As to the qualities of his heart? No one could be more human, more faithful to his friends, more respectful of another's ideas than Léon Blum. His only weakness may be a certain excess of generosity and sensitivity—he believes stubbornly in the good faith of his enemies and has never accustomed himself to the vulgar wickedness of the reactionaries. There is no one more generous than he; having inherited a respectable fortune from his parents, he gave it all to his political party and to the poor and unfortunate, with the result that he had nothing but the income from his books when he was thrown into prison.

Because of the qualities of his character and mind, because of the nobility of his thought, and the dignity of his life, Léon Blum has been for me the most French of our contemporary statesmen, while remaining the least nationalistic and the most European. The two guiding principles of his political activity have been peace and justice. Love of peace made him the opponent of Poincaré and the champion of Franco-German rapprochement in the days when Germany was a democracy. He became the champion of collective security when the weakness of the Western democracies allowed the growth of the Fascist menace. His love of justice placed him at the head of French Socialism, whose soul he became after the death of Jaurès in 1914; he thought that justice in society was not achieved without violent conflicts, and to attenuate the violence of these clashes, he believed that the workers should exhaust every means democracy offered them to realize their historical mission and transform society. One need not accept Léon Blum's policy in its entirety, but I defy anyone to find in it an element of baseness or ugliness. I defy the historian who examines Blum's ideas on disarmament, reparations, collective security, and the necessary means for checking Fascist activity, not to conclude that in most cases this man was right.

Concerning the governmental policy and achievements of Léon Blum, I shall say nothing; history alone will be the judge. The Riom trial has added stature to his actions by contrasting them with those of his predecessors and successors. Still more, the Riom trial emphasized his nobility as against the mediocrity of his adversaries.

In the eyes of the French people, Léon Blum incarnated the Popular Front; if the people were free, they would turn to the Popular Front and acclaim him once more as their leader.

The great honor of Léon Blum is that those who had for so long repeated the slogan, "rather Hitler than Léon Blum," were the same men who betrayed their country in 1940. At that moment, Blum became the symbol of French democracy.

176

The Military Preparation of the War

6

I N DEFENDING DALADIER against Vichy's charges, I do not mean to approve his entire policy; I am afraid he will remain the man of Munich. I would not even dare to approve his military policy and I disagreed fully with his general conception of our national defense. He underestimated the role of aviation in modern warfare and did not take energetic steps against Fascist propaganda within the Army. I refused to join his cabinet in 1938 out of loyalty to the spirit and the principles of the Popular Front, which the Senate had broken. I disapproved of the appointment of Georges Bonnet as head of the Ministry of Foreign Affairs, and of the divergence from the social and economic policy of the Popular Front. From 1938 until 1940 I opposed the policy of the Daladier cabinet on more than one occasion, and, although at times I regret supporting him on certain issues during that period, I have never regretted any of the votes I refused him or any of the speeches or articles in which I attacked him. The general policy of Daladier, in 1938 and 1939 when he was Premier, must be judged with the utmost severity.

Daladier's general policy, however, was not the one criticized during the Riom trial. He was not indicted because of his attitude at Munich or because he did not put a stop to Fascist propaganda. The man accused by the Vichy government was the Minister of War of the Popular Front, Pétain's lifelong opponent, who fought to neutralize the influence of Pétain in the Army. In spite of his general policy in 1938 and 1939 and his mistakes as Minister of War and National Defense, Daladier has redeemed himself. He opposed the demand for an armistice in June, 1940; he never considered the idea of a separate peace. On the contrary, he sailed aboard the *Massilia* with Mandel, Campinchi, Delbos, and several members of the Chamber of Deputies to organize resistance in North Africa—and when they landed in Morocco, he was arrested by General Auguste Noguès and sent back to France. Last, but not least, before the Riom Court, his courage and steadfastness revealed him once more as the man whom, ten years before, the French people had loved as one of their best soldiers in the battle for democracy. He contributed to the rehabilitation of French democracy by his daring stand against Hitler and Pétain. He proved greater in adversity than in the days of political success.

According to the Vichy government, the French Army was defeated because it had been poorly prepared for the war—the morale of the troops, their military training, and, above all, their equipment were said to have been inadequate. If this thesis were generally accepted, the question would still remain whether these deficiencies could be attributed to the governmental action of Daladier or to the Army's military leadership.

DECADENCE OF THE ARMY

Daladier was not Commander-in-Chief of the Army; he was Minister of War and National Defense. His responsibility did not extend to military questions in the strict sense of the word—such as the choice of strategic plans or the training of officers and troops; it was limited to his ministerial function, which was the general orientation of national defense and the direction of the War Department. Was he so incapable a Minister of War as to justify the verdict of the Council of Political Justice that "he betrayed, by his inefficiency, the duties of his office"?

The best answer is to compare the action of Daladier as Minister of War with that of his predecessors. This comparison is all the more interesting because Marshal Pétain was one of these predecessors. Pétain was Minister of War in 1934, while Weygand was Chief of the General Staff. Before 1934 Pétain had been, almost without interruption, Inspector-General of the Army, the highest post in the military hierarchy. His influence on French national defense prevailed from 1918 to 1936.

After the German defeat in 1918, the French Army was for many years the most powerful and well equipped in Europe. This superiority derived largely from the absence of any serious competition. The German Army had been reduced to a mere hundred thousand men, deprived of modern armament, and most military experts refused to take seriously the efforts of the Red Army. In 1936, before Daladier became Minister of War in the Blum cabinet, the French government had occasion to weigh the strength of the Army prepared by Pétain and Weygand. On March 7, 1936, Hitler, acting against the advice of his generals, annulled for the first time one of the territorial clauses of the Versailles Treaty and ordered his troops to occupy the Rhineland. This was a serious blow to French security, as it gave the German Army a powerful position. Albert Sarraut, then Premier, immediately affirmed that "France would not tolerate that Strasbourg remain within the reach of German guns." After consulting with his military experts, he was compelled to change his tone; he learned that the French Army had not one anti-aircraft gun, not one anti-tank gun, and that it was incapable of partial mobilization and of active resistance to Hitler. The only thing the French Army could envisage was a war of coalition. Such a step would have necessitated previous agreements with allies, but Sarraut found that Laval's policy during the

Ethiopian War had compromised the Anglo-French understanding to such an extent that an appeal to the League of Nations was impossible.

Three months later, when as Minister of War in the Popular Front government Daladier asked for reports on the modern fighting equipment of the French and German armies, he learned that Germany had a thousand tanks, while France had nothing but the antiquated equipment of the war of 1914. The French Army had no anti-tank mines and only 34 modern tanks; the Maginot Line had not a single anti-tank gun; the General Staff had as yet been unable to select a suitable model for anti-aircraft guns; the equipment of the field artillery was fifty years old; and the Air Force (then in a relatively better condition than the Army) had only 607 airplanes that were less than three years old.

The decadence so brutally disclosed by the events of March 7, 1936, started in 1918. The French Army was a victorious one, and the German Army, a defeated one, thirsty for revenge. The small German Army authorized by the Versailles Treaty was organized rapidly into an elite force, which became the core of the new Reichswehr. It rid itself of the old leaders, such as Hindenburg and Ludendorff, and was guided by intelligent and ambitious officers in its search for new war methods. These leaders studied the causes of the individual setbacks and of the ultimate breakdown of the first World War. They decided to avoid the mistakes of their predecessors, and at every stage of the military hierarchy, they superimposed on the traditional "Prussian" discipline a new intellectual discipline—the need for thought before command. All the while, the French Army was resting on its laurels and the illusion of superiority. Army leaders felt no need to abandon methods which had helped them win the war, and, with the methods and equipment of 1918, they remained the marshals and generals of 1918, conservative of everything and everybody—of armaments and of men. While the German Chief of Staff, a man under fifty, with only 100,000 soldiers to lead and train, could devote eight hours a day to planning and a few minutes to the chores of administrative work, his French colleague, a man over sixty, at the head of 600,000 men and several millions of trained reserves, had to spend eight hours a day on questions of administrative detail with only a few minutes left for thinking and meditation. The one was preparing for the future; the other was buried in the present.

Furthermore, the French Army lacked the spur of a great ambition. Saturated by the Versailles Treaty and a vast Colonial Empire, France had nothing left to claim, desire, or conquer. The General Staff was satisfied with asking the government to build the Maginot Line, and then went to sleep behind this new Chinese wall, lulled by its illusions, laziness, and belief in the permanence of existing political, social, and military institutions. Had it been less reactionary in its origins and traditions, the French High Command could have found a new field of activity in the League of Nations; it could have become the military arm of the League, the brain of collective security, the organizer of an International Police Force. It could have seized the numerous opportunities given by the Fascist dictators and troublemakers—in Manchuria, in Ethiopia, in Spain, in Central Europe—to uphold international law, to support the League of Nations, and thus to acquire practical experience and training for the eventual defense of the country; it could have easily become the leader of all anti-Fascist forces. Military planning and leadership for controlled disarmament, mutual insurance, and international police would have won France more glory than the greatest military triumph. But such aims were far above the intellectual level of the French generals. Satisfied to watch ramparts that no enemy threatened overtly and to conserve obsolete traditions, the French Army sank into routine.

The troop officers became indolent in the ease of garrison life, while the staff officers split into rival factions. The most famous hostile cliques were those of Foch and of Pétain—two men who detested each other, Foch contemptuous of Pétain and Pétain jealous of his rival. These two "mother" cliques, in the course of a permanent ambush warfare, gave birth to further divisions. There grew up the Maurin clique against that of Debeney, the Gamelin clique against that of Weygand, and finally the Georges clique against that of Gamelin. There arose the fight between Army and Air Force and that between Air Force and Navy. In 1930, for instance, the Air Force antagonized the Navy, which was attempting to retain control over its airplanes, by copying the Navy uniform; two years later the Navy retaliated by copying the Air Force cap; in turn the Army changed the color and design of its uniform and created a special dress uniform for gala occasions. Such were the pastimes of many a general, whose task should have been to prepare for modern warfare.

These petty intrigues deprived the Army of some of its most valuable elements. A number of career officers, discouraged by the mediocrity of their surroundings, resigned and turned to industry, civil service, or business. Those who left had, in general, the best intellectual background and training. For more than a century, France has had two military schools, of very different standards: Polytechnique, which has been one of the world's foremost scientific schools, and Saint-Cyr, a military academy, which neither in its entrance requirements nor in its curriculum has been concerned with serious intellectual training. The comparative merit of these schools is illustrated by the fact that Joffre and Foch graduated from Polytechnique, Pétain and Weygand from Saint-Cyr. From 1919 to 1939 the proportion of Polytechnique graduates in the French Army decreased as the relative number of Saint-Cyr graduates rose. The military profession was rapidly losing its nobility and grandeur in the eyes of young Frenchmen; only the prospect of a career in the Colonies or in aviation saved it from attracting merely mediocre elements. But colonial operations resembled modern warfare less and less, and military aviation was daily becoming more of a sport and less of a military pursuit.

In short, the progressive decadence of the French Army from 1918 to 1939 was largely the consequence of an intellectual and moral crisis in the ranks of the officers.

This general cause was heightened during 1934-1935 by an unfortunate circumstance: the War Department was headed by old and indolent men without political experience.

From a military point of view 1934 and 1935 were the crucial years. Long ere this, the Reichswehr had started its reorganization and intellectual renaissance; its leaders had lost no time. Under the Weimar Republic their work had been one of schooling, research, and experimentation. Only with Hitler did they receive the industrial and financial means which they needed to create a new war machine. In 1933 Germany officially left the League of Nations. In 1934 the first units of the modern army that was to smash the old French military system were created—two Panzer divisions were organized and ready for service in 1935. In 1934 and 1935 were published the important books of Major-General Erfuhrt and Major Guderian, which were to determine the orientation of the tactics applied in 1939-1940, and which were tested in 1936-1937 during the Spanish war.

In 1934-1935 it would have been easy for France to imitate Germany and follow the same tempo in modernizing her Army. As a result of the Versailles Treaty and in spite of the intellectual laziness of its leaders, the French Army was still in a good position to match German progress. It had three or four times more trained officers and abundant war matériel and equipment. The gap between French and German industrial capacity, which was to become as 1:3, was then only as 1:1.75. France had a solid network of political agreements in Central Europe, and the first steps towards the Franco-Soviet Pact already had been made. The creation of two armored divisions in 1934 and 1935—even with a six months' lag behind the German Panzer—would have indicated to Hitler that France was unwilling to grant him a monopoly on methods of modern warfare. To build nothing new, on the other hand, was to condemn oneself to an irretrievable delay—in view of Germany's superior industrial power—and to admit the defeat of French military thought by its German rival.

Not only did France fail to create anything new, but the crucial years of 1934 and 1935 were characterized by a complete lethargy in French military thought and activity. While war budgets were being increased all over the world, the French war budget actually was reduced in comparison with preceding years. A certain effort was made in the Air Force, where the Air Minister, General Denain, executed the "Plan" decided upon by the Daladier cabinet in the fall of 1933. But nothing was done either to keep pace with other countries or to compensate by international agreements for the relative decline of the French Army.

Neither Daladier nor the Popular Front nor General Gamelin was responsible for this indifference. In 1934 and 1935 the French Chief of Staff was General Weygand, a man of sixty-eight, on the eve of retirement; in 1934 the Minister of War was Marshal Pétain, seventy-eight; in 1935 the Minister of War was General Maurin, seventy-two, chosen by Pétain as his successor, when he felt too tired and old to remain a cabinet member (in the Flandin and Laval cabinets). When Maurin took office, he was a retired officer on the payroll of an armament firm—a dubious qualification for a man who was to represent the state against private armament industry. Pétain and Maurin were not only old, they were military leaders without knowledge of politics. Like most French generals, they believed in "order," they had a strong reactionary tendency, and they held to the childish idea that citizens in general and workers in particular must be handled the same way as privates in a regiment. Becoming cabinet members when over 70, they had to learn a new profession, always an arduous enterprise for old people.

Experience in France has shown repeatedly that generals always make poor ministers of war. They tend to defend the Army against all criticism; they are hampered in action by the burden of habits and allegiances, and often by rancors and prejudices as well. They are never equipped for their ministerial functions with the impartiality and the sense of perspective that long experience in public life develops. Unable to overlook details and tackle the central problems, distrustful of the masses who resent their authoritarian tendencies, they either exaggerate or underestimate the difficulties of governmental rule. This is how it always has been, at least in the democracies, and it could hardly have been otherwise, for the training of the military is too different from that of statesmen to permit a general to assume suddenly the functions of a cabinet minister or a chief of state.

It was a great misfortune for the French Army to be headed during those crucial years by such men. In Germany, the Minister of War was Goering, a man of forty, with ten years' experience in revolutionary action; the German Chief of Staff was not a World War general, but a man of fifty who had been ripened by the defeat. In France, the Minister of War and Chief of Staff were old men whom age and political bias rendered incapable of grasping the political and technical trends of modern warfare.

The period in which Pétain was Minister of War can be summarized in a single word, inertia—the inertia of the French Army as contrasted with the activity of the German. Inertia, like all negative factors, generally escapes observation and is difficult to prove. But in the case of Marshal Pétain, it was overt, deliberate, and obstinate; it expressed itself in categorical refusals to act and to modernize the French Army; it was the inertia of a stubborn old man. Four instances were particularly symptomatic.

First, the refusal of Marshal Pétain and of his successor, General Maurin, to act. This was apparent from a document signed by General Weygand and contained in the dossier of the Riom Court. In February, 1936, General Weygand, having reached the age limit, was replaced as Chief of Staff by General Gamelin. Before relinquishing his post, Weygand, in an attempt to absolve himself of responsibility, drew up a report on the deficiencies in the French Army and on the armament program. At the hearings Daladier read the following lines from the conclusion of Weygand's report: "Since May 17, 1934, the date on which I submitted to the Minister of War [Marshal Pétain] the reasoned opinion of the Supreme War Council regarding the needs of the

Army, I have repeatedly urged the convocation of the Council so that it may make its recommendations on the measures to be taken in order to remedy the deficiencies set forth in that opinion. Such a meeting, the only effective means to action, was never called."

Nor was the Supreme War Council summoned after the departure of General Weygand. Indeed, it did not meet during all the time that Marshal Pétain and General Maurin were at the head of the Ministry of War. The measures proposed by General Weygand were not taken until Daladier became Minister of War in the Popular Front government. But General Weygand's request was dated May 17, 1934, and the government of the Popular Front was not formed until June 6, 1936. Marshal Pétain and General Maurin wasted two years; they set up no reform project, no plan of operation, no armament program.

Second, Marshal Pétain curtailed war budget appropriations at a time when Germany's expenditures for national defense rose from 299.5 million dollars in 1933 to 2,600 millions in 1935 and to 3,600 millions in 1936. When Pétain took office in February, 1934, he found a budget which had been established by his predecessor, Daladier, at the end of 1933 and approved by vote of Parliament. It provided 600 million francs for construction of modern war matériel, a sum which Pétain reduced by 200 million francs. In the same fashion, he curtailed all proposals for the 1935 budget that came to him from his Chief of Staff and the various divisions of the Ministry of War. The war budget for 1935 was even lower than that of 1934 (only the Minister of Aviation, General Denain, was granted increased appropriations). What is more, as Controller-General Jacomet testified at the hearing of March 12, 1942, and as the *Journal Officiel* can verify, Marshal Pétain and his successor did not even utilize fully the meager credits which Parliament had voted upon Pétain's recommendation: 30 per cent of the 1934 credits and 59 per cent of the 1935 credits were voided by not being used. The French Army was incapable of action in the Rhineland and Daladier found no modern equipment when he succeeded Maurin, because Marshal Pétain so willed it. The Riom Court, if it had dealt out equal justice to all, would have had to call such lack of action "a betrayal of the duties of ministerial office."

Third, Marshal Pétain opposed the extension of the Maginot Line to the North Sea. The Maginot Line was a group of permanent fortifications facing Germany; these fortifications were begun in 1928 by Paul Painlevé, then Minister of War, and were developed by his successor, André Maginot. The question of where to end the Maginot Line had first been submitted to the Supreme Council of National Defense in January, 1931, at the request of Minister of War Maginot and of the Chief of Staff, General Debeney; it came up again in May, 1932, when Pietri was Minister of War and General Weygand, Chief of Staff. Maginot, Pietri, Debeney, and Weygand were all in favor of extending the line of fortifications to the North Sea, behind the Belgian border. But Marshal Pétain was at that time the highest military authority in France; he was Vice-President of the Supreme Council of National Defense (whose nominal President, according to the law, was the President of the Republic), and in that capacity would have been Commander-in-Chief in case of war. He fought the proposals of Maginot and Pietri with arguments which are in the minutes of the Supreme Council. These minutes were read at the Riom trial; according to Pétain, the extension of the Maginot Line was not necessary because, "if the Belgians fortified their frontier against Germany, the French Army would have to be moved to that frontier; in the opposite case, the defense would depend on mobile troops and field fortifications." Unfortunately, the Supreme Council of National Defense, by a majority vote, adopted Pétain's viewpoint, which was to govern operations in 1940 when the French Army moved into Belgium. In 1934 it became evident that Germany was rearming, and the problem was raised again by the General Staff and brought up before the Military Committee of the Senate. There Marshal Pétain appeared, on May 2, 1934, to defend the same thesis which in 1931 and 1932 he had upheld before the Supreme Council of National Defense. He added that the Ardennes Forest covered the French border sufficiently and thus provided an obstacle equal or superior to the best fortifications. With this belief, Pétain canceled the programs in preparation for the fortification of the Sedan region. This measure was extremely serious as the Ardennes pass, in the general direction of Namur, Charleroi, and Sedan, has always been the most vulnerable point on the French frontier and the route of all military invasions. The German columns, in May, 1940, passed through the Ardennes Forest without difficulty, crossed the Meuse at Sedan, and thus upset the entire defense strategy of the French Army. Many military experts believe that France lost the war then and there.

Pétain's decision prevented the French from protecting the most threatened sector of their frontier. A network of fortifications would have kept a local defeat from becoming a national disaster. By their inertia, Pétain and Maurin rendered France incapable of opposing the Germans in the remilitarization of the Rhineland in March, 1936, and in the crossing of the Meuse in May, 1940, which meant abandoning the two most important outposts of her defense. Had these not been lost, France could not have been defeated and Marshal Pétain never would have established his dictatorship.

Fourth, Marshal Pétain offered passive but stubborn resistance to every attempt at intellectual reform of the Army. I shall have more to say about this when I examine Pétain's role in the stabilization of French military doctrine. Everyone may make mistakes, and in the domain of the intellect men over eighty should be treated with particular indulgence. Pétain was not a criminal because he had a wrong and antiquated conception of warfare, but for those in power to obstruct the development of thought and suppress every new idea as heretical is a sin against the spirit. It is a sin which the German General Staff did not commit. One is amazed, in reading German military literature of the past twenty years, by the freedom with which German officers expounded their own opinions and discussed the theories of their superiors. The same liberty reigned in the military academies of the Soviet Union, where doctrinal controversy and dialectical exercises were encouraged. In France the narrow and reactionary policy of Weygand and Pétain caused every officer who did not subscribe completely to the official doctrine to be treated as a dangerous element and deprived of chances for advancement. In 1934 and 1935, when Pétain had reached the zenith of his power, the *Revue Militaire Française* published several articles which attempted to warn the High Command of the disadvantages of such conservatism and pointed out the merits of the new German and Russian methods. Such attempts were soon discouraged, as official favor was reserved for the admirers of Pétain and his ideas.

A young officer, Charles de Gaulle, then a commandant, who had been impressed by the German doctrines and driven to despair by the inertia of French leaders, tried to arouse the generals of the General Staff from their slumber by addressing the public directly. De Gaulle proposed a complete reform of the French military organization, the abandonment of the vast national army and of compulsory military service in favor of a small "professional army" of 100,000 highly trained men, equipped with modern matériel, and grouped in six motorized divisions, with important scouting units. De Gaulle developed his ideas first in the *Revue des Vivants,* a magazine directed by Senator Henry de Jouvenel, and later in his book, *Vers l'Armée de Métier.* The result was that De Gaulle was regarded as a revolutionary and his book as guilty of lese majesty. Only a few political men, notably Paul Reynaud, De Jouvenel, and Philippe Serre, were startled by De Gaulle's suggestions. They attempted to interest Marshal Pétain and the General Staff in these important, although debatable, ideas, only to be repulsed by a triple barrage—conservatism, old age, and hierarchic prejudice. On March 31, 1935, during debates on military credit appropriations in Parliament, Reynaud suggested to the Minister of War the creation of an "armored corps," consisting of armored divisions. General Maurin replied in one sentence: "France's plan of mobilization rests on the principle of defense." It was a definite rejection of De Gaulle's ideas.

The Irretrievable Delay

The attitude of the ministers of war, and particularly of Marshal Pétain, from 1934 to 1936 was all the more unpardonable as neither ministers nor their governments entertained any illusions about Hitler's intentions. More internationally-minded statesmen, partisans of the League of Nations and collective security, would have viewed the situation differently; they would have sought international solutions for the problem of French security. Neither Pétain nor Maurin had the slightest hope or desire for these solutions. It was the Doumergue cabinet, in which Pétain was Minister of War, which caused the closing of the Disarmament Conference by its diplomatic note of April 17, 1934. The note was issued against the advice of Foreign Minister Louis Barthou, the cabinet's champion of collective security, but upon the formal recommendation of Pétain. It put an abrupt end to all negotiations for disarmament and declared that France alone would attend to the needs of her defense. Pétain thus knew that no international agreement on armament limitations would ever be reached and that the armament race was on in

Europe. The normal thing, upon his return to his office after the cabinet meeting on April 17, would have been to summon his Chief of Staff, examine the means of reinforcing French defenses, and then ask Parliament for additional appropriations. Pétain did just the opposite. He refused to call a meeting of the Supreme War Council and declared, before the Military Committee of the Senate, that extension of the Maginot Line to the North Sea and fortification of the Sedan region were unnecessary. Whether it was stupidity or treason only history will decide.

If Pétain had no hope of disarmament in 1934, he should have had no illusions about the chances of France in the armament race. He could not have failed to realize that French industrial capacity never could compete with Germany's in building modern armaments, because it was in 1934 and 1935 that French economy disintegrated while German economy developed. Yet Pétain never opposed the economic and social policy of deflation which led to that disintegration. Furthermore, he could not expect France, if attacked by Germany, to be supported by Soviet Russia or England. He was a confirmed adversary of Russia—as a military leader, full of contempt for the Red Army, as a conservative, afraid of Communism. He always approved the foreign policy of Laval, which separated the cause of France from that of England. He thus faced quietly and calmly the prospect of France opposing alone Nazi Germany and Fascist Italy because he was blinded by his admiration for Hitler and Mussolini. As far back as 1932 he expressed this admiration, which equaled his disdain for England.

Henry Torrès in *La Machine Infernale,* a book about the activities of the Fifth Column in France, relates how he submitted to Pétain, then Minister of War, a dossier covering the activity of Mussolini's agents in the Alpes Maritimes region, whose representative he was. As this region borders on Italy, it was obviously Pétain's duty to launch inquiries and take the necessary measures. But Torrès found Pétain an unwilling listener.

"It is quite possible," Pétain said, "that the propaganda you speak of does not emanate from true Fascists, but is the work of anti-Fascists who, in their efforts to create division between us and Italy, will resort to ingenious stratagems; frankly, I should be surprised if the Fascist authorities know anything about it."

When Torrès continued, specifying and proving his allegations, Pétain answered: "I am more and more surprised. I cannot tell you how graciously, with what friendship and respect, I was received in the Italian capital. My wife, who accompanied me, was the object of the most exquisite attentions. Nowhere was her room decorated with better care and taste. Those are small details, but they reveal an attitude and a mentality. I am not a politician, M. Torrès, but for my part I have faith in Italy. We must avoid offending her and seeming to look for trouble. That is how I understand the French interest."

"Marshal Pétain," said Torrès, "I am here to inform you about something that regards you personally as the leader of our Army. Italian espionage is being intensified every day. Our means of protection are sadly inadequate.

Must I resort to interpellating the government and alarming the country?"

"By no means do that," said Pétain, "please, let's have no incidents."*

Of Pétain's admiration for Hitler's Germany many examples might be cited. Characteristic was his behavior toward Marshal Goering at the funeral of Marshal Pilsudski in 1935. Pétain, who represented France, showed himself so eager to please Goering that he had to be reminded discreetly of the proprieties demanded by his rank and function.

Thus, while the deflation policy of conservative cabinets was weakening French economy, Marshal Pétain and General Maurin disarmed France and Pierre Laval isolated her. It was as if Pétain, Laval, and the partisans of their policy had determined to allow France no alternative but co-operation with the Fascist nations and acceptance of a reorganization of Europe under Hitler's tutelage. From Hitler's viewpoint no French War Minister was better than Pétain.

Daladier's Efforts to Overcome the Errors of His Predecessors

It will not be difficult to show that Daladier was a better Minister of War than his predecessors.

Daladier's achievement in the domain of national defense cannot be denied. He could, indeed, pride himself at the Riom hearings of February, 1942, on the "intensity of my effort to ensure the French Army matériel that would be equal in quality and only slightly inferior in quantity to that of the German Army, despite Germany's great industrial superiority over France. . . . No Minister of War, no Premier, has ever devoted greater effort to national defense or has ever secured larger credits or more matériel for the French armies. I took the initiative in August, 1936, when I caused the adoption of an armament program unprecedented in our history. To assure its execution, to speed up French labor, I did not hesitate, as head of the government, to break by the force of law and civic action whatever resistance endangered public safety. . . . In September, 1939, and on May 10, 1940, the Army was equipped with such matériel as should have made possible a victorious resistance to the German offensive."

It is a fact, verifiable in the *Journal Officiel,* that only in 1936, under the Popular Front government, had France entered upon a rearmament effort comparable, although inferior, to that of Germany. From 1934 until the middle of 1936 France spent about 20 per cent less on her Army than in 1933. During the same period the German national defense budget was increased by 800 per cent. But during 1937-1938 the French war budget was increased 110 per cent, while the German budget rose only 22 per cent. In 1939 France increased her budget another 20 per cent, but Germany raised hers only 10 per cent. All the witnesses at Riom admitted that until 1936 no attempt at rearmament was made in France, that not a single armament pro-

* Henry Torres, *La Machine Infernale* (New York: Brentano's, 1942).

gram was approved by the General Staff nor put into action by the Minister of War.

Next must be emphasized the impact of the 1934-1936 period on the 1936-1939 period. The policy of Marshal Pétain and General Maurin gave Germany a priceless advantage. France never could hope to retrieve in the armament race the time she had lost. Germany had launched her rearmament effort as early as 1933 and systematically pursued it for six years before her assault on the world. Launching her program in 1936, France had only three years instead of six. With French industrial inferiority, three years was not enough to turn out modern armaments, create a new war industry, build new plants, and obtain adequate machinery. Modern mass production cannot be improvised. The lack of equipment in 1939-1940 was partly due to lack of production in 1934-1935, but mostly it was due to past inertia, inertia that prevented truly large-scale production in 1937 and 1938. As Daladier said, answering a question of the Prosecuting Attorney at the hearing of February 28, 1942: "You need time to make cannon. No country can do without time. Three years of research and tests is necessary for the construction of one large caliber cannon; after that, another fifteen or eighteen months is required before any mass production of cannon may be launched. That explains the present situation in the Pacific." This is particularly true if we remember the French economic situation. When Daladier entered the Ministry of War in 1936, he found the country not only lacking in modern matériel, armament programs, and cannon and tank models for speedy mass production, but also suffering from a disintegrating economy, ill-equipped factories, extinguished blast furnaces, and a shortage of specialists, whom the depression had ruined and dispersed.

Finally, the singularly difficult conditions under which Daladier had to work must be remembered. It was obvious that his policy would have to be the reverse of Marshal Pétain's. Yet the Marshal was still connected with the Ministry of War; vexed and irritated, already a partisan of Fascism, he was ready to adopt a critical and negative attitude toward everything, and to lay snares, wherever possible, in the path of his successor. Pétain's influence on the officers and on the General Staff was very strong. For twenty years not a single important appointment in the Army had been made without his approval and signature. He had been able to place his friends and satellites in all departments, in commanding and controlling positions. As Minister of War in the Doumergue cabinet, he ceased to be merely a military figure; he became a political personality. He declared himself an enemy of the Popular Front, an admirer of Fascism and, after the outbreak of the Spanish Civil War, he prided himself on his friendship with General Franco. He naturally became the center of all the intrigues which grew up within the French Army against the republican government. From 1934 on, he was cited by conservative and Fascist newspapers as the "providential man," the "eventual savior," to whom the country would rally in an emergency. As early as 1936 they spoke of him as the devoted father and loyal patriot, a legend which his followers exploited until 1940, when it became evident that the devoted father was sending his sons to concentration camps and that the loyal patriot was delivering his Communist—or so-called Communist—fellow countrymen to the Gestapo for execution. Pétain rallied all the malcontent and demagogical opponents of the republican regime in the Army. Despite the precautions of President Caous, the Riom proceedings exposed a few of the intrigues to which Daladier was subjected. The hearing of March 25, 1942, brought up the case of General Gerodias, one of the ablest officers of the French Army, who fell into a trap of Fascist propaganda. In 1936 he had been General Gamelin's assistant chief. One day an officer handed him a report on the Spanish war from a high military authority, and asked him to circulate it among the officers. General Gerodias found the report interesting and had copies distributed among the troops. The Ministry of War soon realized that the report was a medium for propaganda most dangerous to the morale of the Army. In reality, it was a political pamphlet based on false information; it attempted to show that Franco's officers had been compelled to revolt for the sake of their own and their families' safety to save the country from "Bolshevism." It was the glorification of the revolt of the military, of the "patriots and champions of order" as against the Popular Front, the "forerunners of the Revolution." Circulated in the name of the General Staff, the report had the character of an official warning.

"You cannot imagine," said Daladier at Riom, "what panic it caused among the French officers. They lived in constant fear of seeing their barracks invaded; they slept with loaded revolvers beside their beds, expecting at every moment to be attacked by their own men. The report in question was subsequently published by a newspaper of the extreme Right, l'Echo de Paris, and its publication produced the same effect throughout the country." At Riom General Gerodias admitted, with great honesty, that he had been the victim of a maneuver intended to demoralize the officers. "Who was the officer who handed you this report?" asked President Caous. General Gerodias, according to the correspondent of the New York Times, created a sensation with the reluctant answer, "I received it from an officer who, at that time, was attached to the staff of Marshal Pétain."

This officer was Commandant Loustaleau-Lacau, who was not merely a member of Pétain's special staff, he was his private secretary, his homme de confiance and political associate. In 1940 he became the head of the Legion, a Fascist organization that attempted to make itself the French equivalent of the Rumanian Iron Guard, the Italian Blackshirts, and the Spanish Falange. In 1937 he was one of the leaders of the Cagoule.

The Cagoulard affair was significant in more ways than one. The conspirators had organized an army prepared for civil war. In addition, they were working hand in hand with foreign Fascist powers. The investigation revealed that the larger part of their arms came from Germany or Italy, and that several acts of organized railroad sabotage, the bombings of planes and aviation matériel, and the attack on a Spanish submarine that had taken refuge in a French harbor, were in direct response to orders from Franco. Moreover, the Cagoulards had numerous accomplices in the Army, Navy, and Air Force.

Their scheme strongly resembled the strategy that had permitted Franco, with the aid of Italy and Germany, to launch the Spanish Civil War. Everything indicated that the Cagoulards aimed to establish a military dictatorship in France, and the investigation had reached the point where, to discover the ringleader, it was necessary to question Marshal Pétain and inquire into his political activities. In fact, all the threads of the plot led to Pétain's friends, associates, and immediate entourage. In view of Pétain's rank and personality, the question of whether to pursue the investigation became a problem of general policy which had to be solved by the cabinet.

I have a particularly clear recollection of the Cagoulard affair because of its ramifications in the Air Force and the steps I had to take against certain officers. I had several occasions to discuss the legal and political aspects of the matter with Minister of the Interior Dormoy, who was in charge of police investigations, with Minister of Justice Auriol, and with Minister of National Defense Daladier. We were all aware of the extent of Fascist propaganda in the Army and we knew the sentiments of Pétain; nevertheless, we were stupefied to learn that he might be connected with the Cagoule. The problem was brought before a cabinet meeting and the resulting discussion was the most dramatic and moving I witnessed since the meetings before and after the 6th of February, 1934. Two theories clashed. With Dormoy, Blum, Zay, and several other ministers (whose names I must withhold to prevent Hitler's or Pétain's vengeance), I was in favor of a complete investigation, in which justice was to take its course and Pétain, if the evidence warranted, was to be indicted. The President of the Republic and the Premier, Chautemps, held the opposite view; they were seconded by Daladier, who pointed out that indictment, should it occur, would create a turmoil in the country and the Army. "I am responsible for the nation's defense and for the morale of the Army," he said, "and I cannot permit the prosecution of a Marshal of France, the hero of Verdun, for a plot against the safety of the state—in other words, for treason." He added that if the cabinet decided differently, he would have to resign. By a majority vote the cabinet decided to support Daladier, who was to call in Pétain and appeal to his sense of honor and patriotism. As we left the meeting, I stopped to talk with Daladier.

"You are wrong," I said. "You know better than anyone else that Pétain is not to be trusted."

I can still see him as he stopped and, putting a hand on my shoulder, looked at me fixedly with his blue eyes. "I believe you are right," he said, using the familiar tu, with him always a sign of emotion, "but I could not do anything else. Pétain is almost eighty and no longer quite responsible for his actions. He is still the banner of the Army. And yet, at his age, he is just a toy in the hands of the Fascists." I felt that he was shaken by his own decision and already had begun to regret it.

This incident is mentioned not as an anecdote of French governmental life, but rather as an indication of the conditions under which Daladier was forced to work. I have never known a more sincerely patriotic man than Daladier; he had a truly Jacobin conception of patriotism. France to him was a physical and a moral personality; he loved her for her landscapes as well as for her traditions. His task was heavy: he had to mend the errors of his predecessors, to make up for their inertia; he had to shake out of its torpor a General Staff which still lived in 1918; he had to fight administrative red tape and industrial difficulties obstructing rearmament. And while he was thus working for the security of the country, he found intrigue and treason in his own house, under the banner of a French Marshal. Directly or through the officers of his entourage, Pétain intrigued constantly against the Minister of National Defense, whose efforts he should have supported as a subordinate and a French patriot. That Daladier could succeed in carrying out his program despite these obstacles is perhaps the highest praise that can be bestowed on him.

What specific accusations were brought against Daladier by the Vichy government at Riom? And what remained of those accusations after the witnesses had been heard?

MILITARY MORALE

If Vichy counted on the Riom trial to confirm the legend of the demoralization of the country under the Popular Front and of the Army under Daladier, it was sadly disappointed. Not a single witness could be found to support it. Instead, the testimony proved that the morale and the courage of the soldiers of 1939-1940 were worthy of their predecessors of 1914-1918.

Morale of the Troops

The hearings demolished the thesis that the Popular Front had caused the moral disintegration of the French people and left them incapable of fighting a war and resisting the German armies. It was a legend carefully circulated by Vichy to justify its abdication and the behavior of the officers. The testimony given on this point deserves keen analysis. The most valuable depositions were not so much those of the high officers, whose judgment relied on the accounts of their subordinates, but rather those of the commanders of small units who could speak from direct personal experience.

Several of the witnesses—notably among commanders of armies or army corps—had been influenced by Vichy propaganda; yet a sense of honor forbade them to perjure themselves, and their testimony may be summarized as follows: We have been told that the morale of the troops left much to be desired; the troops under our command, however, were excellent and fought in exemplary fashion. This was the gist of the testimony given by Generals Besson and Blanchard on March 17, 1942. Similarly, General Lenclud spoke of the ill effects of the "revolutionary agitation of the years 1936 and 1937"—whose causes he obviously had not analyzed—but when asked how his troops had stood up in actual combat, he declared that they had been admirable and that he had nothing but praise for their courage and spirit.

Other witnesses limited themselves to accounts of what they had seen, without encumbering their testimony with general comments. "The spirit of the troops was as good as in 1914," was the testimony on March 25 of General Gerodias, who had commanded a division of Alpine troops. "The conduct of the elite troops who served in the armored divisions was admirable," said General Martin on March 31. "The men were fully confident of succeeding, which was perhaps not true of the entire Army," he said, pointing his remark at the General Staff officers who had lacked such confidence. "Those people who, before the war, maintained that things were going badly were mistaken," said General Préaud, former Commander of Saint-Cyr; "from the beginning of the war, the morale of the troops was excellent." Even Generals Conquet, Mittelhauser, Sicard, and De la Porte du Thiel (leader of the Vichy-organized *Chantiers de la Jeunesse*), Colonels Ragaine and Perré— all those who actually led the French soldiers into combat—were full of praise for the "bravery," the "courage," the "pluck," and the "unreserved loyalty" of their men.

At the hearing of March 25 General Andray, the commander of the French troops at Dunkerque, gave a picture of the French soldier which, according to the correspondent of the *Neue Zürcher Zeitung,* confirmed and summed up the statements of the other witnesses: "The French soldier is not without his faults; he is not very fond of discipline and likes to complain; the military spirit, properly speaking, has waned since the last war. But when the time comes to fight, the Frenchman is incomparable; he becomes a warrior capable of every sacrifice. He is a soldier rather than a military man, but as regards courage and self-abnegation, there is nothing you cannot ask of him." Here is the very definition of the citizen soldiers of the French Revolution, the *soldats en sabots* whose valor aroused the enthusiasm of Goethe; the very definition of the *grognards*—the veterans of the Napoleonic wars—and of the soldiers who in 1916—at Verdun—supplied the laurels on which Marshal Pétain was to rest for so long. The soldier of 1939-1940 was worthy of his ancestry.

Among all the eulogies bestowed on the French soldiers of 1939, I should like to mention for their particular importance those of Colonel de Moustier and of General François.

It was inevitable that Colonel de Moustier should be called to the stand. Commander of a tank regiment during the war, he had been in peacetime a deputy of the extreme Right, a fanatic nationalist and outspoken enemy of the Popular Front. He was expected to testify to the demoralization of the troops by the Popular Front. Instead, at the session of March 17, he gave unreserved praise to the "courage and confidence of his men" and concluded by saying that "the outcome of the war could have been different if the soldiers had been better commanded." This was the contention of Daladier, to whose patriotism Colonel de Moustier paid homage when he declared: "I am a man of the extreme Right, a political opponent of Daladier. In Parliament I represent a frontier region, the Department of Doubs, where before 1936 no defenses had ever been constructed. I informed Daladier of the deficiencies in our defenses and he immediately took the steps which the situation demanded." Marshal Pétain had failed to fortify the gap in the Jura mountains, just as he had opposed the fortifications of the Ardennes pass, and Daladier had remedied the mistake.

The testimony of General François was awaited with no less impatience. The Council of Political Justice had accused Daladier of having "offered facilities to foreign invasion in peacetime, chiefly through the admission to French soil of hundreds of thousands of dangerous Spaniards and their leaders." During the war, these "dangerous Spaniards and their leaders" had fought in the ranks of the Foreign Legion, in which General François had commanded a mixed division of Colonial troops and Legion volunteers. It could be hoped that he would confirm the "clear, complete, and perfectly motivated" conclusions of the Council of Political Justice. However, on March 18, after declaring that "his Morocco troops had been above all praise," General François added that they had been surpassed in courage only by the "Legion troops which, even after a heavy battle, had stormed to the front to continue fighting rather than obey the order to retreat." In fact, the "Red" Spaniards, the "bad characters," fought like lions in the 21st, 22nd, and 23rd regiments of the Foreign Volunteers; 9,000 men went into battle and fewer than 500 returned; their valor aroused the admiration of their French commanding officers.

What had become of the accusations of the Vichy government? An Army that could command such praise on the part of the generals who had led it into battle was hardly one corrupted by politics and demoralized by anti-patriotic propaganda. There were, it is true, certain rotten elements, but the whole was sound, because the French people were sound. And whenever the High Command's orders permitted French troops to measure themselves against the enemy, they were not only courageous but successful, even after an initial disadvantage. When they retired, it was, in most instances, because they had been ordered to do so, or because the blunders of the High Command had caused them to be outnumbered one to twenty. General Mittelhauser in his testimony described the resistance of his Alpine Army, which, at the outbreak of the war, had been thirteen divisions strong, but which had been reduced to six divisions by General Weygand; it had been attacked by twenty Italian divisions and, in the rear, by German troops sweeping down the Rhône valley. "The German and Italian divisions," said General Mittelhauser, "had arranged to meet at Chambéry and at Grenoble, but they never succeeded in taking these towns; they were so successfully repulsed by the Alpine Army that the latter was gaining the offensive against the Italians, when it received orders to cease fighting because the government had signed the armistice." The Pétain government thus forced the Alpine Army to surrender to the Italian generals, whom it had defeated despite vast numerical odds and German aid. No, the Popular Front had not made cowards of the French people; but those who signed the armistice and stopped the war were not the men of the Popular Front.

Had the proceedings not been interrupted, witnesses for the defense would have confirmed the impression created by the witnesses for the prosecution. There would have been accounts of the soldiers who were sent to Norway, and of the troops on the Maginot Line, who continued fighting for several days after the armistice, disregarding the orders of Pétain and Weygand. Not all the soldiers showed equal courage, for no army in the world is composed of heroes alone. But the witnesses for the prosecution, in speaking of the causes which in some instances had brought about a lowering of morale, did not once incriminate Daladier or the ministers of the Popular Front; all accused the General Staff, with its methods of training and instruction and its operational orders. General Blanchard, while praising his soldiers, declared that the morale of the troops had been lower in May, 1940, "when the moment came for the test, than in September, 1939, at the time of mobilization." He blamed the long period of inaction during the winter of 1939-1940, indicating morale had been endangered more by the influence of the General Staff and its officers during those eight months than by several years of Popular Front rule. According to the testimony of General Conquet, "the Army, though brave, was badly equipped for modern warfare; its officers lacked the necessary instruction; the Army had not been sufficiently trained for co-operation with the Air Force." Other witnesses complained of inadequate training, particularly for noncommissioned reserve officers. All these were obviously the responsibilities of the High Command and the General Staff rather than of the Minister of War.

Finally, General Lenclud declared that "the severest blow to the morale of the French Army had been the order of October, 1939, at the end of the Polish campaign, to fall back to the Maginot Line," after having reached the forest of Waarndt on the way to Saarbrücken in the first month of the war. "The soldiers had been told," said General Lenclud, "that the September offensive was intended to permit the Alsatians to return to the villages they had been forced to leave. The offensive had been costly and the losses great. When the order came to abandon the positions gained, the troops did not understand; they felt senselessly sacrificed." Already some of the troops may have wondered whether the General Staff, responsible for these operations, was composed of Fascists or of incompetents.

Among the various statements on the morale of the troops, two are particularly worth quoting. They do not allude to the responsibility of Popular Front ministers, but to politics in general.

I have already mentioned the first: General Lenclud in his testimony complained of the effect on the soldiers' morale of "the revolutionary agitation of the years 1936 and 1937." But in view of the homage he paid to the conduct of his men in battle, we may conclude that the "revolutionary" policy practiced two years before the war had not affected the fighting mettle of the French soldier.

Similarly, the second allusion to French political life was more significant for certain conclusions it suggested than for the facts it established. General Requin, Commander of the Army of the Vosges, complained of Communist propaganda. According to his testimony, there existed in his army some Communist cells, "although not very numerous." He "had been forced to contemplate certain measures in the event that mutinies should take place." As there were no mutinies, the "contemplated measures" were never enforced and the testimony of General Requin lost its interest. Questioned by President Caous, General Requin declared that before the war he had been forced to take steps against "revolutionary propaganda," but he hastened to add that whatever sanctions he had imposed had always been approved by Daladier. General Requin's testimony, therefore, furnished no incriminating evidence against either Daladier or the Popular Front government. The truth was that the Communists fought as well as anybody—and a great deal better than the Fascists. If Communist propaganda had really affected the morale of the troops, its effects would have permeated the entire front and undoubtedly would have been mentioned by the other witnesses.

The testimony of General Requin reminds me of an incident that revealed the way in which certain military leaders received, or even provoked, the charges of Communist activity. Before the war, the commander of each unit had to issue an annual report on the morale of his troops. In December, 1936, Colonel Delattre de Tassigny—later General de Tassigny, who fought so brilliantly during the war and who revolted against the total occupation by Germany in December, 1942—was commander of an infantry regiment garrisoned at Metz. He had been Weygand's collaborator in 1932-1936, and, although he advocated the Franco-Soviet alliance for reasons that bespeak his vision and patriotism, he could not be suspected of sympathy with the Popular Front. His regiment was largely recruited from workers in and around Paris, many of whom were Communists; their morale and discipline were exemplary and Colonel de Tassigny said so in his report. Immediately afterward he was summoned to the Ministry of War and told: "Your report is incomplete; you have forgotten to point out the 'revolutionary propaganda' of the Communist workers."

"But I have no such propaganda in my regiment," replied De Tassigny. "The morale of my men could not be better."

"I want you to understand," his interviewer went on, "that there is always some revolutionary agitation to report. Many of your soldiers come from the 'Red' districts of Paris and we need a few facts on revolutionary propaganda."

"Even if there are none?"

"There always are. Look at what is happening in Spain. Don't be stubborn, take your report and return it to us amended." Colonel de Tassigny refused. The story was told to me by General Bourret, Commander of the Alsatian Army during the war, and was confirmed later by De Tassigny. It shows that as early as 1936 certain high officers of the General Staff were busily fabricating dossiers to establish that the "revolutionary propaganda" of the Communist party had corrupted the morale of the Army—just as, forty years before, their predecessors had forged documents that were to prove the "treason" of Captain Dreyfus.

The witnesses proved that the morale of the Army was satisfactory. This justifies the conclusion that the Popular Front exercised no demoralizing influence on the Army and that Daladier did not commit a "crime" when he admitted the refugee soldiers of the Spanish Republican Army.

The Fascist Officers

The discussion of Army morale would not be complete without reference to the attitude of the Fascist officers.

Had the defense witnesses been allowed to speak, they easily would have proved that Fascist propaganda had had a devastating effect on both active and reserve officers. It influenced their behavior when confronted with the enemy, and it partly explains why the French soldiers, General Andrey's "incomparable warriors," lacked the leaders and staff they deserved in the crucial months of May and June, 1940.

The French people know, and every war correspondent has confirmed, that while the majority of active officers showed great courage, many reserve officers did not live up to their task. Incapable of inspiring their men in actual battle or of taking the independent action that a specific local situation demanded, they were far too often ready to yield, instead of encouraging their troops to resist even an equal opponent. The French reserve officers, both in quality and moral stamina, could not compare with the German reserve officers.

How are we to explain that difference? During 1914-1918 the French troop officer had been equal, or superior, to the German; the battle of Verdun was won not so much by the orders of Marshal Pétain as by the courage of platoon leaders, company and battery commanders, who resisted valiantly and under the most devastating attacks preferred to die on the spot with their men rather than yield the few feet of ground that had been entrusted to them. Even if we take into account the disadvantages of the French officer of 1940, the inadequate training he had received from a lazy and ill-informed General Staff, even if we consider the element of surprise at German methods of warfare for which the ignorance of his superiors had left him unprepared, and if we make allowance for the fanaticism which spurred the German officer to super-human effort, the deterioration of the French officer since the first World War still remains difficult to understand.

The only plausible and satisfactory explanation for this phenomenon is a political one: a large number of French reserve officers, either by outspoken sympathy or through anti-democratic bias, were Fascists.

I am not implying that the Fascist regime breeds softness and cowardice. We hardly need the example of Germany to teach us that Fascism relies on the fanaticism which drives men to sacrifice their lives. But the French Fascists were not engaged in a fight *for* Fascism; they were expected to fight *against* Fascism and for a democracy they despised. Their situation was very different from that of the French reserve officers of 1914-1918 or that of the German reserve officers of 1940; their heart was not in the war they had been ordered to fight. They were not less brave than the Germans. But two men of equal courage, whether Fascist or not, will fight differently according to the conviction of each that the cause for which he is fighting is a just one. The French officers thought with Marcel Déat that they ought not to "die for Danzig"; they believed with Pierre Laval that "France had declared war on Germany"; and they repeated with General Weygand that "France had been steered into another war because the interest of the Anglo-Saxon powers had won over that of the French." They believed it all, because their daily papers never ceased to repeat or at least to imply it. They detested Hitler as the leader of a Germany whose strength they feared, but secretly they admired him and envied the German people their political regime. Although their love for France took precedence over political convictions, they hated their democratic government, which represented the French people. Realizing that France was fighting a Nazi Germany, they still clung to their old belief that the true enemies of France were the "Bolshevists" and fervently hoped that it all would end in a war of the "civilized powers" against Communism. Fascist propaganda had developed in them a hidden and generalized moral opposition to any war against Italy, Spain, or Germany.

Much of this was explained to me in May, 1940, by Colonel Jean Vautrin, a member of the General Staff and one of the ablest officers of the French Army, who escaped from France in 1943 and joined the forces of General de Gaulle. He had been commissioned by General Headquarters to make the first inquiry into the reasons for the weak resistance of the French troops at Sedan and had been struck by the bad conduct of the reserve officers. I asked him what he thought was the cause of this and he explained: "When officers have lived together for eight months with no intellectual food other than reading *l'Action Française, Je Suis Partout,* and *Gringoire,* it is not surprising that each one, when the time comes for him to do his duty, has a moment's hesitation. Add up all those moments, and you will understand why so many of the officers were the first to retreat, without blowing up the bridges or firing a shot. They were corrupted by Fascist propaganda." I did not feel it necessary to point out to him that the newspapers he had just named had supported Pierre Laval, praised Marshal Pétain, and covered the Popular Front ministers with calumnies and insults.

I changed the conversation to another aspect of the question, the attitude of General Corap, a commander in charge of troops defending a particularly dangerous sector. "The man is either an imbecile or a traitor," said Vautrin, "or, more likely, an imbecile *and* a traitor." General Corap, a militant member of l'Action Française, was stationed in Morocco shortly before the war but proved so mediocre that General Noguès asked to have him transferred. There is only one explanation for allowing the career of such an incompetent man to continue: his government's fear that, by refusing him the usual advancement, it might seem to be discriminating against him for his political views. It was this curious scruple, born of an old tradition of liberal courtesy, which caused a man wholly unfit for the responsibility, to be placed at the head of an army. This sort of courtesy was the antithesis of the harshness necessary for the struggle against Fascism.

There were so many Fascists among the French reserve officers because they were, in general, recruited from among the young bourgeois; they were students and engineers, lawyers, and businessmen. The French bourgeoisie, as we know, tended more toward Fascism than any other section of the nation. Furthermore, the Fascist organizations, in particular the Croix de Feu, had systematically disseminated their propaganda among the reserve officers as they counted for their assumption of power on the general mobilization that would place their members in commanding positions. Finally, the leaders on the General Staff, who had been exposed for a long time to the clerical and reactionary influence of Weygand and Pétain, ousted, wherever possible, the "republican reserve officers." For these reasons the Fascist reserve officer had come to be the rule, and the republican officer the exception. This had been apparent since the 6th of February, 1934, when groups of reserve officers had indulged in political manifestations that were clearly Fascist.

Deplorable also, from a professional as well as from a political viewpoint, was the recruiting of reserve officers from the upper classes. Reserve officers usually became troop officers (commanders of platoons, companies, etc.), and as such had to be good teachers as well as leaders; but to train and guide men successfully, one has to know them, to feel and think like them, to share their pleasures, regrets, and memories. For that reason, the best reserve officers always have been the small businessman, the village notary, the factory foreman, the trade-union secretary, or the official whose professional life centers in a modest community. But such popular, democratic recruitment from the ranks of the petite bourgeoisie was not to the taste of men like Weygand and Pétain; they wanted "men of the world." As a result, France was defeated.

The Army of the French Revolution had established the military reputation of France. The democratic Army of 1914 had amazed the world by its bravery and sacrifice. The Fascist officers of 1940 were worthy neither of their predecessors nor of their men.

Politics in the Army

Had Daladier been accused of failing to purge the Army of its Fascists, he would have been forced to plead guilty. But when the Vichy government undertook to prove that Daladier had demoralized the Army by his political prejudices, there was not a single witness who supported the charge.

According to the Council of Political Justice, Daladier had "morally disarmed France . . . by his criminal submission to political influences and his inefficiency with respect to the moral support of the Army in peace and war." The witnesses corrected this accusation by testifying to the high morale of the troops. And on April 1, 1942, General Stehlé, the former Director of Infantry in the Ministry of War, flatly denied all allegations of the Council: "There has been talk of political influence. I hereby emphatically protest against any insinuation which might convey the impression that politics had entered into the Army; it is a duty which I owe to my Minister." To appreciate the implications of General Stehlé's statement, we must relate it to the incident described by General Gerodias at the hearing of March 25 and to the statement of Colonel Vautrin. The Fascists, not the partisans of the Popular Front, tried to break the morale of both the French Army and the people. Daladier not only did not inject "politics" into the Army, but he made every effort to exclude it and to restore to the Army its national and popular character. When the Popular Front insisted on the necessity of purging the Army of its Fascist officers, it was to improve and not to weaken the morale of the rank and file. Witnesses and documents proved that the French Army was weak because it had Fascist officers and not because it had Popular Front privates. To be sure, democratic France did not have Germany's army of fanatics, ready for every act of courage and for every crime, with blind obedience and disregard for the individual. Democracy develops not the military but the civic spirit. The soldier of the Third Republic was a citizen, not a slave; he was the heir of the heroes of the French Revolution. Beneath his uniform he remained a man, capable of understanding, judgment, and devotion; he was not the tool of an ambitious dictator, but the son of liberty.

To do them full justice, let us remember that the vast majority of those courageous and disciplined men, who were so much braver than their officers, were real democrats, partisans of the Popular Front and faithful to its ideals.

THE STATUS OF MATÉRIEL

Most of the generals who commanded armies in the field complained of the inadequacy of war matériel at their disposal. Only General Gerodias declared that his troops possessed sufficient equipment to repulse the enemy's attacks. Most witnesses insisted there was a shortage of tanks, cannon and particularly, aircraft. From there to the charge that the Popular Front ministers had failed to supply the Army with the necessary arms was only one step. The conclusion was drawn by Marshal Pétain and his Council of Political Justice even before the beginning of the public hearings.

The question is obviously far more complex. If the Vichy government merely wanted to prove that Germany, a large industrial nation under a totalitarian regime, was able to muster on the battle front more divisions and matériel than France, with her smaller industry and population and her democratic prerogatives, there was no need for a political trial; a few statistics would have been enough. To establish the exclusive responsibility of the ministers of the Popular Front for the inadequacy of French matériel required some work of minute deliberation. Before passing judgment, one had to know what advice the ministers had received from their military advisers, what information they had on the power and preparedness of the Reichswehr, what operational plans had been prepared by the General Staff, and what armament programs were appended to such plans; in short, who had done his duty and who had not.

To determine this, it was first necessary to take into consideration French industrial capacity—the measure and limit of French armament.

Let us suppose that everybody, from Blum to Pétain and from Daladier to Gamelin, had done his duty after June 6, 1936. Even then, it would have been folly to hope that France could match the number of German divisions and German equipment. "God is with the stronger battalions," said Napoleon; were he alive today, he would add, "and with the larger factories." The French battalions and factories, for reasons so basic that neither three nor even twenty years would have changed them, could not approximate the German battalions and factories. France lacked both the human and the material resources of Germany. It is easy to ascertain what human resources were available for the war effort. The last statistical data published go up to December, 1937, in Germany and to March 8, 1936, in France. At that time, Germany—with Austria—had 17,580,000 men between fifteen and forty years of age, while France had only 8,630,000 (with the proportion of females substantially the same as the male population in both countries). France had half Germany's manpower for her factories and Army. Granting that France was able to recruit in her Colonies approximately one million Colonial soldiers and half a million workers, the French forces could, under the best of conditions, have reached only 65 per cent of Germany's manpower.

Even more serious was the problem of the comparative industrial capacity of the two countries. Here the figures are somewhat more difficult to obtain, but may be arrived at by either of two methods. We may take as a basis the study made in 1935 by the German *Institut für Konjunkturforschung;* if we correct the coefficient given by the *Institut* to take into account the changes of subsequent years, (such as differences in labor supply, variations in the indices of production and unemployment), we find that the productive capacity of the German factories during the period 1936-1939 was approximatively three times that of the French. We arrive at the same conclusions if we compare the output of the most essential raw materials for armament production, as seen in the table below. It may be argued that France could have constructed new machinery and equipped new factories; and, indeed, she did. But Germany, too, was building factories in large numbers. Moreover, if

TOTAL PRODUCTION FOR THE YEARS 1934-1939 IN THOUSANDS OF METRIC TONS[1]

	France	Germany[2]	Ratio
Steel	39,000	119,000	1:3.0
Aluminum	209	711	1:3.4
Coal	229,000	788,000	1:3.4

[1]Source: *Statistical Yearbook of the League of Nations.* Production in 1939, for which no figures are known, has been assumed to equal that of 1938.
[2]Germany, including Austria, but not Czechoslovakia.

France had utilized more of her industrial capacity for the building of new plants, she would have had to do it at the expense of her armament production, under the limitations of her supply of labor, energy, and steel. There is no denying that France's maximum capacity for the production of armaments was one-third that of Germany's.

If France had engaged in as strenuous a war effort as Germany, allotting to her factories and Army the same percentage of total manpower and equipment, she could still not have hoped to muster more than 65 divisions (Colonial troops included) for every hundred German divisions, nor more than one gun, one plane, and one tank for every three guns, planes, and tanks of the enemy. This ratio does not apply to the matériel left over from the war of 1914-1918, but only to modern equipment.

Two French to three German divisions, one tank to three, was all that could be accomplished. Under such conditions, it was evidently impossible to pass to the offensive. Yet, with the aid of Britain's small Army and the powerful Royal Air Force, it would have been possible to offer fierce resistance, and to make the invasion of France a costly and thankless undertaking, by falling back step by step toward southern France and North Africa and leaving the invaders nothing but blown-up railroads and bridges, filled-in springs and "scorched earth." The Germans would have been compelled to pursue the French Army to Africa, and the crossing of the Mediterrarean controlled by the French and British Navies would have been a far more difficult proposition than the crossing of the Meuse River. France would have lost a battle and her metropolitan territory, but an Allied victory would have been ensured by her sacrifice.

The above proportions must be borne in mind to appraise justly the responsibility of the Popular Front ministers and the ethical level of the Riom trial. It will be seen that, generally speaking, French armament as a whole was one-third that of Germany's, both at the outbreak of the war in September, 1939, and at the beginning of the German offensive of May, 1940. The ministers of the Popular Front, and particularly Daladier, had utilized the human and material resources at their disposal as competently as Germany had used her resources.

Before reaching definite conclusions, the Riom Court had a second problem to consider: repartition of armaments.

The amount of armament produced and the amount actually at the disposal of the troops during May and June, 1940, were not necessarily the same. Through stupidity or treason, only part of the available troops and matériel was thrown into battle. During the winter of 1939-40 General Weygand, Commander-in-Chief of the French troops in Syria, had requested and received additional divisions and modern equipment to enable him to attack Soviet Russia should the occasion arise; a considerable army was being maintained in North Africa and at the Italian frontier in the Alps and some troops had been sent to Norway; guns, tanks, planes, and equipment for twenty divisions were being kept in munition dumps and depots, either by mistake or by Fascist plotting, instead of being allotted to the combatant units in the decisive hour of the battle. Marshal Pétain and General Weygand decided in June, 1940, not to throw all their force into the battle against Germany, thereby gaining an instrument for their coup d'état under pretext of saving for the government "the means of ensuring order and forestalling the Revolution." The inevitable result was that two divisions of French soldiers— "incomparable warriors," not supermen—had to face not three, but five German divisions, and there were five German tanks and six planes to every French tank or plane. Conditions made the defeat inevitable. Obviously no responsibility of Blum's was involved in this situation, for Blum had not been a member of the government since 1938; nor could any blame fall on Daladier, for the direction of military operations was solely a matter for the General Staff. The authors of these errors and betrayals emerged as those truly guilty of the defeat of France—the generals who issued unwise orders and the friends of Germany who first inspired and later benefited by those orders.

If the judges of the Supreme Court had been free and unbiased, the case against the Popular Front ministers could have been clearly formulated and easily resolved. The first question would have been whether the governments of the Popular Front and of Daladier had succeeded in supplying the Army with matériel equal to one-third of the German war equipment; if they had, their responsibility would automatically have been excluded. The next question would have been whether the matériel thus produced met the requirements of modern warfare; if it did not, the succeeding step would have been to investigate whether this was because of the General Staff's failure to request in good time the necessary equipment, or whether the cabinet had let political considerations prevail over technical decisions. The final question would have been whether the matériel requested by the military authorities and produced by the Minister of National Defense had actually reached the French soldier; a negative answer would have led to an investigation into the nature of the orders, the errors, and the treachery which caused this vital equipment to be diverted from its legitimate destination.

Daladier a Match for Goering

The trial revealed that Daladier was as capable and as successful as Goering. The comparative strength of the French and the German Armies in 1939-1940 is explained by circumstances which have nothing whatever to do with the competence or intelligence of either Daladier or Goering, or with any difference between National Socialism and the Popular Front in their capacity to prepare for war. The difference in power between the German and the French Armies was the reflection of profound differences in the economy, size, and structure of the two countries and in the strategy of their General Staffs.

This is made clear by the official communiqué of the Vichy government, dated February 20, 1942, in which an attempt was made to show "the inadequacy of French armament at the outbreak of the war and in May, 1940." Let us consider only the Army. At the beginning of the war, France had 110 divisions in the lines and 2,108 tanks; in May, 1940, she had 115 divisions in the lines and 3,000 tanks, to which must be added, in accordance with documents submitted to the Riom Court by Colonel Rivet, Chief of the Information Service, 369 tanks in North Africa. Germany had 120 to 130 divisions in the lines and approximately 4,000 tanks at the beginning of the war, as against 180 divisions and 7,000 to 8,000 tanks in May, 1940. Daladier thus had placed at the disposal of the General Staff about half the quantity of matériel that Goering was able to give the German Staff. Neither the Popular Front generally nor Daladier in particular can be held responsible for these fundamental differences in the human and economic resources of the two nations.

Daladier's achievement becomes all the more remarkable in light of the political and social difficulties and obstacles that were constantly raised by the opponents of the Popular Front government, and of the state of the French Army in June, 1936. The relatively high ratio of French to German armaments—it was one to two, as compared with a productive capacity of one to three—is explained by the fact that France had preserved considerable quantities of armaments, particularly Army equipment, from the first World War, whereas Germany had been forced to destroy her stocks in accordance with the military clauses of the Treaty of Versailles. With fewer rifles, machine guns, and trench mortars to produce than the Germans, French war industry was able to concentrate more heavily on the manufacture of tanks and anti-tank guns. The balance sheet of all the conditions with which Daladier had to cope in his effort to equip the French Army shows it was only by a combination of tenacity, patriotism, and vision that, within four years, he succeeded in mending the errors of his predecessors and forging a military instrument which, had it been more ably manipulated, would have permitted France to avoid defeat.

To forestall the threat that the proceedings might reveal Daladier's merits as general purveyor of war materials to the Army, the Vichy government, on the eve of the trial, made an attempt to deceive, not the judges, but public opinion at home and abroad by issuing the communiqué of February 20, 1942. Instead of publishing wrong figures and false documents as in the Dreyfus case, they preferred the crafty presentation of exact figures; they juxtaposed the total number of German divisions with the number of French divisions stationed in Europe, omitting the divisions and the equipment which had been deliberately left in North Africa and the Colonies; similarly, there appeared, opposite the figure for German planes of every category, the number of first-line planes of the French Army engaged on the northeastern front, excluding those in depots, in Syria, Morocco, Algiers, and on the Alpine frontier; and it was the same with all the other matériel which the troops had found so scarce.

On the day of the hearing, however, President Caous, refusing to take part in this malicious stratagem, gave Daladier permission to read aloud the official documents compiled jointly by the Ministry of War (Colonel Rivet) and the Ministry of Aviation (General Redempt, Director of Military Matériel). It was learned that France had approximately 4,000 tanks (French and British) in May, 1940, and more than 6,000 planes at the time of the armistice—more matériel than the German Army had utilized to defeat the French. The witnesses then confirmed that Daladier had provided the Army with matériel amounting roughly to 50 per cent of the equipment of the German Army. Nobody could have done more. Daladier, in comparison with Goering, was in the position of an industrialist with half the number of workers and one-third the machine tools and capital, who earns great merit by producing half as much as his rival.

The witnesses heard at Riom were unanimous in praising the quality of French war matériel. These men had used, or at least had seen, the matériel in actual battle, having commanded troops or inspected units in action; their testimony was consequently of the greatest value. In all the armies of the world, the men who handle war matériel frequently blame its deficiencies on the technical services. Nevertheless, all the officers who appeared before the Supreme Court lauded the equipment. Generals Langlois, Martin, and Keller, and Colonels Ragaine and Perré pronounced the French tanks superior to the German. According to General Martin, the Germans soon realized their own disadvantage and avoided battle even when they had numerical superiority (hearing of March 31, 1942). The German tank forces defeated the French only by superior strategy. At the hearing of March 17 General Blanchard, who commanded the Northern armies, which included five armored divisions, stated: "The matériel was so excellent and the men so courageous that the front was never broken. It was only because I found my flank exposed that I was forced to retreat. . . . " And because President Caous insisted, he added: "At first, we had the impression that our matériel was superior; it was only when the Germans sent in their heavy tanks that we found the matériel of both sides to be equal in quality."

Generals Sicard, François and Gerodias, who commanded infantry divisions or army corps, concurred in these statements. As the modern arms employed by the French Army had been constructed between 1936 and 1940, it could not be maintained, after the Riom hearings, that the measures of the Popular Front had disorganized war factories, laboratories, and research bureaus. Neither general industrial development nor the General Staff's armament program was hindered by the nationalization of the war industries and the social reforms of the Popular Front. The excellence of French armament production was all the more noteworthy as France had long since ceased to be a great industrial nation. Whether or not one approves of the Popular Front and nationalization, one cannot gainsay the quality of the arms which came from factories nationalized or controlled by Daladier.

Industrial mobilization—the transformation of a section of peacetime industry into war industry—is always a delicate operation. All economists recognize that totalitarian states have a definite advantage over capitalist democracies in the organization of their industrial mobilization, for the simple reason that the peacetime economy of a totalitarian state differs little from its war economy; with so much shorter a road to travel to put itself into a state of war, it is inevitable that the totalitarian state should outdistance the democracy. In England and the United States as well as in France, the industrial mobilization had encountered hesitations and delays. Daladier could not work miracles. As had to be expected, the Council of Political Justice taxed him with "inefficiency in the preparation of industrial mobilization," and Pétain added this "inefficiency" to the list of Daladier's "crimes." The only witness before the Court to allude to the production of war matériel in wartime was General Keller, a tank inspector, who stated that the rate of tank production rose from one to two in Germany during the war, and from one to five or six in France (hearing of March 31, 1942). We must not conclude from these figures that democratic France out-produced Nazi Germany, but merely that Germany in September, 1939, was already in a state of complete industrial mobilization. It is none the less true that France would have been unable to step up her production so rapidly if her industrial mobilization had been prepared badly. Arms production throughout the war was under the direction of Raoul Dautry, Minister of Armaments. In May, 1940, General Piquandar, Director of Artillery in the Ministry of War, acknowledged that all the programs set up by the General Staff and given to Dautry had been carried out according to schedule. The war factories were not troubled by strikes or sabotage; indeed, the workers voluntarily gave up such social reforms as might have retarded the manufacture of arms.

In truth, the French industrial mobilization would have been better had it not been hampered by the demands of a General Staff, which preferred large effective forces to the development of modern arms. A policy of large forces and a policy of modern armaments are to a certain extent contradictory. Modern war is total war; at every step in its preparation and conduct one must know where effort is to be concentrated—the same man cannot simultaneously be in the factory and in the army—and how human and material resources are to be apportioned to the military and industrial sectors. A war can be lost because the army has depleted the factories, and vice versa. In France men were poorly divided between Army and factory. During the winter of 1939-1940 France had about as many men under arms and in the training camps as Germany. This necessarily decreased the labor supply for French factories. In Germany, however, the distribution of manpower permitted her to keep about four times as many workers in her factories as France, and subsequently to produce four times as much equipment, other things being equal. The conception of the "war of men" as opposed to the "war of machines" grew out of the general military conception, which had been evolved by the General Staff, the Supreme Council of National Defense, and Marshal Pétain. Daladier and Dautry, who had not contributed to it, were faced with its existence. If Daladier did not prepare industrial mobilization better, and if Dautry did not direct the industrial war more successfully, it was because both passed their time fighting the conservatism of the military. They made the best of a situation for which they were not responsible; they furnished the General Staff the men it demanded, using all the human resources left at their disposal.

The ratio of one to two between the matériel of the French and German Armies is a round, average figure; it holds true only for the total and not for the various categories of armament. The communiqué of February 20, 1942, showed that this ratio was approximately correct for tanks; France had about 2,000, Germany 4,000, in September, 1939, and about 3,500 to 7,000 or 8,000 at the beginning of May, 1940. But other types of equipment showed differing ratios. The witnesses for the prosecution insisted on the more damaging figures. According to the hearings, the anti-aircraft artillery was in the worst situation; France lacked anti-aircraft guns more than planes or tanks. On April 3, 1942, General Marescaux, Director of Aerial Defense (anti-aircraft artillery) in the Ministry of War, informed the Court that France had needed 12,000 cannon of all calibers for defense against enemy aircraft, and that she actually had 2,000—600 for the protection of the armies and 1,400 for home defense—less than a sixth of the necessary number. Similarly, the ratio of French to German aircraft was about one to three; in June, 1940, France had 6,000 military aircraft, of which 2,100 were first-line planes, as against Germany's 16,800 aircraft, which included 6,850 first-line planes. The Maginot Line equipment was not mentioned at Riom, but its armament was comparable in quantity and quality with that of the Siegfried Line. The general conception of the Siegfried Line was, in my opinion, better than that of the Maginot Line, which was more rigid, more "linear," and less graded in depth; but the importance of the Maginot Line was as great, and the accumulated arms represented about the same expenditure of work and raw materials. Nor was anything said about the Navy; but in 1936 France had a Navy twice as important as the German—533,000 tons as against 243,000—and had under construction 170,000 tons as against increased German construction of 275,000 tons, or a ratio of 1 to 1.6. In the same way, the general equipment of the 115 French divisions (uniforms, shoes, food, arms, and individual equipment, means of transportation and communication, medical supplies, etc.) equaled more than half the general equipment of the 180 German divisions, even if one considers only matériel manufactured since the last war. It was impossible to include in a general ratio of one to two (representing the total balance sheet of French and German armament) certain more favorable factors without also listing less favorable items. In short, it was impossible to have a Maginot Line as powerfully armed as the Siegfried Line, 115 divisions instead of 180, and at the same time to construct one anti-aircraft gun, one anti-tank mine, and one field radio set for every two that Germany was building.

Finally, it was just that matériel of which France had the least that proved to be most important in the course of the war. In a sense, the French Army never had an opportunity to use those arms of which it had the greatest amount. The French Army was not defeated in a series of operations opposing the Maginot Line to the Siegfried Line, or its infantry divisions to the German infantry divisions; it was beaten in the open field, in operations involving the use of matériel which it possessed in a proportion of less than one to two. As the witnesses were unanimous in stating that the French matériel was equal in quality to the German, they established, thereby, the ability of French technicians and war factories (nationalized or not) to produce the matériel which the Army needed; it would have been as easy to construct more anti-aircraft guns and anti-tank mines as to construct more special cannon for the

Maginot Line. The only impossibility was to build more of both. It would, consequently, have been as easy for Daladier before the war, and for Dautry during the war, to construct more tanks and less fortification matériel, more mobile arms and fewer fixed arms.

When the problem is thus stated, it can be seen that Daladier was able to put at the disposal of the French Army, matériel equal in quality, and inferior in quantity by only one-half, to that which Goering furnished the German Army. But France erred in her choice of the arms to be manufactured. Daladier should not have been asked: "Why did you build so few arms?" The questions should have been: "Why did you build this type of armament? Why did you build so many arms for a war of position which never developed, and so few arms for a war of movement which came instead?" Had these questions been asked, Daladier would undoubtedly have replied: "Because, instead of listening to Colonel de Gaulle, I followed the advice of Marshal Pétain." The Riom hearings threw some light on the real cause of the inadequacy of French armament, the result of an ill-advised choice.

Armament Programs Determined by the Doctrine

Daladier gave the French Army the war matériel which the General Staff had demanded. He could not have done otherwise. The armament programs of modern armies are never set up by Ministers of War in accordance with their political opinions, but by the heads of General Staffs in accordance with their operational plans and general conceptions of war. The technical complexity of the art of modern warfare makes this rule apply with equal force to democracies and totalitarian states. The proportion of specialized tools, in comparison with general equipment, has grown ever larger in the modern army just as it has in modern industry. It is no longer true—if it ever was—that the same arms can be used equally well in offensive and in defensive strategy, in war of position and in war of movement. The general of today is like an industrialist who cannot convert from the manufacture of automobiles to the manufacture of airplanes without transforming his machinery, whereas his predecessor, the artisan, could build plows, carriages, or artillery caissons with the same primitive tools. To a certain extent, specialized armament creates the specialized soldier, as specialization in industrial machinery leads to specialization of the worker. The modern army becomes the "professional army" of De Gaulle and the "army of mobilized technicians" of Germany and Russia. The Germans and Russians were the first exponents of the specialized army, when they created large attacking units (armored divisions and parachute troops) and other units trained in the consolidation and defense of conquered territories. Specialization of armament leads to specialization not only of the individual soldier but also of entire military units.

Before setting up an armament program a military leader should know what he will have to do, in what theater he will deploy his army, what kind of strategy he will be able to use against his presumed enemy, and what kind of warfare he can expect from that enemy. He must have settled on his war doctrine and determined his general plan and method of war. The commander-in-chief of the most powerful army, supplied by the wealthiest country, cannot afford the risk of preparing for all eventualities without running the danger of being prepared for none; because if he prepares for all, he will divide his resources and be weak on each front. These considerations have a particular importance for a country inferior to its enemy in human and material resources, for such a country can afford even less the expensive luxury of hesitation or error. If a plan of war has not been adopted, an armament program can be no more than a sample catalogue, providing for the manufacture of models to be tested, and postponing to a later date the actual armament program. It follows that it is easier to prepare for an offensive war than for a defensive war, because the offensive strategy offers better chances of forcing a desired type of warfare on the enemy. The strategy of offense is excellent for poor countries with young and bold generals, while the strategy of defense is appropriate for rich countries having elderly and timid leaders, who are generally the losers. Here again, the lasting laws of war have been reinforced by the evolution of industrial technique, because armament has become more difficult to construct and is more quickly outmoded: a tank built ten years ago or a three-year-old plane is of no value. Consequently, a commander-in-chief has greater chances of victory if he knows in advance, long before the outbreak of war, both where and when his troops will fight. The policy of aggressor Fascist states have many advantages over the policy of democratic and peaceful states in the preparation and conduct of war. Crime is easier than virtue in a society without police.

Every armament program is therefore bound to a war plan on whose merit its value depends. Events have shown that the French war doctrine and war plan were deficient; the calculations of the French General Staff were inferior to those of the German. The path of war in 1939-1940 was the one the German General Staff had planned and prepared, not what the French General Staff had desired or expected. The French armament program depended on the theory of the continuous front and the German armament program on the pincers movement. Each of the two programs was well conceived and correctly executed, but they grew out of opposing views. Thus, while the German armies were supplied with matériel that was adapted to the needs of the war as it was actually fought, the French armies were equipped for a war which did not take place.

Reasoning establishes the dependence of the armament program on the war plan; the hearings of the Riom trial confirm it. This interrelation and its unfortunate effects were effectively demonstrated by General Mittelhauser, former member of the Supreme War Council, at the hearing of March 18, 1942. General Mittelhauser exposed the "hesitations and vacillations" of the General Staff and the Supreme War Council in establishing a war doctrine and an armament program. "From 1936 on," he said, "the Supreme War Council discussed the importance and the use of tanks and airplanes, but without arriving at any agreement. In 1935 the Germans already had two armored divisions completely organized and prepared to take the field, while we had not been able to organize even one division by the beginning of the war. . . . The Germans and Italians used the Spanish war as a testing ground for their matériel and methods of warfare . . . but the French General Staff was unable to interpret the lessons of the Spanish war and changed neither its conceptions nor its programs. . . . The French High Command had no clear policy regarding the use of tanks or airplanes or the types of matériel to be ordered."

This opinion was confirmed by the depositions and discussions concerning certain matériel of which there had been particularly inadequate supplies. The "vacillations of military doctrine" and the "hesitations of the General Staff" had constantly retarded the setting up of programs and the manufacture of armaments. It was also revealed that Daladier had struggled untiringly to overcome the apathy of the General Staff. Significant examples were given at Riom. Witnesses who had commanded troops in battle complained about the lack of aerial support and the shortage of anti-aircraft guns. The French Army urgently needed airplanes to direct artillery fire and fighter planes for infantry and tank attacks. On March 16, 1942, Colonel Verdurand, liaison officer between the War Ministry (Direction of Artillery) and the Ministry of Aviation, explained to the Court why the construction of planes for the direction of artillery fire had not been begun before November, 1939. The need for these planes had appeared as early as 1937; but, since the beginning of 1938, the General Staffs of the Army and Air Force had been discussing the problem of whether the planes should be paid for by the Ministry of Aviation or by the War Ministry, and the High Command had been unable to reach any solution. Daladier himself had to cut short the dispute. Artillery planes began to appear at the beginning of 1940. "The situation improved," said the witness, "but it was too late." The discussion and hesitation of the military authorities had wasted two invaluable years. At the hearing of March 18 Daladier stated that attacking planes had been written into his armament program in 1937 by the Ministry of Aviation, but that this order was canceled at the request of the General Staff, which did not believe in the efficacy of aerial action in land fighting. His statement was confirmed on March 19 by General Hering, who pointed out that the Supreme War Council in March, 1937, had refused to create the "attacking aircraft" proposed by Daladier. Finally, at the hearing of April 2 Daladier entered into a discussion with a witness, General Marescaux, Director of Aerial Defense in the Ministry of War. Daladier declared that the French Army could have had 25 mm. anti-aircraft guns in construction since 1925, and 88 mm. guns since 1935; although the models existed, these guns were not included in the armament programs because "the General Staff was unable to agree on means of anti-aircraft defense. At last," Daladier added, "I had to take it upon myself in 1938 to order 90 mm. Navy guns so that the D.C.A. (anti-aircraft defense) might have some equipment."

No witness for the prosecution accused Daladier of having delayed the execution of the programs of construction. As we have seen, the social legislation of 1936 and 1937 did not interfere with these programs. At the hearing of February 27 Controller-General Jacomet, in charge of war manufactures, showed that "the armament program set up by the General Staff was six months ahead of schedule on January 1, 1939." Nor did any witness maintain that the armament program was reduced by Daladier; it was learned, on the contrary, that in September, 1936, Daladier had undertaken to have the government approve a rearmament program of twenty billion francs, whereas the program of General Colson, Assistant Chief of the General Staff, amounted to only twelve billions. If the French soldier had to go without the matériel he needed, it was because the General Staff had not included him in its programs.

Matériel Kept for the Germans

The Riom Court was stupefied to learn from the witnesses that important quantities of armament and equipment had been left behind in depots and dumps instead of being thrown into battle; part of this matériel was later captured by the Germans and used against the English and Russians. The amazement of the Court was great because this was the matériel most needed by the French Army. The statements of the witnesses gave the impression that some members of the General Staff, acting like faithful agents of the Fifth Column, had wanted to keep in reserve a part of the matériel ordered by the Ministry of War and manufactured by French factories.

The information collected by the Court in the course of its examination was made public by Daladier. When he was questioned, he stated that approximately 2,000 French tanks were thrown against the Germans. But according to documents furnished by Colonel Rivet, the French Army had approximately 3,500 tanks. It was also learned that the Air Force had used 1,125 planes against the Germans; but Colonel Chatelain, assistant to Colonel Redempt, then Director of Aviation Matériel, revealed that France had on June 28, 1940, 4,238 planes (of which 1,739 were first-line planes) in the unoccupied zone, plus 1,800 planes (of which 300 were first-line planes) in North Africa. Daladier announced that the Court's files showed that the Germans had captured 700 anti-aircraft guns in the depots. To appreciate the importance of this figure, one must recall the deposition of General Marescaux, Director of Aerial Defense, that the protection of the armies in the field depended on 600 anti-aircraft guns. Consequently, in the battle which decided France's fate, the High Command used approximately 55 per cent of its tanks, 45 per cent of its first-line planes, and 45 per cent of its anti-aircraft guns (excluding the guns of the Maginot Line and those used for the home defense); the rest was held in reserve—and delivered to the Germans.

More damaging than the statement of Daladier and the documents submitted to the Court was the testimony of the witnesses, which at last made the Vichy government decide to suspend the trial. On March 27 Colonel J. Janson informed the Court that at the end of the war, the arsenal of Gravanches (Puy-de-Dôme) contained eighteen to twenty tons of machine guns. On

April 1 General Keller complained of the shortage of radioelectric sets and optical instruments in the armored and motorized divisions. On April 3 the testimony of General Hureaux, former head of the Army Geographical Service, revealed that great quantities of these materials had been left at Saint-Denis, on the outskirts of Paris; there, in a storehouse, were enough stocks to equip twenty-five divisions. Generals Requin, Lenclud, and Andrey complained of the lack of boots and blankets from which their men had suffered. The official communiqué of February 20, 1942, had presented the same complaint, and the lack of two million blankets had been offered by the Council of Political Justice as one of the most incontestable proofs of "inefficiency." Other witnesses also spoke of the lack of boots and uniforms, but Quartermaster-General Bernard refuted these accusations in sensational testimony on April 30.

"In a single depot at Troyes," he declared, "there were two billion francs' worth of blankets, boots, and uniforms, while the troops were in need of them. . . . The commissarial stocks had been inadequate, but that was in 1935 [when Marshal Pétain was War Minister]. These blankets, still lacking at the beginning of the war, were manufactured rapidly, the commissariat having assured the supply of a million new blankets monthly after October, 1939. The same speed of manufacture was reached for uniforms, boots, and other necessary equipment, so that everything had been supplied by the beginning of 1940." The depositions of General Hureaux and Quartermaster-General Bernard obliged General Gamelin to admit that the High Command and the General Staff were responsible for the allocation of the stocks of armament and equipment. Bernard also pointed out that forty thousand horses had died of hunger in the winter of 1939-1940 because fodder had not been provided. These examples proved that the High Command and General Staff had refused, or neglected, to furnish the forces with the matériel that Daladier had obtained for them.

Once again we are faced with the fundamental question: incompetence or betrayal? History will decide, and probably will discover in the complexity and quantity of errors, a surprising mixture of stupidity, conceit, vanity, treason, and gross negligence. Too many Fascist officers were only half interested in the war, and too many Cagoulard officers were traitors. If Vichy, frightened by the march of truth, had not suspended the Riom trial, other revelations would have been added to those of Generals Bernard and Hureaux, and Colonels Janson, Rivet, and Chatelain. Modern cannon, light and heavy, were left in the depots at Bourges, while divisions were sent into battle with old 75 mm. guns, dating from 1914 and invented in 1887, and this is but one of many instances. All that can be said in extenuation of the French General Staff was that it was so utterly surprised by the German methods of warfare that its leaders lost their heads; most of them had no idea of what was happening. Some understood, but their reactions had been conditioned in terms of another type of warfare. The habits of twenty years cannot be transformed in a day, especially when these habits are founded on intellectual laziness and smugness. In its *Kriegspiel* the French General Staff had spent much time showing that a battle of tanks and airplanes was inconceivable and that De

Gaulle was wrong. It was unable to improvise a defense against tactics whose possibility it had denied. The more rapid a war, the better must be its preparation.

Everything thus compels us to ask how the generals planned and directed the war. The responsibility of the political men recedes more and more into the background, while attention centers increasingly on the military and the General Staff. The question becomes one of knowing whether the French defeat was a military defeat provoked by the unwise policy of the Popular Front, or a political defeat caused by the inferior preparation of the Army by the military. To answer this, we shall have to determine how military operations were executed and how the general conception of warfare—or, to use the French term, the general war doctrine—of the General Staff was put into practice.

The Riom trial proved that Daladier was a better Minister of War than his predecessors Pétain and Maurin; he was, other things being equal, a better Minister of War than Goering. The morale of the French soldier cannot be praised enough. If these men had been led by officers who thought and felt like them, if they had been inspired by the great idea of the international fight against Fascism, if their leaders had given them some conception of modern warfare, they would have astonished the world as did the soldiers of Valmy. Without Fascist officers and guided by competent leaders, the French Army would have been a match for the Reichswehr. The French Army received from the nation and from the Minister of War the armament which the General Staff had ordered. It cannot be said that Daladier by negligence, or the workers by laziness, failed to produce what the soldiers needed; they manufactured what was asked of them.

The one charge that can be laid at Daladier's door is that he did not purge the Army of its Fascist elements. Stalin's various purges of the Red Army did not weaken it; they saved it. To fight Hitler's Fascist army, one must have an anti-Fascist army. When the Cagoulard plot was uncovered, instead of shielding Pétain, the knife should have been plunged into the wound; the moment had come to rid the Army of the Camelots du Roi and the Croix de Feu, whose very presence in positions of leadership was a danger to democracy. Such a purge would have been in accord with the feeling of the nation, and was included in the Popular Front program, but national sovereignty under the Third Republic was held in check by the conservative majority of the Senate. The Popular Front ministers, Daladier in particular, erred in not understanding that they were in a revolutionary situation, and in not establishing the dictatorship of the majority—the only means by which democracy could have been achieved in France at that moment.

Daladier was not asked to explain this error. He was not blamed for retaining Fascist elements in the Army, but for mistakes he had not committed and for deeds for which he did not bear the responsibility. Having furnished the General Staff the matériel it had demanded of him, having given the Army "remarkable soldiers," "courageous warriors," Daladier had the right to ask the military leaders: what did you do with these men and these arms?

The Role of the Military in the Defeat

G ENERAL GAMELIN'S silence during the hearings makes it difficult to analyze military responsibilities in the preparation and conduct of the war. Progressive and conservative tendencies existed in all armies, including the French, before 1939. Certain military leaders wanted to transform organization, armament, and combat methods, so that the Army might take advantage of modern technical resources. Others were fearful of change, cautioned that "nature makes no leaps," and considered the experience of the last war still valid. In Germany the progressive tendency won the day, and the Nazi Army of 1939 had little in common with the Imperial Army of 1918. In France the conservatives triumphed, and the Army of Gamelin and Weygand had the same general organization and war doctrine as the Army of Marshal Foch. The reform tendencies of the Popular Front failed to touch the French Army, whereas the revolutionary spirit of National Socialism brought youth and strength into the German Army.

If General Gamelin, instead of keeping silent, had limited his evidence to the preparation of the war, we should have been able to learn who were the champions of conservatism or of progress in the General Staff and in the Supreme War Council; but his obstinate silence permitted those who were responsible for the military inertia to escape whatever explanations might have been required of them. This silence obliges us to lump together for collective reprobation men of very different caliber, some of whom fought valiantly against the red tape of the rest. Fortunately, it is a provisional reprobation. The publication of the military archives will allow us to do justice to certain generals and to judge more severely the reactionary elements. Certain distinctions are already possible, thanks, in part, to disclosures made at Riom.

The strictly military responsibilities for the defeat were to be sought either in the poor preparation of the Army by its leaders or in the inefficient conduct of operations.

In terms of French law, the direction of operations of war was exclusively the task of the military authorities; the government could take no part. For better or worse, this rule had been adopted as a consequence of the events of April, 1917, when the Premier had intervened to put a halt to the offensive of General Nivelle. The "law on the organization of the nation in wartime" drew the line clearly between military and governmental action. Entirely responsible for the military conduct of war, the High Command in peacetime had complete control over the general organization of the Army, the elaboration of the war doctrine and war plans, the training of officers and men, and the formulation of armament programs. Not even the Minister of War could overrule the High Command on purely military questions in peacetime, since the High Command carried sole responsibility for operations in wartime. The French High Command thus enjoyed more power in peacetime than those of Russia, Germany, England, or China, because the law burdened it with greater responsibilities in wartime. We must therefore examine how the Army was prepared for its task by the High Command and how military operations were subsequently conducted. Only then shall we be able to allot the responsibilities for its poor preparation and ineffective use.

THE FRENCH MILITARY DOCTRINE:
THE CONTINUOUS FRONT

The evidence submitted to the Court not only showed that the French Army had been poorly equipped for modern warfare, but also explained the reasons for this inadequate preparation. Most of the witnesses attributed it to the war doctrine which still prevailed in high military circles in 1939. One witness alone, General Touchon, undertook to defend this doctrine; all the rest criticized it for the poor organization of the Army and the inadequate training of men and officers. Their evidence may be summarized as follows:

The Army, prepared for a war of position, found itself faced by a new form, a war of movement, of airplanes and tanks. The criticism of General Mittelhauser was continued at the hearing of March 19 by General Hering, another former member of the Supreme War Council. "I had always advised," said he, "the creation of large motorized units; unfortunately, I succeeded in winning only one disciple, General von Brauchitsch. . . . The success of the Third Reich is due to the co-ordination of German forces more than to superiority in men or matériel." On March 26 General Conquet declared: "Our army had received no instruction which permitted it to resist the attack of modern engines of war."

A few days later, General Préaud, former head of the Military Academy of Saint-Cyr, while recognizing that "much had been done to modernize the Army under the direction of General Gamelin" (in other words, after Pétain was no longer Minister of War and Weygand no longer Chief of Staff), attacked the "defensive doctrine" of the French Army. On March 20 General Sicard stated that "this doctrine was erroneous." On March 31 General Keller said: "Our doctrine, not our numerical inferiority, was the determining cause. We followed defensive tactics, and we were in error." On March 17 General Besson, who had commanded a group of armies during the war and had also been a member of the Supreme War Council, developed more fully the question of a "lack of doctrine in the employment of tanks." On March 20, returning to the same subject, Colonel Ragaine deplored that "in accordance with our doctrine, the tank had been attached to the infantry." On March 31 General Martin investigated the same problem: "Whereas after 1935 the Germans and British had arranged their tanks in large, maneuverable units, our doctrine governing the employment of tanks remained, until the beginning of the war, one in which the tank's mission was to support the infantry, to maintain liaison with the foot-soldiers. . . . Our military regulations had been drawn up with this orientation in 1933, and they were not changed."

On April 1 Colonel Perré recalled that Germany had created her *Panzer-divisionen* in 1935. "We French," he continued, "remained attached to our outmoded conceptions until the Supreme War Council's meeting on December 2, 1938, which voted the creation of two armored divisions for the month of October, 1940. . . . These were the unfavorable conditions under which we entered the war." At the meeting of March 20 M. Ribet, Daladier's counsel, had General Lenclud confirm the deposition which he had made before the investigating body: "Our conception of the employment of tanks lacked boldness and breadth. We were wrong to disperse them in the face of the German concentration." On April 1 M. Ribet reminded General Langlois of his deposition: "The subordination of the tanks to the infantry was the cause of all our misfortunes. . . . It was the tragedy of the war. France chose a strategy of scattering her forces, Germany one of concentrating hers."

Thus the Riom trial offered the curious spectacle of a single witness in defense of the French official doctrine, while all the rest exposed its errors and its evil influence on the preparation for, and consequently the fighting of, the war. And these were the witnesses for the prosecution, some of whom had sat in the Supreme War Council and had helped formulate the official doctrine, while others had held important positions on the General Staff. They did not say: our doctrine, our plans of war, and our programs were good, but the application of the doctrine and the execution of plans and programs were compromised by the policy of the Ministry of War. On the contrary, they denounced the official doctrine; it was an act of courage, for this doctrine had the support of Marshal Pétain.

The French Conception of War

The French General Staff had a conception of a long war, which would take the form of a war of coalition. Based on the idea of defense, it was to lead to a war of position and the establishment of the "continuous front."

This general theory was based on the lessons of the first World War, which the General Staff still considered completely valid. It may be summarized as follows:

1. Conscription (compulsory short-term military service with periodic training of reserves, as practiced in most countries of continental Europe) and

mass production have created the mass army, which, in the largest countries, amounts to several million trained and mobilizable men. These armies are more unwieldy and less maneuverable than the older professional armies, but they permit the High Command to establish along the frontiers continuous firing lines, consisting of barrages of automatic arms and artillery. These lines are generally formed by means of bases, staggered in depth, but close enough to be able to flank each other and cross their fires. They function under the cover of passive obstacles, from permanent fortifications to field fortifications, modernized to allow for such new weapons as tanks and airplanes. As long as the continuous line of fire holds, invasion of the territory is impossible. It is extremely difficult to break through such a line, for the attacker is deprived of the two classic devices—flanking attack and surprise. The continuous line of fire cannot be flanked, for there is no flank. Nor can the continuous front be taken by surprise, because it is made up of a series of obstacles under heavy fire. Any attack presupposes the destruction of obstacles or the neutralization of fire at one or several given points; this cannot be achieved without the use of heavy artillery, whose arrival on the battlefield cannot be concealed. Under these conditions the preparation of attack requires a period of time which the High Command of the defending troops will use to send reserves to the endangered points and to organize supplementary positions, also staggered in depth, so that if an attack should succeed, the attacker quickly would have to halt his advance in order to bring up his heavy artillery and begin a new offensive action. The operation of the continuous front forces the enemy to make successive attacks, which, at best, would absorb his margin of superiority and give him only Pyrrhic victories. In other words, the continuous front is a consequence of the mass armies and the balance of forces in Europe, and its effect is to render impossible the war of movement with its unexpected turns, and to transform any European war into a war of position.

2. The continuous front is not only the most probable (perhaps the only possible) form of war for France; it is also for her the most advantageous method. The continuous front war is the normal form of the long war, of the war of attrition, whereas the war of movement may be short. Because of her economic, demographic, geographic, and political situation, France has more to fear from a short war than from a long war, which alone would permit her to utilize the resources of her Colonial Empire. Moreover, the only war which France can envisage is a war of coalition. France is menaced seriously in Europe only by German power; isolated, she cannot hope to fight Germany, and her security therefore depends on the state of her alliances. France's likeliest and most indispensable ally is England. The economic resources of the British Empire are immense, but slow to be transformed into military power; its military might is potential rather than actual. The short war gives the advantage to the totalitarian powers, which pursue a policy of aggression and conquest, whereas the long war offers a certitude of victory to coalitions that possess control of the seas and access to raw materials. The role of the French Army is to prevent a short war, and it can do so only by the organization of a mass army.

3. In the course of a long war, the time will come for the French Army to pass to the offensive and thus to the war of movement. This will happen only in the second phase of hostilities, when the coalition armies will have been brought together and organized under an inter-Allied command, and when the enemy armies will have been sufficiently weakened by attrition and blockade to be given the coup de grâce. It would be suicidal to plunge prematurely into the war of movement. The object of French strategy at the beginning of a war consequently should be to force the enemy into the war of position; it must be a defensive and linear strategy, to avoid drawing from the garrisons of the continuous front the men needed for offensive maneuvers. This could be achieved by (a) a network of alliances in Central or Eastern Europe (preferably Czechoslovakia and Poland) obliging Germany to divide her forces and preventing her from concentrating more than 120 divisions against the French Army; (b) a French mass army, capable of mobilizing 100 divisions and covering the frontiers rapidly with an uninterrupted line of continuous fire—a mobilization which should be possible with the aid of covering troops and permanent fortifications established along the frontier (the Maginot Line); and (c) training this mass army for the war of position. It follows that the French General Staff ought to concentrate its efforts on the preparation of the war of position, as the most probable and most desirable form of war; it is unnecessary to prepare in peacetime for the war of movement which would come only in the second phase of operations. The instrument for the coup de grâce that will bring an inter-Allied victory should be forged during the war of position. In other words, 1918 should not be prepared for in 1913; and it has been pointed out that if the French Army had adopted a defensive strategy in 1914, ten départements would not have been invaded.

Such was the doctrine of the continuous front.

The ideas of coalition, mass army, and continuous front were constantly linked in the thinking of the French General Staff, which could not conceive of a mass army capable of maneuvering against another mass army that was strongly entrenched on a continuous front. These three ideas formed a homogeneous bloc, and anything that might challenge this theory was considered illusory. The general conception of war thus took on the appearance of a "doctrine"—and, in fact, the French General Staff spoke of a "war doctrine," whereas the Germans and Russians spoke of "methods of war." At the heart of the French doctrine was the postulate of the continuous front, which soon became a dogma.

It was believed that this dogma had been found in the lessons of the first World War. The continuous front war had at that time been a necessity; it was born of facts, not of theory. The continuous front had been the outcome of a group of accidental circumstances: the equilibrium of the forces on the eastern front; the effect of industrial techniques on armament and equipment; and the impossibility of maneuvering on fronts extending from the North Sea to the Swiss Jura and from the Tyrol to the Adriatic. The doctrine of the continuous front had been the expression of the methods best adapted to these circumstances. Nor had it been a peculiarly French doctrine, for all armies, German, Italian, and British, had adopted it. It had not been a matter of preference, but of necessity—a simple historical fact.

The French General Staff established a dogma on a set of circumstances that no longer existed. Because the first war of mass armies had been a con-tinuous front war, the General Staff imagined that the continuous front was the logical consequence of the mass army. It did not understand that other forms of war, impossible in 1914-1918 for technical or political reasons, had become possible for mass armies that were equipped, armed, and organized in a different way. It did not begin to realize that the knell of the continuous front had sounded as early as 1918, and that a certain tendency had existed even then toward the war of movement of mass armies. It remained faithful to the doctrine of the continuous front, which had won the war in 1918. This mistake resulted from its leaders' lack of intellectual power and scientific training, and from the general orientation of the French mind, which is more dogmatic than pragmatic, prefers abstract logic to the rigors of observation, does not allow sufficiently for evolution, and generally reasons on the static, instead of the dynamic, level.

The consequences of this dogmatism in military organization resulted in an organization of the French Army that remained as nearly as possible what it had been in the first World War, for it best suited the requirements of the continuous front. This organization was built around the infantry division, composed of three infantry regiments, divisional artillery, etc. To allow for technical advances, certain modifications were affected in arma-ment and equipment, but were integrated into the existing general frame-work and thus put at the service of the continuous front. The result was that the infantry division, which had already been unwieldly in 1918, grew still heavier; its command had to face not only all the earlier problems, but new ones arising from the use of airplanes and tanks. The means of repairing possible breaches in the continuous front were divided among the large units charged with assuring the defense of this front, in order to have them as near at hand as possible; tanks and airplanes, in particular, were divided into "small packages," at the disposal of the infantry divisions, instead of being organized into large armored or aerial units, capable of mass action. The doctrine of the continuous front taught that a breach made by the enemy had to be warped immediately to prevent the enemy from exploiting his success— that it was better to be able to launch a counterattack immediately with a battalion of tanks and the infantry of the line than to prepare a counter-offensive in a week's time with armored divisions and motorized infantry. Consequently, numerous "small packages" of reserves (composed principally of tanks) were placed at the disposal of army corps; no strong reserves were in the hands of commanders of army groups or of the commander-in-chief—reserves which could be sent to all points of the front for large strategic operations. The General Staff remained faithful to the method used by Foch, without realizing that these were no longer the days of 1918.

218

Organized, equipped, and trained for a continuous front war, the French Army was not very different in 1939 from what it had been at the end of the last war. It was a modernized, not a modern, Army.

The German Conception of War

It was natural that modern methods and conceptions of war should have developed in Germany and Russia rather than in France or England. The Red Army was a revolutionary army, formed in the days of the civil war; and civil war, with its ambushes, guerrilla fighting, and incessant maneuvers, was to prove a better preparation for modern warfare than did the continuous front war of 1914-1918. Then, too, the Red Army, shortly after its inception, had had to fight the Polish Army; and the Polish war, marked by 25-year-old Mikhail Tukachevsky's daring raid to the very gates of Warsaw, was the antithesis of a war of position. Thus the Red Army's tradition of warfare was one of movement rather than of position. The German Army, for its part, was a conquered Army, but it rid itself of its old generals, and its young leaders studied the causes of the defeat of 1918 in order to avoid, wherever possible, the errors which had proved fatal for their predecessors. These leaders were not only younger than those of the French Army, but their thinking was different, because of a basic difference in mentality. It was slower and heavier, but less dogmatic, less bound by formal logic, more receptive to change, and aware of realities—the spirit of Hegel as opposed to the spirit of Descartes. Moreover, World War I had not been exclusively a continuous front war for the German military leaders; they had been constantly forced to move their armies from the western front, held by the French and British, to the eastern front against the Russians. These "maneuvers on the interior lines," as General Von Taysen observed, preserved them from the illusion of the continuous front. Unlike the French, they had unhappy memories of the continuous front—the front of defeat—and they were versed in large mass transports, which were to be the basis of the modern war of movement.

It is more important to compare the French conception of war with the German rather than with the Russian, because the French Army was beaten by the German Army. Let us note, however, that the German military leaders admitted in their writings that they borrowed freely from the Russians. Thus the contribution of Russian military leaders was at least as important as that of the Germans in the preparation of modern war.

To understand the evolution of German military thought from 1918 to 1939, we must divide it, somewhat artificially, into three stages.

The first was marked by a violent reaction against the theory of the continuous front. The German military realized that the continuous front war, especially if fought on two fronts, was bound to be long, the most dangerous form of war for Germany. To combat the discouragement of the Army and of the country, they undertook to escape from the double specter of the continuous front and the two-front war. They advocated a rapprochement with the Soviet Union, which became the consistent policy of the German General Staff and the reason for the military leaders' opposition to Hitler's anti-Communism. To the same end, they praised the war of movement, which they considered the only possible form of a short war. "For multiple reasons," General Reinhart wrote, "we must prefer the war of movement of the future to a rigid defense, in which the enemy can methodically bring into play his heavy engines of war, superior to ours." It was during this first period of the German military renaissance that many books were published dealing with the ideas and "war plans" of General Schlieffen. These plans, based on the principles of the war of movement, had the object of annihilating the French Army in a few weeks; as a result of their publicity, the rehabilitation of the war of movement was ultimately attributed to the theses of General Schlieffen, whom the German Army considered the greatest strategist of modern times. This project was headed by important men, such as General Groener, Minister of War in the Weimar Republic; Wolfgang Foerster, Archivist of the Ministry of War; and Karl Lustrow, one of the best minds of the German General Staff. After studying what he called "the will of Count Schlieffen," General Groener wrote: *In der Bewegung liegt der Sieg* (in movement lies victory)." At about the same time, General von Seeckt advanced his theory of the *Blitzkrieg*, which aroused the interest of all military circles and the enthusiasm of the young officers. This enthusiasm was no mere passing fancy; only a few years before the second World War, Captain Dingler reiterated the state of mind of the younger military generation when he wrote in the *Deutsche Wehr*: "It is better to take a chance on winning a war in a few weeks than to be certain of losing a war of several years." These ideas did not remain isolated; they quickly penetrated the military organism itself, and their influence was already visible in the *Regulations Concerning the Conduct and Combat of All Arms* (commonly called *Tug*), published shortly after the last war.

The second period was marked by a certain reaction against the enthusiasm for the *Blitzkrieg* and by advanced studies of modern war. Some writers demanded that the lessons of 1914-1918 not be forgotten, and that the conditions of the *Blitzkrieg* and its possible consequences be studied before any decision was made. These appeals to prudence bore fruit; instead of envisaging the *Blitzkrieg* as a form of war opposed to that of the continuous front, German military thought turned towards a more complex form of war, "total war," in the course of which, periods of *Blitzkrieg* and of *Sitzkrieg* alternate. After 1932 Germany increased her efforts beyond the military field to the spheres of politics and economics. In the political sphere, the importance of geopolitics was emphasized, and the idea of total war was revealed to the public by General Ludendorff. In the economic sphere, a General Staff of Economic Warfare was created under the leadership of General Thomas. In the strictly military sphere, tactics and organization were studied as well as strategy. The wealth of documentation offered even to line officers by military reviews such as the *Deutsche Wehr* and the *Militärwissenschaftliche Rundschau* was impressive. The most important work, and the one which contributed the largest number of new ideas and ingenious solutions, was *Der Kampfwagenkrieg* (*The War of Tanks*), published in Munich at the beginning of 1934 by the retired Austrian General von Eimansberger.* A partisan of the war of movement, he pointed out that the modern tank revolutionized the art of war; he foresaw both anti-tank defense and the tank offensive. For offensive action he recommended the organization of tanks into large armored units, the *Panzerdivisionen,* which were to include 250 tanks— 150 medium tanks and 100 light tanks—motorized infantry and artillery, an aerial unit, etc. For anti-tank defense he asked not only that the ordinary infantry divisions have strong anti-tank artillery—seventy-two cannons per division—but that special divisions, the *Kraftdivisionen,* be organized and powerfully equipped. The *Kraftdivision* was to be able to resist the action of enemy tanks on a twenty kilometer front; it was to include three infantry regiments (each with three battalions, each battalion to have six anti-tank cannons), two anti-tank artillery regiments with fifty-four anti-tank cannons each, an artillery regiment which could be used in anti-tank and other opera- tions, an engineers' battalion, a battalion of specialists in anti-tank mines, a squadron of observation aircraft, etc. Von Eimansberger's organization was capable both of creating powerful defensive fronts against enemy tanks and of undertaking offensive maneuvers and operations. Von Eimansberger was not the inventor of the armored division; this honor belongs to an Englishman, General Fuller; but von Eimansberger was the first to envisage a new organiza- tion of the army based on the use of tanks in large units and the specialization of certain units in defense. His work had great importance in the evolution of German military thought.

The third period in the development of German military thought deserves 'longer study; it was a period of synthesis, of organization, and of perfection. It was dominated by an ever vaster conception of warfare—a conception which was, as the Germans put it, colossal.

On the basis of studies which were political, economic, historical, and geographical as well as military, the German General Staff realized that it could avoid neither a long war nor a war on several fronts—an eastern front against Russia and another against France and England. This General Staff had to take account a new factor: the advent of Hitler. It knew that Hitler would soon quarrel with the whole world, or rather with everyone who did not accept his doctrine. But the General Staff understood that it could, without direct opposition to Hitler, transform a long war on several fronts into a short war, by means of modern methods. The war on several fronts which Germany could not fight was a war on several *simultaneous* fronts; but Germany could readily win a war on several *successive* fronts. The long war which Germany could not permit herself to fight was a war without raw materials, but Germany could win a long war after certain political, economic, or military operations which would assure her the raw materials she needed.

* L. R. von Eimansberger, *Der Kampfwagenkrieg* (Munich: J. F. Lehmanns Verlag, 1934).

Thus the German General Staff envisaged a general war which would break down into a series of partial wars and campaigns. The shorter campaigns would be waged first to obtain the materials needed to continue the war, thus fortifying German economy and weakening that of Germany's eventual adversaries. Since the economic resources of Germany were inadequate, supplementary resources would have to be obtained by resorting to diplomacy, politics, or, if necessary, to arms. Munitions from Czechoslovakia, nickel from Norway and Greece, iron ore from French Lorraine, copper from Spain and Yugoslavia, bauxite from Hungary and France, coal from Poland—all would be absorbed by a series of operations preliminary to the war itself. This would make possible campaigns to secure the unlimited resources of the Soviet Union, the wealth of the Near East, and the products of the African continent. Germany could then laugh at America and impose her order on the New World as on the Old. The motto of such a war should have been *vires acquerit eundo*—war shall feed war. A general plan for such a war could not be merely one of military operations; political and economic strategy had to accompany military planning. The principal object of the political strategy was to be the division of Germany's eventual adversaries for as long a time as possible. In this respect, National Socialist politics, disadvantageous in many ways to the General Staff, had advantages. By developing and exploiting the fear of Communism, it would be possible to separate France from the Soviet Union. In the same way American isolationism would be fostered to avoid the possibility of the United States entering the war before Germany could dominate the European continent. The economic strategy was to have three objects: the transformation of German economy, which had to be protected from blockade by development of synthetic raw materials; the furnishing of arms and war materials needed for the preliminary short wars and the first short campaigns of the long war; and the equipment and organization of territories annexed by politics, subjected by persuasion, or conquered by arms. The economic strategy was to prepare and organize, first in Europe, then in Russia and Africa, a New Order, whose resources would be equal or superior to those of the American hemisphere.

A successful synthesis of the most important ideas developed during the first three periods, and the adaptation of these ideas to the political and economic needs of a Nazi Germany was the task of the German High Command and of the Berlin *Kriegsakademie*. The basic elements were furnished by the military reviews, which pursued their work of investigation. Two men deserve mention—General Guderian, a specialist in tank warfare, and General Erfuhrt, director of the *Militärwissenschaftliche Rundschau*. In the first issue of the latter, Guderian published an article which placed him among the leading theoreticians of modern warfare. He expressed his admiration for De Gaulle's ideas, ideas which influenced him, but which he did not entirely adopt. Guderian, closer to the conceptions of von Eimansberger, envisaged an offensive system based on the organization of armored divisions, the close alliance of the tank and airplane, and the creation of specialized units, *Kraft-*

fahrkampftruppen, for defense against enemy armored divisions. The man who was to lead the attack on the French lines at Sedan in 1940 revealed in 1936, in all its details, the war doctrine which was to overcome the French Army.

In 1938 and 1939 General Erfuhrt published a series of articles which outlined the whole Polish campaign. If the leaders of the French Army had bothered to read the German military publications, they would have known in advance who would attack them and how they would be beaten if they persisted in their outmoded views. As early as 1935 the new edition of the *Tug* revealed the essential features of German military thought: the Army was trained both for the war of position (every German soldier had to be a "pioneer") and for the war of movement. Outlining German tendencies in the *Revue Militaire Française* in July, 1935, Colonel René Altmayer indicated that "its offensive maneuver, as much in strategy as in tactics, aims at overwhelming and encirclement. . . . It seems that that is the maneuver which will be attempted in the first operations of the next war, from the battalion to the group of armies. . . . The High Command should always aim at the flanks or the rear of large enemy concentrations. The *Schwerpunkt* must be in the flanks, whether it is a question of a tactical operation or of a strategic maneuver." In all the echelons of the German Army it was forbidden to fight while maneuvering, and the recommended maneuver was the classic one of encirclement by the flanks.

Having defined its general conception of war, the German High Command proceeded to organize its army. The great modern strategists—from Napoleon to Schlieffen—were all great military organizers. The army that the German General Staff planned was not a professional army but a mass army. The German High Command avoided the errors of the French High Command, which confused the mass army with the continuous front and identified the war of movement with the professional army. The mass army prepared by the German General Staff was an army capable of offensive as well as defensive maneuvers, of the war of movement as well as the war of position. Anticipating various forms of war, the Germans constructed a diversified military machine based on specialization of troops. The large units were specialized by their armament, their composition, their equipment, and the training of their personnel for a definite task; units were created for the destruction of obstacles and fortifications, for attack, for exploitation, for defense, or for the occupation of fortresses. Formations and divisions were specialized, just as in the course of military history, the infantry, the cavalry, the artillery, and the engineers had been specialized. This was achieved by degrees after 1934—at the time when the French Army was lulled by Marshal Pétain's faith in the doctrine of the continuous front, the Maginot Line, and the impenetrability of the Ardennes Forest.

The years 1934 and 1935 were decisive; by 1935 the first two armored divisions were entirely equipped and capable of action. In March, 1935, the

Militär Wochenblatt restated with improvements von Eimansberger's central idea, and published a plan for a complete organization of specialized arms, including units for the break-through and the offensive in force; units for the exploitation of the break-through and the maneuver of encirclement— armored and motorized units transported by amphibian vehicles and including machine-gun regiments and light artillery; defense units—the old infantry division with barrage units (*Sperrbanden*); and various special units—reconnaissance, pioneers, fortress troops, etc. Thus the German military organization was becoming as specialized as large industry; it could be used for the offensive and defensive operations of the war of movement, thanks to its armored divisions and defense divisions, just as it could be employed for the operations of the war of position and for those of siege warfare.

Even after determining its doctrine and creating its organization, the German Army did not go to sleep; it used every opportunity to hold large maneuvers and to make life-sized experiments. Before September, 1939, it had tested its system of transports—while invading the Rhineland in 1936, Austria in 1938, Bohemia in the spring of 1939. No other army had such training. The most important experiment was in Spain during the Civil War. Through the so-called German "volunteers," the General Staff tried out its organization, its combat methods, its airplanes, and its tanks. It realized at that moment that "Goering was not worth Daladier" nor, especially, Stalin, for the German tanks and airplanes turned out to be inferior to certain foreign war matériel to which they were opposed (Russian airplanes, in particular). New matériel was manufactured in terms of these lessons. The trial period even continued during the war: in his speech of July 20, 1940, celebrating the victory of his armies over the French, Hitler admitted that before attacking France he had made changes in his Army on the basis of the Polish campaign. In its turn the French campaign made possible a new perfection before the opening of hostilities with Russia. But before attacking Russia the German General Staff needed a longer period of time; fortunately for the Allies, Hitler's impatience hastened this invasion. Because they had not understood the character of war, because they had all repeated, one after the other, "it can't happen here," because they had practiced isolationism instead of collective security, the nations of Europe were, each in turn, guinea pigs for the German Army. If Soviet Russia had not been more farsighted than the rest, she would have suffered the same fate.

Through perseverance the German General Staff created and constantly improved its modern war doctrine. It thought, worked, experimented, thought further, and worked again. It abandoned the doctrine of the continuous front, which corresponded to neither its desires, needs, nor possibilities. But it did not lose itself in the clouds of the *Blitzkrieg,* or rather it saw in the *Blitzkrieg* one form of modern warfare and not modern war itself. The German General Staff forged the best instrument of modern warfare out of many parts; unfortunately, this instrument was used by Hitler in the service of the worst of causes. When the leaders of the German Army, after measuring their war methods in the field with those of the French generals, conquered the victors of 1918 after a six-week campaign, they must have felt that they had reaped the rewards of their work.

Conservatism of the French General Staff

Compared with German ideas, the French conception of modern warfare was not only timid, but lazy and conservative—stubbornly conservative; the General Staff and Supreme War Council refused to take notice of the warnings which came to them from all sides.

The French military authorities could not be unaware of what was being prepared and organized in Germany. Although the volume of preparations was unknown, and the Hitlerian regime made the work of the information services very difficult, German conceptions, ideas, doctrines, and plans were published in the military press. One had to do no more than read the abundant German military literature or follow German military reviews, to know what was happening on the other side of the Rhine. The *Revue Militaire Française* kept up with this literature. I have already referred to Colonel Altmayer's article in this *Revue* on "The German Doctrine" (July, 1934). I might also mention a very complete analysis of von Eimansberger's book, *The War of Tanks,* in the *Revue Militaire* (June, 1935). In 1934 and 1935, the Popular Front had not yet come to power; the influence of Marshal Pétain was sovereign in the French Army and General Weygand was Commander-in-Chief. The military authorities knew that if war broke out between France and Germany, the French Army would be faced not by an improved version of the army of 1918, but by a modern army, conceived and built on new principles. As late as August, 1939, the Russians put at our disposal all their information concerning the German Army—information which was far more extensive than ours. Lastly, during the Spanish war the Republican government gave all possible facilities to our Military Attaché in Madrid, Colonel Morel, to obtain information on German organization and combat methods.

Certain progressive and reform tendencies existed in the French Army itself; but instead of being favored by the High Command, they were either discouraged or denounced as heresies. I have quoted the bitter words of General Hering during the Riom trial, when he said that he always had been a partisan of large motorized units, but that he had had only one disciple, General von Brauchitsch. During the trial, Daladier paid tribute to General Doumenc, "inventor of motorization," and to General de Gaulle, whom he "was proud to have named general, and the youngest general in the French Army during the war." At the same hearing he refered to Generals Billotte and Bourrette as advocates of armored divisions in the Supreme War Council. The military leaders therefore included a minority which had been won over to modern ideas. An even stronger minority existed in the ranks. Young officers fidgeted with impatience at the jobs they were forced to do, like thoroughbred horses harnessed to rubbish carts. If French military literature offered neither the richness of thought nor the abundant solutions of the German, it was because it required courage to fight the dogma of the continuous front. Numerous officers had that courage. At the beginning of 1934, in an article in the *Revue Militaire Française,* Colonel Arguerolles foresaw the creation of motorized divisions containing a regiment of tanks with three battalions; he was praised neither by his Minister of War, Pétain, nor by his Chief of Staff, Weygand, but his plan was lauded by the editor of the *Militär Wochenblatt.*

In October, 1935, Lieutenant-Colonel Lançon published "Some Reflections on Tactics" in the *Revue Militaire Française.* "The idea of large mechanized units is in the air," he said. "To be convinced of it, one has only to read military publications, especially foreign ones. The Austrian General von Eimansberger has recently published a book on tank warfare, which has created a deep impression." In April, 1936, Lançon published, in the same *Revue,* an article called "Motorization and Maneuver." In it he again called for the organization of "units of the type necessary" for the rational use of modern armament, and the adoption of "tactics and strategy conforming to the necessities and possibilities of motorization, which, generally speaking, imposes itself on our age in every field." In February, 1938, the same note appeared in an important article by General Velpry published in the *Revue Militaire Générale.* Velpry pointed out the dangers of the official doctrine outlined in the *Instructions Concerning the Tactical Use of Large Units*—the French equivalent of the German *Tug.* He quoted this sentence from the *Instructions:* "As a general policy, and especially at the beginning of a war, one must avoid open battle." What was still more important, he quoted the opinion of General von Eimansberger: " 'The tactical use of tanks advocated by these *Instructions* constitutes a monstrous unawareness of realities.' " Thus the Germans themselves warned French leaders that they were on the wrong track!

Lastly, there was an article by De Gaulle, published in February, 1934— before General von Eimansberger's book—in the *Revue des Vivants,* and his celebrated book, *Vers l'Armée de Métier,* published at the end of 1934. At the Riom trial Daladier criticized De Gaulle in a friendly way "for connecting the formation of armored divisions with the *armée de métier.*" Daladier was correct in the sense that the *armée de métier* was not a good solution for the modern army; the Germans and Russians were wiser in integrating armored divisions into the mass army, and reorganizing the mass army without returning to the professional army.

If the French General Staff and High Command had not been blinded by the fetish of the continuous front, they would have synthesized the different ideas which, as Lançon put it, "were in the air," as the Germans synthesized the ideas and criticism expressed by their officers. They would have retained what was new and constructive in De Gaulle's book and in the various articles in the military reviews; they would have asked De Gaulle and the other critics to work, revise, consider all objections, and seek inspiration from foreign publications. As head of such a group of young officers, Commandant de Gaulle would have furnished French military thought with the elements of its revival and rejuvenation. But no one in France paid him any attention. Only the German General Staff profited by his ideas; the German military reviews took his book seriously. The *Revue Militaire* gave him a review of twenty-five lines, after which his name was shrouded in silence. Moreover, after Paul Reynaud had called the attention of the Minister of War and of Parliament in March, 1935, to the solutions advocated by De Gaulle, the military leaders condemned the young officer to a kind of ostracism and irrevocably rejected his book. In January, 1937, in an article in the *Revue Militaire Générale,* General Weygand spoke against the *armée de qualité,* the professional army, which he opposed to the mass army; and on the very eve of the war, Marshal Pétain in an exposition of his "war doctrine" hurled his thunderbolt against the author of *Vers l'Armée de Métier,* in the name of the doctrine of the continuous front.

It was with full knowledge of the case that the French military authorities, swollen with pride and doomed by conservatism, refused to change their general outlook. Neither the examples of Germany and Russia nor the arguments of partisans of motorization shook the doctrine of the continuous front. The General Staff wanted neither the motorized divisions of General Doumenc and Colonel Arguerolles nor the armored divisions and the professional army of Commandant de Gaulle. Between 1930 and 1939 the French Army, alone among the great European armies, did not set out boldly on the road of sweeping structural reforms; it slumbered in the shelter of its fortifications while the war clouds gathered. It was still built around the infantry division. To the partisans of the continuous front, the infantry remained "the queen of battles," and the tank and airplane were only auxiliaries in the service of this queen.

Even the Spanish war brought no change in ideas; the General Staff refused to be dragged out of its torpor. At Riom Daladier stated that the French military authorities had tried to find confirmation of their theses in the Spanish war, which they interpreted as a defeat for mass action of armored divisions (because of the Battle of Guadalajara), as a defeat for the intervention of air power in land battle, and as proof of the inefficacy of anti-aircraft artillery and aerial bombardments of open cities. General Duval in *The Lessons of the Spanish War* (1938) and General Chauvineau, in *Is an Invasion Still Possible?* (1938) expressed precisely that interpretation. General Duval's book contained a preface by General Weygand, and General Chauvineau's book, one by Marshal Pétain.

General Chauvineau's book was rightly considered a development of the official doctrine. It was the last book on military doctrine published in France before the war, and it became recommended reading for the Army. It extolled the superiority of the defensive over the offensive, and sang the praises of the continuous front; it contradicted De Gaulle's ideas and opposed the formation of armored divisions. "The command of large mechanized units destined to act in isolation," Chauvineau wrote, "poses insoluble problems because of the dispersion and rapid movement of the participants. Such command would require an intuition and presence of mind that no one possesses." According to Chauvineau, tanks should be considered not as instruments of a strategic offensive or counteroffensive (as the Germans, Russians, and De Gaulle maintained), but as elements of defensive maneuver. "As mobility is the raison d'être and even the safeguard of a caterpillar engine," wrote Chauvineau, "it is fitting to use it only in defensive maneuvers involving movement. . . . In these maneuvers the tank, instead of penetrating the enemy lines and engaging in close fight, which may prove fatal to it . . . withdraws from all its enemies and is content to fire on the vanguard of the infantry or to counterattack with limited objectives. . . . The tank and the infantry, operating in close association, thus seem best qualified to bar the way to an advance. . . . Every infantry battalion should include a tank company and an anti-tank company."* It was the thesis of dispersion pushed to the extreme and even to absurdity. In May, 1940, the French Army had about 3,500 tanks and 1,000 infantry battalions; the application of Chauvineau's ideas would have caused the High Command to organize the tanks in small groups of three or four, to fight the German armored divisions. "Good Lord," the French soldier would have said, "get rid of those marshals and generals with their continuous front, and I'll take care of the *Panzer-divisionen*."

Consequences of French Military Conservatism

With its erroneous conception of modern warfare, it was impossible for the French military to forge an effective instrument of modern war. Neither Daladier's "incompetence" nor the general policy of the Popular Front nor even Fascist betrayal had anything to do with it. The brutal fact is that Germany created an army for a war of movement, which took place, while France created an army for a war of position, which could no longer take place. The false conception of the French High Command compromised the entire military preparation for the war. It influenced simultaneously the organization, armament, and equipment of the Army, and the training of officers and men.

Because of this, the French Army could at best be one of an improved 1918 type. The general organization of the Army was antiquated and outmoded. Until after Munich there were no armored divisions and only three light mechanized cavalry divisions (of which two formed a "cavalry corps"), comprising nine hundred tanks. In his disposition of April 1, 1942, Colonel Perré revealed that it was only on December 2, 1938, that the Supreme War Council, revoking its earlier decisions, decided to create two armored divisions, but not to organize them until 1940—whereas the first two German armored divisions had been decided on in 1934 and created in 1935.

* N. Chauvineau, *Une Invasion Est-Elle Encore Possible?* (Paris: Berger-Levrault, 1938).

To overcome the Supreme War Council's repugnance to the creation of armored divisions, it had been necessary to wait for Marshal Pétain's disappearance from the military picture; he was named Ambassador to the Nationalist government of Spain before December, 1938. Fortunately, Daladier did not wait for 1940 to create armored divisions; in August, 1939, the first armored division was completely formed and equipped, and the second was being organized.

The French Army received armament and equipment corresponding to the general conception which had dictated its formation. Germany, starting with a mobilizable male population almost double that of France— 17,580,000 men from fifteen to forty as against 8,630,000 Frenchmen plus a million mobilizable colonials—and an industry which in the preceding six years had produced three times as much steel and aluminum and three and one-half times as much coal as France, had 120 to 130 *modern* divisions in September, 1939. By applying the same methods and using the head start she obtained from the Versailles Treaty (particularly from the point of view of small arms and equipment), France might have had about 60 divisions as modern as those of Germany, but she could not have had 110 *modern* divisions. The French High Command preferred 110 divisions of an improved 1918 type to 60 divisions of the German or Russian type, because it needed large numbers of men to garrison its continuous front. The French High Command committed once more its mistake of the last war: it preferred a policy of men to one of matériel. In 1912 the achievements of the German Army had raised the question in France whether it was better to ask Parliament for credits to increase the number of men (by raising the period of compulsory active service to three years and lowering the conscription age by one year), or to increase the matériel (especially machine guns and heavy field artillery). The French General Staff chose to increase the number of men. General Debeney, then a professor at the École de Guerre, taught that "our regiments have enough and even too many machine guns." Similarly, on the eve of the present war, with the human and economic resources and the credits put at its disposal by Parliament, the General Staff could have organized a modern army of sixty divisions, including six armored divisions demanded by De Gaulle; but the conservatives of the General Staff preferred an army of 110 divisions, armed and equipped for the continuous front war, to one which would have assured the security of the Allies' "western battlefield."

Finally, the officers of the French Army were trained for the continuous front war, those in the active Army as well as the reserves. Most of the career officers were competent, attentive, and conscientious. One must, however, make a reservation with respect to their political opinions, which separated them from the masses (who constituted the rank of the French Army), isolated them within the country, made them members of a caste rather than officers of a national army, and prevented them from engaging wholeheartedly in a democratic war against Fascist powers. The line officers were good professional soldiers, expert in the routine they had learned. They could have acquired the routine of the war of movement as easily as they learned that of the war of position, but they could not be expected to know the former when they had been taught only the latter. Their regulations for maneuvers, their manuals of instructions, their military schools, their required reading, their work—all orientated them in terms of the continuous front. They had confidence in the ideas of their leaders and the doctrine of the General Staff. After the death of Foch, four great military leaders succeeded, in turn, to the leadership of the Army: Pétain, Maurin, Debeney, and Weygand. All four published magazine articles or books and none of their writings challenged the validity of the continuous front doctrine. The leading military writers occupied an important place on the General Staff—Loiseau, Duval, and Chauvineau, for example—and all were partisans of the continuous front. How, under these circumstances, could that doctrine have commanded anything but respect from the line officers? It was known that the leaders of the Army were divided and jealous of one another, but it was also known that they were unanimous on the form of the future war. After 1935 there was De Gaulle's book, to be sure. But the important men of the Army—those in charge of inspections and those who controlled promotions—spoke with scorn of his book, which only few line officers had read. Those who might have been touched by doubt always found within reach some officer sent by the General Staff to point out the deficiencies of De Gaulle's book and to remind them that a good military man with proper regard for his career should prefer the doctrine of a marshal to that of a commandant. Why should the line officers have felt doubts when everything had been done in the course of their careers to destroy their critical sense? Doubt is the basis of philosophic thinking, but not of the military mind, as French traditions define it. If some subaltern officers permitted themselves personal ideas about the doctrine, the officers' corps as a whole thought that the General Staff, the marshal, and the generals were there to think for them, and that everyone should stay in his own place. There was no chance for such officers, trained since youth to regimental discipline, to escape the infection of conformity.

It was fatal for reserve officers and men to be poorly prepared for the war of movement. To quote General Conquet at the Riom trial, "the men had not been trained to meet the attack of modern engines." Generals de la Porte du Theil and Trolley de Prevaux tried to attribute the inadequate training to the democratic law of one-year military service. This argument does not hold. French reserve officers, noncommissioned officers, and men had spent, on the average, more time than the Germans in the barracks and training camps. In May, 1940, the least trained French soldier had done one year of military service and had been mobilized since September, 1939; his officers had had twenty months to teach him. For an Army that had 4,000 more career officers than the Germans, such a period of time was more than sufficient.

The officers and men of the French Army should actually have been better than the officers and men of the German Army, especially since French social structure—unfavorable though it was to economic preparation for modern warfare because of France's lack of heavy industry—was adapted admirably to the military training of a modern army. France, much more than Germany, was a country of artisans, small industrialists, and entrepreneurs— men accustomed to head "small teams" of workers and to make decisions. The modern war of movement conformed both to the general professional training of the average Frenchman and to his temperament; for he has always been a man of action more than one of patience, more intelligent and resourceful than disciplined, a better fighter than a military man. If the High Command had chosen its reserve officers from the town councilors and village artisans, it would have been able to build and train a modern army within the one-year military service; but it preferred the young bourgeois of the Croix de Feu, whose political opinions were those of the High Command to the natural leaders of the French people. A better understanding of the social morphology of the people would have provided the High Command with an instrument for the creation of a modern army superior to that at the disposal of the German High Command.

The French High Command made no effort to understand. It remained the prisoner of its class prejudices and of its doctrine. The malady which attacked the French Army before the war and put it into a state of least resistance during the war was a malady of the intellect and the spinal marrow, striking first at the brain, extending to the nervous centers, and causing, at last, a general paralysis of the organism.

The misuse of the Army during May and June, 1940, even more than the inadequate preparation revealed the crisis in French military intelligence and the failure of the General Staff. With its absolute freedom of operations, the High Command could not escape by confusing political and military responsibilities. It was plainly responsible, because it alone was responsible. Hence the Vichy government tried to avoid mention of the military operations at the public hearings at Riom. It did not succeed entirely. The accused were clever enough to ask the witnesses questions on both the military preparation and the conduct of operations, and President Caous was loyal enough to resist, if only temporarily, the expected policy of covering up the truth.

Military operations were thus drawn, however incompletely, into the discussion. The evidence of Daladier and the witnesses would be inadequate if we had to pronounce definitive judgment on the action of the General Staff in the Battle of France; but this evidence reveals the procedures and methods of the Staff through the military operations. These operations should be considered a test, to permit us to weigh the responsibility of the military authorities.

The war was badly conducted because it had been badly prepared, and it was badly prepared because it had been poorly conceived. A very general comparison of the plans and methods used by the Germans and the French will bear out this statement.

THE GERMAN MILITARY DOCTRINE:
THE SCHLIEFFEN PLAN

In the attack on France the Germans used the plans of General Schlieffen, remodeled and adapted to the techniques of modern warfare.

Schlieffen's basic conception was that Germany must avoid a two-front war by fighting the French Army and the Russian Army in turn. Before risking war with Russia or in case of a war involving all of Europe, Germany was first to dispose of France, and only then send her armies against an eastern front. For only a war against France could be a short war. To liquidate the French Army, France was considered as an immense fortress which had to be surrounded. The east of France, along the German frontier, was well protected by the strongholds of Nancy, Toul, and Verdun; these defenses were to be overwhelmed by a broad strategic movement of encirclement to overcome— *einrollen*—the entire French Army.

To realize the idea on which he had worked since 1897, Schlieffen set up the following plan of maneuver in 1905: the German Army should be deployed, facing France, around the fortress of Metz. The Army should include two flanks of unequal strength, one extending from Metz to the Swiss frontier, and the other from Metz to the North Sea. The right flank, on the northwest of Metz, should be the marching flank. Widely staggered in depth, this flank was to send its columns toward France, crossing Belgium along the Antwerp-Namur line (and, said Schlieffen, "crossing Holland if diplomacy permits it; otherwise, in order not to arouse the fear of England, the way through Belgium would have to do"); the marching wing was to cross the Meuse, penetrate into France, and head toward the area of Abbeville-Saint-Quentin to overcome the left flank of the French Army. This action would begin by describing an almost perfect semicircle around the pivot, Metz; the radius of this semicircle was then to be prolonged, and the circle would become an ellipse. The German right wing was to cross the Seine in the direction of Rouen, to cut off the French Army from any English forces which might be sent to its aid. This wing would then swerve toward the south and fall back toward the east while continuing to destroy the French left flank. It would thus force the French Army to retreat toward the frontiers of the Jura. Nothing would remain for the German Army to do but march straight ahead in open terrain, leaving Paris to the north. This would enclose the French Army "in a sack," force it to fall back to the strong points of Verdun, Toul, Nancy, and Belfort, and deprive it of the space necessary for any maneuver, cutting it off from the rest of France and holding it between the two claws of a huge pincer. Rendered incapable of receiving reinforcements and supplies, the French Army would be impotent and quickly reduced to the point of capitulation.

Schlieffen's plan was the outline of a great chess game which would culminate in the checkmate of the French Army, less by battle than by a series of marches. Like Napoleon, Schlieffen based his plan on the maneuvering abilities of his army and on "the legs of the infantrymen." To free the men needed for his encircling maneuver and to assure the necessary rigidity for the semicircle which he intended to trace with his armies on the map of Western Europe, Schlieffen decided to fortify his right wing, at the expense of his left. The left wing served only to fix French troops—fix them rather than hold them—by retreating, if necessary. Schlieffen coldly envisaged the possibility that this wing might be taken and Alsace and The Palatinate invaded, believing with Frederick the Great that "one must know how to lose a province to win the war." In the distribution of his army corps, he gave his marching wing sixty-nine infantry divisions, eight cavalry divisions, and twenty-two Landwehr brigades, while allotting the left wing only ten infantry divisions, three cavalry divisions, and one Landwehr brigade, besides the garrisons of Metz and Strasbourg—a total ratio of seven to one. The marching wing itself was formed of three unequal groups of which, once more, the right group was the strongest, having thirty divisions, whereas the left group had sixteen, and the center thirteen. Thus the mass of the German maneuver was to be concentrated at its extreme right wing, prepared to throw itself into the great adventure and sweep across the countryside of France like a great wave carrying everything in its path.

Schlieffen later modified his plan to take into account the offensive tendencies which the French General Staff was showing under the influence of Colonel de Grandmaison, head of the Troisième Bureau (Operations). Schlieffen drew up a memorandum in 1912 in which he prophesied the possibility that the French, anticipating the Germans, would be the first to reach the Antwerp-Namur line. It would then be necessary to make a tactical break-through before proceeding to the strategic maneuver; this break-through in the French front would be enlarged to permit the German Army to charge and execute the encircling maneuver. To force the French to divide their forces, attacks were to be staged along the whole front. Because of the terrain and the existence of French fortifications in the east, Schlieffen pointed out that the break-through should be made in Belgium and the Meuse should be crossed at Sedan. Afterwards, the mopping-up armies would head for Abbeville, Saint-Quentin, and Rouen, according to the plan of 1905. The reader will understand the importance of these details when we come to the account of the march of the German armies in May and June, 1940.

Failure of the Plan in World War I

The Schlieffen plan failed in 1914, not because it had been poorly conceived, but because it was poorly executed by Schlieffen's successor.

The plan to be applied was not that of the 1912 memorandum, but that of 1905. For the execution of the 1912 plan—tactical break-through preceding the strategic maneuver—Schlieffen had foreseen the need to create new army corps, and these corps had not been formed. The 1905 plan, however, was applicable in 1914, because the German armies, having penetrated into Belgium by surprise, had reached and passed the Antwerp-Namur line before the French. These armies could consequently carry out their encircling maneuver without a tactical break-through, but the plan was badly executed. Count Helmuth von Moltke the younger, the Commander-in-Chief of the German armies, was a man without energy or character, a kind of German Pétain, completely lacking in the daring and imagination which make great captains. Fifteen years younger that Schlieffen, he had succeeded him at the head of the German General Staff partly because he had won Wilhelm II's confidence by flattery; he was as much a courtier as a military man. Ludendorff revealed in his memoirs that Moltke believed in occultism and consulted the stars before offering battle. This timid man did not follow Schlieffen's "will" in his decisions. He replaced the ratio of seven to one in the division of forces between his right and left wings by a ratio of four to one, then of three to one. He could not face the possibility of seeing French troops on German soil, and feared the outbursts of Wilhelm II. Before the war, Schlieffen, who knew Moltke well, was already disturbed by these tendencies, which threatened to compromise the success of his plan. Obsessed by his marching wing, the great Schlieffen repeated even on his deathbed, "Give me only a powerful right wing."

Moltke did not create such a wing. Cut in half, the German marching wing no longer had the means of seeking in Normandy the large spaces which were to assure its freedom of maneuver; it was still able to pass the French right wing, but it could not overwhelm it powerfully enough to catch it and pull it to the east. It still retained the initiative in operations, but its point was blunted; it could no longer dare to cross the lower Seine north of Rouen, and encircle Paris, a maneuver that would have dealt a powerful blow at the beginning of the war to the morale of the French nation by dislocating governmental, administrative, and economic life. Nevertheless, the Schlieffen plan was so strongly marked by military genius that, although distorted and poorly carried out, it gave the German High Command a margin of superiority that permitted it to dominate the French Army and to impose its will. At that time it was the superiority of the French High Command over the German that saved the French Army, or rather the superiority of Joffre—an old republican soldier, the son of a cooper, with no use for occultism—over Count von Moltke.

The escape of the French Army was accomplished on two different occasions and was the result of two factors: the wisdom of Joffre and the nervous timidity of Moltke. The first occasion was the clever retreat of the French Army. Keeping his wits about him, Joffre refused to give battle under unfavorable conditions and withdrew his troops, not letting himself be overwhelmed by the Germans. He thus forced the troops of the German marching wing to wear themselves out in pursuit—for Moltke, as a consequence of his initial error and by abandoning the famous seven-to-one ratio, could no longer send fresh troops to relieve those charged with carrying out the maneuver. By his retreat Joffre forced the Germans to lengthen their line, to extend themselves, a thing which they could have done under the original Schlieffen plan, but could not do with a Schlieffen-Moltke plan except by thinning and weakening the line. The second instance was the Russian attack in East Prussia in answer to Joffre's SOS to Russia through the French government. The intervention of the Russians saved the French Army. The Russian Army had not yet finished mobilizing, and all the German calculations had been based on the inevitable delays in the mobilization of a mass army in a country where distances are huge and means of communication quite poor. But the Russians understood in 1914 that to win a war of coalition, an ally must be prepared to lose a battle and launch an offensive under unfavorable circumstances, in order to avoid still greater misfortunes. They attacked with great courage, certain of defeat, and paid no attention to rules of prudence or to the art of war.

To oppose this attack, the German High Command had to withdraw two army corps from the western front and send them to the eastern front. Moltke was forced into a war on two simultaneous fronts, which Schlieffen had advised against and which will always offer a fatal threat to Germany. Moreover, the French now attacked in Alsace and Lorraine, in an attempt to "pinch off" all the German troops not charged with the encircling maneuver. Moltke fell into Joffre's trap; he withdrew the two army corps for the eastern front from the marching wing, which was already weak, and deprived himself of any possibility of bringing his maneuver against the French Army to a successful conclusion. "I admit," he wrote in his memoirs, "that the error committed at that moment was paid for on the Marne."

The punishment for Moltke's mistakes and the reward for Joffre's cool-headedness both came, indeed, on the Marne. Instead of continuing its march toward Rouen, the German right wing drove back toward the east and passed north of the entrenched camp of Paris, directly before the French armies, instead of being on their flank or rear. Aerial reconnaissance (the first in military history) informed the French General Staff of this change in direction. Joffre understood that the moment had come to halt his retreat and to counterattack. General Joseph Simon Galliéni, military commander of Paris, sent troops to Joffre's aid in Paris taxicabs which he requisitioned (the first use of motorized troops). Joffre ordered the attack, and the Battle of the Marne began. The French offensive changed the course of destiny by forcing the German troops to halt their advance, dig trenches, and take shelter. After the long retreat, the French Army no longer had fresh troops or strong enough artillery to throw back the German divisions. It was then that the folly of the French General Staff became manifest; it had preferred large numbers of men, which it obtained by the three-year conscription law, to the construction of extensive heavy field artillery. But Joffre was able to hold his adversaries, deprive them of the benefit of the initiative, and avoid encirclement. The calm genius of the French general caused the Schlieffen plan as carried out by Moltke to fail.

Most historians believe, with reason, that Joffre on the Marne and in his collaboration with the Russians won not only the battle but the war. His maneuver had drawn Germany into a war on two simultaneous fronts of almost equal importance—a war which Germany was fated to lose for geographic as well as military reasons. The strategic exploitation of the Marne victory by Joffre was another proof of his coolheadedness. He drew up the balance sheet of his own forces and of the enemy's; then, instead of exhausting the slight margin of superiority that his maneuver had given him by trying to take back a few more square feet of French soil, and instead of charging straight ahead in what a German author was to call "buffalo strategy," Joffre began the "race to the sea." As Foch said, it was really a "race to the enemy," with Frenchmen and Germans both trying to avoid the overflowing of their northern wings and both lengthening their lines. Joffre understood that, in a war which was becoming a long and two-front war for his enemies, the essential problem was to establish a strong liaison between the French forces and the British Army still in the process of formation. Here again, he was improvising his maneuver and making the best use of his resources. He created a new cavalry corps out of elements which had not been formed into divisions (army corps regiments and divisional squadrons); at the same time he used all the means of transportation at his disposal to send his troops toward the north—thus two divisions at Paris were sent toward Le Havre and Cherbourg and transported by sea to Dunkerque. He maneuvered on the arc of a circle while the Germans used the chord. When the French troops had reached the sea and rendered the enemy stationary in the Battle of Flanders, Joffre, a former engineering officer, brought his whole army into the field and gave a brilliant demonstration of trench warfare. The war at that point became a trench war and on the western front became a war of attrition. The Allies won this war of attrition thanks to the resistance of the Russians and to the arrival of American troops at the front. Russian resistance was all the more admirable if one considers that the Russian General Staff and the Russian government were rotten with Fifth Column activity at a time when the term had not yet been invented and that Czarist Russia had no industry to manufacture sufficient quantities of armament and equipment.

Joffre had been able to force a continuous front war on his enemy because he was not possessed by the specter of the continuous front. This old anti-clerical with his scientific and Voltairian mind believed in no dogmas. He arrived at a continuous front by way of maneuver—the only instance of a large-scale maneuver on the western front. He succeeded because his mind was more modern and flexible than that of his adversary. The common man in the service of the French Republic overcame the aristocrat in the service of the German Empire because he had fewer prejudices; he was victorious because of his reconnaissance squadrons and the "taxis" of the Marne— the aerial and motorized forces of his day.

After the Battle of the Marne and the race to the sea, the war became a matter of routine. None of the large attacks staged by the French, English, or Germans succeeded in breaking the line of steel of the continuous front. "What are you doing?" Joffre was asked by the impatient. "I am nibbling them away," he would answer in his voice of a peasant from the Pyrenees.

Unfortunately, Gamelin, Pétain, and Weygand mistook the continuous front for a gift of Providence and "buffalo strategy" for the last word in the art of war.

The New Version of the Plan and Its Application

The failure of the Schlieffen plan in World War I did not daunt the Germans. Between 1919 and 1939 German Army leaders and the General Staff studied Schlieffen's work with renewed vigor. With the methodical patience of the German mind, they carefully considered all the factors and eliminated what could not be used.

A mysticism grew up around Schlieffen in Germany, just as one developed in France around the continuous front. Among the German military intelligentsia Schlieffen had many partisans and few opponents; he was compared to Napoleon, Clausewitz, and the elder Moltke; his plan, broken down into its elements and resynthesized, became the *pons asinorum* of the German General Staff. The Germans continued to believe that in case of another World War it would be necessary to dispose of the French before attacking the Russian Army, more powerful than the old Czarist Army; and that it would be imperative to flank the eastern fortifications to invade "the fortress of France" through Belgium. The French continued to ignore Schlieffen's ideas. A translation of the plan was published in France with a dry and impersonal preface by General Weygand that made no comment on Schlieffen's ideas. In French military literature there was only one study of any importance, a mere historical account in the form of three tedious articles by Commandant Courbis in the *Revue Militaire*. French Army leaders derided the Schlieffen plan and the interest it aroused on the other side of the Rhine. In his book *War and Men* (1937) General Debeney, Weygand's predecessor as Chief of Staff, assailed General Schlieffen with his irony; he invented a dialogue in Hades between Schlieffen and the younger Moltke in which the latter demonstrated to "poor Schlieffen" that his plan had failed because it had been unfeasible and always would be. "I saw nothing to object to," added Debeney, "in the German High Command's adherence to [the Schlieffen plan]. Nor do I object to the Germans' continuing belief that this doctrine proved itself in 1914 and 1918. That is their affair." Such was the superior and detached tone taken by one of the leading French military authorities just two years before the present war in speaking of the intellectual effort of the German Army. It is true that in the same book General Debeney added: "It was the coexistence of modern matériel and vast numbers of men in the leading nations which created the continuous front." In an earlier book, *Concerning the Military Security of France* (1929), he fought the idea of the professional army and the short war.

The study of the Schlieffen plan served as a central theme for Germany military thought and proved to be the best plan which the German General Staff could use against the French Army. Modern techniques and armament offered greater hope of carrying out the plan than those of 1905 or 1912; the airplane and tank were better for strategic maneuver and tactical break-through than Schlieffen's heavy artillery, infantrymen, and cavalry divisions. And the Germans equipped themselves with the necessary modern armament. The plan as carried out in 1940 was the original plan plus the internal combustion engine.

The general and military policy followed by the French General Staff, particularly under Marshal Pétain's influence, not only facilitated the setting up of this plan, but in a sense demanded a return to it. On the military level, this policy gave the German High Command the three most favorable elements for the encircling maneuver advocated by Schlieffen. The construction of the Maginot Line drew the French right wing to the Franco-German frontier, furnishing the German left wing with the pivot it needed. The decision of the Supreme War Council, at Pétain's request, not to extend the Maginot Line beyond the Belgian frontier facilitated the enveloping maneuver of the marching wing, giving it (in the plains of Flanders and northern France) the open spaces necessary for its deploy. Lastly, Pétain's refusal to allow the Ardennes region and the passages from the Meuse to Sedan to be fortified created a zone of least resistance at the very spot chosen by Schlieffen for his tactical break-through. Similarly, under Pétain's influence, the general policy of the military circles favored the enemy—their hate of Communism caused the rupture of the Franco-Soviet Pact (through the agency of Bonnet); Franco-Italian amity prevented answering the German maneuver by a French attack through Italy (Laval's work); and narrow patriotism, based on admiration for the *ancien régime,* finally rendered French military men incapable of conceiving a broad strategic retreat involving the withdrawal of the French Army to North Africa, when it was necessary to abandon metropolitan France to win the war. Thus the general and military policy of Pétain eliminated the only efficacious strategic parries.

The plan, curtailed by Moltke in 1914, was broadened by Hitler's generals. The use of all of the Low Countries, Holland included, to deploy the columns of the marching wing, as recommended in the early plan, was self-evident, since England supported France. To parry a British counterattack that might come from the sea, the occupation of Denmark was added; and to protect both the flank and the rear, Norway was invaded. The invasion of Norway was intended to immobilize several French and British divisions, just as the Finnish War was later to immobilize Russian troops and Italy's entry into the war after the beginning of the encircling maneuver was to immobilize the French Army in the Alps. The enlargement of the Schlieffen plan gave the maneuvering army the freedom and territory required. It was obviously the 1912 memorandum rather than the plan of 1905 that was to be used. For one thing, there was little chance of success for a strategic surprise which would make possible the occupation of the Antwerp-Namur region and the crossing of the Meuse before the French could recover themselves; before attacking France, it was necessary to get rid of Poland and Czechoslovakia, and the disposal of these two countries, however cleverly managed by Hitlerian diplomacy, was bound to arouse the attention of the French. Besides, France and England were bound by a powerful solidarity of interests as well as by the Locarno Pact.

In 1914 the German General Staff had overlooked the "negligible English Army." In 1940 a British Expeditionary Force on the European continent had to be expected as soon as operations against France began. For these reasons, as Schlieffen had foreseen in 1912, it was vital to precede the strategic mopping-up with a tactical break-through, preferably in the area of Sedan. For this the General Staff built an army that Schlieffen could not have envisaged in 1912. The maneuvering mass was composed of modern engines (bombers and attacking planes, parachute troops and tanks) arranged in large specialized units capable of effecting both the tactical break-through (by means of armored and aerial divisions) and the strategic mopping-up operations (using mechanized divisions, motorized infantry, light bombers, and parachutists). The German General Staff had facilities unknown to Schlieffen. In his time cavalry divisions could not be used for breaking through, and the break-through of infantry presupposed the use of heavy artillery, whose slowness excluded the element of surprise. The new plan was based on the idea of a tactical break-through, accomplished in part by a surprise action that would facilitate its strategic exploitation.

This exploitation was to be developed on both sides of the breach. Certain mopping-up units (whose importance would depend on the disposition of Franco-British forces) were to drive the extreme left of the French armies and the British Expeditionary Force toward the sea, while other units were to overrun Paris, move toward the lower Seine, and then return to the east, accomplishing the large enveloping maneuver. The double objective was to outflank the fortifications of the Maginot Line and to release toward the southeast, elements which could join the Italian Army, whose attack would come at the opportune moment.

The general object of the new plan was the division of the Franco-British armies into three fragments, and the encirclement of these fragments by large movements of motorized troops. The northern fragment (the Franco-British Army of the far left) was to be driven to the sea; the central fragment (the troops of the Maginot Line) were to be bottled up in their own fortifications and destroyed by attacks from all sides; the southern fragment (the Army of the Alps) was to be attacked by the Italian Army, aided by German columns coming down the Rhône valley and returning by way of the upper Rhône valley and the valleys of the Isére and the Romanche. The essential maneuver, the cornerstone of the operation, remained the one advocated by Schlieffen, but it was an enlarged and motorized Schlieffen plan, on the scale of Hitler's ambitions, beginning with moves into Norway and ending with operations which pushed the German divisions to the shores of the Mediterranean.

The 1940 version of the Schlieffen plan was carried out masterfully, with a precision indicating the accuracy of the General Staff's political forecasts and the degree of training in an army that, in addition to the usual maneuvers, had been prepared by actual experience in modern warfare in Spain and Poland.

According to Daladier (hearing of March 27, 1942), the Germans trapped the French by drawing them into Belgium. The French line was lengthened according to the principles of the lineal strategy so dear to Marshal Pétain and his disciples, because this line was supposed to form a continuous front. A continuous line, however, cannot grow longer without growing thinner. The front was broken at Sedan with such ease as must have made the German High Command laugh. An invading army with armored divisions, under the command of General Guderian, drove the Belgian, English, and French armies at its right toward the sea. These armies were trapped and bottled up. The Belgian Army capitulated, and the Franco-British troops, surrounded and threatened with annihilation, embarked at Dunkerque for the British Isles under cover of the fleet and air force. Thanks to the wisdom of its commanders and the courage and discipline of the troops, this mass evacuation aroused the admiration of the world.

But one should not be deceived: the embarkation at Dunkerque was conclusive proof of the Franco-British defeat. The German High Command had achieved its objective: the separation of the Franco-British forces of the north from the main body of the French Army, which was chained to the Maginot Line, and the elimination of these forces from action during the entire time required for the principal encircling movement executed by a wide swerve around Paris. This maneuver remained the essential feature of the plan. It was carried out without difficulty because the French High Command, unable to foresee anything, was equally incapable of improvisation. The encircling maneuver was facilitated by local break-throughs or gains, which were effected along the entire front (notably at Champagne) and had been anticipated in the Schlieffen memorandum of 1912. In 1940 the German High Command did not err as in 1914; instead of moving east too soon, it moved backwards a little and then on towards Rouen and the lower Seine, certain not to find any serious resistance in the west of France—in Normandy, Brittany, and the Loire valley. Moving now straight ahead and now towards the lines of least resistance, armored and motorized divisions crossed the Seine and Loire, pushed their vanguards through Brittany, and detached some units toward Paris, without ever giving the French High Command time to recover and reassemble its forces. Certain columns then proceeded along the Atlantic coast, and others moved up the Loire valley, driving before them the remnants of the French Army. The maneuver continued until the final onslaught, which in its vastness was unprecedented in modern military history.

The Battle of France lasted less than six weeks. As Victor Hugo said of the defeat of the *Grande Armée* at Waterloo, the French regiments "melted away like wax" in the sun of the summer of 1940. This battle left dreadful memories in the hearts of all Frenchmen—memories of incompetence and of betrayal. But because of these memories, a Frenchman must recognize that the Battle of France was a credit to the knowledge of the enemy leaders who conceived, prepared, and conducted it.

The campaign did no honor to the French General Staff. It was a chess game which the German High Command won in a few moves, not because it held more pawns than its enemy, but because it was better acquainted with the rules of the game of war and with the rules for the employment of modern matériel. The Battle of France proved that French technicians were no less capable of producing good war matériel than German technicians, and that Daladier was able to obtain proportionately as many tanks from a given quantity of steel and aluminum as had Goering. The Battle of France proved that the French soldier had lost none of his traditional qualities; the British and Americans will not forget that 125,000 French soldiers gave their lives for the cause of liberty. The Battle of France proved that the line officers were courageous and led their men under fire as well as did the German officers. But the Battle of France also proved the incompetence of a General Staff which did not know how to make the most of the human and material resources entrusted to it.

We need not wait for publication of the military archives to attest to that incompetence, but the archives will help to establish the particular errors and individual responsibilities and, above all, will help to distinguish among treason, ignorance, and vanity. For a general judgment, there is sufficient evidence in the proceedings of the Supreme Court, in certain public statements made by General Weygand since the armistice, and in the declarations of Lord Gort, Commander of the British Expeditionary Forces in France.

THE FRENCH DEFENSE

The following general view is based on the disposition of French forces in May and June, 1940, and particularly on the disposition of the troops sent by the High Command against the German invaders.

Scattering of forces characterized the general disposition of the French armies. Corps and divisions, instead of being concentrated for a definite action, were spread out along the frontiers, from the Mediterranean to the North Sea, by the linear-meter method—so many soldiers, so many cannon, and so many machine guns to the meter.

Shipment of a powerful army to Syria, at the request of General Weygand and under his command, had begun the scattering of forces. His idea was "to open an eastern front," either by invading Central Europe or, preferably, by attacking Russia, whom he called the faithful ally of Germany. France, he contended, had nothing to fear from Italy. This idea was so preposterous that I must cite my sources. In a speech at Dakar before the officers and noncommissioned officers after the abortive landing attempt of General de Gaulle and the British, Weygand said: "In order to open hostilities with a country of eighty million inhabitants, which possessed an enormous and highly perfected war matériel and had prepared itself minutely in every field for a war to be fought at a time it would choose, a country obeying a single leader, it was necessary for a nation of only forty million inhabitants and relatively little war matériel to assure itself of an eastern front. I worked for the creation of a Mediterranean front, but I did not succeed in persuading the responsible men to do what would have been necessary for the creation of such a front." The General Staff published and distributed copies of this speech. Early in 1940 Weygand traveled from Syria to Paris and on April 3 proposed to the war cabinet that the government profit by the Russo-Finnish War to attack Germany from the south "and thus deprive Germany of the oil of Rumania and of the Caucasus."

Weygand's great idea was to attack Russia. Historians will learn the reasons for such a proposal, which can be explained only by ignorance or by a criminal desire to substitute a war against Soviet Russia for a war against Fascist Germany. France obviously could not fight the Soviet Union and Germany at the same time; a war against Russia would be a means for France to propose to Germany the organization of an anti-Communist crusade. The Chamber of Deputies met in secret session while Weygand was in Paris, and Flandin and Tixier-Vignancourt, pro-Fascist deputies, asked that France aid Finland by attacking the Soviet Union. Weygand's proposal thus formed part of the Fifth Column's plan of action. Daladier, then Premier, and Reynaud, who succeeded him a few days later, rejected Weygand's proposals. Weygand's influence on the General Staff, however, was strong, and a large army of elite troops was sent to Syria; more than fifteen divisions were kept on the African continent, but none was ever used against the Germans.

In a further scattering of forces, thirteen divisions were sent to the Alps, facing Italy. In September, 1939, when the German Army was fighting in Poland, an ultimatum could have been sent to Italy, demanding that she clarify her position; invasion of the Italian peninsula and liberation of the people from dictatorship could have followed an unsatisfactory reply. This proposal actually was made to the French government by Count Carlo Sforza, an anti-Fascist leader then in Paris. Italy's Army was in no position to fight at that time; the frontier was poorly fortified on the Italian side, and the Italian people, weary of Fascism, would have hailed the French as liberators, just as they hailed the Americans and British four years later. Count Sforza's proposal was approved by General Gamelin, and the French Army of the Alps held itself ready to march on Italy. On the insistence of Georges Bonnet and Anatole de Monzie, the French cabinet preferred to appease Mussolini. All that winter France supplied the oil and iron ore Fascist Italy needed for armament manufacture.

Finally, there were the troops opposing the German armies. Although under the immediate command of General Georges, they were actually the maneuvering mass that Gamelin, and then Weygand, were going to use. They included the Maginot Line garrisons, almost as large as those of the Siegfried Line, and about sixty divisions divided into three groups of armies: Billotte's in the north, behind the Belgian frontier; Pretelat's in the center, behind the Maginot Line, and Besson's in the east, guarding the Swiss frontier, whose violation was expected. Another fifteen divisions were held in reserve.

A general distribution of this sort was unwise, in that it gave too little importance to the northern frontier where the attack was most likely to occur. Reserves aside, almost half the French troops in line were in Syria, the

Alps, behind the Swiss frontier, or behind the Maginot Line, while four-fifths of the German Army was available for execution of the new version of the Schlieffen plan by way of Belgium. Even before the attack the French Army was in an inferior position as a result of its poor distribution—the fault of its High Command.

This initial disadvantage increased in the course of battle. As soon as the scope of the German High Command's plans was revealed by the invasion of Denmark and the Low Countries, the French High Command had to choose between going to the aid of the Belgian Army and letting it receive the first shock while French troops massed behind the Franco-Belgian border on familiar soil prepared in advance. Gamelin decided to go into Belgium, which had the advantage of shortening his front. This decision made, he had to choose between two possible maneuvers, both of which had been studied in peacetime: the l'Escaut maneuver, which consisted in advancing the right wing of Billotte's group toward that river, and the Dyle maneuver, which was a penetration of all Belgium by the Billotte group, the area of Sedan serving as a pivot. Gamelin decided on the latter strategy, and Billotte's divisions entered Belgium to meet the German troops.

Billotte's group was composed of five armies. From the North Sea to the Sedan-Longwy region, where the Maginot Line began, were the Seventh Army (Giraud), the British Expeditionary Force, the First Army (Blanchard), the Ninth Army (Corap), and the Second Army (Huntzinger). The Belgian forces were assigned to General Billotte and were to serve as a shock absorber for his troops. According to General Weygand, Billotte had forty-six divisions at his disposal (twenty-four Belgian, thirteen French, nine British) plus the majority of the French mechanized divisions and the British armored division. Gamelin was said to have given Billotte his best troops and matériel.

Only specialists on military questions can one day decide whether Gamelin was right or wrong in going into Belgium. His decision was certainly influenced by the desire of the British to see the Belgian coast defended. But the prerequisite for the Dyle maneuver was the creation of a solid bolt for the "hinge" of Sedan, and the adoption of the measures necessary to oppose the crossing of the Meuse by German columns debouching from the Ardennes Forest. It was not necessary to have studied Schlieffen's plan to appreciate the importance of the gap at Sedan and Ardennes. All French boys and girls in elementary school knew that the French Army had been beaten at Sedan in 1870, and the veterans of 1914 remembered that the invading armies had passed through the Ardennes region before reaching the Marne. History and geography both marked this spot, even to those ignorant of military matters. The two armies defending the area of Ardennes and Sedan were commanded by Generals Corap and Huntzinger, and comprised in large part cavalry and reserve divisions. Huntzinger (who was to become Minister of War in the Vichy government) was considered a good general. But General Corap, a militant member of l'Action Française, was justly considered an incompetent leader. Since the French General Staff expected the principal German drive at the extreme right of its forces toward the North Sea, the best parts of the Billotte group had been brought under the command of General Giraud, while the poorest of the French armies and the most incompetent general were stationed in the Ardennes sector. Gamelin's error was in believing what Marshal Pétain had so often said, that the Ardennes region was impenetrable and that the Meuse could not be crossed. Everything took place as if General Gamelin (whose honesty and patriotism are unquestioned) had been advised by Fifth Column agents to choose the alternatives most favorable to the German armies.

The Germans decided to break the French front between Sedan and Carignan—the very point indicated by Schlieffen—and found themselves opposed by an inferior general and insufficient troops. On May 12, 1940, the armored force of General Guderian, preceding two other armies charged with supporting his maneuver, attacked the French line. Guderian's vanguard drove back the cavalry which Corap had caused to advance into Belgian territory. Specialized attacking troops crossed the Meuse and established a bridgehead under cover of attacking aircraft; the operation was quite easy, for General Corap had failed to blow up the bridges of the Semois (a small river in front of the Meuse) and those of the Meuse itself. On May 13 the bridgehead was consolidated and the two lips of the breach in the French forces were widened. On the 14th, forestalling Corap, who was thinking of counterattacking, the *Panzerdivisionen* drove into open country; they took, in passing, the headquarters of General Corap, who fled with his General Staff, leaving his papers, documents, and plans behind. French-speaking German officers immediately took over the telephones and radiophones and transmitted to the French troops orders which increased their confusion. In the meantime, troops specialized in defense strongly entrenched themselves on the edges of the breach in order to oppose any possible French counterattacks. Abandoned without orders to the onslaught of the Germans, dismayed by a type of war for which nothing had prepared them, demoralized by the attack of the Stukas and the charge of armored engines, the Corap army fell to pieces. Colonel Conrad H. Lanza, an observer for the United States Army, published a very well-documented report on the history of the Corap army and the tragedy of Sedan in the *Field Artillery Journal* (February, 1941): "Officers . . . could not remember anything in the Regulations which applied to a situation like this. They rallied their men . . . took emergency measures, hoping to the last that someone would come along with an intelligent order. It never came. The confusion became hopeless. . . . They had been abandoned by their own headquarters. They gave up. Men threw away their arms and joined the hordes of refugees which crowded the roads."

The public debates at Riom threw one ray of light on this tragedy. General Etcheberigaray testified at the hearing of March 27 that three reserve divisions and no active divisions had been placed at the "hinge." Daladier observed that the French reserve divisions (like the troops of the German Landwehr) did not have the modern armament of the active divisions. To the most threatened point of the front, the French High Command had sent its most poorly equipped troops to face the elite troops of General Guderian. Etcheberigaray added this comment, so compromising for the General Staff:

"The invasion of German armored units on May 13 and 14, 1940, could not be absorbed because we received the shock where we did not expect it. . . . The circumstances of the enemy attack were not what we had anticipated." Colonel Lanza, in the previously mentioned study, confirmed this viewpoint: ". . . in the Sedan campaign, the Allies made an erroneous assumption as to the enemy's intentions. He did not make his main effort on his right, but on his left. The erroneous assumption was fatal—it led to catastrophe. . . ."

Broken at Sedan, the French front could not be reconstituted. General Gamelin, his armored divisions dispersed, lacked the elements for a large-scale counterattack to cut off the Guderian army from its bases. One French armored division had been sent to the north with the Giraud army; another was in the rear, to guard the bridges of the Oise and the Sambre Canal; a third was with the Huntzinger army to defend the Argonne. Only the fourth armored division, commanded by De Gaulle, was available. Once more the method of "little packages" had prevailed. Led by De Gaulle, the fourth armored division performed prodigious feats, but it could not remedy the situation single-handed. All of Gamelin's counterattacks met the resistance of troops specialized in defense, which played as decisive a role in the Battle of France as the armored divisions and the attacking aircraft. While the Guderian army continued its advance, the second and twelfth German armies, which were following his armored and motorized divisions, penetrated to the right and to the left of the constantly widening breach, and undertook to drive the French troops to the north and south. The first part of the battle of France was won by the German Army.

The Mistakes of the High Command

Following Gamelin's failure, the Reynaud cabinet gave General Weygand supreme direction of operations. After his appointment, one seeks in vain for even the shadow of a strategic idea in the decisions of the French High Command. If there had really been any sincere desire to continue fighting, the means were not lacking. An important battle, not the war, had been lost. Two principal solutions were feasible as well as a whole gamut of compromise solutions combining the principal alternatives.

One was suggested by General de Gaulle, who had been named Undersecretary of State in the Ministry of War. He wanted to withdraw toward Brittany what could be saved of the French Army, to keep, if possible, a bridgehead on French continental territory. This bridgehead would have had the support of the English and French fleets, whose big guns and antiaircraft defenses would have helped the troops in a territory particularly favorable for defense. "If we cannot resist in the *réduit Breton,*" said De Gaulle, "our troops will embark for North Africa." This solution offered the advantage of retaining in France the bridgehead necessary for a landing of Allied forces. Perhaps it was too ambitious in view of the forces remaining to the French Army, but it deserved to be tried. If it succeeded, it would have left France and the Allies North Africa as well as a foothold on the continent—certain guarantees of victory. It was to General De Gaulle's honor that he proposed it. Weygand rejected the plan and offered nothing in its place.

The second solution would have had the whole French Army, from the Vosges to the North Sea, fall back in order to evacuate the largest possible number of divisions to North Africa from the Atlantic and Mediterranean ports. This strategic withdrawal would have been possible if everything was destroyed in the course of the retreat, if all the bridges, crossroads, aqueducts, cities, factories, and railroads were blown up—the scorched earth policy so effectively used by the Russians. The Germans would have been left in possession of a desert, without shelter or water, where rear guards with the aid of the civilian population would have kept up guerrilla warfare and where the constant and omnipresent danger of revolution would have threatened to set a match to the European powder keg. In this kind of France the German Army would have lost its initial speed of penetration and blunted its point. "War would no longer have nourished war." This second solution was proposed by Winston Churchill, when he asked for a coalition of all the resources of the British and French Empires, putting the English fleet and merchant marine at the disposal of the French High Command for evacuation operations; it was recommended by General Noguès, Commander-in-Chief of the territory and troops of North Africa. With the aid of the French and British fleets and the airplanes we then had, North Africa would have been protected. In light of the Germans' unsuccessful attempt to cross the Channel in late 1940, they would certainly not have been able to cross a Mediterranean in Allied control. This strategic maneuver could have been accompanied by an attack on Italian possessions in North Africa. France and England at that time had many airplanes and twice as many troops in North Africa as Italy; moreover, the Allies had absolute control of the Mediterranean. It would have been relatively easy to answer the victory of German armies on the European continent by the victory of Anglo-French armies on the African continent.

Weygand accepted neither alternative, nor had he a strategic plan of his own. In his Dakar speech he merely stated that the idea of holding Brittany was "absolutely unfeasible." He evaded the African solution by saying that "we had no industrial resources [in Africa] which allowed us to continue the war." This, when it was easier for England to provision French North Africa than Egypt, and easier for the Allies to send arms to Morocco and Algeria than for the Italians to send them to Tripolitania!

What did General Weygand do? Instead of taking the long view and giving ground temporarily, he sought immediate tactical solutions, forgetting that the best tactics are powerless in the service of poor strategy. He thought neither of North Africa nor of Brittany; he did not even think of withdrawing his troops behind the barrier of the Seine or the Loire; he did not maneuver, he merely defended whatever points the enemy chose to attack. He sent his remaining divisions to the rivers that flow north of the Seine, in an attempt to re-establish a continuous front. "The High Command," he said at Dakar, "gave orders to form a barrier to the North Sea." He admitted that this barrier was inadequate: "At the end of May the French front consisted of a line of troops without depth or organization." He then tried to maintain himself on a line from the Somme to the Aisne. "I had the opportunity," he declared, "to see officers whose units had withstood the shock of the *Panzerdivisionen,* and I realized that these German units marched only on the roads and did not waste their time in going across country. The way was opened up for them by airplanes. We therefore adopted a system to establish a series of points that the men had to hold with their lives—which they did. But it would have been necessary to be able to continue the battle in depth, and we lacked reserves." The "system" of points and centers of resistance was not a new idea; it had been described long ago in the regulations of the German, Soviet, and Czech Armies. The application of this method would have yielded good results under only two conditions: the insertion in a more general tactic of resistance *à outrance*—including guerrilla warfare, a call for the rebellion of the popular masses, and the scorched earth policy—and its use in the service of a strategic idea—for example, to give French units the respite they needed to reach Brittany or points of embarkation for North Africa.

As these two conditions were not fulfilled, the tactics of defending strong points merely retarded the disaster by a few days. After his puerile attempt to establish a continuous front from Alsace to the Somme, Weygand did nothing; in military matters, at least, he ceased to think or act, and spent his time drawing up orders to retreat, worded in general terms. He made no attempt to understand what was happening and what could be done. At that time I received much information from a former German General Staff officer (now in London), who had left Germany because he was known for his anti-Fascist political ideas. He was well acquainted with the German plan for he had helped prepare it; every day he told me what would happen the following morning. On several occasions I requested through Colonel Vautrin, a liaison officer between the cabinet and the General Staff, that this informed anti-Fascist be heard by the Information Service. I obtained no satisfaction, but received this answer: "General Weygand is certain that the Germans are not using the Schlieffen plan. Contrary to your information, he believes that the German columns will not head for Rouen and the lower Seine." That day I learned once more that none are so deaf as those that will not hear.

Weygand tried no strategic plan because he had given up the idea of a fight to the death. As early as May 27 Weygand had informed the members of the cabinet that the situation appeared very grave to him. Certain ministers, among them Lamoureux, concluded from his explanations that "there was nothing to do but ask for an armistice." Weygand admitted at Dakar that on May 29, realizing the inadequacy of his oral summary, he had sent a written statement to the Premier paraphrasing the words of a German general who had maintained that "when an armored column penetrates twenty miles be-

247

yond the front, it has won." Weygand "explained" in his note "that this general was, unfortunately, correct." According to his Dakar speech, it was he who "together with Marshal Pétain proposed on June 12 that an armistice be asked of the Germans." It has been rumored that the proposal for an armistice was made by Vice-President Chautemps, in Pétain's name. One must render unto Caesar what is Caesar's: until we have proof to the contrary, we must assume that the initiative for the armistice which dishonored France was taken by General Weygand in agreement with Marshal Pétain. *Habemus reum confitentem.*

This rapid review of the main lines of French strategy in May and June, 1940, shows us how badly Gamelin and Weygand did their work. The two French Commanders-in-Chief proved inferior to von Brauchitsch and von Keitel. History will determine whether they failed because they were unskilled in their task, never having dreamed of this kind of war; because they preferred an alliance with Nazi Germany to the dangers of a people's war; or because they were handicapped by an instrument adapted to the war of position rather than the war of movement. Yet the question of tactics of the High Command was opened at Riom in connection with the question of tanks, when it was disclosed that the armored formations had been used injudiciously.

During the preliminary investigation, numerous statements concerning the tank battle were collected by the Supreme Court. To conform to the order of the Vichy government, the Court refused to allow these statements to be examined during the public hearings. But the testimony given by defendants and witnesses made it possible to reconstruct with fair accuracy the manner in which the French armored units were organized and used against the German armored divisions.

In September, 1939, the German Army began the war with five armored divisions—the famous *Panzerdivisionen*—and, in all probability, with five light armored divisions. Two armored divisions had been created after the Munich Pact with the aid of matériel the Germans had taken in Czechoslovakia or ordered manufactured in Czech factories. Without the appeasement policy of Chamberlain, Halifax, Daladier, and Bonnet, the war might have begun with two armored divisions less for the Germans, and two additional ones at the disposal of the Allies—a ratio of mechanized forces much more favorable for the Allies than existed in 1939. At the beginning of the war the French Army had one operating armored division, another in process of organization, and three light mechanized divisions (armored cavalry divisions). The English sent one armored division to the continent. The armored divisions had only about 1,000 of the French Army's tanks; the remainder was grouped in battalions, at the disposal of the infantry units. According to the statements of Daladier and the testimony of General Stehlé and Colonel Perré, the French Army had forty battalions of modern tanks plus ten battalions of older tanks. At the hearing of March 31 General Martin said that the French tanks totaled 32,000 tons and the German 39,000, a ratio of four to five. At the hearing of April 1 General Stehlé contended that the total tonnage of French tanks was equal to the German tonnage. It would have been possible to organize a larger number of tank battalions into armored divisions and to oppose the German armored and mechanized divisions with a maneuvering mass approximately equal in size.

"The Polish war," Daladier declared, "had shown the tremendous power of the German armored divisions. The Poles did, indeed, destroy many more German tanks than has been told; the German armored divisions suffered heavy losses. But in spite of everything, they broke the Polish military organization and certainly determined the victory for Germany. The example was therefore an eloquent one, and after the month of September [1939], since we had more than 4,000 tanks [available], it would not have been difficult to organize armored divisions."

De Gaulle, then a colonel in command of the tanks of the Fifth Army (the Army of Alsace), proposed such an organization. He sent a note to the High Command. "He based his argument on the experience gained in the first engagements of French tanks," said Daladier, "and on the use of German armored divisions in Poland. He showed that the rules governing the use of our tanks and their organization did not correspond to their real possibilities or to the existence of armored masses organized by Germany. He sent a note to his leaders, telling them: 'Don't you find the truth inescapable? The engine upsets your doctrines; the engine will also upset your fortifications. Armored divisions must be created. We have excellent matériel; we must organize it as the Germans do, and we shall have the superiority over them.' He sent this note to his leaders; it went through the hierarchy . . . and was sent on to General Headquarters by General Bourret, commanding the Fifth Army, with his approval. . . .

"Curiously," continued Daladier, "we encountered the same opposition and the same difficulties as before the war. . . . General Georges, Commander-in-Chief of French troops on the northeast front [that is, of all French troops opposing the Germans], made a note on De Gaulle's report: 'Interesting, but the reorganization is not of the quality of the criticism. Have this studied.' The Troisième Bureau of General Headquarters—Operations—studied it. The Bureau upheld the thesis that the Polish experience did not make a revision of the French system necessary, and on December 3 General Dufieux, former Inspector-General of tanks, addressed a vehement criticism of De Gaulle's suggestions to General Gamelin, concluding: 'I think that Colonel de Gaulle's conclusions should be rejected.' . . . I could allow myself the essentially artificial and irrelevant pleasure of reading you articles attacking the use of armored divisions, articles written as late as January 1, 1940, by General Dufieux, one of my principal accusers, and by others. You have these articles; they were sent to the Court. . . . 'A new school,' wrote General Dufieux, 'came into existence a few years ago; it foresees large units of tanks crossing the enemy front in an irresistible wave, annihilating batteries, destroying bases of the command, their staffs, and munitions depots, overpowering the reserves before they can even be brought into action, and cutting communications, thus ruining, in a few hours, every possibility for an army to stage an effective comeback. The example of Poland is inappropriate. Who can think that such will be the situation between adversaries possessing comparable numerical and material strength? How can it be imagined that these armored units will be able, as in Poland, to drive alone against the enemy's forces and penetrate them without risking almost total destruction?' That is what he wrote. And I could multiply quotations."

As a consequence of De Gaulle's report, General Gamelin was confronted by two contradictory reports—General Billotte's, favoring the armored divisions, and General Dufieux', advising against them. Although the Troisième Bureau of his own General Staff opposed it, General Gamelin called a meeting of the Supreme War Council to settle the question. The members met at the end of December, 1939, and, "in spite of the horribly confused discussion," said Daladier at Riom, "decided to create four armored divisions."

As a result of these decisions, the French High Command had at its disposal in May and June, 1940, the following armored forces: four armored divisions—one first reserve division at the disposal of General Headquarters, two second reserve divisions, and one "reinforced armored division," organized shortly before the beginning of the offensive and under the command of Colonel de Gaulle; four light mechanized divisions—two divisions formed a cavalry corps, an independent division sent to Belgium with the Giraud army, and a division organized at Saumur in May, 1940; and battalions of independent tanks which were not organized into armored divisions. The German forces were also opposed by a British armored division and tanks of the Belgian Army. Omitting the latter, we can see that the French High Command had at its disposal nine armored divisions; the Germans, according to a Vichy communiqué, had twelve armored divisions, or a ratio of three to four.

Were the French and German armored divisions equally powerful? It appears from the Riom debates that the three French light mechanized divisions had 900 tanks in all. The German armored divisions were certainly stronger, in spite of the opinion of Colonel Perré, who said: "During the war we organized into armored divisions a total of 3,000 tanks of a quality superior to that of the *Panzer* divisions which also were formed with 3,000 tanks." According to Colonel Perré (hearing of April 1, 1942), the armored division which he had commanded included 210 armored vehicles, of which 155 were tanks. "If I rely on a communiqué of D.N.B., the official German news agency," said Daladier, "the figure of 300 tanks to a *Panzer* division would be nearer the truth . . . the rest of the division being composed of motor machine guns." But it would have been easy for the French High Command to correct this numerical inferiority by assigning to its armored divisions a few tank battalions destined for the infantry. The elements of information given at Riom showed that the Germans had about 6,000 tanks on their western front, while the French, British, and Belgians had about 4,000, and that German tanks were lighter in general than the French.

In my opinion the relative weakness of the French mechanized force was due more to its tardy formation than to its numerical inferiority. Three armored divisions out of four had been created after September, 1939; a light mechanized division was formed during the battle, equipped at Montlhéry, near Paris, and used immediately. All these divisions were led by chiefs who knew little about the weapon under their command. "Before the war," declared General Mittelhauser at the hearing of March 18, "none of our armored divisions had been in maneuvers." General Martin, inspector of tanks, added in an effort to excuse his associates on the General Staff that "external events had offered an obstacle to the organization of such maneuvers." The explanation was invalid, as "external events" could not block the maneuvers of armored divisions any more than they did the maneuvers of ordinary divisions, which took place that very year. The truth was simply that the French General Staff had not organized large maneuvers of armored divisions because it did not believe in the utility of these divisions, and concentrated its efforts on other problems. Only the first three light mechanized divisions were well trained. The Germans also had created new armored divisions during the war, but their organization as a whole had been built more rationally and methodically. The German armored divisions had profited by the experience of the Spanish Civil War and the lessons of the Polish campaign. The German High Command had been able to correct the defects. Given equal men, leaders, and matériel, the French armored instrument of war still could not measure up to the German because of the erroneous conception of modern warfare which dominated the French General Staff. The Germans had a slight numerical superiority, the French, a slight qualitative superiority (in weight and armament). The German advantage lay in their superior organization, in the method which their General Staff had used in preparing for war.

In addition to mismanaging the organization of the armored forces, the French High Command erred in its use of what armored force there was. Instead of grouping the armored divisions, the French High Command used the fatal method of "little packages."

I was in London in August, 1940, with French officers who had served in the British armored unit as interpreters or liaison officers. They all praised the excellence of its matériel, the courage of the men, the competence of the officers; after fulfilling the mission to which it had been assigned, the British division was able to cross Normandy and Brittany and embark for England. Its exploit showed that General Weygand could have withdrawn to the south of France and sent some of his armored divisions to North Africa, if he had not decided, with Marshal Pétain, to cease fighting.

All depositions and documents confirmed the fact that the French armored divisions were used under the worst of circumstances. They were in the hands of a General Staff that did not believe in their efficacy; the Troisième Bureau had opposed them from the beginning and remained certain, with General Defieux, that their creation was a mistake. It was not displeased to see a maneuver of armored divisions suffer the defeat which it had prophesied, and which, it thought, justified its doctrine. This General Staff, accustomed to a war of position, was incapable of directing a war of movement with armored forces.

"All that," declared Daladier, "was in the hands of men who did not believe in the formation of the armored division, and who, in spite of all the orders given to them, employed this arm under conditions which General Keller described in a document which is to be found in the dossier. . . . [In this report] he says: 'French tanks were scattered from Dunkerque to Belfort, one battalion and one commandant of a tank company at the disposal of every colonel of an infantry regiment.' That is what the operational accounts tell us. And I can readily understand why it was wished that the operational accounts might not become the object of a public debate. Yes, I understand. . . ." And Daladier, by leaving the sentence unfinished, let it be understood what high officials would otherwise have been charged.

"But the armored divisions themselves," he continued, "the four divisions that were created—how were they used? According to General Billotte's plan? According to the plan of General de Gaulle, whom I am proud to have named general and who was the youngest general in the French Army in action? According to Colonel Perré's plan? Did this enthusiastic and energetic young army [the army of armored and mechanized divisions], which I salute for its magnificence on the battlefield, have an opportunity to show its competence, its capacity? No, gentlemen, for these mechanized divisions were thrown into the Battle of Belgium too soon. These armored divisions had been placed so far in the rear that, to enter the battle, they were obliged to make a trip of such length as to put them into a position of minor importance.

"The first division arrived in the neighborhood of Charleroi, and its first units had hardly left the train—for it had been transported by rail— when it was thrown piece by piece into the furnace; the division was not reformed, its leader was never in command of all its elements. And yet it was heroic. If I remember correctly, it was commanded by General Buisson, a man whom I had had with me as chief-adjutant of my military cabinet, the son of a teacher, an admirable soldier with the passion of the warriors of '93 [the French Revolution]. He behaved like a hero. His armored division, which had been given 130 tanks [by the General Staff] when it should have had twice or three times as many, fought for three days against 1,500 German tanks, held them during that time, inflicted on them losses greater in number than its own, and gave way only when it became impossible, with 130 tanks, to resist such a massive onslaught.

"As for the second armored division, Colonel Perré has put into the dossier [of the Court] the result of his inspection: 'A magnificent engine of war commanded by a leader worthy of the name! . . . [but] on the front of the Somme and Aisne, certain generals had the curious idea of setting out tanks as sentinels on the bridges, depriving them of all support, instead of sending the armored division into battle in mass formation and according to clear and precise plans. The armored divisions were wasted, scattered, broken up; that explains why the efficacy of our machines was so different, although we had as many tanks or armored cars on the battlefield as the Germans."

It was at this point that President Caous interrupted Daladier by declaring that "this demonstration is outside the scope of the trial . . . [which] deals with the inadequacy of the military preparation for war and not with the conduct of operations." The demonstration was becoming dangerous. All the witnesses who had taken part in tank engagements were to reinforce Daladier's statements and to confirm the accounts of General Keller and Colonel Perré, through examples drawn either from their own experience or from official reports of operations they had conducted. At the hearing of April 1 Colonel Perré, after pointing out that the Germans had thrown no more tanks into the battle than the French, came out with a statement most damaging to the General Staff and the High Command. "And yet," he said, "we had to fight one against twenty."

The unforgivable mistakes that were made in the use of tanks have been treated in a study recently published in the United States by Daniel Vilfroy, a military critic who as a line officer had participated in the engagements of a French mechanized division. An expert as well as an eyewitness, Vilfroy stressed, as did the officers who testified at Riom, the dispersion of tanks, the scattering of armored units, and the deplorable conditions under which they were used; at the same time, he paid tribute to the courage and technical skill of the men and the line officers.* Were it still necessary, Vilfroy's study would remove the last remnant of doubt as to the contributing factors in the defeat of the French Army, an Army as courageous and almost as well equipped as the German, but infinitely poorer in leadership. No future testimony or document will ever be able to challenge General Keller's concluding words at the hearing of March 31: "Generally speaking, it may be said that our tanks were inferior in number to those of the Germans, but it was not numerical inferiority which determined the outcome of the war. Our inferiority was to be explained partly in terms of an erroneous military doctrine. We were pursuing purely defensive tactics. . . . We ought to have realized that a defensive strategy requires a huge numerical superiority. . . . Since we were numerically weaker than the enemy, we ought to have concentrated all our tanks to enable us to launch, at the proper time, the necessary counteroffensive."

The French Command held in its hands the instrument for the counteroffensive but was incapable of utilizing it; in fact, it wasted that instrument. What good did it do that General Gamelin and the Supreme War Council at the end of 1939 finally adopted the ideas of Billotte and De Gaulle and organized new armored divisions, when at the moment of decisive battle these divisions were engaged not in mass maneuvers, but one by one and piece by piece, and were "scattered," as Colonel Perré put it? Napoleon I won his battles with the legs of his infantrymen and through the concentration of artillery fire—through the combined effect of vast troop movements and the powerful massing of arms. The French Command, however, adhered to the strategy of those inferior generals of the first World War, who failed to concentrate the artillery of their divisions or army corps and, instead,

* Daniel Vilfroy, *War in the West* (Harrisburg, Pa.: Military Service Publishing Co., 1932).

placed their groups and batteries at the disposal of regimental commanders or infantry battalions. It ignored two elementary principles of the art of war: movement and the concentration of forces. With 9 armored divisions against 12, 4,000 tanks against 6,000, and 3,500 first-line planes against 6,000, it should have been possible to resist an enemy forced to stagger its forces throughout Denmark, Holland, and Belgium, not to mention the occupation of Norway. Joffre in 1914 had faced a less favorable balance. It was imperative to plan a retreating action while allowing the deep and destructive advance of the German columns into France. At the same time an appeal should have been made to the French masses to harass the invaders by guerrilla warfare and sniping, to fight under the revolutionary banner the battle against Fascism for the people and with the people, like the Spanish republicans of 1936-1938 or the Chinese and Russians of today. The defense of Paris should have been entrusted to the workers, who themselves suggested holding the city as an excellent obstacle to the enemy's advance, instead of declaring it an open city merely to save some private property from destruction. Reversing the psychological current, France should have presented to the world an example of determination to sacrifice everything rather than cease to be what Daladier once called "the trench of freedom." Reserving the mass of armored divisions for the ultimate counteroffensive, the retreat could have been accomplished by infantry tank battalions, which would have forced the *Panzerdivisionen* to use up part of their munitions and supplies. Once the German divisions were engaged in devastated enemy territory, that was the moment for a counteroffensive. The object should have been to cut off the German divisions from their bases with the aid of light mechanized divisions, and then to force them to meet the French under unfavorable conditions, in a battle in which the armored divisions would be used. Such a maneuver would have reversed the balance of forces; in an actual battle it would have given the French an opportunity to utilize their superior armored power—superior both in position and in weight, according to General Stehlé's statement that the total tonnage of French tanks was at least equal to that of Germany.

Even more than Foch, Joffre would have been capable of evolving such a counterstrategy to the new Schlieffen plan. What he did in 1914 was more difficult still. Moreover, with his background, his convictions, and his loyalty to the spirit of the French Revolution, he would have been able to launch the necessary appeal to the masses and, in the manner of the Convention, declare "the motherland in danger." Gamelin and Weygand were incapable of such action because they were ignorant of the language of the people and untouched by the spirit of the Revolution. If Joffre addressed his orders of the day to the "soldiers of the Republic," Gamelin and Weygand spoke to the "soldiers of the French Forces." Joffre believed in the people; Gamelin distrusted them; Weygand hated them. The generals of 1940 were prudent and timorous sons of the bourgeoisie, not of the people. Instead of concentrating their troops for a maneuver that would have kept France in the war of the democracies, they scattered them; the mechanized divisions were sent into Belgium; the armored divisions, instead of being placed on the flanks where they could be moved easily, were concentrated at the center, in the Laon region, where they engaged only in sporadic, ineffective action.

The employment and the leadership of the French Army in May and June, 1940, merely confirms the diagnosis based on the study of military preparations: through the fault of its leaders, the Army was exposed to conditions that made resistance impossible; its disease was one of the intellect. It remains to be seen who were the carriers of that disease.

Military Leadership

In dealing with this question I have no intention of countering the charge of the Riom Court with an indictment of my own. We are not yet in possession of the documents that will reveal whether those guilty of the defeat were guilty under criminal law. The final indictment will one day be drawn up "in the name of the French people."

The responsibilities to be examined here are moral as well as political and professional. Did those men entrusted by the government of the Republic with the preparation and conduct of the Army fulfill their duty?

Let us begin with those who carry the heaviest share of responsibility because of their failure in the military preparation of the war. Those in charge of the actual operations were able to say, with a certain amount of justice, that it was difficult to conduct a successful war with an instrument so poorly adapted to the exigencies of modern warfare. The others, however, who, until the eve of the war, preached and enforced the dogma of the continuous front, who failed to create a modern army when it was still possible to build one, remain without an excuse.

The ones to blame are not the authors of the continuous front doctrine in the first World War, but those who so stubbornly upheld it after it had become obsolete. The intellectual disease that infested the French Army was its conservatism, which developed all the better since it found fertile soil among the high dignitaries of the Army for several reasons: (1) an inherent conservative tendency, for conservatism, be it political or military, is but the expression of a particular mentality and turn of mind; the human brain is not divisible into watertight compartments by means of which a man may be the prisoner of a doctrine in one domain, yet unprejudiced in all others; (2) that self-complacency of which I have already spoken; the French military's satisfaction at having won the first World War was accompanied by an inferiority complex deriving from an obscure feeling that something more than their own intellectual merits had brought about victory; (3) the low ebb in critical talent owing to the decline in scientific schooling, which was bound up with the predominance of Saint-Cyr over Polytechnique graduates; and (4) old age; between 1920 and 1940, the average age of French Army leaders was ten to fifteen years above that of German and

Russian leaders. In his memoirs, edited by his collaborator Jean Martet, Clemenceau wrote on the eve of his death: "The age limit of our generals [in 1918] was sixty-one. It was raised to sixty-two, then to sixty-six, and finally to seventy. One day the country will have to pay dearly for that."* Need we recall that during the second World War the situation was worse, General Weygand being seventy-five years old?

Let us now look at the chief agents of conservatism, the men who were responsible for maintaining the doctrine of the continuous front.

The military doctrine of the Army was laid down in the *Règlements de Manoeuvre* (regulations for operations) and reflected further in the general organization and operational plans established by the General Staff in accordance with the directives and decisions of the Supreme War Council. The authority ultimately responsible for the poor military doctrine and, consequently, the inadequate preparation of the war was therefore the Supreme War Council. Its members made decisions by majority rule on the basis of files and reports submitted to them. However, these members were appointed upon recommendation by the Chief of Staff and actually, if not legally, with the approval of Marshal Pétain, at least until 1936.

After 1932, the year before Hitler assumed power, the guiding spirits of the Supreme War Council were Weygand, 1932-1935, Gamelin, 1935-1938, and Pétain, whose influence lasted from 1918 to 1938. Two other influential members were General Debeney, Weygand's predecessor at the head of the General Staff, and General Maurin, the successor of Pétain in the Ministry of War. These men adhered to the strategy of defense based on the continuous front. While the ideas of Debeney, Maurin, Weygand, and Pétain were known from their published writings, those of Gamelin escaped publication. According to Daladier's statements at Riom, Gamelin tried to give the Council a more modern orientation after 1938; thus he obtained the decision permitting the creation of two armored divisions. It was a belated conversion which, as we shall see, must be attributed largely to the influence of Daladier. The man who embodied the doctrine of the continuous front and represented the main pillar of conservatism was, without question, Marshal Pétain.

Pétain's Influence

In the last chapter I spoke of Pétain as a bad Minister of War, of his political influence on the officers, and of his activities at the center of Fascist intrigues, which sabotaged Daladier's recovery project. Pétain's military activity, in the formulation of French military doctrine, was equally disastrous. The position he occupied in the Army was exceptional. In recognition of services rendered in the first World War, he had been kept on the staff without regard for any age limit. Immediately after the 1918 Armistice,

---

* Jean Martet, *Georges Clemenceau* (London, New York: Longmans, Green & Co., 1930).

he was appointed Vice-President of the Supreme War Council—which meant that in the event of war he would take over the command as chief of the armed forces. In 1922 his powers were augmented still further by a decree naming him Inspector-General of the Army. From that moment on, he controlled the Army both in war and in peace and dominated the General Staff. In 1931, at the age of seventy-five, he resigned as Commander-in-Chief in favor of General Weygand, then Chief of Staff; at the same time he was appointed Inspector-General of Aerial Defense, an honorary post which it was thought would satisfy a man of his age. However, in 1934 he became Minister of War in the cabinet formed by Gaston Doumergue immediately after the 6th of February; and when he left the Ministry in 1935, he had his successor, General Maurin, reappoint him a member of the Supreme Council of National Defense of the Supreme War Council and of the High Military Committee, a committee supposedly limited to the Ministers of National Defense and Chiefs of Staffs of the Army, Navy, and Air Force. None but Pétain ever exercised so many functions or occupied so high a place in the military hierarchy for so long a time.

The prestige which Pétain enjoyed in military circles during the ten years preceding the war cannot be overestimated. After the death of Foch, Pétain's star had risen constantly. In the words of Henry Torrès, "he had become a living legend." Foch's personality during his lifetime had eclipsed Pétain's. But Foch's death, not long before that of Joffre, coincided with the gradual disappearance from public life of all the men who had been at the head of the government during the war—notably Clemenceau and Poincaré. Most of those who had observed Pétain during the first World War knew him for what he was worth—a good troop leader, but a commander without character or imagination and, furthermore, a weakling and a pessimist.

"Pétain's talent lay in execution, whereas Foch's lay in action," Clemenceau used to say. Joffre, in his memoirs,* referred on several occasions to the "pessimism" of Pétain. "In the course of a tour through the headquarters of the Second Army which I made with Pétain in July, 1916," wrote Joffre, "I was struck by his pessimism, and shortly afterwards was confirmed in my impression of that state of mind. Already in June, the firm confidence of Foch, who had come to General Headquarters, had calmed excessive fears; Pétain, in fact, alarmed everybody once more by his limited confidence in the possible length of resistance of Verdun." Poincaré, in his memoirs,† that inexhaustible source of information on French governmental life during the first World War, related Loucheur's opinion of Pétain: "Loucheur, the energetic and farsighted Minister of Armament, is greatly dissatisfied with Pétain, whom he considers a dyed-in-the-wool defeatist, and who, a few days ago, said to him, 'We ought to begin peace negotiations.' When the Minister repeated those words to Foch, the latter said: 'It would be madness to ask for peace.' " Elsewhere in the book, Poincaré continued: "Foch says that Pétain

* Joseph J. C. Joffre, *The Personal Memoirs of Joffre* (New York: Harper & Bros., 1932).

† Raymond Poincaré, *Au Service de la France, Neuf Annees de Souvenirs* (Paris: Plon., 1926).

lacks character . . . that in a secondary position, like that of communicating orders, [Pétain] would be perfect, but that his fear of responsibility disqualifies him as Commander-in-Chief." Poincaré also reported the opinion of Clemenceau who, on December 18, 1917, during his tenure as Premier, confided his misgivings to Poincaré, then President of the Republic: "A second cause for concern is Pétain. Things aren't going so well there. You heard him the other day, when we asked him: 'Can you hold out?' He did not answer: 'I shall hold out under such and such conditions'; he said: 'I shall not hold out unless. . . .' There you have the man." In June, 1918, Clemenceau took Poincaré aside and said to him: "Pétain is irritating and provoking in his pessimism. Can you imagine, for instance, that he told me the Germans would beat the English Army in the open field and after that would defeat us. Ought a general to pronounce such words or even think them?" Lloyd George, who used to see Pétain at inter-Allied council meetings, had the same impression. "Pétain never gave me the impression," he wrote, "of a general whose personality or genius could lead huge armies to victory. He was a *Fabius cunctator*."* Thus Pétain, then twenty-two years younger, had already indicated what he proved to be in May and June, 1940: an irritating pessimist, a man afraid of responsibility, a defeatist through and through, and—to cite Joffre again—a man with a tendency to "accept the will of the enemy." But during World War I Pétain held less power and was not admitted to cabinet meetings. No one followed his advice to abandon the English and negotiate a speedy peace with the Germans.

With the great witnesses of the first World War gone (except for Weygand, whose ambition bound him to Pétain after he had first been attached to Foch, who had despised Pétain), the Marshal's star rose steadily on the military horizon. Pétain was clever and insisted on popularity; a team of collaborators under General Laure (today, Secretary-General to the Presidency) worked relentlessly to increase the reputation of the "hero of Verdun." As the only marshal in active service in the French Army, he was the highest military authority of the country. Even before Doumergue made him a Minister of War—which carried his vanity to the point of a paroxysm— nothing in the Army was done without his advice or approval. All important nominations and decisions passed through his hands. He was considered the wise man, the prophet, and the oracle. Even under the Popular Front he remained a member of the Supreme Council of National Defense and of War, and of the High Military Committee, because any attempt to dislodge him would have resulted in a scandal. According to General Laure, his confidant and authorized biographer, "Pétain succeeded, thanks to his attitude which was that of a prudent, extremely clever man, in gaining a powerful influence in the course of the meeting of the High Military Committee." And, still quoting Laure, he became and remained "a high military councilor attached to the Premier." In the conformist and conservative circles of the French Army, nobody would have dared to question the validity of his

* David Lloyd George, *Memoirs of the Peace Conference* (New Haven: Yale University Press, 1939).

opinions or attack his general conception of war. He had the power to exercise an intellectual dictatorship over French military thought—a mere prelude to the political dictatorship which this enemy of democracy was to impose on all of France in the interest of defeat.

As a member of the High Military Committee from February, 1933, until February, 1934, and again from June, 1936, until January, 1938, I witnessed Pétain's work. It was in this Committee, after 1936 called the Permanent Committee of National Defense (*Comité Permanent de la Défense Nationale*), that the general issues of French military policy were decided. The Committee met, as a rule, once a month. Never did any of the generals called before the Committee dare to criticize Pétain's opinions. Never, on his part, did Pétain protest, as should have been his duty if he disagreed, against the general orientation of French military policy. He supported on December 15, 1937, the Committee's decision not to consider the plan for the extension of the Air Force that had been submitted by the Ministry of Aviation. During 1936-1937 he presented to the Committee a single proposition: the creation of a General Staff of National Defense, superior to the three General Staffs of Army, Air Force, and Navy. This seemed senseless, in that it established a supplementary organ at the head of the Army. However, Pétain was stubborn. In February, 1938, Daladier finally gave in and the General Staff of National Defense was created; Gamelin was placed at its head, and General Georges took over the direction of the Army General Staff. As might have been expected, all the witnesses at Riom, when asked about the organization of the High Command, complained of the disadvantages of that system and the incessant conflicts of jurisdiction between the staffs of Gamelin and of Georges. Nobody pointed out that the system had been adopted at the request of Marshal Pétain.

Pétain's most consistent bias was in favor of a defensive strategy and the continuous front, the two ideas which, without exaggeration, formed the basis of his reputation. During World War I he had represented the principle of stationary resistance as against that of dynamic maneuver held by Joffre, and the spirit of defensive warfare as against the offensive warfare represented by Foch. In the eyes of the public, the glory of Pétain derived from the Battle of Verdun, and Verdun had been a defensive battle, won by the resistance and sacrifice of troops which held their ground, and not by the maneuvers of the High Command. Verdun remains the only great battle in military history which was won without maneuvering. "They shall not pass," Pétain had said in a famous "order of the day," and the Germans failed to pass either on the right or left banks of the Meuse, hurling themselves vainly against the defensive organizations or improvised positions of the continuous front. According to Joffre, at that time Commander-in-Chief of the French Army, the true victor of Verdun was not Pétain. "If history," wrote Joffre in his memoirs, "permits me to judge the general officers who served under my orders, I must say that the true savior of Verdun was Nivelle, with the valuable aid of Mangin." But legend is often stronger than history, and Pétain owed his halo to Verdun. Old and crowned with honors, Pétain remained stubbornly faithful to the ideas he had professed and practiced in the first World War.

This inflexibility had disastrous consequences. I already have mentioned General Chauvineau's book, *Is an Invasion Still Possible?* (1938), in which he sang the praises of the continuous front and opposed the creation of armored divisions. Marshal Pétain wrote a long preface for this book. To understand the weight of this fact, one must know that Pétain wrote very little, and that the book was published shortly before the meeting of the Supreme War Council in which the proposal to create two armored divisions was discussed.

Pétain, siding publicly with General Chauvineau, spoke out in favor of the continuous front and against the armored divisions. He supported Chauvineau's general idea against that of "the professional army"—the plan of Colonel de Gaulle, whose ideas he attacked without naming their author. "Less ambitious than the professional army," he said, "it [Chauvineau's plan] seems more certain, and, after all, more useful. In short, General Chauvineau's views on the opening of land operations are full of wisdom. . . . The continuous front is not an accident which one can cast off like a bad habit. At the beginning of a war, it is the weaker belligerent's only way of guaranteeing the defense of his counrty. . . . The continuous front is an inevitable consequence of the increased forces of the armed nation and of the technical progress of arms. . . . The professional army is above all an offensive weapon; the quality of its matériel and men makes it an irresistible instrument in the eyes of its author. It would be somewhat imprudent to adopt his conclusions. . . . It seems that the technical possibilities of tanks and of the command of armored divisions have not been sufficiently studied. . . . General Chauvineau's idea seems to answer better both the technical possibilities of today's armored engines, their use in the face of mines and anti-tank arms, and also the healthy strategic conceptions which require the immediate and sure occupation of a defensive field before one can think of a strategic offensive." This, after Munich, which had saved Germany from the menace of the Czech Army, which was more modern and more maneuverable, if smaller, than the French Army; this, in spite of the creation of the German *Panzerdivisionen,* in spite of the lessons of the Spanish war, which Pétain's friend Franco had just won. Pétain told the General Staff and the entire French Army: "Take care! Attempts are being made to draw you on to the wrong road. The author of the idea of the professional army is mistaken; his idea is poorly thought out, and it would be imprudent to adopt his conclusions. The thesis of General Chauvineau, adversary of the armored divisions and partisan of the principle of scattering tanks, seems to me closer to reality."

Pétain went further; he did not want his true intentions to be misunderstood. After analyzing and approving Chauvineau's work in general terms, he added a section to the preface, which he called "Elements of a War Doctrine." With frequent reference to Chauvineau, who thus became the official interpreter of his ideas, Pétain developed in this section his general conception of modern warfare. According to this, modern war had to be a continuous front war: "Battlefields prepared and reinforced by permanent fortifications permit the achievement of two essential results—the creation of a continuous barrier, which could not otherwise exist, at least at the beginning, and the realization, for the defense of this barrier, of the greatest savings for the benefit of the elements placed in reserve. If the preparation of the battlefield is adequate and its occupation rapid, the enemy will be forced to stage a methodical operation, *his hopes of bringing a quick end by means of a sudden attack will be frustrated.*" Pétain considered the war of movement dangerous: "One still finds some tendencies to return to the doctrine of the war of movement from the beginning of operations, according to the ideas in vogue before 1914. The experience of the war was too costly for us to return with impunity to old and erroneous notions. . . . It will be General Chauvineau's rare merit to have shown that the continuous front is based both on the lessons of history and on the technical properties of armies and fortifications. . . . General Chauvineau's study does not hesitate to rehabilitate the continuous front, which is little studied in peacetime and which bears the weight of general reprobation, as if it were the product of an inferior art of war, whereas it actually is the consequence of large numbers of men mobilized by the armed nation, and of the technical properties of arms capable of laying down barrages that are impenetrable to men and tanks."

Marshal Pétain went on to study the use of aviation, which Chauvineau had not considered, and just as he condemned the armored divisions, so he condemned the direct use of aviation in land battle: "We find no fundamental error in the account [of Chauvineau], but merely certain omissions concerning the use of aviation. Aerial forces have an important influence on land battle. However, their direct action in battle is hazardous, as the troops involved are stationed to give and receive blows. It is by indirect action on the rear that aerial forces will most effectively be employed." (Unfortunately, the Chief of Staff of the Air Force followed Pétain's advice, and French aviation, employed only in rear attacks, was not involved in the land fighting.) Thus stating the most recent development of his doctrine, Pétain concluded: "General Chauvineau establishes himself on the solid and unassailable base of technical fact; the continuous front is a reality which one denies at one's peril. The system recommended corresponds perfectly with the political, geographic, and demographic situation of France, and with the fortifications that have been built on her frontiers."

Such, in his own words, was Marshal Pétain's war doctrine. It was conservative, reactionary, anachronistic. Pétain was the first, last, and most eminent doctrinaire of the continuous front. No work on military doctrine was published in France after General Chauvineau's; not another line was written by Pétain after his "Elements of a War Doctrine." Under these circumstances the improvement of the Army became extremely difficult and almost impossible, for it would have presupposed a General Staff and a Supreme War Council capable of standing up against the authority and advice of the Marshal.

Having kept the French Army in the rut of the continuous front doctrine,

Pétain could take the road to Burgos, certain of a warm welcome from Franco. The German armored divisions had nothing to do but break the continuous front with the aid of air power "directly engaged in the land battle"; that done, Hitler rewarded Pétain by helping him assume power in France.

Thus the poor preparation of the Army as directly caused by the French war doctrine, was the fault of Marshal Pétain.

Gamelin and Weygand

The men to whom the government entrusted the leadership of the armies in battle were, first, Gamelin, and then, Weygand. Both proved inferior to their task. Weygand was infinitely guiltier than Gamelin, for while Gamelin erred in action, Weygand refused to act.

Gamelin and Weygand were not, as non-Frenchmen sometimes believe, Commanders of the Army; they were Commanders-in-Chief of the Army, Navy, and Air Force. The land and army air units opposing the Germans were under the command of General Georges, the naval forces under Admiral Darlan, and the Air Force under General Vuillemin. The particular field of Gamelin and Weygand was not tactics or the maneuver of a particular army, but the supreme direction of forces—strategy in its most general terms. They alone could prepare a plan that would include the armies of North Africa and the Colonies as well as those of continental France, the Navy, and the Air Force. If they failed to set up a general plan, no one could do it in their stead. They had to concentrate on strategy, leaving the solution of tactical problems to the various commanders. They had to remain strictly within the domain of general strategic action, never descending from it to lose themselves in details of execution or to try to direct the politics of the nation with the incompetence characteristic of men of their circle and profession. To be good strategists, they had to be nothing else; for there was enough to be done in that field.

It was in such terms that Joffre understood his position in 1914. When the French Army was beating a painful retreat, when most of the generals, surprised by the German maneuver, were losing their heads, when Parliament and the cabinet were leaving for Bordeaux in great anxiety, Joffre kept his head; in the course of the retreat and during the Battle of the Marne, he ate and slept at regular hours, in order to be able to win his chess game with Moltke. Neither Gamelin nor Weygand gave proof of such mastery; they were incapable of dominating the situation and of pulling the Army together.

Let us grant that it would have been more difficult to revitalize the Army in 1940 than it had been in 1914. For one thing, in 1914 events could move only with the velocity of infantry columns; the speed of the German advance had therefore given the French High Command time to assimilate new factors and adapt itself. In 1940 events moved at the rate of armored divisions and lightning war; because of the poor organization of the French Army, the headquarters of regiments and divisions were thrown into confusion and many of them were captured. The General Staff was deprived of its organs of information and liaison, and had no communication with the troops; disorder sprang not from the confusion, but from the absence of orders. Moreover, the French officers were better in 1914 than in 1940. They were technically superior, especially in comparison with the German officers, much more realistic, and closer to their men. Politically, they had greater integrity because the officers of the French Army had been purged after the Dreyfus affair, and because the High Command contained few determined enemies of the democratic regime. No such purge had been attempted by Daladier after the Cagoule affair. Finally, in 1914 the line officers had identified themselves with the nation as a whole, and commanded the affection of their men; in 1940 too many officers hated the Popular Front electors, and the republican soldiers distrusted their Fascist officers. The direction of the men under fire under unforeseen circumstances was consequently more difficult.

An army cannot free itself in a moment from habits formed during twenty years of constant error. If we but observe in ourselves the persistence of professional habits, we shall be more indulgent toward certain generals who obstinately insisted on carrying out the methods of war that Pétain had taught them. The leaders of the French Army reaped what they had sown; when they wanted to fight the war of movement with an army prepared for the war of position, they realized that the nerve centers were paralyzed, that local orders were no longer in harmony with the supreme command, and that neither General Staff officers nor line officers understood what was expected of them.

To overcome this general paralysis, a great impetus would have been required; the war would have had to be transformed into a people's war. Joffre would have understood and obeyed that necessity. Gamelin did not understand this, at least not soon enough. Weygand understood, but decided to ignore it.

The honest and gentle Gamelin did his duty, although poorly; he tried to stop the German horde, but failed. Events revealed him inferior to his task. Compared with the remodeled and rejuvenated Schlieffen plan, his plan of defense was mediocre.

Gamelin was a man with an open and subtle mind, with a flexible intelligence, but he lacked broad vision and authority. Of average height, somewhat stout, with short arms, a rather mottled complexion, and a somewhat hesitant manner of speech, he looked like a scholar disguised as a military man. He certainly lacked the temperament of a military leader. He had been placed at the head of the General Staff in 1935 by General Maurin, then Minister of War, on the departure and the recommendation of Weygand, and with the assent of Pétain; once more, these three men, Pétain, Weygand and Maurin, had been mistaken in their judgment. But Gamelin had undeniable qualities, and not the least was his loyalty. He had no clear-cut political opinions, but he was incapable of betraying the Republic, for his conception of duty differed from that of Pétain or Weygand.

After 1936 his patriotism had been shocked by the intrigues of Pétain and his followers, and by the extent to which Fascist propaganda had spread among the officers. He was disturbed by Pétain's fiery defense of his war doctrine, for if Gamelin still adhered to the continuous front, his faith was shaken, and he had begun to doubt. Encouraged by Daladier and by Generals Bourret and Decamp, who were collaborators of Daladier, he tried to fight Pétain's influence; but he did so in his own way, which was gentle and timorous, the way of a scholar and not of a military man. It was he who caused the creation of two armored divisions in December, 1938, when four or six were needed, and when Pétain wanted none at all. In the days of Munich Gamelin showed foresight; he drew up a circumspect but firm report, asking that Czechoslovakia be supported, not abandoned. As some of the reserves were mobilized at that time, he observed that the defeatism of the Croix de Feu officers contrasted sharply with the enthusiasm of the popular masses and anti-Fascist soldiers, and he would say to all who wanted to hear him: "I now know on which side the 'patriots' will be in case of war." The Fascists never pardoned him for this statement. Nor will they ever pardon him for having declared during the winter of 1938-1939 that a military alliance with Russia was the only way of preserving peace and of winning the war.

To try to parry the German attack Gamelin sent an army to Belgium. Was he right or wrong? Would it have been better to establish the Anglo-French troops in positions prepared during the winter, to let the Belgian Army alone absorb the first shock, and to wait for the arrival of armored divisions on a known terrain? No one can tell, given the present state of information. During the Riom trial General Besson claimed that the troops would have been able to resist on the French frontier if they had not received the order to go into Belgium. Daladier replied that Gamelin's maneuver in Belgium would have succeeded if the generals charged with holding the Ardennes gap had done their work properly. Gamelin remained silent, apparently withdrawn from this debate which concerned his own plan. Gamelin, who was badly served both by circumstances and by some of his subordinates, did what he could and showed his measure, but he was incapable of halting the German advance. He lost the battle through his own error. But he lost neither the war nor his honor.

The same cannot be said of Weygand. Weygand lost the war by refusing to fight in the *réduit Breton* or in the Colonial Empire. He dishonored himself by giving the cabinet false information—the news of a Communist revolution in Paris—to frighten the government and induce it to ask for an armistice.

Following Gamelin as Commander-in-Chief, Weygand had as his task the formulation of a strategy corresponding to the situation—to dispose his forces inside or outside France to obtain the best possible result. He was not asked to handle details of execution and tactics, which were the problems of his subordinates; he was asked still less to concern himself with politics, which was the problem of the government. Weygand had no strategic ideas; he dabbled with tactics, trying to re-establish the continuous front and to organize centers of resistance; and he engaged in much political activity. He acted not as the servant of France but as the servant of Pétain, who was aspiring to the role of dictator. Gamelin's plan is open to discussion, but Weygand's is not, for it did not exist. Gamelin can be defended; Weygand cannot.

On June 12 at Cangé, when Weygand asked the cabinet to treat with Germany, he was reminded that he still had many troops—nine normal and nine light divisions intact, the forces of the Maginot Line, and ten divisions in the Alps. And the depots were bursting with men and matériel. He had enough divisions to assure the retreat of a part of his Army, if not to the *réduit Breton* where the fight would have been difficult, at least to North Africa where there existed a powerful Colonial army. He returned a dry answer to the ministers who favored resistance, who asked him to draw up the balance sheet of his forces: "I need my troops to re-establish order in case of disturbances." He preferred order—a bourgeois and pro-Fascist order—to the welfare of his country. He knew at that time that France possessed airplanes, cannon, warships, tanks, fifteen divisions in North Africa, and a Colonial army. But he had made his decision; the war of the democracies against Fascism did not interest him. His only thought was to maintain "order."

How can General Weygand's attitude be explained? Old age, sterility of mind, inability to judge situations in broad perspective or to rise above detail, or the desire to play a part in the "National Revolution" which the Cagoule had prepared and of which Pétain wanted to be the beneficiary?

Until more complete information is available, I tend to think that Weygand's attitude can be explained in terms of personality and political prejudice.

Weygand had none of the qualities needed by a Commander-in-Chief. Despite his remarkable gift for executing operations, he was only an excellent second-rater. Dry and methodical, he lacked humanity, sensitivity, and imagination. His small, shriveled frame enclosed a narrow and uncultured mind. Belgian by birth, he entered Saint-Cyr as a foreigner without examinations, and later could not enter the higher institution of the École de Guerre. As a cavalry officer, he seems to have been a good horse trainer. He was unable to understand the common men, of whom modern armies are composed. He carried his hussar's whip through life. His brain was just a machine, and from the time he reached the age of seventy, a rusty machine, in the service of a petty ambition. "He has a curious resemblance to a weasel," said Painlevé; still more, he resembled an old woman. He was famous in the Army for his ostentatious bigotry, not piety. He was more clerical than Catholic, with the intransigeance of a fanatic. General Sarrail called him "the Tartuffe of the General Staff." The reports which he read to the Permanent Committee of National Defense in his flat voice resembled catalogues; all the details and figures were there, but never a general idea, never a spark of genius. Once, with the habits of my brief professorial career, I observed that one could take a report by Weygand, invert the order of the parts or even of the sentences, and the report remained the same, always good in the same mediocre way, telling everything and explaining nothing, because it was merely a mosaic of information and fact, held together by no unifying strand. And I said to Daladier: "You can see that it has neither head nor tail." A mere glance at his articles, his few books, and his prefaces to military books will confirm that impression of iciness and pettiness. It was because Weygand's report on the role of aviation had "neither head nor tail" that we decided, against his advice, to create the Air Force in April, 1933.

This evaluation does not detract from Weygand's accomplishments in the first World War or since that time. He was and will always be a good subordinate, a competent bookkeeper. His reputation in the Army was a reflection of his collaboration with Marshal Foch, an unquestionable military genius, who had a horror of detail. Foch conceived great strategic ideas, which he based on the information supplied by Weygand. Weygand was charged with shaping these ideas into battle orders and supervising their execution. Weygand, "who knew everything but understood nothing," was a valuable collaborator for Foch, who could have found no one more scrupulous or more perfectly adapted to the task. In his office at General Headquarters, the tall, irritable and nervous Foch paced up and down, smoking his pipe and consulting the maps hanging on the wall; without stopping, he gave his general instructions in elliptical and generally incomprehensible formulae. Weygand, always methodical, precise, attentive, and unimaginative, gathered up Foch's ideas, classified and translated them into decisions for army commanders or proposals for the government and the Supreme Allied Council. His position with regard to Foch was analogous to Marshal Berthier's with Napoleon. Berthier, "one of the stupidest men in the Grand Army," was indispensable to Napoleon, because he, too, knew minutely the situation of the troops, the condition of provisions, arms, and munitions, and because he was able to interpret the master's ideas; but if Berthier had been told to lead the Grand Army, this perfect subordinate would have been incapable of making a single independent decision.

Weygand's attitude is explained also by his political prejudices. He has never defended himself for admiring Fascist regimes and hating democracy. In speaking of him, Clemenceau said: "Weygand? Intelligent, but dangerous and ambitious! If the Republic is ever overthrown by a coup d'état, it will come from him." The masses have always considered Weygand a reactionary with clerical ideas and monarchist tendencies. When he left the Army in 1935, instead of living honorably on his pension, he accepted a position as administrator in the Suez Canal Company; he was extremely well paid although obviously incompetent in business matters. The company had merely bought the name of Weygand, ex-Commander-in-Chief of the Army, for its advertising. It was the first time that a former Chief of Staff in the French Army had consented to sell himself in such a way. Weygand, never liked, now felt himself actually despised by the people. He returned their scorn with hatred. This hatred, as much as his reactionary and clerical tendencies, made him a Fascist. In 1937 General Duval, another Fascist sympathizer, published his *Lessons of the Spanish War.* Weygand wrote a preface for this book; speaking of the Spanish republican government, he stated that "victory cannot come out of anarchy and ignorance," and he eulogized the "little handful of men who had decided to free their country from an intolerable servitude." Hating democracy, he particularly detested the League of Nations. In an article in the *Revue des Deux Mondes,* he had celebrated as a victory the defeat of the Disarmament Conference. In the *Revue Militaire Générale* for January,

1937, he began an article on "The Unity of the Army" with these words: "Beside the reasons for anxiety which assail us, there appears a cause for comfort . . . the ideology of Geneva has become merely literature." Fearing the French masses, he particularly detested the Popular Front and its leaders.

This enemy of the Popular Front and of French democracy hated the Anglo-Saxon democracies as much as he did the Soviet Union. In his Dakar lecture he gave free expression to this feeling: "In 1918, to obtain full advantage of the victory, it was indispensable to make the Rhine the frontier of Germany; but America and England wanted to keep France from having too great an influence in Europe. . . . *It is no exaggeration to say that if we once more found ourselves at war, it was because the interests of the Anglo-Saxon powers overcame the interests of France.*" (Italics are in the text of the speech.) He repeated the thesis of Nazi Germany and of Vichy concerning the responsibilities for the war: "Our diplomatic weakness showed itself particularly when it became a question of entering the war as England's ally." One cannot be surprised that General Weygand refused to envisage solutions permitting France to remain in the war with Great Britain; he made some attempt to resist the German Army; but he was not troubled by the end of a war which had forced him to fight those whose doctrines he admired, for a French people whose ideals he hated, and allied to a democratic and liberal Britain whose foreign policy he had condemned since 1919 and considered responsible for the war.

Dominant among Weygand's idiosyncrasies was his fear of revolution, which led him to the edge of treason. He had supported rapprochement with the Soviet Union in 1933 for strictly military reasons; but when a journalist mentioned this fact in 1936, he cynically replied: "I changed my mind when I saw the growing strength of Communism," which meant: I prefer that France run the risk of being wiped out rather than see her adopt economic or political formulae which displease me. This fear and his dislike for the people caused his dishonor, for it was responsible for his refusal to take the French Army to North Africa, for his insistence on keeping his reserves to subdue the people if necessary, and especially for his attempt to sway the cabinet with false news.

Weygand's responsibility is thus greater than Gamelin's, and as grave as Pétain's. Whatever Gamelin's errors or lack of genius, it would be a mistake to put him in the same class with Pétain and Weygand.

Daladier

Could not Daladier, who had been Minister of National Defense and of War from June, 1936, until the beginning of May, 1940, have opposed the development of Pétain's doctrine and have kept better watch over his General Staff? Is he not at least indirectly responsible for the inadequate preparation of the war?

Let us observe, first of all, that Daladier had no part in the request for an armistice or in the naming of Weygand. Daladier was not a member of the government in June, 1940, when the fatal decision was made, and he—like

Blum, Herriot, Jeanneney, and many others—opposed this decision. It was Reynaud who replaced Gamelin with Weygand over Daladier's objection, just as it was Reynaud who appointed Pétain Minister, again over Daladier's protest. Daladier had good reason to distrust Pétain and Weygand. Reynaud, a clear but insensitive mind, had shown foresight by recommending in 1935 the creation of the armored divisions advocated by De Gaulle; he had demanded in 1938 that France support Czechoslovakia, and in 1939 he had insisted on a military alliance with the Soviets. But he was a bad choice for a Premier: while he judged events well, he judged men poorly. Surrounded by reactionaries and intriguers, he placed Weygand at the head of the Army and appointed Pétain, Baudoin, and Prouvost as members of the cabinet. He made the same mistake in dismissing as General Secretary for Foreign Affairs, Alexis Leger, a former collaborator of Briand and the key figure in Anglo-French co-operation, whose crime consisted of displeasing the partisans of Franco-Fascist collaboration. Reynaud, imprisoned by Marshal Pétain, is paying for mistakes which he did not commit; his courage earns him the admiration of his friends and his adversaries. I was his friend, but I remain certain that if Daladier had been Premier and Gamelin Generalissimo in June, 1940, the war would have gone on in North Africa and would have ended in 1942 with an Allied victory.

Moreover, in May, 1940, when he was still Minister of War, Daladier could neither legally nor actually intervene in the direction of military operations. The legal question is indisputable, for the "law concerning the organization of the nation in time of war" is explicit. And if Daladier had tried to influence the decisions of the men responsible for such action, he would have exceeded his powers and betrayed the confidence of the government of which he was a member. On May 10, 1940, when the German attack began, Reynaud was Premier; he alone, conferring with the Commander-in-Chief, could exercise any influence on the decisions of the High Command—and no one can blame him for not having blossomed out as a strategist.

Daladier's indirect responsibility can therefore be formulated only in terms of his influence on the preparation of the French Army before 1940. It goes without saying that such responsibility as he may have can be only political, and not criminal.

Daladier's sphere of action as Minister of National Defense included not only the direction of the Ministry of War, but also all problems concerning the security of the country and the preparation for the war; he was in charge of co-ordinating the action of the Ministers of War, Air, and Navy, of preparing the anti-aircraft defense of the land (which depended in part on the Ministry of the Interior), the industrial mobilization, and so forth. From 1936 to 1940 Daladier was the specialist on national defense in the government; if he had suggested to the cabinet that Gamelin be replaced by a general with more modern ideas, his colleagues certainly would have followed him. In four years he could have exercised a sobering influence on the Army, and orientated it towards the war of movement and armored divisions, away from Marshal Pétain's cherished principles.

268

But these are theoretical, not practical, objections; and to evaluate Daladier's conduct, we must take into account both the actual circumstances and the man's temperament.

To fight the continuous front doctrine, certain preliminary conditions had to be fulfilled. A man capable of heading the General Staff would have had to be found. Gamelin had been named Chief of Staff in 1935, and his replacement would have been considered a political maneuver of the Popular Front. It would have been necessary to find a man with sufficient authority over the entire officers' corps. It was impossible to think De Gaulle, then a lieutenant-colonel who lacked the necessary weight and experience, in spite of his excellent ideas. Billotte or Bourret might have been considered, but, as they were both good republicans, the choice of either inevitably would have brought loud protests. The name of General Georges was occasionally mentioned; but he was physically disqualified, since he had been dangerously wounded at Marseilles in the attack which cost the life of the King of Yugoslavia. Nor was he truly an adversary of the continuous front; at that time the war of movement and armored divisions could not claim as a supporter a single great military name who would have been acceptable to the public and the Army.

It would also have been necessary both to change the Chief of Staff and to fight against the highest military authorities, particularly Pétain and the Supreme War Council. Nothing significant could be done in the way of Army organization or the preparation of operational plans or armament programs without the advice of the Council; a complete reformation of the French military system could not be undertaken with a hostile Council. The appointment and dismissal of members of the Council were surrounded by such guarantees as would have required a change in the law before the composition of the Council could be altered—and such a change presupposed the approval of the Senate.

Daladier was not the man to carry on such a huge battle because he was hampered by his conception of his role, by his temperament, and by his policy. He was not a technician, and did not consider it part of his duty to replace the ideas of the leaders of the French Army with his own. Personally, I feel that Clemenceau's epigram, "war is too serious a matter to be left to the military," contains a profound truth. Modern warfare is not solely a technical problem; to entrust the military with the direction of the war would be as great a mistake as to entrust economists with it, on the pretext that war has an economic side. As modern war is total war, its direction and preparation ought to be the work of the government, and the military leaders should be only the agents of execution. This does not alter the fact that in the sphere of execution technical problems will arise which must be solved by technicians. A minister can break up a quarrel between two specialists, but it would be imprudent for him to substitute his opinion for theirs; and all the more so when they are in agreement. Daladier did not have a revolutionary or dictatorial conception of his ministerial function; he did not consider himself infallible, and would not assume the right to oppose his military ideas to those of his generals, especially when he knew that these generals—and not he—would be in charge of the war and its operations.

Questions of temperament are also involved. Daladier is honest, intelligent, and cultivated, but weak; he is a man of transaction and compromise rather than a man of decision. He has only the mask of authority. He is more rough than headstrong, more choleric than resolute, violent in his words but hesitant in his ideas. The roughness of his manners tends to conceal the indecision of his nature. Born of modest parents (his father was a baker) in a little southern town, he offers an astonishing mixture of peasant shrewdness, provincial bon-homie, Latin intelligence, and timidity. A former Professor of History at the Lycée de Grenoble, he knows and loves his country passionately. Hence, per-haps, his political success; for no one knows better than he does the soul of the French people; no one values and enjoys more the traditions and virtues of France. The baker's son in politics remained a petit bourgeois intimidated by people of the world, whom he both scorned and feared; he never felt com-pletely at his ease before an industrialist, an Academician, or a Marshal. This thickset little man, who looks and talks like a *Provençal,* lacked confidence in himself. He had neither the vast erudition of Herriot, the finesse of Briand, that prelate of European politics, the culture of Painlevé, the intelligence of Blum, nor the methodical precision of Poincaré. He had only average and robust qualities, which he skillfully exploited—the love of work, a sense of balance, the art of judging men, and common sense. He was a southerner, but a southerner of the type which is at once cold and passionate, raised in the Rhône valley, where the freezing mistral blows. His strength lay in his famil-iarity with the petite bourgeoisie, of which he was the perfect representative. Such a man could direct the Ministry of War and guide the generals, but to enter into open combat with them was too much to ask of him.

Let us make no mistake. The Riom debates showed Daladier's best side—his presence of mind, his skill in improvisation, his physical and moral courage when, with his back to the wall, he faced his enemies. But the Riom trial did not show Daladier, the good boy, frightened by life, tortured by hesitation, undecided, weighing all opinions but trying to reconcile them all, afraid to make a mistake and returning in the morning to the solutions of the night before. He has been called conceited, but how wrongly! Had he only been more so! He hid his weakness under an appearance of severity, and, occasion-ally, of arrogance. He always conveyed the impression that he was going to say no; as a matter of fact, he began by saying no, after which he would say per-haps, and finally compromise, if he did not give in altogether. Like most weak men, he was susceptible to flattery; he was surrounded in the lobby of Parlia-ment by a circle of mediocre deputies and senators, whom his southern friend-liness, patriotism, and republican faith attracted; but the presence of these flatterers drove from Daladier those men who, loving him for his virtues and in spite of his weaknesses, attempted to put him on his guard. In spite of these contradictions he remained superior to most of those who criticized him. He was a man of good faith; but a man of authority was wanted. He was the Ledru Rollin of his day; but France needed a Gambetta. To finish this portrait of the man who directed our national defense for so long, I should like to add that he married an admirable woman, an uncompromising and passionate democrat, an intransigant enemy of all forms of reaction; she was both his conscience and his character. Mme. Daladier died of consumption in 1933; she left him her conscience, but she could not leave him her character; and Daladier, growing weak, went under.

Finally, it was Daladier's general policy from 1936 to 1940 which prevented him from entering into open conflict with the General Staff. Here again, the death of Mme. Daladier had unhappy consequences. I knew and liked Daladier before this sad event; from then on I noted his evolution, not toward Fascism but toward a kind of social conservatism. To use the language of the Revolutionary Assemblies, he went from the Jacobins to the Girondins. When he entered Parliament after the last war, in which he had fought courageously, Daladier had belonged to the Left wing of the Radical-Socialist party. He fought not only against the narrow nationalism of Poincaré and Tardieu, but often also against Herriot and Briand, whose personalities dwarfed his, but whom he accused of being "too moderate," too inclined to make concessions to the Right. He was, at that time, the champion of the "union of the Left," an alliance of all democratic elements against the forces of reaction. On February 6, 1934, he defended the republican order against the uprising organized by the Croix de Feu and the Camelots du Roi. From 1934 to 1936, with Blum, Herriot, Paul-Boncour, and a few others, he was one of the *bêtes noires* of French Fascism. But those who knew Daladier were already fearful of a certain tendency in him to "put water into his wine," as the French people say. Shortly after he had been appointed Minister of National Defense and of War in the Blum cabinet, he turned toward the policy of appeasement, which, to his misfortune and ours, he was to practice from 1938 to 1940. In the field of foreign policy, appeasement took him to Munich and made him neglect Franco-Russian amity.

In the domestic field, appeasement of the Right brought about his break with the Communist party in 1938, and with the organizations of the working class in 1939. To come to terms with the Right that hated him and betrayed the nation, Daladier moved away from the Left, which was fighting against Fascism and whose political instincts corresponded to the interests of the country. This new policy was to prevent Daladier from fighting the high French military authorities, particularly Pétain, because they belonged to the reactionary and conservative milieu which he was trying to appease. In order to inherit the political succession from Blum, Daladier, a man who came from the Left, had to reassure the moderate elements of the country, and to accomplish this he had to be on good terms with the Army leaders. Unfortunately, the Army leaders were enemies of democracy, sympathizers with Fascism, and partisans of the doctrine of the continuous front.

I have often wondered what were the basic reasons for Daladier's political development. I certainly would not exclude personal ambition. Daladier wanted to succeed Blum and Chautemps, Popular Front Premiers; consequently, he was eager to appear a lesser evil to the adversaries of the Popular Front. But this reason would not have been sufficient; even without the moral support of his wife, Daladier was not a man to put his ambition above his duty.

The most plausible and human explanation seems to be that Daladier had been completely upset by the events of the 6th of February; he had done his duty, but this duty had been painful for him. He was stricken with remorse and with grief, because he had been head of the government when the police had to use arms to preserve order. I was beside him during the tragic night of February 6, and was one of the few witnesses of his reactions; he was haunted by the specter of civil war, as so many brave, farsighted, and patriotic veterans of the first World War, both in Europe and America, have continued to be haunted to the point of becoming isolationists and defeatists. I hasten to add that this explanation, which most charitably accounts for Daladier's conversion to the Right, is no excuse. As I have already said, all Frenchmen were more or less at fault in the years preceding the war. Daladier was guilty—if of nothing else—of not carrying on the fight against the Fascists who were corrupting the French Army. By purging the Army of members of the Croix de Feu and of the Cagoulards, he would have assured its political, intellectual, moral, and, consequently, military rehabilitation. I do not hesitate to denounce this grave error: first, because it carries no penal responsibility; second, because there is no fear of Vichy's holding it against Daladier; and finally, because Daladier redeemed himself at Riom in the eyes of every enemy of Fascism by his magnificent defense of the republican regime and by his vigorous denunciation of Hitler and Pétain.

It is apparent, then, that Daladier was not the man to combat the doctrine of the continuous front. He was, however, too intelligent not to see the reaction and red tape in this doctrine. He had always distrusted Pétain. I must admit that before February 6, 1934, I had made a distinction between Pétain, whom I considered an upright though somewhat aged man, and Weygand, the clerical general. Daladier, with whom I was then on excellent terms, told me: "Pétain is the more dangerous, because he is less intelligent and more ambitious than Weygand."

What did Daladier do in 1936 to fight the evil influence of Pétain and to orientate the military authorities toward a more intelligent conception of modern warfare? He used his favorite methods, appeasement and compromise. Instead of attacking the obstacle head-on, he tried to flank it; instead of offering open battle to the Supreme War Council, he tried first to neutralize it, and then to come to terms with it. After pointing out the erroneous principle of his action, we must admit that he pursued his appeasement policy more cleverly in the military field than in the sphere of internal and foreign policy. He took advantage of the vacancies caused by retirement in the War Council to promote to the higher posts of the French Army such generals as Billotte, Bourret, Doumenc, and Garchery, who were the least reactionary and most intelligent. He considered it clever to appoint Pétain Ambassador to General Franco, not realizing that in ridding the Army of this intriguer, he encumbered our foreign policy. Thanks to Daladier, the French Army, which in 1936 had had two mechanized divisions and no armored divisions, possessed in the fall of 1939 three mechanized divisions, two armored divisions, and enough matériel and officers to organize two additional armored divisions and one more mechanized division during the winter of 1939-1940. Such action would have been impossible, had the Minister of War been Pétain.

But this action was not enough. Aided by Gamelin, who was just as weak, Daladier did his best to effect reforms; had he been aided instead by Billotte, he might have revolutionized the very bases of the Army and changed its structure and general organization. Instead of creating a new weapon, he contented himself with improving the one bequeathed to him by Pétain and Maurin. When it became obvious during the war that the instrument was deficient, it was too late to create another. Experience has shown that one may correct a system while under fire, but not change from one system to another. The French Army could not do in a few months under war conditions what it could easily have accomplished in a few years of peace.

Historians will ask whether it was possible to do anything else, or rather, under what conditions it would have been possible to do something else. To revolutionize the Army would have meant revolutionizing the country. More radical methods were employed in the field of aviation with the result that the Fascist and reactionary forces attacked the reformation of the Air Force more savagely than they did the improvements effected by Daladier in details of the Army. What France needed was a spirit of daring, not of timidity.

Prepared, organized, and led by young and unprejudiced men, the German Army was victorious; its doctrine expressed audacity. Prepared, organized, and directed by old men according to outworn formulae, the French Army was conquered in spite of the courage of its men; its doctrine reflected timidity.

Neither Daladier nor Goering had anything to do with the elaboration or application of the French or German war doctrines. Neither of them can claim the credit or bear the blame for these doctrines and their consequences. If Hindenburg and Ludendorff, in the German Army of 1925-1935, had played the role that Pétain and Weygand played in the French Army from 1930 to 1940, it would have been impossible to construct a modern German Army, based on modern principles and capable of exploiting all modern techniques. What Germany could never have done with a Marshal and General who were survivors of the first World War, France could not do with Pétain and Weygand.

Fascism was responsible for the moral and political defeat of France, and Pétain and Weygand, representatives of Fascism in the French Army, were the men chiefly guilty for the ineffective military preparation and the poor employment of the forces.

Were they traitors in the legal sense of the word? I cannot think so. Until proof is available, no Frenchman has a right to accuse fellow Frenchmen of treason. Until that day, we can judge their conduct in the words spoken by Daladier—a Daladier grown in stature in the course of the Riom trial—at the hearing of March 31, 1942: "The hatred of novelty, the hatred of intellectual daring, the hatred of everything modern led the French Army to its ruin."

These words epitomize Pétain and Weygand.

Aviation and the French Defeat

8

THE BATTLE OF FRANCE demonstrated the importance of air power in modern warfare; it proved that an army can do nothing without the support of an adequate air force.

Until that time, the military use of aviation had not produced the struggles which many had prophesied. The bombing of large cities, such as Madrid and London, had not resulted in the panic that might have been expected, and aerial struggles lacked the spectacular aspect of naval battles. But aerial warfare was still in the process of development. From more recent experiments—in England, Russia, North Africa, Italy, and continental Europe—one may conclude that if aviation alone cannot win the war, it has, nevertheless, become a decisive element of warfare. The actual war is by no means an aerial war; it is a total war, to which the increasing participation of aerial forces gives its peculiar character and its rhythm.

The easy conquest of France by the Wehrmacht in May and June, 1940, was largely due to the perfect collaboration of armored divisions and aerial forces. The absolute necessity for this collaboration has been the true lesson of the French defeat. The military correspondent of the *London Times* was quite right in writing (July 15, 1940), "there is no doubt that it was, in the main, the combination of tanks and aircraft which not only broke through each successive organized line of defense, but also smashed every extemporized center of resistance. . . . It has been reported that, again and again, when a tank or even a few motorcyclists met with opposition, the dive bomber came to their support within thirty to forty minutes." Such excellent co-ordination of effort and movement cannot be improvised on the battlefield; it is the result of minute preparation, long training of soldiers, and especially of the adaptation of the military organization and machinery.

Neither the French Army nor the French Air Force was organized for this total warfare, because the French High Command before 1939 did not believe in the alliance of the tank and the airplane. It continued to consider the Air Force an auxiliary arm like the engineering corps and the baggage train, charged with important but secondary duties and subordinated to the needs of the fighting forces. These duties were long-range scouting and strategic reconnaissance, surveying and photographing of the battlefield, rapid communication between separated centers, and, especially, the regulation and observation of artillery fire. The French General Staff admitted the *indirect* use of air power in warfare, particularly in attacking supply columns and harassing lines of communication, but not its *direct* participation on the battlefield.

All witnesses interrogated at the Riom trial complained of the inadequacy of French air power and of the insufficient co-operation between land and aerial units; all mentioned the extensive participation of German aircraft in the battle. "Our troops were unable to fight airplanes," said Generals Mittel-hauser and Lenclud; and General Requin, answering La Chambre's claim that large numbers of French airplanes existed, said on March 19: "I do not know where these airplanes were; all I know is that they were never seen on the battlefield."

The question of the location and use of these French airplanes during the battle is one of the most interesting aspects of the problem of responsibilities for the war and the defeat; unfortunately, this question was never raised during the Riom hearings. I do not emphasize it because of the accusations made against me, but because the organization and use of the Air Force, more than the organization and use of the Army, revealed the true causes of the French defeat. With respect to the Army, the General Staff can be charged with having failed to create the organs of modern warfare—armored and de-fensive divisions. The situation in the Air Force was worse; the organs had existed—aerial divisions and parachute units had been created in 1936 and 1937 by the Popular Front, but they had been abolished in 1938 and 1939 at the express request of the General Staff. Similarly, in 1936 and 1937 the Minister of Aviation had proposed the creation of an "attacking air force with light multiplace airplanes, to be used in land warfare"; he had proposed exten-sion of the Air Force and the development of anti-aircraft artillery—in short, everything France lacked in 1940—and the Permanent Committee of National Defense had rejected these proposals.

The short history of French aviation in the last six years permits an accurate measurement of the harm done French national defense by the conservatism of the military leaders. A division of this history into two periods will supply answers to the accusations which the Vichy govern-ment and its Council of Political Justice brought against La Chambre and me. I was Minister of Aviation from June 4, 1936, to January 13, 1938, and I assume entire responsibility for the domestic and foreign aviation policy of the Popular Front. La Chambre was Minister of Aviation from January, 1938, until March, 1940; it was his responsibility to prepare the Air Force on the eve of war and to supervise the manufacture of matériel used by the Air Force in the Battle of France. As the average life of an airplane in time of war is less than a year and a half, none of the airplanes ordered or built under the Popular Front could be used in May and June, 1940; the Popular Front could be charged with only an indirect and remote responsi-bility for the material or moral preparation of the war. It is also easy to show that the charges against La Chambre were as unjustified as those against Daladier; France had all the airplanes which the General Staff had con-sidered necessary for her defense. As for the charges against me, I intend to demonstrate that some were so vague as to make a reply impossible. Others were political acts for which I certainly do not mean to seek excuse: the nationalization of the aeronautic industry, the fight against the Fascists who infested the Air Force, the reorganization of the Air Force on modern and democratic bases, the creation of popular aviation—so much for domestic policy; the sending of certain matériel to the Spanish republicans, the organization of collective security by agreements with Czechoslovakia and negotiations with the Soviet Union—so much for the foreign policy. If those are the "crimes" of which I am accused, I intend to acknowledge them proudly; and I am waiting patiently to render an account of this policy to the French people, who alone have the right to place the blame.

AIR POWER IN THE BATTLE OF FRANCE

The French and British Air Forces took part together in the Battle of France. To evaluate their role in that battle, one must consider three factors: the strength of these forces, the use made of them, and the reasons that prevented the French Army from having at its disposal on the battlefield the airplanes which were at the rear.

The power of an air force depends on the quality of its personnel and matériel, the number of planes which it can put into active service, the productive capacity of the industry which feeds this force, and, last but not least, its general organization.

Quality of Personnel and Matériel

Let us first consider quality. All evidence indicates that the superiority of German aviation was quantitative and not qualitative. Every time that the French or British aviators met German aviators in equal numbers or even two against three, they were victorious.

The succession of these victories, recorded in the official communiqués, established, first, that the morale, training, and aptitude for battle of the French crews left nothing to be desired. These, like the British crews, were superior in training to the German. France and England, with convenient access to the sources of petroleum products, had been able to give their pilots, bombardiers, and mechanics more flying experience. Furthermore, the victories proved that French matériel, taken as a whole, was satisfactory. Not having prepared for war at a definite date, French aviation could not be expected to have the best machines in every category; but its average was respectable and tended to improve, thanks to the prototypes built after the nationalization of the aeronautic factories. At the beginning of the war this average was based on the Morane 405 (single-seater pursuit plane) and the Potez 63 (light fighter-bomber); to these were added later the D520 and

Bloch 151 (pursuit planes) and the Leo 45, the Bloch 135, and the Bloch 174 (fighter-bombers).

The average quality of French aircraft was the result of a combination of airplane bodies which were somewhat superior to foreign models with engines which were slightly inferior to foreign products. In the course of the war the most modern French airplanes were outclassed only by the English Spitfire and the German Messerschmitt, the best pursuit planes in the world, so that the Anglo-French bloc always had at least a qualitative equality in aeronautic matériel. The French Air Force also had in service several hundred American machines which were entirely satisfactory, especially in view of the perfection of the American engines. Nor did Germany have superiority in armament. The French planes were armed with cannon, machine guns, and bombs; their cannon were somewhat better than the German; their machine guns were slightly inferior; their bombs had the edge in destructiveness on German bombs of the same weight, and the precision of French bombing was satisfactory. In short, the French Air Force, like the French Army, had qualitative parity in matériel. The Popular Front technicians and workers had conceived and built these machines; the plane crews had been recruited just before or during the Popular Front period, and they had been trained under the Popular Front. We may therefore conclude that the Popular Front had not perpetrated the alleged ravages on the matériel and morale of the Air Force.

Keeping these diverse elements in mind, one can say that one French and one British aviator could fight three Germans.

Quantity of Planes in Active Service

On the other hand, a fatal quantitative inferiority existed. With three times fewer men in her factories and an industrial potential three and a half times smaller, it would have been impossible for France, even under dictatorial rule, to produce the same number of planes as Germany. All that could be hoped for was that England would make up for the numerical inferiority. While part of the armament of the Army could be drawn from stocks left over from 1918, such was not the case for the Air Force, which could use only planes built in 1938 and 1939. The hearings disclosed that in June, 1940, France had about three and a half times fewer planes than Germany.

The truth came to light in spite of Vichy's efforts. The communiqué of February 20, 1942, alleged that France possessed, on May 10, 1940, 1,730 combat planes, of which 1,130 were first-line planes; the communiqué added that Germany had, at the same time, 16,800 planes—without giving more specific information. These figures were intended to give the impression that French aviation had been impotent; it was necessary to explain to the soldiers why they had seen so many German planes in the sky and so few French; it was also necessary to support Marshal Pétain's justification to the French people that "French aviation was forced to fight outnumbered one to six."

The Riom hearings revealed that the figures of the communiqué issued by the French Agency of Information were exact, but incomplete. Vichy had studied the proverb, "there are three degrees in lying—the lie, the woman, and statistics." The following information was gathered by the Supreme Court of Justice and read aloud in public hearing: (1) The figure of 16,800 included all German military aircraft; according to the Information Service, Germany had about 6,200 first-line planes in May, 1940, of which 5,200 were in the French campaign and the rest at the disposal of the Navy, on the Russian frontier, in Norway, etc. (2) The figure of 1,130 French aircraft included only the 600 pursuit planes and the 530 bombers and observation planes used against the Germans; this figure corresponded to the General Staff's operational plans, but did not include the 600 airplanes assigned to the infantry divisions, the 350 at the disposal of the Navy, the 300 first-line planes in North Africa, or the reserves of matériel in France and North Africa. (3) A document brought before the Court by Colonel Chatelain, assistant to General Redempt, who was Director of Matériel in the Ministry of Aviation, gave a detailed account of the situation of the French Air Force on July 28, 1940, after the armistice. In spite of the 2,000 planes that had been lost, destroyed, or abandoned in the course of the fighting, the Air Force still had 4,238 airplanes (1,739 first line) in France, and 1,800 airplanes (300 first line) in North Africa—a total of 6,038, of which 2,039 were first-line planes—plus 1,400 combat planes in reserve and 350 at the disposal of the Navy.

General Redempt's figures are beyond dispute because he was responsible for the war matériel of the Air Force. These figures are in line with those given the Air Commission at the beginning of June, 1940, by Laurent-Eynac, then Minister of Aviation, and with the résumés handed every two weeks to the British authorities in London by the French mission which remained there until the armistice. As a member of the Aeronautic Committee of the Chamber of Deputies, I had been apprised of Laurent-Eynac's figures, and I obtained in London a copy of the last report given our Allies, on May 24, 1940. This shows that during the Battle of France French aviation might have had 2,100 fighter planes in line (1,800 on the continent and 300 in North Africa) as against 6,200 German planes (5,200 on the French front and 1,000 on other fronts); and that the total figure of armed and equipped aircraft (to use the term of the reports) was 3,500 as against 13,865 German aircraft. If only 1,130 airplanes were thrown into battle, as Vichy contended, the High Command failed in its task, for 3,500 combat planes were available.

The ratio of first-line planes was, then, about 1 to 3, and that of combat planes (first line and reserve) about 1 to 4; the ratio of first-line planes on the Western European front and that of the total number of planes was still more favorable. The French Air Force was what it should have been, all that it possibly could have been, if one remembers the relative power of production and foreign supply facilities of France and Germany. These figures were La Chambre's best defense—the only one he should have presented before the Supreme Court—and he might have asked the Prosecuting Attorney how Marshal Pétain could have done better with the means at his disposal.

It was patently impossible for France to fight Germany alone when her numerical disadvantage was so great. But to the French Air Force was to be added the Royal Air Force. British participation in the air war should have been greater than British participation in the land war, for very simple reasons. Because of their geographic situation and their differing economic structures, it was normal for France to favor the development of her land forces, and England her naval and air forces. If Great Britain did not have many more men of military age than France, she had about twice as many industrial workers (ten million in mines and industry, against five million in France and seventeen million in Germany, Austria, and Czechoslovakia), and her industrial might was two and one-half times as great; it was to be expected that France could put more divisions in the field and that England could have more airplanes over continental Europe. Omitting the British air squadrons which were in the Mediterranean area from Gibraltar to Egypt and those put at the disposal of the Navy, England's aerial forces on the European continent and in the British Isles in May and June, 1940, numbered 1,900 first-line planes. Thus France and England could have sent 3,700 first-line planes against the 5,200 which the Germans used. If 500 first-line planes had been withdrawn from the defense of London, Paris, and other vulnerable points (without speaking of reserves), a ratio of 2 to 3 for first-line planes and of 3 to 4 for reserves would have existed—a more favorable ratio than existed on land for the tanks, whose ratio was about 2 to 3, reserves included.

Productive Capacity Feeding the Air Forces

In September, 1939, Germany's productive capacity had a slight margin of superiority. This shifted to the Allies in May, 1940. The control of the sea and the support of American industry also favored the Allies. According to the reports given by the Minister of Aviation to the Aeronautic Commission in February, 1940, French factories in 1939 had produced 2,497 combat planes and about 800 training planes, transport planes, aircraft for export, etc., or an average of 250-280 planes per month (not including those furnished by the United States and assembled in French plants). Although general mobilization had disorganized production during the first weeks of the war, the steady increase in production since the beginning of the year absorbed the the temporary decrease. The volume of French production on the eve of the war can thus be estimated at about 250-300 planes per month. At the same time the production of English factories was estimated at 800 planes per month, approximately three times that of France. To the output of French and English factories were added the shipments of planes ordered from the United States. Although 300 machines per month had been expected, the volume of imports from the United States did not exceed 100-150 airplanes per month in the first months of the war. The Allies could count on 1,200-1,300 planes per month, of which 800-900 were combat planes.

The most reliable estimates of German productive power indicate that at the beginning of the war Germany was producing 1,300-1,400 planes per month, of which 900-1,000 were combat planes. This production figure was reached by instituting an industrial demi-mobilization before the war. In the spring of 1939, according to information released by Major George Fielding Eliot, the French *Revue de l'Armée de l'Air,* and the English publication, *Aircraft Engineering,* German production was estimated at 600-700 planes per month. Thus in the six months preceding the war Germany had doubled her production, while England and France had increased their production 50 to 60 per cent. At the outbreak of hostilities Germany profited by a slight margin of superiority which was to be absorbed in the Polish campaign.

As the experts had foreseen, the productive capacity of the Allies increased more rapidly than that of Germany: the industrial resources of France and England were about as great as those of Germany plus those of Austria and Czechoslovakia; Germany had begun her industrial mobilization before her enemies; and the Allies could appeal for help to American industry, whereas Germany could appeal only to Italian industry. Normally, after the time necessary for industrial mobilization, Franco-British production should have equaled German production, and the American complement should have been almost a net profit. These prognostications based on economic realities turned out to be almost exact. The "war plan of aeronautic production" set up by the services of the French Ministry of Aviation was very ambitious. This plan was disclosed by the Minister to the Aeronautic Commission of the Chamber of Deputies in February, 1940: "Our war plan leads to the ultimate production of 1,600 planes per month, after passing through a stage of producing 750 planes per month. We expect to reach this stage next spring, and we intend to arrive at a production of 1,000 planes per month toward the end of 1940, achieving the final figure in 1941." The Minister stated that the aeronautic industry had sufficient stocks to build 641 warplanes and 71 training planes during the month of May, 1940; 700 combat planes, 132 training planes, and 41 aircraft for the Navy during the month of June, etc. These forecasts proved to be incorrect. The Minister cannot be blamed for that. The United States and England need only compare the curves of their own forecasts with their actual results during the same period to appreciate that in aeronautics anticipations are frequently frustrated.

In May, 1940, French factories reached a monthly output of 400-450 planes —350 warplanes plus 50-100 training planes. To this figure must be added about 125 American aircraft, partially assembled, armed, and equipped in French factories. At the same time British production rose to about 1,300 planes per month, to which we can add the equivalent of 125 American machines in the form of planes or plane parts. The production feeding the Franco-British aerial forces totaled 1,900-2,000 planes per month. German production had risen from 1,300-1,400 planes in September, 1939, to 1,600-1,700 per month in May, 1940. Allied production outdistanced German production for several months after January, 1940. Italy's entrance into the war on June 10, 1940, gave the Axis an additional 300-400 planes per month, and restored equality between the two blocs. The fall of France in June, 1940, upset this equilibrium. With France no longer a part of the Allied bloc, the Axis capacity of production was greater. Only in the middle of 1941 was the equilibrium re-established; Russian participation in June, 1941, gave the Allies a considerable advantage, which even Japan's entry in December, 1941, was unable to destroy.

These statements show that France and England had every interest in throwing into battle all their reserves during May and June, 1940. Since these reserves, when not in use, declined in value from day to day, the Allies had every reason to sacrifice planes to make Germany sacrifice them, too. The Allies might have established a numerical superiority by reciprocal attrition. This was indicated since the average of German losses was higher than that of Allied losses. In May and June, 1940, the draining-off of aerial forces would have given France and England an unquestionable advantage, for American production would have made up their losses. France pursued exactly the opposite policy, saving when she should have spent; she signed the armistice with approximately 6,000 airplanes on hand. Furthermore, these statements reveal that the ratio of French productive power to Germany's was approximately 1 to 5 at the beginning of the war and 1 to 3.7 in May, 1940; the ratio of French to English production was and remained 1 to 3.

Organization of the Air Forces

Of all factors, the importance of air force organization in aerial might is the least known to the public and is sometimes neglected by specialists; and yet it seems to me the most important. Aviation is characterized by the rapidity and breadth of its movements. There is no advantage in having the best matériel, the best-trained crews, the largest aerial fleets, if the lack of an efficient organization interferes with their proper employment. Everything said about tanks in the preceding chapter is still more true of combat planes; separation weakens, while concentration increases, their power tenfold. In modern warfare aviation represents the highest degree of motorization; an air force is a super-motorized army. Only the airplane can transport firing units (machine guns, light cannon, bombs), not only from one point on the battlefield to another but behind the lines of troops in battle; the airplane adds a vertical dimension to warfare. The continuous front means nothing to the airplane, limited as it is only by its radius of action. But an aerial force is more difficult to direct than an armored force. To have a thousand planes at a given moment and in a given place, to engage and withdraw aerial divisions and corps in combat, requires a mechanism of command, liaison, and control which cannot be improvised. Here maneuver and organization are closely allied; a good organization of aerial forces multiplies their power, whereas a poor organization reduces them to auxiliaries of the infantry.

In the air as on the ground, the Germans had an organization adapted to the needs of the maneuver they had planned. They had large aerial units, capable of mass action whenever their intervention was needed. They had combat squadrons, which could take a direct part in land fighting by using bombs, cannon, and machine guns against enemy infantry. These attacking squadrons—the famous Stukas—had been specially trained to support armored divisions and tank attacks. Furthermore, the Germans had parachute units which could be used for many purposes, from combat and maneuver to espionage and Fifth Column activity. And German anti-aircraft defense was as good as their aerial organization. Believing in the efficacy of aviation, they had taken care to defend their troops against air attack; they understood that a plane lost in battle has paid for itself, but a plane destroyed on the ground because of poor camouflage or lack of other protection has been wasted.

The French and English had taken no precautions. To defend themselves, two against three, they would have needed an organization equal or superior to that of the Germans. The bases of this general organization should have been the following: (1) A High Command of Anglo-French aerial forces; without a unified command English and French Air Forces could have undertaken concerted operations, but not the type of operations carried out under a single leader capable of pooling all available resources. (2) The close concentration of their forces and the inclusion of large aerial units (divisions and corps) essential for large-scale aerial maneuvers. (3) The formation of parachute units. These would have been more useful to the Allies, operating on the defensive, than to the Germans, who were on the offensive, because German armored units had great difficulty in maintaining liaison with the supply columns and motorized divisions which followed them. Parachute units could have increased these difficulties and retarded the German advance. English or French parachutists who had to operate on French or Belgian soil would have been aided by the civilian population, which was not true to the same extent for the Germans. (4) Sufficient anti-aircraft defense to cover the Allied armies in battle and to protect their aerial formations.

The Anglo-French Air Forces lacked such organization. The first months of the war could have been used to create an Anglo-French Air Command and aerial divisions. To quote General Billotte on the subject of armored divisions: "It is easy to create these units when the matériel and the personnel are available," and to quote General Keller: "Because we were inferior in numbers, we had to concentrate our resources." But in May, 1940, there were no unified command, no aerial divisions, no parachute units, no suitable anti-aircraft defense. The large majority of the French Air Force was divided into small units, escadrilles, or groups assigned to defend "vital points" of the land or to units of the Army—each infantry division had an escadrille, each army a group, etc. The only organized elements were a few heavy bombing squadrons for use in "reprisal" operations in Germany and for long-distance scouting to obtain strategic information. For the most part, French aviation had in 1940 the same organization as in 1918.

With such an organization the Anglo-French forces, and particularly the French Air Force, could not be used effectively.

Although the French Air Force could place about one plane in the air against three German planes, its poor organization made its "fighting value" four times less than that of the German Air Force. The power of the French Air Force as compared to that of Germany was about 1 to 4, the number of planes 1 to 3, the productive capacity 1 to 4.5, and the general organization, 1 to 5. The weakest point of French military aviation was its bad organization, which led to the misuse of this fighting arm.

Starting from a slightly different basis, the annual supplementary edition of the *Encyclopaedia Britannica* arrived at similar results for the end of 1939. It gave the following coefficients for the number of planes belonging to the great European Air Forces: Germany, 10; Soviet Union, 8; Great Britain, 6; France, 3. The air power was rated as follows: Germany, 10; Soviet Union, 7.6; Great Britain, 5; France, 2.5.

THE EMPLOYMENT OF THE AERIAL FORCES

Actually, the use made of French aerial forces was even worse than that of the land forces. No attempt was made to recover lost time—as Gamelin had tried to do by sending an army into Belgium in May, 1940. General Vuillemin, as Chief of Staff for the Air Force, did nothing to change its organization. Although inefficient, he was an honest man and a patriot, who fought with all his might against Weygand's armistice proposals. Consequently Vichy did not call him as a witness for the prosecution at the Riom trial, and Pétain, appointing the Chiefs of Staff of the Army and Navy to the Ministries of War and Navy, did not appoint Vuillemin as Minister of Aviation.

France and England would have been capable of sending two planes against the enemy's three, even three against four, if they had chosen to endanger their large cities in order to save their armies and win the war. This proportion was large enough to make resistance possible. In air warfare more than in land and sea battles, "defense is the strongest weapon," for the defending air force uses bases prepared and equipped in times of peace, and works under the protection of its anti-aircraft artillery. This is an indisputable fact, since we have witnessed the British fliers' performance in 1940-41, and that of the Russian and German fliers in 1942-43. After the fall of France the Royal Air Force was outnumbered one to three; early in 1942, the Soviet airmen were generally outnumbered one to two; finally, the German aerial forces available for the defense of western Germany when the bulk of the German air fleet was engaged in Russia certainly did not represent half the Anglo-American air forces massed around the European continent. In May and June, 1940, the general balance of aerial forces was more favorable for the French than it was to be for the British, Russians, and Germans, respectively. Experience proved once more that the numerical factor, as in the time of Napoleon, was less significant than the factor of strategy. The air battle was lost not because the French and English airmen were less numerous or less courageous than the Germans, but by the errors of the French Command; one can hardly say that the battle was lost—it was never fought.

A comparison with German strategy will furnish the most vivid illustration.

German Methods

German aerial strategy was marked not by genius but by common sense. It was without imagination but impeccable in execution. It revealed the organizational talents of General Milch, formerly a specialist in commercial aviation, who was the veritable creator of the German Air Force.

This strategy was subordinated to, and formed part of, the general plan which accomplished the destruction of the armies of Western Europe in six weeks. It was a concentrated strategy, massing all aerial forces and putting them at the disposal of the invading armies. During May and June, 1940, German airplanes did not penetrate the French lines except on two occasions: a raid on Paris and another on the Rhône valley. And these two operations were related to the requirements of the German High Command. The raid on Paris was carried out on the eve of the day when the question of defending or abandoning the capital was being discussed; its object was to freeze defending air forces, which would have been more usefully employed fighting General Guderian's armored divisions, and to frighten the French population in order to facilitate the work of the Fifth Column. The raid on the Rhône valley was a reconnaissance in force, intended to explore the terrain that the motorized columns would follow on their way to join the Italian armies, and to show the French that nothing could stop Hitler's airplanes. The German Air Force was, above all, the arm of the German armored forces. The airplane was the hunting dog, the watchdog, and the sheepdog of the tank. Aerial forces served the armored divisions as scouting and liaison units and as heavy artillery. Theirs was the role formerly played by cavalry and long-range artillery; but this modern cavalry could advance at three hundred miles per hour, and this artillery threw projectiles whose wind could put a twenty-ton tank out of commission. The French armies were broken by the combined action of aerial and armored forces.

German tactics were still better than German strategy, for here General Milch and his subordinates did use imagination. Remarkable liaison was established not only between aerial units in action and their command, but also between aerial and armored units. The co-ordination of effort at every level was the result of long training and of excellent organization: everyone knew exactly what he had to do, every leader had available the transmission facilities needed for the reception of information and the sending of orders. The airplanes were charged with a sort of rapid cleaning-up of the battlefield; they destroyed or neutralized the defensive organizations which Marshal Pétain considered impassable. They came to the aid of armored units as soon as

these units met any resistance; they broke resistance by bombing field fortifications, and attacked enemy tanks with cannon; in short, they neutralized the
enemy forces. The ruthless attacks of the Stukas forced the French troops to
take cover for the few moments needed for the passing of the tanks. The planes
worked, in general, in successive waves, organizing a kind of endless chain
over the battlefield, which gave the soldiers the impression of both power and
permanence. The co-ordination of the aerial and tank operations had been
planned in detail on the basis of the lessons learned in the Spanish war and
the Polish campaign. When German planes attacked French troops on the
road, they carefully avoided destroying the roads or tunnels which their
motorized units were later to use; they dropped bombs on both sides of the
road until the explosions stopped the columns by blocking the road at several
points. Then they attacked with cannon and machine guns.

To perfect their method of fighting, the Germans had combined the art
of warfare with elements of mob psychology. They knew that the direct
intervention of aviation in land fighting was more terrifying than deadly—all
the more so since they knew that the French troops had not been trained for
this type of warfare. They were more concerned with smashing the nerve of
the French soldier than with killing him. Many observers affirm that the
German bombs were supplied with giant whistles to increase the terror.
Whether or not this was so, the Germans did try to terrify their enemy.
Lucien Bossoutrot, President of the Aeronautic Commission of the Chamber
of Deputies, learned from the French General Staff of the Air Force that the
Germans followed up planes engaged in land battle with other planes,
often outmoded and without armament, manned by crews not sufficiently
trained to take part in the fighting. These planes remained behind or above
the combat zone and were protected by the action of the aerial forces engaged
in battle; but their presence in the background, giving the impression of a
numberless, irresistible, inexhaustible force, caused the French soldiers to
repeat: "The sky is black with German planes. Where are ours?"

The German parachute units also helped the German advance, especially
in the march through the Netherlands and Belgium; a fort in Liége was surprised and taken by a parachute group. In France either the activity of these
troops was somewhat limited or information on its extent has not yet come to
light. Small groups of parachutists in civilian dress or disguised as French soldiers were used to throw panic into the refugees who crowded the roads, or to
occupy bridges and crossings before they could be destroyed. But there seems to
have been no real maneuver by parachute units. Either the Germans had
not sufficiently developed their methods for using parachutists and preferred
to study the lessons of the actions in Belgium, or they intended to save their
parachute units for another phase of the campaign—the phase which did not
take place. When the French Army, discouraged and exhausted, might have
turned toward the réduit Breton or the ports of the Atlantic coast, it would
have found in its way destroyed bridges, crossings captured and held by automatic arms, traps and ambushes; it would have believed itself betrayed, and the

retreat would have become a rout. Thanks to Weygand, the German High Command did not have occasion to use this *ultima ratio*.

German air power in the French campaign was characterized by concentration of forces, the co-ordination of aerial and land maneuver, and the perfection of execution.

French Methods

French aerial strategy was one of dispersal, as opposed to the German strategy of concentration. It corresponded to the general scattering of forces which characterized French planning under Gamelin and under Weygand. This strategy was even more unpardonable in the field of aviation, in view of the possibilities of maneuver open to an air force because of its mobility.

There was no inter-Allied strategy, no unified maneuver of British and French Air Forces, nor was there any thought of organizing a Franco-British Air Force. Nothing significant had been done to achieve these in the years preceding the struggle, and the Allies did not profit by the ten months of the "phony war." Instead of sending a force of 3,000-4,000 planes against the German air fleet, a small number of squadrons and groups, working without order or organization, were sent up. The French General Staff asked only that the Royal Air Force put at its disposal a certain number of aerial formations, which the English did with very good grace. Winston Churchill, replying to Marshal Pétain in a public address, said that if the aid of British air power had been inadequate, it nevertheless had been greater than that for which the French General Staff had asked. Five hundred British bombers and two hundred British pursuit planes were stationed in France. Other formations that had remained in England also took part in the battles of May and June, some going into action over Belgian or French territory (the evacuation of Dunkerque, for example) and others bombing the Ruhr at the request of the French Command. These operations, however, were not connected with any idea of maneuver or any general plan.

The French aerial forces were scattered from Syria to the North Sea. Pushing its doctrine to absurdity, the French Command applied the continuous front even to aviation. The largest part of the Air Force had been divided at the time of mobilization among the large units of the Army, so that each general of an infantry division or an army corps had his half-dozen planes. This dispersal precluded the possibility of any important maneuver. During the French campaign, when French air power should have been concentrated against the armored divisions, 700 first-line planes (including many American machines) were left in the Mediterranean basin, 300 in North Africa at the disposal of the Army, 350 at the disposal of the Navy, and 200 behind the Alpine frontier. Thus in May, 1940, France set aside 900 first-line planes, approximately 40 per cent of her force, to watch Italy, who had not yet declared war. If we add to the French aircraft the British forces then in the Mediterranean area, we arrive at this paradox, the crux of Anglo-French aerial strategy: France and England, fighting only Germany, used the same ratio of aircraft against *both* Germany and Italy—two Anglo-French planes faced three Italian planes and two Anglo-French craft faced five German planes! Moreover, several hundred French aircraft were left behind the Maginot Line—where German air activity was zero—or assigned permanently to the defense of Paris and certain "vital points," whose destruction was to be much less significant than that of the French Army. Given such a division of forces, it was impossible to win the war.

With more planes than their opponents, the Germans threw five out of of every six into the battle, while the French and English did not even send one out of two. Vichy's communiqué was correct when it said that France had sent 1,130 first-line planes against the German forces; but it did not speak of the 700 British aircraft sent to France, and it assuredly did not mention that a different strategy would have made use of 3,500 first-line planes and relatively more abundant reserves. Figures were juggled to deceive public opinion and to hide the errors of the General Staff.

The Anglo-French Air Forces were used under the most deplorable conditions. A single bloc comprising the 1,130 French and the 700 British planes should have been thrown against the German armored divisions or sent to the aid of the French armored units, which were without aerial support. Similarly, a striking force might have been improvised with the reserves of the Air Force, which had a large personnel and much matériel. It would, of course, have been less efficient than the German forces, but it could have retarded the advance of the *Panzerdivisionen* by forcing the enemy tanks to leave the roads and by dispersing their supply columns. For example, the French Air Force had in its reserve 300 Dewoitine 501's armed with cannon and machine guns, which were as fast as the Stukas; if these had been fitted out with bomb racks (which could have been done in a few hours), the Dewoitine 501's could have carried light bombs, permitting them to attack enemy tanks and their convoys. Under the protection of Anglo-French fighters, these improvised attacking planes could have protected the retreat of the French divisions toward the embarkation ports. But nothing was attempted, because such action contradicted the doctrine that aviation could not engage directly in land warfare. While the German Air Force, three times as powerful as the Anglo-French Air Forces stationed on the European continent, did not bomb cities and factories in the interior of France in order to save all its strength for the land battle, French and English formations bombed the Ruhr and German industrial centers. This fact is hardly credible, but it is proved by official communiqués published in all newspapers. In a speech delivered at Geneva, Henry Bidou, semi-official interpreter of the French Command, revealed that 75 per cent of the Anglo-French bombing forces had been used for such missions. The stupidity of the French General Staff won out over simple common sense.

French air power also lacked adequate anti-aircraft protection for its bases and fields. Here the Air Force paid for the errors of the General Staff of the Army. As this General Staff did not believe in the intervention of aerial forces in land battle, it assigned the largest part of the anti-aircraft guns to home defense instead of to the defense of the armies. According to the statement made by General Marescaux, Director of Aerial Defense, before the Court of Riom, 600 cannon were assigned to the army zone and 1,500 to the interior. It was considered more important to protect property than fighting men; yet it was the men who were attacked by the German aerial forces, not the interior of the country. The result of the General Staff's miscalculation was that the French Air Force lost more planes on the ground as a result of German bombings than in aerial combat. Information submitted to the Aeronautic Commission and transmitted to British authorities showed that the French Air Force lost 650 planes between May 10 and May 28: 120 lost in aerial operations, 150 destroyed on the ground by enemy bombing, and the others lost from "divers accidents" (piloting and mechanical accidents, collisions on the ground, etc.). In a book* published under the control of the Vichy censorship, Henry Bidou gave the figures of the losses of the French Air Force in May and June, 1940: 757 planes were destroyed—306 brought down or destroyed in combat, 229 destroyed on the ground, and 222 lost by accident.

One can cite as an example the odyssey of a pursuit squadron headed by Major de Marmier, an admirable reserve pilot and militant supporter of the Popular Front, who fought for the Spanish Republic and joined the Fighting French Forces of General de Gaulle in 1940. De Marmier's unit was in battle uninterruptedly from May 12 to June 17, and occupied seventeen airdromes in succession. At none of these stations did he find any anti-aircraft; consequently, in five weeks of fighting, he lost nine aircraft on the ground as against only four in combat, inflicting at the same time far more severe losses on the Germans. The inadequacy and poor distribution of anti-aircraft artillery cost De Marmier twice as much as the German numerical superiority cost him.

In this parallel between French and German methods, we cannot speak of French parachutists, because France had none. The French Army, which had had parachute units under the Popular Front, had dispersed these formations, whose creation was attributed to "Communist influence."

It would hardly be an exaggeration to say that French air power was not beaten; it never fought. Half its formations remained far from the scene of battle. With more than 6,500 aircraft on May 1, 1940 (for after the armistice, after all the losses, and after the destruction of matériel to keep it from falling into German hands, about 6,000 machines remained), the French Air Force lost in the service of France 757 aircraft, of which a small percentage was destroyed in combat! The percentage of losses in men was still more insignificant. In peacetime the Air Force had 2,000 officers and 40,000 noncommissioned officers and troops, whose ranks were swelled by a larger number of reserves after the mobilization. The losses were: 117 dead, of which 57 were officers (less than 1 per cent for the officers and a smaller percentage for the men); 191 wounded, of which 79 were officers (again less than 1 per cent for the officers); 371 missing, of which 149 were officers (less than 2 per cent of the total number of officers); in other words, 206 officers killed or captured out of more than 8,000. One must seek far in military history for an army whose

* Henry Bidou, *La Bataille de France* (Geneva: Éditions du Tour du Monde, 1941).

leaders ordered it to cease firing under such conditions. To the honor of the air men it must be said that they had no responsibility or share in this shame. They fought their infrequent and useless battles, outnumbered, not, as Pétain asserted, one to six, but one to ten, because they were badly commanded. With leaders of average quality, they might have fought in the ratio of two to three; with good leaders, the ratio would have been one to one. Only their courage made it possible for them to inflict greater losses than they suffered. They avenged their dead; they saved their honor; but those who commanded them did not permit them to save France.

THE CAUSE OF THE DEFEAT IN THE AIR

The answer to the general problem of why France was defeated in the air involves several questions: Could France have had more airplanes to send against Germany? Could she have had foreign aid? Could the French Air Force have been used more effectively?

Economic Factors

To be able to send more airplanes against Germany, France would have had to build them in her factories or obtain them abroad.

It would have been impossible for France to build more airplanes in her factories before and during the war without changing the bases of her military policy. With her human resources (industrial and military manpower), with her financial resources, with her raw materials, her plants and tooling, France could not have hoped to have a fleet of 533,000 tons, an Army of 115 divisions, a Maginot Line, and a powerful Air Force. The French military leaders had to choose. As Lucien Bossoutrot put it, "France had not the Air Force she needed, but the Air Force her credits purchased, the credits of her war programs, and the programs of her miltary doctrine." The aeronautic production of a country always depends on her industrial possibilities, the credits allotted to this production, construction programs set up by the military authorities, and the special features of the industry engaged in this production.

French industrial possibilities should be evaluated by comparison with those of Germany and England. What must be determined is the general capacity of such industrial production as could have been employed for the construction of such aircraft as could have taken part in the Battle of France. Modern air-craft becomes outmoded so rapidly that all planes actually in line in May, 1940, must necessarily have been built after the beginning of 1938, that is, after the fall of the Popular Front. They were built, it is true, in factories nationalized by the Popular Front and according to prototypes chosen during that period, but they were of excellent quality and their technical conception and execution have never been criticized. The only question is whether the factories constructed the quantity of planes corresponding to the country's general productive capacity in 1938, 1938, and 1940.

Capacity of Production

This general capacity must be determined on the basis of labor supply and the production of basic raw materials. The personnel employed in industry and factories represented about five million workers and technical and administrative employees in France as against ten million in England and fourteen million in Germany (the last figure was swelled in 1939 by two and one-half million Czech workers). We must also bear in mind the general organization of industry: France was a country of small industries and artisans; the number of "independent employers and workers" in industry (mines included) represented, in France, 31 per cent of the total number of salaried workers, whereas it represented 13 per cent in Germany, 14 per cent in Czechoslovakia, 7.5 per cent in Great Britain, and less than 5 per cent in the United States. It was normal for French "small industry" to produce relatively less than the "big industry" of Germany, and especially of England or America. During the three years under consideration French industry produced 3.6 times less aluminum, 3.3 times less steel, and 4.1 times less coal than German industry, as the following table shows. The ratio of German industrial production to French production can therefore be estimated at 3.7; the ratio of British industrial production to French production would be 2.7.

INDUSTRIAL CAPACITY OF FRANCE AND GERMANY IN THOUSANDS OF METRIC
TONS DURING THE YEARS 1937-1939

Year	Aluminum		Steel[1]		Coal[1]	
	France	Germany	France	Germany	France	Germany
1937	35	132	7,900	20,000	44,300	184,700
1938	45	156	6,200	23,500	46,500	186,500
1939	50	186	6,200	24,400	46,500	193,500
Total	130	474	20,300	67,900	137,300	564,700
Ratio	3.6		3.3		4.1	

[1] As the figures of production for the year 1939 are not known, the figures for 1938 have been taken and increased by the number corresponding to half the Czech production for 1939; this method of calculation is more favorable to Germany than to France.

These figures should be studied carefully, as they give an exact statement of the possibilities of French industry on the eve of hostilities and during the war. They demonstrate that even if France had assigned the same proportion of her industrial resources to the development of her aeronautic production as Germany did, she could not have had more than one plane to Germany's four at the moment of trial. These elementary facts and their inevitable con-sequences must not be overlooked. The General Staff of the Air Force was not unaware of these realities. It had been warned. General Armengaud had com-plained in an article in the *Revue Militaire Générale* (May, 1939) that the ratio of French to German aerial forces was one to three. He was answered in an editorial in the following issue of *l'Aéronautique,* the only serious French periodical of its kind: "The ratio of one to three is the ratio of normal strength, at normal rates, between French and German industries. And if the actual ratio of production between the two industries were, at this moment, 1 to 4 or 1 to 4.5 —which we think nearer the truth—that would mean either that the German leaders have favored aeronautic production in their distribution of the resources of war production or that Germany already had availed herself of the first steps of industrial mobilization. How can we doubt that this second hypothesis is cor-rect, when we know the facilities that a dictatorial regime has in such matters?"

The figures revealed at the Riom trial proved that France possessed in Europe and North Africa at the moment of the armistice, approximately 6,000 military aircraft, of which approximately 2,000 were first-line planes. If we take from this total about 1,000 American airplanes, which were added to the Air Force in May, 1940, and which included about 300 first-line planes, we see that French factories furnished a total of 5,000 military aircraft. It would have been natural for Germany to have at the same time four times as much aircraft in every category, or about 8,500 first-line planes and a total of 24,000 military aircraft but Germany had only 6,850 first-line planes out of a total of 16,800. On the other hand, the ratio of 1 to 4 exactly represented the comparison be-tween French and German aircraft production from 1938 to 1940.

To determine whether France could have produced more airplanes, we must consider the strength and capacity of the aeronautic industry. Was French industry capable of accomplishing a greater effort, of constructing a larger number of airplanes? The answer is yes, had it been granted adequate credits. It was incapable of a full effort, however, with the limited appropriations of the years 1937-1940.

The experience of the war proved that the French aeronautic industry was able to turn out good machines. During this period it lacked neither skilled workers and technicians nor competent industrialists; but it still lacked credit appropriations. It had resolved its most difficult and basic problems—the choice of good prototypes and the organization of mass production. Everything else was a question of financing industrial development. It is no more difficult, indeed, it is at times simpler, to produce two hundred planes of one type than it is to make one hundred. The shift from an output of one hundred to two or three hundred planes is not a question of aeronautic technique, but of industrial technique, which could be solved by competent industrialists, even by those with little knowledge of aeronautic production. The aeronautic industry could have been expanded if industrial means and resources had been diverted from other uses to its development.

The aeronautic industry did suffer from numerous imperfections, but none of these would have hampered the stepping-up of production from one hundred to two hundred planes of one type. Had the necessary funds been made available, we would have seen an industry imperfect but well developed, instead of one that was both imperfect and undeveloped. La Chambre made some statements at Riom on the incompetence and egotism of financiers, industrialists, and manufacturers which on many occasions had paralyzed airplane production. He was right. But the flaws which he pointed out were not peculiar to the aeronautic industry; they were characteristic of French mechanical industries as a whole and of the entire class of French employers. The same deficiencies existed in the shipbuilding industry, in machine-gun manufacture, and in the motor-car industry. Both Daladier and Jacomet gave similar evidence. Nor was the aeronautic industry affected more heavily than other industries by the repercussions of the social and political agitation.* It would have been no more difficult, from an industrial point of view, and more important to the national interest, to build additional airplane factories than to open new shipyards.

We arrive at the same conclusion if we examine the chief bottlenecks that threatened to strangle aeronautic production. The first of these was the military authorities' clumsy interference with the process of production; forgetting that "the better is the enemy of the good," the General Staff requested frequent changes in production plans and prototypes, often in the very middle of the mass production process, without considering that this necessitated constant modifications in machinery and entailed heavy costs for the industrialists. Another bottleneck was the red tape of French bureaucracy, which accumulated control of industry; the Ministry of Finance, in particular, which had arrogated to itself control of the entire administration, applied to aviation certain methods dating back to horse-and-buggy days. In a field requiring continual technical evolution, the Ministry of Finance saw nothing reprehensible in delaying production for six months. A single incident will illustrate this. In June, 1937, the Ministry of Aviation required the authorization of the Ministry of Finance to order planes for delivery in 1938; it was a formality, a simple matter of administrative routine. Despite repeated attempts to impress upon the Ministry of Finance the urgency of this order, the authorization was not received until October—and, at that, with a 50 per cent curtailment that led to three more months of negotiations.

A third bottleneck was the inadequate co-ordination of all branches of production. Plane parts—bodies, engines, armament, and numerous accessories (navigation instruments, landing gear, etc.)—were manufactured by different producers, so that the delay of any one manufacturer slowed the entire process. In 1937-1939 motors were turned out less speedily than were bodies; in 1937 the delivery of planes to military formations was held up by a delay in cannon and machine-gun construction; and finally, during the war plane production was hampered by the slow output of landing gears.

The nationalization law helped remedy, to some extent, the bottlenecks of aeronautic production, particularly through the establishment of a "general

* See Chapter 3.

production plan." Bottlenecks existed in Germany and England, too, but their existence was not an impossible obstacle to conquer. Even if things had come to the worst, the production of a series of two hundred planes would have suffered no greater delay than a series of one hundred, and in the last analysis more planes and motors would have been turned out. Moreover, in 1937-1939 French aeronautic industry did not at any moment work to the limit of its capacity. In September, 1937, the Investigating Committee on Production issued a report on the aeronautic industry; in it, the reporter, M. Roos, pointed out that "without new investments, the productive capacity made it possible to meet a demand far larger than that which could be expected in the near future." Thus production was limited by "demand"—by the programs of the General Staff, and not by the insufficient output of the factories.

As no insoluble industrial or technical problem prevented an increase in aeronautic production, it would have been sufficient to allocate more credits and resources to the aviation industry. But neither larger nor better results could be expected as long as industrial and financial resources were dictated by the plans of the General Staff; La Chambre was only the "purveyor" who had to respect the orders of his "client."

The Volume of Credits

Under a liberal economy the distribution of the means of production is accomplished by the manipulation of credit. By giving her aeronautic production comparatively larger credits than did Germany or England, France might have improved the relative condition of her aeronautic industry by reducing other branches of production. But the volume of credits allotted to the Ministry of Aviation for the manufacture of new aircraft obviously depended on the programs set up by the military authorities, and these programs were not inclined to favor air power to the detriment of the Navy or Army.

The study of the credits allotted to the Ministry of Aviation shows how French aviation was administered. Whether the Ministers of Aviation were good administrators actually goes back to the question of whether they made the aeronautic industry reach the maximum production possible with the sums put at their disposal. The examination of this problem depends on a comparison of the relation between credits and production in France, Germany, and England during the period preceding the war. The comparison of the English and French figures is particularly important: the economic and financial systems of France and England were more alike than those of France and Germany; moreover, when one deals with Germany, one must rely on estimates, whereas with France and England one has, at least for the years before the war, verifi-able official figures. As the aeronautic industry could not spring out of the ground by magic, a comparison of credits, if it is to be truly revealing, should deal not only with the period of aircraft construction (about two years before the opening of the French campaign), but with the period of the organization and equipping of the factories—about two additional years; the comparison should, in fact, go back to June, 1936, to the advent of the Popular Front.

CREDITS IN MILLIONS OF DOLLARS SPENT BY THE MILITARY AIR FORCES OF FRANCE, ENGLAND, AND GERMANY FROM JUNE, 1936, TO SEPTEMBER, 1939

Year	France	England	Coefficient in proportion to France	Germany[1]	Coefficient in proportion to France
1936[2]	81	140	1.7	315	3.9
1937	170	420	2.5	920	5.4
1938	230	600	2.6	1,050	4.6
1939[3]	230	600	2.6	1,155	5.0
Total	711	1,760		3,440	
Average			2.3		4.7

[1] The estimates correspond to 23 per cent of the figures given by the *Foreign Policy Report* of October 1, 1938, for the total expenses of German national defense for 1937, and to 25 per cent of the total credits for 1938 and 1939.
[2] Credits spent from June through December estimated at half of the credits spent in 1936.
[3] Credits spent from January to September estimated on the credits spent in 1938. For Germany, these credits have been increased by 10 per cent to allow for the absorption of Czech airplane factories.

Here again, the figures justify the French Ministers of Aviation. With approximately one-fifth the credits of Germany and less than half the credits of England, they equipped an Air Force capable of mobilizing one-third as many planes as Germany and almost two-thirds as many as Britain; they equipped an aeronautic industry producing about one-fifth the number of planes that Germany was turning out at the beginning of the war (that is, when Germany had already begun her industrial mobilization), one-fourth the number Germany was producing in May, 1940, and a third as many as England (whose general industrial organization was better than France's). The French aeronautic industry was as well adapted as the German to the needs of the force which it was to feed, since one-third of the German production was easily achieved by adding to the production of French factories a normal complement of American shipments. Thus the French ministers had done their duty, by assuring an Air Force one-third the size of the German force and replenishment equal to one-third of German production. To achieve this result, they had spent in the preceding four years one-fifth as much as General Milch.

To convince those who are still amazed by the so-called inadequacies of French aeronautic production, one need only cite, in addition to the credits set aside for aviation, those which were allotted to the Navy by France and England. The French Navy received about one-third the credits of the British Navy, and no one found it scandalous that the French fleet began the war with 533,000 tons in service and 171,000 tons under construction, whereas the British fleet had 1,350,000 tons in service and 675,000 tons under construc- tion. The same causes cannot produce different effects, and there cannot be one truth for the Ministers of the Navy and another for the Ministers of Aviation.

The truth is that the French Ministers of Aviation could not construct more with the credits they were given. Bossoutrot was right: if France did not have the Air Force she needed, she had the one her credits had purchased.

Distribution of Credits and Resources

These credits corresponded to the programs of construction laid down by the Services of the Ministry of Aviation to carry out the "Air Force Plans" as formulated by the military authority. The financial control exercised by the Ministry of Finance made it impossible to allot to the Ministry of Aviation larger credits than the execution of these plans required. The programs of construction were prepared by the Technical Services, but approved by the General Staff of the Air Force—in other words, the men who fixed credits by determining the programs were the military authorities themselves. They refused to favor aeronautic production although they had complete knowledge of the situation. Aeronautic production could be favored only by diverting to the credit of the Air Force part of the men (soldiers, technicians, and workers) and means of production already allotted to other industries. Given the general resources of French industry, it would have been easy to increase the productive capacity of aircraft factories more than was done by beginning in 1937—for it takes time to build or change machinery—and by reducing the naval construction program, for example. Such a shift in credits and resources would have benefited French security. At the beginning of the war France was able to build 280 planes per month and Germany 1,400, a ratio of about 1 to 5; but France had under construction 171,000 tons of warships and Germany 276,000, a ratio of 1 to 1.6. The ratio of naval construction was much more favorable to France than the general ratio of industrial production, which was about 1 to 3.5. This was compensated by the less favorable ratio of aeronautic construction: 1 to 5, instead of 1 to 3.5.

It would have been better to begin the war with an additional 1,000 planes and a greater capacity for aeronautic production than with such a big naval program, since England, too, was building more ships than planes. In September, 1939, England had 675,000 tons of warships in her shipyards, more than Germany (276,000 tons) and Italy (242,000 tons) together, while her aero- nautic production was weaker than Germany's by about 33 per cent. Not only did the Allies have more naval tonnage under construction, but the French and British Navies already were considerably stronger (1,350,000 plus 583,000 tons) than those of Germany and Italy (243,000 plus 458,000). But the combined French and British air fleets were much weaker than the German. The distribution of resources and credits among the different divisions of French national defense was therefore most unwise.

The distribution of credits and resources was a problem of general military policy, which could be decided only by the military organs of national defense, and the military authority had rejected on several occasions in 1936-1937 the Ministry of Aviation's request for a redistribution in favor of aviation.

Similarly, after the Munich Pact, which had further shifted the balance of aerial forces in favor of the Fascists by giving them the Czech planes, factories, and bases, Léon Blum demanded in a series of articles in *le Populaire* that naval construction be slowed down in order to accelerate aeronautic construction. Again, the military authorities refused to open their eyes to the aerial peril and to understand that French national defense, by making itself uselessly strong on the sea, was condemning itself to a dangerous weakness in the air.

In 1940 the High Command had at its disposal only the modest Air Force it had asked for—the Air Force of its plans and programs. It was just what had been envisaged by the decisions of the War Council and Air Council—the technical organs of national defense. Neither General Gamelin, Chief of Staff for the Army, General Vuillemin, Chief of Staff for the Air Force, nor Marshal Pétain, high military adviser of the government, had ever asked for an additional plane or escadrille.

The Riom hearings conclusively established this point. Generals Besson and Lenclud* complained of the inadequacy of the aerial forces put at the disposal of their armies, but admitted that these forces were precisely the ones for which the High Command had asked. It seemed as though La Chambre was being reproached for not having been more royalist than the king, for having failed to furnish planes that the military authorities had not requested and for which no funds had been allocated.

During his examination La Chambre stated that, although in September, 1939, a small number of observation squadrons had not yet received the matériel intended for them by the plans of the General Staff, they had received it in May, 1940. At the hearing of March 5, 1942, La Chambre read aloud two letters from General Vuillemin. In one, dated February 7, 1940, the Air Force Chief of Staff declared that "the shipments [of aeronautic matériel] had corresponded to the plans"; in the other, written at the same time, he added that "by the spring of 1940 the Anglo-French aerial forces will match the German forces." Vuillemin had made the same statement at a meeting on August 23, 1939, called to discuss whether the French armies were able to wage war. Colonel Chatelain, who was in charge during the war of French military planes as head of the *Entrepôt Spécial* of the Air Force, testified before the Riom Court that he had delivered all the planes which the High Command had demanded from September, 1939, to June, 1940. Thus the hearings set forth that (1) the High Command of the armies engaged against Germany had received from La Chambre the planes it had asked for; (2) the armament programs had been carried out according to the plans of the General Staff; and (3) the Chief of Staff for the Air Force had reassured the government that he had forces strong enough to assure the aerial security of the country.

* See Chapter 6.

These forces were the ones that figured in the "Air Force Plan" set up by the military authorities and known as "Plan V." This plan had been proposed by General Vuillemin himself in February and March, 1938, and had been approved by the Air Council and the Permanent Committee of National Defense. Plan V involved the organization of an air force with 2,400 first-line planes and 1,600 first reserves. The first-line planes consisted of 600 light defense and pursuit planes; 600 heavy defense planes (bombers, scouting planes, etc.); 600 observation planes to co-operate with the Army; and 600 planes intended for North Africa and the Navy. Plan V, however, had two weak points. It failed to include an attacking air force capable of taking part in land warfare, and it emphasized the permanent disposition of planes to infantry divisions. In the course of the Riom hearings Daladier and La Chambre stated that an attacking air force had figured in the plan originally submitted to the military authorities but had been dropped. The High Command had considered an attacking air force useless, and thought the credits and industrial resources necessary for such a force might better be used, for example, in naval construction.

I must add my own evidence to the declarations of Daladier and La Chambre. Plan V was a new version of proposals made in 1936 and 1937 by the Ministry of Aviation to increase the part of aviation in national defense. These proposals included the formation of an attacking air force. The prototypes of these attacking planes had been studied by the Technical Services of the Ministry of Aviation and by the research bureaus of the National Construction Societies. After the Munich Pact I again demanded, in my book, *l'Armée de l'Air,*[*] the creation of such a force. That it was not created in time was not because of forgetfulness or negligence on the part of the Ministers of Aviation, but because of the refusal of the military authority to understand modern warfare. The dispersal of planes to infantry divisions accounted for a third of the aerial forces stationed on the European continent—600 first-line planes—and a still larger proportion of the planes allotted to North Africa; the German equivalent, on the contrary, included exactly one-sixth of the first-line aerial forces. This excessive emphasis was the logical consequence of the French conception of warfare. To be able to throw in a large number of infantry divisions, the High Command wanted a large "observation" air force. The doctrine of the continuous front thus weakened the bombing forces and prevented the creation of an attacking air power. Thus the authors of Plan V, and not the organizers of the aeronautic industry, are to be blamed.

Diplomatic Factors

In its foreign policy as well as in its domestic policy the military authority was again guilty of shortsightedness. It followed policies which proved to be least beneficial to France.

[*] Pierre Cot, *L'Armée de l'Air* (Paris: Grasset, 1939).

France was not solely dependent on the planes that she could produce herself. There were two channels through which to procure whatever additional forces were needed: military agreements and commercial negotiations.

International Air Agreements

A General Staff aware of its responsibilities would have urged the government to support collective security, and would have seized every opportunity to adapt its plans to those of the friends of France. The preparation for a defensive war of coalition was particularly important to aviation. The strength which France could not draw from her factories had to be sought from the Soviet Union and from England.

From the standpoint of aerial warfare an agreement with the Soviet Union was most desirable. Until 1938 Soviet aviation was equal or superior to German aviation, and until the war it was stronger than the British. In 1936 and 1937 efforts were made to establish a link between the French and the Soviet Air Forces. For political rather than military reasons this link was forged primarily by way of Czechoslovakia, the natural bridge between the French and Russian forces. Czechoslovakia was the keystone of the Franco-Soviet alliance, and this keystone was destroyed by the disastrous Munich Pact. Until then the combined strength of the French, Czechoslovakian, and Russian Air Forces was greater than the combined strength of the German and the Italian Air Forces. If France had succeeded in drawing England into this bloc, Hitler and Goering could never have disturbed the peace of the world. Taking off from Czech bases to land in France, and vice versa, French, British, and Soviet bombers would have been in a position to strike at all German military and industrial centers under constant cover of their fighting squadrons, that is to say, under the most favorable conditions. Berlin, Munich, Dresden, Vienna, Chemnitz (the seat of the chemical industries), and the industrial and mining regions of Silesia and the Ruhr could have been reached within two flying hours, which would have made possible the concentration of aerial forces and large-scale maneuvers. Germany would have been obliged to scatter her anti-aircraft defenses over her entire territory. The Munich agreements permitted her to concentrate these defenses in the west.

The duty of the Chief of Staff of the Air Force was to draw the attention of the French government to these elementary facts. General Féquant, Chief of Staff in 1936 and 1937, fulfilled that duty. General Vuillemin, who succeeded him, had a completely different conception of aerial security. In September, 1938, greatly impressed by the German air power—for he had been the official guest of General Milch only a few months earlier—and incapable of any wider international vision, he counseled appeasement. This appeasement policy crushed Czechoslovakia and permitted Germany to increase her Air Force 80 per cent within a single year, while Franco-British air power increased only 50 per cent. La Chambre might have mended this grave error by demanding a policy of close military co-operation with the Soviet Union in 1938-1939; no documents indicate that he did. On the contrary, in reviewing the book in which I recommended that preparations be made for a war of coalition and for a Franco-Soviet alliance, the *Revue de l'Armée de l'Air,* published under the control of the General Staff, declared that there were grave reasons for doubting the aerial strength of the Soviet Union.

With respect to Czechoslovakia and Russia the General Staff did nothing after 1938 to prepare for an aerial war of coalition. La Chambre unfortunately adopted an even more rigid attitude than did his Chief of Staff.

With regard to England the situation was somewhat better; here, at least, the responsibility was evenly divided between the French and the British authorities. Negotiations were first begun in 1937 by General Féquant, who found the British little inclined to enter into a policy of actual military collaboration. Féquant was persistent in his attempts, and we both went to London in June, 1937, he to see the Chief of Staff of the Royal Air Force, and I to meet the Minister of Aviation. The Englishmen were cordial but reserved. We came up against the wall of their polished manners each time we broached the subject that was our chief concern—the organization of a defensive coalition against the aggressor nations. A few months later the Chief of Staff of the Royal Air Force returned Féquant's visit, but it was again impossible to move beyond the sphere of courtesy, in other words, of triviality. Such visits, to be sure, were not useless, but at that time conservative England did not clearly realize the danger of Hitlerism. Franco-British relations improved only after Munich; they finally led to the agreements which in 1940 assured France the support of the Royal Air Force. But they did not achieve the organization of a joint Franco-British air force under a unified command, which would have been the only means of resisting the forces of General Milch.

The French General Staff did not fulfill its duty in the east. It acted somewhat better in connection with the British problem, but still accomplished nothing substantial for lack of precise plans and proposals.

French Purchases Abroad

It was evident that in the event of war France would have to obtain supplies from abroad. This aspect of the war had to be prepared in peacetime. French crews had to be given an opportunity to grow accustomed to foreign materials, and technicians' squads had to be trained in the conservation and repair of these machines. This process could not be improvised, if only because the units of measurement in Anglo-Saxon countries were different from those used by French manufacturers. New blueprints had to be drawn, the lettering changed, and certain new implements provided. Moreover, only a purchasing plan spread out over a number of years could enable foreign producers to provide the specific equipment required by the Allies. It was essential not to restrict our industrial mobilization to the capacity of French industry, but to organize it within a far larger framework.

This policy was worked out under the Popular Front government. In 1936 and 1937 missions of technicians and manufacturers were sent to Russia and the United States to explore the possibilities of obtaining supplies from the only industrial powers capable of opposing Germany. As the Franco-Soviet Pact was then the cornerstone of collective security, the French Air Force had to be familiarized with Russian matériel, for any inter-Allied air maneuver was bound to bring Soviet planes into France, just as French planes would be landing in Czechoslovakia. In addition, the only war that France could envisage presupposed the aid of Great Britain and the freedom of the seas. Hence the utilization of American productive resources had to be carefully organized. After a minute study of the entire problem, the conclusion reached was that the commercial policy of French aviation would have to consist of (1) a technical exchange program with the Soviet Union; (2) an arrangement with the United States whereby matériel would be purchased over a period of several years; and (3) a program for the construction of airplane factories in Canada financed and controlled by French capital.

Blum approved this general project. But intrigues forced the Popular Front government to cut down on the technical exchange with Russia. As early as 1937 a French group was organized under Henry Potez to acquire shares in certain Canadian enterprises. At the same time the Ministry of Aviation was buying licenses for American motors, and its technical missions reported that American industry would be able to supply about two hundred fighter planes, some training planes, and five hundred motors during 1938. Georges Bonnet, then Minister of Finance, refused to endorse the necessary credits for the purchase of these materials. The question was submitted to Premier Chautemps in a report dated December 6, 1937. In principle, Chautemps received the plan favorably, but he, too, had to reckon with Bonnet's objections. The result was that no decision was reached before the collapse of the Popular Front (January, 1938). In 1938 La Chambre abandoned the exchange program with Russia and showed no interest in Franco-Canadian collaboration, but he succeeded in obtaining from the new Minister of Finance, Paul Reynaud, the credits for purchases in America. La Chambre ordered not only motors and planes that American industry could deliver in 1938, but also 315 bomber planes for delivery in 1939 plus a sizable number of training planes, spare parts, motors, etc. According to his statement at Riom, La Chambre placed approximately 1,605 orders for American planes before and during the war. "I sincerely feel," he said, "that I utilized to its maximum the productive capacity of the United States during that period." This result was due largely to the support of William C. Bullitt, then the United States Ambassador to France. The policy, incidentally, benefited the United States as much as it did France, for the orders placed by La Chambre helped the development of American factories.

One might assume that the High Command would have favored a policy that presented the twofold advantage of increasing supply possibilities for the Air Force and of freeing forces at home. Yet, as La Chambre revealed at the Riom hearing of March 4, the General Staff constantly opposed any projects for the purchase of foreign planes. The power of red tape was stronger than the exigencies of modern warfare.

Fortunately, La Chambre overrode the General Staff's objections. Thanks to his policy of buying abroad, the French Air Force was in a position to mobilize successfully several hundred American planes in May, 1940. There were some American planes in North Africa, and some had remained at Martinique. La Chambre increased by about 25 per cent the possibilities of supplies to the French Air Force, a percentage which continued to grow.

The conditions under which the French Air Force had to obtain its supplies clearly shows the injustice of the accusations brought against La Chambre.

La Chambre—with industrial resources that were about one-fourth those of Germany and half those of England, and with credit appropriations one-fifth the amount that General Milch enjoyed and less than half the amount at the disposal of the British Minister—succeeded in creating (1) an air fleet of 2,100 first-line planes (1,800 in France, 300 in North Africa), about one-third of what Germany had and two-thirds of what the British had; (2) 6,000 military aircraft, more than a third of the German force; (3) an industrial capacity that guaranteed the delivery of 500-600 airplanes per month and this compared favorably with the 1,700 planes produced by German industry during the same period, or even with the 1,350-1,400 planes which were turned out by the combined British production and American supplies.

All this was accomplished by factories that had been equipped or created by the Popular Front. La Chambre did not mention this at Riom; he even intimated that the development of the French aeronautic industry had been subsequent to the Popular Front. But the experience of England and the United States has proved that more than two and a half years is necessary for the realization of an industrial program that includes everything from the construction of factories to the building of airplanes. Under the best of circumstances, the French planes used during the war had been constructed in factories set up in 1938, that is to say, on the basis of production and equipment plans dating from 1937. As a matter of fact, all the factories which built La Chambre's planes had figured in the Popular Front's program of June, 1937, for the expansion of the aeronautic industry. This program (except for several delays caused by the General Staff) remained in force without modification until June, 1940, when the new production chief, M. Meny, evolved a new plan.

Both La Chambre and I made many mistakes. But who, in our place, could have constructed more planes with the same limited financial and industrial means? If one compares the curves of credit and production of France with those of the great industrial nations—Germany, the United States, Great Britain—for the years 1936 to 1940, it is evident that we did as well as the Air Ministers of those countries.

Military Factors

The most serious obstacle to the development of the French Air Force was raised by the General Staff. As the testimony of the witnesses proved, in 1940

France had roughly all the planes provided for under Plan V and requested by the military authority. In the field of aviation the General Staff carried a heavy burden of responsibility. It set up inadequate plans. It willfully refused to construct an attacking air force. And it permitted without protest the shattering of the very bases of French security in the Munich Pact.

The Doctrine of Air Warfare

The doctrine of aerial warfare merely applied Pétain's general conception to the field of aviation. He had been Inspector-General of Aerial Defense from 1931 until 1934, and had developed an entirely false notion of the possibilities, the dangers, and, consequently, the function of modern aviation. He believed that aviation ought to play a triple role: (1) at the outbreak of hostilities to stage large-scale raids on the interior of enemy countries to paralyze their mobilization and break civilian morale; (2) during the war to serve primarily in small units as auxiliary arms to infantry units; and (3) to participate indirectly in land warfare by bombardments outside and behind the battlefields, to extend, but not replace, artillery action.

These ideas were not original. They had been given to Marshal Pétain by his usual advisers on aviation matters—Colonel Vauthier, General Dusseigneur (a Cagoulard leader), General Watteau (later a judge at the Court of Riom), and General Pujo (Minister of Aviation in the Pétain cabinet after the armistice). Of these men, Pujo was the most intelligent. Profoundly reactionary by education and temperament, he was quite timorous but had a refined and honest mind; unfortunately, his entire career had centered on aviation as a supporting arm for the other forces, a prejudice strengthened by his friendship for Pétain. The Pujo-Pétain doctrine was opposed to the exaggerated concepts of Italy's General Douhet—defensive land war, total aerial offensive war—which had had its partisans in the Air Force, especially after General Tulasne's translation of Douhet's book. The Pujo-Pétain doctrine was also opposed to modern conceptions of organization and use of forces—sometimes called Russian conceptions because the Russians had shown them to French aviators when the first air mission had gone to Russia in September, 1933. The Russians had studied the double maneuver of using parachute troops and fighter planes for dive-bombing airplane formations and for attack at low levels; they had developed their ideas at several conferences held at the Military Academy in Moscow. The contact with Russia had aroused the curiosity of French military thinkers. In spite of this spur, in the years 1934-1936 when nothing counterbalanced the influence of Marshal Pétain at the head of the French Army, the General Staff of the Air Force refused to change its doctrine and organization. In 1935 General Pujo had been appointed Chief of Staff for the Air Force; and in February, 1936, Captain P. Étienne expressed a widely-held view when he wrote an article on "The Official Doctrine of the Air Force" for the Revue de l'Armée de l'Air: "In spite of the replacement of materials and the improvement in quality, the same doctrines relating to their use that were in force twenty years ago have been *strictly* [italics his] adhered to."

The Popular Front attempted to get out of the rut. Under General Féquant, Chief of Staff of the Air Force, a new organization of the Air Force was created, experiments in dive bombing and with attacking air forces were made, new ideas were put into circulation, and the Pujo-Pétain doctrine was abandoned. Modern and progressive in his thinking, Féquant surrounded himself with a group of enthusiastic young officers determined to create a modern air force. On the intellectual plane the reorganization began in September, 1936, with an article in the *Revue de l'Armée de l'Air* by Engineer-in-Chief C. Rougeron, entitled "Low-Altitude Bombing." This article discussed the intervention of the airplane in land warfare and opposed the classic doctrine. Shortly afterwards came the creation of the School of Aerial Warfare and the Center of Advanced Aerial Studies for the study of tactical problems introduced by the use of aviation. In March, 1937, Rougeron published a second article, "L'Aviation et les Chars de Combat," again in the *Revue,* in which he explained the *direct* use of the airplane in land warfare; he recalled the theories developed abroad, chiefly by the Italians, as well as the experiments of the Russians, and developed the ideas which inspired the new General Staff group, ironically called "the brain trust" of the Aviation Ministry. "The intervention of the airplane in mechanized war," wrote Rougeron, "will completely change the conception which we have of it today. . . . The airplane is the best anti-tank weapon."

In February, 1937, while explaining my views on the use of aviation to the Chamber of Deputies, I had declared myself in favor of the concentration of aerial forces as opposed to the dispersal and assignment of aerial units to army units. "We want to be ready," I said, "either to throw ourselves into land fighting with all our forces or to co-operate with the Navy with all our forces or, if necessary, to fight the air war with all our forces. . . . We are concentrating on the use of parachutists, dive-bombing, and low-altitude bombing, which permit us to attack enemy columns with lightly-armored aircraft, in the expectation of paralyzing the advance of motorized units."

On December 11, 1937, I again explained the general broad rules—the need to increase the importance of aviation in national defense, particularly the development of heavy bombers; and the need to create an offensive air force capable of attacking armored units. This doctrine was approved by a large majority. Only the most reactionary elements of Parliament did not concur. The leaders of national defense, however, preferred to follow Marshal Pétain's theories, and the new doctrine was abandoned when I left the Air Ministry in January, 1938.

With the dissolution of the Popular Front, General Féquant and his principal collaborators were removed in disgrace; their error had been to believe, with Napoleon, that "one must know how to change tactics every ten years." A more conformist Chief of Staff, General Vuillemin, was appointed, and in spite of the resistance of the Aeronautic Commission of the Chamber of Deputies, the Air Force returned to its old ideas. The classic doctrine of

Pujo and Pétain triumphed again. La Chambre accepted this change of orientation without realizing its consequence, for he had never dealt with the problem of aviation; he had been President of the *Army* Commission of the Chamber of Deputies, and he brought to his new duties the spirit of the Army, a spirit favorable to the use of aviation as an auxiliary arm of the infantry, and unfavorable to the concentration of aerial forces. Moreover, La Chambre was the political enemy of the Popular Front, which had tried to build a modern air force. A return to the classic doctrine was marked in the directives published in the *Revue de l'Armée de l'Air*.

The official doctrine was expounded in 1938 in two articles by General Maginel, the new Director of the Center of Advanced Aerial Studies, that appeared in the *Revue Militaire Générale* (an official publication of the Ministry of National Defense) and were the last doctrinal statements on the use of aerial forces published before the war. These articles attacked Rouger-on's thesis on the use of air power against the tank and in land warfare. According to General Maginel's conception, "aviation should be used pref-erably in the rear. . . . Aviation should extend artillery fire and not replace it, except in special circumstances. . . . The enemy's rear constitutes the Air Force's normal field of intervention, because it allows it to use its essential qualities to the utmost, and assures it a maximum effort with minimum losses. Why wait to attack until the enemy forces have deployed and protected themselves with firing bases, when by crossing an insignificant distance one can surprise them in columns on the roads?" It was the very doctrine of Marshal Pétain: no direct intervention in the battle, no attack of armored or other formations engaged in battle, no substitution of aircraft fire for artillery fire; aviation must be used on the rear columns and not on the vanguard. With such a doctrine, the way for the German armored divisions was easy; they ran no danger from a concentrated air attack.

Those Responsible for the Misuse of the Air Force

General Maginel cannot be held responsible for the misuse of French air power; he had the right to be mistaken, and he was mistaken in good faith. Those really responsible for the misuse of the French Air Force were the men at its head, following the dismissal of General Féquant and his group. Three names must be mentioned: Vuillemin, Tétu, and Bergeret.

Of these the least guilty was General Vuillemin. He had all the gifts a leader of men needed, but none of the qualities required in a Chief of Staff. One can say of him what Stendhal said of Napoleon's generals: "It is a mis-fortune that generals of divisions are recruited from generals of brigades." It is one thing to lead troops in combat and another to plan maneuvers. An excellent soldier and a magnificent pilot, General Vuillemin had won most of his honors during the first World War by his astonishing courage, and after the war, by his work and the seriousness of his character. His mis-fortune was that before his appointment as head of the Air Force, he had always served with the soldiers, and, never having attended any large military school, he did not even know routine General Staff work. He had spent a large part of his military life in the African bush, which he knew to the smallest details, and it was a great mistake to take this incomparable leader from the men who adored him and shut him up in an office to do work foreign to his temperament. He was the banner of the Air Force; an attempt was made to make him its brain.

Vuillemin had no idea of modern aerial warfare and was content to "let things go and let people talk." During the war he showed neither initiative nor imagination, and was merely a tool in the hands of Generals Gamelin and Weygand.

General Tétu cannot claim the same indulgence. He was intelligent and energetic, but he hated new ideas. Although he cannot be considered a criminal in the legal sense of the word, he was an incompetent general attached to outdated conceptions. As chief of the aerial forces he was charged with organizing and preparing the Air Force during the eighteen months preceding the war. By September, 1939, he had destroyed the organization created by General Féquant under the Popular Front.

It was evident from Tétu's background that he would not accept any Popular Front theory. He was more than a reactionary. In 1936, some months before the discovery of the Cagoulard plot, he was in charge of the air base at Chartres. He organized a large reception for General Dusseigneur, one of the Cagoulard leaders, and declared before all his officers: "We know what is being prepared, General, and you can count on us; command, and we shall obey." I summoned Tétu at once and asked him what he had meant; he gave me a vague explanation. The Cagoulard affair was as yet unknown and General Féquant could only shift Tétu to another post. When La Chambre succeeded me, I told him about the Chartres affair, adding: "Beware of Tétu. He is a Fascist and a plotter; give him no position in which he will have any control over the Air Force." I was stupefied to learn, some weeks after this warning, that General Tétu had been given the second highest position in the hierarchy and had become the real head of the Air Force under General Vuillemin.

General Tétu had the end he deserved. Entrusted by the Vichy government with the defense of French Equatorial Africa, he fell prisoner to the Fighting French Forces of General de Gaulle; he did not find the opportunity to fight the Nazis in 1940, but he did fight against the French soldiers of liberty.

General Bergeret was the man actually responsible for the misuse of the Air Force during the war. As head of the Bureau des Opérations, he was in charge of planning aerial strategy and tactics; both his strategy and tactics were poor. The Bureau of the Air Force was even worse than that of the Army (which opposed the creation of armored divisions in December, 1939). Bergeret did not learn anything from the Polish campaign, he did not even suggest the organization of an Anglo-French Air Force, and he refused to re-establish the aerial divisions and the units of parachutists which General

Tétu had broken up. He made no effort to improvise an attacking air force during the battle; he understood nothing—and he accepted the Air Force's defeat without fighting. Coming from the man who agreed to become Marshal Pétain's Air Minister and who delivered the French air bases in Syria to the Germans in 1941, such an attitude was suspicious—although it may be explained by the arrogance and lack of imagination which characterized him.

General Bergeret has always been an adversary of democracy. In 1940-1942 he was a fervent advocate of Franco-German collaboration. When Germany started to stagger from the blows inflicted by the Anglo-Russo-American coalition, he suddenly became anti-German, but remained Fascist. He joined General Giraud in North Africa and became his main collaborator. His appointment was so scandalous that General Giraud was obliged to dismiss him under the twofold pressure of the Americans and of French popular feeling.

The Fascist and reactionary generals who formulated the policy of the High Command will find it most difficult to justify their actions as "patriotism" in face of the evidence accumulated against them.

Aviation Policy of the Popular Front

9

Examination of the Popular Front's aviation policy and its moral responsibilities for France's defeat in the air continues the study begun in the preceding chapter.

When I cleared Guy la Chambre by showing that the men of the High Command were to blame for the defeat in the air, I justified the Popular Front as well, proving unquestionably that it could not be held legally responsible. If the Air Force had the types and quantities of aircraft in May and June, 1940, that the High Command had ordered, how could the Popular Front, which had had nothing to do with French aviation for two and a half years, have been responsible for the defeat? Plan V, the air policy followed during the war, was conceived by the Air Force Chiefs, approved by the General Staff, and implemented by the Director of Technical Services and Production in the Ministry of Aviation, all of whom came to power after the Popular Front. Even if the Popular Front aviation policy had been deplorable, it could have had no direct influence on the defeat.

All the factors so far discussed—volume of credits, industrial capacity, the need for international agreements, the antagonism of the military responsible for defense, and comparison with similar problems in other countries—have shown that the Popular Front, however limited and in face of constant opposition from a bourgeois minority, did a far better job of protecting France than did either its predecessor or successor.

In fact, development of the Air Force from January, 1938, to May, 1940, was retarded rather than accelerated by measures requested by the General Staff, which opposed all reforms instituted by the Popular Front. Thus, the aircraft industry, which did not have a single strike from the time of the Matignon Agreements until I left the Ministry of Aviation, became troubled repeatedly by social unrest provoked among the workers by the recrudescence of Fascist agitation.

A favorite contention of Fascist propaganda has been that the Popular Front weakened French aviation. With all its contempt for truth, the Council of Political Justice could not parrot this statement; it merely declared that the Popular Front, "in spite of repeated warnings [we are not told from whom] had failed to give France the Air Force she needed."

We already have answered both contentions with facts and figures, but a broader outline of the Popular Front's aviation policy is essential for a true picture of its efforts to revitalize the Air Force.

It is best to let figures determine the validity of this statement. The following table shows that from June, 1936, to January, 1938, the strength of the Air Force increased by about 200 per cent, and the productive capacity of the aircraft factories by about 115 per cent. In January, 1938, the French Air Force had not only more machines, manned by a better-trained personnel, but the planes were much faster, better-armed, and more powerful than those of June, 1936; the increase in power resulting from the combination of speed and firing-power was more than 200 per cent.

GROWTH OF THE AIR FORCE UNDER THE POPULAR FRONT

	June 1, 1936	January 1, 1938	Percentage Difference
Squadrons in line	134	175	+ 30
Airplanes in line	607	1,350	+122
Total, "armed and equipped" military aircraft, including all reserves	1,500	3,157	+110
Weight of bombs carried (in tons)	296	852	+187
Motor power in service (in h.p.)	850,000	2,150,000	+153
Automatic arms (cannon and machine guns)	2,197	7,581	+145
Officers in service	2,051	3,163	+ 54
Capacity of airplane production (in tons)	3,200	6,900	+115

One would, of course, have wished for even better results; but to do more would have required more credits, and to obtain more credits from the Minister of Finance would have presupposed the military authorities' approval of an increase in the size of the Air Force and an extension of its function in national defense, as well as the establishment of more far-reaching programs.

POLITICAL ASPECT: THE FUNCTIONS OF THE AIR MINISTRY

It must be remembered that the French Minister of Aviation, as in most other countries, had no absolute powers; he was not an air dictator, but merely a member of a cabinet that functioned according to constitutional rules and custom. His action was confined to a framework whose limits he could not alter; within it, he had to solve problems conditioned not only by international policies which determined France's place on the world chessboard, but by the amount of credits allotted to aviation and by the military policy fixed by the Supreme Council of National Defense. International agreements, credits, and a general military policy did not depend on the Minister of Aviation, or at least not on him alone. His role was double; like his colleagues in the cabinet, he took part in the orientation of the general governmental policy, that is, in determining the framework within which he was to exercise his particular authority. In that respect, he had a collective responsibility with all members of the cabinet; aside from that, as head of the Ministry of Aviation, he was confined to this framework and here alone could his personal responsibility be involved. These rules were fixed not only by the Constitution but by equity; they are expressed in a short sentence of the Constitutional law of February 25, 1875: "The ministers are collectively responsible before the Chambers for the general policy of the government, and individually for their personal acts." Moreover, there could not be the slightest doubt concerning the legality of acts performed by a French minister and their attendant responsibilities, personal or collective. Acts of general policy were discussed either in the Council of Ministers or by several ministers acting as delegates of the Council; in practice, these acts took the form of decrees countersigned by the President of the Council and all the ministers in charge of their execution. The personal acts of a minister, on the contrary, bore only the signature of that minister, or, in the case of decrees, only his own "countersignature." Thus the formal criterion of signature or countersignature was added to the real criterion, which shows the essential nature of the act.

My Work as Minister of Aviation

The aerial policy which I favored was founded on the following ideas: (1) Preparation for a war of coalition, chiefly by the development of agreements between France and the Soviet Union. The war of coalition envisaged was obviously a defensive war against aggressor nations. The co-operation of the Soviet Union, which then (1936-1937) possessed the most powerful military Air Force in the world, was indispensable to the security of a country like France, whose general capacity of industrial production was one-third that of her principal potential enemy, Germany. (2) Increase of the role of aviation in French national defense, through modification of the basic distribution of credits and resources for national defense among the Army, Navy, and Air Force; in 1936 the Air Force received the inadequate proportion of about 22 per cent of the credits and 5 per cent of the men. (3) Reorganization of the Air Force along modern lines, including, particularly, large aerial units (aerial divisions and corps) and parachute units. (4) Reorganization and extension of the aeronautic industry, in which the power given the state by the law nationalizing war industry would be used to break private resistance, modernize machinery, and give the Air Force the necessary industrial foundation.

Even a reader unfamiliar with questions of governmental policy will understand that the execution of such a program did not depend exclusively on the Ministry of Aviation. For the realization of points (3) and (4), I had a certain degree of autonomy. Points (1) and (2), however, were almost entirely out of my hands: in this field, I could propose but not act. I could propose the strengthening of bonds between France and Russia—but the direction of foreign policy belonged to the Ministry of Foreign Affairs. I could propose an increased share for aviation in national defense—but the determination of general military policy was a matter for the Ministry of National Defense, which had to consult the technical organs of National Defense in order to change plans. The cabinets in which I held the Aviation portfolio—the Blum cabinet of June, 1936, to July, 1937, and the Chautemps cabinet of July, 1937, to January, 1938—had a Minister of National Defense whose task it was to co-ordinate the action of the Ministries of War, Navy, and Aviation. These departments were charged with carrying out a general policy conceived in the Ministry of National Defense by the Minister of National Defense and by two technical organs, the Permanent Committee of National Defense and the Supreme Council of National Defense. The Minister of National Defense in the Blum and Chautemps cabinets was Daladier, who was also Minister of War. I have often thought, and have said as much in my book, *l'Armée de l'Air,* that it was an error to give the same man two such important functions. Not that Daladier was incapable of rising above the rivalries and jealousies of the different Chiefs of Staff, but he was too much absorbed by the direction of the Ministry of War, one of the most difficult of administrative tasks, to be able to concentrate on the larger problems of modern warfare; he could not take a broad perspective and think of national defense as an entity whose constituent parts were subject to adjustment and change.

The functions of the Minister of National Defense and of the Minister of War were not only distinct, but could at times become contradictory. Their union under one head had the effect of making Daladier both a judge and an interested party when it was a question of fixing the relative importance of the Army and the other services or of establishing the order of the respective needs of the various arms in the division of resources, credits, and men. We need not dwell on the character of Daladier—his difficult and occasionally irritable side—but it must be said that he, like everyone else, had a kind of functional deformation as a result of his long service as Minister of War under various administrations; he was inclined to consider the needs of the Army—his Army—over those of the Air Force. He would have been an excellent Minister of National Defense, had he been only that. One cannot reproach him for his inability to fulfill two contradictory tasks or for having preferred in 1937 the suggestion of his military advisers to the proposals of General Féquant, who, like myself, asked for an extension of the allotments to the Air Force.

A single man in the French military organization was placed above the Army, Navy, and Air Force, independent of all three: Marshal Pétain. His role as an official of the Republic was to take part in the work of the Permanent Committee of National Defense and the Supreme Council of National Defense. By his rank and functions, he was to play the role of an arbitrator for the various tendencies and disputes of the Army, Navy, and Air Force and their Chiefs of Staff. A high military adviser of the government, with greater leisure than Daladier and with the full confidence of military leaders, it was his duty to think of war as a vast entity, to keep himself informed, to make a synthesis of needs and doctrines, and to propose solutions. Unfortunately, Pétain proved inferior to his task. In the first World War he had been what Clemenceau called him, "a man of execution and not of action." On the eve of the second World War he revealed himself a man of political ambition, without ideas or imagination. During all the time I was a member of the cabinet and of the Permanent Committee of National Defense, no general report prepared or signed by Marshal Pétain was ever addressed to the French government—and I am in a position to say that the same was true after 1938. The only reforms undertaken, the only progress achieved in the general organization of national defense, were the work of Daladier. The principal obstacle to these reforms, the greatest check on progress, was Pétain—not by any direct action, for he lacked even the courage for open opposition, but indirectly, by continual criticism and generalized ill-humor, because this narrow-minded military man remained obstinately attached to the conceptions of 1918. He represented conservatism in its heaviest and most obtuse form—the immobility of the mind.

As head of the Ministry of Aviation, I attempted with the inadequate credits allotted me to ensure French air security. The results obtained during the Popular Front period were, if not miraculous, certainly significant.

To begin, I must point out my share of collective responsibility in the establishment of the framework that was imposed on the Ministry of Aviation in 1936 and 1937. In order to obtain larger appropriations for aviation, it was my duty to warn the military authorities (the Permanent Committee of National Defense and the Supreme Council of National Defense) and the political authorities (the Minister of National Defense and the Premier) that the country needed a revision of the bases of her national defense. I believe that I fulfilled this duty. If my efforts were often fruitless, it was because they clashed, especially after Chautemps had replaced Blum as Premier, with the holy alliance of military conservatism, of which Pétain was the symbol, and financial orthodoxy, whose guardian was Bonnet. The facts and documents offer sufficient proof.

At the beginning of September, 1936, Germany had established a two-year compulsory military service, which Daladier, Minister of National Defense, decided to answer by a general rearmament effort. As a substitute for Plan I (1,000 airplanes in line and 200 in reserve) which was then in operation, I suggested to the Council of Ministers the adoption of Plan II (1,500 airplanes in line and 900 in reserve). My proposal was accepted without opposition. There was no need to consult the technical authorities of national defense in taking this decision. Some months earlier General Denain, a conservative and patriotic Frenchman, had caused the military authorities to adopt the principle of Plan II, in preparation for the eventuality in which the international situation might oblige France to develop her aerial armament. The credits needed to replace Plan I by Plan II were at once granted by the Minister of Finance, Vincent Auriol, an intelligent and farsighted man, who anticipated the action of Germany and Italy in the Spanish Civil War. The volume of credits requested by the Ministry of Aviation was not such as to necessitate a general revision of the bases of our national defense.

In the fall of 1936 I asked General Féquant, new Chief of Staff of the Air Force, to make a study of the international aviation situation. On December 20 of the same year I addressed to the Permanent Committee of National Defense a report based on the conclusions of General Féquant, in which I proposed new plans for the Air Force. These were Plans III (reorganization and increase of anti-aircraft defense) and Plan IV (extension of the Air Force). Unlike Plan II, these plans could not have been addressed directly to the cabinet because their adoption required a change in the entire conception and organization of national defense. The Ministry of Aviation, in addition to its usual resources (calculated in terms of Plan II), would have been allotted 3,000 officers, 30,000 men, and the equivalent of 870 million dollars to be spent in three years—which, in practice, amounted to doubling the manpower and the budget of the Air Force. Moreover, in wartime the Air Force was to receive a larger number of reservists (3,540 officers and 154,000 men for Plan III alone), and a larger number of French factories was to take part in supplying this force. Such a development could not come without a complete revision of the French military system, for it was impossible to allot the men, credits, and industrial resources necessary for the execution of these programs without withdrawing them from the allotments to the Army or Navy; and these allotments were limited by the demographic and economic situation of France. The proposal to create more aerial divisions and more regiments of anti-aircraft artillery indirectly involved the mobilization, in case of war, of fewer infantry divisions and the construction of fewer warships—a change in the very structure of national defense. The proposals of the Ministry of Aviation were studied by the Secretariat of the Permanent Committee of National Defense, by the General Staffs of the Army and Navy, and by Marshal Pétain, and were rejected by all of them. The question was discussed by the Permanent Committee of National Defense on February 15, 1937: the Committee decided unanimously that "*there was no need to modify or extend the plan for increasing the Air Force.*"

Both Pétain and Darlan were important members of the Permanent Committee and participated in the decision—the most fatal decision ever made, in my opinion, by the military authority. In the light of the war and the defeat, I consider the rejection of Plans III and IV as fatal in the military sphere as the Munich Pact in the international sphere. Undoubtedly Plans III and IV were imperfect; they had been prepared by the General Staff of the Air Force only from the point of view of the Air Force's needs. They required further study by higher authorities before they could be adjusted to the needs of the other services. General Féquant and I considered them a design, an outline, on which the Permanent Committee could improve and even build new plans. The Committee, however, requested the Air Force to retain Plan II. Indifference and ignorance cannot explain this decision. It was a refusal to change the general conception of national defense. Pétain and Gamelin knew that, to comply with the new plans, they would have to reduce the number of their infantry divisions, thus eliminating the doctrine of the continuous front. Darlan realized that the execution of the plans would absorb credits and industrial resources, and would lead to the reduction of present or future programs for naval construction. The ancient hatred of the Army and the Navy for the Air Force triumphed over the interests of France. The proposals of the Minister of Aviation were progressive; their adoption would have given French national defense a new direction. The decision of the Permanent Committee saved the established order and the military status quo. The fate of Plans III and IV proved that nothing could pull French national defense out of the rut into which its leaders had steered it. The Popular Front Air Ministry and General Féquant were begged not to disturb the slumbers of their superiors. De Gaulle had received the same rebuff in 1935.

When we left the meeting of the Permanent Committee of National Defense, I said to General Féquant: "Well, we've been defeated." He answered: "France has lost today the first battle of the war." During 1937 General Féquant frequently attempted to sway the opposition we encountered, but was always silenced by the doctrine of the continuous front.

Having failed with the military authorities, I decided, together with General Féquant, to return to the Minister of Finance. Unable to achieve the modification of Plan II, we tried to obtain financial means which would permit a more rapid execution of this plan and, at the same time, the development of the aeronautic industry. In the spring of 1937 the bureau in charge of aerial construction in the Ministry of Aviation set up a complete program for the development of the aeronautic industry, from raw materials necessary for production to measures for an industrial mobilization that would correspond to this general development. Unfortunately, the Blum cabinet was overthrown in the meantime, and Bonnet succeeded Auriol as head of the Ministry of Finance. I was as much out of sympathy with the political ideas of Bonnet as I had been in sympathy with Auriol's. Bonnet believed that it was his duty as Minister of Finance to subordinate everything to the defense of the franc, whereas Auriol believed in the defense of the franc *after* the defense of France and the French people. During the period between June, 1936, and January, 1938, the "provisional credits" (permitting the placing of orders for the following year) requested by the Ministry of Aviation for the development of aeronautic production (prototypes, series, works and installations, industrial mobilization) were reduced by 1,300 million francs (76 million dollars) and the "definite credits" were reduced by 1,900 million francs (96 million dollars). The reader will have some idea of the importance of these figures if he considers that 1,900 million francs represented at that time the cost of two thousand warplanes; in other words, the credits requested would have permitted France to have 50 per cent more airplanes in her squadrons, and a productive capacity increased by 50 per cent at the outbreak of the war. The financial policy of Bonnet added another obstacle to those which military conservatism already had put in the way.

Having failed with the Minister of Finance and with the military authorities, I decided to take the first favorable opportunity to speak directly to the

Premier. On various occasions I had called the attention of the cabinet to the inadequate credits allotted to aviation; but with the decision of the military authorities and the policies of the Minister of Finance against me, I had been unable to do anything. My opportunity came when Chautemps returned from a trip to England, greatly impressed by the figures he had been given on the production of British aircraft factories. (The figures had been supplied not by British authorities but by Frenchmen living in England.) On December 6, 1937, I handed him a report summarizing the steps I had taken in the past year and a half for the adoption of a new military program and the obtaining of adequate credits; and, after comparing the situation of France and England, I demanded most urgently a "supplementary credit" of 11 billion francs (about 360 million dollars) to be spent in three years, to increase the productive capacity of French aircraft industry. The program submitted to Chautemps would have made it possible to realize the industrial plan set up during the summer and rejected by Bonnet. This program involved the construction of attacking airplanes and dive bombers—aircraft which France lacked in June, 1940. In a general way this plan corresponded to the needs of an air force of 2,500 first-line planes—or about half the air force which Germany then had under construction, an increase of 80 per cent over Plan II. The report to the Premier also asked that France immediately order planes from America to make up for the delay caused by the refusal of my previous requests. The Premier answered that it was impossible to plan for the execution of this program before the vote on the budget. He promised favorable action in the near future, but the Popular Front government was overthrown before the credits had been granted, and I left the Ministry of Aviation in January with nothing more than this oral promise.

At the same time (December, 1937) I addressed a report on the situation in the Mediterranean to the Permanent Committee of National Defense, asking for the creation of four aerial squadrons and four aerial groups (twenty-two escadrilles in all) in North Africa. I based my request on the presence of German and Italian aerial forces in Spain and on the collusion thus revealed between the Fascist dictators. I specified that this force should be stationed in North Africa as part of the general organization of the Air Force, so that it might be engaged, in case of need, in the theater of operations where it would be most useful. The military authorities did nothing; no decision was taken, no investigation was made while I was in the Ministry of Aviation.

The facts speak for themselves. I repeatedly requested the increase of our air strength and the development of our productive forces. If my proposals had been followed, France would have had 3,000, not 2,100, planes to send against the 6,850 of Germany in May and June, 1940; and what is still more important, France would have had 500 attacking planes and dive bombers with which to fight the armored divisions.

My proposals, requests, and demands are verified by the reports, plans, programs, and requests for credit addressed in 1936 and 1937 to the Permanent Committee of National Defense, to the Premier, and to the Minister

of Finance. In accordance with the rules and the accuracy of French administration before June, 1940, all these documents were registered and thus several
copies exist in the archives. Even if the Vichy government had wanted to
follow the traditions of the Dreyfus affair, it would have been dangerous
to destroy all proofs of my insistence on the extension of the Air Force and
the development of the aeronautic industry. Many officers of the General
Staff of the Air Force, many aeronautical engineers, many control service
officials and experts under the controller-general had taken part in the
elaboration of Plans III and IV, in the setting-up of the programs of construction, and in the calculation of the credits necessary for carrying them out.
The Riom hearings themselves revealed that the plan put into execution
by La Chambre was Plan V, and that the plan in operation in 1936 and 1937
was Plan II. But what had happened to Plans III and IV? Dictatorial regimes
can change many things and hide many truths, yet they can't keep three and
four from coming between two and five. Furthermore, my plans for extending
the Air Force had been revealed in outline to the Aeronautic Commission
of the Chamber of Deputies before their rejection by the military, and the
reporter of the budget for aviation in the Chamber's Finance Commission
also knew of them. It would have been awkward for Vichy to deny the
existence of documents known to so many persons.

As for the documents themselves, I wish to emphasize the report submitted
to the Premier on December 6, 1937, in which I stated, "to legitimize my
request [11 billion francs of supplementary credits to be spent in three years],
I consider it my duty to place it in the context of the efforts I have made in
vain since June, 1936, to obtain the necessary means for the enlargement of
the Air Force." I consider the report the best reply to the "clear, precise, and
perfectly motivated conclusions" of the Council of Political Justice.

A careful perusal of the report* will make clear my attitude and permit
an accurate evaluation of my efforts to make the military comprehend international dangers and the perspectives of modern war.

The accusation of the Council of Political Justice that I had "limited"
aviation credits (an accusation not repeated by the Supreme Court of
Justice) was based on a legal error, for the requests for credit addressed to the
Finance Commissions of the Chamber and the Senate were signed not by the
Minister of Aviation alone, but by the Ministers of Aviation, Finance, and
National Defense, and by the Premier. These requests did not express a personal
action of the Minister of Aviation, for which his personal responsibility might
be called in question, but a general and collective policy of the cabinet, which,
according to the principles of public law, could involve only a collective responsibility. The accusation also rested on a factual error: the requests addressed to
Parliament were not the same ones which I had requested of the Minister of
Finance and the Premier, and their "limitation," at a given level, was not my
doing, but an act of the entire government. Bound by the rules of ministerial
solidarity, I was forced to defend before Parliament a budget and credits whose
inadequacies I had denounced—a situation that occurs daily in every govern-

* See Appendix II.

mental system because the work of government is by its very nature a collective task. Moreover, and most important, these credits were "limited" by the Air Force plans, which the military authorities had refused to change. If there was a "crime" in the limitation of the credits, it was committed by the Minister of Finance—Georges Bonnet—or by the Permanent Committee of National Defense.

It would be as paradoxical as it would be unjust to blame the errors of the military authority on a minister who did his best to show them that they were on the wrong track, and who suggested plans which would have steered them in the right direction and helped build a modern air force. It would be equally absurd to reproach De Gaulle for not having obtained the creation of armored divisions and the *armée de métier,* which he was demanding about the same time. I mention this analogy for those partisans of General de Gaulle who have remained, through lack of information, the adversaries of the Popular Front and of its air policy.

Why I Didn't Resign

Inasmuch as my efforts to obtain new plans for the expansion of the Air Force were frustrated by the red tape of the military authority, there arises the question of whether I should have resigned my post and left the Popular Front cabinet. The question has often been put to me by French and American friends: it is particularly well formulated by Louis Levy in his excellent book *Vérités sur la France.**

To resign as Minister of Aviation in 1937 would certainly have been in my interest; yet even in the light of events which have since taken place, I think that it was my duty not to resign. To justify my course I might invoke the French governmental tradition: a minister did not resign unless he was in disagreement with the general policy of the cabinet of which he was a member. Louis Barthou did not resign as Minister of Foreign Affairs when the Doumergue cabinet compelled him to send the notorious note of April 17, 1934, in which France broke off the disarmament parleys, although he disapproved of this note, the international consequences of which were to be more disastrous than the limitation of the aviation credits. Paul Reynaud, Georges Mandel, Champetier de Ribes, and César Campinchi did not resign at the time of the Munich Pact, whose tragic side they understood.

If France had been menaced by a serious danger as a result of the inadequacy of her aerial armament or because of the military authority's refusal to increase the size of the Air Force, it would have been my duty as well as my right to resign. Such danger, however, did not exist, because France was not isolated, and it would never have arisen, had France remained faithful to the international agreements which then guaranteed her security. France could not by any hypothesis hope to defend herself alone against German aggression; the problem of French security therefore had to be viewed, in the field of

* Louis Levy, *Vérités sur la France* (England: Éditions Penguin, 1941).

316

aviation as in all others, on an international scale, and in terms of the aerial and military forces of the political bloc to which France was attached. France was bound by political and military agreements to Czechoslovakia and by political agreements to Great Britain and the Soviet Union. French aerial security would have been imperiled only if the combined air strength of France, Great Britain, Czechoslovakia, and the Soviet Union had been in danger of becoming inferior to the air strength of the Axis. Such danger did not exist in 1936-1937 or in 1938; it was created by the appeasement policy practiced at Munich, which deprived France of Czech planes and air bases, and led to the destruction of the Franco-Soviet Pact. Given this foreign policy, French aerial security would have been compromised even if the Popular Front had built twice as many planes. Without the policy of appease-ment and isolationism, however, French aerial security would have been unimpaired, had the Popular Front built half the number of planes.

This is my answer to the charge of the Council of Political Justice that I deceived Parliament and the country by false affirmations and subterfuges, thus bringing France to believe her aerial security assured. The Riom Court absolved me of this charge, which, indeed, corresponded badly with the decla-rations I had made before the Parliamentary Commissions and before the Chamber of Deputies. As long as I was in the Ministry of Aviation, the aerial security of the political bloc of which France formed a part was assured. Statistics furnished by the Information Service of the Ministry of Aviation, as well as the strategic superiority which the anti-Axis powers derived from their possession of the "Czech bastion," from the possibilities of American supplies, and from the safe remoteness of Soviet centers of produc-tion, prove this.

AERIAL STRENGTH OF THE COMBINED FORCES OF FRANCE, GREAT BRITAIN, RUSSIA, AND CZECHOSLOVAKIA COMPARED WITH THAT OF GERMANY AND ITALY.

Date	Planes in Line		Total Military Aircraft		Monthly Capacity of Plane Production	
	Allies[1]	Axis	Allies[1]	Axis	Allies[1]	Axis
July 1, 1936	3,107	2,500	5,250	3,430	350-450	350-450
January 1, 1938	5,190	3,768[2]	9,107	6,600[2]	500-600[3]	500-650
September 1, 1938 (before Munich)	5,750	5,000[2]	16,360	11,800	900-1400[4]	950-1250

[1] 3/5 of the forces in line and the reserves and 2/3 of the production—to allow for the threat of Japan.

[2] Not including 300 Italian airplanes immobilized by the Spanish Civil War and compensated for by an approximately equivalent number of Loyalist aircraft.

[3] After four to six months of industrial mobilization, taking account only of exist-ing factories.

[4] American supplies not included.

Resignation in 1937 would have been a spectacular gesture without practical effect. Even if followed by a public debate in the Chamber of Deputies, it would not have given our military policy the jolt it needed. The most certain result of resignation would have been to reveal to the public, doubtless to Hitler's satisfaction, the disagreement between General Féquant, Chief of Staff of the Air Force, and the French Army leaders.

My resignation would also have created political repercussions whose extent it was impossible to foresee; it would have involved a change, possibly a permanent dislocation, in the Popular Front. I still believe that the Popular Front policy was the best the French people could have followed at that time.

I confess that I thought of resigning much more in protest against the insufficient support we were giving the Spanish Republic than because of the outdated military policy inspired by Pétain.

Since I chose to remain at my post, it was my duty to make the best of a poor situation.

SOCIAL ASPECT: AERONAUTIC REFORMS

The creation of "Sections of Popular Aviation," open to all young Frenchmen without regard to origin, opinion, class, or wealth, was not one of the most important reforms of 1936-1937, but it aroused reactionaries of every stamp against me, and the Council of Political Justice had it in mind in accusing me of having "sacrificed the interests of the country to my partisan preferences."

The idea of Popular Aviation had been advanced before the elections of 1936. Until then the state had appropriated large credits for the development of private aviation, but the distribution of the subsidies was so organized that only the rich could profit by it. Generally they went to exclusive Aero-Clubs in which social considerations and, after the 6th of February, 1934, political considerations often predominated. Private aviation was a luxury, and in a country where wealth was unequally distributed, it became a class luxury. Despite the subsidies, the purchase price and the upkeep of private planes remained so high that only a small minority could afford them. Thus the nation as a whole was made to pay for a pleasure restricted to the rich. Besides this injustice, it seriously limited potential recruits in number and character. Instead of training young people on the basis of their aptitude, it confined flying to the wealthy; others could not learn except by enlisting in the Air Force. Other countries, particularly Germany and Russia, were making every effort to transform aviation into a popular sport, accessible to all youth. And this was what the Popular Front tried to do in creating Sections of Popular Aviation in each province. The young people who wanted to fly were divided according to age and education into three categories: general instruction in the principles of aviation, glider instruction, and flying and navigation. All participants in Popular Aviation received technical training—study of the airplane and its motor, meteorology, navigation, and radio operation. Flying became the reward for effort, and selection by merit replaced selection by wealth. Co-operation of the schools—especially technical schools—and the trade-unions proved extremely successful. The Ministry of Aviation soon was unable to fill requests for teaching matériel—gliders, planes, and instructors— and a new handicraft industry specializing in small sport planes grew up to supply the needs of French youth. Popular Aviation aroused general enthusiasm at the same time that popular interest in sports was being promoted by Leo Lagrange, Undersecretary of State for Sport and Leisure. Just as France had never before seen workers indulge in "upper-class" pleasures such as swimming, skiing, hiking, and bicycling, she now saw for the first time young workers using their leisure to learn flying or parachute jumping. The first Congress of Popular Aviation in 1937 brought thousands of enthusiastic young people to Paris.

One of the unexpected consequences of this reform was a severe blow to the Fascist organizations. After the 6th of February, 1934, the Croix de Feu had made good use of the subsidy system to create party aviation, ready for conversion into a civil war force. It was led by two Fascist aristocrats, the De la Roziere brothers, who were connected with big business; one later became private secretary to Pétain's Minister of the Interior, Pucheu, a Fascist banker, who was responsible for the delivery of many anti-Fascist hostages to the Gestapo. The real menace of Croix de Feu aviation was not in its sport planes but in its powerful connections with the Air Force. It had placed at the head of the Association of Air Force Reserve Officers one of its own men, Reserve Major Heurteaux, World War I ace, who had done nobly for the Croix de Feu during the Fascist uprising; and it had close contacts with many officers of the Air Force in active service, especially through General Dusseigneur. These facts counted for nothing in the creation of Popular Aviation; their importance was revealed only in the investigation following the discovery of the Cagoulard plot. But the Fascist organizations suspected me of a greater political shrewdness than I actually possessed, and imagined that Popular Aviation had been planned to forestall their enter-prises by introducing democratic elements into French aviation. Among the members of the Council of Political Justice was the Vice-President of the Croix de Feu, Deputy H. Valin. Consequently, there is no reason to be astonished at the Council's accusation that I had "partisan preferences." I admit unblushingly that I "preferred," and still prefer in an altogether "partisan" way, the Popular Front to Fascism and the French people to a handful of semi-professional agitators. I simply obeyed a desire to open to all Frenchmen the doors of aviation, which had too long been restricted to the rich.

After the fall of the Popular Front attempts were made to destroy its work. It would have been impossible to eliminate the existing Sections of Popular Aviation without arousing strong resentment. Popular Aviation, therefore, became "aerial military preparation." The great stream of enthusiasm was gone, however. To be sure, young Frenchmen were eager to serve in the

Air Force, but they felt that what they had created was being taken from them. They no longer enjoyed the same confidence; they were called upon to obey, not to show their initiative. There was less joy and singing on the airfields.

ECONOMIC ASPECT: NATIONALIZATION
OF THE AERONAUTIC INDUSTRY

On the subject of the aeronautic industry, the Supreme Court of Justice agreed with the decision of the Council of Political Justice and accused me of having "aggravated the inadequacy of aeronautic production by the application of the law nationalizing war manufactures." To this principal accusation, the Council and the Court added the one they already had raised against Blum and Daladier—"weakness with respect to revolutionary intrigues."

The law nationalizing the war industries was published in the *Journal Officiel* on August 12, 1936. The principle of nationalization was part of the Popular Front program and had been inserted in the "Ministerial Declaration" which the Blum cabinet submitted to Parliament with its rise to power. After the nationalization law had been passed without opposition by the Chamber of Deputies, after intensive study by competent Commissions, and after public hearings, it was examined by the Senate in public meeting on August 7 and 8. At the first session, on August 7, only one senator was against nationalization—M. H. Lemery, Senator for Martinique (after June, 1940, Minister of Justice in a Pétain cabinet). His opposition was based not on arguments arising from national defense but on the "inviolable and sacred" character of the rights of property. What the Senator for Martinique objected to in the proposal was the tinge of the Popular Front, which he feared endangered those "rights." At the meeting of August 8 the Senate modified the Chamber's text by adding two amendments, one presented by M. Fallières, and the other by M. Pernot. These amendments dealt with the regulation of the indemnities to be paid the owners of nationalized factories. The Senate wanted to assure these owners the most complete guarantees: the reservations of M. Lemery were not forgotten. The modified text came back to the Chamber, which adopted it without discussion and by a show of hands on August 11, 1936— the very day that the newspapers announced the appointment of von Ribbentrop as Ambassador Extraordinary and Minister Plenipotentiary of the Third Reich to the Court of St. James's.

The text voted by Parliament was general in its application, including aircraft, munition, and cannon factories: the reports of the Parliamentary Commissions and the explanations given in the course of the discussions leave no doubt on this point. I had sketched before the Senate, at the meeting on August 8, the general lines of the plan I intended to apply to the nationalization of the aeronautic industry. What the Council of Political Justice and the Supreme Court termed "a betrayal of the duties of the ministerial office" was thus the most legal and regular of acts. The Senate adopted the law of nationalization with the same lack of enthusiasm it displayed toward other reforms proposed by the Popular Front; the Senatorial Aeronautic Commission, when consulted, had said only that "it was not opposed to the Chamber's vote on the plan." But no one, either in the Senate or the Chamber, voted against it. The conservatives were under no illusion about the will of the people; at that moment the nationalization corresponded to a moral necessity, to a categorical imperative of the national conscience. For reasons deeply rooted in their conception of social life, the French people had increasingly revolted against the profits of the armament industry. The cause of these profits, which they considered immoral, had shocked them even more than their extent. Before making heavy sacrifices to national defense, they wanted to be sure that some men would not make fortunes from the same things that caused other men misfortune. They demanded equality of burdens and sacrifices. Nationalization had been called for in the course of the electoral campaign not only by the partisans of the Popular Front but by democratic organizations in general and by the immense majority of war veterans. If ever a law conformed to the will of the people and was imposed by the conscience of the people, it was that law which the Council of Political Justice and the Supreme Court blamed Blum, Daladier, and me for having enforced.

The Council and the Supreme Court might, it is true, have attacked the application of the law rather than its principle. Such criticism was theoretically possible, but then the procedures which would have made a *good* nationalization possible would have had to be defined. Other plans and other methods would have had to be suggested in lieu of the plans of nationalization which were enforced under the control of Parliamentary Commissions and administrative tribunals. Other plans had not existed in 1936 and 1937. From that point on, it would indeed have looked odd for the accusers to give the Popular Front government a posteriori lessons in nationalization. No such demonstration was attempted.

Reorganization of the Aeronautic Industry

To explain how the nationalization permitted the reorganization of the aeronautic industry, three questions must be answered: Why did the French aeronautic industry require reorganization in 1936? How did the law of August 12, 1936, permit this reorganization? What were the practical effects of the reorganization and the nationalization?

The aeronautic industry had to be reorganized because it was not adapted to the needs of a modern air force. It was an industry permeated by the spirit of routine; its capacity was inadequate. Plan I, although modest, had been started in the spring of 1934, and in June, 1936, the aircraft industry had been able to deliver only 607 of the 1,200 combat planes called for—scarcely 300 per year. The industrial capacity can be measured by the total output of the years 1933, 1934, and 1935: the production of airplane bodies had been

4,835 tons, or an average of 1601 tons per annum; the production of motors had been 1,580,000 h. p., or an average of 526,666 h. p. per annum. In 1936 the aeronautic industry still had three defects: inadequacy of machinery, its dangerous concentration in the neighborhood of Paris, and a certain degree of favoritism and corruption.

The inadequacy of machinery had assumed striking proportions. Experts' analyses at the time of nationalization fixed the total value of the expropriated machinery at less than sixty million francs, a figure smaller than that of the annual profits. This machinery represented 80 per cent of the French aircraft industry. The equipment of engine factories was more satisfactory, but that of the equipment and accessory factories even poorer. French industry after the end of the first World War had remained in a kind of handicraft state; it absorbed relatively too many workers, a situation which, given the limited industrial resources and social structure of France, was especially dangerous. Because of laziness and the desire for immediate profits rather than for lack of capital, most of the industrialists had failed to develop their machinery. The large profits earned by airplane builders would have enabled them to make all desirable improvements, if only they had had a different sense of their responsibilities. Immense fortunes had been made by French aircraft industrialists. But these men preferred to exploit a sheltered section of French production, which they had gradually transformed into a monopoly. They discounted the regular orders of the state and divided them among their factories by means of agreements and subcontracts, which frustrated any effort of administrative surveillance. Moreover, the way in which the state distributed its orders hardly incited the industrialists to renovate their machinery: sale prices in the state markets were based on cost plus 10 per cent to cover profits and general expenses—thus, the higher the cost price, the higher the profit. Under such procedures the best airplane, from the point of view of the builder, was a complicated one built with rudimentary machinery and at a high total of labor costs, a combination of "qualities" bound to yield the largest profits.

The industry's second major defect, its concentration in the Parisian area, had been favored by a sound economic principle, since the environs of Paris contained the best qualified labor. At the beginning of 1936, 65 per cent of the factories manufacturing bodies and 90 per cent of the factories manufacturing engines were in or near Paris, less than one flying hour from the eastern frontier. The Ministry of Aviation had tried for ten years to obtain decentralization of the factories, placing "decentralization credits" at the disposal of the industrialists and organizing a "general decentralization fund." Interests and habits were too strong; experience proved that one could hardly count on the patriotism of the capital involved in the aircraft industry.

The corruption affecting the industry was almost invisible and generally unconscious, the corrupter being aware of it, but not the corrupted. Most of the civil and military officials of the Ministry of Aviation were honest people, who would have resisted every bribe. But it was impossible to establish watertight bulkheads between administration and purveyors; social or family relations and friendships grew up and destroyed the absolute independence that should have existed. When General Dusseigneur, the unscrupulous salesman of a construction firm, recommended such or such a plane to his former subordinates, it was difficult for them to refuse to listen to his arguments. Thus corruption slowly took root. As to favoritism, it showed its ravages in the administration's tendency to take account of positions acquired and services rendered in the past rather than to recognize present qualifications; the "pioneers" of the aeronautic industry—who had built good planes before or during the first World War and had been covered with honor and money for it—thought that they had a lifetime or hereditary right to partake of the manna of state orders. Their bankruptcy would have been considered scandalous and, although their techniques were long since outmoded, they received orders which were euphemistically called "orders of support." These orders were large enough to allow ten families to live in luxury without producing anything; natural selection was unable to operate. Nepotism was another of these vicious customs, the oldest firms (which were often the worst) being filled with sons, nephews, and sons-in-law, all of them parasites who extracted a heavy toll from French aviation.

Obviously, all the airplane factories were not run in the same way. The French aeronautic industry had not only technicians as good as any abroad, but competent and honest industrialists, who deplored the practices which gave them an undeservedly bad name. Moreover, the general level of morality in the field of aviation had risen after the prosecution of the directors of the *Aéropostale* had shown that money and political connections were not a strong enough armor. Fear of the law had indeed been the beginning of wisdom. Yet on the whole, the industry added the typical vices of monopolistic capitalism to the inadequacies of a semi-handicraft organization. The development of the industry had to begin with a complete housecleaning, involving the re-equipment, regrouping, and decentralization of the factories. This was accomplished by nationalization.

There were two methods of nationalization: the creation of arsenals under the administrative system or of national firms operating under the framework of private law.

The first way seemed simpler. It consisted in the expropriation of the aircraft factories within the limits of the credits voted by Parliament and the transformation of these factories into state arsenals headed by government officials. This method had its advantages, but it would have created difficulties and delays in manufacture. For one thing, the Ministry of Aviation, unlike the Ministries of War and the Navy, never had possessed arsenals of its own; its officials and engineers hadn't the training to permit them to be transformed into industrial leaders. For another thing, the rigidity of administrative law in France was not adapted to the necessities of aeronautic production; aeronautic technique, constantly being improved, needed flexibility and liberty.

The second method was to create National Societies for Aeronautic Construction, controlled by the state but functioning according to commercial law. This was inspired by ideas which had long been advocated by the General Confederation of Labor (C.G.T.) under the name of "industrialized nationalization"; it permitted utilization in various forms of experiments made abroad. It was quite similar to the methods used in 1933 when commercial aviation was reformed and the Air-France Company created. Industrialized nationalization could be more easily employed for a reorganization of the aeronautic industry than for the transformation of private factories into arsenals. Its application led to the acquisition, by means of the law of August 12, 1936, of actual and potential elements (such as factories, research bureaus, machinery, patents, inventions, etc.) necessary to carry out a general plan of production and extension of the aeronautic industry.

The most characteristic features of the new system were: (1) not to create a monopoly of manufacture for the profit of the state, but to organize a reasonable competition within and around the nationalization; (2) to make this competition an integral part of a general plan, so that it might operate to the interest of the public and not against it. How could these ideas be reconciled?

The bases of the new system were the National Societies of Aeronautic Construction (five societies for airplane bodies and one for engines). These were formed by the state with the means of production (factories and machinery) that had been acquired. Instead of completely expropriating certain enterprises, only some elements (plants, tools, etc.) were expropriated and gathered into regional groups based on strategic locations, so that there was a National Society for each region. This was done to facilitate the organization of production by concentrating the enterprises, and to let each Society become a center for industrial mobilization. Holding the majority of the shares, the state could impose its general directives on the National Societies, while leaving them sufficient liberty of operation; it chose the best aviation industrialists to head the societies, and, as there were more candidates than positions, it eliminated those whose industrial methods or techniques were outmoded. The only important change in the customs of French commercial societies was that the state appointed a trade-union representative (which meant, in practice, a man chosen by the C. G. T.) to the board of directors of each National Society.

Competition was created among the various National Societies and between them and private enterprises; these enterprises continued to exist, because not all factories had been expropriated and because new private factories came into existence after the nationalization. As no monopoly existed, these private enterprises also submitted bids for the manufacture of planes which the state needed. In each National Society the directors and the technicians were given a share in the profits, so that they had the same personal interest in running their business well as did the directors of private enterprises. The largest part of the profits was used to remunerate the technical and administrative personnel and the workers, either by bonuses or by social benefits, so that the entire personnel had a direct interest in the success of a National Society. The Popular Front also set up a state arsenal which specialized in the most secret works of national defense, but which also could compete with both private and nationalized industry. Thus the new program made possible a constant comparison of the results obtained by the three different organizations; and at the same time it introduced a maximum of competition and honesty into the aeronautic industry.

This system was completed by the creation of "common organs" of nationalization, which added the advantages of a planned economy to those of competition. The "plans of production" and the "program for the extension of the aeronautic industry" were to be established above the National Societies by the bureaus of the Ministry of Aviation after consultation with the National Societies, which were charged with executing them. The National Societies, while remaining competitors, had many interests in common, such as problems of labor, raw materials, and finance, and needed a co-ordinating body to combine their efforts.

The "common organs" were committees which included representatives of the Ministry of Aviation and of the National Societies or filial societies of the National Societies. The most important were: (1) Financial Committee, charged with the study of financial and economic questions involving all the societies, such as a general treasury, plans of production and expansion, collective purchase of raw materials, machinery, accessories, etc.; it created a filial society for collective purchases. (2) Committee on Labor and Social Questions, which included representatives of factory and office employees to study all questions of labor—especially the problem of apprenticeship—and those raised by the enforcement of the new social legislation (collective bargaining, paid vacations, etc.). (3) Center of Documentation and Research, headed by a General Inspector of Aeronautics, to direct the work of research bureaus and laboratories; it tried to avoid overlapping and assure a better co-ordination of technical effort. (4) General Export Office of Aeronautic Material.

This was the general nationalization plan which the Council of Political Justice and the Supreme Court termed criminal. It was actually the only attempt at systematic organization accomplished in French industry before the war. It was not without shortcomings; it could not produce a magical transformation in an industry inherited with all its defects. Like every new system, it had to adapt itself, correct its initial errors, and replace certain organs by more efficient ones. Nevertheless, it represented a degree of industrial organization far better than any preceding system. It made possible a plan for increased production and for the extension of the aeronautic industry. To mention only one example: before 1936 it had been impossible to create a liaison between the various research bureaus of private enterprises, whose insistence on individual research caused a particularly distressing waste in a country with a limited number of technicians; the Center of Documentation and Research created such a liaison, while continuing to respect secrecy and freedom of research. When I look back at the work undertaken in 1936 and 1937, I think that its weak point was not excessive, but rather insufficient, nationalization. At that time, when it was possible to bring together in the National Societies about 80 per cent of the factories manufacturing airplane bodies, nationalization affected only 20 per cent of the engine industry and did not touch accessories (equipment, navigation instruments, landing gear, etc.). This difference resulted from the fact that the nationalization was accomplished by degrees;

after July, 1937 (fall of the first Blum cabinet) it was retarded, and stopped completely with the fall of the Popular Front. In 1936 we had begun by nationalizing the manufacture of bodies, an industry which was more disorganized and less well equipped than the engine industry. After the first National Society for engines was created in 1937, the nationalization met the immovable opposition of Bonnet, the Minister of Finance. His opposition was all the less justified, as the experiment with the manufacture of bodies had achieved savings in airplane manufacture, according to the reports of MM. Jardel, Bourgier, and Picot, all officials of the Ministry of Finance. For lack of sufficient credits, we had to restrict ourselves to one Society for engines and to the organization of a system of financial control for the other enterprises. Thus the nationalization remained incomplete. In fact, before and during the war most of the delays in manufacture which affected the Air Force came from the engine and accessory industries—those branches which had not been nationalized.

Effects of Nationalization

When the Council of Political Justice and the Supreme Court condemned nationalization as a crime, they maintained that it had disorganized production and prevented the Air Force from obtaining the planes it needed. To determine whether this accusation was valid, we must examine the effects of the nationalization from three angles: the economic, the technical, and the social.

From the economic point of view, nationalization facilitated the solution of the most important problems of the aeronautic industry—decentralization, improvement of machinery, development of the capacity of production, and price control.

Decentralization. After 1936, all new factories were built in the provinces and some plants in the Parisian area were transferred to less exposed regions. The decentralization and reorganization of the factories caused a few insignificant delays in manufacture—delays which were blamed on nationalization by its enemies, whereas they were actually the inevitable result of a measure demanded by the General Staff. Before nationalization, 60 per cent of the aircraft factories were in or near Paris, and 40 per cent in the provinces; at the end of 1937 the proportion had been reversed. At the beginning of the war, as a result of the plan initiated by the Popular Front, 80 per cent of the factories were scattered throughout the country. Forty per cent of the aircraft industry had been decentralized in three years, whereas it had previously required five years of fighting private interests to decentralize only 15 per cent.

Machinery and equipment. The National Societies ordered 170 million francs' worth of machinery in 1937, and more than 500 million francs' worth in 1938. If one allows for a normal rate of depreciation, it can be said that the machinery was quintupled in three years.

The plan for the extension of aeronautic industries. A complete plan, covering everything from the providing of raw materials and semifinished

326

products to the manufacture of accessories, was drawn up by the Ministry of Aviation in 1937. This plan served as the basis for all credits requested from the Ministry of Finance and for the report of December 6, 1937, to the Premier. It included the creation of large modern factories scattered throughout France, particularly in the central sections (extension of the factories at Bourges, new factories at Chateauroux, a repair plant at Clermont-Ferrand, etc.), in the west (Nantes-Bouguenais, Bordeaux, etc.), and in the Colonies (Algeria, Morocco, and repair and assembly plants in Indo-China). The plan was retained after the fall of the Popular Front and put into operation by stages in 1938 and 1939. Its execution increased fivefold the productive capacity of the factories, whose output rose from 2,400 tons per annum in 1935-1936 to 11,000 tons on the eve of the war, with industrial mobilization theoretically able to triple production within eight months. During the same period the number of workers rose from an average of 20,000 to 60,000—an increase to 300 per cent in labor for 500 per cent in production. Thus, by reorganization of factories and transformation of machinery, French aircraft production grew from a small industry concentrated in or near Paris to a large industry scattered throughout the country. At that time no other branch of French economy, including the armament industry, showed itself capable of such progress.

Price control. The coexistence of a private and a nationalized sector permitted comparisons of prices and production rates, which were to the advantage of the nationalized sector. For example, in 1937 orders for the same quantities of bombers were given to the National Society of the Center and to the Renault Company, which many experts considered one of the best construction firms in France. Renault's prices were 20 per cent higher and the period of delivery 40 per cent longer than those of the National Society. I published these facts to show the results of the nationalization, and drew the hostility of many industrial leaders. In 1938 I wrote in my book, *l'Armée de l'Air:* "If in 1937 the national factories had been directed like the private factories, production would have gone down instead of up; prices would have risen sharply instead of becoming stabilized; the delays in carrying out Plan II would have been at least equal to what they were in 1935-1936 for Plan I—50 per cent, instead of 10 per cent. If the mason is judged by the wall, the national mason built better, faster, and more cheaply than the private mason." I have had no reason to revise this judgment.

Nationalization also yielded good results from a technical point of view. In 1936 the more or less disinterested adversaries of nationalization had made gloomy prophecies. As they were obliged to concede that planned economy in mass production and decentralization of factories had certain advantages, they contended that state intervention would transform inventors into officials and that technique would be submerged in bureaucratic routine. The opposite was true. French technique had been on the downgrade; it was outdistanced by English and German techniques at about 15 per cent for pursuit planes and 20 per cent for bombers. This inferiority had three causes: (1) The deflation policy followed from 1934 to 1936 had brought a reduction of the credits available for research and the study of models (the proportion had fallen from 18 per cent of the total volume of credits before 1934 to 13 per cent in 1934 and 6 per cent in 1935). (2) During the same period the General Staff of the Air Force had not set up, or even planned, any new program of models; technicians, who had not been consulted and had received no orders, could hardly study new models without knowing whether their studies corresponded to the Air Force needs. (3) The indifference of the military with respect to innovations found support in the ignorance of the General Staff and even of the technical services of the Ministry of Aviation concerning industrial and economic questions. The new machines were chosen for performance alone, without consideration of the difficulties of construction or upkeep. Thus, at the beginning of 1936 an excellent pursuit model was chosen—the Morane 405—the mass production of which required two years of preparation and 15,000 working hours per machine, whereas the manufacture of the Messerschmitt 109, which was being studied in Germany at that time, required one year of preparation and 10,000 working hours. Only after 1936 was a serious effort made to catch up. For the light and heavy bombers the delay was made up; for the pursuit plane there still remained a delay of 5 to 10 per cent (instead of 10 to 15 per cent in comparison with Germany and especially with England), caused by the insufficient strength of French engines. Although the improvement in aeronautic technique was evident in the Air Force after 1939, the credit for it goes back to the Popular Front, since a period of two to three years was needed to perfect prototypes. In short, the Popular Front's achievements in aviation can be appraised when we observe that in 1936 and 1937 the Ministry of Aviation was obliged, for lack of better prototypes, to order machines inferior to those made abroad, whereas in 1938 and 1940, thanks to the nationalization, domestic planes were as good as those produced abroad. With only one exception (the Amiot 351 bomber), all the planes that gave satisfaction during the war had been designed and built by the nationalized sector of the aeronautic industry.

Nationalization facilitated the regulation of social questions and greatly eased employer-worker relations. Here again, reactionary propaganda has invented a legend of labor troubles and semi-permanent strikes in the national factories. This legend was accepted by the Council of Political Justice and the Supreme Court of Justice which blamed me for having shown "weakness with respect to revolutionary intrigues." However, no indication of the nature of these revolutionary intrigues was given. The best means of destroying legends is to compare them with the facts. In 1936 the relations between the leaders of the aeronautic industry and their personnel were strained. When the Popular Front came to power, all the aircraft factories were on strike and occupied by the workers—a situation left me by Marcel Déat, my predecessor. Negotiations were promptly begun on the initiative of the Ministry of Aviation between delegates of employers and workers. An acceptable solution was found, a collective contract negotiated, and work resumed in all the aircraft factories even before the signing of the Matignon Agreements which applied to the whole of French industry. From that time until January,

1938, there was not one strike, nor the threat of a strike, in the national aircraft factories. During this period only two short strikes occurred in *private* enterprises: the Latécoère factories in Toulouse and the Renault factories in Paris. These were quickly settled by arbitration, and in both cases the arbitrator agreed that the employers were at fault. My "weakness with respect to revolutionary intrigues" consisted in using arbitration to settle, in the shortest possible time, social conflicts which might have retarded production. I did not hesitate to threaten certain industrialists with the requisitioning of their factories, should they refuse to obey the law or bow before the decision of the arbitrators. To maintain the authority of the state above the authority of the employer did not mean giving in to "revolutionary intrigues." It was, rather, the refusal to yield to the unpatriotic and anti-democratic intrigues of the large industrialists. These intrigues, and no others, were revealed to me in 1936 and 1937.

I can draw no general conclusions from an experiment limited to one sector of French production. But so many Frenchmen and foreigners believe themselves capable of judging what happened in French factories in 1936 and 1937, on the basis of superficial impressions or second-hand information, that it seems to me useful to offer my evidence. The French aeronautic industry formed part of the metallurgical industry, and 80 per cent of the metallurgical workers, those handling bodies and engines, was concentrated in the Parisian area. Although these workers were known for their radicalism, they caused no serious difficulty during the entire Popular Front period. The only disturbances came from two employers, one of whom was Renault, an important financial backer of Fascist organizations and later an ardent collaborationist.

During 1938 and 1939 strikes occasionally broke out in the aeronautic industry. While they were troublesome, they were not illegal, and they were quickly settled by arbitration, causing neither disorder nor delay in manufacture. As I do not know the causes of these strikes, I have no right to judge them. But from their mere existence, I permit myself the conclusion that my methods were better than La Chambre's, and I am still convinced from my experience that social peace is most easily preserved, and work and production best assured, by a government that possesses the confidence of the popular elements. The fact remains—to the credit of nationalization and of the Popular Front—that from June, 1936, to January, 1938, the aeronautic industry was the branch of French economy in which labor and social problems were settled with greatest facility; nationalization improved the social climate of production, even more than it improved the equipment of factories.

It was, without question, because of this transformation that the Council of Political Justice declared nationalization "criminal." If it actually was a crime, I claim the honor of having been the criminal who preferred national to private interest. Nationalization was not only an important industrial experiment in the economic history of France, it was also humane: the gradual elimination of traditional worker-employer animosity in favor of collaboration in a common national enterprise; co-operation in the search for new and better relations among the different factors of production; an effort to reconcile freedom of initiative, competition, and control of production through an authority capable of setting up general plans of industrial manufacture and extension—a step toward a form of industrial management which will conform to the requirements of modern technique, the dignity of the worker, and the interest of society.

The formulae of 1936 and 1937 have today been left behind by more recent events; but at the time of their enforcement, they were symbols of progress and hope for the future.

MILITARY ASPECT: ORGANIZATION
OF THE AIR FORCE

In discussing the Popular Front government's organization of the Air Force, the word *organization* must be taken in its broadest sense, as applying not only to the military machine itself but to measures for the education and training of Air Force personnel. The Council of Political Justice accused me of having "disorganized the Air Force." The Supreme Court of Justice (which could hardly reject all the theses of the Vichy government) merely blamed me for having shown *impéritie* in the constitution of the Air Force. *Impéritie* is an old French word which has fallen into desuetude; it means incompetence. Let us examine the degree of my incompetence by comparing my record with those of my predecessors and my successor. Again, to evaluate the work of the Popular Front, one must know what existed before June, 1936.

The truth is that practically no organization existed. In June, 1936, France had military aviation, but no Air Force; her aviation had remained, in its main lines, what it had been from 1914 to 1918—an auxiliary arm of the infantry division, charged with the surveillance of the battlefield and the direction of artillery fire.

The creation of the Air Force had been decided on in 1933, against the advice of General Weygand. The decree of April 1, 1933, defined the role of the Air Force in the following way: "It should be capable of taking part in aerial operations, in combined operations with the Army and Navy, and in the aerial defense of the land. The Air Force is organized, inspected, taught, and trained for this triple purpose." Although a poor specimen of French prose, the text was perfectly clear; it ordered the formation of an Air Force "organized . . . and trained" for participation in all operations of modern war. The decree sprang from the conception of *"l'air intégral,"* an independent force participating in war operations either separately or jointly. Beginning in 1933 the Ministry of Aviation had studied the organization of such a force and had begun several reforms. But after the 6th of February, 1934, General Weygand, supported by Marshal Pétain, had no difficulty in breaking the will for reform among the Air Force's partisans, and General Denain, Minister of Aviation in the Doumergue, Flandin, and Laval cabinets, had offered no resistance. As a flagrant disregard of the decree of 1933 would have provoked Parliament, the military authority created the semblance of an Air Force without its substance. They organized a peacetime Air Force, which in time of war would give way to a model 1918 organization, adapted solely to the needs of continuous front warfare. This stratagem succeeded because the mobilization plans were not under Parliament's control; it was only when I returned to the Ministry of Aviation in June, 1936, that I discovered the truth and revealed it to Parliament.

Instead of the independent force decreed in 1933, French aviation was merely a juxtaposition of small aerial units, squadrons, and groups. In peacetime, for convenience of administration and command, these small units were organized into air fleets or escadres, consisting of two groups of two squadrons, and into brigades, consisting of two air fleets. When the day of mobilization should come, 86 per cent of the air fleets and brigades were to be dissolved and their squadrons divided into pursuit groups and observation escadrilles, at the disposal of the commanders of land armies, or into escadrilles of co-operation, at the disposal of commanders of army corps and divisions. Only two brigades, representing 12.5 per cent of the aerial forces—16 squadrons out of 134—were to remain grouped, at the disposal of the High Command for serious aerial operations. The mobilization of all other aerial units was bound to the mobilization of the large army units. It became extremely difficult to separate from the army units with which they were associated, the aerial formations that were to be used alone or assigned to other units. Such a system lacked flexibility and made it impossible for French aviation to participate in operations in which the Army would not be engaged at the same time, such as international police operations (this was illustrated at the time of the remilitarization of the Rhineland in March, 1936, when it proved impossible to mobilize the *whole* Air Force without mobilizing the *whole* Army); or in aerial coalition operations, such as the formation of an inter-Allied air force; or the use of massed aviation on a selected point of the front or for a specific aerial, naval, or land operation (a mass attack on enemy armored divisions, the pursuit of an enemy fleet, etc.). The Air Force had not the necessary organs of command and administration for any of these operations. The system in force from 1934 to 1936 was suited only to the needs of a continuous front war and was in absolute contradiction to the spirit and letter of the decree of 1933.

The offensive strength of the Air Force was about nil at the time when most European air forces were developing their heavy bomber formations (for attack on economic and military centers) and light bomber formations (for attack on tanks and warships). In June, 1936, the French Air Force, faithful to its old formulae, was still divided in the following way: pursuit, 34 per cent; co-operation (observation), 41 per cent; bombardment, 25 per cent.

Finally, the personnel of French military aviation had been trained only in terms of an outmoded form of warfare. Most of the regulations in force in June, 1936, dated from 1923, and had been drawn up according to the precepts of the first World War. No longer adapted to the performance of the matériel in service, these regulations had fallen into disuse, but had not been replaced. Certain officers, more daring or more curious than their comrades, had developed new combat methods, but these were not generally accepted or codified; the training of the troops and the education of the staff were far from systematized. The Air Force lacked a doctrine governing its disposition, although after 1933 young officers had been satisfactorily trained at the Air School—which I had created in spite of the opposition of the General Staff of the Army. The superior officers, however, headed for the highest rank were studying at the Center of Advanced Studies of the Army, and the officers who were candidates for General Staff commissions were sent to the Superior War School of the Army, so that both groups learned to lead large army units, but not to direct large-scale air operations. Special courses and exercises for aviators had been added at these schools, but this instruction was limited to the accepted doctrine of aviation.

This sketchy description of the state of things in 1936 shows why it was necessary to organize the Air Force. Beaten in 1933 on a question of principle, General Weygand had been clever enough to prevent the creation of a real Air Force.

The aim of the Popular Front was to carry out the decree of 1933 by organizing an Air Force capable of independent action. To transform the aerial formations of Plan II into such an Air Force required that the small units permanently assigned to large army units be reduced to a minimum and that the other formations be reassembled into units large enough to execute every type of maneuver required by modern warfare.

The Popular Front formed regional aerial groups, which gradually replaced most of the observation squadrons that had been organic parts of the army units. The regional aerial groups differed from these squadrons in that they were composed not exclusively of personnel in active service, but included reservists. This new organization satisfied the Army and permitted the conversion of certain observation squadrons into bombing squadrons. At this time (1937) the Ministry of Aviation suggested to the Army General Staff that an artillery air force be organized; this offer was rejected. It was not until the beginning of 1940 that the General Staff got around to doing this.

To create a large independent force, aerial units, aerial divisions, and air corps were formed. Most of the pursuit squadrons were combined into a light air corps, with the special duty of assuring aerial coverage in case of mobilization; following this, the divisions, squadrons, or groups could either remain together for tactical maneuvers or could be assigned individually to different protective or defensive missions.

A bomber corps was formed, containing in mixed divisions (heavy, medium, and light formations) the two heavy bomber brigades in existence before 1936, six medium and light bomber fleets (escadres) created from the observation squadrons released by regional aerial groups, and new bomber formations created by Plan II. Thus the greater part of the Air Force stationed in metropolitan France could be collected for mass action if the High Command deemed it necessary. Through creation of the bombing corps, the total weight of bombs carried rose from 296 to 880 tons in eighteen months.

The organization was completed by the creation of an aerial infantry and an attacking air force. We made use of Russian experiments in this work, and were greatly aided by the advice of Russian technicians. Three parachute groups were organized under the command of an excellent officer, Commandant Geille. At the end of 1936 five groups were planned, which were to become battalions immediately upon mobilization. At that time Germany still had no parachute units, and, thanks to the Popular Front, France was the second nation in the world—after the Soviet Union—to create an aerial infantry. Commandant Geille's groups took part in the Air Force maneuvers of July, 1937, in the southeast of France and in the Army maneuvers of September, 1938, in Normandy. The Army generals viewed the parachutists with skepticism and disdain; but, on the second day of the maneuvers in Normandy, Commandant Geille turned this disdain into fury by capturing the general of a division with his entire staff. The first attacking air force was set up in 1937 under Commandant Crochu, and experiments proved the efficacy of this type of attack on armored and motorized units.

Preparations for a war of coalition also were made. Within the French Air Force, the General Staff of the Air Corps could, in case of need, direct the action of inter-Allied forces. In the new organization the General Staff was complete and free, and could furnish command and liaison organs for an inter-Allied air force organization. Thus, within the limited means of the Ministry of Aviation, everything was done to make France able to defend herself.

All this was obviated by the military authorities after the fall of the Popular Front. Instead of correcting the faults which new creations were bound to have, everything was destroyed. The aerial divisions and air corps were abolished in spite of the opposition of the Aeronautic Commission of the Chamber of Deputies, which was more farsighted than the military authorities, even with respect to the parachute units. When Bossoutrot, President of the Commission, protested the abandonment of these units, General Vuillemin answered: "Parachutists are only fit for the circus." The military authorities were not satisfied until they had regressed to the methods and organization which had prevailed before 1936. We know the consequences of this return to the past: in 1940 the High Command was unable to put French air power into play and lost the battle without a fight. If I showed *impéritie,* it was in not perceiving how far the stupidity of the military authorities could go.

To put our new Air Force organization into active operation, officers capable of doing the job were needed. It was less a problem of training the men—who knew their business—than of training the staffs which were to direct them. The number of commissioned and noncommissioned officers had to be increased 50 per cent, thus proceeding from Plan I to Plan II; whatever increases other plans of extension required had also to be considered. And measures had to be taken to fight the Fascist propaganda spreading dangerously among certain Air Force groups. To solve the personnel problem, the staff had to be rejuvenated, democratized, and trained to conduct modern air warfare.

The average age of Air Force officers was much higher in France than elsewhere; other things being equal, a force trained and commanded by old generals is always defeated by a force trained and commanded by young men. A decree lowered the age limit by three years, thus permitting the appoint-ment of Air Force leaders only slightly older than those of Germany and Italy and somewhat younger than those of England. These salutary measures provoked the fury of the old generals who were forced to retire, although it had been decided to continue their pay for three years before pensioning them. These generals had their revenge when the Council of Political Justice declared that I had "discouraged the Command"—a charge which the Supreme Court of Justice dropped. If I had only "discouraged" them thoroughly by bringing still more young blood into the staff!

It was also imperative to democratize the Air Force. The Air Force officers had been particularly infected by the Fascist virus, especially by the propa-ganda of the Croix de Feu. Some did not even trouble to conceal their hatred for the Republic, whose pay and decorations they continued, however, to accept. Officers who took part in political intrigues were severely punished, and the arrest of General Dusseigneur after the discovery of the Cagoulard plot reminded certain military leaders where their sense of honor and their duty lay. The Council of Political Justice was referring to the measures taken against these Fascist officers when it accused me of having "favored insubordination"; but, here again, I do not regret my share in purging the Air Force of its Fascist elements, whose actions coincided too strikingly with Hitler's interests to be above suspicion.

The democratization of the Air Force was aided by the increase in the num-ber of officers. To supply 1,100 additional officers, it was necessary to draw on the reserve ranks and the corps of noncommissioned officers; four hundred non-commissioned officers were appointed to second lieutenancies in 1937. These men were promoted after passing an examination that was based only on merit. They belonged to a healthier section of society than did their superior officers. Like the crews of the French Navy, the noncommissioned officers of the Air Force, generally recruited from among artisans and workers, had defended themselves more successfully against Fascism than had the young officers of aristocratic or bourgeois origins. In fact, I have rarely known a social or profes-sional group more competent, more devoted, and more intelligent than the noncommissioned officers of the Air Force. Not "insubordination" but merit was favored when the officers' corps was swelled by these men of the people, who were not ashamed to believe in democracy. The Air Force became a more national force—a more truly French force. If in 1940 it had had leaders worthy of its rank and file, it would have played a more successful part in the battle.

Preparation of a staff to wage a modern war posed two problems: the organization of advanced aerial teaching and the formulation of new regu-lations for maneuvers. A School of Aerial Warfare to train General Staff officers and a Center of Advanced Aerial Studies to train the staff officers of the Air Force were created and were in operation from 1937 on. New teaching methods were adopted; the tacticians were instructed not merely to explain the official doctrine, but to contribute by their research and teaching to the development of methods for the use of air power. A circular of November 17, 1936, prescribed the organization in all Air Force formations of lectures and demonstrations during the winter to increase the technical information and general knowledge of the officers. We tried to institute "laboratories of ideas and of technical and tactical conceptions," and to stimulate progress through work. New regulations for maneuvers were drawn up. As with all reforms and innovations, they were criticized. I did not know, nor did most of the critics, whether they were good or bad, as regulations were the concern of the General Staff and were outside the competence of the Air Minister. But this much was clear—it was better to have drawn up imperfect regulations, which could be amended, than to retain perfect regulations, dating from 1923 and based on lessons of the First World War, which had become inapplicable and obsolete.

In May, 1940, France went into battle without aerial divisions and parachute units, which, created in 1936-1937, could have been developed in 1938-1939. In January, 1938, the Air Force was not yet powerful but it was in existence; its construction had hardly begun but the foundations had been laid. The new General Staff, led by Vuillemin and advised by Tétu, destroyed this foundation. Their purpose was obvious when the expansion plans and construction programs were changed. At the beginning of 1938 the orders placed at the end of 1937 for bombers and attacking planes were withdrawn, and orders for pursuit and observation planes were substituted. From Vichy's own testimony, the 1,800 first-line planes stationed in Europe in May, 1940, were grouped into 700 pursuit planes, 304 scout planes, 96 bombers, no attacking aircraft, and 700 observation planes. The program of the Popular Front provided a more essential distribution: 600 pursuit planes, 300 attacking planes, 150 heavy bombers, 450 medium bombers, and 300 observation planes.

The program to popularize aviation, the nationalization of the aeronautic industry, the democratic organization of the Air Force in terms of modern war—all aroused the wrath of the Fascists, who went to great lengths, through vicious propaganda both nationally and internationally, to substitute false legends for the genuine progress made by the Popular Front.

The activities of the Air Ministry were not limited to industrial and military problems; they necessarily touched the field of foreign affairs. While I was Air Minister, I considered it my duty to participate in the international struggle against Fascism as well as to purge the Air Force and air industry of their most dangerous elements. As an advocate of collective security, I did my best to help the Spanish Republic and to initiate a military alliance between France and Soviet Russia. According to my adversaries, these attempts were criminal.

POLICY TOWARD THE SPANISH REPUBLIC

One of the principal complaints made against me by the Council of Political Justice was that I supplied planes and other war matériel to the Spanish Republic, and it was one of the three charges which the Supreme Court of Justice retained.

If I attached any importance to the prosecution and decisions of the Vichy government, my defense would be short and simple: none of the matériel sent to Spain by the Popular Front could have been used against Germany or Italy in 1940. Most of the planes exported in 1936 and 1937 had long since been outmoded and had been withdrawn from military formations even before September, 1939 (Potez 25, Potez 54, Dewoitine 37, etc.). In 1940 the General Staff had in the rear many planes of more recent categories, which it never thought of sending into battle. Those which had been fit for use in 1936, but were antiquated in 1940, never entered into the question of the defense of France.

Only *three* planes (two Dewoitine pursuit planes and a Bloch 210 bomber) sent to Spain were models built in 1936. If they had not been sent, they would never have been used by the French Air Force, as they had been built for export before the beginning of the Spanish Civil War. Only the Bloch 210 belonged to a type ordered by the Ministry of Aviation, and construction was immediately begun on another machine which was delivered to the French Air Force in the spring of 1937. The effect of shipments to the Spanish Republic was a six months' delay in 1936-1937 in supplying a *single* bomber.

Much ado about nothing! If these shipments had not been made, the Air Force would still not have gained a single plane that it could have used in 1940. It follows, therefore, that the supply of planes or munitions to the Spanish Republic had nothing whatsoever to do with the defeat of France.

These shipments constitute, on the contrary, a political act for which I want to claim the responsibility and the credit. More than anything else in my political life—with the possible exception of my firm stand for collective security through a Franco-Soviet alliance—this aid to republican Spain inflamed Fascists and reactionaries against me; it was at the source of the press campaigns which pictured me as the disorganizer of French aviation and which, after the French defeat, followed me even to the United States. In 1936 I became for many Frenchmen a kind of symbolic figure representing the support given by the French masses to the Spanish Republic. Maurice Pujo, in l'Action Française, and Henri de Kerillis, in l'Echo de Paris, proclaimed that I should be tried for treason, and they proved to be good prophets. By repeating these charges the Council of Political Justice and the Supreme Court rendered me a great service, for they revealed that they had nothing against me except the fact that I had been the champion of the Spanish Republic and the enemy of Fascism at home and abroad. My only ambition is always to deserve such charges.

The policy of the Popular Front government toward the Spanish Republic earned the Blum cabinet and, in particular, its leaders, reproaches from the most liberal elements of international public opinion. Today it is apparent that the nonintervention policy in Spain was disastrous; intended to preserve peace, it allowed Hitler greater freedom in preparing for war. It is nevertheless important to understand under what conditions and subject to what pressure the Blum cabinet adopted and practiced this policy, As one who always fought nonintervention and who, in spite of severe limitations, did his best to supply the Spanish republicans, I feel obliged to reveal certain facts which will permit a more balanced judgment of Blum's conduct. I cannot mention the names of those Frenchmen—ministers, officials, technicians, and military men—who helped supply the Spanish Republic, without exposing them to the fury of the Fascists in control of Europe. Their names shall be published at a later date, to the honor of French democracy. The following pages do not even attempt to give a complete résumé of the Popular Front's policy; they are a simple account of the reasons which weighed so heavily on the Blum cabinet, obstructing its freedom of judgment and obliging it to make decisions that corresponded neither to the feelings of its leader nor to the will of the majority of its members nor to the desire of the French people.

Acceptance of the Nonintervention Policy

The causes of the nonintervention policy must be sought in its historical development. It was the result of a compromise between the inclinations of the Popular Front government and the tendencies of the British Conservative government; it was accepted in order to avoid what then seemed the greater evil, the threat of a general war.

The Spanish Civil War broke out on July 17, 1936, with a military uprising started by General Franco in the Canaries and Morocco and by General Mola in Burgos and other Spanish cities. The Spanish government understood the gravity of the situation: this was no mere military revolt in the tradition of the *pronunciamientos,* but a vast plot, long prepared by all the reactionary forces within the country with aid from abroad. Hitler and Mussolini knew what they stood to gain from a Spanish Civil War: at worst, they would divide public opinion in the Western democracies which, with Soviet Russia and Czechoslovakia, offered the greatest obstacle to their imperialist plans; at best, they would replace a Spanish Popular Front government, friendly to France and the Soviet Union, by a military dictatorship that owed its power to them; in any case, they would test with impunity the strength of resistance and the cohesion of the nations united in collective security. The Spanish government tried to obtain on the European market the arms it needed to re-establish order. On July 21 it sent an appeal to France, its neighbor and friend; this was natural, since a commercial agreement, signed in December, 1935, during the Laval Ministry, gave Spain the right to purchase armaments in France. Blum unhesitatingly accepted the principle of the Spanish request, which he could not have rejected without violating international law. Daladier and I, for the Army and Air Force, respectively, were told to determine how we could best satisfy the Spanish requirements. The Spanish government asked Fernando de los Rios, then in Geneva, to go to Paris to settle the judicial and technical questions raised by the forthcoming shipments. De los Rios made a stop in London, and arrived in Paris on July 24.

The rebels had friends in the Spanish Embassy in Paris—especially the Counselor of the Embassy and the Military Attaché, who shortly afterwards resigned to join Franco. As soon as the request of the Spanish government arrived in Paris, it was turned over by treachery or indiscretion to the French Fascist and reactionary press. A campaign against the legal government of the Spanish Republic was at once unleashed, and praises were sung of the revolt of the military against the people. *L'Action Française* and *l'Echo de Paris* were in the vanguard of this campaign, whose extent proved the international solidarity of the forces of social and political reaction. "Will the French Popular Front dare to arm the Spanish Popular Front?" asked *l'Echo de Paris* as early as July 23.

The Blum cabinet attached no importance to these snarlings. But Blum—unfortunately for Spain and for France—had gone to London on July 22. His trip had been planned long before the revolt of the Spanish generals; he wished to establish personal contacts with the British leaders, and was going to join Yvon Delbos, Minister of Foreign Affairs, who was representing us in London at a conference of England, France, and Belgium. The object of this conference was to examine the consequences of Germany's remilitarization of the Rhineland in March, 1936. The French and English ministers were exchanging opinions on the international situation in general and Blum was anxious to find out where the British stood with regard to the Spanish Civil War. To his surprise, our Ambassador in London, M. Corbin, indicated that there was strong pro-Rebel feeling in the British cabinet; the cabinet quite naturally reflected the opinion of conservative circles, which were intimately allied, financially and socially, with the Spanish conservatives. The British financial circles feared that the Spanish Republic would nationalize the mines and heavy industry, and the British aristocracy was full of pity for the "Spanish grandees," who were threatened with the division of their estates among the peasantry. At that moment even the more liberal British conservatives, who were most aware of the Fascist menace, preferred Franco to the Republic, an indication of how social prejudice affects the intellectual equilibrium of the best minds.

Blum returned to Paris on the evening of July 24. That same night he summoned to his home the ministers who were to deal with the requests of the Spanish government: Yvon Delbos, Vincent Auriol (Minister of Finance), Daladier, and myself. We arrived at ten o'clock and found De los Rios there. He explained the situation with intelligence, feeling, and subtlety. His task was not difficult; we all realized the danger of having a new Fascist government on the French frontier; we all knew that the security of our country—one-third of whose Army was in North Africa—required the maintenance of a friendly government in Spain; and none of us had any illusions about the feelings of the Spanish anti-democrats toward French democracy. Contrary to the reports published in the reactionary press that Daladier's attitude was opposed to mine, Daladier was as aware as anyone else of the peril which menaced us; he judged the situation not only as a man responsible for national defense, but as a historian who appreciated the importance and implications for France of the Spanish question. Of the four ministers present, only Delbos, impressed by his conversations with the English, was reticent—asking that precautions be taken not to alarm international public opinion unnecessarily. We examined the moderate requests of the Spanish government: batteries of field artillery, a few hundred machine guns, several thousand rifles and munitions, about fifty planes. All this could have been taken, not from the Army reserves, but from discarded equipment or from matériel manufactured specifically for export. De los Rios left us at midnight. Blum told us what he had heard in London and Delbos repeated his advice to be cautious; but both felt strongly that the arms requested had to be sent. It was decided to convoke the cabinet the next day. In the meantime I was to see De los Rios again and go over certain details with him. When I arrived home, I telephoned him, who, for safety's sake, joined me there, and we worked a good part of that night.

The next day the press campaign reached new heights. "Will the French airplanes handed over by Pierre Cot go to Madrid?" asked l'Echo de Paris, adding, "Madrid no longer has a regular government. The Spanish capital has fallen to a Communo-Anarchist Soviet. M. Léon Blum, M. Pierre Cot, and M. Édouard Daladier are actually sending supplies to the Communists." The author of the article, Henri de Kerillis, attacked me in particular, and emphasized the danger involved if Germany and Italy should intervene: "The government's act is criminal and abominable. . . . Germany and Italy are showing nervousness and anger, as their newspapers indicate. Neither of them has any interest in seeing Communism triumph in the Mediterranean area and in the west of Europe. The interference of France is such as to provoke their own." It was the thesis which the Vichy government was to restate before the Supreme Court.

M. de Kerillis was undoubtedly sincere. At the time of the Munich crisis he took a firm stand against National Socialism. But from 1934 to 1938, like others in the same social group, he was dominated by his hatred of the Popular Front.

The evening of July 25 the cabinet examined the question of Spain in its entirety. Aid to republican Spain was opposed, and very weakly, by a small minority which expressed formal reservations and counsels of prudence rather than actual dissent. Delbos dutifully reported the opinion of the British ministers. Chautemps, who was to become the cabinet's champion of non-intervention, told us of the effect created on the conservative circles of the Senate by the campaign of *l'Echo de Paris*. We wished, of course, to take into consideration the attitude of the British; but there was no doubt in our minds as to the danger for both France and England in allowing an anti-democratic and pro-Fascist government to establish itself at the western outlet of the Mediterranean, on the Iberian peninsula, and in Spanish Morocco. Moreover, we knew that the success of a military coup d'état might similarly inspire certain French generals and thus do great service to the Fascist cause in our own country and in all Europe. As a debate on domestic policy was to take place in the Chamber of Deputies, the cabinet adopted the following resolution:

(1) The shipments of arms requested by the Spanish government were to be collected and prepared, which would require a period of eight to ten days.

(2) This period was to be used for a debate on foreign policy in the Chamber, so that the world, and England in particular, might learn the true position of the French public as expressed by its representatives.

(3) A General Staff technician was to explain to the British authorities France's vital interest in not permitting the Spanish republican government to be replaced by a government with Fascist tendencies; as this problem was above all a naval one (involving the security of our maritime transports across the western Mediterranean and along the Atlantic Coast, and the danger that powers hostile to France or Great Britain might use the Balearic or Canary Islands), it was decided to send Admiral Darlan to London.

(4) It was agreed that the cabinet would re-examine its policy toward Spain after the debate on foreign policy, unless shipments of arms to the rebels from Germany or Italy should cause us to speed up our own supplies in order to prevent the defeat of the Spanish Republic.

The possibility of denouncing the treaty which allowed the Spanish government to buy arms in France was never considered for a moment at the meeting of July 25.

On July 30 an unexpected event took place. "Unknown" military aircraft destined for General Franco landed in French territory in North Africa, thinking they had already reached the Spanish zone controlled by Franco. An investigation was promptly ordered; in view of the geographic situation, there was at least the presumption that the "unknown" aircraft had taken off from an Italian base.

On July 31 the debate on foreign policy began in the Chamber of Deputies; it was obvious that a large majority was in sympathy with the Spanish Republic. The deputies who spoke in favor of the rebel generals— saying that "they were fighting the attempt to sovietize their country"—were the same men who, without exception, were to support Marshal Pétain's policy in 1940; the policy of nonintervention in 1936 became the policy of collabora- tion four years later. Answering the interpellators, Delbos stated that "the Spanish government was a regular government, whose legitimacy no one could contest . . . and, moreover, a government friendly to France. . . . France would in no way violate the principle of nonintervention in the affairs of another country by furnishing arms to this government. . . . This delivery of arms would not be a violation of international law, for it would be made to a regular *de jure* and *de facto* government." He added that we had not actually shipped arms—which was strictly true at that time—"in order not to give even the appearance of a pretext to those who might be tempted to support the insurgents with arms." Alluding briefly to the planes that had landed in North Africa, he merely indicated "that an investigation of the incident was under way," thus reserving to the government freedom of judg- ment on the results of this investigation. During the subsequent debate, in spite of requests from the partisans of nonintervention, he refused to commit himself.

On August 1 the report of the investigation directed by General Denain arrived at the Air Ministry. A conservative, thoroughly loyal to the Republic, he could not be accused of being anti-Fascist or anti-Italian. Denain's con- clusions were formal: the aircraft were military planes, withdrawn from forma- tions of the Italian Air Force with such haste or carelessness that their military logbooks had not been removed; they had been sent by Mussolini to Franco. What was still more important, the investigation proved that the shipment had been decided upon before July 17, as the planes had been collected and prepared as early as July 15. Thus, on July 30, before any French shipments had been made to the Spanish Loyalists—and long before any shipments had come from Russia—Italy was publicly convicted, not only of intervening in the domestic affairs of another country, but of giving support to factious military men in revolt against their legitimate government. Hence the belief of opponents of the Popular Front government that France's intervention in behalf of the Spanish government might cause Germany and Italy to aid the rebels was not only legally inacceptable but actually inaccurate. I telephoned General Denain at Algiers, asking him to come to Paris to submit his report to the Parliamentary Commissions. I knew my adversaries, and I was aware that, if I did not take this precaution, they would claim that I had drawn exag- gerated conclusions from the report. This report was of considerable importance for a balanced judgment. With proof of Italian intervention, the situation was growing clearer and simpler: to let Italy supply the rebels while we denied the Spanish government the benefits of the commercial treaty of 1935 would amount to a violation of international law. Far from indicating our respect for the principle of nonintervention, it would mean, on the contrary, that we *were* intervening in Spanish affairs, by refusing to let the legitimate government exercise its right of purchasing arms and by basing this refusal on a question of domestic affairs. On a foundation of nonintervention, we would be establishing a judicial thesis which might become fatal to all nations threatened by Fascism. Blum decided to convoke the cabinet the following day, August 2, to make possible an analysis of the political and legal consequences of the situation.

With a few exceptions, the ministers who met on August 2 were determined to support the rights of the Spanish government; all were indignant at the intervention of Italy; not one wanted to sacrifice Spanish democracy and French security to the mirage of appeasement. Delbos again explained the position of the British cabinet: the British conservatives continued to prefer the rebels to the republicans and, in the name of Anglo-French amity, we were advised unofficially not to take sides and to observe strict neutrality. It was either at this meeting of August 2 or at one on August 8 that we were informed of the failure of Darlan's mission. Darlan had been rejected by the *esprit de corps* of the British Admiralty, which was scandalized that mere sailors, faithful to their country's government, had refused to obey the orders of rebel officers, had taken over warships, and had returned them to their legitimate owner, the legal government of Spain. In the conflict between discipline and law, the British Admiralty had taken sides with discipline, a decision that outweighed all considerations of French security in the Mediterranean. In spite of Darlan's shifts and reversals from June, 1940, to December, 1942, I persist in thinking that he carried out this mission correctly; in 1936 he was still a loyal officer, mindful of the vital interests of his country; in 1939-1490 he was corrupted, partly by Laval, Weygand, and Pétain—who were neither his moral nor intellectual equals—partly by his own ambition.

In spite of some opposition and President Lebrun's advice to be "prudent," the cabinet understood that its first duty was to permit the Spanish Republic to be supplied in and through France. Blum declared: "Our duty requires that we aid our Spanish friends, whatever the consequences of this support may be." On Delbos' proposal, and in consideration of the British position, the cabinet agreed to send out an appeal to the wisdom of the European nations, which would lead to the adoption of "common rules of nonintervention"; but it was clearly stated that if the rebels continued to receive arms, the French frontier would remain open to the Spanish government.

Although this decision safeguarded France's rights, it was not reached without discussion. It was unsatisfying, in that it transformed the Spanish government's incontestable right to buy arms in France into a kind of retaliation for the Italian government's violation of a no less unquestionable rule of international law—the prohibition against furnishing arms to rebels. We accepted this compromise because we considered it to the interest of the Spanish government that we should remain on friendly terms with England, while giving her time to reach a fairer judgment of the situation; but the condition which made the compromise acceptable was the maintenance of the Spanish government's right to receive what arms it needed.

The decision of the cabinet was expressed in a communiqué of the Ministry of Foreign Affairs, dated August 3. It stated that (1) the French government had decided to "send an appeal to the leading governments, to obtain the adoption of common rules of nonintervention"; (2) the French government declared that it had not sent any arms, "even in fulfillment of contracts con-cluded before the outbreak of hostilities"; and (3) "the fact that military sup-plies were coming to the rebels from abroad caused the French government to reserve its freedom of judgment for the enforcement of the above decision," in other words, to retain its freedom of action.

The communiqué set off an explosion of fury in the pro-Fascist and reactionary press. The reaction was all the more violent because, foreseeing new difficulties, Daladier and I had hastened to live up to France's agree-ments, and had sent the Spanish Republic everything we could. These deliveries, although entirely legal, were denounced as criminal by the French friends of Franco, Mussolini, and Hitler. The Cagoulards, l'Action Française, and l'Echo de Paris organized a veritable spy network to keep watch on exports intended for Spain. Later the system was perfected and surveillance became action— planes whose destination was suspect were blown up. I became a target for mud-slinging, when it was learned that within a few days I had succeeded in sending to Spain more than fifty planes—thirty reconnaissance planes and bombers, fifteen pursuit planes, and about ten transport and training planes. These made possible the first defense of Madrid. They saved the Spanish capital and at the same time the honor of French democracy. The events of the 6th of February, 1934, had successfully hardened me against slander; but the importance of the reactionaries' attacks on me lay in the fact that they were repeated and developed in the German and Italian press, and aroused some anxiety in British conservative circles. Our Ambassador in London and the English Ambassador in Paris echoed that feeling. We were informed that we were in danger of compromising our general appeal to the European nations. To that we replied that by not sending arms we were running the dan-ger of compromising the Spanish Republic and the security of France and European democracy.

Although these exchanges of opinion were courteously phrased, they showed conclusively that the Spanish affair and the shipment of arms from France to Spain were far from beneficial to Paris-London relations. The campaign of Franco's friends in France was devilishly clever. It was rumored in the corridors of the Chamber and Senate that our attitude threatened to earn us the displeasure of both the British and the future government of Spain; even Pertinax, usually so well informed of the danger of Fascism, fell for a while into the trap of reactionary propaganda and wrote in l'Echo de

Paris: "The nationalists have won. . . . Madrid is in the hands of Communists and Anarchists." Steps to have Delbos apply a policy of "complete nonintervention and neutrality" were taken by Henry Berenger, President of the Senate Foreign Affairs Commission, and Jean Mistler, President of the Chamber Foreign Affairs Commission—two men who were to play disastrous roles at the time of Munich and in June, 1940. Special pressure was brought to bear on Blum and on Lebrun. I have never seen a more complete mobilization of conservative and reactionary forces, a more perfect collusion of the defenders of the existing social order and the adversaries of democracy. For their part, the French masses demonstrated as best as they could their attachment to the democratic cause; on August 5, speaking in the name of the C. G. T., Léon Jouhaux denounced absolute neutrality as an anti-French position. "The defeat of the Spanish workers," he said, "may well become *our* defeat, not only from the social point of view, but actually the defeat of our country." On August 8, at the regular meeting of the cabinet, the question of Spain was again raised—and this time France took a definite step toward nonintervention.

At this meeting, the cabinet reversed the position (which had been, on the whole, acceptable) that it had taken on August 2, and, by a decision to suspend all arms exports, nullified its previous understanding in favor of a provisional nonintervention policy.

The communiqué published after this meeting spoke in the following terms: given "the almost unanimously favorable replies which it has received on the question of the principle involved," as a result of its proposal that common rules of nonintervention be adopted, "the government has decided to suspend exports of arms to Spain." Jean Hutin, diplomatic editor of *l'Echo de Paris,* added this commentary, which corresponded only too well to the position of the government: "Although the communiqué does not state it precisely, there is no difficulty in ascertaining in government circles that our neutrality is not absolute but conditional, and that if Germany or Italy send arms to the partisans of Franco, we should reclaim our freedom of action." Some days later Delbos confirmed this interpretation by emphasizing in a public address that "neutrality ought not to be a fraud." And on September 5, 1936, addressing the Socialist Federation of the Seine, Blum stated: "The suspension of arms exports [to Spain], which was proclaimed on August 8, was conditional." Such was the thesis of the French government. Unfortunately, France never exercised her right to reclaim her freedom of action and was caught in the toils of nonintervention.

It was only after a long debate that the cabinet had agreed on "the suspension of exports with the privilege of reconsideration." Proposed by Delbos, this idea revolted Blum, who can be said to have resigned himself to it rather than to have adopted it. Among those who fought it, I can mention only Maurice Violette, Secretary of State, because he is dead and beyond Fascist vengeance. The cabinet was divided into three unequal camps: the partisans of nonintervention, a weak minority; the opponents of nonintervention, a more numerous group; and the undecided, who finally agreed on

nonintervention with the privilege of reconsideration and with the reservation of the right for retaliatory action to avoid what seemed to them the
greatest danger. There is little point in re-examining the arguments of the
opponents of nonintervention; the course of events has proved they were
right to believe that nonintervention would become a "fraud," with Spain as
its first victim and France its next. It is far more important to reveal the
argument which swayed the decision of Blum and the majority of the cabinet.

In was first of all the argument of Anglo-French solidarity, which Blum
considered the cornerstone of collective security, and consequently of French
security. This cornerstone had been shaken so badly by the policy of Pierre
Laval in 1935 that, upon the occupation of the Rhineland by German troops
in March, 1936, England had refused to enforce sanctions against Germany—
just as France had refused England's request a year before to apply such a
policy to Italy. In answer to Laval's flirtation with Mussolini, Great Britain
had signed an agreement with Germany to limit naval armaments, without
consulting France. British conservative circles contained a strong faction
favoring a European policy based on an Anglo-German entente, and this
faction had been strengthened by the conservatives' distrust of the French
Popular Front. As soon as Blum came to power, he had set out to remedy
this situation with great intelligence and perseverance, and his partial success
can be attributed to his frankness and to the position he had taken at the beginning of July in the League of Nations. But on August 8, 1936, the cement
he had poured had not yet hardened, and Anglo-French solidarity required
discretion. It was quite obvious that the British cabinet disapproved of the shipments of French arms to the Spanish Republic. The English wanted France to
adopt a policy of neutrality toward the conflict which was tearing Spain apart;
failing that, they suggested helping General Franco, a policy which would
have compromised collective security and the League of Nations forever.
That was what Blum had been given to understand when he had gone to
London on July 22, and it had been repeated still more frankly to Admiral
Darlan in naval and military circles; nor did the dispatches of M. Corbin,
our Ambassador in London, leave any doubt as to British feeling. The Spanish
affair threatened to become a stumbling block for Anglo-French solidarity, on
which Blum counted as a guarantee for the peace of Europe and against the
devaluation of our currency which was threatened by the speculation of financiers who opposed the Popular Front.

There was certainly no question in Blum's mind of any bargaining between
France and England with the Spanish Republic as the stake; but he feared
to see France run the risk of war before having strengthened the political and
psychological ties which bound her to England. This argument had already
been presented by Delbos on August 2. If Blum and the majority of the
cabinet accepted on August 8 what they had refused on August 2, it was
because an almost unconscious reflection had magnified the information
received from London on the state of British opinion; rightly or wrongly, it
looked as if the nonintervention policy would be the only way of preventing
England from aiding Franco.

Certain considerations of domestic policy also made themselves felt. We knew that a majority of the Senators desired a policy of neutrality and non-intervention; moreover, it was undeniable that the Blum cabinet was at this time (July-August, 1936) meeting great difficulties in the Senate. The position of the cabinet with respect to the Senate would have been weakened still more if we had continued to furnish arms to the Spanish government. A serious political conflict might have arisen, had it been felt that the cabinet was endangering Anglo-French solidarity. I must say, however, that when this argument in favor of nonintervention was advanced by Chautemps in the course of the discussion, it was haughtily rejected by Blum, who was not a man to accept a vicious foreign policy for reasons of internal policy. The feeling of the French people, had it been upheld by the government, would have overcome the opposition of the Senate. In 1936 the Senate was preoccupied with blocking the enforcement of the social legislation demanded by the country; with regard to Spain, the French working class and the masses instinctively understood that the fate of European democracy was at stake and that the Spanish Civil War was but the first act of the European war. They would willingly have given up the advantage of an unquestionably just social legislation to help the Spanish Republic. It must be said to the honor of the French Communist party that exactly such a suggestion was made by one of its leaders. It would therefore have been possible for us to conquer the hostility of the Senate by sacrificing the workers with the workers' own permission. But these considerations of internal policy actually played no part in the decision of August 8. If Blum accepted that day a proposal which he had previously rejected, it was solely because of the English position; I know how his conscience suffered because of that compromise.

After four years, with the double perspective of time and exile, I still believe that the decision of August 8 was the wrong one, for the following reasons:

(1) The legitimate government of Spain had the right to buy arms in and through France, and the decision of August 8 denied this right.

(2) Leaving the French frontier open to the Spanish republicans would have been their salvation. Germany and Italy would not have sent many more arms to the rebels than they actually did, for they sent all they could. With a French frontier almost entirely closed, the Spanish Republic resisted for two years the onslaught of Spanish Fascists and their Arab mercenaries and Italo-German legions. With an open frontier, the Spanish Republic would have won, or at least continued its resistance into 1939. It would have become one of the Allied Nations and the whole aspect of the present war would have changed.

(3) The risk of international war which the partisans of nonintervention flourished before us was real enough; but it was a minor risk, far less to be feared than that of a Fascist victory in Spain; it would have been better for the World War to have broken out in 1936 than in 1939. In 1936 the German Army was weaker than the Red Army, and the Italian Army had been exhausted by the conquest of Ethiopia; the French Army, together with

the Czechoslovakian and the Red Armies, would have had nothing to fear from Germany and Italy.

(4) England would not have abandoned France in case of actual danger, because her interests would have forbidden such a move; it would have been impossible for her to remain out of a European war that was bound to result in a redistribution of international political and military power. She would have followed us unwillingly, but she would have followed. Instead of an Anglo-French policy directed by the English conservatives and suffered by the French Popular Front, we would have had an international policy oriented by the Popular Front and suffered by the English conservatives. Democracy and the peoples of the British Empire would have gained by the change.

Speaking at a meeting organized at the beginning of the winter of 1939 by the International Peace Conference, Delbos admitted that the nonintervention policy had been a mistake. French democracy was not alone in committing it. If politics is an art of foreseeing and choosing between evils, it must be said that on August 8, 1936, the French cabinet was unable either to foresee or to choose properly. But it would be most unjust to consider that cabinet the principal author of an historical error, in which it was joined by the majority of European and American democracies. Except for the Soviet Union, Chile, and Mexico, all the great powers erred in the Spanish war. Blum made the same mistake that Churchill and Roosevelt made—and he had many more excuses than those two statesmen; he resigned himself to a policy which his intelligence condemned and his heart rejected. In comparing the attitude of the French Republic with that of the other democracies—which had greater freedom of choice—few nations will be in a position to censure the French Popular Front cabinet.

The results of the decision of August 8 are well known. France, embroiled in nonintervention and having subordinated her policy to that of the British cabinet, found it more and more difficult to recover her independence. We are always prisoners of our past mistakes: having accepted the demands of Germany in September, 1938, France and England could not prevent Hitler from entering Prague in March, 1939; having recognized the Pétain government in 1940, the United States had to negotiate with Darlan in 1942.

Development and Consequences of the Nonintervention Policy

On August 11 the Soviet Union agreed to send no more arms to Spain after August 20; on August 21 and 24 Italy and Germany, respectively, took similar decisions. The European powers appeared to have answered France's appeal, and toward the end of the month the "Committee of Co-ordination" was created in London. While England, France, the Soviet Union, and the other democratic states respected their pledges, Germany and Italy continued to supply Franco, and nonintervention became a huge farce. This farce was denounced, and evidence presented, by representatives of the Spanish Republic in September of the same year before the Assembly of the League of Nations.

347

The Soviet Union demanded in vain an international investigation of violations of nonintervention. Germany and Italy opposed this investigation, and,
on October 24 Soviet Russia reclaimed her freedom of action, while continuing to demand the enforcement of controlled nonintervention. The decision
of the Soviet Union was in accord with international law; she was the only
country to oppose the intrigues of the Fascist powers. A certain number
of us asked the French cabinet to adopt the same attitude and to return to
the principle of August 2—nonintervention with the privilege of reconsideration. The cabinet was divided and again concerned itself with ascertaining
the position of the British cabinet, instead of following the instinct of the
French people. In January, 1937, France agreed to forbid the departure of
volunteers for Spain. Thus by degrees we descended the ladder and sank
into the policy which was to allow Franco to impose his dictatorship on the
Spanish people.

What were the political consequences of nonintervention?

I believe that we lost in Spain one of the most decisive battles of the
present world conflict; with a little daring the democracies might have won.
The Spanish Civil War was for them a test of weakness, and for the
Fascist states a test of strength. Moreover, the Spanish war allowed the
German generals to make their first life-size maneuvers and to experiment
with combat methods and matériel: the Polish campaign was prepared in
Spain, just as the French campaign was prepared in Poland.

The domestic consequences were no less important. The moral unity of
the French Popular Front was broken over the Spanish question. After July,
1936, the French masses had shown a profoundly healthy reaction; they
understood that the triumph of Franco, after that of Hitler and Mussolini,
would complete the political encirclement of French democracy and would
sign the Republic's death warrant. There was never in France a more popular
cause than that of republican Spain. The will of the people expressed itself
in the most moving ways; thousands of young men crossed the frontier to
fight Fascism. The spirit of the volunteers of the French Revolution lived
again in these young heroes. Refugee women and children were adopted by
French families; in all large and small towns committees were formed to
study how civilians could help the Spanish republican cause. But the French
masses became discouraged and demoralized by the nonintervention policy.
Not only the unity of the Popular Front, but the democratic principle was
imperiled by a policy obviously opposed to the will of the French people, who
became aware that the democratic machinery had been breaking down, that
their will was no longer sovereign, and that the state was dominated by
conservative influences which were as powerful as they were sinister. The
Popular Front government seemed impotent under the control of British conservatives and paralyzed by the worst elements of a French bourgeoisie, whose
decadence the people could already see. The masses realized that the governmental system was bad, and that the Third Republic had reached that stage
of development where conflicts break out between the democratic and the
capitalistic principle. Majority rule had become inoperative. And when the

French people were called upon in 1939 and 1940 to defend national and democratic liberties, some shrugged their shoulders, saying, "What for?" Their faith in democratic institutions was weakened.

The large majority of the people, aware of the Fascist and Franquist danger and shocked by the activities of the reactionary Right, overflowed the ranks of the Popular Front. After July, 1936, all that was good and generous in France was on one side of the barricade. The Spanish Civil War became the touchstone for patriotism and liberalism. We must pay particular homage to those Catholics who, braving all insults, refused to let their faith be confused with the cause of the Spanish bishops, monks, and fanatics who supported Franco. I want to mention specially Cardinal Verdier, Archbishop of Paris, and many Dominicans; Jacques Maritain, Georges Bernanos, François Mauriac, and Georges Bidault, among the writers; Raymond Laurent, Ernest Pezet, and Philippe Serre, among the deputies. Emile Buré, Geneviève Tabouis, and Pertinax (who, after his errors of judgment, soon rediscovered the true direction of French interest), among the conservative journalists, and a few conservative statesmen, such as Paul Reynaud, Georges Mandel, and Champetier de Ribes, also refused to take part in the comedy which made Franco a champion of "order" and a friend of the French people.

We cannot denounce too strongly the rage with which most of the French reactionaries tried to transform the Spanish Civil War into an instrument against the Popular Front and democracy in general. Certainly it was the right of the French enemies of democracy to prefer Franco to Negrin, to side with power against right; but to this preference they brought a revolting partiality, a complete absence of intellectual and patriotic scruples, and, above all, a spirit of hate which was dishonorable. This partiality and hatred transformed the French friends of Franco, sometimes without their knowledge, into accomplices of Hitler and Mussolini. Their press campaigns, their public speeches, their appearances before Parliament were designed to prove by every means that the rules of nonintervention established in London were being violated by Blum and me rather than by Hitler and Mussolini. The demonstration of these charges preoccupied them more than the search for truth or the defense of national interest. Their speeches and campaigns gave the governments of Germany and Italy the pretexts they needed to supply the rebels while they continued to have representatives in the Committee of London; they furnished the arguments which von Ribbentrop used to attack and denounce France. There was at that time a systematic campaign of slander against the leaders of the Popular Front, and what was said about our attitude toward republican Spain was only a part of this campaign. Blum was accused falsely of sabotaging French economy, Roger Salengro, of desertion during the first World War, and I, of sending the Spanish Republic the most modern airplanes intended for the French Air Force. "French aviation has not yet been supplied with this perfected matériel" and "the Anarchists and Communists will be served first," printed *l'Echo de Paris,* December 23, 1936. These statements weakened the reputation of France abroad and struck at the morale of the Air Force, many of whose officers read this paper. On January 29, 1937, it was proved before the Chamber of Deputies that no airplanes intended for the Air Force had been sent to Spain—and that these articles, reprinted in the German press, had fed the fires of Dr. Goebbels' propaganda. Other Fascist and reactionary newspapers used the same arguments, the same devices, and the same campaigns. On October 15, 1936, Maurice Pujo wrote in l'Action Française: "Almost all the aviation matériel and fliers of the Madrid government are French." At the beginning of 1938, another editor of l'Action Française, Pierre Héricourt, published a book, The Soviets and France: Purveyors of the Spanish Revolution.* In another work, Why Franco Will Win, the same author wrote that the assistance given to Franco by Germany and Italy "had never been as great as had been claimed and had been much less than that of France and the Soviet Union."† The same thesis was upheld before Parliament on December 5, 1936, by certain nationalist deputies, who, vouching for the loyalty of Franco, declared: "France's interest is to support Franco. . . . At the beginning of the Spanish Civil War there was not a German in Spain. . . . When the French government committed the folly of sending important aeronautic matériel to Spain from the very first day of the war, Germany and Italy hastened to take the place we should have taken [in supporting Franco]. . . . The French government has permitted 12,000 French volunteers to cross the frontier . . . the International Brigade is formed largely of Frenchmen."

General Franco was eulogized as "the defender of the Christian faith against Bolshevism." The same group of so-called defenders of order organized a public fund and sent a sword of honor to General Moscardo, "the hero of Toledo." General Weygand praised the "little handful of men who are determined to free their country from an insupportable servitude," thus legitimizing in advance the military coup d'état against democratic power. One need merely open the reactionary and Fascist newspapers of those days or consult the record of the Chamber of Deputies for further examples of the baseness of the French Right. Not even in the days of the Dreyfus affair or the White Terror had French reaction stooped lower.

The Spanish Civil War, more than any other event, drew the real dividing line in French politics. An abyss was formed between the French people and the reactionary bourgeoisie—because the Spanish Civil War proved that the reactionary bourgeoisie was prepared to commit any crime to check the power of the people. I wonder when and how this abyss can be bridged; the resistance of the French workers to Fascism and Hitler and Pétain makes me think that the abyss still exists. Nor should one be surprised. With rare exceptions—and Henri de Kerillis is a notable example—those who supported Franco in 1936 were to fight and betray the French Republic in 1940; and those who most energetically defended the cause of the Spanish Republic were to fight against the collaboration policy invented by General Franco's friend, Pétain. Moreover, after 1936 strong bonds existed between French and Spanish Fascism. These were revealed when the Cagoulard plot was

* Pierre Héricourt, Les Soviets et la France: Fournisseurs de la Révolution Espagnole (Paris: Baudinière, 1938).

† Pierre Héricourt, Why Franco Will Win (Paris: Baudinière, 1936).

discovered. Certain of the outrages committed were intended either to paralyze the sending of supplies to the Spanish Republic (the bombing of airplane hangars at Toussus-le-Noble under the pretext that they contained airplanes intended for the Spanish Reds, the bombing of certain engineering works on the railway lines between France and Spain, etc.) or to facilitate criminal operations which Franco ordered carried out on French territory. I shall give only one example of these operations: a Spanish government submarine, while in harbor at Brest, was attacked on September 19, 1937, by a band of men armed with machine guns; they succeeded in coming aboard and tried to steal the vessel. The coolheadedness of the sailor on guard frustrated the attack, and the men took flight. They were caught and arrested by the French police. The authors of the attack were Spanish Fascists, commanded by Major Troncoso, the Military Governor of Irun, and French Fascists, commanded by Reserve Commandant Chaix. Arrested among Troncoso's and Chaix' accomplices were Spanish and Italian terrorists, some known to our counterespionage services as Gestapo agents. They had been involved in other acts of terrorism on French territory. Although the French government had abstained from intervening in the internal affairs of Spain, Franco had no such scruples; democratic solidarity did not aid the Spanish Republic, but Fascist solidarity aided Franco, as it was to aid Hitler in 1939 and Pétain in 1940. After the events of 1936 and 1937, it is indeed difficult for a French democrat to believe in the patriotism of the Croix de Feu and the Cagoulards.

Aid to Republican Spain

By aiding the people of Spain, the French people attempted wholeheartedly to mend the government's error. As shipments of arms were forbidden, the people sent milk for the children, food and clothing, trucks and ambulances, and until 1937, volunteers; French blood was shed once more for the cause of liberty, this time on Spanish soil. Ingenious devices were invented to furnish Spain everything compatible with the rules of nonintervention—even a little more. Moreover, the Popular Front administration and people's groups tried to intercept what contraband the Fascist organizations were attempting to send Franco through the Basque territory. In the traditional fashion of French politics, this fight occasionally permitted the expression of the people's sense of humor. Thus it happened that three pro-Franco deputies, on their way to present the sword of honor to General Moscardo, were stopped at the frontier by a customs officer who told them gravely that "as traffic in arms was forbidden, he could not take it upon himself to permit a sword to pass, and that the nonintervention administrators would have to be consulted." The consultation caused the ambassadors of l'Echo de Paris to miss their train.

The time has not yet come to tell the full story of the French Popular Front's work for Spain; I can speak at this time only of my own efforts, to answer the charges brought against me.

I fought the decision of August 8 with all my power, and thereafter constantly demanded the exercise of the "privilege of reconsideration." But I was limited by the principle the cabinet had adopted, and I had no intention of helping Nazi propaganda prove that France did not keep her pledges—whatever *l'Action Française, le Jour,* or *l'Echo de Paris* might have said. I considered it France's duty and to her interest to aid the Spanish Republic and to facilitate the work of "the regular government, the friend of France"—to use the expression of Blum and Delbos. To reconcile these two aims, I appealed to the rules of international public law. The decision taken on August 8, 1936, by the French government derogated both from common law and the provisions of the commercial treaty of 1935; it had to be interpreted strictly, but we could do everything it did not expressly forbid. I expounded this idea to Blum, certain that he would raise no objection, and decided to make it the basis for my action. It was particularly easy to do this without risking France's reputation, since the control of nonintervention was in the hands of international commissions. It was not my duty, even with respect to aeronautic supplies, to interfere with the functions of the commission in charge of guarding the frontier of the Pyrenees. As that commission praised the way in which France had respected her pledges, the French government's interpretation must be regarded as correct; one may well be surprised that the Supreme Court of Justice placed more stock in the opinions of *l'Echo de Paris* and *l'Action Française* than in the decisions of the International Control Commission.

Once I had decided on a strict interpretation of the rules of nonintervention, there remained the other part of my duty: our Spanish friends had to be aided to the fullest measure of our abilities.

How many planes were sent to Spain? How many foreign planes flew across France to Spain? The most fantastic figures were cited in the French press and in Parliament by Franco's friends. Henri de Kerillis declared on December 31, 1936, that the Spanish "nationalists" had already brought down 69 French planes since the beginning of the war—which, on the basis of a reasonable percentage, would have implied shipments of over 200 planes in five months, obviously an impossibility. According to Pierre Héricourt, editor of *l'Action Française,* of 729 foreign airplanes sent to the Spanish "Reds" during the first eight months of the war and identified by Franco's forces, 212 were French; of 147 planes shot down by "nationalist" artillery and identified, 100 were French. The same journalist claimed on October 12, 1937—fifteen months after the outbreak of the Civil War—that of 700 planes brought down by the troops of Franco, more than 200 were French. During a visit to the "nationalists," he himself "recognized" the debris of 172 French, 313 Russian, 157 American, and 72 Czech planes, and he had seen matériel recovered on the battlefield by Franco's men which included 615 French machine guns, 72 French pieces of field artillery, 16 French pieces of heavy artillery, 53 French infantry cannons, numerous French tanks, and a considerable number of French rifles. Lastly, speaking at a meeting of the Chamber of Deputies in December, 1937, M. Tixier-Vignancourt informed the public opinion of France and the world that France had sent the Loyalists 540 more military planes than Soviet Russia (which, according to Tixier-

Vignancourt, had sent 437), 110 more than Holland, 78 more than the United States, and 40 more than England. The contention of the French friends of Franco, from Héricourt to Tixier-Vignancourt, was that I had been the main purveyor of Loyalist aviation.

These figures were false. If the laws of the Vichy government condemn people for their intentions as well as their deeds, I am certainly guilty. Had I not been hampered by the rules of nonintervention, I would have contributed for the defense of democracy against Fascism all the planes "identified" by Héricourt and listed by Tixier-Vignancourt and De Kerillis. A brochure published in London by the Spanish Press Center of Franco, under the title *I Accuse France,* charged me, somewhat more modestly, with having sent the republicans in 1937, 129 planes, of which 83 were warplanes. I suppose these figures are approximately correct. In their partisan hatred the French nationalists attacked one of their compatriots more bitterly than did the Spanish followers of Franco!

The strict interpretation I had placed on the decision of August 8 made it possible to send these planes, however indirectly. Some fifty aircraft had already been sent before August 9. Since the decision applied to actual war matériel, I refused—wrongly or rightly—to designate transport planes, sport planes, and training planes as war matériel, although some of them, of course, could be transformed by the Spaniards if they wished. The decision in no way prevented us from sending warplanes to foreign countries whose hands were not tied by nonintervention agreements and were not represented at the London Conference. Nothing prevented the King of Hejaz, the Finnish government, or the Brazilian government, for example, from buying warplanes in France—and when I authorized the departure of planes from a French airport, the intentions and destination of the pilot were none of my concern. I was not obliged to know whether an airplane en route to Hejaz by way of Spain was going to remain in Spain or not, because my ministerial function did not make me the policeman of the London Committee.

I applied similar rules to certain foreign planes that passed across French territory and used our airdromes. Somewhat ironically, my "strict interpretations" often brought me the reproaches of Delbos, the Minister of Foreign Affairs and faithful guardian of the decision of August 8; but these reproaches always came after the enforcement of my interpretations, and I discovered with pleasure in 1936-1937 that the application of international public law is a matter of imagination. I always bowed before the judgment of the Minister of Foreign Affairs—after the deed—but I had a tendency not to consult him before taking action. Delbos jestingly called me a "smuggler," and I claimed to be nothing but a "jurist," prepared to demonstrate that the common law on war contraband could not apply unqualifiedly to the particular case of Spain and aeronautic matériel. I admit that I did not apply the theory of the "continued trip" in the same way to both the regular Spanish government and the rebels, but I think I had the law on my side. Only the profound legal ignorance of my adversaries could transform my actions into a violation of the rules of nonintervention; to give me as opponents the retired cavalry officers who discussed these problems for the Fascist newspapers was to stack the cards in my favor. Once again the traditional behavior of the French reactionaries—who were not merely "evil men"—favored the democrats.

Since I am confessing my "crimes," I must add that sending French or foreign planes was not the only means of legally aiding the Spanish Republic, even in the field of aviation. As our Spanish friends lacked training planes and instructors, I put at their disposal some French training centers and schools. Similarly, it happened that Loyalist aircraft (especially pursuit planes with a limited radius of action) had to be refueled at our airports, in order to cruise from Catalonia to the Basque country. This refueling was, in principle, forbidden as an act of assistance in favor of the Loyalists. But I was satisfied with the explanation that certain pilots committed "errors of navigation." I did not consider it my business to verify from where they came or where they went. Lastly, with the aid of the Air Ministry, an aerial navigation society, "Air Pyrennées," was created and I understand that it rendered many services to the cause of liberty.

Nor did I limit my efforts to France. The Fascist countries aside, the center of opposition to the Spanish Republic was in the conservative circles in London; there, it was necessary to show the liberals and conservatives what a new Fascist victory in Europe really would mean. Many British conservatives and liberals had understood that the fate of democracy and international order was being decided in Spain, and that their country had to defend principles rather than interests on the Iberian peninsula. Lord Robert Cecil, Lord Lytton, and the Duchess of Atholl, among the conservatives, and Lloyd George and Archibald Sinclair, among the liberals, quickly joined the ranks of the defenders of republican Spain, side by side with the laborites who were headed by Philip Noel Baker. The International Peace Conference, of which Lord Robert Cecil and I were co-presidents, and which was then very power-ful in Europe, mobilized all its forces for Spain, and the associations supporting the League of Nations did the same. I went to England several times to co-ordinate our efforts with those of our British friends. Among the British conservative leaders, two in particular seemed to me capable of changing the viewpoint about the Spanish question: Anthony Eden and Winston Churchill. I had come to know Eden at Geneva, when as young cabinet members we were representing our countries at the League of Nations. But in 1936-1937 he was Minister of Foreign Affairs, and I would have aroused the legitimate irritation of Delbos by discussing with Eden problems relating to the foreign policy of England and France—especially on a point where I disagreed with the official opinion of the French cabinet. I therefore preferred to discuss the Spanish question with mutual friends who could report to him on my ideas and inform me of his personal views as a supporter of collective security and not of his official opinions as Minister. On the other hand, I discussed the ques-tion of Spain with Churchill on several occasions. As a good conservative, Churchill had begun by confusing Franco's cause with that of the social order. I was in London when we learned of the terrible bombing of Guernica, and I think it was this straw that broke the camel's back, for Churchill then realized that Spanish Franquism was using the same methods as Italian Fascism and German Nazism.

These visits to London had still another interest for me as a French Minister who defended the Spanish Republic in the Popular Front cabinet. I was anxious to find out how the stand of the French government was being interpreted by the Nonintervention Committee. We were represented on this Committee by our Ambassador, M. Corbin, an entirely honest and loyal man, but a career diplomat and a conservative. The Blum cabinet had, in reality, resigned itself to nonintervention to avoid a gulf between its foreign policy and that of the British cabinet; I therefore considered it the duty of our representative to defend the rights of the Spanish Republic as strongly as possible within the framework of the nonintervention policy. It was his task to keep a middle course between the position of the Russians, who were giving Spain every possible legal aid, and that of the English, who were prepared to let the Spanish Republic die. I realized, however, that M. Corbin was adopting the position of the British conservatives much more than that of the Popular Front cabinet. The result was that Popular Front France seemed to be drawing England into nonintervention, whereas the Blum cabinet and Blum himself had accepted this solution only to avoid breaking Anglo-French solidarity. The interpretation which our Ambassador adopted did not give a precise picture of the opinions of his government. M. Corbin undoubtedly acted in good faith, but his attitude proved that France was, in practice, dominated by its high officials who, as a result of their conservative education and their attachment to the capitalist system, were incapable of translating the will of the French people into governmental decisions.

When I returned from London, I addressed a report to Blum and Delbos in which I indicated what I thought could be done to aid the Spanish Republic without compromising our friendship with Britain. This report was drawn up in June, 1937, at a time when I began to notice a certain change of attitude in Eden toward republican Spain. But we hadn't time to extricate ourselves from the glue of nonintervention, for a few weeks later, Blum, a Premier *resigned* to nonintervention, was overthrown by the Senate and replaced by Chautemps, a determined *partisan* of nonintervention.

When Spain and France are free again, it will be possible to pay tribute to the Frenchmen who helped republican Spain and were aware of their real duty. "Help Spain! Save Spain! Cannon and airplanes for Spain," were for months and months the cries of true France. Those who supported the cause of the Spanish Republic from 1936 to 1938 are united everywhere in the world by an invisible bond.

During the winter of 1940-1941 I was asked to speak at Hamilton College, in New York State. My speech ended quite late at night. It was snowing heavily and the roads were blocked. When my talk was over, two men came up to me—dark, lean, fine Spanish types, with shining eyes and sharp features. They were former soldiers in the Loyalist Army, who, like myself, were now refugees in the United States. They were simple workers; they had walked ten miles in the snow to shake hands with me, because I had supported the Loyalist cause. At midnight they went back on foot in the deep snow. This handshake repaid me a hundredfold for the attacks which the Fascists and reactionaries—French and others—have leveled against me.

COLLECTIVE SECURITY AND RAPPROCHEMENT WITH THE SOVIET UNION

The last question to examine in this review of the foreign aerial policy of the Popular Front is that of rapprochement with the Soviet Union. My efforts in this field were more game for Fascists and reactionaries to attack. The first offensive launched against me in the press and in Parliament after I became Minister of Aviation in 1936, was directed against what *l'Echo de Paris* called my "Sovietophilia." Hitler in his speech of September, 1938, blamed me for having tried to create an alliance of French and Russian air power through Czechoslovakia. My policy towards the Soviet Union was the essential cause of my adversaries' animosity; the Spanish question did the rest. My work in the Air Ministry, or rather the caricature they presented of it, were mere pretexts with which to strike at me.

I need not apologize for being a "Sovietophile" in 1936 and 1937. A French Air Minister who had been anything else would have failed in his duty. The Red Army was then the only European force that could compare with the German Army; events have shown that a military alliance between France and Russia would have guaranteed the peace. Today, civilization is indebted to the Red Army. We may like or dislike these facts, but we should bear them in mind when judging the different political, social, and economic systems in the world.

Russian support was particularly necessary to French security in the field of aviation. In 1936-1937 Russian military aviation was the strongest in the world; Russia had more planes and crews than Germany, and the Spanish war proved that the Russian Air Force compared favorably in quality and tactics with the German. Russian combat methods—especially parachute units and dive-bombing—were the most modern; the industrial capacity of the Soviet Union was at least four-fifths that of Germany. A Franco-Soviet alliance was all the more indispensable because the French military leaders persistently failed to recognize the significance of the airplane in modern warfare; the daring farsightedness of Soviet Russia would have made it possible to compensate for the stupidity of French generals. Lastly, a military alliance, as another step in the direction of a Franco-Soviet rapprochement, would have had political as well as military repercussions. If it had fitted into the framework of collective security and the League of Nations Pact, and if it had been opened to all nations resolved to resist attempted aggressions, this alliance would have given Popular Front France and Soviet Russia the leadership in a new policy of peace and progress in Europe and throughout the world. This policy would have had the immediate support of Beneš and of Titulescu (then Rumanian Minister of Foreign Affairs); it could have avoided the Spanish Civil War, the annexation of Austria, the destruction of Czechoslovakia—all the preliminaries of the final catastrophe. There is not a single friend of peace and liberty who does not realize today than an international policy directed by Blum and Litvinoff would have benefited humanity.

The Russians had informed us on several occasions in 1936 and 1937 that they were disposed to extend into the military field the Franco-Soviet Pact, which the French Parliament had just ratified when the Popular Front came to power. I upheld the necessity for a Franco-Soviet alliance in the cabinet and in the meetings of the Little Council—Ministers of State, National Defense, Foreign Affairs, and Finance. This group was charged with the study of all questions relating to foreign policy and French security. Frequently, General Gamelin, Chief of Staff, and Alexis Leger, General Secretary of the Ministry of Foreign Affairs, took part in its meetings. I tried to force the issue on several occasions, particularly in 1936, when Hitler instituted his two-year compulsory military service, and in 1937, when it became clear that Germany was entering upon an armaments race.

Difficulties in Negotiating a Franco-Soviet Alliance

Both military and diplomatic reasons, however, blocked the negotiation of a Franco-Soviet military alliance in 1936 and 1937.

The military reasons derived from the fact that the Supreme War Council was seriously divided on the question of the strength of the Red Army. The reports of our missions and attachés, especially those of Colonel Maindras, Military Attaché at Moscow, left no doubt about this strength. But most of the generals, prisoners of their social and political prejudices, remained skeptical. The idea of a Franco-Soviet rapprochement was violently attacked in military circles by Weygand and Pétain; both denounced the Franco-Soviet Pact in press interviews. It is curious and revealing that their hostility was based on political rather than military arguments; they claimed that Russia was incapable of mobilizing, and that we had everything to lose and nothing to gain from a rapprochement with her. Their influence in military matters was considerable. Besides, the charming and smiling William C. Bullitt, who became Ambassador to France during the summer of 1936, after having represented the United States in Moscow for several years, conveyed in his conversations an impression of Russia which strengthened the thesis of Pétain and Weygand. Bullitt was intelligent, but he had obviously seen Russia through the wrong end of his opera glasses. He had great influence over Daladier. I recall that in 1937, when I was insisting on the necessity of a military agreement with Russia, Daladier answered me with his usual bluntness: "Bullitt claims that you are the only one who believes in Soviet air strength"—which may be a distortion of what his American friend said. Be that as it may, I found no one among the leaders of the French Army who shared my belief in the power of the Red Army.

The true reasons blocking a Franco-Soviet alliance at that time were diplomatic. They were the same reasons that caused the Popular Front cabinet to adopt the nonintervention policy in the Spanish war—the fear of compromising Anglo-French solidarity. The "technicians" of the Quai d'Orsay and the diplomatic corps constantly repeated that the British cabinet would frown on a military extension of the Franco-Soviet Pact. They were right. It remains to be seen whether the political conclusions they drew from the feeling of the British were justified. Opinions differed on this point in the cabinet and the Little Council—in which Maurice Violette in particular upheld with me the advisability of an alliance with Russia, whereas Chautemps and Paul Faure warned us against the dangers of such an alliance. The opinion of Blum was that we should consolidate the two bases of our foreign policy: friendship with Britain and friendship with Russia. Under the particular circumstances, he was in favor of cementing Anglo-French solidarity first, to prevent the Baldwin cabinet from following the advice of Sir John Simon or Sir Samuel Hoare (rather than that of Eden) and from embarking on a policy favorable toward the Fascist states. If the prejudices of the British conservatives could have been dissipated by the "wisdom" of the Popular Front, we should then have been able to proceed to a military alliance with Soviet Russia and with all nations determined to resist by force, if necessary, the spread of Fascism. In 1936-1937 it was possible to envisage calmly a foreign policy in two stages. Blum was consistent in 1938-1939. When Anglo-French solidarity had been assured, he became the advocate of a military agreement with Russia. I had a different conception of the problem in 1936, because, as Air Minister, I could see better than Blum the value of Soviet aid. I thought it necessary to explain at once to the British cabinet why a Franco-Soviet alliance was an essential feature of French policy. This explanation given, it was up to us to begin Franco-Soviet negotiations immediately, insisting always that the projected alliance be within the framework of collective security. The British cabinet would not have thanked us for thus confronting it with its responsibilities; but it would not have changed the bases and general orientation of its European policy, for British policy has always been formulated in terms of the interests of the British Empire, and not because of the social or political prejudices of certain ministers. At the worst had it been necessary to choose between Russia and England, it should have been observed that in 1936-1937 the military co-operation of the Soviet Union was more vital than that of Britain; it would have been better to begin the war in 1939 with Russia as an ally of France and England neutral rather than with England as an ally and Russia neutral—and no one can seriously think that England would have allied herself with Nazi Germany. Such was and still is my opinion on the outlook for a Franco-Soviet alliance in 1936 and 1937. Obviously the realization of such an alliance would have involved much discretion and care; it could hardly have been arranged in so categorical and undiplomatic a fashion as that in which I have had to summarize my views.

The Popular Front cabinet adopted, in general, the position of Blum; it attempted to base its foreign policy on a parallel development of Anglo-French solidarity and of Franco-Soviet collaboration. To say that the Russian aspect of this policy was subordinated to the British would be to misinterpret it. This subordination came about only in 1938 and 1939 after the fall of the Popular Front, when Daladier became Premier and Bonnet, Minister of Foreign Affairs. It led us to Munich, to appeasement, to a rupture with the Soviet Union, and, finally, to war under the worst of conditions. Popular Front France tried to keep an equal balance between the English and the Russian partners; she only refused to develop Franco-Soviet solidarity to the point of compromising Anglo-French solidarity, and vice versa. Every official speech of our Minister of Foreign Affairs affirmed the value of the Franco-Soviet Pact, to the fury of Hitler and the annoyance of the British. Blum's policy of collective security was based on Russia, and Blum intended to turn toward Moscow after having put into port at London. In any case, the Popular Front again planned and acted more constructively than its enemies. I am well enough acquainted with Blum's ideas to be able to say that, if the Popular Front had not fallen in 1938, France, instead of signing the Munich Pact in 1938, would have concluded a military agreement with Soviet Russia and Czechoslovakia; and the course of the world would have been changed.

Importance to France of Aerial Collaboration with Russia

In 1936-1937 Soviet aviation had more to teach us than to learn from us. Some of our prototypes and experiments could interest her; but, in return, she had mastered mass production problems which our aircraft industry had not even dreamed of before the coming of nationalization; moreover, she had developed combat methods and types of instruction infinitely more modern than ours. Information furnished by Russia could help us gain time to organize our parachute units and reform our industrial methods. In June, 1936, after speaking about the problem with Blum, I approached the Russian Ambassador and Military Attaché in Paris to find out what could be done in the interest of our countries.

As was to be expected, our Russian friends were anxious for the negotiation of a complete military alliance; they wanted the problem of Franco-Soviet collaboration to be treated in its entirety rather than in detail. But until such negotiations became possible, they agreed to help us; the principle of "technical collaboration" and technical exchanges was easily established. We arranged for two French missions to go to Russia, one of parliamentarians and the other of technicians. The parliamentary mission included members of the Air Commission, recruited from all parties; its object was to report to Parliament on the strength of Soviet aviation. The technical mission was intended to reveal to French industrialists and engineers Russian industrial power and methods; it was to show our technicians the importance of Franco-Soviet collaboration for the development of our aeronautical industry. The missions went to Russia in July and August, 1936; both returned with valuable information. Good connections between French and Russian aviation were established. The technical exchanges were organized and developed. Unfortunately, the change in the orientation of French foreign policy after the fall of the first Blum cabinet and especially after the fall of the Popular Front prevented France from profiting fully from this collaboration. Again, a bold Popular Front policy, conforming to the will of the French people and oriented toward the Soviet Union, would best have served the nation's interests.

Collaboration with Russia was fought constantly and maliciously by the French reactionaries, who were opposed to everything the nation desired.

At the end of June, 1936, we were about to organize parachute units, and asked the Russians to give us the benefit of their experience. The documents and other information they furnished made it possible for us to do in six months what otherwise would have taken us more than a year to achieve. For their part, the Russians asked our authorization to buy the patent of an airplane cannon, manufactured by the French firm of Hispano-Suiza. This was the Oerlikon cannon of Swiss origin, whose patent the Hispano-Suiza Company had acquired; it was manufactured in the Hispano-Suiza factories by a Swiss engineer. It was, therefore, not even a question of a French invention that was the sole property of the French government. The cannon had been adapted to an Hispano-Suiza engine, the patent to which had been bought by the Russians before the Popular Front came to power; having the engine, the Russians wished to buy the cannon which was its complement. France had an interest in seeing a reliable ally acquire an arm that could increase its strength. I did not hesitate for a moment to give the authorization, thinking that if we had parachute battalions and the Russians a good cannon, everyone would be satisfied except Hitler.

My granting this authorization served as the excuse for a grand reactionary offensive against me, or at least against my management of the Air Ministry. Not hesitating to betray his professional duty to the profit of his political friends, an officer of the Air Ministry had informed l'Echo de Paris that I had given this authorization. The pro-Fascist officer obviously failed to mention that the policy of technical exchanges had already begun. On July 6 l'Echo de Paris, in a two-column article, denounced my "Sovietophilia" (the first use of this phrase) and accused me of "sending the Soviets the most valuable secrets of our national defense. . . . Have we already fallen under Russian dependence? Are we a dominion of Moscow?" demanded the author. Other anti-democratic papers followed suit. On July 11 I was interpellated in the Chamber of Deputies by a conservative deputy concerning the alleged "sending to Russia of armaments which national interest required to be kept secret." It was the first time in French parliamentary history that such an accusation had been leveled against a minister taxed with national defense—and I need hardly say that this campaign wrought havoc with the morale of the French officers who thought that the Popular Front had betrayed them. The attack was defeated in public debate. I could obviously not reveal to the Chamber what information we had received from the Soviets in exchange nor could I acknowledge publicly the Soviet government's aid in the organization of our parachute units; but I proclaimed the right of the French government to organize technical exchanges with the nations that were bound by collective security pacts, and I explained the importance of this policy for the development of our aviation. My opponents' case was so poor, and their methods so objectionable, that the debate was closed with the largest vote of confidence that the Blum cabinet had yet received, 403 to 152. Even many Rightist deputies, enemies of the Popular Front, had been shocked by the possible impact of such an attack on the country's morale.

After I had furnished the Aeronautic Commission with more detailed explanations concerning Franco-Soviet collaboration, the Commission, which included representatives of all political parties, unanimously approved my conduct. Nevertheless, the newspapers continued their campaign; things came to the point where certain nationalist deputies wrote a public letter denouncing "the thoughtlessness and violence" with which l'Echo de Paris had attacked me. In spite of this, the campaign did not stop; it continued until the day that the reactionaries and Fascists found it more convenient to concentrate their attacks on my shipments of planes to the Spanish Republic.

The campaign of l'Echo de Paris against my "Sovietophilia" not only tended to paralyze Franco-Soviet collaboration, but to envenom Anglo-French relations, by making the English believe that we had mysterious agreements with the Soviets; moreover, it troubled the consciences of Air Force officers. Already well prepared by Croix de Feu propaganda, these officers were only too ready to accept as gospel truth the rumors of the anti-democratic press. I bear no grudges and should like to believe in the good faith and naïveté of certain editors of l'Echo de Paris. But if I may pass a broad judgment on the demoralization of French officers from 1934 to 1939, I must say that the campaigns of l'Echo de Paris were more pernicious than those of l'Action Française, Gringoire, and Flambeau, the outspokenly Fascist papers. The slander which wears the mask of virtue is the most dangerous. L'Echo de Paris profited from an old reputation of patriotism—for, by insisting on their own patriotism, the men of the Right had finally convinced the French bourgeoisie that they had a monopoly on it. It was the "newspaper of the clergy and the soldiers" and thus addressed itself to an honest but credulous audience; it had famous retired military leaders on its staff, such as General de Castelnau, and it passed as the interpreter of General Staff ideas. More than half the officers of the French Army read it. When this paper had repeated ad nauseam that the Air Minister was sending "the most valuable secrets of our national defense to the Soviets" and "the best airplanes ordered from the Air Forces . . . to the Spanish Anarchists and Communists," even decent people who lacked critical sense imagined that France was being betrayed by the Popular Front government. They fell easy prey to the Fifth Column and sincerely believed they were doing their duty by taking part in the plots which were being hatched against the French Republic. L'Echo de Paris also published the famous document which the testimony of General Gerodias revealed to the Riom Court—a document handed over by Pétain's collaborator, Commandant Loustaleau-Lacau, which, in the words of Daladier, was destined to "ravage the morale of the officers."

These campaigns had no effect on my acts or decisions; they merely made my task a little more difficult. They prevented France from taking full advantage of Russian collaboration; they provoked against me the kind of hatred that was to drive others to suicide. I was not affected by being called traitor by the Fascists. The technical exchanges between France and the Soviets continued; it was not my fault that they were not developed further.

In the political sphere, aeronautic collaboration between France and the Soviets was to be an extension of technical collaboration.

France was bound to the Soviet Union by an agreement conceived only in general terms, and it was my duty as Air Minister to see how this pact could be enforced in case of war. This was a delicate task, since France refused to negotiate a formal military alliance as long as diplomatic preparation had not been arranged with England. But as time passed, German rearmament proceeded and the need grew for the development of Franco-Soviet political and military collaboration. When in February, 1937, the Permanent Committee of National Defense had decided that "there was no need to extend the Air Force plans," I told Blum that only an aviation agreement with the Soviet Union would permit us to stand up to the German forces. Blum agreed with me about the blindness manifested by French Army leaders with respect to aviation; but, faced with a technical problem—the relative importance of different armaments in national defense—he had to take into consideration the position of the Permanent Committee and the attitude of Daladier. I told the Premier that if we did not wish a direct agreement with Russia, we could arrange one through the medium of Czechoslovakia; for we had military agreements with Czechoslovakia, who, in turn, was bound to the Soviet Union. I wrote to Beneš, explaining the necessity and the difficulty of France's allying herself more closely with Russia. Czechoslovakia was herself in a difficult situation; even more than France, she was obliged to take account of the policy of the British conservatives, whose tendencies toward appeasement she foresaw; and in her effort not to irritate England, she had to avoid any move which might irritate Hitler. But the Czechoslovakian democracy had more courage than the French, because her constitution was more explicitly democratic and her political system less dominated by the forces of economic reaction.

Beneš sent to Paris a man whom he trusted implicitly, Rybka, now Minister of Foreign Affairs in the Czech government-in-exile. We studied the existing agreements between France and Czechoslovakia as well as the relations between the Soviets and Czechoslovakia. We found it possible to use, that is, to adjust, these agreements in such a way that in case of need they could serve as a basis for military collaboration among France, Czechoslovakia, and Russia. It was, indeed, a narrow basis, but it was the only means of preparing the way for a military alliance, and in 1937 there was always a possibility and expectation that it could be broadened. As it was, it permitted us preparatory work, which was immediately undertaken by the General Staff of the Air Force; we considered the possibility of action in the sphere of aviation which the coalition of French, Soviet, and Czech forces would afford us. The position of Blum, Beneš, and Litvinoff on collective security is so well known that it is hardly necessary to say that the sole object of these studies was to determine what we would do in case an aggressive war was directed against one of the nations signatory to the League of Nations. It would be absurd to think that we were planning to attack Germany, which was Hitler's contention.

The logical outcome of this policy was to be an aviation pact signed by France, Czechoslovakia, and Russia. When I left the Air Ministry in January, 1938, everything was in readiness for this pact. After the fall of the Popular Front, these projects were abandoned. My successor in the Air Ministry lacked imagination on an international scale and nourished the usual prejudices of his circle against Soviet Russia. Besides, Delbos had been succeeded by Bonnet, about whom nothing further need be said. Instead of turning toward Moscow, France's foreign policy turned toward Berlin, with the success to which the events of September, 1938, and March and September, 1939, bore witness.

Finally, my efforts to activate Franco-Soviet collaboration extended to the military sphere.

In 1937 I had realized that the leaders of the Permanent Committee and the Supreme Council of National Defense were blind to the importance of Soviet Russia and of air power in modern warfare. Their hostility to Russia could be explained by reasons of domestic policy; thus Marshal Pétain, in an interview published in *Flambeau,* the official organ of the Croix de Feu, on the eve of the general elections of May, 1938, had said of the Franco-Soviet Pact: "In extending our hand to Moscow, we have extended it to Communism. . . . We have let Communism enter the circle of avowable doctrines. We shall very likely have cause to regret it." With actual reasons masked under military pretexts, I concluded that the best way to break resistance would be to establish indisputably the importance and necessity of a Franco-Soviet alliance.

Each year the Centers of Advanced Military Studies of the Army and of the Air Force took up one major military problem. These two Centers were attended by the young colonels who were destined to fill the highest positions of the General Staff—so much so that the Centers came to be called, somewhat ironically, a "school for marshals." In 1937 I suggested that in their program the question of a war of coalition with Russia against Germany and Italy be included. My proposal was considered scandalous. Until that time the General Staff had taken for granted that Italy would be on our side in a European war, or at least, that she would not be on Hitler's. Marshal Pétain, in particular, declared it inadmissible that one could ever envisage a war between France and Italy, both Mediterranean powers, allies in the World War, bound by Latin fraternity, etc. I let him talk, and held fast. When the programs of the Army and Air Force Centers came up for approval, I obtained the permission of Daladier—who was far more intelligent than his military leaders—to have the hypothesis of a German-Italian coalition chosen by the two Centers. For an entire winter the elite of the French Army studied this problem and based its exercises on the information that the General Staff had collected. When I left the Air Ministry in January, 1938, I asked that the conclusions of these studies be communicated to me confidentially. The students concluded that (1) it was impossible for France, even with the aid of England and Czechoslovakia, to overcome a German-Italian coalition, especially in the air—the Allies could resist, but not triumph; and (2) a relatively easy victory was certain if the Allies obtained the aid of Russia.

This information has never before been published. Before the French defeat I could not have revealed it without informing Germany of the limitations of the French Army and the weakness of the Anglo-French coalition. But there is no longer any reason not to underscore the importance of the work done by our two Centers of Advanced Military Studies in 1937-1938. As a result of these studies alone, the French General Staff should not have rested until it had obtained a military alliance with the Soviets. The General Staff of the Air Force in particular, knew that such an alliance meant a guarantee of victory in the air. The Air Minister did nothing to bring about such negotiations, behaving as if his own experts had not demonstrated that the aid of Soviet aviation was a matter of life and death for France.

Answers to Vichy's Accusations

A judgment cannot be based on hypotheses. But I was so intimately involved in the fight against Fascism, in the action of the Popular Front government, and in the Franco-Russian rapprochement that I may safely call the fall of the Popular Front a tragedy in this respect. If Blum had remained in power in 1936, if the strength of the Popular Front had grown instead of diminishing, there would have been no Munich; instead, France would have signed a military agreement with the Soviet Union in 1938, and the peace of the world would have been preserved. When I left the Air Ministry, French and European aerial security were guaranteed, thanks to the collaboration of France, Czechoslovakia, and Russia; after my departure, it disintegrated.

I do not claim that my work was perfect; it had its good as well as its bad side. I am merely awaiting the demonstration that, given the political, social, and military circumstances of France in 1936-1937, it was possible to do better. My work was at once a fight against the growth of Fascism in the Air Force and against the conservatism of the military leaders, who preferred battalions and warships to airplanes; it was a fight for the Spanish Republic and for Franco-Soviet collaboration, in other words, for the defense and construction of that collective security without which France was condemned to fall.

Of all the accusations which my enemies marshaled against me—in the course of a campaign of slander which has not yet ended—the Supreme Court of Justice retained only three complaints. It blamed me for having shown "incompetence" in the organization of the Air Force: I might reply that the organization of the Air Force depended on the General Staff and not on the Minister of Aviation, but I prefer to answer that the organization of 1936-1937 included younger officers, aerial divisions, and parachute units. The Court blamed me for nationalizing the factories and showing weakness toward the workers: I might reply that the law voted almost unanimously by Parliament had decreed the nationalization, yet I prefer to say that the nationalization achieved the decentralization of industry and the improvement of machinery and quintupled production between 1936 and 1939; as to my alleged "weakness" toward the workers, it may be judged by the fact that while I was Air Minister, there was not a single strike in the national factories. The Court blamed me for having sent airplanes to republican Spain: I might retort that these airplanes could not have been used in 1940, but I prefer to express my bitter regret that the nonintervention policy limited my shipments. I might answer all the accusations of the Supreme Court with judicial arguments: I prefer to say that I regret none of the acts for which I was blamed. I am sorry only that I did not carry out the Popular Front program more fully, for it expressed the will of the people and the interests of the country.

My aerial policy, too, had its advantages and disadvantages. It is open to criticism in all its details. But no one can deny that it tended toward the organization of an invincible European bloc by means of the collaboration of France, Czechoslovakia, and Russia and the support of nations attacked by Fascism. I am waiting to see my policy compared to the petty ideas and enterprises of those who preceded or succeeded me. Above all, I cannot think it will suffer by comparison with the great betrayal by the Fascists and collaborationists. The French people alone have the right to make these comparisons and to judge.

In their eyes I shall remain the man who fought for the support of Spain, for an agreement with Russia, for recognition of the importance of aviation in French national defense. My attitude in these matters will continue to bring me, as in the past, the confidence of the people and the hostility of the French haute bourgeoisie. My work has been praised without exception by the representatives of the working class, by all who incarnated the spirit of the French Revolution; and it has been criticized, likewise without exception, by every admirer of Fascism, by all the enemies of the people and of the French Republic. If it is true that a man has the friends and enemies he deserves, I should be satisfied. I am content not to be the friend of the generals, bankers, and aristocrats who betrayed France; for I am the friend of Édouard Herriot, Léon Blum, and Maurice Thorez, who are to me the true representatives of the French spirit.

PART III

CONCLUSION

"The French Republic is as invincible as reason; it is as immortal as truth. When liberty has made a conquest like France, no human power can dislodge it."

"Force can overthrow a throne, but only wisdom can be the base of a Republic. . . . The founding of the Republic is not a child's game."

ROBESPIERRE: Speech at the Convention on the Principles of the Revolutionary Government, December 25, 1793.

"Article 35—When the government violates the rights of the people, insurrection is for the people and for every section of the people, the most sacred of rights and the most indispensable of duties."

DECLARATION OF THE RIGHTS OF MAN AND OF THE CITIZENS, 1793.

11

I T IS UNNECESSARY to dwell on the judicial outcome of the Riom trial: it was won by the accused and lost by Pétain's government. By adjourning the trial *sine die* in 1942 and by suppressing it completely in 1943, Vichy admitted itself incapable of proving the guilt of the men it had indicted and denounced as responsible for the war and the defeat—men whom its leaders had condemned in advance without a hearing. Pétain and his ministers bear the shame for imprisoning at Portalet or turning over to the Gestapo, men whom their own judges did not dare pronounce guilty.

SIGNIFICANCE OF THE RIOM TRIAL

The political consequences of the Riom trial cannot be overemphasized. The trial was the touchstone for French resistance to Fascism. No single event contributed more to the revival of a public opinion that had been crushed by the defeat and then led astray by Vichy propaganda. In spite of the orders to the press, there emerged two opposing conceptions of law, justice, government, politics, and authority, and their relations to the individual. For the first time since Pétain's coming to power, two men, Léon Blum and Édouard Daladier, were able to uphold the democratic doctrine of the French majority against the dictatorial doctrine of the Vichy government. These two conceptions were not new, but they were stated in new terms, and the clash took on a tragic character from the circumstances of the moment. This clash brought home once more to Frenchmen the historic conflict that had been going on for a hundred and fifty years, dividing the nation into two factions—irreconcilable, in my opinion—the partisans of the French Revolution and the partisans of the *ancien régime*.

Whether they wanted to or not, all thinking Frenchmen have been forced to take a stand in this conflict of the "Two France's" (the striking title which Professor Roger Soltau applied to a study of the factions in his book *French Political Thought in the Nineteenth Century*). No generation has been able to refrain from partisanship; our fathers had the Dreyfus and Boulanger affairs; their fathers had the Commune and Marshal MacMahon's attempted coup d'état; and their grandfathers had the Revolution of 1848 and the coup

369

d'état of Napoleon III. The previous generation had fought the Restoration or supported its inglorious disciplines, and those who preceded them had been the men of the Revolution or of the Empire. Riom is merely the last link in the chain. The trial showed the observer of ideological currents in contemporary politics that Hitler and Pétain have been able neither to arrest nor alter the march of French thought.

The conflict between the French Revolution and the *ancien régime* will last as long as do the circumstances which engender it. So long as one social class is privileged by comparison with the others, and holds economic power and all the attendant advantages in ever increasing concentration, this class will try to preserve the status quo beneficial to it and so will come into conflict with the rest of the nation. The ideological conflict between the partisans of dictatorship and the partisans of political liberty masks the reality of class struggle in its most elementary form, and this reality becomes daily more naked as it grows more brutal. The differences between the interests that the privileged class wants to defend and those that the majority of the people tries to uphold are not only *quantitative* but *qualitative,* as the founders of French democracy pointed out. "The interest of the common people is the general interest," said Robespierre in 1791, "the interest of the rich is a particular interest."

The Riom trial showed how much more powerful social reality is than political appearances. It was not only the French Republic—a political regime —which was called to trial before the Supreme Court of Justice; it was the Popular Front—a movement which was as much social as political, the desperate attempt of the French people to realize an economic and social New Deal by democratic methods. By setting the problem of the Popular Front in its entirety, by explaining its origins, accomplishments, and failures, Blum showed that government by the people's representatives is merely an illusion when not accompanied by control of economic power. It follows that a democratic government cannot adjust itself to the present class system, and that political liberty presupposes the achievement of social equality.

In Blum's mind—and those who heard him could not give a different interpretation—these declarations supported the Marxist interpretation of history and of social phenomena. It demonstrated from recent French experience that political power is fatally dependent on economic power; that the state is a *superstructure* based on the social *infrastructure;* it reinforced the conception that the modern state can only be an instrument of domination in the hands of the class group holding economic power, not an independent arbiter between class antagonisms. This demonstration was particularly convincing in a country where military dictatorship had just suppressed public liberties to impose the corporatist hierarchy. Pétain's policy fortified Blum's arguments. These arguments had a strong impact since the Marxist theses were familiar to a large proportion of the French nation, where Socialism and Communism always played an important role in politics and in the labor movement.

Thus the Riom trial has contributed to the regrouping of political forces in France. It has proved to all democrats that it is impossible to base a democracy on anti-democratic institutions. Translated into present day terms, the hereditary conflict seems to be not a conflict of doctrines but a conflict of classes; the hopes echoed since the French Revolution will not be realized until class hierarchies disappear. Democracy postulates Socialism.

The Riom trial also revealed the differences of value and quality that separated the common people from the haute bourgeoisie in France.

"If all the leaders had been as good as the common soldiers," said Robespierre in 1793, "Europe (monarchistic and counterrevolutionary Europe) would have been conquered long ago." These words are still true; they apply not only to the military but to the civil leaders, to the financiers and industrialists as well as to the generals. If the social class that dominated the Army, the national economy, and the administration had been as good as the common people, there could have been neither defeat nor dictatorship.

Englishmen or Americans who traveled in France before the war had few contacts with the peasants and petits bourgeois, and almost none with the workers; they saw only one side of France. Similarly, the large majority of Frenchmen who settled outside their country and almost all the refugees from French Fascism belong to the haute bourgeoisie; they have the defects and the qualities of the milieu that produced them. The Committee of National Liberation in Algiers is composed almost entirely of men who are bourgeois by origin, education, and mode of life. This gives an untrue impression.

In every country, I could almost say in every human being, there are two great ideological currents fed in turn by several streams: the progressive (which sometimes takes a revolutionary form) and the conservative (which sometimes takes a reactionary form). Everywhere the common people are progressive, and the bourgeoisie, conservative. But between the French common people and the bourgeoisie the gap is greater than that between the two classes in other countries, assuming the same degree of political maturity and the same social organization. This is due in part to the revolutionary form which the political struggle for French democracy has taken in the past; it is conditioned also by the structure of French society, which is more stratified, more ossified, less fluid than in any other country.

The common people of France are intelligent. It was of them that Charles Péguy wrote: " 'What a pity,' observed God, 'when there are no more Frenchmen, there will be no one to understand some of the things I do. . . . You French people, the peoples of the earth call you frivolous because you are quick. . . . You reach the goal before the others have even started.' "

The common people of France are generous; they have championed all the great causes of history. No one has fought more relentlessly against tyranny; in the Spanish Civil War the French furnished the largest proportion of volunteers for the International Brigade.

The French people, like other individuals, have their defects. They are impulsive; their love for logic makes them overlook the historical and philosophical aspects of things; their love of clarity pushes them into excessive simplifications, into dangerous abstractions. As De Tocqueville noted, they are "full of contrasts, constantly doing worse or better than what was expected of them, at times above, at times below, the level of mankind. . . never so free as to go beyond the reach of slavery nor so enslaved as to be unable to break a yoke. . . . The most brilliant of all European nations, the most fitted to become in turn an object of admiration, of pity—but never of indifference."

Largely under the domination of a privileged class, the children of the French common people have been unable to develop fully their inner resources, and are admirable raw material. Just as they are, with their faults and virtues, the French people take their place with the best of the Old and New World. Their political experience has ripened in social conflict. For a century and a half they have known instinctively the best solutions; but the imperfections of the French economic system and the defects of the French constitutions have rarely allowed them to express their views on public affairs. In my political experience I have found more wisdom and knowledge of men in the mayor of a village, in a schoolteacher who is also town clerk, and in a trade-union secretary—those three pillars of French democracy—than in the generals, financiers, and industrialists at the top of the social hierarchy, who claim today, as in the past, the leadership of French politics and of the nation.

By the French common people I mean not only the workers and peasants but that part of the middle class which has remained faithful to the spirit of the French Revolution; the artisans and civil servants, the small businessmen and technicians, the members of the liberal professions, who derive their income from their own work and not from inherited wealth, speculation, or the exploitation of the labor of others. Placing human values above material goods, they consider themselves of the same class as the French worker, of the same human race as the natives in the Colonies; they dream of a society in which the hierarchies of capitalism will be replaced by the social equality of free men—in short, I refer to all those who, by allying themselves with the masses, created the Popular Front and made the fight against Fascism possible.

I have some right to speak of this class, both city dwellers and country people. I represented them in Parliament for twelve years, and they upheld me in my political endeavors, the surest sign, perhaps, that I correctly interpreted their will. The most dynamic element of the French people is its working class, which carries in its wake the timid petite bourgeoisie. In the political education and the traditions of the workers are found the best reasons for thinking that France has not ceased to be a great nation.

Conversely, the French bourgeoisie is one of the worst, the most corrupt and egotistical in contemporary history. It is no longer the Third Estate—which fought the nobility and the clergy—but a caste that clings fiercely and viciously to the defense of its privileges. This judgment applies to the bourgeoisie taken as a whole and considered as a distinct class; it does not necessarily apply to all the individuals of this class, the majority of whom have been conditioned by their education and mode of life, without even being capable of understanding what has happened to them. "Unless he is a genius," wrote Péguy, "a rich man cannot imagine poverty." This congenital lack of imagination prevents the French bourgeois from taking a broad view of his time. In saying this, I am not forgetting the eminent role which the bourgeoisie has played in the material and intellectual development of modern France. Nor do I forget to distinguish between the haute bourgeoisie, isolated in its ivory tower, and the petite bourgeoisie, in touch with the masses. All rules have exceptions: Blum, Herriot, De Gaulle, and many others are bourgeois. But considering general behavior, it is evident that this class can no longer exercise its power of leadership without serious danger to France. Events have left it far behind. More than ever it deserves the lashes with which Balzac and Zola scored its egotism. France will take her place in the vanguard of progressive nations, she will contribute once more to the progress of man-kind—only if she frees herself from the domination of the bourgeoisie.

Since June, 1940, the people have fought, the "rich" have collaborated. For the most part, the resistance to Fascism and Hitlerism is, or has been, popu-lar and democratic. This resistance includes two elements: the passive element, consisting of almost all Frenchmen who were furious to see their country occupied by German troops with the support of the Vichy government; and the active element, leading the underground battle of sabotage and civil war. Eighty per cent of those who have upheld Vichy's policy of collaboration belong to the haute bourgeoisie. Eighty per cent of those who form the active element of resistance belonged to Popular Front organizations before 1939. Most of the hostages, the so-called criminals, executed by the Gestapo or the Vichy authorities—50,000 in two years, or one every twenty minutes—supported the Popular Front. When the balance sheet of resistance and betrayal is compiled, it will show that the workers were in the vanguard of the fight for liberty, while the haute bourgeoisie formed the battalions of the Fifth Column. The honor lost by Marshal Pétain and his collaborators is being saved by the common people.

Here again, the opposition of the "Two France's" is entirely natural. The French masses continue the battle against Fascism which began on the 6th of February, 1934; the present war against the Gestapo and Vichy is for them the logical and tragic continuation of the old fight against the Croix de Feu and the Cagoulards. Those who placed their hatred of Socialism above their respect for national sovereignty continue to fear that the collapse of Fascist dictatorships in liberated Europe will release everywhere the forces of progress and revolution. It is as normal for a militant supporter of the Popular Front to engage in sabotage and active resistance, as it would be paradoxical for a former Cagoulard to participate in such activities. The defeat of Hitler means for the latter only the material liberation of French territory; the former expects not only this liberation, which is ardently desired by all Frenchmen, be they of the Left or of the Right, but also the political, moral, and social liberation of the people. The patriotism of the one is checked by his Fascist ideology and his class interest; the patriotism of the other is intensified by the identity of the national interest and his political philosophy and conception of history.

Thus the Riom trial has recalled the elementary truths of French politics. It reveals the permanent conflict hidden beneath the cloak of contemporary events, and shows that this conflict, in its last analysis, is only a class struggle between the bourgeoisie, which collaborates to preserve its privileges, and the common people, which resists to allow the French nation to progress.

"What's past is prologue," wrote Shakespeare. The Riom trial helps us not only to understand the policy of the Popular Front—the recent past—but enables us to appreciate the efforts of the Committee of National Liberation of Algiers—the present.

THE ALGIERS COMMITTEE OF NATIONAL LIBERATION

If it is true that the battle of resistance to collaboration is the present form of the battle between the "Two France's," one may well be astonished at the political and social composition of the Committee of National Liberation formed at Algiers in May, 1943.

To direct a civil war actually fought by petits bourgeois and workers, it would have been desirable that the National Committee be constituted to give a true picture of underground resistance, or, at least, that its political tendencies conform to those of the resistance. The Algiers Committee includes no workers or peasants. Its members are honest, courageous, patriotic, and devoted to the public welfare. They have undertaken a difficult task, and it is the duty of every democrat to second their efforts. Each is a good technician—but government by technicians is by no means a form of democratic government. Most of these men are unknown to the French people. Since political opinions cannot be used as a criterion for classifying them, their professions must be used—and their professions are revealing. The miner from the Pas de Calais, the farmer from the Landes, the teacher from Savoy, the mechanic from the Parisian suburb certainly have been surprised to find their resistance represented abroad by a syndicate of generals, businessmen, and officials.

The absolute loyalty of the president and members of the Algiers Committee and the democratic feeling of the majority of its members give sufficient assurance that the basic interests of the French people are safe. But the composition of the Committee is a cause of weakness.

This was apparent in its first acts. As soon as General de Gaulle tried to purge the Army and administration of Fascist elements, he encountered the objections of Generals Georges and Giraud, and, more particularly, counsels of moderation from the conservative elements within the Committee. As in the days of the National Union cabinets, one could see the congenital weakness of a coalition which, under pretext of unity, has brought together men of radically opposed political ideas. The Algiers Committee has been driven to half measures which satisfy no one and cannot keep pace with events: *nascitur ridiculus mus!* Instead of sending up for trial men guilty of so many arbitrary arrests—crimes punishable under criminal law—they were merely asked to resign; the guiltiest, Peyrouton, received a letter of thanks, which will serve as a precedent for all of Pétain's and Laval's collaborators. An investigating committee has been named to consider sanctions to be taken against the former collaborators; its decisions must be awaited with confidence, but the committee will have difficulty in reaching some of them—intimates of General Giraud and the Cagoulards who came to Algiers under his aegis; it will be unable to reach the ex-collaborators of the Vichy government who have become important members of the De Gaulle organization—and if these big Fascist fish slip through the net, why should the minnows be caught? Instead of putting democratic leaders at the head of the Army—or, if enough could not be found, appointing *commissaires* to deal with political questions, thus reviving a tradition of the Army of the First Republic—the anti-De Gaullist Fascists were replaced by pro-De Gaullist anti-democrats, a shrewd move for the present, but one which may prove fatal. Such men do not inspire any more confidence among democrats than do the monarchists who surrounded General Giraud when he went to Algiers. Public life in North Africa has not been revived but kept dormant. Even now, a distinction unworthy of the French spirit is maintained between North African "Jews" and "Frenchmen."

We should not, of course, judge too soon the work of the Algiers Committee, which at the time of this writing is barely three months old. It deserves all the more credit because the majority of its members have no experience in political affairs; they must learn their new work. But one cannot help thinking of the role the Committee could have played in contemporary politics if, instead of including so many representatives of the General Staff and of the high financial bourgeoisie, it had included men of the masses. A truly representative National Committee would have increased France's stature in the eyes of the world. It would have given French resistance a world-wide importance, instead of restricting it to the defensive reaction of an invaded people against its invader. It would have taken up the tradition of the French Revolution, and would have dealt with colonial, international, and social problems—the three major problems of our time.

In the name of Liberty, such a committee would have revived Briand's ideas of a European Federation and thus would have put France at the head of the little nations of Europe, tying the future of the world to French ideals.

In the name of Equality, it would have made an appeal to all colored peoples to join the battle against Fascism, thus establishing a link between the conservatism of the British Empire and the movements of liberation appearing in the Far East, India, in the Arab world, and among the black peoples.

In the name of Fraternity, it would have fought the anti-democratic corporatism of Marshal Pétain, prevented the dollar speculation of French bankers and their excessive influence on the Colonies, and begun economic and social democracy. This action would have wiped out the memory of the delivery of refugees and hostages to the Gestapo, the barbarous treatment of Jews and Spanish republicans, and all the dishonorable acts for which Vichy stands guilty before humanity.

The social and political composition of the Algiers Committee prevents it from undertaking this rehabilitation. To achieve it, the majority of its members would have to burn what they had adored and adore what they have burned; such abjuration runs counter to human nature.

The composition of the Committee is not only the cause of its democratic impotence; it also limits its powers and reduces its competence.

The formation of the Committee corresponded to the necessities of the war, but no one has the right to maintain that the Committee corresponds to the political sentiments of the French nation. Under these circumstances, Committee powers cannot outlast the duration of the war. To decide otherwise would be to act arbitrarily and run the risk of substituting another dictatorship for Pétain's. Dictatorship could be forced on France if the Committee, backed by Giraud's army, opposed the manifestations of the popular will which will take place after the defeat of the German Army.

Generals de Gaulle and Giraud, President Roosevelt, and Prime Minister Churchill have all affirmed that the French people will be free to choose their regime and their representatives. For these affirmations to become a reality, this choice must be exercised not *after* the total liberation of the territory but in the course of this liberation. It should begin by the organization of local governments, for it would be dangerous to leave this in the hands of Vichy-appointed civil servants or other partisans of collaboration. Even summary elections or spontaneous manifestations of the will of the people will permit the reconstruction of a democratic public life on a basis of reality.

By itself, liberation will be *fait nouveau;* it will create a political situation different from that which led to the formation of the Algiers Committee. The true political forces of France will appear and the leaders of the underground will become known. It is doubtful that these forces will accept the guardianship of the Committee in its present form. They probably will demand an enlargement and alteration of the basis of the Committee; similarly, they will require that the local assemblies (the municipal councils and general councils) and the underground organizations be used for the provisional administration of the country and for the organization of elections that will express the national will. The political forces and the leaders of the underground must have complete freedom. It would be prejudicial to permit a non-elected committee to act indefinitely on behalf of the French people.

These considerations have been reinforced by legal arguments—particularly those of international public law. Certain Frenchmen in Algiers, London, and the United States were worried by the delay in recognizing the Algiers Committee. Their impatience was natural. The United States would have profited by the early establishment of a formula of recognition determining the Committee's legal status. But one must observe, first, that Roosevelt, Churchill, and Stalin have had more urgent problems to consider; the delay in opening a second front was more important, even for the French. In addition, the composition of the Committee has made difficult the choice of a satisfactory formula.

What is the Algiers Committee? It is obviously not a legitimate government which could be recognized *de jure.* Nor is it a *de facto* government of the French nation, as its power does not extend to metropolitan France. It could be considered the *de facto* government of the Colonies, having accepted its authority and official representation of French interests. According to its communiqués, however, the Committee claims to be the "trustee" of the French nation. The term is incorrect, unless it is explained that the trustee is a "self-appointed trustee," or what French law calls a *gérant d'affaires*. Even if it were demonstrated that the Committee had received full power to be the representative of the underground organizations, its legal capacity would not be changed; these organizations are without doubt the noblest element of the French nation, but they are not the nation, the sovereignty of which is indivisible and cannot be delegated. The Committee is not a substitute for the legitimate authorities of the Republic; it is merely the representative of the Republic abroad, and manages the affairs of the Republic for the period of time and on the territory where the legitimate authorities cannot exercise their power because of circumstances beyond their control. This preserves the principle of national sovereignty and prevents the identification of the Committee with the Vichy government, which is not a *gérant d'affaires* but an usurper. It allows the widest interpretation of the recognition given by the governments of the United Nations. In the concert of the United Nations the Committee is the representative of France; it is the administrator of those French overseas territories having joined it; it has the right to lead the French war effort within the framework of inter-Allied collaboration; it represents the interests of the Republic through its diplomatic privileges. But it is for the French people themselves to establish at the proper time their government and constitution.

As the powers of the Committee are thus limited *ratione temporis*, its competence is reduced *ratione materiae*. As a *gérant d'affaires*, it must limit itself to "acts of administration and conservation." Its functions are administrative rather than governmental. It cannot change laws. It can, and must, organize an army, take part in military operations against the Axis powers—for in its mission is involved the liberation of France—administer the French Colonies, enforce the laws of the Republic, especially with respect to the former collaborators of Vichy who have committed crimes punishable by these laws.

The Committee can participate in all negotiations for an armistice or for the establishment of a provisory treaty of peace. It must represent the French Republic in the concert of the United Nations, but it cannot sign a peace treaty setting up a new international regime, as its members cannot substitute their will for that of the French people in matters dealing with problems as important as disarmament, the colonial regime of the future, European organizations, modifications to be made in the sovereignty of the state, etc. This limitation of competence stems from the facts as well as from the law. When General Giraud declared in Canada that there is much that is "good" in National Socialism, he cautiously avoided explaining what he meant by "good," and General de Gaulle has never told us whether the "Fourth Republic" of his dreams is a soviet republic, a Socialist republic, a parliamentary democracy, or a capitalist state. When they venture to discuss the problems of the future, the two most important men of the Algiers Committee limit themselves to generalities, which anyone might interpret as he wishes, and offer no solution. For them, this is expedient; more precise statements could not satisfy both the anti-Fascists who form 80 per cent of the "active resistance" and the anti-democrats who are still on the staff of Giraud's army.

This general discussion of public law makes it easier to understand the composition of the National Committee of Liberation, which corresponds to the duties of a *gérant d'affaires* and not to the needs of a provisory government. The Algiers Committee is a commission of experts, not a government council. It is therefore natural that it be composed of technicians of the Civil Service, Army, and business, and not of representatives of political parties. To avoid all misunderstanding, its decrees should be worded not "in the name of the French people by the Committee of Liberation," but "in the name of the French people for the government of the Republic 'in bond' by the Committee of Liberation."

The limitation of the Committee's competence *ratione materiae* has created a situation which worries all democrats. Unable to speak a language which would conform to the political thought of the majority of Frenchmen, the Committee is reduced to placing the accent on nationalism, and it is a short way from nationalism to chauvinism. This nationalism is the dangerous type much encountered in Europe, and should not to be confused with the nationalism of the American political scene, which does not attempt to promote the good of one nation at the expense of others. European nationalism, through the excessive zeal of its adherents to obtain a dominant position for the nation concerned, has had much to do with causing wars, and has discarded the democracy and liberalism which were once part of its precepts.

The Algiers Committee emphasizes the "national" side of the resistance, instead of its human character. By entering on the path of nationalism, it gives grounds for fear to all those who want to see France participate in the organization of international life. In unofficial propaganda this nationalism has sometimes taken the shape of arrogance. This shrinking from humanism to nationalism may lose for France the great opportunity offered by events.

Unable to rally the French masses around a political ideology suited to their temperament, the Committee tries to unite them around a man. As in primitive or decadent societies, hero worship replaces the discussion of ideas. Hero worship, when added to a nationalist urge, is no sign of political health. A certain type of "De Gaullism" is developing which is only a deviation, a hypertrophy, of the gratitude which patriotic Frenchmen feel for General de Gaulle. De Gaullism springs into being as did "Boulangism," from an abdication of criticism, from a triumph of instinct over reason, coinciding with a period of national trial. The danger of this deviation should escape no one—it should escape General de Gaulle least of all, for he runs the risk of becoming its victim rather than its beneficiary. The best remedy for the malady of De Gaullism is in a reawakening of democratic political life in North Africa.

It would be unjust to blame the composition of the Algiers Committee on the political inexperience of its organizers. Statesmen more familiar with governmental practice would have avoided many errors; they would have made up for the presence of certain military and financial figures by naming qualified representatives of workers' organizations. But one should not forget that General de Gaulle, the true head of the Algiers Committee, did not have a free hand; he had to contend with several obstacles.

There was the Empire Council formed by General Giraud and composed exclusively of reactionary and pro-Fascist elements which had remained faithful to the ideal of Pétain's "National Revolution." For military reasons, which were explained at length in the American press, it had the support of the occupation authorities and of Washington. The Algiers Committee was formed, after long and painful negotiations, by a fusion between the National Committee of London (the De Gaulle Committee) and the Empire Council. General de Gaulle had to agree to let Giraud appoint half the members of the new Committee, and he had to proceed cautiously to drive out the most Fascistic elements of the Empire Council—Peyrouton, Bergeret, and Boisson. He succeeded, but he was obliged to throw ballast overboard, accepting other elements not too friendly to democracy. The Algiers Committee is therefore not a political emanation of the resistance; it is not representative of the French people; it is a compromise between the tendencies of the old National Committee of London and of the old Empire Council.

There was also the spirit of the African Army. Led for more than two years by Vichy-appointed commanders, especially by General Weygand, this Army included a large proportion of anti-democratic officers. Moreover, during the spring of 1943 several hundred officers, including General Georges, arrived in North Africa. Patriotic and animated by a sincere desire for revenge, they wanted to fight the German Army, but they remained openly faithful to the person and spirit of Marshal Pétain. They detested De Gaulle as much as they did the republican system, refusing to pardon the one because he had betrayed his caste in revolting against his superiors, and the other because it had wanted to subordinate them to the will of the people. One of the first tasks of the Algiers Committee was "to bring the French Army back into the war at the side of the Allies"; the governments of London and Washington desired the rapid formation of a French Army capable of taking part in projected or current military operations. They advised General de Gaulle not to alienate the men whose aid was considered necessary for the preparation of this Army. Contrary to French tradition and democratic doctrine, contrary to the feelings of the French people, the political tendencies of the officers' corps weighed heavily in the formation of the Algiers Committee.

With these handicaps and organized by two generals hostile to each other, the Algiers Committee could not be composed in any other way. Under the circumstances, it is apparent why the democratic and anti-Fascist organizations of the underground decided to support the Committee. These organizations are the political expression of the underground resistance and actually of the French nation. They have formed a National Council of Resistance to direct their activities, composed not of technicians but of representatives of the political forces of the resistance. Representatives of the democratic political parties and the labor unions are the most influential members.

The leaders of the Council of Resistance are not children. They have more political experience than the members of the Committee of National Liberation, and they understand better the necessities of the underground resistance than do their compatriots abroad. They accept the Committee's authority because it actually participates in the fight against the invaders of France. It helps wipe out the stain made on French honor by Marshal Pétain and his collaborators. The support they give the Committee cannot be overestimated.

Tomorrow, to build a new France and extirpate the roots of Fascism, other men and other methods will be required; but today, the French anti-Fascists have only one goal: to drive out the armies of Hitler and their accomplices in Vichy. By supporting a Committee in which the conservative elements hold the upper hand, the underground organizations show the quality of their patriotism. Their attitude contrasts with that of the "patriots" of the Right who refused during the war to agree to the formation of a cabinet in which Blum would have had a seat.

Not to support the Algiers Committee would be to abandon De Gaulle, and his popularity is a fact of which the organizers of the resistance are fully aware. It is too important to be observed only through the distorting prisms of De Gaullism or anti-De Gaullism.

For most Frenchmen, General de Gaulle is not a political figure whose doctrinal conceptions and governmental aptitudes provoke sympathy or opposition—he is a national hero. He is not the leader of a party but the symbol of resistance. The impenitent collaborators aside, all Frenchmen are grateful to him for raising the banner of revolt in June, 1940, when so many hesitated over which way to take. The anti-Fascists of the resistance have decided it would be a mistake to let the popularity of General de Gaulle be used to forward a little clique of patriotic reactionaries and the shrewd Croix de Feu. They act realistically. They are partners of De Gaulle without worrying too much about his former political opinions. They give him the shock troops and staffs for his work within the country, asking him in return to respect their ideals and convictions. Thus they have caused an evolution of his thought. It would be puerile to think, however, that by cheering De Gaulle, the Communists have ceased to be Communists, that the Freemasons have become clericals, and that the democrats have rallied to the doctrine of personal power. The heroic destiny of General de Gaulle has not changed to so great an extent the bases of French politics. The conflict of the "Two France's" still exists. Under the Croix de Lorraine which covers the walls of France are found Phrygian caps, hammers and sickles, more often than fleurs-de-lis.

Since December, 1942, the underground organizations have used the name of General de Gaulle as a rallying point for the democrats as well as a national symbol. This crystallization of anti-Fascist opinion resulted from methods used by the American authorities in North Africa, particularly the deals with Darlan, Giraud, Boisson, and Peyrouton. These were explained to international public opinion as occasioned by the "stress of battle" and the desire to save American soldiers. Nevertheless, they provoked in democratic circles a reaction favorable to De Gaulle. General Giraud was considered a man of great courage and solid virtue, but politically, a friend of Pétain. At Algiers he appeared to be the pivot of a political operation directed against democracy. This operation had been planned while Giraud was still a prisoner in Germany by officers in the entourage of Weygand, by Royalists in the entourage of the

Count of Paris, and by former Cagoulard leaders. Its object was to save Pétain's "National Revolution" in the event of a German defeat. It was part of a huge political maneuver begun after the armistice and probably prepared before the war. The first step was the overthrow of the republican regime, thanks to Pétain's collaboration with Hitler; the second step was to prevent the return to democracy, thanks to Giraud's collaboration with the Americans. Giraud was chosen when Weygand could not be used. The Americans were approached because it was believed that they would be more interested than the British in the preservation of the capitalist order and less informed about the exact balance of French political forces. The Americans listened to the song of the siren that promised them the aid of the French Army for their landing in North Africa. The maneuver gave real cause for alarm in disclosing that the conspirators still could obtain support by using as a rallying cry the bogeyman of "Bolshevism." Pertinax, an accurate observer of French politics, thinks that Giraud acted with the assent of Pétain (once more playing a double game). After long conferences and many secret deliberations, the representa-tives of all the French reactionary forces slipped out of France with suspicious facility and went to Algiers. The economic forces—the 200 Families, the Comité des Forges—were the most active. Their agents surrounded Giraud, whose candid honesty and innocent patriotism could not even suspect the role he was to be made to play. The political operation was supplemented by a financial operation intended to "revaluate" in terms of the American dollar the large private fortunes which had been reduced by the war; emissaries camou-flaged as friends of democracy appeared in Wall Street and Washington. Lastly, the constitution of a powerful army, composed of native troops, staffed by pro-Fascist officers, and provided with American matériel, was to furnish the instrument which would be needed to muzzle the people after the departure of the Gestapo and the victory of the Allies.

To defeat this operation, the anti-Fascist elements of the resistance assem-bled around General de Gaulle. He was the battering-ram to be used against the wall which the Cagoulards were building at Algiers. By showing that they preferred De Gaulle to Giraud, the leaders of the resistance caused those Anglo-Saxons who were preparing to support Giraud to reconsider. They countered the ambitions of the Giraud entourage by emphasizing the threat to French unity in the disappointments and apprehensions apparent in De Gaulle's entourage. As human nature is the same everywhere, it was not forbidden to oppose the Fascist tendencies of the Empire Council with the professional jealousies of the National Committee of London. The gathering around De Gaulle of the anti-Fascist forces was spontaneous, and the leaders of the resistance made good but cautious use of it; from December, 1942, on, every democrat who left France went to De Gaulle because all the French Fascists went to Giraud. The democrats thus supported De Gaulle rather than Giraud —while deploring the excesses of a quarrel which did not contribute to the rehabilitation of the French military. At the same time the Anglo-Saxons understood that to remain in contact with the French underground, it was necessary to bring about the formation of a new committee which would include both De Gaullists and Giraudists.

Anti-Fascist support of the Algiers Committee is loyal but determined by the necessities of the war and limited to the war's needs and its duration. The underground organizations agree with Generals de Gaulle and Giraud and with the governments of the United Nations that the Algiers Committee's only objective must be the liberation of France, her territory and her people; the reconstruction of France will be the work of the French people. Two formulae characterize this attitude. The first was used at Algiers by one of the leaders of the De Gaulle movement: "We shall follow the Committee and its leader with our eyes open, not shut." The second was launched as a general warning by the Communist deputies who were freed from concentration camps: "The people of France will not accept the dictatorship of a new Boulanger any more than that of a new Bazaine or a new MacMahon."

The National Council of Resistance has made it known that it does not consider itself subordinate to the Committee of National Liberation. It considers the Algiers Committee an agent to carry out the will of the underground. It takes precedence because it is a more direct and democratic expression of national feeling. The origin and composition of the Committee and of the Council fix the respective competence and the order of their relations. As soon as circumstances allow, the Council will come to the fore. It will speak and act in the name of the French people. The problem of national representation then will emerge in clearer terms, and the Council can, if necessary, be recognized de facto as the provisory government of the Republic.

We see in these facts the progressive elaboration of a democratic government of transition corresponding both to the will of the people and to circumstances. In such a regime, sovereignty continues to belong to the people, but is exercised by the Council until free elections allow the formation of a national assembly. The Algiers Committee is the executive organ of the Council, and is, therefore, responsible to the Council.

The fear that the functioning of such a regime might create a conflict between the Council and the Committee has been subdued by the declarations of Generals de Gaulle and Giraud and the loyalty of the Committee itself. The Committee knows that if it were in discord with the underground, it would no longer be followed by public opinion and would have no support other than General Giraud's bayonets. It is as an agent of the resistance that the democrats accept the Committee's authority.

The main duties of the Committee of National Liberation and the attitude of the democrats who support its action also must be analyzed. The duties are easy to name but difficult to carry through; they fall into three groups.

The first duty is that of liberating French territory. This implies building a democratic army. If the army were not democratic, it could become the tool for a coup d'état after the war. The liberation of the territory also implies the delivery of supplies to that army of saboteurs and partisans who struggle inside France—an army more important politically and as useful militarily as General

Giraud's—as well as the utilization of all moral and material resources in lands controlled by the Committee. This task is purely administrative. The civil administration has been less corrupted by Fascism than the Army; nevertheless, measures should be taken to bring back to their republican duties those civil servants who have been led astray.

The second duty is the liberation of the French people. This implies the applications of the laws of the Republic and the return to a normal democratic life in North Africa. The Committee is not entrusted with directing the political thought of the French people. It is in the diversity and the clash of opinions that this thought will thrive anew. The Committee should not impose the one-party system on the French, but should favor their political re-education and encourage free discussion. Censorship must be limited to military questions; it should become as natural to criticize De Gaulle in Algiers as it is to criticize Roosevelt in Washington.

The liberation of the people postulates the establishment of a "project to return to political liberty," applicable as each bit of territory is liberated. This should be studied by representatives of the political parties, trade-unions, and underground organizations. Its publication would be the best answer to the criticisms of anti-De Gaullists and anti-Giraudists. When France will be liberated, partially or completely, the Committee and the Council of Resistance will be in charge of her provisory administration. The *gérant d'affaires* is, in fact, obliged to continue what he has begun until the rightful "master" is able to assume the responsibility. The primary object of any plan which would guarantee a return to political life must be to assure the transmission of powers now held by the Committee to the French people. This could be done by applying the Treveneuc law of February 15, 1872, which provides for the temporary administration of the country by *conseillers généraux* and the organization of elections with the least delay when the regular government is unable to function. This law is not perfect; but it can be ameliorated by measures justified by circumstances—principally the imprisonment of those *conseillers généraux* who have been accomplices of the Vichy government. As it is, this law provides the simplest means for establishing a government under which legal elections would culminate in the creation of a constituent assembly capable of expressing normally the sovereign will of the people.

The liberation of the people necessitates the preparation of a program of material rehabilitation, dealing with food, lodging, transport, health, and the right to work. Men are not free when they are cold and hungry. It is not a question of having this program applied by the Committee—which would delay too long the formation of a democratic provisional government—but of preparing research files to be transmitted by the Committee to its successor.

The third duty of the Algiers Committee is to strengthen the international friendships which France needs for her liberation as well as for her reconstruction. This is most important. The place France will occupy tomorrow depends on the sympathies she acquires today. The kind of recognition accorded to the Committee by the United Nations is less important than the quality of personal relations between General de Gaulle on one side and Roosevelt, Churchill, and Stalin on the other.

The French people alone, after their liberation, will decide France's foreign policy. The duty of the Algiers Committee, like that of all Frenchmen living abroad, should be not to jeopardize this freedom of choice by awkward attitudes or stinging words. Every friend made for France is a valuable asset. We have the right to fear the reactionary tendencies of certain foreign circles; we have the right to warn our friends in London, Washington, and Moscow of the traps laid by the French Fascists; but we cannot always be satisfied with the policy of other countries, nor they with ours. If we take contemporary politics as a whole, considering what France has given and what she has received in the fight for liberty, we must admit that the dominant feeling of patriotic Frenchmen toward Great Britain, the United States, China, and the Soviet Union should be one of modesty.

By our dignity in misfortune we will prove that we know how to remain among the greatest nations.

Foreign policy is a cold-blooded proposition in which there is no place for vanity. When Frenchmen not well acquainted with international customs imply that De Gaulle does not receive the credit due his courage, it is difficult to contradict them: they are right. We must remind them of the treatment given Beneš or Negrin and accepted without protest. These two great Europeans have served the cause of liberty more faithfully than anyone else in our generation. They were the first to fight National Socialism. From 1938 to 1940 Beneš was pushed aside by the Allied governments; even today, Franco is preferred to Negrin. The injustices suffered by some Frenchmen are neither important nor exceptional. What really matters is to try to win for France as many friends as possible.

France needs the world as much as the world needs France. The presence in the Algiers Committee of certain men whose reputations abroad are as legitimate as in France will permit in the near future the words, gestures, and, perhaps, the reconciliations necessary for harmony between France and the world. The misunderstandings will disappear through the common action of the adversaries of Fascism.

In the hierarchy of obligations, the duties toward the French people come before the duties toward the Algiers Committee. The first care of democratic Frenchmen abroad should be the maintenance of the necessary international friendships. The action of expatriated individuals and groups should complete that of the Algiers Committee, and everyone should cultivate the field closest to him. That the Catholics on the Committee have tried to turn their co-religionists in Canada and South America away from Pétainism can only be praised. The role of the anti-Fascists is more important; it consists in reminding everyone that the French masses are ever faithful to the ideal of the French Revolution.

It is imperative that democratic Frenchmen offer their services to the Algiers Committee, according to the physical and professional aptitudes of each. The Committee needs democratic soldiers for Giraud's army and the underground movement; it needs civil servants, magistrates, jurists, professors, propagandists, and missionaries of democracy. On the day that mobilization of all competent persons becames an actuality, the effectiveness of the Algiers Committee will be doubled.

Finally, democrats must watch carefully the political activities of the Algiers Committee and so help its democratic members, who are doing their best. It is all the more necessary as the Committee—at least up to the time of this writing—has not organized a democratic control for its acts. In *Combat,* a De Gaullist weekly, Professor René Capitant, a specialist in constitutional law, wrote in July, 1943: "Authority has not been democratized; the dictatorship of a committee has replaced the dictatorship of a man."

Giraud and De Gaulle have promised the formation of a Consultative Assembly. The powers of this Assembly are to be of the same nature as those of the Committee. As long as its composition and character are not known, one cannot say to what degree the Assembly will realize the "democratization" of the power. It is to the interest of the Committee to permit a formal expression of criticism and opposition, qualities necessary to all democratic organisms.

I have been a member of many cabinets and I know from experience that if opposition is often irritating for those in power, it is always more beneficial than harmful. In this respect, a small group of Socialists and democrats—the Jean Jaurès group in London—has rendered more services to De Gaulle than all the partisans around him. Without the courteous but firm opposition of the Jaurès group, De Gaulle would have remained attached to the formulae of 1941. In the same way, the New York France Forever Committee, largely under the influence of the famous Professor Henri Focillon, formally stated to M. Pleven, De Gaulle's envoy to the United States in 1941, that an organization which did not include in the text of its program the term "French Republic" would have no chance of success. Better to have keenness in democratic opposition than servitude in dictatorship.

Opposition has its duties as well as its rights. It must be constructive, especially during the war. Its present aim should be to help the best elements of the Algiers Committee who are defending the "interests of the Republic."

The vigilance of French democrats must never be relaxed. They must work toward a democratic army free from Fascist officers, officers who may be eager to liberate French territory, but who, with the same eagerness, will oppose the liberation of the people. Ever present is the threat that they may find support among conservative Anglo-Saxon elements as well as in the French reactionary nucleus.

Today, De Gaullism signifies patriotism. It must be watched closely, nevertheless, for the very word is dangerous. No democrat should permit the use of his name to define a political movement. Karl Marx himself said, "I am by no means a Marxist." Marxism indicates only philosophic and economic concepts, not the political party founded by the author of *Das Kapital.* Montesquieu's saying that even virtue has its excesses may well be applied here.

Deviations toward nationalism and, consequently, Caesarism do exist. Among De Gaulle's supporters are fanatics, chauvinists, and anti-Semites.

Some cunning partisans are trying to transform De Gaullism into pro-Fascism. Their principal organ, *Résistance,* would have a sick France swallow a new Fascism through the classical themes of "national community," the "chief," and the "elite." Fervent democrats, who have been in London since June, 1940, or who more recently have risked their lives to come out of France to fight for freedom are increasingly worried by this deviation. Their uneasiness has been echoed by British liberals and international democratic movements. We would lack intellectual probity, democratic courage, and loyalty to De Gaulle if we discounted this uneasiness.

The danger lies in a possible fusion of the various pro-Fascists. A combination of the Fascist De Gaulle groups, the African Army, and, quite likely, certain groups around Pétain would allow new political maneuvers on the part of the reactionary forces who, after backing Pétain and then Giraud, would rally to De Gaulle either to use him or to imperil his standing.

The pre-Fascist atmosphere still existing in Algiers must be cleared. It may be that De Gaulle, absorbed by multiple functions, has not measured the force of the current separating him from the French masses. It is up to the democrats who have upheld his patriotic effort to make this clear and to warn him and the anti-Fascists inside France and abroad. As in June, 1940, and in 1941, when he joined with the anti-Fascist forces of resistance, De Gaulle is at the crossroads; the liberals hope that he will again take the democratic road; they will know how he has chosen, and will take their stand accordingly.

General de Gaulle's career, his fight against the General Staff, his revolt against Pétain, his political evolution, his alliance with the anti-Fascist resistance, recall Jung's saying about historical personalities: "Their greatness has never consisted in their unconditional subjection *to* convention, but, on the contrary, in their liberating freedom *from* convention." To be faithful to what Jung calls "the law of one's being," De Gaulle must sever the last ties binding him to "convention"—in this case, his clerical and reactionary environment. If he does not do it today, how can he resist tomorrow the urge to dictatorship which undoubtedly will arise from that environment?

A Frenchman aware of his national history is wary of generals meddling in politics, especially when this is accompanied by signs of increasing pre-Fascist activity—nationalist exaltation, hero worship, affirmation of the authoritarian principle, and contempt for democratic values. For more than ten years I have fought against Fascism and dictatorships. My comrades in this struggle and my dearest friends are now in the mountains of Savoy and in the underground organizations. I would betray their confidence if I did not point out all the dangers that I see.

The hate of the French people for all manifestations of personal power, General de Gaulle's loyalty, the friendship of the United Nations for the French people, and the vigilance of the democrats must combine to liberate France. If one of these elements should fail, the others would have to tighten their common bonds and continue the struggle.

THE FRENCH PEOPLE

What will the French people do with their restored freedom?

In answering this question, a Frenchman may unconsciously substitute his own opinions for the facts and his own preferences for the probabilities. As for me, I think with G. D. H. Cole, author of *Europe, Russia and the Future,* that the problem of political liberty cannot be solved individually for the different European countries; it is not France or Germany but the whole of Europe which must be organized and purged of Fascism. The formal and static conception of democracy prevailing during the nineteenth century must be replaced by a realistic dynamic conception; democracy must find its roots in the economic order, and equality must exist in the social order before there can be political democracy. Only a lasting entente among all progressive elements will permit the establishment of a society which, through elimination of class hierarchies and privileges, will lead humanity on the road to progress.

These concepts or those of other Frenchmen living abroad have practically no importance in a discussion of the future. Ideas of former ministers or of members of the Algiers Committee do not count. What the French people *want* and what they are *able to do* will be the deciding factors.

What the French people *want* will depend largely on the changes occurring in their environment, and their ability to understand them. What they will be *able to do* depends largely on the modifications in the social and economic structure during and after the war. Their desire will be subordinated to the psychological reactions provoked by war, defeat, military dictatorship, German occupation, French resistance, and the civil war which will follow the German collapse. Their power will be subordinated to material conditions and to the attitude of the Allied governments and other European nations.

The conditions which will determine the behavior of the French people are many. Among these is the question of political leadership.

It may happen that France will have to submit to dictatorship under military masters, who will continue the anti-democratic work started by Pétain. If France is free, however, her leaders will be new men, unknown to the public, men not to be found on the Algiers Committee nor among the emigrés. They will rise from the political underground organizations inside France and will take control during the period of struggle after the departure of the German troops and the collapse of the Vichy government. Their popularity and their authority will be based on the confidence of the people. To achieve liberation and participate in the organization of a new Europe, France needs audacious leaders; she will find them among the members of the National Council of Resistance and among those who are actively participating in the internal struggle. Certain members of the Algiers Committee and certain refugees, because of their technical competence or their friendly ties in foreign countries, could be used, if necessary, by the future government of France; but to think that they could exercise any active function in the government or take political leadership would disclose political insensitivity or historical ignorance. The leadership will belong to younger men more directly involved in the battle against Fascism.

The deep meaning of things is hidden from us at present by a "patriotic screen." The struggle for the liberation of the territory is more important than the battle for liberation of the people—the first enemy to crush is Hitler. It is natural that this battle be fought in the name of the French people by generals outside the territory occupied by the Germans. When Hitler's regiments have been disposed of, the struggle for the liberation of the French people will become the only struggle. This battle will be political; it will take place inside France; and a team formed outside the metropolitan territory cannot possibly lead it. The control of large industrial towns, such as Paris, will be worth more than the administration of the overseas territory or the legal status of the Algiers Committee. The highest military chiefs will be overshadowed by political leaders, who, because of their training and background, will be more capable of understanding and directing the popular enthusiasm. These leaders will not be found in the old government personnel —although the latter is more popular than is believed abroad—but in the ranks of the anti-Fascists. If a symbolic figure is needed, he will be chosen from among the veterans of the anti-Fascist battle rather than from among those associated with the war against Germany.

This would be neither fickleness nor ingratitude on the part of the French people: new conditions demand new leaders, and the anti-Fascist struggle began in February, 1934, not in June, 1940. In 1918 Clemenceau was the victorious leader and the liberator of the territory; in 1919, his task completed, he left the limelight. In spite of his popularity and the immense services he rendered, he could not have continued in power without imposing a dictatorship which would have led to civil war.

To ask what the French would do if they were free to make a decision, that is, what do they want to do, is to oversimplify the problem, but this is a necessary step for analytical purposes. Assuming an ensemble of favorable circumstances—a German Army conquered and driven out of France, a Vichy government promptly liquidated, a French Army respecting the will of the people, and Allied governments wise enough not to intrude in French domestic affairs—what would be the most probable course of French politics?

According to reliable sources to which I have access, free elections would result in a Popular Front majority stronger in number, more unified, more radical than in 1936. Data indicate a move toward the Left—a natural event, since the Pétain experience, the German occupation, and the policy of collaboration have largely discredited Fascism, whereas the economic evolution, accelerated by the war, has precipitated the proletarization of the people. Furthermore, admiration for the Soviet Union is developing throughout Europe, not only because of the victories of the Red Army, but because of the general behavior of the Soviet peoples and government during the war. War prisoners and workers sent to German factories by Laval and Pétain will return to France with hate in their hearts for their military leaders and for the social class which supported the Vichy government. For these reasons, all the serious-minded statesmen who recently have escaped from France believe that no republican government can now be formed without the participation of Communists. It is impossible to estimate the actual strength of the Communist party in France; but it has forced the admiration of its adversaries by its active participation in the resistance.

A new Popular Front will transform the social and economic structure. In the economic field Socialism will have to be reckoned with, since it will be difficult to realize a rehabilitated Europe—including France—without a global plan or without governmental control of economic activity. In a planned and controlled economy, Socialism is the democratic alternative to corporatism and Fascism. Nationalization of the key industries will be facilitated by the fact that they are at present controlled by Germany; for control by Hitler's officials, the French people will substitute control by their representatives. Partisans of the capitalist regime must refrain from wishful thinking and look squarely at the facts: there is no private capitalism in Europe. As it is impossible to maintain what is no longer there, the question is whether the people will want to rebuild it. The majority of the conservative liberals would hesitate to launch an enterprise so contrary to the laws of history; a Popular Front majority would certainly not do it.

A Popular Front majority would establish a democratic but authoritarian government; it would have to impose its laws on the minority. France will not accept that debonair and tolerant republic which allowed her adversaries the freedom to seal her doom. Public life will be difficult in France and in the rest of Europe. On a less extensive scale, France will have to deal with the same problems as Germany. She will have to eliminate all traces left by Fascism and re-educate her youth poisoned by anti-democratic propaganda. In France the reactionary forces, especially militarism and clericalism, will unite to plot against the majority. "Dictatorship of the majority" will be the necessary form of democratic government for a limited period. Men of my generation may regret it, but the prospect of a return to political liberalism is as unlikely as a return to economic liberalism. "The founding of the Republic is not child's play," said Robespierre. Always tending toward liberty, the new French Republic must seek greater inspiration in the constitutions and the practices of the First Republic than in the Third Republic. It will be submitted to the law but will draft laws able to protect itself.

Is it possible for France to choose her fate freely? I see great obstacles and several circumstances that can modify the course of her popular will.

France will be affected by what happens in the rest of Europe. It is not an exaggeration to say that she will be influenced as much by the happenings in Berlin as by the happenings in Paris. If Germany is Communist, then France and perhaps all of Europe will follow suit. If Germany succumbs to military dictatorship and practices a reactionary policy, it will be difficult for France to escape the contagion, and the nationalist fever will rise again in Europe. Between these two extremes, intermediary solutions will find their place, but all will react on French politics.

France is not immune from nationalism and dictatorship. These germs

389

exist in Algiers—where, until now, more has been done to encourage them than to fight them. These germs can develop in the entourage of a Giraud as well as in that of a De Gaulle. In North Africa there is being equipped an army of 300,000 men, mainly natives, who obey whoever happens to give the orders. If two-thirds of this army occupies France, its leaders may be tempted to "maintain order." And what the military calls "order" will be impossible for some time, as the French people will not get rid of the Pétain regime without breaking some window panes. If order should be re-established by the underground organizations before the arrival of the African Army, we can count on the Right to provoke the necessary skirmishes. After the Pétain-Laval government is abolished, danger of civil war will not come from the Left or the Extreme Left; the Communists wish for nothing more than a peaceful evolution of European politics. The danger will come from the Machiavellism or the shortsightedness of French reactionaries. Small groups of fanatics and Cagoulards will try to get control of the town halls and of the important strategic points: certain documents gathered by the Intelligence Service of De Gaulle's army leave no doubt on this score. Such action and the reaction which it will provoke among the people can furnish the African Army the necessary pretext for intervention.

If this should take place and is not immediately checked by a provisional government of the people, France will be torn by civil war. What the result would be no one can foretell. Considering the opposing forces—the people on the one side, the armed forces on the other—the drama of the Commune could well be re-enacted. More likely the issue of civil war in France will be linked to what takes place at the same time and for the same reasons in the rest of Europe. There would be large international armies of civil war which would overrun the continent as the first generation of the Red Army and the army of the White generals overran Russian territory. Modern European history would take a new turn, bringing in its wake untold suffering.

Certain aspects of the Anglo-Saxon policy in North Africa and Sicily force us to take into account the hypothesis of foreign intervention. I am convinced of the good intentions of the British and American governments. I have seen enough of the political and social evolution of England to know that British democracy will not lend itself to a policy of opposition to the will of European peoples. Having lived in the United States, I have great confidence in President Roosevelt's declarations guaranteeing independence and liberty of choice to the French people. I do not attach more importance to the friendly words addressed yesterday to Pétain than to those addressed to the House of Savoy or to Otto of Hapsburg; courtesy is not to be confounded with politics. With the assurances of Roosevelt, Churchill, and De Gaulle, I have nothing to fear. If American officers are trained in the knowledge of French customs and French administrative law, I can only be thankful; learning European political history, these officers will understand that their country will gain nothing from meddling in French domestic conflicts. They will come to France as friends, as liberators, as guests, for the very important humanitarian job which will consecrate America in the eyes of the world.

Certain circles lean toward the desire to use the great American force for rebuilding in Europe the social order which existed before the war. The reactionary spirit of the Congress of Vienna is not dead. Capitalism is so deep-rooted in American society that men without historical perception confuse capitalist solidarity with international democratic collaboration. Furthermore, there are several kinds of intervention in the domestic policy of a foreign country: direct intervention finds few partisans; but the process of indirect intervention, by the backing given to certain national groups, is more subtle, less visible, and more perilous. It was this process of indirect intervention that France used after the first World War when she foolishly backed the Rhineland separatists.

A clumsy intervention in European politics could achieve the unity of Europe in its most dangerous form—a continental European bloc as opposed to a continental bloc of the Western Hemisphere.

Among the factions which could provoke foreign intervention in favor of European reactionary forces is the Vatican. Many Catholics are on the front lines in the struggle against Fascism; but because of its hierarchical organization and its political doctrine, the Vatican cannot easily accept a total liberation of the peoples. The difficulties encountered by the democratic forces on the American continent lead me to fear this danger more and more.

Americans have a tremendous role to play in the world. They have a country rich in material and human resources. They must know that all European peoples have their eyes turned toward them. Their popularity in France cannot be overestimated. The recriminations of certain refugees, more complacent in the comfort of American hospitality than grateful for it, should be disregarded. Americans should ignore the susceptibility of certain French newspapers and the nervousness of the official propaganda from Algiers or Brazzaville. *De minimis non curat praetor!* The captive and suffering French people trust them. The French nation, as a whole, has complete confidence in the official declaration of the government of the United States. For them America is not a country of businessmen in search of markets or of conservatives with their eyes turned toward old-fashioned formulae; it is the country of Thomas Jefferson, Abraham Lincoln, Woodrow Wilson, and Franklin D. Roosevelt; it is the land of refuge and liberty; it is the vanguard of democracy.

This immense faith would crumble if the French people sensed that the United States intended to impose upon them certain fixed economic and social directions and, above all, to forbid other courses. Disappointed in her love for America, France would turn to the east of Europe for a new hope. Every time Americans deal with European reactionaries, they help Communism to spread.

The most conservative of American liberals have nothing to fear from an evolution of French politics toward the Left. In the past the heirs of the French Revolution, the men of the Left—for instance, Herriot and Blum—have fought against the Right and the Extreme Right for international collaboration and Franco-American friendship. A glance at the Algiers press or at the underground papers printed in France shows that this spirit is still alive. No matter what her economic regime may be in the future, France must have an entente with the United States; the reconstruction of Europe depends on the help of American industry. American businessmen will have more solid guarantees if they deal with the French government than if they deal with private capitalists, who only yesterday proved their measure of honesty by attempting to exchange their devaluated fortunes for good American dollars.

The possible dangers of nationalism in Europe must be emphasized. Nationalism is not patriotism but its exaggeration and deviation. When the war is over, nationalist explosions will occur throughout Europe, caused by the legitimate resentment of the peoples submitted to the brutalities of Hitler's soldiers. Led by democrats, this resentment would develop into a salutary anti-Fascism; led by nationalists, it would develop into a dangerous anti-Germanism, opposed to all efforts of a rational organization. Europe would remain divided.

America must realize that Europe is no longer what it used to be. "Moderate" conservative and liberal elements have disappeared almost completely from European politics. French politics have become so polarized that on the Right there are no more conservatives, only reactionaries. These reactionaries can be patriotic, but at the same time they are anti-democratic. French nationalism is an indirect danger for the future of Europe. A France with forty million inhabitants is not in a position to menace world peace, but a nationalist and militarist France would be an obstacle to any new organization of Europe or of the Colonies. French nationalism and militarism would be the pretext and the springboard for a resurgence of German militarism and nationalism. If today we try to prevent the possibility of a third World War, we must open no way and give no place to nationalism; we must fight it everywhere. The experience of the 1919 treaties proves that to achieve general disarmament, it is not enough to destroy the war machine of conquered countries. To give the world peace, all the carriers of nationalist germs must be eliminated from power—even the most honest and the least dangerous.

I wish to point out to Americans and more generally to Anglo-Saxons, that by backing the forces of reaction in Europe they would precipitate only civil war and the cruelest of revolutions. Their intervention would force the democrats to choose not between capitalism and Socialism, but between a new form of Fascism and Communism. The latter would be the only means of achieving Socialism during the civil war period. I know, because I have often discussed it with him, that in such a case so moderate a man as Herriot would not hesitate to choose Communism because in the future of Communism a small flame of liberty is visible, while in the development of Fascism there is only blackest night.

For all those reasons, I ask the Americans not to endanger the chances for political liberty in Europe. In the present chaos these chances may seem small to them. I believe, on the contrary, that they are immense if we are to adapt our democratic ideals to the new political and economic conditions. I may add that they would be still larger if the democratic exiles—German, Italian, Spanish, and French—had found more facilities with which to continue the struggle aganist Hitler and his accomplices. The harm done by the policy of appeasement has spread beyond Europe.

A democratic Frenchman should not find fault with England or the United States. The fate of France and liberty in the world depend on the combined efforts of the Anglo-Saxon democracies and Soviet Russia. Whatever the mistakes of our Allies, they have been less serious than ours.

I ask all the friends of France to keep in mind the misfortune of my country. The French people have been betrayed, and they have been conquered. Innocent of the mistakes of the bourgeoisie and the generals, they are determined to erase by their courage the crimes committed in their name.

The nation that has taken the words "Liberty, Equality, Fraternity" as her motto will not give up a struggle that she has waged for so many years; a struggle that has become her history. Her dead, her hostages, her prisoners, bear witness to her valor.

During invasions conquerors have always chosen hostages from among the "notables" of a country—magistrates, noblemen, priests, political leaders, big landowners, or wealthy merchants. The list of Gestapo victims reveals the French "notables" of our day. I select at random from among the names of those executed at Lille on July 25, 1942: Henri Decroix, mine worker; Victor Mariette, factory worker; Louis Chavatte, mine worker; Marcel Ledent, mine worker; Charles Pauvel, welder; Desiré Druars, blacksmith; Marius Fremaux, mine worker. On that day, twenty-eight men were shot; all were plain workers! This is France's new nobility. These are the names and titles which will be engraved on the honor roll of liberated France.

Those who are defending their country and are preparing for the future are the heirs of the French Revolution. As in 1793, the love of France and of liberty are one.

In their heroic effort for liberation, the French people are constantly in danger. In spite of all decrees, schoolteachers still teach children the Declaration of the Rights of Man and of the Citizen, lest they forget that "insurrection is the most sacred of rights and the most indispensable of duties when the government violates the rights of the people," and that among these rights is "resistance to oppression." Saboteurs and partisans are singing once more the Revolution's *Chant du Depart*:

> "Hear the call of the Republic
> Let us win or let us perish.
> For the Republic a Frenchman must live
> For her a Frenchman will die."

The "citizens" have taken up arms. "Liberty guides their steps." If they alternate the *International* with the *Marseillaise*, it is to signify to the world that their sacrifices will serve the interests of humanity as well as the liberation of France.

France is on the way to a new destiny. Suffering is steeling her soul. The conflict of the "Two France's" is nearing its end. After the France of kings and nobles, after the France of merchants and generals, we see not far off the France of the people, ready to take her place in the family of free nations.

APPENDIX

I

Program of the Popular Front

DRAFTED IN JANUARY, 1936

Liberty! Peace! Bread!

A. Defense of Liberty

1. General amnesty.
2. Against the Fascist leagues:
    (a) Disarmament and dissolution of paramilitary groups, according to law.
    (b) Application of legal sanctions in case of provocation to murder or attack on the security of the state.
3. Purification of public life, particularly of parliamentary inconsistencies.
4. The press:
    (a) Abrogation of unfair legislation restricting freedom of opinion.
    (b) Reform of the press through the adoption of legislative measures:
        (1) Permitting the effective repression of slander and blackmail;
        (2) Ensuring the newspapers normal means of existence; obliging them to make public the sources of their capital; ending the private monopolies of commercial publicity and the scandals of financial publicity, and preventing the creation of press trusts.
    (c) Organization of State radio broadcasts to ensure exact information about the equality of political and social organizations.
5. Trade-union liberties:
    (a) General application of, and respect for, the trade-union law.
    (b) Respect for the rights of working women.
6. Schools and freedom of conscience:
    (a) To ensure the life of the public schools not only by the necessary appropriations but by reforms, such as the extension of compulsory education to the age of 14 and the selection of students for secondary schooling on the basis of merit, essential in a system of free education.
    (b) The guarantee to all, students and teachers alike, of complete freedom of conscience, chiefly by respect for academic neutrality, secularity, and the civil rights of the teaching body.
7. Colonial territories:
    (a) Creation of a parliamentary commission of investigation into the political, economic, and moral situation in the French territories overseas, especially in French North Africa and Indo-China.

B. Defense of the Peace

1. Appeal to the collaboration of the people, particularly the laboring masses, for the maintenance and organization of peace.
2. International collaboration within the framework of the League of Nations for collective security, through the definition of the aggressor and the automatic and joint application of sanctions in cases of aggression.
3. Constant effort to pass from an armed peace to a disarmed peace, first through an agreement on limitations, then by the general, simultaneous, and controlled reduction of armaments.
4. Nationalization of war industries and suppression of private trade in arms.

5. Repudiation of secret diplomacy; international action and public negotiations to bring back to Geneva the states which have left the League, without striking at the constitutive principles of the League; collective security and indivisible peace.

6. Rendering more flexible the procedure provided for by the League of Nations Pact for the peaceful adjustment of treaties dangerous to world peace.

7. Extension, particularly in Eastern and Central Europe, of the system of open pacts, following the principles of the 'Franco-Soviet Pact.

C. Economic Demands

1. Restoration of the purchasing capacity curtailed or paralyzed by the depression.

    (a) Against unemployment and the industrial crisis:

        (1) Institution of a national fund for the unemployed.

        (2) Reduction of the working week without reduction in weekly wage.

        (3) Establishment of an adequate retirement system for old workers, which would attract young men to work.

        (4) Rapid execution of a plan of extended public works in city and country, bringing together state and local efforts.

    (b) Against the agricultural and commercial crisis:

        (1) Revaluation of farm products, combined with an attack on speculation and high living costs, to reduce the disparity between wholesale and retails prices.

        (2) Creation of a national interprofessional office of cereals, to eliminate the 10 per cent levied by speculators on producers and consumers.

        (3) Support to agricultural co-operatives, sale of manure at cost price by the national offices of nitrogen and potash, control and price-fixing of the sale of super-phosphates and other manures, development of agricultural credit, reduction of farm rents.

        (4) Suspension of seizures and staggered payment of debts.

    (c) Until all the injustices involved in the legal decrees can be abolished, immediate abolition of measures affecting the classes whose conditions of life are most seriously touched by these decrees.

2. Against the plunder of savings and to better the organization of the credit system:

    (a) Strict regulation of the banking profession.

    (b) Strict regulation of the balance sheets of banks and limited liability companies.

    (c) New regulation of the powers of administrators of limited liability companies.

    (d) Retired or unattached civil servants are forbidden to belong to the administrative councils of limited liability companies.

    (e) In order to remove credit and savings from the domination of the financial oligarchy, la Banque de France, now a private bank, shall become la Banque de la France.

    (f) Abolition of the council of regents.

    (g) Extension of the governor's powers under the permanent control of a council that shall be composed of representatives of the legislative branch, the executive branch, and the great organized forces of labor, industry, commerce, and agriculture.

    (h) Transformation of capital into bonds, measures being taken to guarantee the interests of the small bondholders.

3. Financial reform:

    (a) Revision of the war markets together with the nationalization of war industries.

    (b) Abolition of waste in civil and military administration.

    (c) Institution of a treasury for war pensions.

    (d) Democratic reform of the tax system, involving a better fiscal organization in view of the economic revival, and creation of new resources by measures reaching the large fortunes (rapid increase in the general tax on incomes over 75,000 francs; reorganization of the inheritance tax; taxation of monopoly profits, while avoiding all repercussions on consumers' prices).

(e) Abolition of fraud in transferable securities by the application of a fiscal identity card voted by the Chambers, accompanied by a fiscal amnesty.

(f) Control of the export of capital and prevention of its escape by the most severe measures, including the confiscation of fortunes hidden abroad or of their value in exchange in France.

II

Report from the Minister of Aviation (Pierre Cot) to the French Premier (Camille Chautemps)

DECEMBER 6, 1937

Ministry of Aviation.

No. 712 CM/R

On your return from England, you were good enough to telephone me to tell me how much you had been struck by Great Britain's achievement in the field of aviation. You compared the figures of English aeronautic production with our own, and were dismayed by their disproportion. As the English had called your attention to Germany's ever-increasing aerial rearmament, you told me that we would be taking a grave responsibility if we did not counter the danger which threatens us. I have the honor to submit to you my opinion on this situation and the concrete propositions which it suggests to me.

I am in complete agreement with you. For a year and a half I have constantly insisted that the share of aviation in our entire national defense is much too small. I should be happy to have credits at my disposal comparable with those of the English budget for aviation. If that seems impossible to you, I should like at the very least to be allotted the credits which should normally be given the Ministry of Aviation in our national defense. And I think, with you, that our responsibility would be gravely involved if we were not to take this tack.

Regarding our part in national defense, it must be said that the French Air Force has at the present time the smallest appropriation. Its budget represents 22 per cent of the budget for national defense.* The British budget for aviation represents 34 per cent.† In Germany and Italy the proportion is still larger.

If the Air Force continues to be treated as a poor relation, it will be unable to achieve the effort you consider desirable, and the awakening threatens to be terrible.

Therefore, I do not hesitate, after our conversation, to ask you for new credits, the total of which, I think, should reach eleven billions in three years. These credits should be divided in the following way:

3,800 millions in 1938; 3,400 millions in 1939; 3,800 millions in 1940.

It would be understood that the sum total of these credits could be used from the first year on, and that the credits could be shifted from one fiscal year to another according to need.

To legitimize this request, I need merely refer you to the efforts I have been vainly making since 1936 [June] to obtain the necessary means for enlarging the Air Force.

---

* Proportion of the 1938 budget plan.
† Proportion of the English fiscal year, March, 1937-March, 1938.

Section 1. Efforts Made Since June, 1936

A. The Situation in June, 1936

The situation of the Air Force was grave. The program in force, called Plan I, included the creation of an air fleet composed of 1,000 first-line planes and [in ratio to that force] a 20 per cent first reserve, 1,200 warplanes in all. I myself [as Air Minister] had elaborated this plan at the end of 1933. Since that time, in spite of the advances of the other European states, my predecessors allowed for no increase.

This clearly insufficient plan underwent further reduction when put into practice, as only 60 per cent of the planes provided for were actually built, although the execution of the plan went back as far as 1934. The Treasury was empty; thirty-seven millions remained to keep industry going until the end of the year. The factories dismissed workers and slowed down production.

A law passed at the request of the General Staff provided for a quinquennial renewal of the air fleet. The factories which had been bequeathed to me had, therefore, to maintain a production of $\frac{1200}{5}$, or of 250 warplanes per annum. To these warplanes had to be added about 200 instruction planes, 100 airplanes or hydroplanes for the Navy, and 200 to 300 planes for private use, merchant aviation, export, etc.

B. Plan II (August, 1936)

From the month of August on, faced with Germany's huge aerial advances, I undertook to substitute a more significant program for Plan I. *This program permitted the doubling of the Air Force in three years.* It involved the construction of 2,400 aircraft (instead of 1,200), a construction rate of 800 warplanes (instead of 250) per annum.

A cabinet decision approved this program, which had been given a credit of five billion francs to be spent in three years in addition to the credits ordinarily granted the Ministry of Aviation. The high price level and the devaluation of the franc caused the Ministries of National Defense to revise their evaluations. It had been understood that we would receive five billions "of the value of August, 1936." This sum later equaled 7,100 million francs.

After this date, this already modest program was cut. In spite of my efforts, our credits were diminished.

The first annuity was to have been 1,200 millions. At the request of the Minister of Finance, I consented to a credit of only 500 millions in the budget of 1937. But it had been expressly agreed that I was to be allotted a supplementary credit of 700 millions in the course of the fiscal year. In spite of numerous attempts, I never succeeded in obtaining this sum.

As the French government had decided to aid the aerial rearmament of Rumania, a sum of 75 millions was deducted from the Air Force's credits. We never obtained the restitution of this sum.

Contrary to the promises I had been given, *the National Societies of Aeronautic Construction were not able to obtain the Treasury funds* which they needed. Yet the State, from the moment it accepted the constitution of these societies, had to concern itself with financing them. The societies had to turn to the banks. This move prevented us from saving about 7 to 8 per cent of the market prices; our credits were consequently again reduced by about 100 millions.

From the month of June on, I informed the Minister of Finance that we needed provisional credits [*credits d'engagement*]; these were necessary to place new orders and to avoid the slowing down of the rhythm of manufacture. You know that many months pass between the ordering of material and its arrival; a period of four to five months is needed to obtain even raw materials. In spite of numerous requests, *I was unable to obtain these credits until October, 1937, instead of June, 1937. Moreover,*

400

my requests [based on a production of 800 warplanes for 1938] *have been cut in half. We must therefore expect a decrease in production for next year.*

This decrease is all the more certain and inevitable *since the credits of payment which I asked for in the budget of 1938 have been curtailed.* The reduction came to more than a billion! You must remember that I protested this reduction before the Little Council and before the cabinet itself. Now, the Minister of Finance has asked me to spread out the execution of my Plan II over an extra year. The credits I have received will not permit me to build 800 warplanes in 1938. Our factories, for lack of sufficient orders, have already had to take measures to spread out their production, and therefore our total annual output will be reduced.

Two figures will allow you to measure the significance of the curtailment of our credits. In the course of the fiscal years 1936-1937, the provisional credits necessary for our production (airplanes, prototypes, works and installations, and industrial mobilization) were reduced by 1,298 million francs, or about 30 per cent; the final credits I had requested were curtailed, during the same period, by 1,852 million francs. It must be remembered that this money was requested for the execution of a program which you consider insufficient.

C. The Plans Proposed to the High Military Committee

In December, 1936, I was convinced, as the result of the cabinet's decision, that the government would give me every facility for proceeding to the operation of Plan II (2,400 planes, or 800 warplanes per annum).

However, from that time forward, the Ministry of Aviation, having been informed about the activity of Germany, England, Italy, and Russia, was busy preparing a more important plan.

1. PLAN III

On December 30, 1936, we handed the Permanent Committee of National Defense a report, No. 10.913 R/E.M.A.A. In this report we showed the necessity for a new and more significant effort in the field of aviation.

We took up in its entirety the problem of the aerial defense of the country and demonstrated: the necessity for a single command of this defense through the General Staff of the Air Force; the importance of anti-aircraft artillery, given the increasing efficiency and development of modern air forces—a conclusion that could be drawn from both the German effort and the Spanish Civil War; the necessity for giving the Air Force the anti-aircraft artillery essential to its own operation (protection of its airfields, etc.), while leaving the Army and Navy the anti-aircraft they required for their own defense.

We therefore requested, in addition to the resources provided for in Plan II: 700 officers; 10,000 men in peacetime, permitting the mobilization for the Air Force of 3,540 officers and 154,000 supplementary troops for the aerial defense of the country; a credit of three billions (beyond the sums requested in Plan II).

There is no doubt that these propositions would have greatly ameliorated France's situation. In fact, these suggestions made for the organization of a very compact network of aerial defense. The existence of such a network, freeing our poor and weak aviation from cumbersome duties, would have permitted it greater maneuverability, the possibility of attacking German or Italian bases, and, consequently, would have compensated for the inequality of our aerial strength.

2. PLAN IV

I did not limit my request there. Believing that the German effort was developing dangerously, I requested the General Staff to work out another plan, envisaging several hypotheses, among others the doubling of Plan II. Plan IV would have given us, in addition to Plan II:

2,000 officers; 20,000 troops; 10 billions of credits in three years.

In all, the ensemble of Plans III and IV would have provided us in three years with a complement of:

3,000 officers; 30,000 troops; 13 billion francs.

I believe that these plans would have permitted us, and would permit us, if they were reconsidered and adopted, to provide France with adequate weapons of defense. I have described them. It is not my fault if they were not adopted. You must recognize that if the Air Force is not at present provided with a program that seems adequate and satis-factory to you, I am not to blame.

3. THE REJECTION OF THESE PLANS

Unfortunately, the contacts of the General Staff of the Air Force with those of the Army and the Navy made us think that the higher military circles did not share our point of view. Wrongly or rightly, I cannot tell which, the Army refused to accept our suggestions for the reinforcement of the aerial defense of the land.

I had already met with more than one check in the Ministry of Finance; you will see later that my suggestions on the necessity of international aviation agreements had also been refused. I thought it undesirable to oppose the Air Force to the other forces, and, on February 15, 1937, having made my propositions and believing in the strength of my suggestions, I accepted the High Military Committee's decision that "there was no cause to modify or extend the plan of the Air Force at the present time."

But today, when people reproach me for not having brought about the increase of our aerial defense, I have the right to recall these propositions.

D. *The Suggestions for International Negotiations and Agreements*

I did more. We in the Air Ministry realized that we could never match the aerial effort of Germany. It is an industrial problem even more than a financial one. Germany has a general industrial potential twice as great as ours. Her technicians, physicists, and chemists are as good (to say no more) as ours. Her social regime, however odious it may be, permits her to give more resources than anyone else to her Air Force. National defense and German economy are directed by General Goering, a former war aviator, who obviously attributes more importance to the aerial factor than do our military leaders. All these elements make it impossible for us in France to envisage an effort comparable to that of Germany.

To compensate for this inferiority, whose tragic side I realize, *I asked the govern-ment to negotiate international agreements.* You know with what warmth I upheld this point of view in the cabinet and particularly in the Little Council, which includes the Ministers of State, Foreign Affairs, and National Defense. Only one nation in the world has an aerial strength superior to that of Germany—Soviet Russia. In quality and in quantity, the aeronautic production of Russia outranks that of Germany. Military or industrial agreements with the Soviet Union would revise the order of the factors in our favor.

My propositions were adjourned, then rejected; it would be vain to regret them, but it is my duty to recall them.

I then turned to the United States. There I clashed not only with political but with financial opposition. Nevertheless, I, alone, was able to arrange two important negotia-tions. One of them permitted us to acquire manufacturing processes which will increase the return of our factories; the other will permit us to combat our grave inferiority in the matter of engines by acquiring the patent rights of the best and most powerful American engines. It is clear that all that will remain valueless if the credits needed for important constructions are not granted to the Air Ministry.

E. *Conclusions*

You will excuse me for having recalled these efforts, propositions, and attempts. I am more desirous than anyone else of respecting the rules of ministerial solidarity, but I

402

think it would be unjust and somewhat ridiculous to reproach me for the small figures of our aeronautic production.

On the other hand, I tried my best, in spite of the difficulties and the inadequate credits, to put into operation the program of the 800 warplanes per annum, which had been approved by the government and Parliament.

On the other hand, I have not ceased to tell the government that the effort in the aerial field was insufficient and that it was necessary either to grant me larger credits to proceed to a revision of our plans of national defense and to a different division of credits, or to plan international agreements which would compensate for our weakness.

Section II. What Must and What Can Be Done

A. Given the Present State of Things, What Can We Do

Some claim, it is true, that we could and should produce more with the same credits. It is said that nationalization has disorganized our industry and that the social legislation is responsible for our weak production.

I have already answered this objection in an earlier note. Undoubtedly the social legislation has its repercussion on the aeronautic industry, as on the whole of French production. But the repercussion has been felt less in the nationalized factories than in the free factories. There has been hardly any decrease in output in the aeronautic industry, except in factories of Morane, Latécoère, Renault, and Hispano-Suiza—the factories which escaped nationalization.

As for the cost price of our airplane bodies and our motors, it is comparable to such prices abroad. In general, the comparison is even favorable to us. Again, to be just, it would be necessary to take into account the very different conditions which prevail in our factories. The French Air Force is unfortunately becoming very small by comparison with the German and English Air Forces; the quantity of planes manufactured each year is three or four times smaller. Any industrialist can testify that under these conditions a price 20 per cent or 30 per cent higher would be justified. In spite of that, we have generally produced at the same price (at times even at a lower price) as British industry, for example:

Light monoplanes	Price	Weight
Morane 405 (Fr.)	965,000 frs	1 T. 8
Dewoitine 510 (Fr.)	712,000 frs	1 T. 6
Hawker Hurricane (Br.)	1,247,000 frs	1 T. 8
Gloster Gladiator (Br.)	900,000 frs	1 T. 5
Three-seater airplanes:		
Potez 63 (Fr.)	1,263,000 frs	3 T.
Bristol Blenheim (Br.)	2,175,000 frs	4 T. 8
Fairey "Battle" (Br.)	1,825,000 frs	3 T. 6

The conclusion is that, in spite of insufficient credits, we shall succeed in carrying out the program which corresponds to the decisions made in August, 1936. At the beginning of 1940, we shall have 2,400 planes in line and the oldest of them will be less than five years old.

B. An Effort Comparable to England's Must Be Made

It is this very program that you consider inadequate, compared with the achievements of Germany and England. I am glad you do.

I think—as I am sure you do—that it is impossible for us to make an effort equal to that of Germany. Germany possesses an industrial potential twice as great as ours, and her active population is double our own. Moreover, she is in a state of industrial mobilization. We cannot dream of imitating her.

On the other hand, we can—and should—follow the example of Great Britain, who has spent four years in bringing her important aeronautic industry to maximum. According to the figures which you have given me, she must now be producing 300 planes per month. That would be quite possible, given the credits which have been put at the disposal of her aeronautic industry for the past three years.

Nevertheless, I must offer two observations concerning this figure.

First, such a volume of production must be very recent. This information supplied by the Deuxième Bureau of the General Staff gives us to understand that the British Air Force now consists of 2,060 airplanes. The same information indicates that the English air fleet has grown by 70 squadrons in thirty months. The Deuxième Bureau adds that the proportion of modern and old planes is about the same in the British and French air fleets, which would give Great Britain an annual production of 500 new warplanes. Even if one bears in mind the planes lost in accidents (of which there are many in the British Air Force, because of its many inexperienced pilots), we are still far from the figure that you quoted.

Nevertheless, there may well be only an apparent contradiction between these figures, because you seem to have been given the total sum of production, which includes not only warplanes, but instruction planes, liaison planes, etc., which in a recently organized force may easily reach 700 or 800 planes per annum. This production also includes the hydroplanes and all Navy aircraft, or another several hundred each year. Above all, the reason for the discrepancy is that the figures of the Deuxième Bureau apply to the production of the fiscal years 1935-1936 and 1936-1937. As England has created a powerful industry in the last three years, this industry can only have begun recently to produce at maximum. In any case, these are points which I shall verify at once.

Second, England specializes in the construction of light planes (fighters and defense planes) and we specialize in medium and heavy planes. Thus, out of 1,550 planes in the mother country, the English fleet includes: 420 light planes (fighters), 880 medium planes (bombers, reconnaissance), and 250 heavy bombers.

The French Air Force, out of 1,350 modern planes in service includes: 450 light planes (single seaters), 170 medium planes (planes for the land Army), and 730 heavy bombers.

A heavy plane represents in cost, working hours, raw material, armament, etc., twice or three times as much as a light plane.

If one bears in mind these diverse elements, if one deducts from the sum total of English production a normal proportion of training and service planes and aircraft for the Navy (about 1,000 to 1,200 per annum), if one bears in mind that 500 French warplanes represent (in constructed tonnage, working hours, and cost) about 800 British warplanes, one comes to the conclusion that the production of warplanes in Great Britain must be, now and in the months to come, between three and a half to four and a half times that of France.

This situation is entirely natural if one considers the disparity between the credits put at the disposal of the English and French Ministries of Aviation in the past three years.

C. What We Would Do with the Same Credits as England

It cannot be doubted that, if the Air Ministry for the past three years had been granted credits as large as those of the British Ministry of Aviation, we should have achieved equal and very likely superior results. We should have entered this race with a personnel and a fund of experience that our English friends lacked in 1932. And contrary to opinion spread abroad by a misinformed or biased press, our production costs, other things being equal, have been smaller than those of the British. Finally, if we determine on such an effort, we should profit by the experience of England.

Supposing that you were able to put at my disposal credits equaling those of the English air budget, let us see what an effort of production that would permit us after the slower starting period, which I shall examine later.

In this hypothetical case, the credits of the Air Force would be raised from 4,731 millions to 12,845,260,000 francs (with the pound sterling at 145), or a difference of 8,114,260,000 francs per annum.

How would such huge credits be used? Their division might be as follows:

PLAN FOR AN ANNUAL DIVISION OF AN AIR FORCE BUDGET OF
13,000 MILLION FRANCS

Warplanes (motors and accessories included)	5,000 millions
Training planes and others (export, etc.)	600 "
Prototypes, research and experiment	400 "
Maintenance, spare parts and repairs	1,000 "
Various technical materials, munitions, armaments, etc.	2,000 "
Works and installations (bases, schools)	1,200 "
Personnel—Matériel and operation of the Services	2,000 "
Industrial mobilization	400 "
Subsidy for gunpowder and gasoline	400 "
	13,000 millions

We should thus have a supplementary sum of five billions for the building of war-planes; at the present time, we have about one billion. Even if production in larger quantities did not cause our costs to go down, we could still produce six times as much as we do now, without difficulty and without having to resort to industrial mobilization. Simply by increasing our resources, we would then produce 3,000 warplanes instead of 800, plus 1,000 training planes, seaplanes, etc. If we adopted the English Air Force's proportion of light and heavy planes, we could have 4,000 warplanes and 1,000 planes for the Navy, for training, export, etc. We should then, on the basis of equal credits, achieve a result superior to that of England.

D. What Shall We Do with Credits Totaling 60 Per Cent of the Credits Allotted to the English Air Force

I am perfectly well aware that such a financial effort, while possible for England, would be ruinous for us. But I must insist most urgently on a considerable increase in the credits granted to the Air Ministry.

At the present time, in all systems of national defense, the share of the Air Force in the national defense budget is more than one-third. We are the one country which makes its weakest effort in this field. Nevertheless, it is my conviction that France, more than anyone else, needs a strong air force. We do not know on what fronts we shall have to fight tomorrow; it is quite possible that we shall have to make a strong effort in the Mediterranean. Only the Air Force, by its mobility and speed, will permit us to act wherever the need arises. By not developing the French Air Force in the same proportion as other armies, we run a great risk of committing once more, on a vastly larger scale, the error we made before the war of 1914, when we neglected machine guns and heavy artillery.

England gives her Air Force 34 per cent of her budget for national defense. If I were granted a similar proportion, I should receive nearly 7½ billions per annum. I am obviously not asking that the credits necessary for the enlargement of my budget be deducted from the budgets of the Navy or the Army. Even with the proposed increase, these credits would hardly reach 60 per cent of those at the disposal of my British colleague. Nevertheless, they would permit me to make an honorable showing.

they will be used and divided in the following way:

It is these supplementary credits which I most urgently request. If they are granted

PLAN OF DIVISION OF A SUPPLEMENTARY CREDIT OF ELEVEN BILLION FRANCS TO BE USED DURING THE YEARS 1938, 1939, 1940, EXPRESSED IN MILLIONS

Divisions	1938	1939	1940	Total
Warplanes (motors and accessories included)	2,000	1,600	1,860	5,460
Training planes and others	380	250	380	1,010
Prototypes	200	200	200	600
Upkeep, spare parts and repairs	80	100	150	330
Various materials	200	250	350	800
Works and installations (bases, schools, etc.)	300	400	300	1,000
Personnel	140	200	300	640
Industrial mobilization	300	200	100	600
Subsidy for powder	200	200	200	600
Total	3,800	3,400	3,840	11,040

The Increase of the Credits for Matériel Would Permit the Yearly Production of 3,400 Planes:

Defense planes	600	Liaison planes, etc.	400
Fighters, reconnaissance planes and dive bombers	150	Planes for training, etc.	1,000
Bombers (heavy)	150		
(light)	450	Seaplanes	200
Observation planes	300		
	1,800		1,600

To achieve this production, I would have to follow the example of England and begin by building factories. We can do so as rapidly as the English have done. But we must allow for a delay of three years until our industrial potential is thus increased. Only in 1940 will our production reach the figure of 3,400 warplanes per annum.

From next year on, if the credits are granted at once, we shall be able to increase the rate of our manufacture to 80 warplanes and 40 planes of other types per month by the end of the year, a monthly production of 120 instead of 70.

To compensate for the temporary insufficiencies in our production, I ask you for the authorization to purchase abroad about 200 warplanes and 500 engines. We shall have to pay more for this matériel than it would cost if we could manufacture it ourselves. The danger seems to me so pressing that I do not hesitate to make this proposition to you. I add that this procedure will give us the opportunity to establish, between our aeronautic industry and those of great neutral states, relations from which we shall profit in wartime.

In concluding this study, I should like to ask you for a similar effort in anti-aircraft and passive defense. Those are questions in the jurisdiction of the Ministers of National Defense and of War and the Minister of the Interior. But if we decide to make a considerable effort for the Air Force, I think that such an effort should be accompanied by a large increase in the resources at the disposal of the anti-aircraft defense of the land. The information on German rearmament which I have succeeded in obtaining leads me to think that these two divisions of our national defense are clearly inadequate.

Pierre Cot

III

Constitutional Act No. 7

JANUARY 27, 1941

(Cf. *Journal Officiel* for January 28, 1941.)

Article I.—The secretaries of State, high dignitaries and high officials of the State will take an oath before the Chief of State. They will swear allegiance to his person and pledge themselves to exercise their duties for the good of the State, according to the laws of honor and decency.

Article II.—The secretaries of State, high dignitaries and high officials of the State are personally responsible to the Chief of State. This responsibility involves their persons and property.

Article III.—In case some one of them should betray the duties of his office, the Chief of State, after an investigation which he will initiate, may levy any civil reparation or fine, and apply the following penalties, temporarily or permanently: deprivation of political rights; confinement to residence in France or the Colonies; administrative intern-ment; detention in a fortress.

Article IV.—The sanctions which may be taken on the basis of the preceding article do not stand in the way of investigations made through the ordinary legal channels in cases of crimes or infractions of the law which may have been committed by the same persons.

Article V.—Articles III and IV of the present act are applicable to former ministers, high dignitaries, and high officials who have held office within the past ten years.

Decree Creating a Council of Political Justice

SEPTEMBER 29, 1941

(Cf. *Journal Officiel* for September 30, 1941.)

Article I.—A Council of Political Justice is created, charged with giving its opinion on questions which the Chief of State will consider necessary to bring before the Council whenever the dispositions of Constitutional Act No. 7 apply.

Article II.—The Council of Political Justice is composed as follows:

M. Audollent, Legion of Honor, Croix de Guerre, repatriated prisoner.

M. Aulois, lawyer at the Court of Appeals in Lyon, commander of the Legion of Honor, disabled in both wars.

M. Drouat, captain of infantry in the reserve, Croix de Guerre (five citations), re-patriated prisoner.

M. le Colonel Josse, senator, president of the Association of Soldiers, decorated in danger of death.

M. Percerou, professor at the Paris Law School.

M. Perretti della Rocca, ambassador of France.

M. Ripert, president of a section in the Council of State.

M. Vallin, deputy, knight of the Legion of Honor, Croix de Guerre.

Article III.—The Council of Political Justice will choose its president and establish its own rules.

Article IV.—The vice-president of the cabinet and the Minister of Justice are charged, each as he is concerned, with the execution of the present decree.

Opinion Expressed by the Council of Political Justice

OCTOBER 13, 1941

ÉDOUARD DALADIER.—Under the Government of M. Daladier, France went to war inadequately prepared. The Supreme War Council was not consulted as it should have been on questions relating to the preparation for war.

There was:

Inefficiency in the preparation of national mobilization and in industrial preparedness.

Inefficiency in the manufacture of armaments and the supply of units, which caused a deficiency of arms, munitions, and means of transportation. Inefficiency in the defense of French frontiers.

Inefficiency in the organization, instruction, and moral support of the Army in peacetime and in wartime and in the quantitative and qualitative value of the staff.

Poor organization of the High Command.

Criminal submission to political influences.

Delivery of numerous airplanes to the Spanish Popular Front while the country lacked them.

Injudicious application of the nationalization law to national defense.

Facilities offered to foreign invasion in peacetime, chiefly through the admission to French soil of hundreds of thousands of dangerous Spaniards and their leaders.

Criminal weakness with respect to labor agitation, to its grave repercussions in war factories, and to unpatriotic propaganda.

As a result of this inefficiency and these capital errors, France was left morally and materially disarmed and without the means indispensable to her leaders for the achievement of her mission in the war.

Thus M. Daladier betrayed the duties of his office.

The Council recommends his imprisonment in a fortress.

GENERAL GAMELIN.—As Chief of Staff of National Defense and of War, General Gamelin was responsible for the preparation of the war and for national defense.

In this capacity, he knew the military and diplomatic situation, and the duty of his office was to ensure France's security.

Through lack of energy and character he failed to repair the growing deficiencies in armament and war preparation.

Through disastrous decisions he disorganized the leadership during the war.

He allowed the Army to sink into a state of material and moral inferiority, thus leading it into decisive operations badly prepared, badly trained, badly armed, and unseasoned.

General Gamelin betrayed the duty of his office.

The Council recommends his imprisonment in a fortress.

LÉON BLUM.—Twice Premier, the first time for more than a year, and Vice-President of the cabinet for more than seven months, M. Blum was in power in the period preceding the war. He was familiar with the diplomatic and military situation, which was beginning to grow worse at the time he took over the government.

He was informed of the deficiencies in national defense. His office imposed on him the duty of giving France the arms necessary to her security. He disregarded this duty, failing to give the armament factories the stimulus which the situation so urgently required; on the contrary, he was responsible for disorganization, and also covered with his authority in this field the sinister activities of his Ministers Daladier and Pierre Cot.

408

Labor reforms, on which the country might have reached an agreement, were diverted by him from their true significance and their national purpose, and became instruments of social struggle. The moral strength of the country, as a result, was dangerously weakened.

He put France into a perilous situation.

Thus M. Léon Blum betrayed the duties of his office.

The Council recommends his imprisonment in a fortress.

GUY LA CHAMBRE.—Minister of Aviation from January 18, 1938, to March 20, 1940, M. Guy la Chambre himself, when he came to power, summarized the situation he inherited from his predecessor as follows: "Insufficiency of quantity, deficiency of quality."

What did he do to remedy so deplorable a situation? A few sound measures on his part, it must be said, could not have yielded immediate results.

Guy la Chambre seems not to have lacked good will, but simply will. His good will and efforts were, in fact, constantly offset by the consequences of his weakness. Guy la Chambre was unable to resist the pressure of his political friends, and the improvement of aeronautic production was thereby hindered.

To conceal the effects of this inadequacy, Guy la Chambre did not hesitate to use the most lamentable subterfuges and to lie before Parliament.

Lack of energy, lack of frankness are the principal complaints that can be brought against the former Minister of Aviation.

It must nevertheless be taken into consideration that Guy la Chambre, who left France in June, 1940, returned spontaneously to put himself at the disposal of justice.

The Council deems, by a majority of six to one, that Guy la Chambre betrayed the duties of his office.

As the Council does not consider Guy la Chambre one of the men principally responsible for the disaster, it does not recommend that the Constitutional Act be applied to him.

CONTROLLER-GENERAL PIERRE JACOMET.—As General Secretary of the Ministry of National Defense and of War with special powers since 1936, Controller-General Jacomet had a decisive effect on the preparation for war, in particular on the manufacture of armaments. In his functions, he gave proof of criminal negligence in the military and industrial preparation of the country.

In the face of political agitation, his weakness in dealing with undisciplined workers contributed to the disorganization of production and thereby to the insufficiency of armaments.

He contributed particularly to the unwise nationalization of war factories.

By silence or deceit, he persistently concealed the truth of the situation, and even maintained in December, 1939, that France was morally and materially prepared in the political, military, and economic fields.

PIERRE COT.—As Minister of Aviation for one year in 1933 and 1934, then for over twenty months from 1936 to 1938, he was responsible for the preparation of French military aviation.

In spite of repeated warnings, he failed to give France the Air Force which the situation required.

He sacrificed the interest of the country to his preferences as a partisan by limiting credits, disorganizing the Air Force, discouraging the leadership, nationalizing the factories, furnishing aviation matériel to the Spanish Popular Front, and favoring insubordination.

He aggravated these sinister actions by his constant false affirmations and subterfuges intended to deceive Parliament and the country. He thus led France to believe that her safety was secure at a time when it was irremediably compromised.

Thus, Pierre Cot betrayed the duties of his office.

He would incur, were he present, imprisonment in a fortress; but as he is a fugitive and this sanction cannot be enforced, the Council deems that, for the moment, it is useless to apply to him Constitutional Act No. 7.

IV

Decision Broadcast by Marshal Pétain

VICHY, OCTOBER 16, 1941.

Frenchmen:

The Council of Political Justice has handed me its conclusions on the exact date which I fixed in my speech on August 12. These conclusions are clear, complete, perfectly motivated.

Composed of distinguished war veterans and great servants of the public good, the Council of Justice has unanimously decided that imprisonment in a fortress, the heaviest penalty established by Constitutional Act, No. 7, should be visited upon MM. Édouard Daladier and Léon Blum as well as upon General Gamelin. I consequently order the incarceration of these three men in the fort of Portalet.

As for M. Guy la Chambre and Controller-General Jacomet, whose responsibilities appear less grave, the Council handed down a different opinion. MM. La Chambre and Jacomet will consequently remain interned in Bourrassol.

But the Council of Political Justice has asked me to preserve judicial power from the encroachments of political power; this respect for the separation of powers forms part of our customary law. I have therefore complied with this appeal, which corresponds to my own feeling. The Court of Riom will continue in power.

I shall even go further; I not only believe that the Court of Riom could not be deprived of its jurisdiction, but that national interest requires it to be able to pass judgment as soon as possible. The gravity of the acts with which those chiefly responsible for our disaster are charged is such that it cannot be masked or hidden by mere political sanctions.

As for M. Paul Reynaud and M. Georges Mandel, who have been subjected to a preliminary examination before the Court of Riom, I have decided, on the advice of a majority of the members of the Council of Political Justice, that the grave suspicions attached to them justify their imprisonment in a fortress. I have ordered this measure to be taken.

A country which feels itself betrayed has a right to the truth, to the whole truth. The disaster is but the reflection in the military field of the weaknesses and the acts of the former political regime. The sentence that will conclude the Riom trial must be in the open. It will strike at individuals and also at methods, customs, and the regime. It will be without appeal. There will be no further discussion. It will mark the end of one of the most painful periods in the life of France. The Court has already accomplished a huge task and the Council of Political Justice rendered spontaneous homage to its work and investigations as well as to the method with which it obtained such decisive results.

The proceedings shall be conducted in the open. As they deal with a great trial in our history and take place during a troubled period, they are not, of course, free from danger. I am not unaware of this fact, but I have weighed the advantages and disadvantages of the debates from the point of view of the nation, and have made my decision; any other decision would have been against the interests of the country.

A first stage has thus been passed on the way to that justice which is due to the nation. Undoubtedly the normal development of judicial procedure would have spared me the necessity of invoking Constitutional Act. No. 7, because the chief culprits, to whom this first sanction is today being applied, may find this sanction transformed into a still heavier penalty by the end of the trial. In times like ours each one must assume his own responsibilities; I am setting the example by assuming my own.

In August I felt that the jurisdictional procedure with its prudence, its delays, and its slow progress, was aggravating the unrest under which the country is suffering. It is that unrest which I am attempting to alleviate by today's decisions. I hereby assure you that if you have been betrayed, you will not be deceived. Keep your confidence in me, keep intact the faith in the destiny of the country.

V

The Ministry of Information's Instructions to the French Press

Orders of the Censorship Office

October 15, 1941

ORDER 488—The official communiqué on the Council of Political Justice must be printed on the first page in a two-column head.

October 16, 1941

ORDER 492—The Marshal's speech and the sentences pronounced must be presented in the following way:

(1) A large headline on the first page, the length of the page, in poster-size print: "The justice of the Marshal."

(2) The rest of the story to follow in at least four columns.

General Instructions on the Eve of the Public Hearings at Riom

1. Keep in mind that the trial is limited to the state of unpreparedness for war existing in France from 1936 to May, 1940, which will become apparent during the hearings.

2. Bring to the public's attention the facts which will be revealed concerning the negligence and errors in organization and equipment of the Army and Air Force, development of fortifications, and preparation for industrial mobilization.

3. Make it clear that the defendants are responsible for failing in execution of their duties during the critical period in which they were in power.

4. Point out wherever possible that the real trial is the trial of the state of things from which the catastrophe resulted, so that the French people, plunged into despair, may judge with a clear mind the methods of government of which they have become the victims.

5. Show that this cannot be the trial of the Army, which, from leaders to soldiers, has been compelled to fight without the weapons necessary to modern warfare.

6. Comment and develop daily the arguments and refutations which the Press Service will furnish the newspapers when required.

7. Especially consider this trust when either the person of the Marshal [Pétain] or his policy is referred to during the trial.

8. Stress that the Marshal's policy has been inspired in every field by the necessity assumed in the following sentence: France is condemned to build a new regime or perish.

Special Instructions After the First Hearing at Riom

1. Publish nothing of the reading in Court by M. le Trocquer [attorney for Léon Blum] of the instructions to the press.

2. In the intervention by a lawyer, the expression "the armistice patched up in fear is forbidden.

3. Instruction No. 1 is abrogated.

4. Cut the intervention of M. Daladier: "Germany impatient to see Frenchmen judged."

5. In M. Daladier's intervention, delete: "The Minister of War in 1934 [Pétain] reduced armament credits."

6. The declarations of M. Daladier on the military defeat (equality of armaments, quality of the equipment) are forbidden.

7. Conclusions of M. Ribet [attorney for Daladier] on the responsibility of the War Ministers from 1930 to 1936 are forbidden.

8. In declarations by M. Ribet, all allusions to the inadequacies of French armament since 1929 are forbidden.

9. In the address of M. Spanien [attorney for Blum], the expression, "the generals in the hands of the enemy," is forbidden.

10. Suppress that part of the address of M. Blum's lawyer alluding to the continuation of the war, beginning: "The coalition of which we are a party is not broken."

11. Suppress M. Spanien's sentence: "We do not want to be submitted to the discipline of the Marshal."

12. In Blum's address, suppress the part in which the responsibility of the governments from 1929 to 1936 is stressed.

13. In the same address, suppress all reference to the strengthening of Germany since 1933.

14. In the same address, suppress the names of M. Doriot and M. Bergery.

The accounts of the Riom trial will be censored at Riom and at Vichy. In addition, the local censorships will also receive instructions and will verify their observations before giving permission for publication. The local censorships will see that the arguments and refutations given to the newspapers by the Press Service are used without delay in original articles conforming to the orientation given by the government, and displayed so as to attract the attention of the reader.

Verbal Instructions to Chief Editors
FEBRUARY 27, 1942

German authorities having invited a certain number of newspapermen in the free zone to go to Paris to visit the anti-Bolshevik exhibition, the Information Secretariat has received many demands for *Ausweis*. These demands have been transmitted to the German delegation in Vichy, which will choose those permitted to go to Paris. As soon as authorizations to cross the demarcation line have been received, they will be sent to the beneficiaries.

Additional Special Instructions

1. In the examination of M. Daladier, allusion to a remark by General Weygand that his request to Marshal Pétain to summon the Supreme War Council had been ignored from 1934 on, is forbidden.

412

2. Suppress the word "comedy" with which M. Daladier characterized the Council of Political Justice.

3. Suppress M. Daladier's answer on the attitude of General Weygand and Marshal Pétain in regard to reduction of officers.

4. Suppress every allusion to the 12 millions reduction in appropriations for training camps.

5. Suppress M. Daladier's sentence: "You mention only names of vanquished generals."

6. Suppress Daladier's sentences: "In 1939 there were strong attacks against Pétain in Parliament," and, "Accused and condemned by those whom I have defended."

7. Suppress Daladier's remark: "If we are to suppose that all our partners were equally sincere," also his use of "wrongfully" concerning Germany.

8. Suppress Daladier's sentence: "France assuring alone its own security and Marshal Pétain alone is responsible for this."

9. Suppress Daladier's remark: "In 1934 armaments appropriations: 600 millions—my appropriations; 400 millions—the Marshal's appropriations."*

10. To sum up preceding instructions, suppress all that concerns the actions of the Marshal.

11. Suppress Daladier's sentence: "The Council of Political Justice limited itself to the reading of the chapter titles of the indictment order."

12. Suppress in Daladier's explanation the sentence: "Vicissitudes of political life are such that perhaps they will be my subordinates tomorrow."

13. In the Daladier explanation, suppress the sentence: "I call authentic documents those documents which were made before the armistice."

14. Suppress the sentence of Daladier: "It is unbelievable that the Germans in their advance gathered up hundreds and hundreds of tanks."

15. Suppress the Daladier sentence: "More than 1,200 caterpillar cars have been left in warehouses, but witnesses will come to say that they were lacking at the front."

16. Do not quote the name of De Gaulle in the Daladier explanations.

17. Suppress the Daladier reference to the use made of three mechanized divisions. Suppress also his analysis of military operations and praise for some generals.

18. Suppress all reference to the role of General Weygand in the Balkans.

19. Suppress the Daladier statement that anti-tank guns had been sent to Turkey on the insistence of General Weygand, and the allusion to the part played by General Weygand in the Near East.

* During 1943 both Daladier and Pétain were War Ministers in different governments.

Confidential Note from the Director of Censorship at Clermont-Ferrand to Newspaper Editors

MARCH 4, 1941

I have recently sent you the instructions of the Censorship Office with respect to the Riom trial. Henceforth, the instructions will no longer be sent to the press for reasons you can well imagine. I shall therefore no longer be able to communicate them to you. Nevertheless, in reading those which have been sent to you, you will have appreciated the difficulty of making a complete report. There are numerous cuts which frequently leave only two or three lines of text per page. This very reason has caused the majority of the papers to stop printing personal reports and even to cut out descriptive accounts. Many doubt that the trial can continue much longer. I must tell you in all sincerity that the defense of Daladier produced a very strong impression.

As for myself, I shall not continue to cover the trial regularly. I have, until now, drawn up a descriptive account, trying to give details which, though not in the Havas report, have been authorized by the censorship in certain cases. This account has been published irregularly. I shall therefore telegraph you henceforth only a sketch of the session, which will be perfectly orthodox."

VI

Letter from Léon Blum to the Supreme Court

OCTOBER 20, 1941

Gentlemen:

You gave me a five-day period to present my defense to the Supreme Court of Justice against the indictment order signed by the Prosecuting General.

I had been informed of the indictment on October 16 at 6:45 P.M., a few minutes before Marshal Pétain announced on the radio the sentence already delivered by him against me. On the morning of the 17th, the reasons for this sentence were also made public through the press, in the form of propositions issued by the Council of Political Justice. The Council declared, and Marshal Pétain sanctioned that declaration by application of punishment, that I had betrayed the duties of my office.

Thus you invite a man already condemned—and condemned on the basis of the same charges—to answer the indictment of your tribunal. Is this not a cruel mockery? What meaning will my answers have? Has not the case already been settled before the world? There has been talk of separation of powers, i.e., of the special nature of judiciary authority and of its independence from executive power. Homage has been paid to this beautiful principle. But in fact you have been forestalled: the case has been prejudiced against you as well as against me. Citing the same facts, and in virtue of the same charges, will you be really free to act or to weaken by your future verdict the character and the motivation of the sentence already given by the supreme authority of the State? I should be embarrassed to stress this point further before French magistrates.

My point will be limited to three observations, or to be more precise, to three points of procedure.

Here is the first. I do not know to what extent the Council of Political Justice was informed of your investigation. I wish to recall, however, the attitude which I constantly and deliberately preserved throughout the procedure conducted in accordance with the Council's secret practice, practices long condemned by French law.

In the course of the three examinations by the investigating magistrate (I do not include the first examination of identity), I systematically limited myself to purely general explanations. I did not call upon a single witness or produce a single document. Nor did I discuss any of the testimony or documents gathered by the prosecution. I did not point out, as it would have been easy to do, the errors of partiality or the contradictions contained in many of them. Explicitly and formally, I reserved such discussions as well as other means of my defense for the day that was to come, for the day of public debate and trial. Hence I wish to register a protest, a complete and absolute protest against the contradictory character of the investigation conducted in my case.

The Council of Political Justice, assuming the none too probable hypothesis that they had knowledge of the record of your proceedings against me, delivered judgment in my case without having given me any opportunity whatsoever to exercise my rights of defense, whether by me or for me.

414

As an office-holder accused publicly of having compromised by governmental action the interests and security of my country, I had a right to public presentation of my case, to self-defense and public reparation. I repeat with regret that I can hope for no protection of my rights from your justice. But I preserve and affirm my right to justify myself before my country, before international opinion, and if I may be permitted to say so, before history.

Second observation. My counsels, M. le Trocquer and M. Spanien, presented the Court with a note which was submitted on January 18. From that time on and throughout the early period of the investigation it became evident that the defeat of French arms could not be reasonably explained by the shortage of means and machines placed at the disposal of the Army. We therefore asked the Court to extend its investigation into the field of conduct of military operations. We pointed out that an inquiry into events such as our Army's entrance into Belgium, the rupture of the front on the Meuse, and the lack of a proper offensive after those events, was obligatory for the Court and, in our opinion, even imperative.

Since January last, and with the gradual prolongation of the investigation, the opinion which dictated the above note of my counsels has practically become a certitude. It is now established that the general program of the armaments for land forces introduced for the first time by the government of which I was the head and the execution of that program were, at the time of our entrance into the conflict, ahead of the original schedule.

It has been established that for the greater part of the mechanical equipment which played a determining part in the battle, there did not exist a decisive numerical disproportion between ourselves and the enemy. Hence, since January, the problems of the methods in which these arms were employed and the strategic conduct of operations called for your investigation with even greater urgency than before that date.

The Court has paid no attention to the note presented by my counsels. The result is that the indictment was arrived at without any inquiry into two groups of facts. These facts, on the day of our defeat, were irresistibly pointed out by unanimous public opinion, opinion of soldiers and citizens alike. One group of facts: the mistakes of our command. The other group of facts: that suspicious combination of conscious or unconscious complicity which unmanned the French forces confronting the enemy and which is called in general parlance "fifth column" and "treason." By this I mean not mere "dereliction in discharge of duties of office," but outright treason.

And now the third observation. It obviously follows from the charges and pronouncement of the Council of Political Justice that the accusations against me are aimed primarily at the laws voted and applied, as well as at the social policies practiced by the government of which I was the head—and are not aimed at any positive act of my own.

I affirm once more with even greater force the declaration made by me in the course of my interrogation: By the republican Constitution of 1875, the sovereignty belongs to the French people and is expressed through general suffrage. This sovereignty is delegated to the Parliament. When criminal responsibility is imputed to a man, to the head of the government, without first establishing or even alleging anything that touches him personally, without adducing a single fact contrary to honesty, to honor, to official application of duty, labor, and conscience; when such a man is incriminated exclusively because he carried out policies commanded by sovereign general suffrage, policies controlled and approved by the Parliament to which the sovereignty had been delegated—then it is not the man nor the head of the government, but the republican system and regime itself that is put on trial. And, in the name of my convictions of a lifetime, I shall be proud to face that trial.

I am, gentlemen. . . .

Léon Blum

VII

Act of Indictment by the Supreme Court of Justice

(Arrêt de mise en jugement)

OCTOBER 28, 1941

1. Daladier, Édouard, former Premier, former Minister of National Defense and of War, held;

2. Blum, Léon, former Premier, held;

3. Gamelin, Maurice, General in the Army Reserve, former Chief of Staff of National Defense and of War, former Vice-President of the Supreme War Council, held;

4. Cot, Pierre, former Minister of Aviation, in flight;

5. La Chambre, Guy, former Minister of Aviation, held;

6. Jacomet, Pierre, Controller-General, of the first rank of the administration of the Army, former General Secretary of the Ministry of National Defense and of War, held;

On the charges:

1. Of betrayal of the duties of their office, in terms of the first article of the decree of August 1, 1940;

2. Of attacks on the security of the state.

In view of the definitive list of charges of the Prosecuting Attorney of October 15, 1941, leading to the indictment of the six above-named accused; in view of the memorandum presented by M. Guy la Chambre, the letter addressed to the Court by M. Léon Blum, the note of M. Toulouse, counsel for M. Jacomet, and the memorandum of MM. Arnal and Puntous, counsels for General Gamelin, the Court has the right to deal with the charges of betrayal of the duties of office:

Whereas it appears from the examination that on September 3, 1939, the date of the outbreak of hostilities between France and Germany, that the French Army and Air Force were not ready to fulfill the mission incumbent upon them; whereas with respect to the Army the evidence received revealed especially the inadequacy of the instructions, the inadequacy of armaments of all sorts, the inadequacy of field artillery matériel, trench artillery, and anti-tank defense, of which the fighting units had not received the regulation supplies, the inadequacy of heavy artillery, the inadequacy of anti-aircraft defense and of the aerial defense of the land, especially at high and low altitudes, the inadequacy of armored equipment, tanks, and motor machine guns, the inadequacy of the stocks of clothing and equipment, the lack of preparation of industrial mobilization, which caused the slowing-down of production at a moment when increase was necessary and the drafting into the armed forces of a considerable number of workers and specialists who later had to be returned to the factories; and whereas with respect to the Air Force, it appears that France had on September 2, 1939, far less modern aircraft than the number which the Superior Air Council had declared to be the minimum figure indispensable to the security of the country; that, in particular; we had not a single modern bomber; that, as a result of declarations made by numerous witnesses, the deficiencies which have just been pointed out could be imputed, in whole or in part, to the accused implicated in the proceedings, they are principally charged as follows:

Édouard Daladier, with having shown incompetence in the preparation of the national mobilization, particularly of the industrial mobilization, in the organization and direction of the Army, in the manufacture of armaments of all sorts, in the preparation of anti-aircraft defense and the aerial defense of the land, in the enforcement of labor legislation, especially in forbidding by a circular dated July 20, 1936, any recourse to overtime in war establishments, although it was authorized by law; with not having assured the manufacture of heavy artillery, with having lacked firmness in the face of a propaganda which compromised the output of factories working for national defense, with having made incorrect declarations concerning our military preparation in the Chambers and before Parliamentary Commissions;

Léon Blum, with having compromised national defense by his enforcement of labor legislation, especially by making virtually impossible any recourse to overtime, with having permitted the law on the nationalization of armament manufacture to be enforced in a way harmful to the interests of national defense, and with having caused a considerable decline in production by his weakness in the face of revolutionary agitation, especially by tolerating the occupation and neutralization of factories [sit-down strikes].

General Maurice Gamelin, with having shown incompetence in the direction of the Army, with not having exercised proper action to assure the manufacture of necessary armaments, especially of heavy artillery, anti-tank equipment, and matériel destined for anti-aircraft use and aerial defense of the land, and the distribution of regulation equipment to units, with not having remedied the inadequate stocks of clothing and equipment, with not having assured the preparation of industrial mobilization, and with having, in the course of hostilities, caused the adoption of a faulty organization of the High Command;

Pierre Cot, with having shown incompetence in the organization of the Air Force; with having aggravated the inadequacy of our production by his enforcement of the law on the nationalization of armament manufacture and by his weakness with respect to revolutionary conspiracies, and with having handed over to the Spanish republican government airplanes destined for the French Air Force, especially modern airplanes;

Guy la Chambre, with having aggravated the inadequacy of production of our factories by his weakness in the face of revolutionary agitation, and with having, on numerous occasions, by cunning presentations of the results of production, lulled the vigilance of organizations charged with assuring the preparation of national defense or with controlling the execution of proper means for its realization;

Controller-General Pierre Jacomet, with having shown incompetence in the execution of war contracts and the surveillance of armament manufactures, in the preparation of industrial mobilization, and in the enforcement of the law on the nationalization of war industries, with having shown excessive weakness with respect to revolutionary agitation, with having tolerated or even favored the action of illegal syndicates, and with having ordered the reinstatement in our factories of many fomentors of disturbances, and with having inadequately enlightened his minister and Parliament on the state of our military preparation, through information furnished in a reticent or misleading fashion;

Whereas, moreover, the investigation reveals that on August 23, 1939, eleven days before the outbreak of hostilities, at the request of the Minister of Foreign Affairs, a meeting of military leaders was held at the Ministry of National Defense and of War under the leadership of Édouard Daladier; and that the military leaders were asked whether France could watch the disappearance of Poland without reacting and whether we had the means of preventing the realization of such a happening; and that General Gamelin, without expressing any reservation and without revealing the inadequacy of our military preparation on any point, answered that the Army was ready; and that Guy la Chambre declared that, by reason of the considerable progress that had been achieved, the situation of our air power no longer had to influence the decisions of the government, as it had done in the crisis of September, 1938; and that Édouard Daladier knowingly permitted General Maurice Gamelin and Guy la Chambre to make these answers, from which the Minister of Foreign Affairs concluded that no consideration based on our military possibilities was of a nature to influence our foreign policy.

Whereas it follows from these facts considered as a whole that there are sufficient grounds that the accused, who have held office within ten years prior to the first act of investigation—

Édouard Daladier being Minister of National Defense and of War and Premier;

Léon Blum being Premier;

Pierre Cot being Minister of Aviation;

General Gamelin being Chief of Staff of National Defense and of War and Vice-President of the Supreme War Council;

Guy la Chambre being Minister of Aviation;

Controller-General Jacomet being General Secretary of the Ministry of National Defense and of War—

betrayed the duties of their office in acts constituting a crime as defined by Article I, Paragraph 1, of the decree of August 1, 1940, and subject to punishment under Article 12 of the law of July 30, 1940.

The arraignment of the above-named on the charges specified having been directed, an order for the arrest of the aforementioned defendants has been issued.

And, in the absence of sufficient charges, there being no cause to follow all of the other counts listed in the indictment in order to institute an inquiry, the trial, as stated in Article 9 of the law of July 30, 1940, will take the form of public debates before the Supreme Court, but the courtroom may be cleared whenever public interest requires it; whereas, if none of the counts of indictment retained by the Court deals with the diplomatic relations of France or with the conduct of military operations, certain witnesses have nevertheless been called in the course of the investigation, and may be called to the hearing to express their views accessorily on these two subjects, and that the considerations of national security are opposed to the publicity of open debate on questions of a diplomatic order.

Whereas, furthermore, the Court has received by law the right to judge only with respect to the acts charged to ministers or their immediate subordinates; and whereas in the armed forces the only immediate subordinates of the Ministers of War and of Aviation were the Chief of Staff of National Defense and of War and the Chief of Staff of the Air Force, it thereby follows that the Court, if it had examined the conduct of military operations, could have involved only these two general officers, while the execution of these operations involved the examination of an indivisible body of deeds which could eventually be imputed in part or in whole to other military leaders; and no indictment could be formulated with respect to the conduct of military operations; and, consequently, a public debate, which could, moreover, harm the interests of the country, could not be instituted on this point before the Court.

Now, therefore, it is ordered that the debates be public, but that the courtroom may be cleared during the hearing if witnesses are to be called to express their views on questions of diplomatic order or questions relating to the conduct of military operations.

It is further ordered that the debates will be held at the House of the Supreme Court of Riom, January 15, 1942, at 1:30 P.M.

So decreed by the Supreme Court of Justice, deliberating and ruling in Council Chamber, October 28, 1941, present and concurring: MM. Lagarde, President; Maillefaud, Vice-President; Tanon, Herr Watteau, Devemy, and Olivier Martin, councilors. Signed: H. Lagarde; signed: E. Paulin.

VIII

First Statements of Léon Blum Before the Supreme Court

First Hearing of February 19, 1942

The Silence of Gamelin

The decision which General Gamelin has made is his alone, but its direction and consequences belong to us all. For my part, I cannot suppress the reflections which it inspires in me.

I shall not feign surprise. The attitude of General Gamelin was long to be expected. Now that it is an accomplished fact—a fact which has just been accomplished before us—I doubt whether there is anyone here who has been able to suppress a feeling of pain. By his act General Gamelin identifies himself voluntarily with our unfortunate Army. But precisely the first consequence which cannot fail to strike you as it does me is that, before this trial has even begun, a yawning void has opened.

The Responsibilities for the Defeat

It is your mission to establish and sanction responsibilities. Responsibilities for what? For a military defeat. By your act of indictment everything pertaining to the conduct of military operations has been eliminated from the debate. For greater safety, you have, in advance, condemned to the shadow and to the silence of the closed courtroom all provisions, charges, discussions in which this type of problem could have been raised, even accessorily. But there remained the person of General Gamelin, Commander-in-Chief of the land forces from the beginning of the campaign until May 19. His presence would invincibly have drawn the debate toward the type of problem which you wanted to proscribe. His contact with officials of every rank who were called as witnesses would have forced discussion, caused sparks of truth to fly out willy-nilly. But he will no longer be present at the debate. For not to take part in the debate, to be there as a mute spectator, is not to be present at it. You had already curtailed the subject matter of the debate; General Gamelin has now withdrawn his person from it. The result is that in the debate on the responsibility for the defeat, the war will be absent.

One can hardly conceive of a more amazing paradox. Why was this tribunal created? Because the French Army has succumbed in an ill-fated campaign, and because the French people wanted to know why the Army has been defeated in this war. No one can deny that the people's instinct attributed this military defeat above all to military causes. And you who are to establish these causes, you who have drawn so many things into the orbit of this trial, you exclude from it the war.

"A Judgment Against You"

For it is you, gentlemen, who have reduced General Gamelin to silence, to absence. He has told you his reasons. He will not protest against a sentence pronounced on him by a chief who has been the leading proponent of our war doctrine; nor does he want to accuse his subordinates in the courtroom. His silence was dictated partly by Pétain's decision and partly by the Supreme Court's act of indictment. As he is the only military defendant, the whole, anonymous responsibility for the military defeat depends on him until we are better informed. He can absolve himself of it only by casting it upon others; he can attenuate it only by passing a share of it to others. Now, this determination of respective responsibilities, and, if necessary, of degrees in responsibility, this clarification, was your mission, your duty. You refused to fulfill it, and General Gamelin refuses today to fulfill it in your stead. By declining your mission as judges, you have obligated him to remain silent or else to appear as the public accuser of men who, for you, are capable of being justified, and who have remained for him companions-at-arms. He has chosen to remain silent. This silence, and the respect he draws, are in reality a judgment against you.

For my part I share this respect, but I insist on telling why we shall not share this silence—when I say "we," I mean the friends who are assisting me as well as myself.

The Indignation of Every Free Conscience

It is not that I am not shocked, along with General Gamelin, both by Marshal Pétain's sentence and by the indictment. When the General declares that he is condemned before even appearing before his judges, he is right—but he is not alone in this unprecedented situation. The fundamental iniquity, the basic fault, affects all the accused present in the courtroom. These men, whom your conscience as judges should obligate you to regard as

419

innocent until the moment of the verdict, come before you already condemned. The highest authority in the state has pronounced them guilty of the same acts, subject to the same criminal legislation, and the sentence it has decreed has already been executed. Here is something that offends both reason and the written law, something which, I believe I can say, particularly violates the oldest traditions of the French spirit. Marshal Pétain's sentence is based on no hierarchial prerogative, although he is head of the Army, but on his position as Chief of State, as holder of the totality of the governmental power. His sentence is not a disciplinary condemnation but a political condemnation, based on the proposals—which have been made public—of a Council of Political Justice. I might even affirm that this political condemnation strikes at political men still more directly than at a soldier.

As for your indictment, if it does not subject us to the same moral standards, it strikes a blow, equally serious and intolerable, at our defense.

The High Command Excluded from the Discussion

You exclude from the trial anything that might involve the military High Command during the war—in other words, everything touching on military doctrines, strategic principles, operations, and the actual utilization of modern equipment. You intend to concentrate the prosecution on the matériel, I might almost say, on the quantitative aspect of armament. Yet even the best prepared, the most generously equipped army, will nevertheless succumb if the mistakes of the High Command have maneuvered it into a hopeless situation or if the weakness of its leadership has failed to inspire it with the will to fight. Again, the matériel, however abundant, cannot abound everywhere at the same time. When the doctrines that determine its employment are defective, when the plans are imprudent, and when speculations prove erroneous, even an army having superabundant matériel may find itself in a condition of irremediable inferiority at the time and place where the enemy's surprise attack has struck. These remarks are obvious to the point of being commonplace, but they are curiously confirmed by your investiga-tion; France and the world will be stupefied to learn the true numerical relations between French and enemy matériel at the outbreak of the war or at the time of the German attack in May, 1940. Hence the question of whether the mistakes of the High Command were not perhaps the ultimate causes of the defeat would have to be settled first. That is the direction which you should be following in your investigation if you want to fulfill your task; and that is what I asked of you so urgently over a year ago, in a note addressed and handed to you. Not only have you failed to pursue this essential and interlocutory inquiry . . . but you have, through your indictment, prevented us from raising it in the courtroom.

"Pétain Has Pronounced Sentence on Us, and on You"

I might therefore say, in my turn: "You have mutilated my defense to the point of making it inert and impotent. Judge me, condemn me a second time . . . I shall remain silent." We shall, nevertheless, speak. We shall not restrict ourselves to drawing the logical conclusion to the situation in which we are trapped. From the very beginning of the trial, we shall join the loyal and persevering effort which will be made to change this situation.

I know very well that there is something against which we are doubtless incapable of struggling—it is the sentence which Marshal Pétain has pronounced on us, and on you. It is res judicata against you as it is against us. You have tried to clear yourselves, to save your independence as judges; you know better than I that you have failed. Or do you, truthfully, feel free to acquit and release the men who, on the same charges, were declared guilty by a Chief of State to whom you have sworn an oath of allegiance? You are aware that he has left you no choice but to punish us even more harshly. But in this respect the case has been taken out of your hands. Judgment has been passed on you as much as on us; an indelible mark has been imprinted in advance on your future verdict. But if we attempt to do nothing useful with respect to the Marshal's sentence and its consequences—they are irremediable—the same is not true of your indictment.

On these grounds we can and must give battle. We can and must try to re-establish the trial in its legality and integrity—and that is what we shall attempt, with the ardent desire of extracting from an emancipated trial all the residue of truth it contains. We shall do it less for ourselves, who are already condemned, than for the country, for universal opinion, and, I may say, for history.

"You Have Refused To Try Those Responsible for the War . . . "

We do not despair of this effort before undertaking it. In his message Marshal Pétain said, at the same time that he presented you with the *fait accompli* of his condemnation: "The proceedings shall be conducted in the open. . . . I have weighed the advantages and disadvantages of it. . . ." Let us arm ourselves with these words as if their purpose had really been to leave to your conscience as judges a free zone. Permit me to tell you, gentlemen, that I, like most of you, have been a judge. For nearly a quarter of a century I was a magistrate. My judicial career was almost completed when, against my wish, I was thrown into public life. I was always attached to the highest courts—the Council of State, the Tribunal des Conflits. I know from experience what the conscience of a judge is, and I dare say I know that of a Supreme Court. Sovereignty for a judge is not so much a comfort and a convenience as a burden. The fact that he feels above himself neither a higher court nor any other power of appeal does not free him; on the contrary, it must only increase his sense of responsibility. Whatever he decides will be definitive, and therefore irreparable. . . . As we appeal to your professional conscience, let us remind you also of your love for your country. Once already your patriotism changed the character of this trial, which was introduced as the trial of those responsible for the war, in other words, as the trial of France. You refused to conduct it in that form. The visible result of your refusal is the absence from this bench of Paul Reynaud and Georges Mandel, whose presence would be essential in a debate on the responsibility for the war, and who were aimed at directly in one paragraph of the document that authorized the formation of the Court; but no investigation has as yet been started against them, nor have they been brought out of their cells at Portalet to keep us company.

The Trial of the Republic

Mind you, however. . . the present trial is no longer that of France—but if it remains what it is, it will prove to be the trial of the Republic. A debate on responsibilities for the defeat from which the responsibility of the military has been deliberately excluded, must needs become not alone a conscious assault on the truth but a suit against the republican regime. The Marshal's message gives reason to fear that this is precisely what is expected of you. Do you believe that such a trial will serve the interest and the wish of a country that desires the truth and has never rejected the Republic?

We shall try, therefore—as we can do no more—to substitute for this partisan trial the courageous and objective investigation which the country expects. We shall suggest to you the means. We hope to succeed with your aid. But if you were to fail us, we should not lose courage—we should still fight on. Our duty toward the nation—which we mean to fulfill even here—would not be affected by your refusal; on the contrary, it would only become more urgent. For such a refusal would clearly indicate that you, in full cognizance of the situation, are maintaining the proceedings within their present limits and character: the trial of the Republic, which is still the legal foundation of the country; the trial of the democratic regime with its customs and its methods; the trial of the policy of social justice and conciliation of the government over which I presided. It would then be our task to prove to France that she is not the degenerate nation which,

421

having believed in liberty and progress, has to atone for this ideal and submit to the punishment. As long as the Republic is the accused, we shall remain at our combat stations as its witnesses and its defenders.

Second Hearing of February 19

Distortion of the Law

I wish to support the statements I have already submitted to the Court by remarks of a somewhat different order.

The text of Article I, Paragraph 1, of the decree of August 1, 1940, is worded so clearly that one would think it beyond all controversy.

It fixes a landmark in time—September 4, 1939.

It aims at two categories of acts concerning this fixed landmark.

First, previous acts: those which contributed to the passing from a state of peace to a state of war.

Second, posterior or ulterior acts: those which aggravated the situation thus created.

For the first category the text fixed Sepember 4 as a limit. For the second category there is no limit.

This granted, what should have been the starting point for the acts of the first category?

The text does not state it explicitly, but indicates it.

These acts of the first category are those which contributed to the passing from a state of peace to a state of war. The infractions at which the text aims are, therefore, necessarily posterior to the state of peace as it was last recognized with certainty; peace existing at a given moment in time, under indisputable conditions, the question is to know how and by the assistance of what acts France passed from this state of peace to war. From that time on, if you have pursued your examination in this direction, until what date should you have carried it? When did an indisputable state of peace exist for the last time before the war between France and Germany? I do not believe that there can be any hesitation on this point. The date indicated by the text was that of the Munich Pact. Munich was not only a special arrangement for a given difficulty, but a general and solemn pledge of peace contracted for a long period of years, with the bilateral obligation of friendly consultations and investigations of all European difficulties that might subsequently arise. The texts are formal, the comments of Chancellor Hitler coincide with those of Mr. Chamberlain and of Édouard Daladier. This recollection may today seem . . . strange. But the fact is there. It was affirmed, promised at Munich, that the Pact meant peace. Your investigation into the passing from peace to war could not have gone further back.

There is the ultimate point of departure fixed for the acts of the first category. For the acts of the second, there is none, and no discussion should be possible, since it is fixed explicitly by the text itself. I shall not return to the unanswerable demonstration that has been given you. To cover in your investigation what you consider "acts of aggravation" but those subsequent to September 4, 1939, it was necessary for the indictment order to suppress in its interpretation the crucial word *subsequently,* and for you to eliminate it from the text itself in your act of indictment. Only this alteration of the text of the law permitted you to go back before September 4, 1939. As the legal point of departure had thus been eliminated by you, what new point were you going to choose?

One alone was admissible. One alone found a place in the logic of your error. . . . In the absence of the date explicitly fixed by the text, in the absence of an implicit indication which, of course, one would seek in vain, there was now only one possible point of departure, one which corresponds to the period specified.

An Arbitrary Choice

The preliminary indictment, in express terms, and the Court, as appears from its own examination, arbitrarily chose the beginning of the 1936 legislature.

Why? I permit myself to ask just as has M. Ribet [Daladier's attorney]. Did the rearmament of France suddenly reveal itself as a duty of ministerial office in June, 1936? Or is it, perhaps, that this duty had been admirably fulfilled until June, 1936?

Let me give a few references.

The Nazi party assumed power in March, 1933. The Third Reich left the League of Nations at the end of 1933 and from that time on rearmed openly.

On March 16, 1935, compulsory military service was re-established in Germany.

I know that the year 1933 marked a certain effort in France toward "peaceful coexistence" with the totalitarian dictatorships. It was the year of the Four Power Pact. But after the beginning of 1934 the offer of quantitative limitation of armaments was rejected by the French government. The notorious note of April 17, 1934, which was sent against the advice of M. Barthou, Minister of Foreign Affairs, said: "France will herself provide for her security." This meant that the Disarmament Conference was practically over and Chancellor Hitler claimed his full liberty. From this moment on it was necessary to rearm in order to maintain the "margin of superiority" which we did not want to give up. There was a strong government that enjoyed full powers: Gaston Doumergue was Premier, André Tardieu, Minister of State, Marshal Pétain, Minister of War. There existed at that time not even a trace of modern matériel in the equipment of our fighting units. And yet, what was done? How large were the credits? What was the volume of actual orders? What work projects were undertaken? Only General Denain, the Minister of Aviation, at once began the immediate execution of a vast program, but the official files show with what precipitation and incoherence. The duties of the cabinet were obvious and imperative. Were they fulfilled?

March 7, 1936

To judge if they were, one need only refer to the events of March 7, 1936, two years later. Remember them, gentlemen. Recall the sound of the first words pronounced publicly by the representatives of our government, and then the subsequent collapse of the French position. A complete investigation would have informed you of the reports made by the technicians on the state of our military forces and of the influence of these reports on the decision—or absence of decision—of the government. This incident, which was to bear such grave consequences, will suffice to indicate in what condition the cabinet of June, 1936, found the Army. Your examination should have drawn up this balance sheet. It will doubtless be done in your place. But what had been accomplished between 1933 and 1936? Was it at any time adequate to meet the necessities and the dangers?

The disposition of available matériel is even more important than its quantity, and during the campaign the decrepitude and inadequacy of military doctrines and strategic conceptions became tragically evident. But these doctrines and notions had hardly been born together with the legislation of the Popular Front. Long before June, 1936—in reality, since the last war—the doctrine of our invulnerable fronts, the absolute faith in our fortifications and in the defense strategy, the distrust of armored cars and, particularly, of the role of aviation in warfare, had been proclaimed, inculcated, and practiced. Documentary evidence abounds, and with what signatures!

The Embarrassment of the Indictment

Why then did not the investigation go further back? The act of indictment is silent on this point. The preliminary indictment of the Prosecuting Attorney resorts to a few peculiarly embarrassed explanations, which might be summarized as follows: "To assume that their predecessors were guilty would not absolve the accused of their responsibility." Indeed an unusual conception of justice and equality! Among those guilty of the same crime, one group would thus be punished, while the remainder would be spared deliberately. What can be the basis for this discrimination, if not a political criterion? Is it not evident that, if our predecessors were found guilty, our mistake would at least be attenuated by the fact that we were carrying the burden of a situation which they had transmitted to us? The records would show, on the contrary, that after June, 1936, we did what no one had done before us; the government which I headed put into action a total program to which in size and significance none of the preceding plans could compare. And the dossier proves, furthermore, that the program did not exist merely on paper, but that it was carried out, that it never lacked the necessary credits, and that it was in advance of the time anticipated for its execution when we entered the war. If it was not, by that time, completed, if it was not undertaken on a more methodical industrial scale beginning at the bases of production, the reason has been that it was launched too late; and this tardy beginning is precisely what leads us to the question of responsibilities prior to June, 1936.

Political Reprisals

Let it not be maintained that this prophetic date of June, 1936, corresponds to a critical period in Franco-German relations. I shall go into no detail on this point, even by way of allusion, but the proof would be easy for me. What, then, does this date represent? It can represent only the coming to power, after general elections which overthrew the [National Union] majority, of the government known under the name of the Popular Front government. To begin investigations for the trial in June, 1936, is to admit that political tactics—perhaps political vengeance—have dictated that choice. I can conceive of no other plausible reason. The intention is obvious. It is an attempt to unload the responsibility for military defeat on the Popular Front and its labor and social policy, and thereby on all democratic institutions.

However, gentlemen, I ask you to think about this. A political phenomenon like the Popular Front is not born like a mushroom in one or two election days. It is bound up with what preceded it, and, in a large measure, it is the outcome of what preceded. It is not an absolute beginning and cannot be isolated at will. I shall, when it becomes necessary, cleanse the Popular Front of all misunderstanding and calumny. I shall show its accomplishments in internal and international peace, and in the material, moral, and political preparation for the defense of the country. If you consider its work harmful, if that is your belief, then your examination should have been extended to those who, either by direct action or inevitable reaction, brought it about. Seek out the principal authors, of whom we were merely accomplices.

The Cagoule

The Popular Front was nothing more than a reflex of instinctive defense. For one thing, against the perils which threatened the Republic, of which the agitations of paramilitary associations and the uprising of the 6th of February, 1934, were the obvious sign. For another thing, against the prolonging of the economic crisis which struck at the working masses, the peasant population, and the middle class of the country, and which was expressed by the slackness of business, by the continuing low level of farm prices and salaries, by unemployment, and by poverty.

The promoters of the Popular Front as a political movement—its godfathers—you will probably be surprised to learn, were M. Doriot and M. Gaston Bergery. But its true authors were those who attempted to overthrow republican institutions—those who by their counter-remedies prolonged and aggravated the universal crisis in France.

Include, therefore, in your investigation the conspirators of the 6th of February and of the Cagoule, the men who closed their eyes to their outrages and who protected them in complicity. They are the ones who provoked the spontaneous coalition of the popular masses, so passionately attached to liberty. The direct repercussion on the defeat can be felt here, for these factious conspiracies aggravated the disunion of the country, sapped its confidence in itself, in its institutions, in its ideal, and, thereby, compromised its capacity of resistance in danger.

Address yourselves, moreover, to the champions of gold-parity at any price and of deflation to the death. They are the men who are guilty of this misery, of this suffering, of this revolt of the working classes, of which the elections of May, 1936, were the expression and the extension. This again is the direct reaction of the country at the moment when heavy rearmament was essential. Here is the cause of a large part of the technical difficulties that offered so great an obstacle for the execution of programs as well as the labor difficulties that we had so much trouble in quelling. Draw up the balance sheet. Count the factories that were shut up, the machinery not kept up or not renewed, the skilled workers and specialists scattered abroad or worn out by unemployment.

We Did Our Duty

They [the reactionaries and conspirators] could and did choose their policy freely. Ours was dictated by theirs. Or rather, we could no longer choose except between the policy we practiced and civil war. Civil war was surely not the best way of accelerating manufacture and it was probably not the best way of avoiding foreign war.

Our duty—the duty of our office—was to anticipate this calamity. . . . It was to renew the country's confidence in free institutions and, consequently, to show ourselves scrupulously faithful to the program which the will of universal suffrage had caused to prevail. It was to revive an exhausted and weakened economy by methods contrary to those whose failure had thrown the country into so fearful a condition. We fulfilled this duty. If you think, like the Prosecuting Attorney, that its fulfillment was harmful to the interests of the country, begin by seeking out those who placed this duty on our shoulders.

"I Challenge the Prosecution"

In scanning the history of the past ten years, you do not have the right to stop where you did. Only the judicial period as specified could give you a point of departure. You will have difficulty in finding any other which can be historically justified. In any case, your point of departure is justified on neither historical nor judicial grounds. My demonstration precludes all debate, it seems to me, and I think that I can challenge the prosecution—whatever the agility of its dialectic—to offer me a valid answer on this point. It can be explained only by a single and unique reason, which I do not wish to repeat, and against which you surely wish to defend yourselves. If you persevered in the system employed in the investigation, the indictment order, and your act of indictment, you would thereby proclaim that this trial is a political enterprise, that you are political judges, and that we should no longer have anything to do except to record the admission of those facts.

IX

First Statements of Édouard Daladier before the Supreme Court

First Hearing of February 20, 1942

The Battle of the Tanks

The Polish war had shown the tremendous power of the German armored divisions. The Poles did, indeed, destroy many more German tanks than has been told; the German armored divisions suffered heavy losses. But, in spite of everything, they broke the Polish military organization and certainly determined the victory of Germany. The example was therefore an eloquent one, and it seemed that after the month of September, since we had more than 4,000 tanks [available], it would not have been difficult to organize armored divisions. Curiously, we encountered the same opposition and the same difficulties as before the war. Colonel de Gaulle, who was a determined partisan of armored divisions (but who was wrong, in my opinion, in connecting them with the creation of the *armée de métier*), sent a note to his leaders, telling them: "Don't you find the truth inescapable? The engine upsets your doctrines; the engine will also upset your fortifications. Armored divisions must be created. We have excellent matériel; we must organize it as the Germans do, and we shall have superiority over them." He sent this note to his leaders; it went through the hierarchy, and a meeting was called at General Headquarters at the end of December, 1939. This meeting was thus preceded by a note from Colonel de Gaulle, then in command of the tanks of the Fifth Army, (that is, of the Army of Alsace) which had, on November 11, 1939, been sent on to General Headquarters by General Bourret, with his approval.

Colonel de Gaulle based his argument on the experience gained in the first engagements of French tanks and on the use of German armored divisions in Poland. He showed that the rules governing the use of our tanks and their organization did not correspond to their real possibilities or to the existence of armored masses organized by Germany. In France tanks were divided into two categories: medium tanks for group maneuvers, under the command of a general of a division; and light tanks, arranged in companies, at the disposal of battalion commanders. There was therefore no cooperation between French tanks!

I shall pass rapidly, gentlemen, to the note of Colonel de Gaulle, which is so important, and when read today, so moving. It insistently demands the creation of armored divisions. General Georges, Commander-in-Chief of French troops on the Northeast front, made a note on Colonel de Gaulle's report: "Interesting, but the reorganization is not of the quality of the criticism. Have this studied."

The Troisième Bureau of General Headquarters—Operations—studied it. The Bureau upheld the thesis that the Polish experience did not make a revision of the French system necessary, and on December 3 General Dufieux, former Inspector-General of tanks, addressed a vehement criticism of Colonel de Gaulle's suggestions to General Gamelin, concluding: "I think that Colonel de Gaulle's conclusions should be rejected."

On the other hand, General Billotte—a great warrior whose accidental death in Belgium was an irreparable catastrophe for France . . . maintained that the Germans would seek to repeat their Polish maneuver in France, west of the Meuse, if not on the Lorraine front where the anti-tank defense was irresistible. Gentlemen, listen to this prophecy of Billotte's: "Once again on the west of the Meuse, breaking through the

Belgian barrages, the Germans will attack with their five armored divisions—about 2,000 tanks. . . . Our superiority over the five armored divisions is incontestable." We had three motorized divisions, one armored division already in existence, and the one I had created. Moreover, we had more than forty independent tank battalions destined for the infantry. "It will be enough," added Billotte, "if we increase the number of the units, since we have the matériel, and we can thus form armored divisions which will give us certain superiority."

This valiant soldier, who had fought not only from 1914 to 1918 but all over the world wherever the French flag was flying, sent with his note—as was his custom, for he was not one to lose himself in the clouds—an excellent plan for the organization of three armored divisions, declaring: "It is easy to create armored divisions when the matériel exists."

Gentlemen, let us not pause for discussion. I could allow myself the essentially artificial and irrelevant pleasure of reading you articles attacking the use of armored divisions, articles written as late as January 1, 1940, by General Dufieux, who is one of my principal accusers, and by others.

You have these articles; they were sent to the Court. I quote from them: "A new school came into existence a few years ago; it foresees large units of tanks crossing the enemy front in an irresistible wave, annihilating batteries, destroying bases of the command, their staffs, and munitions depots, overpowering the reserves before they can even be brought into action, and cutting communications, thus ruining, in a few hours, every possibility for an army to stage an effective comeback. The example of Poland is inappropriate. Who can think that such will be the situation between adversaries possessing comparable numerical and material strength?" wrote General Dufieux. "How can it be imagined that these armored units will be able, as in Poland, to drive alone against the enemy's forces and penetrate them without risking almost total destruction?" That is what he wrote. And I could multiply quotations.

Late Creation of Armored Divisions

But, fortunately, the meeting at General Headquarters decided, in spite of the horribly confused discussion, to create armored divisions: four were formed. You will be told that these divisions included far fewer tanks than the German armored divisions. Only the Germans can tell us how many tanks their divisions contained. I doubt whether they will tell. The documents differ on this point. Did the *Panzerdivisionen* include 500 tanks, as is affirmed? I doubt it. General Gamelin also doubted it. It was therefore a question not of 500 tanks but, let us remember, of some 250 tanks, the rest being motor machine guns. For my part, I do not believe that this was a correct figure for the *Panzerdivisionen*, and if I rely on a communiqué of D.N.B., the official German news agency, the figure of 300 would be nearer the truth.

The number of armored cars in the armored divisions is of little importance if the number of our cars was what is claimed by so many witnesses who built them; accordingly we had enough to organize easily, before the May offensive, four or five armored divisions and several mechanized divisions, and to keep enough tanks to support our infantry and to go into battle, as General Billotte told us, with at least numerical equality, if not, as he said, certain superiority.

Misdirection of the French Armored Divisions

But all that was in the hands of men who did not believe in the formation of armored divisions, and who, in spite of all the orders given to them, employed this arm under conditions which General Keller described in a document which is to be found in the dossier.

Alas, gentlemen, this is yet another cause of sadness for us. General Keller tells you that not more than 2,000 tanks were thrown into the battle, whereas we had at least 3,500. Two thousand were used. . . . I hope he is mistaken, but he says: "French tanks were scattered from Dunkerque to Belfort, one battalion and one commander of a tank company at the disposal of every colonel of an infantry regiment." That is what the operational accounts tell us. And I can readily understand why it was wished that the operational accounts might not become the object of a public debate. Yes, I understand. . . .

But the armored division themselves, the four divisions that were created—how were they used? According to General Billotte's plan? According to the plan of General de Gaulle, whom I am proud to have named general and who was the youngest general in the French Army in action? According to Colonel Perré's plan? Did this enthusiastic and energetic young army, which I salute for its magnificence on the battlefield, have an opportunity to show its competence, its capacity?

No, gentlemen, for these mechanized divisions were thrown into the Battle of Belgium too soon. These armored divisions had been placed so far in the rear that, to enter the battle, they were obliged to make a trip of such length as to put them in a position of minor importance.

The first division arrived in the neighborhood of Charlerio, and its first units had hardly left the train—for it had been transported by rail—when it was thrown piece by piece into the furnace; the division was not reformed, its leader was never in command of all its elements. And yet it was heroic. If I remember correctly, it was commanded by General Buisson, a man whom I had had with me as chief-adjutant of my military cabinet, the son of a teacher, an admirable soldier with the passion of the warriors of '93. He behaved like a hero. His armored division, which had been given 130 tanks when it should have had twice or three times as many, fought for three days against 1,500 German tanks, held them during that time, inflicted on them losses greater in number than its own, and gave way only when it became impossible, with 130 tanks, to resist such a massive onslaught.

As for the second armored division, Colonel Perré has put into the dossier the result of his inspection: "A magnificent engine of war commanded by a leader worthy of the name!" He has retraced its heroic epic, but he tells you: "On the front of the Somme and Aisne, certain generals had the curious idea of setting out tanks as sentinels on the bridges, depriving them of all support, instead of sending the armored division into battle in mass formation and according to clear and precise plans. The armored divisions were wasted, scattered, broken up. That explains why the efficacy of our machines was so different, although we had as many tanks and armored cars on the battlefields as the Germans."

Gentlemen, the demonstration of this point admits of no discussion, and I do not wish to insist on it.

The President: This demonstration is outside the scope of the trial.

M. Daladier: No. . . .

The President: I beg your pardon.

M. Daladier: Why?

The President: The trial deals with the inadequacy of the military preparation for war and not with the conduct of operations.

M. Daladier: I am sorry not to agree with you and I beg your pardon for it, but I am replying to that grave sentence of the act of indictment—grave for me—which states that, if we were unable to form armored divisions, it was for lack of matériel. I shall not insist on this point for the moment, for we shall hear witnesses and discuss the matter at that time. Nevertheless, I could not allow this statement to pass without answering it. I hope you understand?

The Prosecuting Attorney: I hope that General Gamelin will be able answer it. He was the Commander-in-Chief.

M. Daladier: He, too, was a partisan of the armored divisions, and if a division was formed, it was with his aid; but General Dosse and others—I quote from memory, although I have the names in the dossier—were opposed to it.

428

Second Hearing of February 20

The Responsibilities of Marshal Pétain

As M. Ribet said in his observations, I objected at first to the presentation of his conclusions on the legal aspect of the trial. I agree with him, of course, that law, according to our system, has no retroactive effect. But at the beginning of this trial and since that time there have been many other violations of the law, and especially of that human law which is engraved in the consciences of all men of honor and probity even more deeply than it is written in codes.

For seventeen months I have been a prisoner. For seventeen months, without a chance to defend myself, I have been denounced to the French people for having fomented the war and caused the defeat. At a time when I was actually forbidden to answer such attacks, instead of permitting the French press to do its work quietly, without hate and passion, the newspapers with official authorization, the Radio Nationale, even the Chief of State himself, were representing me to France and the world as "the man who, one day in September, without daring to consult the Chambers, had declared a war that was lost in advance" and handed over to the enemy a defenseless country.

That is not all. I appear before you not as an accused, but as one condemned. I was condemned on October 16, 1941, by the Chief of State, upon the suggestions of a Council of Political Justice appointed by him, without an opportunity to defend myself, without even knowing the list of charges drawn up against me. I was condemned four months before the trial which is opening today. Is there in all our history a single example of so much contempt for law and justice?

It is true that in his message of October 16, which announced to the country the sentence before the trial, the Chief of State, in his own words, seriously stated that it was his desire "to preserve judicial power from the encroachments of political power." He immediately proved it by predicting your verdict, before the first hearing of the Supreme Court had even been set. "This sentence," he said . . . must . . . strike at individuals, and also at methods, customs, and the regime. It will be without appeal. . . . Undoubtedly the normal development of judicial procedure would have spared me the necessity of invoking Constitutional Act No. 7, because the chief culprits, to whom this first sanction is today being applied, may find this sanction transformed into a still heavier penalty by the end of the trial. In times like ours each one must assume his own responsibilities; I am setting the example by assuming my own. . . . I thereby assure you that if you have been betrayed, you will not be deceived."

We shall see in the course of this trial where, by whom, and in what manner France was betrayed. But I protest against this arbitrary condemnation which is based on force alone. It will prove an ineradicable stigma on the dictatorial regime which was imposed on a defeated France with the aid of foreign domination, but which shall vanish with the conquerors and be buried in contempt. Three-quarters of a century ago, this kind of sentence was branded by the historian M. de Carne, a member of the French Academy, when he wrote in the *Revue des Deux Mondes,* during the Second Empire: "Cloaking prepared verdicts in legal robes has at all times been the work of certain commissions, whose odious memory would have impaired the honor of French magistracy, were it not that its members, in most cases, had no part in the formation of such political tribunals."

Pétain in the Service of Germany

It is true that Germany was undoubtedly impatient. The condemnation of Frenchmen whom she has the audacity to declare responsible for the war was Germany's first demand when she fixed the conditions for an armistice. She has not ceased to be concerned. In a radio address on October 13, 1941, Dr. Funk, a minister of the Reich, announced to his German listeners that the French government would soon condemn those guilty for the war, thus reaching a new stage on the road to collaboration.

429

[Here the President threatened to clear the Court, but M. Daladier continued].

He received satisfaction on October 16. It has been the aim of Germany to utilize for her propaganda the verdict pronounced by Marshal Pétain, which she expects to be confirmed and increased.

After annexing Austria and destroying Czechoslovakia in defiance of the Munich Pact, after invading Poland without a declaration of war, thereby making war inevitable for the Western powers who were anxious for their honor and their own security, Germany still demands of her victims an admission of guilt. What does she care for words of honor which are violated as soon as they are given. . . .

[The President announced that he would immediately clear the Court if M. Daladier continued to involve a foreign power].

[M. Daladier continued].

And yet it is France who must declare herself guilty. The men who day and night gave all their strength to try to preserve peace, who asked their country to take up arms only after having done everything to avoid war, those men must be condemned. But here we have French judges. In the course of the investigation the crime of which Germany accused me was dropped from the indictment. Nor was it retained by the act of indictment of the Supreme Court. That means that Germany alone is responsible for the war. Such was the first answer of French judges to Marshal Pétain's judgment.

Daladier's Effort

On the other hand, these texts have retained what they term incompetence in the preparation of the war, the responsibility for the defeat. I shall not discuss that for the moment, for it is a trial in itself, but let me say that no Minister of War, no Premier, has ever devoted greater effort to national defense, has ever secured larger credits or more matériel for the French armies. I took the initiative in August, 1936, when I caused the adoption of an armament program unprecedented in our history. To assure its execution, to speed up French labor, I did not hesitate, as head of the government, to break by the force of law and civic action whatever resistance endangered public safety. I can prove that in September, 1939, and on May 10, 1940, the Army was equipped with such matériel as should have made possible a victorious resistance to the German offensive.

I shall reveal the actual quantities of modern equipment which I found in use by the French Army when I took over the Ministry of War. In 1934, after the French note of April 17, 1934 had made it clear that all efforts at an understanding on disarmament had failed, at a time when Germany announced her intention to rearm and was putting into operation a vast armament program, the French Minister of War, Marshal Pétain, reduced the armament credits voted to him by Parliament. A year later, in 1935, barely 40 per cent of the credits appropriated were utilized for the production of war materials. Unfortunately, the balance sheet of modern matériel in use by the Army in the summer of 1936 can be drawn up quickly with respect to tanks, modern cannon, fortification equipment, and other items. I shall show the intensity of my effort to assure the French Army matériel equal in quality and only slightly inferior in quantity to that of the German Army, despite Germany's industrial superiority over France. None of the military leaders then questioned the strength of France.

Mutilated Debate

Why was France conquered? Why a defeat so sudden and brutal that the conqueror himself is still surprised at the rapidity of his victory? How is one to arrive at its causes if the government that is condemning me refuses to communicate the military documents and the accounts of operations so indispensable to this discussion? Where is the respect for the rights of the defense if one forbids investigations into the responsibilities for the defeat as soon as the question is no longer one of former ministers but of the commanders who led the armies into battle? Why were so many French tanks and armored cars senselessly dispersed along the entire front, instead of being grouped and organized for rapid and powerful counterattacks? Why were so many arms and munitions left in depots and arsenals, useless to the country's defense, at the very moment the battle was raging? Why was the French front pierced at Sedan, and later at the Meuse, and how is one to explain that formidable surprise which proved the decisive cause of the defeat?

And how many more painful questions ought to be asked on military operations and on the circumstances under which at Bordeaux, after a dramatic governmental crisis, the decision was made to cease firing and ask for an armistice? After the affirmations, many times repeated, that the French people would learn the whole truth, why now this obstinate refusal to let me introduce the documents which are kept at the Ministry of War and which alone would completely illuminate the true causes of the defeat?

Indeed, it is even stranger when we know that the Pétain government has modified the military code of justice in such a manner as to ensure the impunity of generals who capitulated in open field or who, after their imprisonment, accepted liberation on their word of honor that they would never again bear arms against the enemy. Let us marvel, furthermore, at the declaration of Marshal Pétain's government, which passes a retroactive amnesty where it is a matter of investigating military responsibility, and, at the same time, in the search for responsibility among political men, creates a new type of crime, giving it retroactive effect. Thus, if Gambetta were living today, he would probably be in prison, while Bazaine would be in the government.

Pétain Against the Republic

As Marshal Pétain said on October 11, 1940, "the disaster is but the reflection in the military sphere of the weakness and the acts of the former political regime." The purpose now is to dishonor the Republic, having already destroyed it despite the law voted by the National Assembly. Was it the Republic that reduced the armament credits in 1934? Was it the Republic that prevented the War Minister of 1934 from matching the German armament plan with a French program? Is the Republic responsible for the professional blunders or the moral failings which we shall discuss in the course of this trial? Neither the Republic nor the institutions of liberty led France to her defeat, but the men who would not put into action the arms and war materials at their disposal.

But what of it? The truth will blaze forth in the course of this public trial, in spite of all obstacles put in its path. It is up to you to pass judgment on the violations of the law. As for me, I have never in my official capacities had the honor of meeting the judges who today are sitting in the Supreme Court of Justice. But I have faith in their impartiality and I am sure that they will do honor to the noble traditions of French justice. If I were not at peace with my conscience, if I felt responsible for the disaster, I should not have outlived it, as all those who know me well will understand. But because I am sure I have done my patriotic duty, I shall fight for the truth, without concern for my own fate.

Only knowledge of the truth can give back to the people, who today are being misled by propaganda and partisan feeling, their confidence in the future. Their fighting sons were not cowards. Nor has the French nation forfeited her heroic virtues; her passionate love of freedom has never led to that so-called decadence for which, today, she is asked to atone in resignation. I am convinced that even in this severe and momentous trial, however bitter and painful it may be, the French people will find something to give them hope for their own future.

X

Cablegram Sent to the Supreme Court by Pierre Cot

AT BEGINNING TRIAL ON RESPONSIBILITIES FOR THE FRENCH DEFEAT I DECLARE THAT I TAKE ENTIRE RESPONSIBILITY ALL MEASURES CONCERNING AVIATION AND DELIVERY ARMAMENTS TO

SPANISH REPUBLIC DURING PERIOD JUNE 1936 JANUARY 1938. I WANT LEON BLUM AND DALADIER RELIEVED IN THESE MATTERS FROM ALL RESPONSIBILITY.

LACK SUFFICIENT AVIATION CAME PRINCIPALLY FROM WRONG MILITARY CONCEPTION GENERAL STAFF. BY DOCUMENT NO. 10-913 R.E.M.A.A. I PROPOSED ON DECEMBER 30 1936 PLANS 3 AND 4 WHICH PERMITTED DOUBLING OF AIR FLEET. BY UNANIMOUS DECISION HIGH MILITARY COMMITTEE THIS PROPOSITION WAS REJECTED ON FEBRU-ARY 15, 1937. PETAIN DARLAN AND GAMELIN WERE MEMBERS THIS COMMITTEE. BY LETTER TO PREMIER NO. 712 CM/R I PROTESTED ON DECEMBER 6 1937 AGAINST ATTITUDE HIGH MILITARY AUTHORITIES.

I PROTEST AGAINST ILLEGALITY TRIAL AND WILL SUBMIT TO JUDGMENT COMPETENT COURT WHEN FRANCE HAS FREE GOVERN-MENT CONTROLLED BY REPRESENTATIVES ELECTED BY THE PEOPLE.

PIERRE COT.

This cablegram was sent on February 24, 1942, to the President and Prosecuting Attorney of the Supreme Court, Riom, and the attorneys for Léon Blum and Édouard Daladier, with a copy to Gaston Henry-Haye, Vichy's Ambassador at Washington.

Acknowledgements

Due to wartime restrictions, it has been impossible to consult the following foreign publishers in regard to works of theirs which have been quoted in this volume.

BARTHÉLÉMY, J., AND DUEZ, P. *Traité de Droit Constitutionnel.* Paris: Dalloz, 1933

BIDOU, HENRY. *La Bataille de France.* Geneva: Éditions du Tour du Monde, 1931.

CHAUVINEAU, N. *Une Invasion Est-Elle Encore Possible?* Paris: Berger-Levrault, 1938.

EIMANSBERGER, L. R., VON. *Der Kampfwagenkrieg.* Munich: J. F. Lehmanns Verlag, 1934.

MAGNOL, JOSEPH. *A Study on the Supreme Court of Justice.*

MORDACQ, J. J. H. *Les Grandes Heures de la Guerre.* Paris: Plon, 1938.